The Analogical Imagination

THE ANALOGICAL IMAGINATION

Christian Theology and the Culture of Pluralism

DAVID TRACY

CROSSROAD • NEW YORK

1991
The Crossroad Publishing Company
370 Lexington Avenue, New York NY 10017

Printed in the United States of America

Library of Congress Cataloging in Publication Data
Tracy, David.
The analogical imagination.
Includes indexes.
1. Theology, Doctrinal. I. Title.
BT75.2.T645 230 81-629
ISBN 0-8245-0031-8 AACR1
ISBN 0-8245-0694-4

Grateful acknowledgment is made to Little, Brown and Company in association with the Atlantic Monthly Press for permission to reprint "Entries" by James Tate from *Absences: New Poems*, copyright © 1970 by James Tate.

To
D. McC. and J. J. H.

Contents

Preface *xi*

Part I : Publicness in Systematic Theology 1

1. A Social Portrait of the Theologian:
The Three Publics of Theology: Society, Academy, Church 3
i. Introduction 3
ii. The Public of Society: The Three Realms of Society 6
iii. The Public of the Academy:
Theology as an Academic Discipline 14
iv. The Public of the Church:
A Sociological and Theological Reality 21
v. Conclusion: Theology as Public Discourse 28

2. A Theological Portrait of the Theologian:
Fundamental, Systematic and Practical Theologies 47
i. A Theological Portrait of the Theologian 47
ii. Three Disciplines in Theology:
Fundamental, Systematic, Practical 54
iii. Conclusion: Publicness in Fundamental, Systematic
and Practical Theologies 79

3. The Classic 99
i. Introduction: Systematic Theology as Hermeneutical 99
ii. The Normative Role of the Classics: Realized Experience 107
iii. The Interpretation of the Classics and
the Pluralism of Readings 115
iv. The Production of the Classic: A Thought Experiment 124
v. Conclusion: Systematic Theology as Hermeneutical
Revisited 130

4. Interpreting the Religious Classic 154
i. The Conversation and Conflict of
Interpretations of Religion 154
ii. The Religious Classic 167

5. The Religious Classic:
Manifestation and Proclamation 193
i. The Realized Experience of Truth in Religious Classics 193
ii. Classical Forms of Religious Expression:
Manifestation and Proclamation 202

Part II : Interpreting the Christian Classic 231

Introduction: *A Methodological Preface* 233

6. The Christian Classic I:
The Event and Person of Jesus Christ 248
i. The Event and the Text:
Jesus Christ Witnessed to in the Scriptures 248
ii. The Classic Expressions of the New Testament: A Proposal 259
iii. The Correctives: Apocalyptic and the Doctrines
of Early Catholicism 265
iv. Proclamation as Event and Content 269
v. Narrative in the Gospels 275
vi. Symbol and Reflective Thought:
The Theologies of Paul and John 281

7. The Christian Classic II:
The Search for a Contemporary Christology 305
i. Retrospect: The Forms of the Whole and the
Search for Adequacy 305
ii. Some Questions for a Contemporary Christology 317
iii. Conclusion: The Belief in Jesus Christ 329

8. The Situation: *The Emergence of the Uncanny* 339
i. The Theologian and the Situation 339
ii. The Dialectic of the Classics of the
Contemporary Situation 345
iii. The Self-Exposure of the Classics to and in the Situation:
The Ideal of Dialogue 352
iv. Orientations, Options, Faiths: The Uncanny 355

9. Christian Responses in the Contemporary Situation:
Family Resemblances and Family Quarrels 371
i. Introduction 371
ii. The Trajectories of the Route of Manifestation 376
iii. The Trajectories of the Route of Proclamation 386
iv. From Manifestation and Proclamation to History and Praxis:
Political and Liberation Theologies 390

10. A Christian Systematic Analogical Imagination 405
- i. Classical Theological Languages: Analogy and Dialectic 405
- ii. A Christian Systematic Analogical Imagination: A Proposal 421
- iii. Christian Analogical Imagination: Ordered Relationships, God-Self-World 429

11. Epilogue: *The Analogical Imagination* 446

Index of Principal Names 457

Index of Principal Subjects 465

Preface

The major question this book addresses is a perplexing one. In a culture of pluralism must each religious tradition finally either dissolve into some lowest common denominator or accept a marginal existence as one interesting but purely private option? Neither alternative is acceptable to anyone seriously committed to the truth of any major religious tradition. The need is to form a new and inevitably complex theological strategy that will avoid privatism by articulating the genuine claims of religion to truth.

For those in any religious tradition who reject pluralism, such a complex strategy will be deemed unnecessary. Rather the truth of one's own monism can be restated over and over again in the hope that this messy pluralism will one day go away. Yet as the history of competing monisms in the modern period shows all too starkly, this hope soon dissolves into the pathos of whistling in the dark as we await the inevitable crash. For those like the present author who accept pluralism as a fundamental enrichment of the human condition, hope must lie elsewhere. But where? A simple affirmation of pluralism can mask a repressive tolerance where all is allowed because nothing finally is taken seriously. Or pluralism can cover a genial confusion. To affirm pluralism responsibly must include an affirmation of truth and public criteria for that affirmation. But how? That is the basic question this book addresses.

The argument of the book occurs in four principal steps. In a first step (chapters 1 and 2) the background of the problem for theology is sketched. Theology, by the very nature of the kind of fundamental existential questions it asks and because of the nature of the reality of God upon which theology reflects, must develop public, not private, criteria and discourse. Yet the kind of publicness which theology achieves must also speak from and to three publics: society, academy and church. How can the publicness of theology be achieved in responsible relationship to the often conflicting claims of these three publics? The first two chapters form a single unit. Chapter 1 outlines the problem of publicness in relationship to the three publics. Chapter 2 provides a proposal for the kind of public criteria operative in the three principal sub-disciplines in theology (fundamental, systematic and practical theology).

In chapter 3, the second, foreground stage of the argument is developed. Here the problem of the privatization of religion is related to the equally perplexing issue of the marginalization of art in the modern period. By understanding systematic theology as fundamentally a hermeneutical enterprise, the issue of both the meaning and truth of religion is related to the analogous issue of the meaning and truth of art. The central claim advanced is a claim to both meaning and truth in our common human experience of any classic. There follows the need to develop a theory of the classic (chapter 3) and, related to that, a theory of the religious classic (chapters 4 and 5). Those theories are designed to account for both the reception and the production of any classic. Indeed, the heart of the argument of the entire book may be found in the argument on the phenomenon of the classic. If that argument stands, the rest of the book can follow. If that theory falls, the rest remains, at best, on shaky ground.

If that argument works, however, the systematic theologian would have a necessary but not a sufficient warrant for attempting a systematic theology. For sufficiency, only the risk of an actual interpretation of the religious classics of one's own tradition would suffice. In the third step of the argument, therefore, I take that risk by presenting a theological interpretation of the classic of my own Christian tradition: the classic religious event of Jesus Christ as witnessed to in the classic Christian texts, the New Testament (chapters 6 and 7). The contemporary horizon of that interpretation is also interpreted (chapters 8 and 9) in order to render that interpretation applicable to our situation (chapter 10).

Only then is the fourth and final moment of the argument suggested: that is, the development of the notion of an "analogical imagination." That imagination functions as a contemporary strategy that allows, indeed demands, pluralism without forfeiting the need for common criteria of meaning and truth. My hope is that at the point where that analogical strategy is finally rendered explicit (in chapter 10 and the Epilogue), the reader will not find its entry surprising. Rather one may recognize that an analogical imagination has in fact been operative throughout the entire work. For my fundamental aim (as the title of the book suggests) is to suggest how the strategy of an analogical imagination may serve as a horizon for the genuine conversation open to all in our pluralistic present. Whether that aim succeeds, the reader will have to decide.

One possible practical problem: Several helpful analysts of the present manuscript have suggested that the more methodological discussions of chapters 1 and 2 may discourage some readers who would in fact be interested in the discussions of the rest of the work. I recognize and regret that fact but have not found any honest way to avoid those more methodological background discussions. It may be possible, however, that some readers will wish to begin with chapter 3 and return later to the first two chapters. I cannot, given my own belief in a genuine pluralism of readings, disallow this option. I admit, however, that I continue to believe that the first two chapters maintain their proper place in the wider, four-step strategy.

I am honored to express my thanks to several institutions and individuals for their invaluable aid in the long gestation of this project. The notes indicate some of those from whom I have learned.

I do want, however, explicitly to thank several others. My colleagues at the University of Chicago, both faculty and students, have provided inestimable aid as I have tried to work this project out in seminars, private discussions, lectures and colloquia. I want especially to thank my colleagues in the theology area (Anne Carr, Brian Gerrish, Langdon Gilkey, Larry Greenfield, James Gustafson, Bernard McGinn and Paul Ricoeur) for their literally invaluable advice. My thanks as well to my colleagues in the Committee on the Analysis of Ideas and Methods (especially Wayne Booth, Wendy Olmsted, David Smigelskis and Charles Wegener) for their valuable critical suggestions on chapters 3 and 4.

Several institutions over the past four years have honored me with invitations to speak on one or another aspect of this project. The reality of conversation on those occasions has been invaluable. Rather than naming each of these institutions, I hope that some of the results of these conversations may show in these chapters as one inadequate way to express my thanks. Besides the opportunity to give individual lectures on different aspects of the problem at several institutions, I am especially thankful to the Gregorian University and the North American College, in Rome, for the opportunity to lecture on the whole project in its earliest form. I am also thankful to those journals which have published earlier versions of some of the sections of individual chapters.

I wish to thank publicly as well the American Council of Learned Societies whose generous grant allowed me to finish the research on chapters 4 and 5 as well as begin the research on the "next" project (on the interpretations of religion in modern theologies and in religious studies).

Several persons read earlier versions of this manuscript and helped greatly through their criticism. Among them are the following: Anne Carr, Arthur Cohen, Hugh Corrigan, Mary Durkin, C. Franklin Gamwell, Andrew Greeley, Mary Gerhart, Eric Holzwarth, Werner Jeanrond, Robert Jones, Steven Kepnes, Joseph Kitagawa, Mary Knutsen, Joseph Komonchak, Martin Marty, Susan Shapiro and William Warthling. My thanks as well to Werner Mark Linz, my publisher, and Justus George Lawler and Frank Oveis, my editors. I am especially thankful to Frank Oveis for his extraordinary and untiring editorial skills and his unfailing friendship throughout the entire project. Special thanks also are due to those readers who not only provided many valuable critical suggestions but also developed the excellent index: Mary Knutsen, Mary Gerhart and Steven Kepnes.

My thanks to my mother, Eileen Couch, remain profound. She has continued to give unfailing critical advice and support as well as generous retypings of redrafts throughout the project. For the typing I am also thankful to the skills and generosity of Rehova Arthur, Pauline Doty, Martha Morrow and Vicky Starr.

It is impossible, as every author knows, to give adequate thanks to the many persons who made a work possible. I accept this impossibility with reluctance while trusting that all those, named and unnamed, whose aid I gladly acknowledge will recognize their presence in the work itself.

DAVID TRACY

On the Notes

The figures in brackets refer to the chapter (roman) and note (arabic) in which the work cited is mentioned for the first time. Where only one figure is given, the reference is to the note above in the same chapter. The following abbreviations have been used in the notes:

AAR = American Academy of Religion
BRO = *Blessed Rage for Order* by David Tracy (New York: Seabury, 1975)
CTSA = Catholic Theological Society of America
JAAR = *Journal of the American Academy of Religion*
JR = *Journal of Religion*
RSR = *Religious Studies Review*
TS = *Theological Studies*
TT = *Theology Today*

Part I

PUBLICNESS IN SYSTEMATIC THEOLOGY

Chapter 1

A Social Portrait of the Theologian

The Three Publics of Theology: Society, Academy, Church

i. Introduction

Theology as a discipline has many peculiarities. For some critics, the theologian seems, at best, a useful generalist who wanders too widely; at worst, a narrow particularist. As a generalist, so the argument runs, the theologian can sometimes provide penetrating analyses of trends, principles, symbolic resources and human needs. Too often, however, the theologian as generalist seems, like Mr. Dooley's Supreme Court, simply to follow the election returns. As a particularist (more accurately as a confessional theologian), the theologian speaks for a particular group, community or tradition whose claims to meaning and truth may seem doubtful to a wider public.

These common criticisms of theology have some empirical truth particularly when one considers how undisciplined reflection can hide behind some books and articles published under the rubric "theology" or how special interests do provide the real motivation for some theological claims. And yet, on the whole, the charges are unjust to theology and damaging to the wider culture which needs the particular form of public meaning that genuine theology provides. This book will argue that all theology is public discourse. But before the meaning and warrants for that claim can be argued, it is necessary to examine the social reality of the theologian.

If one is concerned to show the public status of all theology, it becomes imperative first to study the reference groups, the "publics," of the theologian.[1] The fact is that theologians do not only recognize a plurality of "publics" to whom they intend to speak, but also more and more the theologians are internalizing this plurality in their own discourse. The results are often internal confusion and external chaos. Just whom does the theologian attempt to address in theological discourse?

A sociology of theology remains beyond my competence and distinct from the central task of the present work. Still, some initial analysis of the social reality of the theologian must be attempted before the question of theology as public discourse is directly addressed. Like the earlier rise of historical consciousness among theologians, the contemporary emergence of a sociological imagination is, however initially unnerving, crucial for theological self-consciousness.[2] For every theologian, by the very acts of speaking and writing, makes a claim to attention. What is that claim? A claim to public response bearing meaning and truth on the most serious and difficult questions, both personal and communal, that any human being or society must face: Has existence any ultimate meaning? Is a fundamental trust to be found amidst the fears, anxieties and terror of existence? Is there some reality, some force, even some one, who speaks a word of truth that can be recognized and trusted? Religions ask and respond to such fundamental questions of the meaning and truth of our existence as human beings in solitude, and in society, history and the cosmos.[3] Theologians, by definition, risk an intellectual life on the wager that religious traditions can be studied as authentic responses to just such questions. The nature of these fundamental questions cuts across the spectrum of publics. Lurking beneath the surface of our everyday lives, exploding into explicitness in the limit-situations inevitable in any life, are questions which logically must be and historically are called religious questions.[4]

To formulate such questions honestly and well, to respond to them with passion and rigor, is the work of all theology.[5] Yet who, finally, is the addressee of the theologian's reflections on these existentially vital and logically odd questions? By definition, i.e., by the very nature of the question as fundamental for any authentically human existence, any fellow human being. In that sense, theology has always been, as Kierkegaard observed, a question of "the single one" to the single one. Yet who now is a single one? Who now does not recognize that existentialist thought in all its forms, once so promising, still so rich a quarry of passionate reflection, speaks more indirectly than directly to us all? For at its best, as in Kierkegaard, existential thinking speaks indirectly to an ideal reader, a limit-concept of the authentic reader.[6] The concept of the "single one" is the ultimate yet not the penultimate ground for the complex reality of the contemporary self of the theologian.

The pluralism of cultural worlds has enriched us all with new visions of our common lives and new possibilities for an authentic life.[7] Yet it does so at a price we can seldom face with equanimity. For each of us seems to become not a single self but several selves at once. Each speaks not merely to several publics external to the self but to several internalized publics in one's own reflections on authentic existence. The fundamental questions are indeed questions by and to a single one. An individual answer, however passionate or tentative, is ultimately also singular and deeply personal. Yet the addressees of our reflections, including the conflict of addressees in each self, are several.

Each theologian addresses three distinct and related social realities: the wider society, the academy and the church.[8] Some one of these publics will be a principal, yet rarely exclusive, addressee. The reality of a particular social locus will, to be sure, affect the choice of emphasis. The tasks of theology in a seminary, in a church-related university, in a pastoral setting, in a program for religious education, in a small community, in the secular academy, in an involvement in a particular cultural, political or societal movement[9]—each of these realities and others—will affect the self-understanding of any theologian. Sometimes that influence will prove so powerful that it will effectively determine the theology. More often a social location will provide "elective affinities" for a particular emphasis in theology, including the emphasis on what will count as a genuinely theological statement.

The more general question "What is theology?" first demands, therefore, a response to a prior question: What is the self-understanding of the theologian?[10] To ask that question as a personal and in that sense an irrevocably existential one is entirely appropriate. Yet to do so with the questionable assumption that the theologian is clearly a single self—an individual in the Western sense of Burckhardt, Kierkegaard and Nietzsche—is to betray the real demands of the passionate reflection of true individuality.[11] More exactly, one risks ignoring the actual complexity of different selves related to the distinct social locations and therefore to the distinct plausibility structures present in each theologian. Behind the pluralism of theological conclusions lies a pluralism of public roles and publics as reference groups for theological discourse.

Beneath both forms of pluralism, external and internal, lies a common commitment among all theologians to genuine public discourse.[12] Whatever the social location of a particular theology, that common commitment demands a commitment to authentic publicness, the attempt to speak from a particular social locus in such manner that one also speaks across the range of all three publics. In this chapter I have suggested that there are three principal "publics" for a contemporary theologian: the wider society, the academy and the church. In studying each, I have chosen to use certain relatively non-theory-laden analyses. We first need a more descriptive account of the "publics" of the theologian rather than another strictly prescriptive account. For the present, a tentative description of the common social reality of every theologian, whatever the more particular positions or prescriptions, seems in order. The assumption of this analysis is straightforward: However personally committed to a single public (society, academy or church) a particular theologian may be, each strives, in principle and in fact, for a genuine publicness and thereby implicitly addresses all three publics. The very character of the fundamental existential questions which theology addresses provides the basic warrant for this statement as principle. The analysis of representative societal, academic and church-related theologies throughout this book will provide the warrants for the statement as fact.

To refuse to face the complexity of the social reality of the theologian may well prove as damaging as an earlier theological generation's refusal to face historical consciousness. For the results of that refusal lie all about us in the contemporary theological context: a relaxed if not lazy pluralism contenting itself with sharing private stories while both the authentically public character of every good story and the real needs of the wider society go unremarked; a passionate intensity masked as authentic prophecy that resists necessary pleas for empirical evidence while demanding compliance to a particular ideology; a rush to the right for the false security of yet another restoration—too often a restoration which, like that of the Bourbons, has forgotten nothing and learned nothing; a reigning pathos among those who still demand argument and evidence (in a word, publicness) and whose inability to cut through the swamp of privateness may finally force them to become those who lack all conviction. We all know the truth in Kierkegaard's description of the modern intellectual as one become "pathologically reflective" or, for the theologian, the harsh realities in E. M. Cioran's description of many modern intellectuals as "religious minds . . . without religion."[13]

Yet perhaps some explicit reflection on the several publics of the contemporary theologian, indeed of several internalized selves, may aid us all at least to hear one another once again. In that renewed conversation, we may well find that anyone who reflects on ultimate issues is really a "single one," but, precisely as such, one who does not retreat to privateness.[14] Each will attempt, in fidelity to a profoundly personal but not private vision, to find the skills to speak publicly again.

ii. The Public of Society: The Three Realms of Society

Most Euro-American theologians are involved, we have noted, in three publics: the wider society, the academy and the church. The first of these publics may be described by the generic word "society."[15] In highly developed societies (i.e., those advanced industrial, technological societies with democratic polities and capitalist, socialist or mixed economies) the word "society" seems preferable to the other natural choice of "culture." For "society" is a word coined by social scientists as the broadest term available to encompass three realms: the technoeconomic realm, the realm of polity and the realm of culture. In relatively non-theory-laden terms these three realms may be further specified as follows.[16]

1. The realm of the technoeconomic structure is concerned with the organization and allocation of goods and services. This structure forms the occupation and stratification systems of the society and uses modern technology for instrumental ends.

2. The realm of the polity is concerned with the legitimate meanings of social justice and the use of power.[17] This involves the control of the legitimate use of force and the regulation of conflict (in libertarian societies within the rule of law), in order to achieve the particular conceptions of justice embodied in a society's traditions or its constitution.

3. The realm of culture—chiefly, but not solely, art and religion—and reflection upon it in various forms of cultural criticism, philosophy and theology is concerned with symbolic expressions. Those expressions, whether originating (as in art or religion) or reflective upon the symbols (as in art criticism or theology), attempt to explore and express the meaning and values of individual, group and communal existence. More exactly, culture is, in Clifford Geertz's careful definition, "an historically transmitted pattern of meanings embodied in symbols, a system of inherited conceptions expressed in symbolic forms by means of which men communicate, perpetuate and develop their knowledge about and attitudes toward life."[18] The realm of culture, therefore, will provide the clues to both the ethos of a society's life (i.e., the tone, character and quality of life—its "style") and its correlative worldview (i.e., the picture people have of the way things in actuality are, their most comprehensive ideas of order).[19] All cultural analyses, including the theological, will concentrate upon the relationships between ethos and world view: for example, whether in a particular instance ethos and worldview are either confrontational or mutually supportive, and how they relate to alternative possibilities of both.

Whether or not particular theologians are explicitly involved in the tasks of responsible citizenship in so complex a society, they are clearly affected by specific roles in that society. One need not become an orthodox Marxist in order to recognize the obvious and, in some cases, determinative influence of the technoeconomic realm on past and contemporary theologians.[20] One need not accept either Daniel Bell's neoconservative prescriptions for our society, nor Leo Strauss' antimodern "return to the polis" suggestions, nor Jürgen Habermas' claim that our society is one involved in "systematically distorted communication," nor any other theory-laden prescription[21] to agree with this initial description of the three interrelated realms that comprise as complex a society as our own.

Indeed, before one engages in any form of prognosis for the present situation, the following comments may serve as a possible consensus statement across the spectrum of conflicting prescriptions. If any society is a complex one with the three realms of advanced industrial societies, then any member of the society (including the theologian) needs to reflect explicitly on that complexity. Nothing is accomplished by retreats to some romantic notion of the solitary individual unaffected by social reality. We are all, in fact, social selves. We are all in constant interaction with the three realms constituting our present society. Our need is to recognize that fact and its influence on all theology.

In the interests of clarity and brevity I shall state my own assumptions for the description of each realm. The appeal of these assumptions, if any, must be, in accordance with the present limited purposes of this analysis, intuitive or counterintuitive for the reader.[22] My hope is that by stating my assumptions as explicitly as possible, the reader will find it easier to accept or reject them.

1. In the technoeconomic realm, I assume the value of technology but also the disvalue of an all-embracing technocracy for the whole society. In brief, functional or instrumental rationality is both necessary and appropriate for questions in the technoeconomic structure. The standard understanding of instrumental rationality seems appropriate here: a use of reason to determine rational means for a determined end. In the technoeconomic sphere, that "end" is ordinarily some form of success or failure in feasibility or efficiency. The major problem of instrumental reason is also obvious: its relative inability to define *ends* for the polity and culture on other than either an instrumental or a merely intuitive basis.

Except for the strict technocrat, most observers agree that instrumental rationality becomes dangerous to the wider society when its evident successes in the technoeconomic realm encourage us to employ only instrumental reason for articulating and resolving value questions for either the polity or the culture. Here the most difficult questions for the wider society emerge when one reflects upon the societal consequences, in both polity and culture, of technological advance.[23] For if instrumental rationality provides the sole paradigm for public, reasoned discourse in society, then we are not dealing only with a technological society but with an emerging technocracy, where the eclipse of practical reason for political decision and action is assured.[24] Then the more usual alternatives for rational, public discourse on societal issues too often turn out to be either unexamined and naive intuitions on value issues by a technological and bureaucratic or Hobbesian elite, or the conflict of special-interest groups.[25] In either case, a truly public discussion of issues of value for the whole society on other than either an intuitive or instrumental basis is quickly short-circuited.

What John Courtney Murray named "civic discourse" or Walter Lippmann articulated as "a public philosophy" for the society is disowned as perhaps applicable to an earlier and simpler age but clearly inappropriate to our complex technological society.[26] Humanistic reflection on values seems ever more confined to humanistic enclaves in the realm of culture. And that realm can itself become a "reservation of the spirit"[27] wherein a marginalized art, a privatized religion, a scienticized politics, an ineffectual philosophy and cultural criticism may continue their now harmless pleasures. Indeed, like the ancient Sybarites, humanists may even flourish on the assumption that they do not stray too far from the reservation and do not offer other than "personal preference" options to the instrumentalist discussion of values for the society as a whole. Narcissus may be allowed his curious pastimes. The polis, however, is both unaffected and unimpressed.

2. In the realm of polity, the one realm where all the citizens of the polis presumably meet, civic discourse and a genuinely public philosophy grounded in comprehensive notions of rationality and the demands of practical reason are imperative.[28] In American society, one need not romanticize the genuinely public discourse of the "Founding Fathers"[29] nor minimize the vast differences between their basically agrarian society and our own advanced industrial, technological one[30] in order to realize that a public discussion of polity issues appealing to all intelligent, reasonable and responsible persons is a necessity, not a luxury, for any humane polity. In the wider Euro-American society, one need not romanticize the politics of Plato and Aristotle, nor minimize the lack of correlation between the original Greek polis and modern society, in order to realize that the Greek ideal of civilized discussion of issues for the polis remains an exemplary limit-concept even in our present vastly more complex society.[31] If we continue to assume the value of reasoned, public discourse in a critical and argued fashion, if we continue to affirm the related values of individual liberties and equality as shared and often conflicting values for a democratic polity, then the discussion of these conflicts cannot be left to either a technological and bureaucratic elite nor to the happenstance of special-interest groups.

In the Western tradition of ethical philosophy, for example, one finds authentically public ways to discuss policy issues. Whether those ways be based upon teleological, deontological, axiological or responsibility models for ethical reasoning, or upon some "mixed theory,"[32] there seems little doubt that all ethical arguments are in principle open to all intelligent, reasonable and responsible persons. As grounded in comprehensive notions of practical reason, they are public—not private. As a single example in recent American history, one may recall the many discussions of John Rawls' *A Theory of Justice*.[33] Rawls' work, as most critics admit, provides one clear focus for arguing about the concept of justice for a society like our own. Rawls' commitment to the tradition of analytical philosophy does not disallow the discussability of his arguments by alternative ethical traditions (e.g., Marxist or "natural law" traditions). His use of an initial model of "reflective equilibrium" allows all participants in the discussion to make appeals to their own informed intuitions and distinct theories of the good. His use of what is, in fact, a mixed theory for ethical reflection allows any intelligent and rational person to enter the argument on genuinely common grounds without prior commitments to Rawls' own "personal preferences." His distinction between "thin" and "fuller" theories of the good should also allow, in principle, the employment of resources from particular traditions for the wider common good.[34] Nor should this discussion be limited only to professional philosophers. For no reflective person in our society can avoid the issues of present polity, especially those issues grouped under the rubric of social justice and specified for a democratic polity as the complex, conflicting and ever-shifting set of relationships between individual liberties and equality.

These questions affect us all. If anyone, including the theologian, claims not to be thus affected, then that person, as Aristotle long since reminded us, is either a god or a beast, not a human being, a social and political animal.[35] Do we not need to ask ourselves anew whether our society can continue to allow itself the fatal luxury of demanding professional competence in every major area of our communal lives except value issues? Perhaps our awe at the astonishing achievements of technology and our correct and healthy recognition of our individual ignorance in the area of technology tempt us to be too willing to hand over the realm of polity to a technological and bureaucratic elite whose own sense of ethical issues is in fact highly unprofessional.[36] Indeed, that sense is often some form of personal intuition heavily influenced by bureaucratic imperatives. Do we not seem too content to retreat from the realm of polity and retire with whatever remaining dignity we can muster to the sphere of our private lives where "personal preferences" are still allowed to reign?[37]

Yet this attitude cannot but be judged dangerously naive and eventually fatal. In fact, if our society applied only "intuitions" to the techno-economic realm, society would wreck the technoeconomic structure itself with more than deliberate speed. The application of instrumental reason alone to ethical questions (in the manner of some proponents of social engineering and systems analysis) is similarly destructive. Instrumental reason is justly praised for its expertise in determining rational "means" for agreed upon "ends" and in determining "feasibility" rationally, but "validity" only intuitively. Ordinarily that same use of reason is merely "intuitive" in determining "ends" for the common good of the polity itself.

The more comprehensive notions for practical rationality, and thereby for "publicness," articulated in such paradigmatic ideal societies as the ancient Greek polis or the New England town meeting, and refined through centuries of moral reasoning and ethical reflection, need far wider recognition in the realm of polity than present circumstances admit or sometimes even allow. Otherwise we should honestly admit that the present complexity of our society entails a scenario something like this: The realm of culture is, in fact and in principle, to be shunted into the margins of society, into the realm of the private; the realm of polity is to become, in principle, a realm where technocracy and bureaucracy reign and where both mediating structures and institutions[38] along with more comprehensive notions of rationality other than the purely technical one for use in rational policy making are now ruled out as impossible, indeed, as frivolous options. An initial step of clarification in this crucial realm is further reflection upon the full range of what will and will not count as reason-giving procedures.

3. In the realm of culture, intuitive and developed senses of values may be found in the classical symbolic expressions of the major traditions informing the culture.[39] Both ethos and worldview, affectivity, style and cognitive principles of order may be analyzed by appropriate methods in all humanistic studies, including philosophy and theology. It seems correct to observe that theologians, whatever their particular social locus (a particular university, seminary, political movement, base community, etc.), relate principally to the realm of culture and, through that realm and its notions of practical reason, to the realm of polity. Religion, after all, is a key cultural index. Indeed, in its cultural functions, religion serves, to recall Clifford Geertz's widely accepted definition, as "a system of symbols which acts to establish powerful, pervasive, and long-lasting moods and motivations . . . by formulating conceptions of a general order of existence and clothing those conceptions with such an aura of factuality that the moods and motivations seem uniquely realistic."[40] The presence of the religious reality in a culture, whether in the form of a religious dimension to the everyday disclosed in limit-situations and limit-questions or, more usually, in the symbols of explicitly religious traditions, demands careful analysis from all those interested in values, including those interested in "fuller" theories of the good for the polity.

It is in the realm of culture that both participation in and critical reflection upon symbols, including religious symbols, principally occur. The artist, the religious personality, the philosopher, the theologian, the social scientist, the literary critic devote major energy to interpreting participatory symbols, including their relevance to the needs of the whole society. In the original meaning of a "liberal education," that knowledge worthy of a free mind, all informed participants in the realm of culture were both humanists and involved in practical reason.[41]

In earlier and less complex societies, the role of culture in polity was usually more direct than in our own. No doubt the very complexity of present society—a complexity which includes a technology demanding specialized knowledge for informed judgment, and an accelerating centralization of power in an elite bureaucracy which tends to level the power and role of all mediating institutions (family, church, neighborhood, school, etc.)—affects all realms. Those effects are clear: a widespread tendency towards privateness; a diminishment of belief in the possibility of authentic civic discussion in the community; and, finally, the tendency to discourage, in both piecemeal and systematic fashion, any significant role in the realm of polity for those whose principal home is the realm of culture.

Whether avant-garde artists or countercultural movements in our century have chosen or have simply recognized their effective absence from the realm of the public remains a moot point.[42] It is the case, however, that art has become increasingly marginalized in our society. Indeed, as we shall see in later chapters, art seems to live principally as the realm of private taste and omnivorous consumption. The claim that the work of art, often through its powerful conscious or unconscious negations of present actuality,[43] discloses a truth about our common human condition often strikes both artists and the general public as counterintuitive. We have been too well socialized into the belief that the artist is, really, "a bird of paradise," a romantic soul yearning to express some purely private vision of the self.

Unfortunately, the artist can internalize this image and spend too much effort in "advertisements for myself." The same socialization process frees the public to allow these diversions. What, after all, is art but a now attractive, now repulsive expression of another's private self? It all depends, after all, on one's "private" taste. Exhausted by the paramount reality of the everyday, a reality itself ambiguously transformed by the same technology and bureaucracy, we can use the escape route of the artist to effect our own temporary vicarious escapes from our other, our "real" responsibilities. With neither Plato's insight nor his honesty in demanding that we remove the arts from the polis,[44] we effectively force the artist into a romantic and finally private misconception of a role. Thereby do we, contra Plato and his unconscious successors, impoverish our communal lives by evicting the symbolic resources of art from the realm of the public into the world of fancy and privateness. One need not romanticize the role of the artist to realize the truth of Ezra Pound's dictum that artists serve as "antennae of the race." They *are* antennae to new visions of human possibility, new values and forms of personal and communal life, new fuller theories of the good. Indeed, beauty, as I shall argue in later chapters, is a signal clue to truth itself.

In an analogous fashion, one need not (indeed, should not) absolutize the claims of any religion[45] in order to realize that any major religious tradition does disclose in its symbols and in its reflections upon those symbols (i.e., its theologies) some fundamental vision of the meaning of individual and communal existence providing disclosive and transformative possibilities for the whole society. Both ethos and worldview are disclosed in any religion. One need not minimize the need for reasoned public discourse upon all claims to truth in order to recognize the indispensable role that cultural symbols, including the religious, can play in the wider society.[46]

This remains especially true of a society like our own, characterized in fact by cultural pluralism and committed in principle to a democratic polity. Where art is marginalized, religion is privatized. Indeed, religion suffers even greater losses than art by being the single subject about which many intellectuals can feel free to be ignorant. Often abetted by the churches, they need not study religion, for "everybody" already knows what religion is: It is a private consumer product that some people seem to need. Its former social role was poisonous. Its present privatization is harmless enough to wish it well from a civilized distance. Religion seems to be the sort of thing one likes "if that's the sort of thing one likes."

The oft-quoted dictum of Paul Ricoeur is relevant here: "The symbol gives rise to thought, but thought always returns to and is informed by the symbol."[47] In the present context: If society is to employ the resources of the realm of culture for value questions in the realm of polity, then we must find better ways, as a society, to discover, recover and analyze the symbolic expressions in our culture. If one recalls the role of the Calvinist understandings of covenant in its contributions to the American Constitution, if one recalls the theological principles of Martin Luther King's struggle in the civil rights movement, one will realize how religious symbolic resources have in fact functioned as important factors in American society. Martin Luther King, through his personal appropriation of the symbolic resources of his religious and cultural heritages, was able to articulate, and to express in action, otherwise unnoticed and untapped ethical resources for the societal struggle for social justice.

Other intellectuals did not need to share the Protestant commitments of Reinhold Niebuhr in order to learn from his analysis of the dialectical relationship of the Christian symbols of "grace" and "sin" that Americans had ignored a deeper dimension of our social and political life.[48] Nor did one need to share the explicitly Catholic warrants in John Courtney Murray's correlation of Catholic "natural law" theory with the theories informing the principles of the American tradition in order to find new or renewed insights for present polity issues.[49]

It is difficult to envisage King or Niebuhr or Murray willingly accepting a privatization of religion. Indeed it is impossible. Yet it is all too possible to imagine many contemporary theologians eagerly moving to some local "reservation of the spirit." Less obviously, perhaps, than those artists who accept their marginalized status in society, but no less fatally, theologians can also rest easily on the reservation. They can even learn to sing its praises and embrace its privateness. They too can define their public not as the wider public of the society and its current almost desperate impasse on serious reflection on values. Rather they can rest content with the public of some smaller group of equally charming, equally private selves in some particular resting place in the increasingly marginalized realm of culture. If the whole realm has become marginalized, why complain? One will, after all, find civilized persons with whom to share the joys of privateness. With luck, one might even find a religious Bloomsbury.

A major assertion of this book may now be stated as a claim: If any human being, if any religious thinker or theologian, produces some classical expression of the human spirit on a particular journey in a particular tradition, that person discloses permanent possibilities for human existence both personal and communal. Any classic, as we shall see below, is always public, never private. Yet even before studying the warrants for that claim, there is some utility in raising to explicit consciousness the dilemma that all in the realm of culture face. Then, at least, certain realities of our actual situation may surface for serious attention: dissatisfaction with the marginalization of the realm of culture, a discontent with an ever more privatized self on a deceptively harmonious reservation, a recognition of one's responsibility to that wider public we call society and its ever more complex present actuality and sometimes frightening future prospect. Perhaps one may even hope that rendering these realities explicit may impel some theologians, whatever their particular social locus, to recognize their public responsibilities to genuinely public discourse for the society as a whole. If humanists, including theologians, in the realm of culture continue to accept their marginalized status,[50] then the alternatives are the short-run enchantment of self-fulfillment and the long-run despair of societal value bankruptcy. If publicness is to be exhaustively defined by instrumental reason, then the adventures of reason will never again inform an authentically public civic discourse in the realm of polity—the realm where, finally, we all must meet.

iii. The Public of the Academy: Theology as an Academic Discipline

The "academy" serves as a generic word to describe the social locus where the scholarly study of theology most often occurs. The journey from the emergence of theology as a "science" in the medieval University of Paris to contemporary discussions of the place of theology in a university setting is a long and complex one.[51] A helpful focus for the discussion is the modern notion of an academic "discipline." Just as the medieval theologians struggled to articulate the claims to meaning and truth of theology on the model of an Aristotelian science, so too modern theologians attempt to understand theology as an academic discipline.

Various proposals for articulating that question have been espoused in our period, usually under the rubric of discussions of theological method. Among the major proposals, for example, one may note in the Swedish university context Anders Nygren's lifelong attempt to demonstrate the strictly "scientific" character of theology as a mode of "objective argumentation,'' the latter specified by a linguistic philosophy and ''value-free'' motif research.[52] In the German context the major work on this issue is clearly Wolfhart Pannenberg's recent attempt to demonstrate the strictly scientific (in the European sense of *Wissenschaft*) character of theology, leading to his constructive proposal for the reordering of theological studies around the basic rubric of a theology of religions.[53]

In the more pluralistic Anglo-American setting many proposals have been put forward. As a major example, Bernard Lonergan has developed an empirical transcendental method in *Insight,* and correlated his earlier studies on the medieval notion of theology as a science with his later work on the contemporary notion of empirical science and the centrality of method over logic.[54] His method is designed to meet the needs of a situation formed by historical consciousness and the emergence of the many specializations in all modern fields of study, including theology. Lonergan's important constructive proposal for scholarly collaboration in theology consists in rethinking the present range of field and subject specialities as eight functionally related specialties (research, interpretation, history, dialectics, foundations, doctrines, systematics, communication).[55]

Lonergan's extraordinary achievements in methodology, still too widely overlooked, consist principally in employing his own empirical-transcendental method as the key by which the present diversity of field and subject specialties can be transformed into *functional* specialities. Precisely as newly forged functional specialities, the ideal of collaboration in religious and theological studies can become the actuality of functional interdisciplinary work. All these recent proposals have united with recent historical work on past paradigms for theological method to focus the attention of many theologians on formal questions of ''method.''

An influential although not determinative reason for this interest in method is the continuing presence of theology in major secular and church-related universities. Indeed, both Pannenberg's and Nygren's proposals are explicitly related to the crisis of legitimation for theology in the contemporary German and Swedish state universities. The same kind of process of legitimation emerges in the more pluralistic North American scene. Here theology may be done in several distinct academic settings: the church context of the seminary where professional training for ministry is the primary responsibility; the departments of religion and/or theology in the major church-related colleges and universities; the divinity schools of the older secular universities; the departments of religious studies in other private or state colleges and universities. All proposals for theological method are affected by the particular academic location of a particular theologian.

For some the situation seems so confusing that they argue, in effect, that theology, in its confessional and professional modes, belongs solely and exclusively to the churches. Theology should not be present in a university setting where all "normative" claims for a discipline—especially one which seems to possess an "exclusivist" norm—are suspect. Indeed, the choice of the title "religious studies" rather than "theology" for university departments often serves to indicate the distance which its proponents desire from theology's traditionally normative claims. "Religious studies," therefore, indicates an objective, nonnormative scholarly study of religion as distinct from what is viewed as, at best, the theologian's use of special "confessional" criteria or, at worst, special pleading for traditional norms.

Indeed the conventional alternatives for the academic study of religion are sometimes posed in some such manner as the following: Religious studies is a study of religion in keeping with the standards, methods and criteria of all scholarly study of any phenomenon.[56] It cannot and should not allow for the use of special criteria (for example, a demand for personal faith in a particular religion in order to understand that religion). Theology, conventionally understood, demands just such special criteria. As a discipline, theology belongs, therefore, to the churches and its seminaries and possibily to church-related institutions of learning. It does not belong in a secular university in a pluralistic culture. In that sense, this familiar conventional wisdom on the American scene is analogous to the insistence in Sweden, Germany or France that the university setting is not the proper one for normative, especially "confessional" enterprises. Thus does one find the proposals of Nygren and Pannenberg, which effectively both dispute this common misunderstanding of theology and reconstruct theology along the lines of other modern sciences in the modern European university.

In a curious union of unlikely allies, some church leaders agree with the secular critics of theology. Indeed, sharing the same conventional understanding of theology's strictly confessionalist role, these church leaders join some secular academics to insist, for their own distinct reasons to be sure, that theology belongs only in church-related institutions, not in the secular university. In Italy, for example, this position is adopted by some church leaders with the result that there are few departments of theology in Italian secular universities. Even in church-related universities problems of legitimation emerge. There the arguments about theology's relationship to the sponsoring church institution can become acute and usually focus on the issue of academic freedom. The issue then is not the need to legitimate theology's presence as a scholarly discipline. Rather, the issue becomes how to relate the academic "norms" of the theologians to the "ecclesial" norms of church authorities.

Other theologians, myself among them, believe that theology clearly belongs as an academic discipline in the modern university. Impelled by that concern, many university-related theologians (Nygren, Ebeling, Pannenberg, Ogden, Harvey, Küng, Kaufman, Gilkey, Metz, et al.)[57] have been engaged in the construction of proposals for the fully public, here integrally academic, character of theology in the context of the modern university and its internal debate on the character of a scholarly discipline. Other theologians in the same setting effectively enter into various "nonaggression" pacts with their colleagues in religious studies and the wider university. In the time-honored Anglo-American fashion, we hope to muddle through. Fortunately, we are spared some of the legal and political complexities of the French, Italian, German or Swedish scenes, so that by and large we do in fact muddle through. That English, empirical habit is, in my judgment, all to the good. And yet, the very drive to publicness which defines theology's task, the normative status of theological and philosophical discourses, does demand explicit reflection upon theology's constitution as an academic discipline.

One appropriate focus for that discussion is the character of an academic discipline itself. Stephen Toulmin's recent analysis of what constitutes a discipline[58] has helped clarify the otherwise vague term "discipline" in such manner that all disciplines in the university may find a new focus for their endless methodological disputes. Toulmin's analysis, which is marked by careful attention to historical and social realities (for example, the historical emergence of new disciplines and the role of professional organizations and journals),[59] refocusses the discussions from more formal analyses of "method" and more global studies of "paradigm shifts"[60] to more concrete historical and empirical analyses of the actual functioning of the various disciplines. In sum, the Anglo-American empirical approach to these issues receives in Toulmin's work its best exponent. Rather than just "muddling through," we are called upon to study the empirical (i.e., historical and sociological) realities informing every academic discipline.[61]

Toulmin distinguishes three kinds of rational enterprises in terms of their disciplinary status: "compact" disciplines, "diffuse" disciplines and "would-be" disciplines. The paradigm for a discipline is, of course, the "compact" discipline, especially as found in the "hard" sciences. The remaining two forms (the "soft disciplines" and/or the "humanities") diverge in distinct ways from that paradigm.

The "compact" discipline is characterized by five principal features:

> (1) The activities involved are organized around and directed towards a specific and realistic set of agreed collective ideals. (2) These collective ideals impose corresponding demands on all who commit themselves to the professional pursuit of the activities concerned. (3) The resulting discussions provide disciplinary loci for the production of "reasons," in the context of justificatory arguments whose function is to show how far procedural innovations measure up to these collective demands, and so improve the current repertory of concepts or techniques. (4) For this

> purpose, professional forums are developed, within which recognized "reason-producing" procedures are employed to justify the collective acceptance of novel procedures. (5) Finally, the same collective ideals determine the criteria of adequacy by appeal to which the arguments produced in support of those innovations are judged.[62]

"Diffuse" and "would-be" disciplines diverge from the paradigm in several ways. The two most important divergences (applicable to such disciplines as psychology, sociology, anthropology and, I suggest, to both religious studies and theology) are: first, a lack of a clear sense of disciplinary direction and thereby a host of unresolved problems; second, a lack of adequate professional organization for the discussion of new results.

To consider the latter factor first: in contemporary American theology, a university-related theologian is likely to be involved in several professional organizations whose membership includes a de facto diversity of paradigms on the nature of theology. More specifically, in the United States, besides professional responsibility for different journals, an individual theologian is likely to have professional involvement in such societies as the American Academy of Religion, the American Theological Society, the Society for Values in Higher Education or the Catholic Theological Society of America, as well as involvement with particular groupings of theologians and other scholars for specific theological projects. The membership in each group sometimes overlaps but often does not. More importantly, the membership within each group is sufficiently diverse to assure that there is no clear consensus on a particular paradigm for theology as a whole. In fact, there is a constant conflict of interpretations over traditional or contemporary paradigms.

As participation in any national convention of any one of these societies will demonstrate, there exists in theology a host of unresolved problems for its practitioners. More basically still, there exists no clear set of criteria for adjudicating these disputes. There is little doubt for any alert participant in any one of those professional organizations or for any reader of the major journals in theology and religious studies that Toulmin's two signs for "diffuse" and "would-be" disciplines are here amply verified: preoccupation with methodological debate and a tendency to splinter the field into competing "sects." In that fluid situation, the dangers for a discipline are obvious: the continuous diffusion of energies; the unending emergence of sects, schools, paradigms, even fads; too little real collaboration among theologians; too little mutual criticism upon agreed-upon standards, criteria and norms for theological performance.[63]

In that same situation, however, there are genuine possibilities for significant discussion and contributions from those who recognize the complex nature of the problem. Then, the search for criteria of adequacy, the demand for evidence, warrants, backing (in a word, for publicness),[64] the construction and proposal of paradigms for distinct theological disciplines (e.g., fundamental, systematic and practical theologies) can command serious attention from fellow professionals. Like social science, modern theology as a discipline clearly does not possess a "compact discipline" in the way it once seemed to. Neither the medieval theologians' notion of theology as a subalternated science, with its clear Aristotelian criteria and warrants, nor earlier notions of dogmatics now suffice.

The present search for a new paradigm for theology is complicated further by the relative decline in recent years of earlier neoorthodox paradigms in Protestant theology and the decline of neo-Thomism and its clear set of criteria and its genre of the "manual" in Roman Catholic theology.[65] Other complexities intensify this situation: the different academic settings of theology; the plurality and diversity of standards for performance in professional organizations and journals; the positive emergence of the alternative discipline of "religious studies" and its own search for paradigms, with the accompanying debates on the relationship between religious studies and theology; the continuing emergence of sects, individual virtuosi, and often outright fads under the cover of the now leaking umbrella of that once proud discipline, theology. All these factors are present to disorient any theologian in any academic setting. All these factors encourage every theologian to reflect more explicitly upon criteria of adequacy and more deliberately upon the disciplinary character of theology itself.

From this perspective, theology's present diffuse disciplinary status should and often does encourage both bold and tentative proposals for criteria and paradigms for understanding theology as an academic discipline. A major contribution along those lines—indeed, a bold proposal—remains Bernard Lonergan's development of a theological method which understands theology as a collaborative, field-encompassing enterprise constituted by eight functional specialities.

In the present discussion, Lonergan's proposal has certain clear merits. First, it recognizes what might be named the disciplinary autonomy of each speciality. Second, it argues for the possibility of genuine collaboration among the disciplines on a publicly adjudicable basis: the functional relationships among the distinct specialities and their distinct criteria based on an empirical-as-transcendental method.[66] Moreover, Lonergan usually explicates criteria for each discipline[67] that allow for public, critical attention from practitioners of each discipline. Whatever the ultimate fate of Lonergan's paradigm (or alternatives like those named above), the fact remains that every theologian is engaged in making claims to meaning and truth.[68] Every theologian, therefore, should render those claims explicit by rendering disciplinary criteria as explicit as possible. The field-encompassing character of both religious studies and theology (more exactly, the fact that they are constituted by several disciplines) inevitably gives rise to their character as "diffuse" or "would-be" disciplines in constant methodological strife for a more relatively adequate paradigm.[69] The characteristic which distinguishes theology as a discipline from religious studies, moreover, is the fact that scholars in religious studies may legitimately confine their interests to "meaning" while theologians must, by the intrinsic demands of their discipline, face the questions of both meaning and truth.[70]

As the later chapters of this book shall attempt to demonstrate, every theologian must make such claims.[71] Theology's setting in the modern academy and explicit, deliberate reflection upon the character of arguments and criteria in all the relevant disciplines in the academy have helped theology immensely. For that setting has forced theologians to reflect explicitly and systematically upon criteria of relative adequacy, and upon distinct paradigms for distinct theological disciplines and for theology as a whole, with renewed vigor.

Most former models of theology (for example, theology as an Aristotelian science and thereby as a "compact" discipline) are as clearly spent as is the Aristotelian paradigm in science. The present proposals for theology's disciplinary status are, to repeat, still in the realm of "would-be" or "diffuse" disciplines.[72] Some theologians, of course, "solve" this problem by joining a particular theological school or sect and then announcing the presence of a "compact" discipline to their initiates. Most recognize that this is a nonsolution to the difficulty. Theology, like the humanities and the social sciences in the modern university, must and can presently content itself with a "diffuse" or "would-be" disciplinary status.[73] Moreover, theology, like its traditional and similarly normative conversation partner, philosophy, must always struggle in every age to constitute itself anew as a normative and self-constituting discipline concerned with that elusive reality "truth."

That struggle, in the context of the kind of rigorous methodological and disciplinary reflection already existing in both religious studies and theology, may take the route of an explication of criteria of adequacy. Yet whether or not that particular focus develops, theology must take the route of "publicness." Otherwise theology will soon forfeit its right to serious academic attention, and thereby betray its own heritage. To ask the question of the truth of religious claims is not a luxury for theology. Even those theologians who "will not stay for an answer" to that question soon find that the drive to speak a truth about religious meaning—and thereby about the most fundamental, existential questions of our common humanity—will not down.

Despite some confused disclaimers to the contrary, all theologians are in fact involved in publicness. The "public" of the modern academy for theology serves to render explicit, and thereby to clarify, that traditional drive with new disciplinary resources. Across the broad spectrum of different academic settings and different cultures, across the even broader spectrum of different paradigms for theology's disciplinary status, most theologians do recognize their responsibility to produce theological discourse which meets the highest standards of the contemporary academy. In that sense alone, the academic emphasis of much contemporary theology is a fully positive force for both theology and for the university and, through the university, for the wider society.[74] Theology aids the public value of both academy and society when it remains faithful to its own internal demand—publicness. Without that demand for publicness—for criteria, evidence, warrants, disciplinary status—serious academic theology is dead. The academic setting of much of the best theology, precisely by its demands for public criteria in all disciplines, assures that announcements of that death remain premature.

iv. The Public of the Church: A Sociological and Theological Reality[75]

The theologian, therefore, must strive for publicness in both society and academy. Yet the theologian, unlike other intellectuals, must also speak explicitly to a third public, the church. Indeed, on inner-theological terms all Christian theology is, in some meaningful sense, church theology.[76] For the present discussion, however, our primary interest is not in an adequate theology of the church but in the church as a sociological phenomenon, i.e., as one of the three publics of every theology.

In sociological terms, the church functions for the theologian, as do society and academy, as one "reference group" or "generalized other" (in present terms, one "public") to which theological discourse is addressed. More exactly, the church as a public may be considered a "community of moral and religious discourse" which the theologian addresses.[77] Alternatively, the churches are voluntary associations exercising a mediating function between individuals and society as a whole.[78] As voluntary associations, the churches include both communal and institutional components. Indeed, as institutions the churches involve both primary and secondary functions in the process of socialization and the formation of personal identity.[79] Unlike participation in a family, participation in a church is now a strictly voluntary matter. Anyone may join or leave at any time. The ethos and the worldview of the churches affect the larger society usually indirectly. Through their individual members and more rarely through their institutional weight, the churches may directly affect the policies of the society as a whole. At any rate, sociologically the church is a voluntary association and one public of every theology.

The voluntary association of any individual with a particular church is a relationship to the church as "an historically continuous body of persons known as Christians, whose common life is in part institutionalized in churches."[80] Any voluntary church relationship, therefore, is to both a social institution and to an interpersonal community and tradition of shared meanings.[81]

If the theologian's relationship includes explicit commitment to both the institutional and the communal aspects of the social reality of the church, there occurs an ongoing process of personal decision and renewed commitment, including genuine loyalty to the church tradition and acceptance of certain disciplines consequent upon that decision.[82] In that case, the concrete church order of the particular church tradition will necessarily command serious theological attention.

In churches with a highly organized church order, like my own Roman Catholic tradition, for example, responsible participation in that church, like responsible participation as a citizen of a particular society, will demand theological reflection upon the principal questions internal to that church. In the Roman Catholic instance, theologians will address such questions as the nature of magisterium (or magisteria), the Petrine ministry, the principle of collegiality, the relationship of the theologian to ecclesially established authorities, the relationship of different theological models of the church to present ecclesial realities, the reform or conservation of present church structures, practices and teachings, etc.[83] If the individual theologian is in fact related to the communal but not to the institutional reality of the church, then issues like those listed above are likely to receive little or no theological attention.[84] In either case, the theologian, like all others in a pluralist and denominational society,[85] is involved, consciously or unconsciously, in an ongoing process of reflection upon one's voluntary commitment and loyalty to the Christian church and, ordinarily, to some particular church tradition. The theologian must thereby relate that commitment and its attendant responsibilities to one's other commitments and responsibilities to the wider society and to the academy and thereby to their plausibility structures.[86]

Adjudicating these conflicts among plausibility structures from all three publics is the proper task of fundamental theology.[87] That task should be rendered more concrete by theological attention to social-scientific analyses of the relationships of distinct claims to publicness in distinct plausibility structures embedded in the structures of the three distinct social realities serving as both constituencies and publics: society, academy, church.

For some theologians the church seems to function as the sole reference group for theology. Yet this self-definition is somewhat deceptive since both society and academy also function in their theologies as reference groups to various degrees of explicitness. For all theologians, however, including those who are primarily either academic or cultural theologians, the church functions as a genuine public—at least in the minimal sense of a concerned body of critical readership for theological proposals,[88] usually in the fuller sense of one voluntary association to which one is responsibly committed and whose traditions and authentic demands one has internalized.

For most theologians the reality of the church (like the realities "society" and "academy" understood theologically as "world"), cannot be grasped only in sociological terms. Indeed, even before a theological decision in favor of some particular model for understanding the church as more relatively adequate than others[89] (for example, as "perfect society," servant, herald, prophet, mission, people of God, *communio* or prime sacrament), the reality of church is not *theologically* reducible to the status of just another social institution. Rather, in most Christian theologies, the church is understood as "gift," more exactly, as participating in the grace of God disclosed in the divine self-manifestation in Jesus Christ.[90] Moreover, there now exists among ecclesiologists a broad consensus that the church is not identical with the "kingdom of God."[91] The importance of this theological consensus is crucial for undercutting any residual ecclesial triumphalism.[92] The Christian church, in its own self-understanding, stands under the judgment of God and God's eschatological kingdom revealed in Jesus Christ.[93] Any individual's loyalty to the church stands under that same eschatological judgment. To confuse those loyalties is, on strictly theological grounds, to risk idolatry.

Any properly theological understanding of church, therefore, insists both that the church is a strictly theological reality, a grace from God and as such worthy of loyalty and faith, and that the church and one's loyalty to it stand under the eschatological proviso of the judgment of God. For most theologians (including the present author), the "world" is also understood as a properly theological reality. Again in the theological sense, the social realities of both society and academy, as expressions of the theological reality "world," also bear a theological and not merely a sociological character.[94]

As a generalization, it seems fair to observe that in theology the more usual temptation is to understand society and academy primarily as social realities and only peripherally as theological: this despite several eloquent, if global, accounts of theological understandings of "world." The problem with understanding the third public, church, is usually the exact opposite. A theological understanding is almost overwhelmingly operative. A sociological understanding may be implicit but is rarely explicit. The notable exceptions to this rule (Adams, Gustafson, Komonchak, et al.)[95] serve to highlight the need among all ecclesiologists, and by extension all theologians, to explicate and correlate both sociological and theological understandings of the reality of "church." The church is primarily considered, in Christian self-understanding, a theological reality. Even those theologians within a particular church tradition who may be vigorous critics of present teachings and practices of that tradition, like Hans Küng in the Roman Catholic tradition, clearly hold to a strictly theological understanding of church.[96] With equal clarity and force, they argue theologically against any strict reduction of ecclesiological self-understanding to solely sociological terms.

The key concept here is reductionism. Indeed, so frightened by this reductionist prospect do some ecclesiologists seem that they are incapable of undertaking, or even appreciating, strictly sociological understandings of the reality of the church. For this reason, they become trapped in their own form of reductionism. They succumb to what James Gustafson has accurately labelled "theological positivism." Any sociological understanding of the church—as voluntary association, as institution, as community, as social reality—will seem reductionist to some theologians. Yet even without accepting Peter Berger's somewhat confusing phrase "methodological atheism" as descriptive of the sociologist's proper method of studying the church, any analyst can agree with Berger's basic point: The sociologist must examine the church on functional grounds just as one studies any other social reality.

Granted that the church is both a sociological and a theological reality, how may an individual theologian relate these two distinct understandings of the same social reality? Again: The concrete study would have to be of individual theologies to uncover the implicit or explicit concrete and particular understandings of church present in them. As a general rubric, however, the following observation is appropriate: To account theologically for the full spectrum of possible relationships between church as a theological and as a sociological reality, the most relatively adequate model is a correlation model. On the sociological side, the closest analogue would seem to be an "interactionist" model (like that of Max Weber or Ernst Troeltsch.)[97]

The theologian should in principle use a correlation model for relating sociological and theological understandings of the reality of the church in the same way one uses a correlation model for the more familiar relationship between philosophy and theology. On theological grounds, this model can account for the full spectrum of possible relationships between "church" and "world" from identity through transformation to confrontation. On sociological grounds as well, a persuasive case has been made by such distinct sociologists of religion as Peter Berger, Andrew Greeley, Robin Gill and others that some form of Max Weber's interaction model best accounts for the sociological and historical evidence of the complex interrelationships of church and society (and, although there seems to be less social-scientific research here, of church and academy).

The historical and social scientific evidence is notoriously complex and awaits some new Troeltsch to sort it out. In general, the church is always influenced by society; sometimes it is even determined by it. In other instances strictly theological-religious considerations determine the church's relationship to society. The latter is especially so when the church acts as prophetic critic of society or as transformative sacrament of the "world." A sociological interaction model and a theological model of correlation, by covering this full spectrum of possibilities, are also relatively adequate general models for understanding the full spectrum of the relationships of particular theologians to particular ecclesial traditions. Again the empirical data are complex. Sometimes, for example, a particular theologian accepts a particular church's official self-understanding and employs it to "judge" society or academy. At other times, the theologian (often the same theologian) opposes that ecclesial self-understanding and may eventually affect that self-understanding in some minor or major way. In every case the theologian, as an interpreter of tradition, is internally related to the church, one of the principal publics for theology. That relationship usually takes the form of an internalized sense of responsibility to the church, indeed a sense of real loyalty to the church community and its traditions and an internalizing of the plausibility structures and the ethical and religious imperatives of the tradition. That loyalty may assume either a conservative form or a more critical, even prophetic one of "loyal opposition" to present church self-understanding and practice. In either case what Josiah Royce analyzed as loyalty to the community, and Gabriel Marcel as "creative fidelity,"[98] will function as dispositions of the theologian. In sum, the church is always one public as addressee for the theologian and usually also an internalized public as an object of moral, religious and theological loyalty.

Although strictly theological judgments must finally play the major role in adjudicating theological conflicts, any theologian's particular concrete relationships to the other two publics of theology (society and academy) will also affect the theologian's relationship to the public of the church. Any theologian, after all, will function as an interpreter of the church tradition. And any theologian will necessarily interpret the tradition in critical relationship to some explicit or implicit contemporary self-understanding. Even if the theologian's self-understanding does not include an explicit recognition of the publics of society and academy (and thereby of the theological significance of the "world" as a theological locus) the influences from those other two publics remain potent. For the theologian, like any other human being, has been socialized into a particular society and a particular academic tradition and has been enculturated into one particular culture. Even when the relationships to society or academy are negative ones, the theologian will be internally related to the plausibility structures of that society, especially as those structures are formulated and refined into plausibility arguments and criteria of adequacy by the academy.

The range of possible responses to this conflict of plausibility structures is wide indeed.[99] The theologian's conscious or unconscious attitude towards the plausibility structures of the society may, of course, be negative. That route of negation, still best symbolized by Tertullian's dramatic and confrontational proclamation "What does Athens have to do with Jerusalem?" has been taken by many. The theologian's attitude may be less purely confrontational and may take instead the form of a critical challenge to contemporary secular self-understanding: for example, Schubert Ogden's or Langdon Gilkey's transformationist critique of secularism challenge a familiar form of contemporary secular self-understanding.[100] Or the theologian may simply make the plea that ultimately church and culture are identical. This "identity" model may take any form on a wide spectrum ranging from T. S. Eliot's or Jean Danielou's conservative arguments for a "new Christendom" to the Ritschlian liberal arguments for a "cultural Christianity."[101] In every case, some internalized conflict between competing plausibility structures is likely to be present in any particular theologian. Hence the complexity of relating the public "church" to the publics "society" and "academy."

There are, therefore, certain general principles and criteria of relative adequacy which can be articulated for understanding the relationships of church and world (to state it theologically) or the relationships among the publics of church, academy and society (to state it sociologically). And yet, certain central if often overlooked facts remain. Above all, one must note the social reality of the theologian: an intellectual related to three publics, socialized in each, internalizing their sometimes divergent plausibility structures, in a symbiosis often so personal, complex and sometimes unconscious that conflicts on particular issues must be taken singly or "retail," not globally or wholesale. What one can do in a wholesale manner is to argue for general criteria of relative adequacy. One can develop a general model, both a theological correlation model and, akin to it, a sociological interactionist model, as more relatively adequate to the actual complexity of reality than other alternatives. If that case can be shown to hold, then general principles and a general set of criteria of adequacy should inform but not determine discussions of particular conflicts. At the very least, criteria of relative adequacy should help to sort out the exact nature of the conflict and the relevant questions, criteria, and methods for its resolution. Yet no general model or ideal type can be applied in automatic, mechanical fashion to any concrete issue. Even aside from the more properly theological difficulties with a mechanical method, the social and personal complexity of any particular theologian's concrete and sometimes unconscious relationships to all three publics militates against any naively automatic procedures.

Complex as this portrait of the theologian's relationship to the church as social reality necessarily must be, there is no reason to bemoan that complexity. In fact, just as the theologian's presence in the academy helps to focus theological attention upon theology's self-constitution as a discipline, so too the present situation, wherein the church is sociologically a voluntary association, demands continuous personal theological reflection and decision which strengthens religious commitment and serious church participation.[102]

One additional complexity in the relationship of an individual theologian to the public "church" is also worth noting. In particular church traditions, the role of the theologian in the church's actual life differs widely. In the mainline Protestant churches that role is likely to be genuinely influential for the life of the church as a whole because the role of theology itself is deemed crucial. In the Roman Catholic church, the exact nature of the theologian's role is currently under discussion, with no clear consensus in the church as a whole. In some liberally oriented free-church traditions, the communal self-understanding of the reality of the church and its principles of order often makes the role of the theologian seem relatively marginal, at least for the decision-making processes of church policies. In conservative evangelical churches, on the contrary, the role of theology is deemed central but sometimes functions diffusely as debates rage on the role of sociological, historical or philosophical claims in relationship to the tradition. For these reasons, it is sometimes important to understand the particular denominational setting of the theologian and the role of theology in that church's self-understanding in order to understand how the public "church" actually functions in the theology. Similarly, it is important to know the particular academic setting (seminary, college, university, religious education program) of a particular proposal for theology's self-understanding, just as it is obviously important to know the particular kind of society to which the theologian is addressing proposals.[103] The particular understanding of society of those theologians living in advanced industrial societies will obviously be different from that of theologians in the Third World—as the debate between Euro-American "political" and Latin American "liberation" theologies demostrates.

In every case, the church will serve as at least one public for all theological work. In most cases, both church and world will also be understood as properly theological realities. In any particular theology, the intertwined realities of both sociological and theological understandings of church need sorting out before the exact role of this crucial public, the church, can be determined fully.[104] Whatever its more particular roles, the church will always function as one major public for all theology. Whatever the sociological and theological complexities inherent in this reality and however real the frustrations of this relationship may sometimes prove for any theologian, the fact is that the church in its innermost tradition serves the cause of publicness. The memories of the tradition along with the present practices and self-understanding of the church, despite their many ambiguities, recall moral, religious and intellectual resources and demands that always aid the struggle for authentic publicness in all theologies.

v. Conclusion: Theology as Public Discourse

These obvious if often overlooked social realities of three publics should not become the occasion to suggest reductionist accounts of any particular theological proposal. Indeed, it is rare that a theologian's position is so determined by a particular church order, a particular academic setting or a particular relationship to society that the theology is utterly determined by that relationship. But if such were the case the theological position would be not merely particular in origin and expression. It would in fact be particularist and, at the limit, private in meaning and unconsciously positivist in method. But such instances fortunately are rare. The more likely situation will be one where clear or obscured elective affinities exist between the distinct publics and distinct plausibility structures of particular theologies. For example, there does exist an affinity between theology in a seminary-academic base to a clearly defined church emphasis in that theology. There do exist affinities between a university base and an often less clearly defined "church" influence, often allied to a more clearly defined but still academically oriented societal emphasis.

In most cases, in fact, some theological correlation model will be employed to relate these affinities and to adjudicate the conflicts between plausibility structures. In a similar fashion, some interactionist sociological model will usually be employed to understand any theologian's relationships to the three publics of theology: society, academy and church. Sometimes, to be sure, there can be a lack of consistency in the application of the model. Such inconsistencies are often occasioned by a lack of explicit reflection on the reality of the theologian's relationships to the three publics. For example, one can find radical critiques of society allied with surprisingly conservative demands for maintaining the present status quo of a given church order. In those cases, one of the oldest secular political policies finds its theological analogue: external liberalism, internal repression.

To some outside observers, this social portrait of the theologian's internal relationships to three publics may suggest that theologians are involved in, at best, honest but unfortunate muddle-headedness, or at worst, sheer duplicity. As this book will argue, such a judgment is flawed. For the very complexity of the contemporary theologian's social reality can also occasion serious and rigorous reflection relevant to the social role of all intellectuals. The theologian's internalization of the demands and plausibility structures of all three publics may, in fact, prove a good test case for studying the genuine dilemmas of any intellectual in modern society.[105]

Insofar as theologians must render explicit the major claims and counterclaims of each of the three publics, they aid the cause of clarity for the wider public. To the theologian, at least, there is in fact no real choice but explicitness. Unlike their colleagues in religious studies, who *may* but need not render the question of the truth of religion explicit, theologians, no matter what public they have principally internalized, cannot avoid that issue. Then plausibility structures must become explicit. The drive to plausibility arguments will become urgent. The need to reflect critically upon real or apparent conflicts of claims in the different publics becomes crucial. The drive to personal decision and commitment is itself internalized with sometimes disturbing, sometimes liberating results. Every theologian must face squarely the claims to meaning and truth of all three publics: the paradigms for truth in the church tradition, the paradigms for rational enterprises in the academy, the models for rationality in the three overlapping realms of contemporary society.

One focus for these concerns is an explicit recognition of the theologian's responsibility for authentically public discourse. Indeed, the drive to genuine publicness is not an idiosyncratic program of some theologians. Rather, it is incumbent upon every theologian, no matter which public any single theologian principally addresses. Of course, it is not the case that every theologian must make the issue of publicness the principal, explicit focus of theology. Yet it is the case that some theologians must address this question explicitly and systematically on behalf of all. The social complexity is there. The theological complexity will not go away by attempts to ignore it. Those theologians who emphasize the public of the larger society, either through prophetic protest and critique or through integrative theologies of culture, are either purely private visionaries or they should command a public hearing. If the latter is the case, they are making public statements to the society and should be held accountable for the plausibility or implausibility of their advice. Those theologians who emphasize the public of the academy are bound to demonstrate, through public academic criteria and disciplined (i.e., disciplinary) reflection, the plausibility of their claims to meaning and truth and the relationship of those claims to the Christian tradition they try to interpret. Those theologians who emphasize the public of the church should show how and why the publicness, indeed the universality their tradition claims, is related to that tradition's central vision as well as to other claims to publicness. In fact, each theologian implicitly addresses all three publics. To render that reality explicit requires some criteria of adequacy for those kinds of publicness which cross the permeable boundaries of all three publics. The following chapters will attempt some formulations of such criteria.

In the meantime, let us recall the gains that the present social portrait of the theologian may occasion for all theologians. If the kind of fundamental questions on the very meaningfulness of our existence does define the nature of all genuinely religious questions, then any individual's response is ultimately and irreducibly a personal one, a question and a response for "the single one." And yet, however correct this existentialist insight into the irrevocably existential and personal character of religious and theological questions undoubtedly is, alone it will not suffice. In fact, as noted earlier the individualist character of recent existentialist thought tended to obscure rather than clarify the fuller complexity of any "single one." By that failure, existentialism rendered unavailable the truth of its own passionate and enduring insignts into the ultimately and irreducibly personal character of each and all responses to genuinely religious and theological questions.

Each theologian has, in fact, internalized to various degrees three publics, not one. Each has experienced the force of conflicting interpretations and conflicting plausibility structures in any attempt to make sense of reality. Most have experienced the evaporation and eventual collapse of any first naivete toward any religious tradition, while sensing the presence of a second naivete towards that same reality. Many have come to recognize the presence of real doubt in authentic contemporary faith. Many, after an earlier exhilaration with "pure reason" when "bliss was it in that dawn to be alive but to be young were very heaven," have experienced Enlightenment hopes for "pure reason" only to see them become the contemporary bonds of a merely instrumental rationality.[106] Many have witnessed the unmourned collapse of all forms of positivism, whether secularist or theological, as inadequate and eventually poisonous articulations of available meaning and truth. Some have recognized that, on the other side of our enjoyment of the enrichment of each by the pluralism present to all, lies the *fascinans et tremendum* reality of each one's seeming inability to become a single self any longer.[107]

Some have recognized that the complexity of the contemporary situation is a cause not for mourning or retreat, but for resoluteness and even, at times, for joy. For the pressures and questions of our situation will not go away by a refusal to face them. And the giftedness of both church and world will not be experienced as the liberating reality it is if an ever more fragile sense of obligation alone commands our minds and hearts.[108] In authentic Christian self-understanding, we are commanded because we are first enabled and empowered. We are gifted, in creation and redemption, in world and church, by a grace that is radical and universal. That grace does not wait upon our designs. It invites and empowers us to decision. As a single one, each theologian finally must decide on her or his own. But if that decision is not to be merely arbitrary, if its consequences are not to encourage further moves to privateness, the drive to authentically public discourse on the part of all theologians must be encouraged.

The theologian characterized by this portrait will inevitably be engaged in a complex set of strategies designed to be equal to the complexity of contemporary reality. If theologians share the understanding of society presented here, they are likely to share the present author's concern to fight against the privatizing forces which separate the realm of culture from the realm of polity. In sum, they will join other humanists in the demand for a more comprehensive understanding of rationality, in a discourse rationally and responsibly informed in its fuller theories of the good by the symbolic resources of art, philosophy and religion. If theologians share the present concern with the character of all disciplined reflection in any rational enterprise (i.e., the question of the nature of an academic discipline), they are likely to be impelled to reflect upon criteria of adequacy for the different disciplines constituting theology, ordinarily under the rubric of discussions of theological method. If they possess a similar theological understanding of "world" or, alternatively, of "common human experience" as a genuine locus for theological reflection, they are also likely to realize that theological concern with the "publics" of society and academy cannot be dismissed as extra-theological.

In principle, society and academy are not purely external relationships or publics for the responsible theologian. In fact, the socialization process will also assure that they are not merely external to the attitudes of any theologian. If theologians share a similar understanding of church as both a sociological and a theological reality, they are also likely to recognize two further needs. First, they must explicate the basic plausibility structures of all three publics through the formulation of plausibility arguments and criteria of adequacy as a general theological model for informing discussions of apparent or real conflicts on particular issues. Second, they must continue the drive to reinterpret or retrieve the classical resources of the church tradition in genuinely new applications for the present day.

Theology, in fact, is a generic name not for a single discipline but for three: fundamental, systematic and practical theologies. Each of these disciplines needs explicit criteria of adequacy. Each is concerned with all three publics. Each is irrevocably involved in claims to meaning and truth. Each is, in fact, determined by a relentless drive to genuine publicness to and for all three publics.

Notes

1. Representative work in this area may be found in the distinct approaches of Van A. Harvey, Peter Berger, Matthew Lamb and Gregory Baum. For Harvey,

see his essays on Nygren (*RSR*, 1975, 13–19) and Berger (*RSR*, 1979, 1–15). For Berger, among his many works see especially (with Thomas Luckmann) *The Social Construction of Reality: A Treatise in the Sociology of Knowledge* (New York: Doubleday, 1967), *The Sacred Canopy: Elements of a Sociological Theory of Religion* (New York: Doubleday, 1967), (with Brigitte Berger and Hansfried Kellner) *The Homeless Mind: Modernization and Consciousness* (New York: Vintage, 1973), and *The Heretical Imperative* (New York: Doubleday, 1979); for Lamb, "The Challenge of Critical Theory," in *Sociology and Human Destiny,* ed. Gregory Baum (New York: Seabury, 1980); for Baum (ed.), *Religion and Alienation* (New York: Paulist, 1975). In general terms, Harvey and Berger principally employ a "sociology of knowledge" approach; Lamb and Baum principally a "critical theory" approach. All four are, in fact, pluralistic in method and all four are open to the need for more empirical studies. Despite queries to several social scientists, I have not been able to locate a strictly empirical study of theologies in relationship to particular societies, academic settings and church traditions. One illuminating study—again pluralistic in method and empirical in data—is John Coleman's *The Evolution of Dutch Catholicism, 1958–1974* (Berkeley: Univ. of California Press, 1978). It might be noted that the modest effort of this chapter is more in the tradition of the "sociology of knowledge" approaches of Harvey and Berger. My own sympathies with the need for both further empirical, social-scientific studies of theology (like Andrew Greeley's studies of church traditions and society—see below) and revisionary critical theory are expressed in this chapter, and my defense of "critical theory" in chap. 2 (on praxis) and chap. 8 (on the situation). The present chapter, which attempts to be more descriptive than prescriptive, is an exercise in sociology of knowledge applied to my claim that theologies have, in fact, three social referents or publics. The hope is that this exercise does not encourage a reductionism of theologies to their social location but rather fosters a recognition of the need to understand the social realities (as publics) actually operative in different theologies. In the spirit of Karl Mannheim, one can hope for a sociology of knowledge account that shows (in Mannheim's famous distinction) "relationism" rather than "relativism": see Karl Mannheim, *Ideology and Utopia* (New York: Harcourt, Brace and World, n.d.), pp. 78–79, 85–87. This hope may become a reality either through metaphysical or transcendental analysis (cf. Mannheim's suggestive if cryptic comments here: ibid., pp. 88–94) or, as in this work, through nonreductionist accounts of theology and whatever religious event theology interprets (see chaps. 2 through 6). The more inner-theological reasons for this sociological matter of fact may be found in chap. 2. For a helpful study providing a critique of the use and misuse of sociological theories by some theologians, see Robin Gill, *The Social Context of Theology* (London: Mowbrays, 1975).

2. The term "sociological imagination" is from C. Wright Mills, *The Sociological Imagination* (Oxford: Oxford Univ. Press, 1959). The term is intended here as a broad rubric to cover the pluralism of social-scientific methods, from more strictly empirical methods through various normative models for social-scientific research. There is, of course, no pretense here to resolve the conflict of interpretations within social science (a conflict at least as sharp as those in religious studies and theology). For one view of that conflict, see the influential work of Alvin Gouldner, *The Coming Crisis of Western Sociology* (New York: Avon, 1970), as well as a study emphasizing the hermeneutical nature of social science itself: Zygmunt Bauman, *Hermeneutics and Social Science* (New York: Columbia Univ. Press, 1978). On the more general relationships of sociology and theology, see the works of Berger and Baum [1] as well as the essays by Andrew Greeley and John Coleman in *CTSA Proceedings* (1977), 31–55, 55–72.

3. The emphasis on "publicness" for theology in this chapter, it should be noted, concerns the kind of fundamental questions theology addresses as logically entailing publicness. The more inner-theological reasons for that publicness (viz., the affirmation of the doctrine of God and the coaffirmation of church and world) will be discussed in chap. 2. For the present, it is sufficient to note that even before the doctrine of God is mentioned, the kind of fundamental questions to which "God" and other religious doctrines (e.g., "the whole") respond already demand publicness.

4. For a defense of this claim, see *BRO*, pp. 91–120.

5. The methodological observations in Part II will clarify how this personal response in the Christian tradition is also by definition a communal response. In the meantime, for the general point see Martin Buber's splendid essay "The Question to the Single One," in *Between Man and Man* (London: Collins, 1961).

6. Note the interesting observations in Stephen Crites' review of Kierkegaard scholarship: *JR* (1975), 235–47.

7. See, especially, Peter Berger's studies of this "pluralization" phenomenon: inter alia, *The Sacred Canopy* [1], pp. 29–52, 126–71; and *The Homeless Mind* [1], pp. 63–97. The dangers of this model in contemporary American culture have been analyzed by Philip Rieff, *The Triumph of the Therapeutic* (New York: Harper & Row, 1966); and Christopher Lasch, *The Culture of Narcissism* (New York: Norton, 1978). The similarity in the descriptive analyses of Rieff and Lasch is all the more striking given the conservative and elitist prescriptions of Rieff and the democratic socialist sympathies of Lasch. The Augustinian theological tradition here (especially the neo-Platonic strains in Augustine where the self's major problem is self-dispersal dialectically related to a "narcissist" self-concern) could bear the same kind of retrieval as Rieff and Lasch accord the moral (Rieff) and the liberating (Lasch) aspects of Freud's psychoanalytic (not psychological) model. The most important theoretical work on the narcissist personality (in contrast, for example, to the Oedipal) as the dominant personality structure of contemporary American culture may be found in the important revisions of Freud's own analyses of narcissism in the work of Heinz Kohut (for an example, see "Forms and Transformations of Narcissism," *Journal of the American Psychoanalytic Association* [1966], 243–72).

8. In the American tradition, note the important studies of Martin Marty on the notions "public religion" and "public theology" and the intertwining of society and church in different moments of that tradition: see especially "A Sort of Republican Banquet," *JR* (1979), 383–406; and "Reinhold Niebuhr: Public Theology and the American Experience," *JR* (1974), 332–60. For Marty's own analysis of behavioral (or praxis) criteria in American religion, see *A Nation of Behavers* (Chicago: Univ. of Chicago Press, 1976).

9. These social realities are not, of course, simply peculiar to contemporary theology. Consider, for example, the import of the episcopal setting for the theologies of Irenaeus and Augustine, the "academy" setting for Clement and Origen, the monastic setting of Bernard of Clairvaux, or the university setting of Abelard and Thomas Aquinas. For an interesting study here, see Richard Crouter, "Hegel and Schleiermacher at Berlin: A Many-Sided Debate," *JAAR* (1980), 19–45, an analysis of the complex relationships of Hegel and Schleiermacher to their society, churches and academy.

10. One of the most important innovations of Bernard Lonergan's *Method in Theology* (New York: Seabury, 1972) is his insistence, based on his generalized (as transcendental) empirical method, that one can and should study the operations of the theologian via intentionality analysis or horizon analysis.

11. For cultural analyses of the notion of "individuality" in the Western tradi-

tion, see Karl Weintraub, *The Value of the Individual* (Chicago: Univ. of Chicago Press, 1978); and Lionel Trilling, *Sincerity and Authenticity* (Cambridge: Harvard Univ. Press, 1972). For critiques of Lasch as well as his defense of the notion against some of his critics, see *Salmagundi* (1979), 166–202.

12. The work of John Courtney Murray is marked by this defense of the need for publicness in a pluralist society. In Murray's language, we need enough consensus to assure even that our disagreements are real and discussable. For his analysis of that consensus in the American tradition, see *We Hold These Truths* (New York: Sheed and Ward, 1960); and for the pluralism in his situation, see, inter alia, his "America's Four Conspiracies," in *Religion in America*, ed. John Cogley (New York: Meridian, 1958), pp. 12–41. For examples of the critical retrieval of Murray's enterprise in our own more radically pluralistic setting, see "Theology and Philosophy in Public: A Symposium on J. C. Murray's Unfinished Agenda," with John Coleman, Brian Hehir, David Hollenbach and Robin Lovin, in *TS* (1979), 700–15. For myself, Murray's ideal of genuine conversation (as distinct from his analysis of pluralism) is what most needs retrieval today.

13. The Cioran quotation may be found in his essay "Beginnings of a Friendship," in the Eliade *Festschrift* entitled *Myths and Symbols*, ed. Joseph Kitagawa, Charles Long et al. (Chicago: Univ. of Chicago Press, 1969), p. 414. Recall how, for Kierkegaard, the modern intellectual, intrigued by possibilities but incapable of the actuality of decision, is in the "aesthetic" as distinct from the ethical or religious mode of existence. In contemporary literature, the novels of Saul Bellow (especially *Herzog*) often provide a disturbing portrait of this dilemma of many intellectuals (i.e., Herzog in contrast to the achieved if fragile actuality of Mr. Sammler in *Mr. Sammler's Planet*).

14. For an analysis of the phenomenon of the "privatization" of religion, see Thomas Luckmann, *The Invisible Religion* (New York: Macmillan, 1967), esp. pp. 28–41, 69–107; for the notion in "political theology," see Alfredo Fierro, *The Militant Gospel: A Critical Introduction to Political Theologies* (Maryknoll: Orbis, 1975), pp. 3–48. Luckmann eschews a "social-critical" interest (pp. 10–11) in his analysis of privatization; the political and liberation theologians insist upon an "emancipatory" interest in their analogous analyses. A careful study of the misuse of the "secularization" hypothesis by theologians as well as an argument for the proper social-scientific model of "privatization" as one aspect of secularity may be found in John Coleman, "The Situation for Modern Faith," *TS* (1978), 601–32. See also Elizabeth Doyle McCarthy, "A Sociological View of the Current Privatism" (paper delivered to the Institute for Religious and Social Studies, 1979). The complexity involved in sorting out theories of secularization as distinct from the more restricted theory of the privatization of religion can be found even in the classic exponent of both, Max Weber: inter alia, note how both claims are present simultaneously in his famous words, "The fate of our times is characterized by rationalization and . . . the 'disenchantment of the world.' Precisely the most ultimate and most sublime values have retreated from public life either into the transcendental realm of mystic life or into the brotherliness of direct and personal human relations" ("Science as a Vocation," in *From Max Weber*, ed. H. H. Gerth and C. Wright Mills [New York: Oxford Univ. Press, 1946], p. 155).

15. The alternative choice is, of course, "culture" in the broad sense rather than the more particular sense employed here. I have chosen to use "society" rather than "culture" to highlight the peculiarity of our society and the dangers of the privatization (of religion) and the marginalization (of art) from the "realm" of culture in the wider society. In the broader sense of "culture" as employed by cultural anthropologists, this kind of society itself can be redescribed as a "culture." For an informative analysis of the history of the usage of "society" or

"culture," see Maurice Freedman, *Main Trends in Social and Cultural Anthropology* (New York: Holmes and Meier, 1978), pp. 18–33; for a representative contemporary discussion, see *The Idea of Culture in the Social Sciences,* ed. E. Schneider and C. Bonjean (Cambridge: Cambridge Univ. Press, 1973).

16. The major sources for these relatively non-theory-laden analyses may be found in Daniel Bell, *The Cultural Contradictions of Capitalism* (New York: Basic, 1976), and *The Coming of Post-Industrial Society* (New York: Basic, 1973), pp. 339–491. Readers of Bell's work will note that although I basically follow his relatively non-theory-laden descriptions for the first two realms of modern society, I employ Clifford Geertz's analyses along with my own theological analyses for the realm of "culture." Moreover, I do not follow Bell's neoconservative prescriptions for present society. For an analysis and critique of this prescriptive aspect of Bell's work, see Peter Steinfels, *The Neo-Convervatives* (New York: Simon and Schuster, 1979), pp. 161–88.

17. For a helpful analysis of some dilemmas in the realm of contemporary polity as distinct from earlier periods, see Richard Sennett, *The Fall of Public Man* (New York: Knopf, 1977). Note especially Sennett's helpful heuristic description of the realm of the public: "A *res publica* stands in general for those bonds of association and mutual commitment which exist between people who are not joined by ties of family or intimate association; it is the bond of a crowd, of a 'people,' of a polity, rather than the bonds of family or friends." A contemporary interpretation of the classical resources on publicness may be found in the works of Hannah Arendt: especially *The Human Condition* (Chicago: Univ. of Chicago Press, 1969), pp. 22–79; *On Revolution* (New York: Viking, 1965), pp. 111–37; and the essays "Tradition and the Modern Age," "What Is Authority?" and "Truth and Politics," in *Between Past and Future* (New York: Viking, 1968). For an analysis of some contemporary literary resources for publicness, see Nathan A. Scott, Jr., *The Poetry of Civic Virtue: Eliot, Malraux, Auden* (Philadelphia: Fortress, 1976).

18. Clifford Geertz, *The Interpretation of Cultures* (New York: Basic, 1973), p. 89. For Geertz's defense of the intrinsic need of humankind for "culture," see his brilliant essay "The Impact of the Concept of Culture on the Concept of Man," ibid., pp. 33–55; for his analysis of culture as "public" and the hermeneutical character of cultural anthropology, see "Thick Description: Toward an Interpretive Theory of Culture,"ibid., pp. 3–33; see also the essays by analysts in different disciplines in the valuable collection *Myth, Symbol, and Culture,* ed. Clifford Geertz (New York: Norton, 1971).

19. Note how crucial the relationships of "ethos" and "worldview" are for understanding religion as a cultural phenomenon: see Geertz, *Interpretation,* pp. 87–142; and chap. 4 of this work. For helpful analyses of the relevance of Geertz's interpretative approach to religious studies and theology, see *Understanding Religion and Culture: Anthropological and Theological Perspectives,* ed. John H. Morgan (Washington, D.C.: Univ. Press of America, 1979).

20. The description "orthodox" is important here. The school of revisionary Marxist cultural criticism has long since made this case on inner-Marxist grounds. For examples of this, see Andrew Arato and Eike Gebhardt, eds., *The Essential Frankfurt School Reader* (New York: Urizen, 1978).

21. For representative examples, see Daniel Bell [16]; Leo Strauss, "The Three Waves of Modernity," in *Political Philosophy,* ed. H. Gilden (Indianapolis: Pegasus, 1975); and Jürgen Habermas, *Legitimation Crisis* (Boston: Beacon, 1975).

22. The use of the phrases "intuitive" and "counterintuitive" are not intended to indicate a return to intuitionism (and its dangers of privateness) but simply to suggest that insofar as the present analysis strikes the reader as "intuitively" correct or incorrect, the *beginning* of public discussion and adjudication of the

issues may ensue. The discussion itself would have to focus on the empirical and theoretical social-scientific work indicated in the text and notes and its relative adequacy or inadequacy to support these descriptions of society.

23. The interdisciplinary work of such centers as the Hastings Institute of Society, Ethics and the Life Sciences is indicative of the kind of work needed here: see the issues of *The Hastings Center Report* for examples.

24. The analyses of the Frankfurt School have been especially incisive in analyzing the decline of an emancipatory practical reason in both late-capitalist societies like our own and state-socialist societies like the Soviet Union. On the latter, see Herbert Marcuse, *Soviet Marxism: A Critical Analysis* (New York: Vintage, 1961); on the former, Max Horkheimer, *Critique of Instrumental Reason* (New York: Seabury, 1974); Jürgen Habermas, *Knowledge and Human Interests* (Boston: Beacon, 1971); and Trent Schroyer, *The Critique of Domination* (New York: Braziller, 1973).

25. The point on "special interest" groups is not to deny their legitimate place in the polity but to insist that there must also be a common good, a common interest in emancipatory reason and a common commitment to the ideal of authentic conversation within a commonly affirmed pluralism and a commonly experienced conflictual situation. If those "common" possibilities are no longer "communal" realities, then the realm of the polis is well described in Hobbes' famous words as "the war of all against all." Hobbes' *Leviathan* exists as a classic illustration of where the special interest option can lead. On the latter, see Leo Strauss, *The Political Philosophy of Hobbes* (Chicago: Univ. of Chicago Press, 1952).

26. See Murray [12]; and Walter Lippmann, *The Public Philosophy* (Boston: Little Brown, 1955). It is true, as Martin Marty has argued, that present American pluralism post-1965 (and, for myself, especially post-1968) is far more radical than either Murray or Lippmann foresaw prior to the emergence of black consciousness, feminist consciousness, the Sixties' radical options and the Seventies' turn inward and ethnic. What needs retrieval in their options are their ideals of civic discourse and public philosophy, not their proposed and inevitably dated solutions. For Marty's schema for the present religious pluralism, see *A Nation of Behavers* [8]. Note as well the informed and distinct analyses in "Religious Pluralism and the American Prospect" by Sidney Mead, Sydney Ahlstrom and Vincent Harding, and especially the commentary of Robert Bellah: *Soundings* (1978), 303–73.

27. The phrase is Max Horkheimer's: see *Critical Theory* (New York: Seabury, 1977), p. 278.

28. Contrast, for example, the notions of "public man" in the analysis of Richard Sennett [17] and in an analysis of the very different expression of publicness in Latin American cultures: Glen Dealy, *The Public Man* (Amherst: Univ. of Massachusetts Press, 1977). For distinct examples of attempts to establish more comprehensive notions of rationality, see: in the analytic tradition, Stephen Toulmin, *The Uses of Argument* (Cambridge: Cambridge Univ. Press, 1958); in the Aristotelian and Thomist traditions, Bernard Lonergan, *Insight: A Study of Human Understanding* (London: Longmans, Green, 1958); in the social sciences, *Rationality,* ed. Bryan Wilson (New York: Harper, 1970); and *Rationality and the Social Sciences: Contributions to the Philosophy and Methodology of the Social Sciences,* ed. S. I. Benn and G. W. Mortimos (London: Routledge and Kegan Paul, 1976); in history of religions, Jonathan Z. Smith, "I am not a parrot (red)," in *Map Is Not Territory: Studies in the History of Religions* (Leiden: E. J. Brill, 1978), pp. 265–89; in social theory, Jürgen Habermas, *Knowledge and Human Interests* [24], and "Towards a Theory of Communicative Competence," *Inquiry* (1970),

205–18; and on social and political theory, Richard Bernstein, *The Restructuring of Social and Political Theory* (New York: Harcourt Brace Jovanovich, 1976).

29. Note the work of Sidney Mead here, especially *The Lively Experiment* (New York: Harper & Row, 1963) and *The Nation with the Soul of a Church* (New York: Harper & Row, 1975), pp. 1–11, 78–95. The demonstration of Thomas Jefferson's relationship to the "common sense" (note common as communal) Scottish philosophies in Garry Wills's *Inventing America: Jefferson's Declaration of Independence* (New York: Vintage, 1979) is the best recent demonstration of this "public" character of the "founders" of the American Republic.

30. The role of John Dewey's retrieval of the Jeffersonian tradition in a postagrarian, industrial, scientific and technological age is notable: see Richard Bernstein, *John Dewey* (New York: Washington Square Press, 1966).

31. Arendt [17] and Strauss [21]; see also Eric Voegelin, *The World of the Polis* (Baton Rouge: Louisiana State Univ. Press, 1957).

32. In general ethics, see William Frankena, *Ethics* (Englewood Cliffs: Prentice-Hall, 1973). In Christian eithics, note the dominant teleological model of most Catholic "natural law" ethics, the deontological model of Paul Ramsey, the axiological model of Max Scheler and Dietrich von Hildebrand and the responsibility model of H. Richard Niebuhr. For a description of the "mixed theory" model, see John Rawls, *A Theory of Justice* (Cambridge: Harvard Univ. Press, 1971), pp. 315–25.

33. Rawls, ibid. For critics of Rawls' work, see *Reading Rawls: Critical Studies of a Theory of Justice,* ed. Norman Daniels (New York: Basic, 1976).

34. For examples of the use of resources from particular traditions for the wider common good (although not related explicitly to the discussion of Rawls), see Robin Lovin, "Covenantal Relationships and Political Legitimacy," *JR* (1980), 1–16; James Bresnahan, "Rahner's Ethics: Critical Natural Law in Relation to Contemporary Ethical Methodology," *JR* (1976), 36–61; C. Franklin Gamwell, "Reinhold Niebuhr's Theistic Ethic," *JR* (1974), 387–409; David Hollenbach, "Public Theology: Some Questions for Catholicism after John Courtney Murray," *TS* (1976), 290–303; and Douglas Sturm, "On the Meanings of Public Good: An Exploration," *JR* (1978), 13–30.

35. One of the classic resources in Aristotle is precisely his insistence on the intrinsic relationship of ethics and politics—a relationship deeply damaged by the modern public-private split.

36. Although clearly a problem in Euro-American democratic, late-capitalist societies, the same kind of problem emerges in state-socialist societies: see Chris Harman, *Bureaucracy and Revolution in Eastern Europe* (London: Pluto, 1974). For an analysis of the cost in human suffering in both systems, see Peter Berger *Pyramids of Sacrifice* (New York: Basic, 1974); for a defense of democratic capitalism, see the essays in Michael Novak, ed., *Capitalism and Socialism* (Washington: American Enterprise Institute, 1979). For contrast, see Erich Fromm, ed., *Socialist Humanism* (New York: Doubleday, 1965). In theology, the political and liberation theologians ordinarily defend some form of socialism on theological grounds. For a good example of an analysis of the complex relationships between economic theory and political theology, see Matthew Lamb, "The Production Process and Exponential Growth: A Study in Socio-Economics and Theology," in *Lonergan Workshop,* I, ed. Fred Lawrence (Missoula: Scholars Press, 1978), 257–309. For myself, revisionary Marxist theories like those of the Frankfurt School, with their ability to locate the nonidentity of reason and society in both systems, and revisionary American praxis-theories like Richard Bernstein's provide responsible alternatives to both state socialism and late capitalism. What seems

most reprehensible, however, is the "selective humanism" of some right-wing and left-wing thinkers. What I hope to show in a future book on practical theology, what most needs recovery, is practical reason with an emancipatory thrust—hence the appeal, to me, of revisionary theorists like Bernstein and Habermas.

37. That "remaining" dignity may prove ever harder to muster, given the manipulative techniques of a consumerist advertising industry and the continuing pressures in our society against such "mediating" institutions as church, neighborhood and especially family: see Christopher Lasch, *Haven in a Heartless World: The Family Besieged* (New York: Basic, 1979). The use of game theory to observe how little dignity can remain in the rituals and roles humàn beings are forced to "play" in society can be found in Erving Goffmann's work: inter alia, see *Relations in Public: Microstudies of the Public Order* (New York: Harper & Row, 1972) for an analysis of decayed social rituals and still alive (if "perfunctory") interpersonal rituals.

38. The principle of subsidiarity in the Catholic "social justice" theory is often applied to a defense of these presently endangered mediating structures. For a basic collection in this tradition, see Joseph Gremillion, *The Gospel of Peace and Justice* (Maryknoll: Orbis, 1976); for a recent retrieval, see *Faith That Does Justice,* ed. John Haughey (New York: Paulist, 1977).

39. A major example of this in American culture may be found in the "civil religion" debate: see the different contributions to this discussion of Sidney Mead and his defense of the Enlightenment tradition as the major tradition [29]; or Sydney Ahlstrom's articulation of the Puritan tradition in *A Religious History of the American People* (New Haven: Yale Univ. Press, 1972), pp.124–35; and the distinct positions articulating the need for both the Covenantal and the Enlightment traditions in the work of Robert Bellah on "civil religion" (*The Broken Covenant* [New York: Seabury, 1976]) and of Martin Marty on "public religion" [8]. For a good example of several of the major participants in this important debate, see Russell Richey and Donald Jones, eds., *American Civil Religion* (New York: Harper & Row, 1974).

The main debate itself has largely focussed on the mainline American Enlightenment and Convenantal traditions with various candidates proffered as the primary analogue for understanding and retrieving that tradition (roughly: Jefferson for Mead, Lincoln for Bellah, the Puritan heritage for Ahlstrom [and behind him, Perry Miller], Franklin and Lincoln for Marty). Each thinker, it should be noted, also accounts for the alternative options; the suggestion (a "rough" one) for the primary focus is my own interpretation, not theirs. Ahlstrom, for example, seems more despairing of the centrality of the Puritans in his final chapter of *A Religious History of the American People* (pp. 965–1097) than his earlier analysis leads the reader to expect. Still, what Marty aptly names our post-1965 radically pluralistic cultural situation has expanded the candidates of alternative retrievable traditions, like the black, feminist, Catholic, Jewish, radical movements and thinkers (or the candidates within each tradition as the distinct interpretations of the American Catholic tradition by John Tracy Ellis, Jay Dolan, Andrew Greeley, James Hennesey and David O'Brien well illustrate). The point is simply to document how several contemporary thinkers in the realm of American religious culture are presently engaged in important operations of retrieval of the pluralistic American tradition. They attempt to allow contemporary publicness to occur in harmony with the *classic* resources of this pluralistic heritage. For an interesting study here that also employs history of religions methodology, see Catherine Albanese, *Sons of the Fathers: The Civil Religion of the American Revolution* (Philadelphia: Temple Univ. Press, 1976).

40. Clifford Geertz, *The Interpretation of Cultures* [18], p. 90.

41. For an historical study of universities as a social reality, see Charles Homer Haskins, *The Rise of Universities* (Ithaca: Cornell Univ. Press, 1957).

42. See Renato Poggioli, *The Theory of the Avant-Garde* (Cambridge: Harvard Univ. Press, 1968).

43. For an understanding of the negations present in all great art, including "affirmative" art, see Herbert Marcuse, *The Aesthetic Dimension* (Boston: Beacon, 1978).

44. For a recent study, see Iris Murdoch, *The Fire and the Sun: Why Plato Banished the Artists* (Oxford: Oxford Univ. Press, 1978).

45. For a recent study which seems to regret this loss of "absolutizing" the claims of a religion into exclusivist claims, see John Murray Cuddihy, *No Offense: Civil Religion and Protestant Taste* (New York: Seabury, 1978). This often brilliant work fails to understand how a real commitment to a tradition need not take an exclusivist stance: a truth well known to Reinhold Niebuhr, John Courtney Murray, Arthur Hertzburg and Arthur Cohen but lost on John Murray Cuddihy.

46. In cultural anthropology, see the valuable collection, *Symbols: Public and Private,* ed. Raymond Firth (Ithaca: Cornell Univ. Press, 1973), esp. pp. 207–43.

47. Paul Ricoeur, *The Symbolism of Evil* (Boston: Beacon, 1967), pp. 347–57.

48. See Dennis McCann on Reinhold Niebuhr, "Religious Symbols and Social Criticism" (Ph.D. diss., University of Chicago, 1976), and his critical analysis of Niebuhr and liberation theologies and the need for publicness: Dennis McCann, *Christian Realism and Liberation Theology: Practical Theologies in Creative Conflict* (Maryknoll: Orbis, 1981).

49. For a study of Murray, see Donald Pelotte, *John Courtney Murray: Theologian in Conflict* (New York: Paulist, 1975).

50. For an instructive account of cultural analysts in British society, from a perspective sympathetic to Marxism, see Raymond Williams, *Culture and Society 1780–1950* (London: Chatto and Windus, 1958).

51. For background here, see Wolfhart Pannenberg, *Theology and the Philosophy of Science* (Philadelphia: Westminster, 1976), pp. 228–97; Yves Congar, *A History of Theology* (New York: Doubleday, 1968); the valuable papers of Edward Farley (on the role of the nineteenth-century theological encyclopedia) and Robert Lynn (on the history of American theological education) for the Vanderbilt Conference on Theological Education (1979) are as yet unpublished.

52. Anders Nygren, *Meaning and Method* (Philadelphia: Fortress, 1972).

53. Wolfhart Pannenberg, *Theology and the Philosophy of Science,* pp. 301–46.

54. See Bernard Lonergan, *Insight* [28] and *Method in Theology* [10]. Note how Lonergan's empirical transcendental method (or, alternatively, his generalized empirical method) can claim that method does account for both logical and nonlogical operations (e.g., insights) and thereby encompasses logic but is not reducible to it. For a clear statement of Lonergan's analysis of the nature of the shift of scientific ideals, see his essay "Aquinas Today: Tradition and Innovation," in *Celebrating the Medieval Heritage: A Colloquy on the Thought of Aquinas and Bonaventure,* ed. David Tracy, *JR* Supplement (1978), S1–S18.

55. *Method in Theology,* pp. 125–49.

56. For a critique of theology employing the conventional understanding, see Ninian Smart, *The Science of Religion and the Sociology of Knowledge* (Princeton: Princeton Univ. Press, 1973), pp. 24–49.

57. The relevant works of Nygren [52], Pannenberg [51], Harvey and Ogden are cited above; for the others: Gerhard Ebeling, *The Study of Theology* (Philadelphia: Fortress, 1975); Gordon Kaufman, *An Essay in Theological Method* (Mis-

soula: Scholars Press, 1975); Langdon Gilkey, "The AAR and the Anxiety of Nonbeing: An Analysis of Our Present Cultural Situation," *JAAR* (1980), 5–18; Maurice Wiles, *What Is Theology?* (London: Oxford Univ. Press, 1976); idem, "Christian Theology in an Age of Religious Studies," in *Explorations in Theology 4* (London: SCM, 1979). We will return to a discussion of several of these positions in the following, more properly theological, chapter. In the meantime, a reader of all of them may note (1) their common academic referents and drive to publicness and (2) the "conflict of interpretations" within theology itself on its relationship to the secular university. The latter conflict can be fully addressed only on the inner-theological grounds of chap. 2. For a study of theology and religious studies in North America by means of an analysis of the professional journals and from a somewhat puzzled European perspective, see Francis Messner, *Théologie ou Religiologie: Les Revues de Religion aux USA* (Strasbourg: Cerdic, 1978).

58. Stephen Toulmin, *Human Understanding,* Vol. I, *The Collective Use and Evolution of Concepts* (Princeton: Princeton Univ. Press, 1972).

59. Ibid., pp. 200–261 (history), pp. 261–319 (professional organization).

60. See Toulmin's persuasive analysis of the difficulties inherent in the well-known position (or positions?) of Thomas Kuhn in his influential work *The Structure of Scientific Revolutions* (Chicago: Univ. of Chicago, 1962 and 1970). For Toulmin's critical analysis, see *Human Understanding,* I, 98–123; for other analyses of Kuhn's position and his responses, see *Criticism and the Growth of Knowledge,* ed. Imre Lakatos and Alan Musgrave (Cambridge: Cambridge Univ. Press, 1970).

61. It might be argued that the European post-Dilthey discussion of the distinction between *Naturwissenschaften* and *Geisteswissenschaften* is philosophically richer than the more familiar Anglo-American discussion. For myself, that is in fact the case. Yet the more empirical (as both less theory-laden and more sociology-of-knowledge oriented) and the clearer (in the sense of analytic philosophy) realities provided by Toulmin's analysis render his account more appropriate as a candidate for this present attempt at a relatively non-theory-laden description of theology as an academic discipline. For a good account of the issues in a European context, see Matthew Lamb, *History, Method and Theology* (Missoula: Scholars Press, 1978).

62. *Human Understanding* [58], I, 379.

63. The manner in which a call for pluralism (of methods, frameworks, etc.) can easily slide into its caricature, eclecticism, if it does not develop criteria of relative adequacy for adjudicating disputes, is dismaying in contemporary theology. A prime example of the latter is the dearth of truly critical reviewing of many works as distinct from an announcement of a pro or con opinion with no supporting argument. A second example is the emergence of a theological eclecticism based, it seems, on personal tastes for a "little of this position" and a "little of that" masked as constructive theology.

64. For an analysis of the structure of argument (claim, warrant, backing etc.), see Stephen Toulmin, *The Uses of Argument* [28]; for the character of judgment as virtually unconditioned, see Bernard Lonergan's classic analysis in *Insight* [28], pp. 271–319.

65. For the development of the neo-Thomist paradigm, see Gerald McCool, *Catholic Theology in the Nineteenth Century* (New York: Seabury, 1977), pp. 129–268. For the political factors in that development, see Pierre Thibault, *Savoir et Pouvoir: Philosophie thomiste et politique cléricale au XIX siècle* (Quebec: Presses de l'Université Laval, 1972); and James Hennesey, "Leo XIII's Thomistic Revival: A Political and Philosophical Event," in *Celebrating the Medieval Heritage* [54], S185–S198.

66. Lonergan's major warrants for his claim are threefold: first, his own generalized empirical method and its development of the fourfold self-structuring process of human consciousness; second, the traditional distinction of theology into mediating theology and mediated theology; third, the contemporary existence of subject specializations which need but cannot seem to find *functional* relationships—the latter can be provided by Lonergan's own generalized empirical method.

67. The most original and promising of these criteria for a necessary discipline may be found in Lonergan's development of criteria for the discipline he names "dialectics": see *Method in Theology* [10], pp. 235–67. A reader of *Method* should note that even if one does not agree with the material conclusions of Lonergan's own use of dialectics, the criteria for that kind of necessary discipline are spelled out with methodological care in a manner which allows for intelligent, rational and responsible pluralism while displacing eclecticism at the root, i.e., by demanding an engagement in dialectics.

68. It is perhaps worth recalling here that the very nature of the fundamental questions to which religions and theologies are responses demands this.

69. The interpreter can, of course, develop paradigms for the discipline of the study of religion, as in Joachim Wach or Mircea Eliade. We will return to a study of this alternative in chap. 4.

70. This is so on the side of publicness. On the side of the "publics" there is also the obvious difference (discussed below) that theology is also in some manner related to the church and not only to academy and society whereas religious studies is not.

71. See especially chap. 2, sec. i, on the significance of the affirmation of God as an inner-theological reason for this reality.

72. Some commentators would prefer to state, I suspect, that theology is a "has-been" discipline. To do so, however, without further analysis of its actual performance is to mistake conventional (and largely spent) models for theology with contemporary, academy-based disciplinary accounts of its status.

73. The social sciences present a particularly interesting case insofar as many social scientists in the postfunctionalist pluralism of methods appeal no longer to the "hard sciences" for their own disciplinary models but to the humanities, as Clifford Geertz has shown in his recent study of the models of "game," "drama" and "text" employed by Goffman, Victor Turner and Becker, respectively: "Blurred Genres: The Refiguration of Social Thought," *The American Scholar* (1980), 165–79.

74. This registers my own disagreement with the now familiar attacks on "academic" theology: for an example of the latter, see Juan Luis Segundo, *The Liberation of Theology* (Maryknoll: Orbis, 1976), pp.7–39. The legitimate motives and authentic achievements of liberation theologies are examined in chaps. 2 and 9. The attack of liberation theologians on academically based theologies (as distinct from their own positive and constructive proposals for other bases for theology, especially the "basic communities") continues to seem to me ill-conceived and often inconsistent (as when Segundo, in the same book in which he attacks "academic" theologies, appeals not to Karl Marx but to Max Weber for an academically based sociology as an example of the kind of sociology needed by theologians).

75. "Society" and "academy" as expressions of the theological reality "world" are also both "theological" and "sociological" realities—as we shall indicate in chap. 2. I have rendered explicit here that complexity for "church" rather than for all three since the complexities of the church as a sociological and theological reality are more striking and more in need of explication. A fuller

theological understanding of "church" must await the discussions in later chapters, especially the Introduction to Part II and chaps. 6, 7 and 10.

76. This is the case not only for Karl Barth in the *Church Dogmatics*. The favorite *bête noire* of the Barthians, Friedrich Schleiermacher, is equally clear on the church-base of his theology: see *The Christian Faith* (Edinburgh: T. & T. Clark, 1968), pp. 3–12, on proposition 2: "Since Dogmatics is a theological discipline, and thus pertains solely to the Christian Church, we can only explain what it is when we have become clear as to the conception of the Christian Church."

77. The use of the word "community" allows for both organized and nonorganized elements in the social reality of church. For a good summary of some classic sociological studies of these organizational and nonorganizational elements in "religious collectivities," see Roland Robertson, *The Sociological Interpretation of Religion* (New York: Schocken, 1970), esp. pp. 113–50. Note also how James Gustafson interprets the academy as a community of moral discourse in "The University as a Community of Moral Discourse," *JR* (1973), 397–410, and church in a similar manner in the excellent discussion of the church as community in *Treasure in Earthen Vessels: The Church as a Human Community* (New York: Harper & Row, 1961) and in "The Church: A Community of Moral Discourse," in *The Church as Moral Decision Maker* (Philadelphia: Pilgrim, 1970), pp. 83–97.

78. A study of "voluntaryism" may be found in James Luther Adams, "Freedom and Association," in *On Being Human Religiously*, ed. Max Stackhouse (Boston: Beacon, 1976), pp. 57–89; see also James Gustafson, "The Voluntary Church: A Moral Appraisal," in *The Church as Moral Decision Maker*, pp. 109–39; and Dennis McCann's creative use of Habermas' "communicative competence" theory in relationship to the "mainline" churches' responsibility *as voluntary associations* to achieve public discourse for the wider society ("Theology as Public Discourse: A Proposal" [AAR West Division—as yet unpublished]).

79. The studies of William McCready, Andrew Greeley and others at the National Opinion Research Center are invaluable empirical sociological studies of the influence of church traditions on both ethos and world view. Inter alia, see William C. McCready with Andrew M. Greeley, *The Ultimate Values of the American Population* (Beverly Hills: Russell Sage, 1976); Andrew Greeley, *The American Catholic: A Social Portrait* (New York: Basic, 1977).

80. James Gustafson, *Treasure in Earthen Vessels* [77], p. 3.

81. Note the later inner-theological use of the primary roles of community and tradition for mediating the event of Jesus Christ to the contemporary Christian in the Introduction to Part II.

82. The notion of "loyalty" is classically articúlated in Josiah Royce's philosophical theology: see *The Philosophy of Loyalty* (New York: Hafner, 1971) on loyalty and betrayal; and the Pauline concept of the church as Body of Christ in *The Problem of Christianity* (Chicago: Univ. of Chicago, 1968), esp. pp. 229–385.

83. See the careful and constructive Roman Catholic ecclesiological writings of Joseph Komonchak: inter alia, "Ecclesiology and Social Theory: A Methodological Essay, *The Thomist* (forthcoming). Komonchak's work often builds on and develops the magisterial historical and theological work of the major twentieth-century Catholic ecclesiologist, Yves Congar, the methodology of Bernard Lonergan and the social-scientific models of Habermas and Berger-Luckmann: see, for example, his "Lonergan and the Tasks of Ecclesiology" in the forthcoming Lonergan *Festschrift*.

84. See Andrew Greeley, *The Communal Catholic* (New York: Seabury, 1976).

85. For the notion of "denomination," see the classic study of H. Richard Niebuhr, *The Social Sources of Denominationalism* (New York: Meridian, 1970). In Niebuhr's case, see also his theological companion volume, *The Kingdom of*

God in America (New York: Harper, 1959). For Niebuhr's own development of what might be called mutually critical correlations between sociological and theological understandings of the reality "church," see *The Purpose of the Church and Its Ministry* (New York: Harper, 1956). For a more recent sociological study of the role of the denomination in American society, see Andrew Greeley, *The Denominational Society* (Glenview: Scott, Foresman, 1972). For representative essays of modern scholarship on the issue, see Russell E. Richey, ed., *Denominationalism* (Nashville: Abingdon, 1977).

86. For the notion "plausibility structures," see Peter Berger, *The Sacred Canopy* [1], pp. 126–54. Also relevant here is the section "Foundation of Knowledge in Everyday Life," in Berger and Luckmann, *The Social Construction of Reality* [1], pp. 19–47. Note also Van Harvey's analysis of Berger's use of pretheoretical and theoretical "plausibility structures" in "Peter Berger: Retrospect," [1]. See also Robin Gill, *The Social Context of Theology* [1], pp. 43–83.

87. See chap. 2, sec. ii. As the example of H. Richard Niebuhr may already indicate [79], some establishment of mutually critical correlations between sociological and theological understandings of church is needed for a fundamental ecclesiology.

88. For Gordon Kaufman, for example, this would seem to be the only legitimate role that the church could play for theology as distinct from religion: see *An Essay on Theological Method* [57], pp. 3–4. However, my own clear disagreements with Kaufman here can only be warranted (in Kaufman's own public terms) by my later defense of the nonparticularist character of any classic church tradition and any classic church theology: see chap. 3.

89. See especially Avery Dulles' ground-breaking work, *Models of the Church* (New York: Doubleday, 1974); and Richard McBrien, *Catholicism* (Minneapolis: Winston, 1980), pp. 691–728, for two distinct accounts of "models" here. An illuminating companion piece to Dulles' theological models may be found in Thomas O'Meara, "Philosophical Models in Ecclesiology," *TS* (1978), 3–22. O'Meara's comments on the philosophical notion of "sign" and the Heideggerian notion of truth in art and history are especially pertinent to the philosophical side of the theological model of "sacrament" developed in this book. There is need for further similar studies of sociological models of the church-society relationship (as in the work of John Coleman) and of social models operative in the theological models of church (as in the work of Joseph Komonchak).

90. Note that, for the present, only the "gift" character of the reality "church" as "participatory" in the event of Jesus Christ is necessary to establish the strictly *theological* character of church. My interest at the moment is to affirm the reality of the church as a result of grace, not the distinct and further question of church as the means through which grace is mediated. A good treatment of the latter issue in Catholic theology may be found in Jerome Theisen, *The Ultimate Church and the Promise of Salvation* (Collegeville: St. John's Univ. Press, 1976). Readers will already note, I suspect, the clear implication (via the participation language) that in fact I hold to a fuller theological model of church as "sacrament of Christ and eschatological sacrament of world" (Rahner, Schillebeeckx) as the most relatively adequate model—assuming, as I do, that the "sacrament" model can also be interpreted to account for the necessary ecclesial dimensions emphasized in the models "servant," "herald," "prophet" and "institution." One must also assume that the real defects of some traditional uses of the model of church as "sacrament"—namely, aestheticism, ecclesial triumphalism and a sometimes mechanistic notion of the church "supplying" and "causing" grace via efficient and instrumental as distinct from exemplary and symbolic causality—can be undone by the symbolic approach. Note, for example, how Schillebeeckx's sacra-

mental model in his early work can expand to include the more sociocritical faith-praxis demands of his later work without abandoning the model of church as "sacrament of Christ and world." Note also Dulles' arguments for the greater adequacy of the "sacrament" model in *Models* [89], pp. 186–87. My own warrants for this theolgical preference can be established only after further discussion of the church-world relationship (chap. 2), the representative (or sacramental) character of christology (chaps. 6 and 7) and the primary mediating role of church and tradition for theology itself (chaps. 6, 7 and 10). For the present, my concern is simply to show the theological reality of church operative in all fuller theological models of church: viz., its engifted participatory reality in the event of Jesus Christ. To understand that reality is also to understand church as a properly theological reality.

91. On the relationship of church and kingdom, note especially the work of Richard McBrien in *Church: The Continuing Quest* (New York: Newman, 1970) and *Catholicism* [89], pp. 641–729.

92. Note McBrien's analysis of the manual theology of Salaverri (*Catholicism,* pp. 649–61). See also the study of the ecclesiology of the "Roman School" by T. Howland Sanks, *Authority in the Church: A Study in Changing Paradigms* (Missoula: Scholars Press, 1974).

93. See chap. 2, sec. i.

94. See especially Karl Rahner, "Church and World," *Sacramentum Mundi,* I (New York: Herder and Herder, 1968), 346–57, for a theological understanding of the relationship of church and world. A valuable study of Rahner's developments in ecclesiology may be found in the articles of Leo O'Donovan, Peter Schineller, John Galvin and Michael Fahey in "A Changing Ecclesiology in a Changing Church: A Symposium on Development in the Ecclesiology of Karl Rahner," ed. Leo J. O'Donovan, *TS* (1977), 736–63. For an informative study of Rahner's development on the church-world issue, see the unpublished thesis (University of Chicago) of Patrick Lynch, "Church and World in the Theology of Karl Rahner." For alternative political and liberation understandings of the relationship of church and world, see Johann Baptist Metz, *Theology of the World* (New York: Herder and Herder, 1969), pp. 107–140; Jürgen Moltmann, *The Church in the Power of the Spirit* (New York: Harper & Row, 1977); Juan Luis Segundo, *The Community Called Church* (Maryknoll: Orbis, 1973); and Roger Haight, "Mission: The Symbol for Understanding the Church Today," *TS* (1976), 620–49. Rahner's own practical suggestions for church reform may be found in his forthright volume *The Shape of the Church to Come* (New York: Seabury, 1974).

95. The relevant works of Komonchak [83], Adams [78], Baum [1] and Gustafson [77] have already been cited. On the sociological side, note the works of John Coleman [1, 2] and Andrew Greeley [2, 79, 84, 85].

96. For Küng's crucial work here, see especially *The Church* (New York: Sheed and Ward, 1968), *Infallible? An Inquiry* (New York: Doubleday, 1971), and *On Being a Christian* (New York: Doubleday, 1976), pp. 463–530.

97. The general theological warrants for this correlation model may be found in chap. 2; for H. Richard Niebuhr's "mutually critical correlations" model for sociological and theological understandings of church, see n. 85. The *loci classici* for Weber are *The Sociology of Religion* (Boston: Beacon, 1968) and *The Protestant Ethic and the Spirit of Capitalism* (New York: Scribner, 1930). For the debates surrounding Weber's latter thesis, see Roland Robertson [77], pp. 170–81. The classic work of Troeltsch here is *The Social Teachings of the Christian Churches,* 2 vols. (New York: Macmillan, 1950). For some of the recent debates on Troeltsch's church-sect typology, see Robertson, pp. 113–49.

98. Royce [82]; Gabriel Marcel, *Royce's Metaphysics* (Chicago: Regnery, 1956).

99. The classic study of this spectrum remains H. Richard Niebuhr's *Christ and Culture* (New York: Harper, 1951). We will return to Niebuhr's paradigms for fuller discussion in later chapters (see especially chap. 9, sec. i).

100. See Schubert Ogden, *The Reality of God* (New York: Harper & Row, 1966); and Langdon Gilkey, *Naming the Whirlwind: The Renewal of God-Language* (New York: Bobbs-Merrill, 1969), *Catholicism Confronts Modernity* (New York: Seabury, 1975), and *Message and Existence* (New York: Seabury, 1979).

101. On the latter, see the reinterpretation by George Rupp, *Christologies and Cultures* (The Hague: Mouton, 1974), and his defense of "Liberal Christianity" in *Culture-Protestantism: German Liberal Theology at the Turn of the Twentieth Century* (Missoula: Scholars Press, 1977).

102. The sociological notion of "voluntary" is related to but distinct from the theological notion of the "freedom" of the act of faith and the primary mediating role for faith of the community and the tradition. For the moment, the sociological reality of "voluntary" association also has the clear theological advantages noted by Andrew Greeley [85] as well as the theological dangers noted by H. Richard Niebuhr [85]. The theological discussion of church as primary mediator of the Christ event may be found in the Introduction to Part II and in chap. 10.

103. For the role of preunderstanding in all interpretation, see chap. 3; for its role in explicitly theological interpretation, see especially the Introduction to Part II.

104. It seems fair to observe that this "sorting out" should involve at least the following factors: (1) the general model for theology, (2) the general theological understanding of "church" and "world" and their relationship, (3) the fuller theological model for understanding church (as sacrament, institution, servant etc.), and (4) the fuller sociological model for understanding a particular church in a particular relationship to a particular society ("church," "sect," "mystical communion," "denomination," "voluntary association" or "community of moral and religious discourse"). In the present work the following basic factors are operative: (*ad* 1) the general model of mutually critical correlations specified in distinct ways in fundamental, systematic and practical theologies; (*ad* 2) a theological understanding of both "church" and "world" and an assumption of mutually critical correlations between them; (*ad* 3) a primary model of church as sacrament of Christ and eschatological sacrament of world, assuming the possibility of incorporating the primary concerns of the other models; (*ad* 4) the general sociological model of church as "community of moral and religious discourse" as allowing for both organizational and nonorganizational social realities, and the more particular model of "voluntary association" as emphasizing *any* particular church's social reality in a pluralist society. In sum, the sociological realities "society," "academy" and "church" are related here to the theological realities "world" and "church" in terms of the general model of "mutually critical correlations" defended theologically in the following chapter. For a discussion of the further implications for the church-world relationship of the model of church as "eschatological sacrament of world," see chap. 10, n. 29. A recent phenomenological study of faith as social existence (i.e., ecclesial existence) is Edward Farley's *Ecclesial Man: A Social Phenomenology of Faith and Reality* (Philadelphia: Fortress, 1975).

105. For a relevant sociological study of the role of the intellectual in modern society, see Edward Shils, *The Intellectuals and the Powers and Other Essays*

(Chicago: Univ. of Chicago Press, 1972). Shils' work has been employed to provide a sociological study of the Catholic modernists as intellectuals in the Catholic church in the Ph.D. diss. (unpublished) by Lester Kurtz entitled "Scholarship and Scandal."

106. Note Matthew Lamb's phrase "innocent theory" for the difficulty in Enlightenment theory: "The Challenge of Critical Theory" [1], p. 186. The central works of the Frankfurt School on this are Theodor Adorno and Max Horkheimer, *Dialectic of Enlightenment* (New York: Herder and Herder, 1972); and Max Horkheimer, *The Eclipse of Reason* (New York: Seabury, 1974).

107. I have tried to describe the religious dimension of this experience of pluralism in the Catholic tradition in "Theological Pluralism and Analogy," *Thought* (1979), 24–37.

108. For an excellent case study of this decline, see Joseph Haroutounian, *Piety versus Moralism: The Passing of New England Theology* (New York: Holt, 1932).

Chapter 2

A Theological Portrait of the Theologian

Fundamental, Systematic and Practical Theologies

i. A Theological Portrait of the Theologian[1]

If the social portrait of the theologian is marked by a recognition of complexity, the more personal portrait is marked by a recognition of that mixture of good and evil, light and darkness named ambiguity. There is, first, the obvious ambiguity of a single self related in loyalty to three distinct publics. Yet real as that existential situation is, it is more an opportunity for hard thought and creative possibility than for easy *Angst*. The more vital existential fact is that ambiguity inevitably emerges even in our most creative achievements and characterizes even our most profound loyalties.[2] The exact line between loyalty and idolatry is notoriously difficult to mark.

Nor is this situation occasioned simply by that strange kind of free-floating anxiety often characterizing the life of any intellectual in our period. Rather it is caused by a recognition of stubborn fact: One's trust in and loyalty to society, academy and church are real but, if also characterized by the cold eye that should mark intellectual appraisal, inevitably ambivalent. In more strictly theological terms, the situation can be described by understanding the intrinsic ambiguity of both world and church for "faith."[3] Faith is, above all and prior to any articulation of specific beliefs, a matter of fundamental disposition and orientation involving the responses of both real trust and genuine loyalty to the object of faith. For the Christian that faith is always directed to God, the God of Abraham, Isaac, Jacob and Jesus Christ. As Christian thinkers focus on the all-pervasive reality of God, they focus on the person and work of Jesus Christ as their surest, indeed decisive representation of both the nature of the ultimate reality of God and the reality and possibilities of themselves.[4] They recognize that in that singular revelation of God and themselves, the reality of both church and world are coaffirmed as real objects of that same faith in God.[5] On inner-Christian terms, one's trust in and loyalty to the reality of the God disclosed in Jesus Christ finally determine and judge all other loyalties and all trust in all other realities.

In the New Testament itself, the ambivalence of the Christian's relationship to the world is nowhere more clearly seen than in the documents called the Gospel of John and the Johannine epistles. There one can witness Christian ambiguity with clarity.[6] The vision of the "world" portrayed in John includes both profound trust in and loyalty to that world as God's creation and, at the same time, real distrust in that world expressed in denunciation, even in flight from it.[7] The pervasive universalism of John's theological vision[8] is frequently broken by such sectarian notes of exclusiveness and flight from this world of danger and disgust.[9]

As Johannine scholars unravel the Judaic and Hellenistic elements in that extraordinary corpus, they allow a clearer understanding of the particular life settings for this conflict in John. In those documents and most subsequent Christian history, the final relationship of the Christian to the world is and remains an ambivalent one.[10] For myself, the Yahwist and the Christian suspicions of the world do not mandate withdrawal. Indeed, the Christian lives a strange and healing paradox disclosed in John and throughout the scriptures: so deeply into one's existence does the unmasking radicality of the Word strike that the radical contingency and ambiguity of all culture, all civilization, all institutions, even nature itself (in sum, the "world") are unmasked by the same Word which commands and enables work *for* the world, and more concretely for the neighbor. This Christian insight into the conventionality, the arbitrariness, the radical contingency of all culture, all nature and all institutions has a reverse side: the radical ambiguity of all culture, nature, institutions—all the world—and their constant temptation to self-aggrandizement and self-delusion. Yet this very same insight into the radical contingency and real ambiguity of the world posits itself not only by negating all "worldly" pretensions to divinity, atemporality, eternity, but also by positing the command and the possibility of living in and for this contingent, ambiguous, created and divinely beloved "world." Rather than repeating the domesticated slogans that presume to capture this dialectic ("The Christian is *in* the world, but is not *of* it"), it seems more correct to say that the Christian is *released* (the violence of the imagery is exact) *from* the world, *for* the world. The passionate Christian and Yahwist suspicion of the world and its pretensions and delusions—its refusal to face its own contingency and ambiguity—should never become the kind of negation that eventuates in the resentful bitterness of "withdrawal." Rather the Christian should be released for the world *as it really is*: arbitrary, contingent, ambiguous, loved by God and by the Christian. Some sectarian Christians will not abide this ambiguity. They may and will appeal to all those passages in John which denounce and deny the world.[11] Other Christians, like John in his basic ecclesial, not sectarian stance, understand the Christian vision in universal terms, not exclusivist ones.

It is, I suppose, already clear that the present author shares the universalist strand in Christianity as fundamental for Christian self-understanding. Indeed, if one does not, then there is really no problem of three publics for theology. There is only one public: the church, more exactly the exclusive sect of the chosen ones.[12] However, if one does share the Yahwist and Johannine trust in and loyalty to the "world," then the realities of society and academy, the realities of our common human experience and disciplined reflection upon it cannot but enter our theological reflections on strictly theological grounds. The "world" is a theological locus for Christian self-understanding.[13]

And yet the "world" is also, as theology and common human experience alike testify, a profoundly ambiguous reality for any honest observer of the human situation. Is it really possible to live in any society and not observe the blatant injustices, the vicious distortions of truth and decency which human beings and humanly constituted structures and institutions inflict? The corruptions of power, the tragedy at the core of every human life, the ever more subtle exercises in self-justification in each human heart are plain to see. How easily even our best civic virtues can become "splendid vices" is not an insight peculiar to the disturbing genius of Augustine.[14] Is it really possible to live in any academic setting and not note the same passions, the same drives to self-justification at work in the construction of even the most creative products of the intellect and the imagination? Exercises in the genealogy of all our most cherished values and the will to power lurking behind our "purest" truths should not be interpreted as merely an expression of the personal vision of that passionate antitheological theologian, Friedrich Nietzsche.

All these realities seem so incontestably true to experience that it should be unnecessary to cite them once again. And yet it is necessary. So enamored can we become by a correct theological affirmation of the world—and our resultant trust in and loyalty to its concrete expressions like a factual "rough justice" in contemporary American society, and the honesty, integrity and demand for evidence which motivate all intellectual and imaginative work in the academy at its best—that we are tempted to ignore, as John does not, the stark ambiguity of the world. Thereby do we ignore the ambiguity of the publics of society and academy. If such easy liberalism ever had a role in theology, that role is now clearly spent.

And yet a recognition of ambiguity is not a license for easy denunciation, angry sectarianism or, finally, a flight from the Christian affirmation of the world. For ambiguity is, after all, ambiguity. Theologically stated, we must recognize that Christian faith, as trust in and loyalty to God and to Jesus Christ, demands a fundamental trust in and loyalty to the world in all its ambiguity. In the more formal terms appropriate to this analysis, Christian faith demands that every theologian affirm the world and thereby pay heed to the legitimate demands for justice in society and for intellectual integrity in the academy. Except for versions of Christian theology that are explicitly or implicitly sectarian (versions which can always find some peaceable kingdom on that reservation of the spirit which is the modern realm of culture), the universalist thrust of Christian self-understanding demands a real affirmation of the world and thereby a real coming to terms with the publics of society and academy.

The theologian's relationship to the church is characterized by its own ambiguity, itself also occasioned by the ambiguity of the church as an object of loyalty. In Christian self-understanding, to repeat, the church participates in, as primary mediator of, the gift of God in Jesus Christ. The church is a theological reality.[15] As such, the church is an object of faith, of trust in and loyalty to its reality. All passionately sectarian versions of Christianity, as in the exemplary case of Tolstoy,[16] can often treat the reality of the church with the same contempt with which they scorn the world. As Tolstoy makes clear, his honest contempt for the institutional church is occasioned by the same mistrust he accords the world in all its institutions—state, family, economic order. To many sectarians, even those who may lack the passion, genius and single-heartedness embedded in Tolstoy's great refusal, the church can seem and sometimes is simply another corrupt and corrupting institution in a despised world.

Who but a fool would attempt to refute this charge of corruption to the historical reality of the Christian church? An elementary knowledge of Western history alone provides ample evidence for the complicity of the churches, Catholic, Protestant and Orthodox, in the sheer indecencies, the thoughtless injustices, the careless mystifications of our blood-drenched history as a civilization. The ambiguous reality of a combination of goodness and pettiness, of real faith and mean-spiritedness, which we all find in the everyday life of any church should be sufficient evidence that there too one finds real ambiguity. And yet, for Christian self-understanding the church remains an authentic object of faith. The fact that one can and often does experience in the church a genuine community where a word of liberating truth and power is spoken, where a tradition of reverence towards all reality and real faith in God is lived in ritual and in practice, where a call to our best instincts is both empowered and commanded and our consistent attempts at self-justification are exposed with the clarity of the gospel—all these experiential realities are also to be found in the ambiguous life of the church.

Still, it is a theological understanding of church which ultimately counts for each church member. Whatever form its particular church order, however visible or invisible its theological self-understanding, however institutional or communitarian its present actuality, the Christian church remains for Christians an object of trust and loyalty grounded in the gifted reality of that fundamental faith, trust and loyalty to the God of love and power manifested in Jesus Christ. In present, more methodological terms, the church cannot but prove a real public for all Christian theology.

We seem left, therefore, with a dilemma at once intellectual and existential. Each theologian attempts to speak in and to three publics. The demands and the plausibility structures of each public have been internalized to different degrees of intensity in each theologian.[17] That drive to publicness which constitutes all good theological discourse is a drive from and to three publics. Existentially, the theologian accords loyalty to and trust in both church and world.[18] Each strives, as a single self, to recognize that one's fundamental faith and loyalty is to God. Each knows, as a theological interpreter of Christian self-understanding, that faith in God includes fundamental trust in and loyalty to both church and world. Each observes that only God is an ultimate object of loyalty and trust. Each knows that both church and world are as ambiguous in reality as the internal conflicts in the "foul rag and bone shop of the heart." To live with that ambiguity is incumbent upon every Christian. To try to think honestly, critically and clearly in relationship to it is incumbent upon every theologian.

Many theologians, as we shall see below, resolve this dilemma by choosing one of the three publics as their primary reference group. They tend to leave the other two publics at the margins of their consciousnesses. Theologians also recognize, however, that their fundamental trust and loyalty is to the all-pervasive reality of God. Any radically monotheistic understanding of the reality of God, whether classical, process, liberationist or liberal, affirms the strict universality of the divine reality. Whatever else it is, any Christian theology is finally and radically theocentric. This insight into the universal character of the divine reality that is the always-present object of the Christian's trust and loyalty is what ultimately impels every theology to attempt publicness. For God as understood by the Jewish, Christian and Muslim believer is either universal in actuality or sheer delusion. Theology in all its forms is finally nothing else but the attempt to reflect deliberately and critically upon that God. Theology is *logos* on *theos*. Any authentic speech on the reality of God which is really private or particularist is unworthy of that reality. Christianity, when true to its heritage, cannot but recognize that its fundamental faith, its most radical trust and loyalty, is to the all-pervasive reality of the God of love and power disclosed in Jesus Christ.

As individual theologians attempt to understand the many symbols expressive of some major insight into that fundamental faith in God—creation and redemption, Christ and Spirit, sin and grace, church and world—they may be tempted to retreat into the privateness of sectarian views. Yet the existential radicality of that fundamental faith in God should help one see the logical need for universality to correctly understand the divine reality. To speak of a theologian's private universality is, at best, to perpetrate an oxymoron. At worst it is seriously to misunderstand the fundamental reality of God. If this faith in God is serious, then any discourse about it must be universal and public. An understanding of the reality of God finally determines all other theological discourse, just as fundamental trust in and loyalty to God finally determines all one's other loyalties.

Yet rare is the theologian whose theology is always explicitly about God. Indeed, the most God-obsessed thinkers—a Spinoza, a Nietzsche or, in our own period, an Altizer[19]—are often the most violent critics of traditional Jewish and Christian theism. Nor is the failure of a theocentric focus in many theologies simply lamentable. There are, after all, many other central symbols and doctrines in the Christian complex. There are, after all, other real questions and problems which demand theological reflection. And yet, any theological discourse which loses its anchorage to the doctrine of God is no longer theological. That discourse may provide cultural analyses which genuinely disclose some major aspect of the human situation. It may be good cultural discourse. But finally it will not serve as theological discourse.

This theological insight into the radically theocentric character of all theology is, I believe, the insight most needed to inform any theological analysis of the public character of theology.[20] For theologians will and must inevitably speak of many things. They will ordinarily be related to one primary public and secondarily to the other two. Yet if they are not involved, at least implicitly, in speech about God, then they are not involved in public theological discourse. How then does this God-talk relate to the distinct publics and their distinct criteria for publicness? Only a study of the three major disciplines in theology—fundamental, systematic, practical—may free us to see that. For the same kind of public, indeed universal reflection upon the reality of God is distinctly formulated in each discipline with distinct criteria for distinct theological disciplines related to distinct primary publics. In each, the nature of the publicness is finally determined by some understanding of the reality of God. In each that publicness will find distinct formulations and criteria because of the character of the particular theological discipline and the principal public to which it is addressed. And the latter publics—society, academy, church—are accorded theological significance beyond their sociological significance for theology: they are themselves expressive of the theological realities "church" and "world" disclosed as coaffirmed in one's Christian affirmation of God.

To claim the elimination of an otherwise omnipresent ambiguity for the reality of God and God alone must not, of course, be confused with any claim to the adequacy of theological speech about God.[21] Nor may it be confused with any claim that the self's faith in that one unambiguous object and subject of trust and loyalty is itself unambiguous. The assurance of faith never, as St. Paul knew, lacks fear and trembling. Seldom in our age, as Paul Tillich insisted, is real faith unalloyed with genuine doubt.[22] The ambiguity present in each of the public objects of the self's loyalty—church, academy, society—is more than equalled by the irreducible ambiguity in any self, including the self's never-ending struggle to find a loyal and trusting belief in God.

The Christian believes, with Albert Camus, that there is more to admire than to despise in human beings. The very radicality and intensity of the Christian vision of all reality as graced by a loving God heightens a recognition of the giftedness and goodness of all creation, while at the same time intensifying a recognition of the pervasive reality of sin. The Christian understanding of sin is understood *as* sin only in the light of grace.[23] Only then do we fully recognize the horror in the self's eternal struggle to absorb all reality into itself: to force, with both the arrogance of pride and the sloth of self-dispersion,[24] all reality into my needs and my desires or else level it. We make a desert and we call it peace. Only then do I recognize how I am engaged in trying to justify myself constantly before God and all publics: in the final trap, before the ever-shifting publics of my private self. That the self of any one of us is *both* essentially good and actually an uneasy, ambiguous combination of goodness and corruption is a lesson taught by both the Christian tradition and the most radical secular masters of suspicion in our period, Freud and Nietzsche.[25] That lesson is available to anyone still able to believe in either the pure goodness or the unrelieved corruption of the human spirit. The truth is that the reality of the private self is as ambiguous as the realities of society, academy and church. Indeed the latter are but the self writ large. If the shunning of simple nostrums and the recognition of complexity are the hallmarks of the contemporary intellectual, the allied existential recognition of the need to face the essential ambiguity of our actual situation is the hallmark of a sane theological view of reality.

Is it any wonder, then, that theologians will recognize the ambiguous reality of all three publics? We know a society where reason is often reduced to sheer instrumentality, where technology is ever in danger of becoming technocracy—yet a society where the interest of a genuine public good is symbolically, legally and politically affirmed and where a "rough justice" can occasionally prevail. We know an academy where too often Plato is preached while Hobbes is practiced, yet where the interests of critical reason and civilized experience are honored and practiced even in the breach. We know a church where the bureaucrat finds new "outlets" for "input," where mystification and repression can often breathe heavily—but still a public where the gift of God's liberating word is preached, where the sacraments of God's encompassing reality are represented, where the dangerous memory of Jesus is kept alive, where a community of persons who actually live the Christian reality may yet be found. Does it not follow that the theologian should maintain trust in and loyalty to all three publics as experiential-social expressions of world and church as long as loyalty to God remains the first and pervasive loyalty?

In an ambiguous world an ambiguous self can yet find trust. In a broken world where the sense of the reality of the whole often discloses itself as a sense of the eclipse of the reality of God,[26] one can still find a fundamental trust in the very meaningfulness of existence itself and thereby, however indirectly, learn to trust in the reality Christians name God. If that trust is articulated in the properly eschatological terms of Christian self-understanding, then a confident hope for a future clear recognition of God, a hope for a vision of the whole beyond present ambiguity and brokenness is disclosed to Christians in that proleptic illumination named Jesus Christ.[27] A gift that is also a command; an enigma that is also a promise; an ambiguity that is also an assurance—in such terms does the Christian consciousness attempt to understand itself and the encompassing reality.

In the meantime, there is the work of theology for some to do. As they perform that work—now well, now badly—theologians strive for a clarity to illuminate, not dissolve, the mystery of God's reality and the ambiguity of all else. In striving for that clarity, theologians will inevitably strive for publicness. Then they may recognize the reality of three publics of theology grounded in the strictly theological realities church and world, and three distinct but related sets of criteria proper to the claims to meaning and truth in each public grounded in the intrinsic publicness of the affirmation of God. Then they may also decide that some division of labor is necessary. The analysis of one such division—into fundamental, systematic and practical theologies—now demands attention.

ii. Three Disciplines in Theology: Fundamental, Systematic, Practical

Each theologian often seems dominated by a single concern. For some that concern takes the form of a particular thematic focus (salvation-reconciliation-liberation) around which cohere all uses of the broad range of the Christian symbol system and the broad range of experience disclosed by those symbols. For others the wide-ranging symbol system and the equally wide-ranging and more elusive forms of experience and language involved in theological discourse occasion the need to reflect first on the character of theological discourse itself before proceeding to more thematic interests. Moreover, the distinct but related crises of meaning of both Judaism and Christianity in the modern period and, more recently, the crisis of the Enlightenment model of modernity intensify the need for clarification of the character of any claims to public truth. The related phenomena of historical, hermeneutical and sociological consciousness are the chief but not sole forces to occasion the question of the character of theological language at the center of reflective attention for many theologians in our period. The language here is not unimportant. As the first chapter attempted to document, a historical and sociological consciousness *occasions* this reflection; however, as the present chapter argues, a strictly *theological* understanding of the intrinsic publicness, indeed universality of the reality of God present in theological discourse united to the coaffirmation of the publics "church" and "world" in the Christian affirmation of God *causes* this methodological reflection on inner-theological grounds.

This general and familiar set of questions may take the more specific form of seeking ways to express anew the authentically *public* character of *all* theology, whether fundamental theology, systematic theology or practical theology, whether "traditional" or "contemporary." In initially general terms, a public discourse discloses meanings and truths which in principle can transform all human beings in some recognizable personal, social, political, ethical, cultural or religious manner. The key marks of publicness, therefore, will prove to be cognitive disclosure and personal, communal and historical transformation. The fuller meanings of each of these forms of publicness will concern us in this and the following chapters. For example, Christian theological discourse serves an authentically public function when it renders explicit the public character of the meaning and truth embedded in the Christian classical texts, events, images, rituals, symbols and persons.

As we have seen above, when one focusses on the character of theology as an academic discipline one cannot but note certain complexities in the character of the discipline itself. Distinct theologies and distinct disciplines within theology are related to distinct social realities as their primary reference group. It is true, of course, that the university setting of much contemporary theology occasions theological attention upon the public character of any theological statement. The same setting, in its reflection upon theology as an academic discipline, impels the contemporary academic theologian to reflect upon the social realities involved. Since the very choice of the word "public" as a focus for theology logically involves a relationship to those *social* realities called publics, it may prove helpful to continue the earlier analyses by suggesting what differences an emphasis upon one or the other of the three publics of theology actually makes for any particular theology. My hypothesis is that the most helpful way to clarify this complexity is to propose the existence of three distinct but related disciplines in theology: fundamental, systematic, and practical theologies. Each discipline is distinct yet internally related to the other two. Those internal relationships are chiefly determined by the strictly theological needs for publicness (the logical entailment of the affirmation of God) and for attention to the empirical-social-historical realities of three publics (the logical entailment of the coaffirmations of church and world in the affirmation of God). Theology as such remains a single discipline demanding publicness. Theology as focussed primarily on one or the other public may be subdivided into three distinct subdisciplines.

Each of these subdisciplines, moreover, will possess both a historical moment and a constructive one. In short, historical theology, as understood here,[28] is a theological *necessity* and as such internal to each subdiscipline's attempt to be faithful to the "Christian fact." There is a need, therefore, to state the basic meaning of each discipline and the fundamental differences of emphasis that occur in each. The major differences may be grouped under the following rubrics: (1) distinct primary reference groups; (2) distinct modes of argument; (3) distinct emphases in ethical stance; (4) distinct self-understandings of the theologian's personal faith or beliefs; (5) distinct formulations of what primarily counts as meaning and truth in theology.

The first distinction of three "publics" is theologically grounded in the distinction of the coaffirmation of church and world intrinsic to every theology. The last four distinctions are variations on the distinct but related ways by means of which publicness is achieved in each subdiscipline. My claim on the latter, as the entire book will argue, is that these distinctions remain real distinctions, neither separations (the "two-truths" theory of Averroes et al.) nor systematically ambiguous as distinct from analogical. To note the latter as a claim here: the focal meaning for each discipline as a theological discipline is the kind of publicness demanded by the doctrine of God; the distinctions and the relationships occur on the basis of the distinction between church and world as the latter are expressed in the social realities church, academy and society. As will become apparent in further analysis, these real distinctions formulated as distinct disciplines within theology need not lead to the chaos of entirely different understandings of theology itself. A shift of emphasis on any one of the five questions does affect the claims to truth in existing theologies. Whether those same shifts of emphasis lead to real or apparent conflicts only further analysis of each type and its relationships to the other two can determine. My wager here is that to change the more global analysis of conflicting "types" or "models" for theology to a proposal for distinct subdisciplines within theology will lead to clarification of the real and the merely apparent differences among existing proposals for theology.

1. In terms of primary reference groups,[29] *fundamental* theologies are related primarily to the public represented but not exhausted by the

academy. *Systematic* theologies are related primarily to the public represented but not exhausted in the church, here understood as a community of moral and religious discourse and action. *Practical* theologies are related primarily to the public of society, more exactly to the concerns of some particular social, political, cultural or pastoral movement or problematic which is argued or assumed to possess major religious import.

2. In terms of modes of argument, *fundamental* theologies will be concerned principally to provide arguments that all reasonable persons, whether "religiously involved" or not, can recognize as reasonable. It assumes, therefore, the most usual meaning of public discourse: that discourse available (*in principle*) to all persons and explicated by appeals to one's experience, intelligence, rationality and responsibility, and formulated in arguments where claims are stated with appropriate warrants, backings and rebuttal procedures.[30] *Systematic* theologies will ordinarily show less concern with such obviously public modes of argument.[31] They will have as their major concern the re-presentation, the reinterpretation of what is assumed to be the ever-present disclosive and transformative power of the particular religious tradition to which the theologian belongs. *Practical* theologies will ordinarily show less explicit concern with all theories and theoretical arguments. They will assume praxis as the proper criterion for the meaning and truth of theology, praxis here understood generically as practice informed by and informing, often transforming, all prior theory in relationship to the legitimate and self-involving concerns of a particular cultural, political, social or pastoral need bearing genuine religious import.

3. In terms of ethical stances, other real differences emerge.[32] *Fundamental* theologies will be concerned principally with the ethical stance of honest, critical inquiry proper to its academic setting. *Systematic* theologies will be concerned principally with the ethical stance of loyalty or creative and critical fidelity to some classical religious tradition proper to its church relationship. *Practical* theologies will be concerned principally with the ethical stance of responsible commitment to and sometimes even involvement in a situation of praxis. Sometimes, as in appeals to "solidarity," that commitment will be to the goals of a particular movement or group addressing a particular and central issue.

4. In terms of religious stances, certain differences also emerge. Both *systematic* and *practical* theologians will ordinarily assume personal involvement in and commitment to either a particular religious tradition or a particular praxis movement bearing religious significance (often, as in Johann Baptist Metz, Jürgen Moltmann, Gustavo Gutierrez, James Cone, Rosemary Ruether, and Juan Luis Segundo, to both). *Fundamental* theologies in fact ordinarily share that commitment but in principle will abstract themselves from all religious "faith commitments" for the legitimate purposes of critical analysis of all religious and theological claims.[33]

They will insist upon the need to articulate the arguments for theological discourse as openly public arguments in the obvious sense of argued, reasoned positions open to all intelligent, reasonable and responsible persons.

5. In terms of expressing claims to meaning and truth,[34]—claims, therefore, to a genuinely public character—the following differences are also present and will receive the major attention of the present analysis:

Fundamental theologies will ordinarily be principally concerned to show the adequacy or inadequacy of the truth-claims, usually the cognitive claims, of a particular religious tradition.[35] They will do so usually by employing some explicit paradigm for what constitutes objective argumentation in some acknowledged discipline in the wider academic community. Usually that other discipline will be philosophy or the philosophical dimension of one of the social sciences or humanities: hence the frequent use of the phrase "philosophical theology" to describe the same kind of task here labelled "fundamental theology."[36]

Systematic theologies will ordinarily assume (or assume earlier arguments for) the truth-bearing character of a particular religious tradition. They will thereby focus upon reinterpretations and new applications of that tradition for the present. In that sense, systematic theologies are principally hermeneutical in character—although, as we shall see, that focus also raises the questions of both meaning and truth, the latter usually as disclosure through hermeneutical retrieval.

Practical theologies will ordinarily analyze some radical situation of ethical-religious import (sexism, racism, classism, elitism, anti-Semitism, economic exploitation, environmental crisis, etc.) in some philosophical, social-scientific, culturally analytic or religiously prophetic manner. They will either assume or argue that this situation is *the* (or at least *a*) major situation demanding theological involvement, commitment and transformation. In terms of truth-claims, therefore, involvement in transformative praxis and a theological articulation of what that involvement entails will be assumed or argued as predominant over all theological theories. The notion of truth involved will prove a praxis-determined, transformative one.[37]

If the description above is accurate, then it becomes clear that a radical if not chaotic pluralism of paradigms on what constitutes theology as a discipline and thereby on the public character of theology is likely to occur. It is necessary, therefore, to study more closely what kinds of arguments cross the more radical lines of difference, and then what kinds of public discussion of the remaining major differences among various types of theology can profitably occur.

Some Constants and Differences in Theological Discussion

The route from a chaotic pluralism to a responsible one within any discipline demands that all conversation partners agree to certain basic rules for the discussion. In fact, among theologians such agreement does occur in spite of their real differences. Central among those already existing rules would be the following.

All theologians agree to the appropriateness, usually the necessity, of appeals to a defended interpretation of a particular religious tradition and a defended interpretation of the contemporary "situation" from which and to which the theologian speaks. Moreover, even within the very general confines of this fundamental agreement, two further constants are maintained.

First Constant: Interpretation of a Religious Tradition

In keeping with the demand that a theological position be warranted by appeals to a religious tradition, all theologians are inevitably involved in interpretation. This implies that some method of interpretation of religious texts and history will be implicitly or explicitly employed and defended. Since the general issues of hermeneutical and historical interpretation can be argued on extra-theological grounds, it seems imperative for each theologian to render explicit her/his general method of interpretation.[38] Included in that explication should be arguments defending any claim that the general rules of interpretation may have to be changed in order to interpret religious texts or events.[39]

In sum, theologians should feel obliged to develop explicit "criteria of appropriateness" whereby their specific interpretations of the tradition may be judged critically by the wider theological community. For example, consider the present theological discussion in Christian theology between some major forms of "existentialist" interpretations of the New Testament and some major forms of "liberation" or "political" interpretations of the same document. The latter often insist upon the need to employ such Old Testament categories as the Exodus symbol in order properly to interpret the New Testament envisionment of human salvation as communal, political and social liberation. The former often insist that a distinctive characteristic of the New Testament basic vision of salvation is precisely its radicalization of interest in the individual as an authentic self.

All or most of the prevailing differences outlined earlier are in fact usually involved in those conflicting interpretations of the basic understanding of salvation in the same document. Still, if a public discussion of these differences is to occur, it remains legitimate, even imperative that all interpreters agree to bracket all other differences for the moment so that a purely hermeneutical argument can ensue over which particular interpretations the texts support without further extra-hermeneutical backings or warrants. Once that argument is clarified, the conversation partners may then move on to the equally relevant issue of the present truth-status of the interpreted meanings. If that conversation does not occur, however, it is all too likely that not merely hermeneutical differences will be present.

Rather, all the issues at once—and all differences obscuring this crucial hermeneutical constant—will emerge to obscure the adjudicable conflict of interpretations and result in a nonconversation between these different theologies.

Second Constant: Interpretation of the Religious Dimension of the Contemporary Situation

In keeping with the demand that a theological position appeal to some analysis of the contemporary situation, all theologians are also involved in another constant of theological discussion. This second constant is more elusive than the first, since some theologians argue for the admissibility of appeals to contemporary "experience" as warrants for a theological statement while others deny this. On theological grounds, some theologians, as we saw earlier, share the more affirmative and universal understanding of the Johannine understanding of world or, alternatively, of the Jewish and Christian affirmation of the essential goodness of creation. Thereby these theologians consider the world and the contemporary situation a fully appropriate locus for theological reflection. Other theologians are far more impressed with the negative understanding of "world" in the more sectarian and exclusivist aspects of the Johannine tradition or, alternatively, more convinced of the centrality of a sense of radical fallenness than of essential created goodness. The latter will ordinarily reject any appeal to the world (e.g., to "common human experience") as warrants for a theological statement.

Even in the latter case, however, some understanding of the contemporary "situation" and some, even if negative, appraisal of that situation will be employed explicitly or implicitly. The influence of the cultural shock of the post–World War I crisis of European civilization was obviously influential upon (not, of course, determinative of) Karl Barth's rigorous stance against all appeals to common human experience or even to religious experience in the crisis theology of his *Romans*. The shock of an all-encompassing technology is obviously influential upon the stances of such distinct prophetic voices in contemporary theology as Daniel Berrigan, Jacques Ellul, John Howard Yoder and William Stringfellow.[40] Whether positive or negative in the appraisal of the contemporary situation, every theologian is involved in some implicit or explicit assumptions about it. This occurs even when the present culture is judged demonic (which is, let us recall, an explicitly religious category) by certain theological analyses of a religious dimension of the present culture.

Whatever particular interpretation of the phenomenon "religion" a theologian follows, each theologian assumes or argues for an understanding of religion as, in some manner, involving particular responses from a particular religious tradition to certain fundamental questions of the meaning of human existence. This implies, negatively, a reasoned refusal to consider as adequate any strictly reductionist interpretation of "religion":

for example, the position that religion is really "art" or "ethics" or "bad science" without remainder.[41] This position also implies that although theologians will often share specific methodological commitments with their colleagues in "religious studies," the scholar in religious studies may, but the theologian must, bear the obligation of rendering explicit the question of truth. That question bears upon two principal realities: an interpretation of claims to truth in the most pressing, fundamental questions in the contemporary situation; second, the claims to truth in the responses of a particular religious tradition.

Even before the difficult question of what constitutes a genuinely public claim to truth in theology is addressed, there is one common assumption among all theologians. That assumption is the need to provide some analysis of the contemporary situation insofar as that situation expresses a genuinely "religious" question, i.e., a fundamental question of the meaning of human existence. A public discussion within the wider theological community is entirely appropriate, therefore, on two major issues: first, whether the situation is accurately analyzed (usually this proves an extra-theological discussion); second, why this situation is said to bear a religious dimension and/or import and thereby merits or demands a theological response.[42]

To cite a "liberal" example of this enterprise: If available social-scientific evidence refutes the particular model for "secularization" employed in earlier secular theologies like those of Harvey Cox or John A. T. Robinson, then this obviously affects the appraisal of the further arguments on the religious dimension of that secularization.[43] To cite a radically conservative example: If the complexity of present technological society is not adequately analyzed by either Jacques Ellul or by some theologians employing some interpretations of Heidegger's understanding of technology, then this obviously affects one's appraisal of the adequacy of the theological analysis of the religious (here often as "demonic") character of present technology.

Although the presence of these two sets of demands and criteria by no means resolves all the important differences among models for "theology" as a discipline, it does clarify certain crucial constants which cut across theological boundaries.[44] The second set of questions, moreover, may serve to indicate when a position in "religious studies"—whether sociology of religion, psychology of religion, cultural anthropology, history of religions, or philosophy of religion—is *also* on this account an implicitly or explicitly theological position.

The Major Differences: What Constitutes a Public Claim to Truth in Theology

Every theologian provides both interpretations of a religious tradition and interpretations of the religious dimension of the contemporary situation. Every theologian, therefore, provides some interpretation of the meaning and meaningfulness of the religious tradition for the present situation. The logic of those interpretations forces the question of the *truth*—of the questions and the responses in the tradition and the questions and responses in the situation—to the forefront of any genuinely theological discussion.

This is the case even more when one also recognizes that the central subject matter of all theology, the reality of God, demands by the very universality of its claims to meaning and truth a public explication of such claims. On the question of what constitutes truth, therefore, radical pluralism erupts in theology with a vengeance. Yet to pose the question of the claims to truth to all three disciplines in theology seems entirely appropriate if one grants that each theology in fact asserts the "truth" of its position.[45] The constant in this second and more complex discussion, therefore, is the articulation of *some* kind of truth-status to any particular theological position. My wager is that if the distinct models for truth are rendered explicit, then both the truly significant differences and similarities among theological disciplines might surface. Minimally, this explication would allow for a clearer discussion of all claims to truth in the inevitable clashes which will ensue.[46] Maximally, this explication may serve to warrant my proposal that there are three distinct but related disciplines constituting theology.

Fundamental Theology[47]

Fundamental theologies share the two constants articulated above. Yet their defining characteristic is a reasoned insistence on employing the approach and methods of some established academic discipline to explicate and adjudicate the truth-claims of the interpreted religious tradition and the truth-claims of the contemporary situation. With historical origins in the logos theologies of Philo and Justin Martyr,[48] these theologies ordinarily possess a strongly "apologetic" cast, sometimes reformulated as "fundamental" theologies.

The major discipline usually employed is, of course, philosophy or the "philosophical" dimension of some other discipline. Philosophy as a self-constituting discipline continues to be the discipline especially well suited for the task of explication and adjudication of the kind of truth-claims involved in "religious answers" to "fundamental questions." Granted the pluralism of methods and approaches within philosophy itself, still any genuinely philosophical discussion will inevitably raise and explicate the issue of truth.

For example, in recent theologies there exist various implicit or explicit criteria for the truth of theological claims. Some employ a correspondence model—whether verification, falsification or neo-Scholastic.[49] Others employ a coherence model—whether the strict coherence model of Thomas Torrance or the "rough coherence" model of Reinhold Niebuhr.[50] Others employ an experiential model for truth—whether in "softer" ontic claims to existential meaningfulness, or stronger ontological claims to adequacy to human experience.[51] Others employ a disclosure model—whether the modest Anglo-American linguistic model explicit in Ian Ramsey and implicit in several theologies of story, or the strong claims for truth as disclosure-concealment of Heideggerian theologies.[52] Others employ a praxis or transformation model—whether the implied transformation of radical alienation through personal involvement of many liberation theologians, or the explicitly transformational model for religious meaning and truth present in Bernard Lonergan's notion of "conversion."[53] Still others employ in effect a consensus model of varying degrees of sophistication.[54] In any case, an explicitly philosophical analysis of the model implicitly or explicitly employed and its success or failure in application cannot but advance the analysis. Systematic and practical theologies may be more implicit than explicit on models and criteria for truth in theology. Fundamental theologies must prove explicit and will thereby help to explicate the criteria implicitly present in all theological proposals.

In fundamental theologies, therefore, arguments will be formulated in harmony with the rules of argument usually articulated in a particular philosophical approach. The theologian will employ those arguments first to explicate the truth-claims and then to adjudicate them. The most obvious strength of this position is its ability, indeed its insistence, that all theological statements be explicated and defended in a recognizably public way. More exactly, the word "public" here refers to the articulation of fundamental questions and answers which any attentive, intelligent, reasonable and responsible person can understand and judge in keeping with fully public criteria for argument.

The argument for this approach to theology takes various forms. Ordinarily, however, certain standard defenses will be adopted. There are inner-theological reasons for this task. More exactly there exist warrants in the Christian tradition for a task like that of fundamental theology. Above all, the Christian doctrine of God renders explicit a particular interpretation of the whole of reality.[55] That interpretation logically demands public, philosophical analysis of that universalist interpretation by all reasonable persons. Hence the tradition, within theology itself, for arguments on the existence and nature of God.[56] The doctrines of creation and the universal salvific will of God provide further warrants for this exercise. The universalism of the basic Johannine and Lucan traditions, the clear implications of Paul's charge in Romans 1:28ff that all are "without excuse" and the Lucan Areopagus speech in Acts provide classical scriptural warrants for this understanding of theology's task. The emergence of logos theologies in Justin, Clement and Origen, the philosophical theologies of Augustine, Aquinas and the Scholastics, the traditions of different apologetic theologies, natural theologies, philosophical theologies and fundamental theologies throughout the history of Christian theology provide warrants for this task from the tradition itself.

In short, either the public character of the fundamental questions which religion addresses (from the side of the "situation") or the fully public character of the responses that any major religious tradition articulates (from the side of the tradition) demand a theological discipline which will investigate and correlate, through mutually critical correlations, questions and responses in *both* situation and tradition. That discipline is here called fundamental theology.

From the "existential" viewpoint of the fundamental theologian, moreover, even if in fact the theologian is a believer in the tradition, in principle as a fundamental theologian (i.e., as one bound by the discipline itself to interpret and reflect critically upon the claims of both tradition and situation), the theologian should argue the case (pro or con) on strictly public grounds that are open to all rational persons. In all arguments in fundamental theology, therefore, personal faith or beliefs may not serve as warrants or backings for publicly defended claims to truth. Instead, some form of philosophical argument (usually either implicitly or explicitly metaphysical) will serve as the major warrants and backings for the claims to truth. These last two factors (understood in the context of the larger, inner-theological argument) clearly distinguish this model of theology existentially from the two remaining models and just as clearly relate it primarily to the public of the academy where disciplined and critical reflection is incumbent upon all.[57]

Systematic Theology[58]

The systematic theologian's major task is the reinterpretation of the tradition for the present situation. All serious interpretation of the tradition for the situation is called systematic theology.[59] Since there are no reasons why anyone holding this position need reject the two "constants" outlined earlier,[60] disagreements between this position and the first must take a different form. One form of argument for systematic theologies (which are ordinarily also church theologies) can be articulated on public, philosophical grounds. The remaining chapters of Part One of this work will develop the fuller argument. For the moment, however, the skeletal character of that argument and its possibly intuitive appeal need some initial and summary expression.

There are inner-theological reasons for doing systematic theology. Indeed, the same doctrine of God which so informs the fundamental theologian's insistence that public discussion of the reality of God as the referent of both our fundamental trust in the worthwhileness of existence and the reality of the whole articulated in various metaphysical systems also informs the systematic theologian's more "confessional" perspective. Here, however, the understanding of the Christian doctrine of God will yield a different emphasis. Where the fundamental theologian will relate the reality of God to our fundamental trust in existence (our common faith), the confessional systematic theologian will relate that reality to their arguments for a distinctively Christian understanding of faith.[61] Indeed every systematic theologian will agree that Luther speaks for the entire Christian tradition when he stated, "Faith and God—these two belong together."

Like Luther, the confessional systematic theologian will insist that the "faith" in question must be authentic, full Christian faith with its trust in and loyalty to the God of Abraham, Isaac, Jacob and Jesus Christ. Otherwise one will not know (or, more cautiously, will not theologically know) that the doctrine of God articulated in a particular theology is real or an idol. The inner-Christian drive to universality, the common faith disclosed by Christianity and the sense of a whole still present in our broken world drives the fundamental theologian to critical philosophical reflection. In an analogous manner, the biblical fear of idolatry, the biblical sense of a fallenness that affects even reason, the biblical insistence that philosophical wisdom cannot judge the gift of faith, drive the systematic theologian to a confessional position.[62] The confessionalist may appeal for warrants to aspects of John and especially to certain central themes in Paul which the more universalist fundamental theologian will account for otherwise.[63] It would be too strong to say that sin more than grace, radical redemption rather than the good of creation, the cross more than resurrection or incarnation determines the confessional position of systematic theology. Yet usually the sense of sin will be strong and the symbol of cross will play a central illuminative role for major neoorthodox Protestant systematic positions[64] just as a strong sense of the "supernatural" and a "high" incarnational christology will often play equally central roles in confessional Anglican, Roman Catholic and Orthodox theologies.[65]

Nor is the confessionalist position likely to lack resources from the contemporary intellectual situation to warrant its claims to publicness.[66] Indeed, as the most sophisticated model for a confessional theology in contemporary theology, H. Richard Niebuhr's subtle and careful position, demonstrates,[67] a confessional position in theology can unite with a profoundly modern sense of historical relativity without collapsing into the privateness of either Christian sectarianism or secularist relativism. The perspectivism[68] which informs all claims to universality (including those, as the confessional theologian is sure to observe, of all metaphysical systems) is the basic leitmotif in this viewpoint on the present situation. When joined to a strong biblical sense of idolatry grounded in a Christian theological sense of the sovereignty of God,[69] the public plausibility of the confessional position seems secure. Christian theology, therefore, should not hesitate to begin with its own inner history and reflect upon its own special occasion or illuminating event as the properly self-evidencing reality of its real foundation.[70]

Nor will this confessional position be merely private or untested. Not only will it allow for a rational image which permits abstraction of general ideas which are illustrated on other occasions.[71] Not only will it allow the views of others (histories external to the community) to inform but not determine its own self-understanding. It will also demand a constant dialectic (or, as stated above, mutually critical correlations) between formulations of the revelatory tradition and the contemporary experience of the theologian. Christian systematic theology, therefore, is as fully aware of its perspectival character as any other historically conscious position in modern culture. Christian theology, in fact, consists in explicating in public terms and in accordance with the demands of its own primary confessions, the full meaning and truth of the original "illuminating event" (or, more modestly, with William A. Christian, the "illuminating suggestion")[72] which occasioned and continues to inform its understanding of all reality. Claims that a discipline, any discipline, can achieve more publicness than this for its truths are misguided. For all metaphysical or general philosophical claims to universality are, in the confessional view, suspect to a historically conscious mind.[73] All theological claims to the formulation of universal truth must be put under the strictly theological hermeneutics of suspicion of "idolatry." Whatever publicness is humanly achievable to disciplined reflection, so the argument runs, is accomplished by all genuine Christian confessional systematic theology related principally to the "public" of the church and articulated in the public of the academy as one expression of the theological reality of "world."

The systematic theologian might also argue that it is a mistaken judgment to assume that only the model for objective, public argument employed in fundamental theologies can serve as exhaustive of what functions as genuinely public discourse even for the academy. Indeed, as Hans-Georg Gadamer, for example, has argued on strictly philosophical grounds,[74] "belonging to" a tradition (presuming it is a major tradition which has produced classics) is unavoidable when one considers the intrinsic, indeed ontic and ontological historicity of our constitution as human selves. Moreover, tradition is an ambiguous but still enriching, not impoverishing reality. Any serious recognition of the radical finitude of any single thinker's reflection and the wealth of experience, insight, judgment, taste and common sense which enculturation into a major tradition offers enriches all participants willing to be "formed" by that tradition. Any major church tradition meets these general qualifications for an authentic ambiguous and enriching tradition. The reinterpretation of that tradition by committed and informed thinkers in the tradition is the goal and drive of all systematic theology. In that wider cultural sense, such reflection is private, not public.

Finally, the Enlightenment "prejudice against prejudices" (as prejudgments) which is said to inform the earlier model for public truth disallows crucial human possibilities for meaning and truth. In art, as we shall see at length later, this prejudice against prejudgment disallows any experience of the disclosure of the truth by the work of art. In effect, Enlightenment prejudices have destroyed the truth-disclosure of the work of art by removing its event-character as a disclosure of truth. The work of art then becomes merely another object over against an autonomous subject. Since the subject already possesses exhaustive criteria for "truth," he or she feels free to judge all artistic truth on spuriously "unprejudiced" grounds. Eventually all judgments become a matter of "taste."

On this reading, the "enlightened" bourgeois critic with an all-embracing subjective and ultimately consumerist taste is the one guilty of privateness, not the critic who recognizes the essentially public character of any genuine work of art or any authentic religion. Indeed, in the modern situation of technology where appeals to "reason" become defined ever more narrowly until only instrumental reason is allowed, it is all too easy for interpreters of both art and religion to become philistines. There is a long and slippery slope from Schleiermacher's "cultured despisers" to contemporary cultural consumers and their understanding of the entire realm of culture as private and marginal to the wider public of society. Every society's self-understanding in the academy can be affected when the "humanities" become marginal to the "harder" pursuit of reason and truth in the scientific community. The presence of the philistine in art is well recorded since Matthew Arnold's time. The presence of the modern philistine in religion is a story yet to be told. For the philistine by definition must disallow any disclosure of further meaning and truth than that already articulated in the controls of one's ever more "objective" criteria and unfailing taste. The rest is a matter of private taste, personal preference and consumer needs.

In an analogous fashion, religion, like art, discloses new resources of meaning and truth to anyone willing to risk allowing that disclosure to "happen." It will happen, the systematic-as-hermeneutical theologians believe, by faithful attendance to, and thereby involvement in and interpretation of, the truth-disclosure of genuinely new possibilities for human life in any classical religious tradition of taste, tact and common (communal) sense.

On this understanding, the theologian's task must be primarily hermeneutical. Yet this is not equivalent to being unconcerned with truth, unless "truth" is exhaustively defined on strictly Enlightenment and increasingly instrumentalist terms. Rather the theologian, in risking faith in a particular religious tradition, has the right and responsibility to be "formed" by that tradition and community.[75] Then a communal taste, a faithful tact, a reverential and public judgment may be expressed through the reinterpretations of the tradition in new systematic theologies.

Moreover, since every interpretation involves application to the present situation, every theological interpretation will be a new interpretation. The criteria for judging its appropriateness, therefore, will be the general criteria for all good interpretation. The criteria for judging its truth include the "disclosure" possibilities of new meaning and truth for the situation to which the interpretation is applied.[76]

This argument is dependent upon the assumption that "classics"—understood as those texts, events, images, persons, rituals and symbols which are assumed to disclose permanent possibilities of meaning and truth—actually exist. If classics do not exist, we may have *tradita* but not authentic tradition as *traditio.* Since even their most skeptical critics grant that the Hebrew and Christian traditions do include classical texts, the hermeneutical theologians can argue that they perform a genuinely public function for both society and academy analogous to the philosopher's interpretation of the classics of philosophy or the literary critic's interpretation of the classics of literature.

Insofar as the hermeneutical theologians articulate the truth-disclosure of the reality of God embedded in the tradition for the contemporary situation—insofar, therefore, as they provide good, new interpretations of that reality for the present situation—they too provide theological truth and they too employ a model of mutually critical correlations between interpretations of the tradition for the situation.

In sum, if this brief analysis is accurate, then a case can be made for the public character of the systematic theologian's work as a hermeneutical theologian. "Truth" in systematics, as we shall see below, ordinarily functions in some form of "disclosure" model implied in all good interpretation. With that working model for the universality of the hermeneutical task as the task of all disciplined reflection, a fidelity to and involvement in a classical religious tradition ("faith" or "belief in") can function as an appropriate theological stance.

It follows that the primary reference group of the systematic theologian will be the church as the primary mediator of the tradition. It does not follow that this will render systematic work private for either society and academy—provided the case for the authentic publicness of the real disclosure of truth that is always already present in every cultural classic, and some disclosure of the reality of God present in every theological classic, is recognized.[77] The notion of the religious classic as a cultural classic can assure the entry of all theological classics into the public realm of culture. The notion of the theological classic as grounded theologically in the affirmation of the doctrine of God and the coaffirmation of the theological realities of church and world can assure the theological admissibility of the claims to public truth as disclosure in all good hermeneutical, systematic theologies. Arguments for both those claims will be the major burden of the remaining chapters of this work. For the present, this analysis may serve as a statement of a thesis that may prove intuitively correct or intuitively dubious to the reader. If the thesis is wrong, then systematic theology should be eliminated and only fundamental and/or practical theologies should really be allowed to function as theological disciplines. If the thesis is correct, and if it is also correct to defend the disciplinary status of fundamental and practical theologies, then the complex relationships among all three disciplines in theology must be reexamined. The present work will confine its primary attention to the relationships between fundamental and systematic theologies with some attention to the claims to meaning and truth of practical theology, a task to which we now turn.

Practical Theologies

Many contemporary theologians insist that any theory or argument in theology must now yield to the demands of praxis.[78] This insistence has occasioned both an enrichment and some confusion on the contemporary theological scene. One clear negative proposal unites the diverse theologies of praxis. The positive proposals on the meaning of both praxis and theory and their interrelationships, however, are actually diverse if not conflicting. The clear negative proposal is this: Since any understanding of praxis regards human action as what we actually do or probably or possibly can do, any merely technical understanding of praxis as mere practice (more exactly as mechanically and routinely applied theory) must be negated.[79] Hence the employment of the ancient Greek word "praxis" rather than the more familiar "practice."

One clear positive proposal also unites theologians of praxis before the major differences occur: Any proper understanding of praxis demands some form of authentic personal involvement and/or commitment. Any individual becomes who he or she is as an authentic or inauthentic subject by actions in an intersubjective and social-historical world with other subjects and in relationship to concrete social and historical structures and movements. Praxis, therefore, must be related to theory, not as theory's application or even goal as in all conscious and unconscious mechanical notions of practice or technique. Rather praxis is theory's own originating and self-correcting foundation, since all theory is dependent, minimally, on the authentic praxis of the theorist's personally appropriated value of intellectual integrity and self-transcending commitment to the imperatives of critical rationality. In that sense, praxis sublates theory, not vice-versa.

If we desire to determine criteria of adequacy for meaning and truth, therefore, we must understand the foundational role of praxis in relationship to theory.[80] We must, by theory's own internal imperatives, pay constant attention to the authenticity or inauthenticity (at the limit, the radical alienation) of the truth-teller's subjectivity. For some theologians of praxis, the clearest, sometimes the sole test for the authenticity or inauthenticity of the subject's truth-telling is whether one speaks the truth by doing the truth.[81] We can discern the reality of the latter by our actual involvement in some particular social, cultural, economic, political or religious movement where true or authentic praxis lives. The more particular forms of theologies of praxis range from emphases upon involvement in particular cultural-historical activity (as in many "theologies of culture") to liberal sociopolitical reform (as in "social gospel" theologies) to radical Marxist revolutionary praxis (as in some liberation theologies).[82]

The most familiar form of praxis-oriented theologies in contemporary theology are the various political theologies and the theologies of liberation.[83] In the latter case, for example, one often finds the insistence that only personal involvement in and commitment to the struggle for liberating transformation of some particular societal evil (economic exploitation and dependency, sexism, racism, anti-Semitism, elitism, exploitation of the environment) will free the theologian to see and speak the truth by doing the truth in solidarity with all those in the cause. For many theologians of liberation, for example, it follows that the major problematic of most forms of fundamental theology, the problem of the truth-status of the cognitive claims of both Christianity and modernity, cannot in principle be resolved by better theories. For the norms of all theories are, in fact, grounded in the value of theorizing. Those norms include a nonobjectified reality which is not theoretical (viz., the theoretician's own emancipated or alienated subjectivity). Norms are ultimately grounded not in the self-evident axioms of further theories but in the concrete intellectual, moral and religious praxis of concrete human beings in distinct societal and historical situations.

In fundamentally classical, usually Aristotelian formulations of this emphasis upon praxis, like those of Bernard Lonergan or Eric Voegelin, the position will emphasize the constant need for personal transformation or "conversion" in all theoreticians.[84] Indeed, the theologian, in Lonergan's judgment, grounds the truth-status of all properly theological discourse ultimately on the "foundation" of the concrete, radically personal but neither private nor individualist basis of the theologian's own self-transcending subjectivity as one who is intellectually, morally and religiously "converted."[85] The cognitive "therapy"[86] provided by a book like *Insight* must be matched by a moral therapy from satisfactions to values and a religious therapy grounded in the radical and transformative gift of God's grace experienced as a state of "being-in-love-without-restriction."

Philosophical meaning and truth are irreducibly grounded in the intellectual conversion of an attentive, intelligent, rational and responsible self-appropriating thinker.[87] Moral meaning and truth are grounded in the moral conversion of an agent possessing a character that recognizes true values along with a reflective phronesis grounding all moral judgments.[88] Religious meaning and truth are grounded in the gift of God's grace, transforming our "hearts of stone into hearts of flesh" and enabling us thereby to cooperate with that graced state through religious actions and a reflective discernment of spirits. In that sense, Lonergan joins such quite different theologians of praxis as Edward Schillebeeckx and Johann Baptist Metz to insist that orthopraxis must ground orthodoxy. Like them, however, he is careful to insist that "doing the truth" also involves "saying the truth."[89]

In terms of claims to truth, theologies of praxis employ what I believe can be labelled a transformation model for truth. More exactly, they argue that theological truth is ultimately grounded in the authentic and transformative praxis of an intellectually, morally and religiously transformed human subject. Although Lonergan rigorously criticizes Aristotle's formulation of science in the *Posterior Analytics,* he joins the Aristotle of the *Ethics* and the *Politics* to insist upon a transformative ethic of agency, character and phronesis, and joins the mainline Christian tradition in understanding the transformative reality of faith as first a matter of orientation, trust and loyalty (*fides qua*) that grounds all right beliefs (*fides quae*). The imperatives of "speaking the truth" (alternatively, the problem of "cognitive claims") are real. Yet they will be treated as the reality they in fact are only by a transformed subject involved in doing the truth.[90]

The role of the practical theologian in this view, moreover, must not be misunderstood as the application of theological theories worked out elsewhere.[91] For every form of "mediated theology" is, in fact, grounded in the transformative praxis of the authentic intellectual, moral and religious conversion of the individual theologian and community.[92] For Lonergan, only an interdisciplinary collaboration among properly transformed theologians can assure that any individual or communal theological study of concrete issues will pay sufficient attention to the personal and communal self-correcting process of both self-transcending learning and self-transformative action.

Any attempt to formulate criteria for theological truth which ignores the foundational reality of praxis as transformed authentic subjectivity is likely to fail. For inattention to the necessary transformations of the theologian's subjectivity will eventually mean that the foundational and highly personal but not individualist praxis element ultimately grounding the meaning and truth of theory itself will be neglected. The theoretician will then be left with theories which may or may not emerge from these authentic praxis criteria. All theoretical claims to meaning and truth in theology, therefore, must be subject to a dialectical analysis forged to discern the presence or absence of intellectual, moral and religious "conversions."[93] Only radical and enduring personal transformation can assure the presence of truth.[94] This may seem peculiar, Lonergan admits, to those concerned with an objectivity so pure that it does not recognize its own character as a "self-transcending" subjectivity. Yet the destructive innocence of any notion of objectivity ungrounded in the transformative reality of authentic subjectivity is exactly what theologians most need to exercise in their pursuit of truth. Indeed, "interest in praxis in the academy," Lonergan affirms, "is only likely to occur after the age of innocence has passed."[95]

The more familiar use of a praxis insistence for determining the truth-status of theological statements, however, may be found not in such classical understandings of praxis as those of Lonergan, Voegelin and others but in the theological use of some form of Hegelian-Marxist analysis on the dialectical relationships of theory and praxis. Whether concentrating upon infrastructural elements in society as in more traditional forms of Marxism, or upon both infra and suprastructural or cultural-political elements,[96] many "political theologians" in Europe and North America, as well as liberation theologians in both the Third World and among oppressed groups in the First World, employ some variant of Marxist analysis for understanding praxis. Sometimes that form is straightforwardly Marxist, as in attempts to unmask the latent economic and class contradictions present in contemporary society through the critical analysis of present oppressive and alienating structures and their attendant ideologies. Sometimes one finds appeals to the earlier, more "humanist" writings of Marx along with various revisions of Marx's own analysis of the "alienating role" of religion.[97]

Most of these Christian theologians of praxis, whatever their other differences, will employ some form of Christian and Marxist ideology-critique upon present church, academic and societal structures.[98] Often they will demand that theologians be committed to a particular praxis situation (e.g., some "base community") in order to assure the "truth" of their claims that they speak the Christian truth to the powers of the prevailing oppressive ideologies. By either assuming or arguing that Christianity is not ultimately an ideology in the Marxist sense,[99] they will insist that Christian faith, hope and love concretized as justice should situate the theologian in an objective conflict with society, church and academy. Thereby will we actualize the truth of the conflict already present, the contradictions inherent in the situation we in fact face.[100]

The spectrum of praxis positions is wide indeed. Indeed the full range is as wide as the spectrum of specific reformulations of the Hegelian and Marxist notions of praxis; the spectrum of particular symbols or themes chosen from the Christian tradition for critical-hermeneutical use (Exodus, liberation, redemption, social sin); the spectrum of particular issues chosen for the major focus of the situation (sexism, racism, classism, elitism, economic exploitation and dependency, energy or environmental crises, etc.); the spectrum of particular prophetic stances or systemic analyses[101] of the relationships between the alienating or oppressive "situation" in its infrastructural roots and suprastructural fruits and the transformative possibilities provided by Christianity.

Despite these significant differences, all theologians of praxis will implicitly or explicitly insist that personal transformation ("doing the truth") is the key to theological truth as speaking the truth. Far more than alternative Aristotelian formulations of the same basic position, the liberation and political theologians will, of course, ordinarily demand explicit analysis of the infrastructural and suprastructural realities affecting any possibility of personal authenticity. Implicit in this insistence will be some propositions like the following: Insofar as praxis sublates theory, insofar as the speaking of the truth demands doing the truth, insofar, therefore, as truth is always best understood as basically transformative in character rather than either metaphysical or disclosive, praxis theology sublates the claims to truth of all alternative formulations articulated in non-praxis-oriented fundamental and systematic theologies. It may still prove helpful for purely methodological reasons to continue to distinguish fundamental, systematic and practical theologies. Substantively, however, all claims to truth in all forms of theology are determined by alienated or emancipated praxis and should be judged on those transformative praxis criteria.

Such seems to be the implicit and sometimes explicit understanding of truth present in most theologies of praxis. Although a fuller treatment of this issue is not possible here, the analyses of later chapters on the relationships between disclosure and transformation models of truth may aid an initial study of the conflicting claims on the nature of theological truth present across the spectrum of contemporary theologies. For the present, a brief analysis of the same kind of dispute present in one clearer but analogous contemporary philosophical discussion may clarify the more fluid and more confusing theological situation.

Indeed, the recent German discussion between the hermeneutical approach of Hans-Georg Gadamer and the praxis orientation of Jürgen Habermas may be taken as a singularly clear example of a dispute over arguments of relative adequacy for contemporary praxis.[102] For Gadamer's familiar insistence upon the disclosive power of the classical Greek tradition has led him to reaffirm his trust in conversation and in the persuasive power of classical rhetoric as sufficient in the public forum. If Gadamer is correct on this matter, it follows that hermeneutical reflection would suffice not only for questions of aesthetic meaning but also for the more difficult question of a relatively adequate strategy for societal praxis. Yet Habermas' counterargument must also be noted: A purely hermeneutical approach can too often serve simply to affirm a tradition, to disallow the emancipatory function of critical reason and eventually to capitulate to, not transform, the status quo. He argues, for example, that our present social, political and cultural situation is not sufficiently analogous to that more harmonious situation of the Greek polis wherein public discourse, personal phronesis and the power of rhetorical persuasion could still be assumed. Rather we find ourselves in a technologically dominated political and social situation wherein systematically distorted communication on a mass scale seems to hold sway. The persuasive power of classical rhetoric seems well-nigh powerless in that all too easily manipulated situation. We need, therefore, some form of a critique of ideologies that can perform a critically emancipatory function on a societal level by unmasking those ideological distortions in the same way psychoanalysis unmasks the distortions and illusions of any individual.

Just as we no longer assume that a psychotic individual can be radically transformed by intelligent, rational and rhetorically persuasive discourse, so we cannot now assume that a societal situation of systematically distorted communication can be transformed merely by hermeneutical reflection and rhetorical persuasiveness. The criteria for relative adequacy, for truly public discourse and practice in that situation, are ones that demand, for Habermas, the development of both a critique of ideologies and a theory of communicative competence correlating language, work and power into a public whole.[103]

I have presented this extra-theological dispute over criteria of relative adequacy for contemporary praxis largely in the hope that it may serve to illuminate the analogous, if ordinarily less sharply formulated, dispute between hermeneutical and political theologians. Briefly stated, in terms of criteria and modes of argument, several contemporary theological discussions seem to take the following form: Some theologians basically appeal to the disclosive power of the languages of story, myth, symbol, metaphor, parable, analogy, etc. Their position implies the need for the kind of disclosive model of truth outlined in the earlier section on systematics. Their position also implies a trust in the sufficiently persuasive power of good hermeneutical work and rearticulated Christian rhetoric to transform contemporary praxis. Indeed, the same kind of rhetorical persuasiveness which Gadamer wishes to accomplish by means of his retrieval of classical Greek texts is what these systematic theologians effectively argue for by means of their hermeneutical and literary-critical retrieval of classical Christian texts. This position does not lack argumentive force. When analyzed in terms of criteria, in fact, the position constitutes an argument for the relative adequacy, that is, the disclosive and persuasive power of those retrieved Christian texts and symbols.[104] Yet unlike their philosophical analogue Gadamer, the hermeneutical theologians seem too content with a relatively unexamined trust that the rhetorical persuasiveness of those retrieved meanings will prove sufficient to transform individual and societal practice.

The political theologians, on the contrary, seem to assume, like Habermas, that a fair analysis of the contemporary societal situation forces any observer to admit to the relative powerlessness of all rhetorical persuasion in a situation of systematically distorted communication.[105] What will prove more relatively adequate to that situation, they effectively argue, is some form of a Christian critique of ideologies often named liberation or political theologies. It is of no little interest to note that both the philosophers Gadamer and Habermas and their theological analogues, the hermeneutical and political theologians, can unite on certain questions of criteria and argument. For example, these theologians do unite with one another and with the metaphysical theologians to attack various forms of positivism. But they go their separate ways again when further questions emerge about an adequate model for truth, the proper strategy, the relatively adequate arguments and practices needed to transform the present political and societal situation.

As the analysis indicates, there are in fact several distinct kinds of claims present in this theological dispute. The basic dispute, I have suggested, is a fundamental one: What constitutes truth for a theological statement? Correspondence, empirical verification or falsification, coherence, adequacy to proper language use or to common human experience, consensus, disclosure, disclosure-concealment, transformation—or, perhaps, a quiet announcement of a plague upon all these models from a skeptical observer masked as "jesting Pilate"?

A second but often overlooked discussion amidst the theological skirmishings should be more empirical and sociological than theoretical.[106] For example, the empirical evidence for our present situation as systematically distorted (however illuminating the analogy with psychoanalysis may be for many aspects of our felt experience of contemporary life) should not be allowed to assume a descriptive and implicitly prescriptive force in theology without rigorously empirical social-scientific support. I may find Jacques Ellul's analysis of technology illuminating about the contradictions and conflicts I sense or experience in this society. That does not absolve me or anyone else from seeking out empirical social-scientific evidence which supports, qualifies or refutes this "prophetic" insight.

I may, in fact I do, agree with the need to employ some form of ideology-critique in social science, philosophy *and* theology.[107] On the presumption that this agreement is based not on personal preference but on a common methodology, any use of ideology-critique should possess a healthy hermeneutic of suspicion upon its own stance. On any standard, after all, the surest sign of strictly ideological thought is the refusal of that thought—ironically sometimes under the banner of ideology-critique—to face and account for the complexity of conflicting empirical evidence. Thus all claims for the primacy of praxis over theory, if they are to prove consistent, must allow for empirical social-scientific analysis to check all theories against our societal situation.

Another area of dispute among all three kinds of theology is more properly theological. Indeed, it has already been investigated in the analyses of fundamental and systematic theologies. There we noted the distinct appeals to different aspects of the Christian tradition: the universalist strain for fundamental theologians, the confessional strain for systematic church theologians. It is clear that practical theologians may also appeal to the tradition to warrant their position. Is it not the clear and consistent teaching of the scriptural and later Christian tradition, for example, that "conversion" is central to the Christian life, including the life of thought? Is it not the case that Christian faith, hope and love are first praxis realities for a transformed agent and community before they are expressed in cognitive claims or right beliefs? In that sense, is it not the case that orthopraxis does in fact ground orthodoxy? The scriptural and traditional warrants for a transformation model of religious and theological truth, therefore, seems to back the kind of praxis emphasis desired by both the distinct Aristotelian and Hegelian-Marxist modern formulations.

Moreover, the case for the social-political dimensions of Christian faith has equally clear scriptural warrants—especially, of course, in the prophetic and apocalyptic strands of the tradition and their assumptions of God's activity in history for the oppressed.[108] These are public claims, let us note, focussed on God as acting in church and world in publicly intelligible ways. Indeed, the notion of God's activity in history in and through prophetic action in the past, present and future seems to be the chief strictly theological assumption for publicness in these theologies.

Finally, the political and liberation theologians have warranted their positions through uncovering sometimes hidden and masked, sometimes forgotten or half-remembered aspects of the Christian tradition.[109] Their understanding of the crisis in the public of contemporary society (or "world") impels them to search in the church tradition for resources, almost always prophetic and eschatological, often apocalyptic, to help transform, liberate, emancipate, save the present "demonic" situation. Romans 13, it seems, has been allowed to play its theme long enough. It is time to consider Revelation 13. The Constantinian and medieval sacralism implied in models of "Christendom" has (*pace* Belloc, Dawson, Danielou, T. S. Eliot and others)[110] long since been unmasked by many theologians, including political and liberation theologians, as an inadequate model for the church. That same kind of church model, even when recast into more liberal forms, has also been unmasked as really a "cultural Christianity" in unholy alliance with a modern, truncated secularism.[111] Any "mystical communion" model of the church which involves flight from the world has been treated to the scorn of the Marxist charges of rank "idealism" and "alienation." The "sect" model, once so marginal to mainline Christian consciousness, may now be reexamined, retrieved and, to be sure, reformulated into an effective praxis model of "church" as a mission fighting for liberation and emancipation.[112] Thus will Jürgen Moltmann reinterpret the Christian doctrine of eschatological hope and the centrality of the cross to formulate a new and vital form of Christian praxis theology and a new ecclesiology. Thus will Johann Baptist Metz provide rigorous and persuasive criticisms of the "individualism" of much contemporary theology while formulating a praxis political theology and ecclesiology honoring the "subversive memory" of freedom and suffering embedded in the central texts, events and witnesses of the Christian tradition. The black theologians, the feminist theologians, the liberation theologians of the Third World, as we shall see below, all warrant their positions by appeals to often overlooked aspects of the Christian tradition. They aid us all by speaking from and to the concrete conditions of oppression, alienation and suffering in their particular societies. In sum, all theologies of praxis will ordinarily be concerned with society as their primary reference group, yet not without substantial warrants from the church tradition itself.

Some realities seem clear, to me at least, in the complicated disputes raised by theologies of praxis. First, as mentioned above, strictly social-scientific claims are to be judged by social-scientific, not theological, criteria. On those criteria, both strictly empirical *and* theoretical positions (including theories of praxis such as ideology-critique or theories of communicative competence) are necessary. Without that empirical base, the theories are literally groundless as social-scientific evidence and should be treated, and respected, as proposals and hypotheses awaiting empirical testing. Without critical theory and transformative praxis, empirical social-scientific studies are always in proximate danger of simply affirming the present, possibly alienated and oppressive, status quo and in remote but real danger of disallowing any real critique of society (including, therefore, genuinely prophetic theological critiques) in favor of what can become a "fetishism of facts."

Second, the tendency to separate, even dichotomize disclosure and transformation criteria for truth is mistaken. Any real distinction (like those between disclosure and transformation, theory and praxis, faith and faith working through love, between liberation-emancipation and redemption) is never a separation. Distinctions remain distinctions, serving the cause of clarity and a need for emphasis through a process empowered by the necessary and enriching power of abstraction grounding all proper intellectual distinctions. As the too easily despised Scholastics correctly insisted, sometimes *debemus distinguere*.

In present terms: Of course, all good theory is grounded in the authentic praxis of intellectual integrity and cognitive self-transcendence. Of course, all real knowledge is in some sense participatory. Yet those realities—denied only by strictly positivist theories of theory and strictly instrumentalist misunderstandings of praxis as mechanically applied theory—can be distinguished without being separated. "Saying the truth" is distinct from, although never separate from, "doing the truth." *Fides quae* is distinct from, though never separate from, *fides qua*. Cognitive claims are distinct from, though never separate from, their grounding in particular historical situations and social structures. More concretely, there is never an authentic disclosure of truth which is not also transformative. We never experience a transformative truth in authentic praxis without also discerning some disclosure of what is now recognized as the case (i.e., true). To attempt to separate truth as disclosure from truth as transformation is damaging to the fuller understanding of truth itself. If adhered to, it could eventually prove fatal to the more comprehensive, the nonpositivist and noninstrumentalist notions of rationality operative in both models of disclosure and models of transformation.

To distinguish these models of truth is entirely appropriate. Sometimes the distinction is put forward to indicate a shift of emphasis in major concerns. Unfortunately, sometimes this is also misunderstood as an entirely novel, revolutionary notion of truth itself. For example, a plausible case can be made that, since the Enlightenment, theology has been concerned too exclusively with the "crisis of cognitive claims." Theology's single-minded concern, perhaps even obsession, with this Enlightenment crisis may have involved theologians unconsciously in those structures of alienation which reach their apotheosis in instrumentalist notions of reason as purely technical and notions of practice as mere technique and application—notions which the initially liberating Enlightenment concept of "autonomous" reason helped to unleash. In that situation, a shift of emphasis from theory (since theory can seem trapped in positivist and instrumentalist categories) to praxis can be and is emancipating, *even for theory*. This same shift of emphasis can clarify that the major question in our situation is not the crisis of cognitive claims, but the social-ethical crisis of massive suffering and widespread oppression and alienation in an emerging global culture. Again, an emphasis upon praxis helps to refocus theological attention on that situation rather than upon the crisis of the modern Christian intellectual analyzing the cognitive claims of the Christian tradition.

However, if praxis effectively becomes identified with some particular cause, movement or program, then neither praxis nor theory, nor the cause itself, is well served. For praxis soon becomes uncritically mediated practice, of whatever form. And any theories daring to be critical of the cause—even, indeed especially, critical theories generated from within the cause—are too quickly dismissed as prerevolutionary, "bourgeois" or "academic." The cause itself may become yet another hardened ideology, more than open to conflict yet closed to the actuality of critique and even the ideal of conversation. The "eschatological proviso" of most political theologies, to be sure, provides a good theological check upon these temptations (not inevitabilities) of any praxis-oriented theology. The internal developments of most forms of liberation theology seem to be providing the same kind of theological check on the same temptations.[113]

And yet any exclusive emphasis upon praxis for truth needs other checks than the strictly theological ones, as much as alternative theological models of truth need, as they do, the checks provided by models of truth as transformative praxis. In the case of a transformation model of truth, the following realities need to be reemphasized: The very notion of praxis is grounded in a distinction, not a separation; truth as transformation always also involves truth as disclosure; speaking the truth is never separable but is distinguishable from doing the truth; cognitive claims are not simply validated through authentic praxis any more than causes are validated through the presence of martyrs; the crisis of cognitive claims does not simply dissipate when the shift of emphasis to the social-ethical crisis of a global humanity comes more clearly into central focus; the need for argument, criteria, warrants, evidence, the need for certain necessary abstractions from the concrete, the need for the ideal of conversation embodied in most forms of contemporary fundamental and systematic theologies remains in force as necessities and ideals even in a situation that is possibly systematically distorted.

In sum, the emergence of theologies of praxis in our time has aided the search for criteria of truth for all theologians by their emphasis upon truth as transformation. In principle, that emphasis may prove complementary to the emphasis upon disclosure in systematic theologies or the emphasis upon metaphysical and existential adequacy to experience in fundamental theologies.[114] In fact, all these theologies are more often in conflict than in conversation or genuine argument. However, it is also true that the distinction among three major disciplines in theology may yet yield a clarification of both the major differences and the major similarities among all existing theologies. Then the possibilities of collaboration (including, of course, argument over the more relatively adequate theological criteria for meaning and truth) might become real again. Then, as well, there might prove a communal recognition of the real need for all three disciplines in theology: really distinct, never separated, each grounded in and ultimately judged by the drive of *all* to the publicness impelling every theology.

iii. Conclusion: Publicness in Fundamental, Systematic and Practical Theologies

Where, then, has this proposal of three distinct disciplines within theology led us? This much, at least, seems clear: the presence of the two constants in any theological position (an interpretation of the tradition and an interpretation of the contemporary situation) is always present. Moreover, there will ordinarily exist some way of establishing mutually critical correlations between the interpretations of tradition and situation or church and world: explicitly in fundamental theologies, implicitly and sometimes explicitly in systematic and practical theologies. The theocentric character of any genuinely theological statement, whether explicitly or implicitly addressed, drives every theologian to claims to truth which demand publicness and, at the limit, universality. The possibilities of a strictly private theological language, even aside from the notorious logical difficulties with that concept noted by Wittgenstein, are rendered theologically impossible by the very nature of the claims to meaning and truth entailed by the radical monotheism of the Western religious traditions.

Indeed, so intense, if sometimes unconscious, is that drive to publicness in all theological discourse that each theologian feels impelled to speak a truth which states not merely publicness but even universality, sometimes mistakenly clothed as exclusivity.[115] The conflicts of claims among theologies, therefore, can often seem insoluble, short of a capitulation by one of the parties. Indeed, the use in ordinary language of the phrase *odium theologicum* is not without warrants in the writings of contemporary theologians. What good then can one possibly perform by proposing three distinct but related disciplines in theology, if in fact practitioners of each discipline more often than not assume that their position, and their position alone, constitutes genuine theology? The rest is "muddle" or "application" or "merely philosophy" or "mere cultural analysis" or "reductionism" or "fideism."

Perhaps this proposal is, finally, a futile exercise born of an irenic temperament. Yet I think not. It would be if the distinctions developed are simply invalid—ungrounded in the common drive to publicness entailed by the doctrine of God and ungrounded in their distinct relationships to society, academy and church entailed by the doctrines of church and world. Yet we have seen that each discipline in theology does in fact appeal to legitimate if possibly partial interpretations of both the Christian tradition and the contemporary situation, of both church and world, and, sometimes, distinct understandings of God. Perhaps, on the scriptural side, what we really find is a conflict of interpretations over which "canon within the canon" or "working canon" must finally decide the fundamental meaning of the pluralistic New Testament and later Christian traditions. If that is the case, then let theologians be explicit on the matter and let the debate over that canon within the canon—a debate to which we shall return in Chapter 6—become the major focus of the conflicts over interpretations of the tradition.

Perhaps we have an analogous problem in the conflict of interpretations of the contemporary situation.[116] There too, a canon within the canon may in fact function: radical secularization, historical perspectivism, metaphysical analysis; the crisis of cognitive claims or the crisis of massive global suffering; the assumptions of reformism, reaction or revolution; the distinct and sometimes conflictual focusses for the fundamental situational questions, etc. Yet surely here, at least, one may further distinguish the issues. Just as there are few theologians left who would not insist that strictly historical judgments of the tradition must be made on strictly historical grounds, so too social-scientific observations upon current society, academy or church must be made upon strictly social-scientific grounds. Neither assumption hands over theology to history or social science. Both assumptions do insist that the theologian has no more right than any other thinker (that is to say, no right at all) to violate the canons of history, hermeneutics, social science, literary criticism, philosophy or any other mode of disciplined reflection in making one's case.

Theologians, therefore, in collaborative, interdisciplinary work with their colleagues, need to ask what after all is the present meaning and truth of the interpreted tradition and interpreted contemporary situation, by focussing on those fundamental questions constituting religious questions and those fundamental responses constituting particular religious traditions, and on establishing mutually critical correlations between both sets of interpretation. Theologians, moreover, in collaboration with other theologians who understand and accept the central, determinative theological criteria of publicness (via both the doctrine of God and the logic of fundamental religious questions) as well as the publicness of the "publics" (via the coaffirmed doctrines of church and world) need to ask: (1) what constitutes a claim to publicness in each discipline in theology; (2) what differences, if any, the major social referent of that claim (society, academy, church) makes; and (3) how are those differences adjudicable on the grounds of commonly affirmed theological criteria? Are those differences as radically in conflict as they are often understood to be? Or are those differences, as claimed here, in principle complementary and thereby legitimately expressed in terms of three disciplines in the common discipline of theology?

In that endeavor, there are few more central issues than what ultimately will serve as criteria for theological truth in analyzing both questions and responses. We have seen three representative kinds of responses to that question of truth in existing theologies. We have seen that each may, in principle, prove public. Each is principally related to one of the three publics while being implicitly related to the other two. Each is concerned to speak a truth about God that can, in principle, be heard by all. If the proposal that there are three distinct major disciplines in the one field-encompassing field of theology is to be warranted as other than another personal preference, then we need to study the forms of publicness, the meanings of truth, operative in all theologies. In fact, Part One of this work is an exercise in analyzing the claims to publicness of systematic theology from the viewpoint of fundamental theology, just as the analysis of practical theology above was from that same viewpoint.[117]

The remaining major question, therefore, may be refined to read: What, from the seemingly disparate stance of fundamental theology, can one argue on obviously public grounds for the public status of all good systematic theology? If one's answer must finally be that no plausible argument can be made for the public status of systematics, then the latter should be disowned as not really a "confessional" but an entirely private option. If one's answer proves, again on plausible public grounds, that systematic theology in fact possesses a genuine publicness distinct from but related to the obvious publicness of fundamental theology, then a case for at least two distinct theological disciplines and distinct but related general criteria of adequacy for each becomes plausible. The remaining, and real, conflicts between the different analyses of each theological discipline are issues common to each. In principle, they should prove adjudicable by careful attention to the relative adequacies and inadequacies of each discipline's major form of publicness. The question, therefore, recurs: Is systematic theology public discourse?

Notes

1. The aim of this analysis is to provide the inner-theological reasons for the public character of theology. In that sense, this resembles the kind of analysis traditionally called "theological encyclopedia" and today "theological method" (i.e., as theological). The classic instance of the "theological encyclopedia" task remains Friedrich Schleiermacher's *Brief Outline on the Study of Theology* (Richmond: John Knox, 1966). I wish to express my thanks to Mark Taylor and his student and faculty colleagues, especially Schubert Ogden, at Perkins School of Theology for their critical response to an earlier draft of this paper.

2. The ability to show this theologically characterizes an important aspect of the theologies of Reinhold Niebuhr and Langdon Gilkey. For an example in Niebuhr, see *The Irony of American History* (New York: Scribner, 1952), pp. 151–74; for an example in Gilkey, see *Reaping the Whirlwind: A Christian Interpretation of History* (New York: Seabury, 1976), pp. 70–79 (on scientific creativity).

3. For one of the clearest theological expressions of the theological meanings of "church" and "world" and their dialectical relationship, see Karl Rahner, "Church and World" [I/94].

In the present chapter, I am concerned only to establish the theological character of both "church" and "world" and the formal mutually critical correlations obtaining between them (and, therefore, among fundamental, systematic and practical theologies and their primary publics—academy, church and society, respectively).

4. For one of the clearest illustrations of this in contemporary theology, see the work of Schubert Ogden on the nature of theology and its theocentric character: inter alia, *The Reality of God* [I/100], pp. 1–71; "What Is Theology?" *JR* (1972), 22–40; and "The Task of Philosophical Theology," in *The Future of Philosophical*

Theology, ed. Robert Evans (Philadelphia: Westminster, 1971), pp. 59–65. Note, too, how Ogden also relates the reality of God to the logic of religious questions as fundamental questions in a manner similar to the claim for publicness in chap. 1 of this work where "publicness" was philosophically related to the logic of the fundamental questions of religion. In this chapter the claim to publicness is related theologically to the doctrine of God (as the religious referent of those questions in the radically monotheistic traditions). For a defense of the latter position, *BRO*, chaps. 4, 5, 6 and 7.

5. As we shall see in the discussion of christology, in the Christian affirmation of the event of Jesus Christ both church and world are coaffirmed as the primary mediators (as "tradition") of the event itself and of the "dangerous" memory of Jesus: see the Introduction to Part II and chaps. 6 and 7. Indeed the matter becomes yet more dialectical when one notes that "church" is sacrament of Christ and eschatological sacrament of *world* (see chap. 10, n. 29).

6. See especially in Johannine scholarship Rudolf Bultmann, *Theology of the New Testament,* II (New York: Scribner, 1953); Raymond Brown, *The Gospel According to John,* 2 vols. (New York: Doubleday, 1966); idem, *The Community of the Beloved Disciple* (New York: Paulist, 1979).

7. Note Brown's analysis of the distinct Johannine communities and their relationship to "outsiders," in *The Community of the Beloved Disciple*. Recall also H. Richard Niebuhr's appeal to distinct aspects of the Johannine tradition in his types for the "Christ and Culture" relationship, in *Christ and Culture* [I/99], pp. 45–52 (Christ Against Culture) and pp. 196–206 (Christ as Transformer of Culture).

8. Contrast, for example, the classic Johannine text, "God so loved the world that he gave his only Son, that whoever believes in him may have eternal life. God did not send the Son into the world to condemn the world, but that the world might be saved through him" (John 3:16–17), with the frequent disparagements of the world in the First Letter of John (e.g., 1:6; 3:8, 11–15).

9. The words "sect" (in contrast to "church") and "sectarian" are used in the descriptive sense of Troeltsch and not the pejorative, ordinary language sense of "sectarianism."

10. For a cultural account of this defamiliarizing process occasioned by the word, see Herbert N. Schneidau, *Sacred Discontent: The Bible and Western Tradition* (Berkeley: Univ. of California Press, 1976); for a theological account of this dialectic, see Schubert Ogden's introduction in Rudolf Bultmann, *Existence and Faith,* ed. Schubert Ogden (New York: Meridian, 1964), pp. 13–21. We will discuss this question more fully in chap. 5.

11. Recall Niebuhr's paradigm of "Christ Against Culture" and the appeals to First John by the sectarians, in *Christ and Culture* [I/99], pp. 45–76.

12. Even here the logic of the belief in God should occasion the drive to publicness even if the "true God" is claimed to be available only to the "sect" or "church" as *the* sole "public." It is the logic of any radical belief in God (correlated to the fundamental questions to which it is a response) that determines the "universality" or "publicness" of any radically monotheistic religion. We shall make similar suggestions by means of the notion of the "whole" for the universal religions of a nonradically monotheistic kind in chap. 5.

13. In experimental terms, this means that "common human experience" is also such a locus—as argued in *BRO*, pp. 43–46. In sociological terms, this also means that both "society" and "academy" as social realities are appropriate "publics" for theology, along with "church" as both a sociological and theological reality.

14. See the classic Christian theological account of this in Augustine, *The City*

of God, Book IV, chap. iv; Book XV, chap. iv. For Augustine on the world, see R. A. Markus, *Saeculum: History and Theology in the Theology of St. Augustine* (Cambridge: Cambridge Univ. Press, 1970); and Langdon Gilkey, *Reaping the Whirlwind* [2], pp. 159–75.

15. Note that this is a minimal theological claim operative in all theological understandings of church. If one also accepts the fuller model (chap. 10, n. 29) of church as sacrament of Christ and eschatological sacrament of world, this is even more the case.

16. Leo Tolstoy, *A Confession and What I Believe* (London: Oxford Univ. Press, 1961), pp. 1–85, 303–35.

17. Recall that the notion "plausibility structure" can bear two distinct meanings referring to either an everyday structure or a theoretical one. See chap. 1, n. 86.

18. This "existential" recognition may provide our first warrant for the claim of "mutually critical correlations" between analyses of "church" and "world" or their *rough* analogues, "tradition" and "situation" (the analogues are rough since "tradition" in fact does not include *only* "church" and "situation" does not include only "world," yet they remain analogues since church is the *primary* carrier of tradition and "world" the *primary* carrier of "situation").

19. See especially Altizer's recent, important exercise in primal language, in Thomas J. J. Altizer, *The Self Embodiment of God* (New York: Harper & Row, 1977).

20. To repeat: This should also be correlated with the logic of the fundamental questions noted in chap. 1 and thereby with philosophical analyses of those questions and the reality of God. The latter questions are the central questions of any fundamental theology.

21. The biblical *loci classici* here remain the Book of Job and Lamentations 3. Aspects of the Jewish tradition have in fact incorporated the notion of faith-ful arguments with God far more than the Christian tradition has.

22. Paul Tillich, *The Courage to Be* (New Haven: Yale Univ. Press, 1952).

23. A theological point made classically by the great Reformation theologians and captured dialectically in Kierkegaard's notion of "religiousness b": on the latter, see Søren Kierkegaard, *Philosophical Fragments* (Princeton: Princeton Univ. Press, 1967), and *Concluding Unscientific Postscript* (Princeton: Princeton Univ. Press, 1968).

24. It is important to note that this problem of the self need not be formulated only (or even necessarily) as a problem of "pride." The critique by feminist theologians is appropriate here: see, for example, Valerie Saiving Goldstein, "The Human Situation: A Feminine View," *JR* (1960), 100–112. It might also be noted that the neo-Platonic element in Augustine also leads to the notion of self-dispersal in contrast to his emphasis on "pride" in his anti-Pelagian writings.

25. For an example, see Paul Tillich, *Systematic Theology,* 3 vols. (Chicago: Univ. of Chicago Press, 1951–63), III, 86–107.

26. See Martin Buber, *The Eclipse of God* (New York: Harper, 1957). In recent theology note how Wolfhart Pannenberg employs the notion of the "whole" in relationship to his notion of "contextual meaning" in hermeneutics (*Theology and the Philosophy of Science* [I/51], pp. 156–224) and in relationship to the concept of "God" as "the all-determining reality" (pp. 333–45).

27. Recall here Pannenberg's interpretation of the resurrection of Jesus as "prolepsis" for all humanity, in *Jesus–God and Man* (Philadelphia: Westminster, 1968), pp. 53–115.

28. If one formulates the issue in terms of modes of temporality (as I did in

BRO, pp. 237–50), the distinctions will be different. My present formulation, as I hope to make clear, does not entail a lesser role for "historical theology" but rather insists on the intrinsically historical (as hermeneutical) theological character of all three disciplines in theology: fundamental, systematic and practical. Exegesis and church history are, on this reading, also theological, ordinarily as systematic or practical theology. The present division of the three sub-disciplines (all hermeneutical to different degrees) should highlight the necessary character of "historical theology" for all theology. This applies, to repeat, especially to exegesis (as also biblical theology) and church history (as also church historical theology). In short, I believe this is not a substantive change but an alternative and, for the reasons advanced above, more relatively adequate formulation of the role of "historical theology" (understood, as in *BRO*, as *theology* not as the history of theological ideas) in *every* theological discipline.

29. Recall that the major *theological* warrant for this distinction of "publics" or "social realities" is the theological coaffirmation of both church and world in the theological affirmation of God.

30. For the first (appeals to experience, understanding, rational judgment and responsible decision), see Bernard Lonergan, *Insight* [I/28] and *Method in Theology* [I/10], pp. 27–57, where the "fourth level" is explicitly developed beyond *Insight*. For the second formulation into arguments, see Stephen Toulmin, *The Uses of Argument* [I/28], on how the categories "claim, datum, warrant, qualifier, condition of rebuttal and backing" operate in nonformal logic.

31. The use of the word "obvious" may call for some clarification: I assume that the modes of argument present in fundamental theology are obviously public to anyone. The major argument of this book will be to show that the hermeneutical character of systematic theologies, although not obviously "public" in the first sense, is nevertheless public in a distinct but related sense. In more traditional Aristotelian language, fundamental theology deals principally with "dialectics" and "metaphysics," systematic theology with "rhetoric" and "poetics," and practical theology with "ethics" and "politics." Each of the three enterprises can achieve a public status distinct from but related to (in a word, analogous to) the other two. Each is concerned with both meaning *and* truth. In the alternative language of transcendental reflection: fundamental theology is concerned principally with the "true" in the sense of metaphysics, systematic theology with the beautiful (and, as we shall see, the beautiful *as true*) in the sense of poetics and rhetorics, practical theology with the good (and the good *as* transformatively true) in the sense of ethics and politics. The major role of fundamental theology is to explicate these transcendentals in relationship to the religious, the holy or the sacred. Hence Part I of this book is, in fact, an exercise in fundamental theology designed to show the truth status of the claims of systematic theologies. The major focus, therefore, will be on the art-religion relationship in the analyses of the classic and distinctively religious classics (chaps. 4, 5, 6). Every discipline in theology must be concerned with the *truth* of its claims on the inner-theological grounds outlined in this chapter. But that concern, I propose, will operate "obviously" in fundamental theology (i.e., as dialectics or argument) and less obviously but no less really in systematic theology (i.e., *like* poetics and rhetoric) and practical theology (i.e., *like* ethics and politics). The obviously ontological (as metaphysical or transcendental) character of these claims distinguishes this enterprise from Anders Nygren's claim that transcendental reflection provides only purely logical sets of operations (*Meaning and Method* [I/52], pp. 209–27).

32. See Van A. Harvey, *The Historian and the Believer* (New York: Macmillan, 1966), pp. 102–27; and idem, "The Ethics of Belief Reconsidered," *JR* (1979),

406–21. It is clear, I trust, that the word "primarily" is crucial here: for example, creative fidelity to the Christian tradition also demands the ethical stance of honest, critical inquiry. For an example of the latter, see Hans Küng, *The Church—Maintained in Truth? A Theological Meditation* (New York: Seabury, 1980). It might also be added that these shifts of emphasis also occasion the emphasis in fundamental theologies on "criteria of intelligibility" and the emphasis in systematic theologies on "criteria of appropriateness." Both disciplines, however, need both set of criteria.

33. More exactly, beliefs may not serve as either warrants or backings in arguments in fundamental theologies. They ordinarily do serve as eliciting or empowering agents for the expressions of systematic theologies and practical theologies. For an interesting analysis of similar issues in modernity, see Wayne Booth, *Modern Dogma and the Rhetoric of Assent* (Chicago: Univ. of Chicago Press, 1974). For the argument-like character of ethos, see Chaim Perelman and L. Olbrechts-Tyteca, *The New Rhetoric: A Treatise on Argumentation* (Notre Dame: Univ. of Notre Dame Press, 1969). The classic Ambrosian line "Non in dialectica placuit Deo salvum facere populum suum" determines the ethos and persuasive power of Newman's *The Grammar of Assent,* a classic on these and related issues. Indeed an analysis of Newman's project in the *Grammar* in the light of the present distinctions among dialectics, rhetoric-poetics and ethics-politics would perhaps prove a more enlightening setting forth of the complexities at stake than one more round of the W. C. Clifford-William James debate on "the will to believe."

34. The meaning of "truth" involved will necessarily be analogous, not univocal or equivocal (nor, if successful as analogous, will truth be systematically ambiguous), in dependence upon the context (e.g., argument [dialectic], conversation with the classics [poetic-rhetoric] and praxis [ethics-politics]): all claims to analogously related expressions of publicness, i.e., truth). Informing these analogical relationships as well is the logical ordering of "abstract-concrete," not "general-specific." My employment of the former category (e.g., for claiming in chaps. 4 and 5 the greater adequacy of poetic speech, even for truth, over necessary, nonpoetic, abstract metaphysical speech) probably accounts for some of my differences on the relationship of fundamental and systematic theologies with Schubert Ogden. See, for example, Ogden's careful delineation of the role of philosophical theology in relationship to historical, systematic and practical theologies in "What is Theology?" and "The Task of Philosophical Theology" [4].

In spite of these differences, where I understand Ogden's position and my own (and others) to converge is in the insistence upon public truth for theology *because of* the nature of the fundamental questions and the doctrine of God as logically demanding publicness in *all* theological disciplines. Where I believe we may separate is in my claim that poetics, rhetoric and ethical-political praxis provide persuasive truth claims even when not formulated in explicit (dialectical) arguments. Dialectical arguments, as necessary abstractions from the concrete and as formulated in fundamental theology in ultimately transcendental or metaphysical terms, remain true and therefore relevant to claims operative in (and abstractable from) the fuller symbolic expressions of systematic theology and the fuller praxis realities of practical theology. For example, the metaphysical reality of God as the one necessary individual can (and should!) be abstracted from the concrete "Reign of God" symbols of systematics and of practical theology and analyzed on fundamental theological terms—even when those necessary abstractions do not exhaust the fuller concrete reality of "God" in the symbol (on this issue of God-language, see further in chap. 10, n. 7).

35. An exception to the emphasis on "cognitive claims" for fundamental theology may be found in Johann Baptist Metz, *Faith in History and Society: Toward a Practical Fundamental Theology* (New York: Crossroad, 1980). Metz's shift is dependent on two principal factors: first, his arguments for the primacy of praxis over theory (see sec. iii of this chapter); second, his claim that the major situation is massive global suffering not the crisis of cognitive claims occasioned by the Enlightenment—especially given the "dialectics of the Enlightenment" itself.

36. See Friedrich Schleiermacher, *Brief Outline* [1], pp. 29–41, for how "philosophical theology" operates in this fashion. The logic of "abstract-concrete" is employed with singular clarity in Schleiermacher and his most obvious successor, Ernst Troeltsch, in their distinct sorting-out of the full task of theology starting with the philosophical but *not* controlled by it (despite the outcries of Karl Barth and Emil Brunner to the contrary). For an unusually clear formulation of the task of theology for Schleiermacher, see B. A. Gerrish, "Continuity and Change: Friedrich Schleiermacher on the 'Task of Theology'," in *Tradition and the Modern World* (Chicago: Univ. of Chicago Press, 1978). On Troeltsch, see Gerrish's "Ernst Troeltsch and the Possibility of a Historical Theology," in *Ernst Troeltsch and the Future of Theology*, ed. John Powell Clayton (Cambridge: Cambridge Univ. Press, 1976), pp. 100–39; see also the Univ. of Chicago Ph.D. dissertations of Garret Paul (on the role of philosophy of religion in Troeltsch) and Walter Wyman (on the role of *Glaubenslehre* in Troeltsch).

37. The more strictly theological analogues here would be: disclosure is related to transformation as faith is related to "faith working through love." Note again that the paradigm remains the movement from the relatively abstract to the relatively concrete.

38. For my own relationship to the Gadamer-Ricoeur tradition of interpretation, see *BRO*, pp. 49–52, 72–79, and chap. 3 of this work.

39. For some recent studies of interpretation of sacred or religious texts, see Wendy Doniger O'Flaherty, ed., *The Critical Study of Sacred Texts* (Berkeley: Lancaster-Miller, 1979), especially the studies of Joseph M. Kitagawa (pp. 231–43), Roger J. Corless (pp. 257–71), and Paul Ricoeur (pp. 271–77).

40. Inter alia, see Daniel Berrigan, *Uncommon Prayer: A Book of Psalms* (New York: Seabury, 1978); Jacques Ellul, *The Politics of God and the Politics of Man* (Grand Rapids: Eerdmans, 1972); John Howard Yoder, *The Politics of Jesus* (Grand Rapids: Eerdmans, 1972); and William Stringfellow, *An Ethic for Christians and Other Aliens in a Strange Land* (Waco: Word, 1973).

41. This central issue on the nature of religion is discussed more fully in chap. 4.

42. For the notion "religious dimension," see *BRO*, pp. 91–121.

43. See Andrew Greeley, *Unsecular Man* (New York: Delta, 1972), and "Sociology and Theology," *CTSA Proceedings* (1977) [I/2]. Readers may note that, as Greeley correctly observes, my own work in *BRO* also partly employed this disputable social-scientific theory. Perhaps a word of clarification is in order. I believe now, as then, in the theological import of the concept of "secularity," not "secularism," on inner-theological grounds. But I did too hastily employ the distinct social-scientific theory of secularization as additional (and insufficiently supported) warrant. Hence I stand corrected. I continue to hold, however, that even on social-scientific grounds there is sufficient evidence to suggest that some sort of secularization process has occurred: clearly for the intellectuals, less clearly but actually for the wider society. Greeley, in fact, denies neither of these but accords them different evaluative status in the first case and more sophisticated and nuanced social-scientific descriptive status (minus, that is, the "theory of secularization") in the second. My social-scientific warrants for the problematic

of the first chapter of this book come, moreover, not from a "theory of secularization" but from the theory of the privatization of religion in modern society; see also John Coleman, "The Situation for Modern Faith," *CTSA Proceedings* (1977), which makes an analogous defense of "privatization" and critique of the general model of secularization.

44. I use the words "cut across" here to indicate the presence in any theology accepting these two "constants" of what is, I believe, a third (if usually implicit) constant. To render it explicit: there will ordinarily exist a correlation model to relate these two interpretations. More exactly, in Schillebeeckx's language, there exist "mutually critical correlations" which the theologian should establish between the interpretation of the situation and the interpretation of the tradition. The mode of establishing these correlations is, of course, context-dependent: i.e., dependent upon the modes of argument of fundamental, systematic or practical theology. For Hans Küng's challenge to this "correlation model" in favor of a model of "confrontation," see his "Toward a Consensus in Catholic (and Ecumenical) Theology," in *Consensus in Theology? A Dialogue with Hans Küng and Edward Schillebeeckx,* ed. Leonard Swidler (Philadelphia: Westminster, 1980). My own response to Küng's alternative argues that logically "correlation" can account for the full spectrum of possibilities ranging from "identity" through continuities, similarities and analogies to radical nonidentity (and hence confrontation), whereas the reverse is not the case. I have not included this "correlation model" as a "constant" among all theologies in the text because, unlike the other two constants, it is not explicitly allowed by all theologians. In fact it is sometimes explicitly denied. However, these present remarks may serve to show that, whatever the de facto situation, de jure any theologian who has interpretations of two distinct phenomena (tradition and situation) must somehow correlate those interpretations: whether through claims for identity, radical nonidentity, similarities, continuities or analogies. There is no way of deciding which of these correlation factors is appropriate to a particular instance prior to the study itself. What can be known is that some mode of correlation (including confrontation) is necessary and that the expression "mutually critical correlations" is more likely to alert the reader to the logical presence of the full spectrum of possibilities from identity through analogy to confrontation than the more general expression "model of correlation." At any rate, some form of correlation of the meanings and truths of both the questions and the answers of tradition and situation can be stated here as a third, if usually implicit, constant of theology. One need not agree with Tillich's original formulation of the "model of correlation," or with my own distinct one for fundamental theology (*BRO*, pp. 45–47) or with Schillebeeckx's formulation in order to accept the general need for some kind of correlation of these two interpretations. Even Barthians correlate, if only ordinarily in the form of *Nein*, to the extra-theological interpretations of the situation!

45. It may be worth recalling that the notion of "truth" here is neither univocal nor equivocal but analogical; see n. 34. Any truth claim needs establishment by the context-dependent procedures appropriate to a discipline (here fundamental, systematic and practical theologies). If a pluralism is forthcoming it will be established by both those context-dependent procedures and by the inner-theological warrants common to any theological discipline as theological (e.g., its publicness from the affirmation of God; its relationship to three publics, and thereby its relationship to interpretations of both tradition and situation, by the coaffirmation of church and world). The pluralism, in short, will be an analogical one (partly the same, partly different, basically similar; more briefly, a similarity-in-difference) and should not be confused with pluralism's caricature (and its temptation!), an

eclecticism based on either personal taste or preference. Nor should pluralism be confused with a weak form of "consensus theory" which in effect counts how many prominent theologians or exegetes hold a position (as distinct from their warrants for holding it) and then announces the result as theological "truth." For reflections on the pluralism of readings that accompanies the present model of interpretation, see chap. 3, secs. iii and iv.

46. Some further rubrics for adjudicating possible disputes between the results of fundamental and systematic theologies will be noted after the fuller analysis of systematic theology.

47. Alternative names for this discipline include apologetic theology, natural theology and philosophical theology. I continue to employ the word "fundamental" as preferable to these alternatives for the following reasons: "apologetics" can often imply a defensive tone; "natural theology" a rationalist tone too often related to that elusive phenomenon beloved by Enlightenment thinkers, "natural religion"; "philosophical theology" often carries too many distinct meanings—i.e., it can be either fundamental or systematic theology. I recognize and regret that the word "fundamental" bears its own set of difficulties. It can seem to imply (and I gather it does for many) an imperialist tone of "setting down the law" or "foundations." But if one keeps the abstract-concrete schema in mind, one can note that fundamental theology is concerned with the *most abstract possibilities and necessities* that *are* fundamental for understanding some of the necessary presuppositions of systematic and practical theologies. Abstractions are necessary to correct confusions in the concrete. Abstractions never replace the concrete. For fundamental theology, thus considered, to replace systematic and practical theologies would prove not merely imperialistic but a prime instance of the "fallacy of misplaced concreteness."

48. On Philo, see Samuel Sandmel, *Philo of Alexandria* (New York: Oxford Univ. Press, 1979); on the Apologists, see Robert Grant, *The Early Christian Doctrine of God* (Charlottesville: Univ. Press of Virginia, 1966); idem, *The Letter and the Spirit* (London: Oxford Univ. Press, 1957); Henry Chadwick, *Early Christian Thought and the Classical Tradition* (London: Oxford Univ. Press, 1966); and H. A. Wolfson, *The Philosophy of the Church Fathers*, I (Cambridge: Harvard Univ. Press, 1956).

49. On verification and falsification models, see *BRO*, pp. 120–24.

50. For Torrance, see Thomas Torrance, *Theological Science* (London: Oxford Univ. Press, 1969); for Niebuhr, his essay "The Truth in Myths," in *The Nature of Religious Experience*, ed. J. S. Bixler (New York: Harper, 1937).

51. Note here Langdon Gilkey's shift of interest from ontic claims in *Naming the Whirlwind* [I/100] to ontological concerns in *Reaping the Whirlwind* [2], pp. 300–318 (on God). See also Schubert Ogden, *The Reality of God* [I/100]; and David Tracy, *BRO*.

52. For Ramsey, see *Religious Language: An Empirical Placing of Theological Phrases* (New York: Macmillan, 1963); for Heidegger, see, inter alia, "On the Essence of Truth," in Martin Heidegger, *Basic Writings*, ed. David Krell (New York: Harper & Row, 1977), pp. 113–43.

53. See the discussion of "practical theology" in this chapter for references.

54. Refined theories of consensus (like Habermas' in philosophy) argue for some determination of criteria for competence in the consensus shapers; unrefined consensus positions (like some in theology) are really disguised eclecticisms (see n. 42).

55. See Wolfhart Pannenberg, *Theology and the Philosophy of Science* [I/51], pp. 309–14.

56. For example, I assume here the more traditional interpretation of Thomas Aquinas' "five ways" as engaged in this kind of enterprise as distinct from the "negative way" interpretation of Aquinas in Victor Preller, *Divine Science and the Science of God: A Reformulation of Thomas Aquinas* (Princeton: Princeton Univ. Press, 1967).

57. This implies, of course, not that this kind of reflection occurs *only* in the universities but that it must occur there. The "academy" refers to the whole community of inquirers, not only those who happen to be in the "groves of academe"!

58. Alternative expressions include confessional theology, dogmatic theology and constructive theology. I prefer the term "systematic theology," not to emphasize the *systematic* character of the enterprise but as a relatively less history-laden term than the alternatives. Historically, the closest approximation to the task I name systematics is the notion *Glaubenslehre* in Schleiermacher and Troeltsch (see n. 34).

59. The full implications of this descriptive definition will have to await the results of the studies in chaps. 4 and 5. For the moment, it is worth noting that every good interpretation is a new interpretation involving application to the situation: see Hans-Georg Gadamer, *Truth and Method* (New York: Seabury, 1975), pp. 274–305. It is important to note even here, however, that both text and reader (as well as their dialogical interaction) are realities-in-process, never purely static constants. All three realities (text-reader-interaction) include the ambiguities intrinsic to the human situation. Interpretation is, by definition, an ongoing process related to these realities-in-process. Even classic texts exist as classics only when actually read; the reader exists as a good reader only by allowing his or her present horizon to be provoked or vexed by the classic text into dialogue.

60. Nor, insofar as systematics is genuinely hermeneutical, will it reject the "third constant" of some form of correlation (n. 42), in this case as a *new* interpretation involving application to a new situation. Although this procedure is rarely described explicitly as correlation, in fact, as always *new* interpretation, systematic theology implicitly always involves some form of correlation as well (see n. 44).

61. See H. Richard Niebuhr, *The Meaning of Revelation* (New York: Macmillan, 1960), esp. pp. 38–43. Two helpful studies of Niebuhr's position on confessional theology may be found in the Ph.D. dissertations (Chicago) of Douglas Ottati and Martin Cook on H. Richard Niebuhr. Ottati's thesis, at this writing, is completed; Cook's is in the process of completion. Both have informed my appreciation for the fuller subtleties of Niebuhr's program. In the text I have tried to interpret Niebuhr's own confessional position faithfully, even on issues (e.g., metaphysics) where I clearly do not agree with that position. My lack of agreement on such issues does not disallow, I trust, a reformulation of Niebuhr's complex and intriguing position at its strongest.

62. Note that the differences are differences in emphasis: like the classic differences in emphasis between the "sapiential" theology of Thomas Aquinas and the "existential" theology of Martin Luther documented in Otto Pesch, "Existential and Sapiential Theology: The Theological Confrontation between Luther and Thomas Aquinas," in *Catholic Scholars Dialogue with Luther,* ed. Jared Wicks (Chicago: Loyola Univ. Press, 1970), pp. 61–71. The article is an abstract of Pesch's well-known work on Luther and Aquinas.

63. The abstract-concrete distinction is important to recall here. Insofar as the fundamental theologian explicates the general, abstract, necessary (i.e., metaphysical) characteristics of any coherent concept of God (e.g., as the one

necessary individual and as dipolar—see *BRO*, pp. 172–204), that analysis should inform and, where necessary, correct the fuller, more concrete expressions of systematic theology. Alternatively, that fuller, more concrete expression (e.g., Luther's "hidden and revealed God" or Karl Rahner's "comprehensible-incomprehensible God" or Eberhard Jüngel's "present-absent God") should develop in the direction of greater concreteness (which, in the case of the reality of God, also means a greater sense of radical mystery) the abstract, metaphysical notions of God established in fundamental theology. Rubrics worth recalling: we understand mystery *as* mystery only on the other side of comprehensibility, just as we understand obscurity *as* obscurity only on the other side of clarity. Similarly, we understand the concrete *as* concrete only on the other side of the enriching clarifications and corrections provided by necessary abstractions—including the *abstract* notion of the "concrete."

64. Recall H. Richard Niebuhr's criticism of liberal theologies: "A God without wrath brought men without sin into a kingdom without judgment through the ministrations of Christ without a cross" (*The Kingdom of God in America* [I/85], p. 193).

65. Recall Karl Rahner's analyses of "the supernatural existential" and his retrieval of Chalcedonian christology. Linguistically, the notion "supernatural" may suggest the obscurantism, mystification and two-storied universe of biblicism and fundamentalism; in which case it should be rejected. (For that use of the word "supernaturalism," see John Dewey, *A Common Faith* [New Haven: Yale Univ. Press, 1934].) However, the word can also refer, in mainline Catholic theology, to a theorem to account for our concretely graced state—as, in distinct ways, the word "supernatural" is used (and is meant) in the work of Henri de Lubac, *The Mystery of the Supernatural* (New York: Herder and Herder, 1967); Karl Rahner, "Some Implications of the Scholastic Concept of Uncreated Grace," *Theological Investigations,* I (Baltimore: Helicon, 1961), 319–46; idem, "Nature and Grace," *Theological Investigations,* IV (Baltimore: Helicon, 1966), 165–88; Carl J. Peter, "The Position of Karl Rahner regarding the Supernatural: A Comparative Study of Nature and Grace," *CTSA Proceedings* (1965), pp. 81–94; and Bernard Lonergan, *Grace and Freedom* (New York: Herder and Herder, 1971), pp. 13–19. For an analogous use of supernatural in Jewish theology, see the important work of Arthur Cohen, *The Natural and the Supernatural Jew,* 2nd rev. ed. (New York: Behrman, 1979). In this second sense, the "supernatural" should, of course, be affirmed. My own belief remains that linguistically the word "supernatural" is so laden in ordinary discourse with intimations of the first sense, that the word is probably best avoided to prevent unnecessary confusion. It need prove no disparagement of the medieval theoretic achievement on the theorem of the "supernatural" to find more disclosive linguistic alternatives to disclose the same reality—viz., our concretely graced state. For an example of the latter, note Bernard Lonergan's interpretation of the medieval theoretic categories for grace in contemporary categories of interiority, in *Method in Theology* [I/10], pp. 285–92.

66. Note, therefore, that despite systematic theology's emphasis upon tradition (and therefore on criteria of appropriateness) there are also appeals to the situation (and therefore to criteria of understandability).

67. H. Richard Niebuhr, *The Meaning of Revelation* [61], pp. 1–43.

68. "Perspectivism" should be further distinguished into "soft perspectivism" (like Niebuhr's) and "hard perspectivism" (like Alan Richardson's). The claims of the latter are far more difficult to defend than those of the former; see Van Harvey, *The Historian and the Believer* [32], pp. 204–46. Note also Bernard Lonergan's

important and creative distinction between "perspectives" (in the functional specialty "history") and "horizons" (in the functional specialty "dialectics"): *Method in Theology* [I/10], pp. 214–24.

69. The tradition of the "sovereignty of God" is, of course, especially representative of the Reformed tradition from John Calvin through Jonathan Edwards and H. Richard Niebuhr to, more recently, the retrieval of that tradition in the constructive theology of James Gustafson: see chap. 1 of his *Ethics in a Theological Perspective* (Chicago: Univ. of Chicago Press, 1981).

70. H. Richard Niebuhr, *The Meaning of Revelation* [61], pp. 59–95 (on inner history), pp. 109–113 (on the "special occasion").

71. Ibid., pp. 125–6.

72. William A. Christian, *Meaning and Truth in Religion* (Princeton: Princeton Univ. Press, 1964), pp. 93–113 (on the notion of "suggestions").

73. This seems to be the general assumption of the confessional theologians. I state it as an assumption since it is probably empirically true (i.e., de facto most contemporary theologians probably share this belief), yet it is rarely argued for. For a persuasive argument against the common assumption that historical consciousness has discredited metaphysics, see Emil Fackenheim, *Metaphysics and Historicity* (Milwaukee: Marquette Univ. Press, 1961). For an explicit argument by a confessional theologian against metaphysics (an argument articulated on philosophical grounds, not general cultural assumptions), see Anders Nygren, *Meaning and Method* [I/52], pp. 29–65. For my own critical reflections on Nygren's understanding of metaphysics, see *BRO*, pp. 157–60.

74. Hans-Georg Gadamer, *Truth and Method* [59], pp. 245–74.

75. In Catholic theology, this insistence has been made often—especially in the Tübingen School and in the work of John Henry Newman and Maurice Blondel. For a historical-critical analysis, see Yves Congar, *Tradition and Traditions* (New York: Macmillan, 1963); and James Mackey, *Modern Theology of Tradition* (New York: Herder and Herder, 1962).

76. Recall that "disclosure" is related principally to rhetoric and poetics and that "application" is not added to interpretation but intrinsic to it.

77. The failure even to consider this option—indeed to assume, not argue, that church-traditions are by definition particularist—seriously mars the argument of Gordon Kaufman's *An Essay on Theological Method* [I/57], esp. pp. 8–11. The argument between Kaufman's position and the present one could occur on grounds acceptable in principle to Kaufman—i.e., obviously public grounds. This is the case since the present work does not assume the public character of particular classic church traditions (which would merely be the opposite of Kaufman's assumption of "sectarianism") but argues for it on non-church-warranted (or fundamental theological) public grounds. I also recognize that a second major difference between my position and Kaufman's would also need further discussion: viz., the acute and probably irreconcilable differences between his Kantian understanding of metaphysics and God and my own (in *BRO* and here). However, even granted these crucial differences, Kaufman's *Essay* deserves far more critical attention than it has received from most theologians because of the argumentative strength of the work in clarifying the need for *any* theologian to show the fully public character of the truth-claims involved in *all* theologies and the intrinsic correlations of the concepts "world" and "God."

78. Background work on the concept includes Nicholas Lobkowicz, *Theory and Practice: History of a Concept from Aristotle to Marx* (Notre Dame: Univ. of Notre Dame Press, 1967); Richard Bernstein, *Praxis and Action* (Philadelphia: Univ. of Pennsylvania Press, 1971); idem, *The Restructuring of Social and Political Theory*

[I/28]. In theology, see the several essays on this theme of Matthew Lamb, especially "The Theory-Praxis Relationship in Contemporary Christian Theology," in *CTSA Proceedings* (1976), pp. 147–78; Johann Baptist Metz, *Faith in History and Society* [35], pp. 48–88; Helmut Peukert, *Wissenschaftstheorie–Handlungstheorie–Fundamentale Theologie* (Frankfurt: Suhrkamp-Verlag, 1978). On the latter work, see Rudolf Siebert, "Peukert's New Critical Theology," *The Ecumenist* 16/4, pp. 52–58; 16/5, pp. 78–80.

79. See Lamb [78], pp. 150–52.

80. For most of the practical theologians (clearly for Baum, Metz, Lamb and Francis Fiorenza), this also implies some form of primacy to practical reason.

81. Notice, for example, the relative ease with which Gregory Baum can move from the praxis-oriented Blondelian "method of immanence" of *Man Becoming* (New York: Herder and Herder, 1971) with its concerns for individual, personal self-transcendence to the praxis-oriented social-critical work of *Religion and Alienation* [I/1].

82. Note, moreover, how in each of these instances the praxis involved is *faith* praxis transforming personal, social and historical praxis. This reality in the American tradition need not prove merely an import from German and Latin American sources. Indeed one of the dominant characteristics of much of the American philosophical tradition is the emphasis on praxis—whether largely individual (as in William James) or social-historical (as in John Dewey). On the latter, note Bernstein, *Praxis and Action* [78], pp. 165–230; and William Shea, "Matthew Lamb's Five Models of Theory-Praxis and the Interpretation of John Dewey's Pragmatism," in *CTSA Proceedings* (1977), 125–42. Moreover, not to appreciate the "political" theological character of many of the classic American theologians is to miss a native resource worth further exploration: note, in American Protestantism, Martin Marty's essay on Reinhold Niebuhr [I/8] and his essay "A Sort of Republican Banquet" [I/8]; note as well the legacy of both the Social Gospel theologians and of Reinhold Niebuhr in the recent work of Langdon Gilkey, *Reaping the Whirlwind* [2], and "The Political Dimensions of Theology," in *JR* (1979), 154–69. In the American Catholic tradition, note especially the positions of J. R. Ryan and John Courtney Murray. For interpretations of the latter, see John Coleman, "Vision and Praxis in American Theology," *TS* (1976), 3–40. As Andrew Greeley has correctly observed, moreover, the extraordinary praxis of the American Catholic immigrant church is one well worthy of reflection by contemporary theologians. Furthermore, the American tradition in figures like Abraham Lincoln and Martin Luther King is strongly praxis-oriented (in contrast to the largely theory-oriented political theories of many European political theorists). On Lincoln, see William Wolf, *Lincoln's Religion, This Almost Chosen People* (Philadelphia: United Church of Christ Press, 1963); Reinhold Niebuhr's tribute to Lincoln as America's classic theologian (of praxis) in *The Irony of American History* [2], pp. 170–74; and the creative use of Lincoln's vision for a theology of liberation in Peter Hodgson, *New Birth of Freedom: A Theology of Bondage and Liberation* (Philadelphia: Fortress, 1976). The work on King's relationship to the praxis tradition (as distinct from other aspects of King's thought) is, to my knowledge, yet to be written. I do not mention these American resources in a chauvinist spirit to suggest that American theologians do not need to continue to learn from European and, more recently, Latin American theologies in these matters, nor to suggest that these praxis traditions are identical—which they are not, as any reader of both Dewey and Habermas or Niebuhr and Metz soon discovers. I do mention them, however, to observe a curious American irony: What was once considered a major "failure" of American theology by European commentators and their American

followers—viz., its "practical character"—is now largely ignored rather than reclaimed by many recent American "political" and "liberation" theologians in favor of denouncing the "academic" and "theoretical" character of American theology. *Plus ça change?*

83. For an excellent analysis of the similarities and differences of these theologies, see Francis Fiorenza, "Political Theology and Liberation Theology: An Inquiry into Their Fundamental Meaning," in *Liberation, Revolution and Freedom: Theological Perspectives,* ed. Thomas McFadden (New York: Seabury, 1975), pp. 3–29.

84. For Bernard Lonergan, see *Insight* [I/28], *Method in Theology* [I/10] and his explication of his own praxis position in "Theology and Praxis," *CTSA Proceedings* (1977), 1–17. For the article upon which Lonergan reflects, see Eric Voegelin, "The Gospel and Culture," in *Jesus and Man's Hope,* ed. D. G. Miller and D. Y. Hadidian (Pittsburgh: Pittsburgh Theological Seminary Press, 1971).

85. *Method,* pp. 267–71. Lonergan's "conversion" language, I assume, can be changed into "transformation" language (i.e., the radical transformation of the subject's "horizon," occasioned by intellectual, moral and religious transformation, not mere development).

86. The expression is David Burrell's as applied to Lonergan's work.

87. Note how Lonergan can appeal here as well to his own earlier interpretation of Thomas Aquinas in *Verbum: Word and Idea in Aquinas* (Notre Dame: Univ. of Notre Dame Press, 1967). Metz could also appeal to his own earlier interpretation of Aquinas' "anthropocentric" (in contrast to "cosmocentric") horizon to show how his later political theology is in continuity with his earlier more "individualist" and "metaphysical" work; see J. B. Metz, *Christliche Anthropozentrik: Über die Denkform des Thomas von Aquin* (Munich: Kösel-Verlag, 1962).

88. In Lonergan, *Method,* pp. 47–55. For a creative study retrieving "character" for Christian ethics, see Stanley Hauerwas, *Character and the Christian Life: A Study in Theological Ethics* (San Antonio: Trinity Univ. Press, 1975).

89. Bernard Lonergan, "Theology and Praxis" [84].

90. A good overview of Lonergan's position on the subject may be found in his *The Subject* (Milwaukee: Marquette Univ. Press, 1969).

91. It is worth recalling here the praxis character of interpretation itself.

92. Note the implicitly social reality operative from the ecclesial character of faith to the collegial or collaborative character of theology. The first Lonergan develops through his notion of "mediating theology" whereby, in dialectics, "religious conversion" is not solitary but communal. The second Lonergan develops through his notion of theology as a collaborative enterprise encompassing eight functional specialties.

93. *Method in Theology,* pp. 237–45.

94. For a development of this theme from resources in Lonergan, Voegelin, Gadamer and Strauss, see Frederick Lawrence, "The Horizon of Political Theology," in *Trinification of the World* (Frederick Crowe *Festschrift*), ed. Thomas Dunne and Jean-Marc Laporte (Toronto: Regis College Press, 1978), pp. 46–70.

95. Quoted in Matthew Lamb, "The Theory-Praxis Relationship in Contemporary Christian Theologies" [78], p. 172.

96. The key remains here the revisionary Marxism of the Frankfurt School: see Matthew Lamb, "The Challenge of Critical Theory" [I/1]; for background works, see Martin Jay, *The Dialectical Imagination* (Boston: Little, Brown, 1973); Susan Buck-Morss, *The Origins of Negative Dialectics* (New York: Free Press, 1977); on Habermas, Thomas McCarthy, *The Critical Theory of Jürgen Habermas* (Cam-

bridge: MIT Press, 1978). On Marxism, see Leszek Kolakowski, *Main Currents of Marxism,* 3 vols. (Oxford: Clarendon, 1978), esp. Vol. III, *The Breakdown,* pp. 341–420; Shlomo Avineri, ed., *Varieties of Marxism* (The Hague: Nijhoff, 1977); Alvin Gouldner, *The Two Marxisms* (New York: Seabury, 1980).

97. For some examples here, see the study by Peter Hebblethwaite, *The Christian-Marxist Dialogue* (New York: Paulist, 1977).

98. See Johann Baptist Metz, *Faith in History and Society* [38], pp. 119–35, for an excellent analysis of the dialectical relationship of redemption and emancipation. It bears repeating that almost all the political and liberation theologians are clearly not reductionist: faith praxis transforms Marxian and other forms of ideology critique. In the language of the present work, Metz establishes mutually critical correlations between the praxis-informing ideology critique and Christian faith praxis.

99. Juan Luis Segundo, for example, uses the word "ideology" in an explicitly non-Marxist sense to speak of faith and ideology, in *The Liberation of Theology* [I/74], pp. 97–125. For a recent study of the generic characteristics of ideology (as both positive and negative), see Alvin Gouldner, *The Dialectic of Ideology and Technology: The Origins, Grammar and Future of Ideology* (New York: Seabury, 1976). For an informative history of the complexities of the concept "ideology" (in both its pejorative [distorted consciousness] and more positive senses) in Marxist thought from Marx and Engels to the present, see Martin Seliger, *The Marxist Concept of Ideology: A Critical Essay* (New York: Cambridge Univ. Press, 1977). For a positive, cultural anthropological view of "ideology" as a "symbolic template" for periods when the "received tradition" is called into question, see Clifford Geertz, "Ideology as a Cultural System," in *Interpretation of Cultures* [I/18], pp. 193–234. For a creative and clarifying use of the work of Gouldner and Geertz here to determine the "genre" of "liberation theology," see Charles Strain, "Ideology and Alienation: Theses on the Interpretation and Evaluation of Theologies of Liberation," *JAAR* (1977), 473–91.

100. For expressions of this conflict orientation, see Charles Davis, "Theology and Praxis," *Cross Currents* (1973), 154–68; and Gustavo Gutierrez in *CTSA Proceedings* (1978) 30–35.

101. For an example of the latter, see Rosemary Radford Ruether, *Liberation Theology* (New York: Paulist, 1972).

102. See *Hermeneutik und Ideologiekritik* (Frankfurt: Suhrkamp, 1971). Part of the exchange is published in *Continuum* (1970). For two commentaries, see Paul Ricoeur, "Ethics and Culture," in *Political and Social Change,* ed. David Stewart and Joseph Bien (Athens: Ohio Univ. Press, 1974); and Dieter Misgeld's analysis in *On Critical Theory,* ed. John O'Neill (New York: Seabury, 1976), pp. 164–84.

103. The "negative" moment of ideology critique is represented in Habermas' early work, *Knowledge and Human Interests* [I/24]. The more recent, complex and still developing positive proposal on criteria for communicative competence is carefully analyzed in Thomas McCarthy [96], pp. 272–387. A use of Habermas' positive proposal for communicative competence to develop a public theology may be found in Dennis McCann [I/78]. Metz and Lamb tend to make more use of the more "theological" thinkers of the "early" Frankfurt School, especially Adorno, Horkheimer and Benjamin. Note also Peukert's [78] appeal to both "early" and "late" schools.

104. As suggested before (n. 31) this position is basically an appeal to poetics and rhetoric as distinct from dialectics (in fundamental theology) and ethical and political praxis (in practical theology). The praxis of the value of theory and argument is also operative in fundamental theology and the praxis involved in all

interpretation is operative in systematics. The real difference between the third position and the first two, therefore, is not that only the third appeals to praxis but that the third accords a *primacy* to praxis and indeed to a specific form of praxis—faith praxis with an ethical-political emphasis (or, as Metz and Lamb name it, mystico-political praxis). One way of formulating arguments among these three distinct but related forms of praxis would be in terms of the abstract-concrete distinctions introduced earlier. In those terms, practical theology is the most concrete yet should, by it own criteria, be open to the necessary correctives provided by the authentic praxis informing the arguments and theories of fundamental theology and the authentic praxis informing the disclosures of systematic theology. (Gadamer, for example, is singularly clear on the reality of praxis—and thereby of ethical and political philosophy—in his insistence on the inner relationship of *intelligere, explicare* and *applicare*: note, for example, his appeal to Aristotelian *phronesis* as praxis in "Hermeneutics and Social Science," *Cultural Hermeneutics* [1975], 308–19, and in "Hermeneutik als praktische Philosophie," in *Zur Rehabilitierung der praktischen Philosophie,* ed. M. Riedel [Freiburg: Rombach, 1972], pp. 325–44). Practical theology can, I believe, sublate the other two disciplines as long as the sublation also includes the truth claims operative in fundamental and systematic theologies. In more strictly theological terms, "faith working through love and justice" (the mystico-political praxis of practical theology) does sublate "faith" only by really including that faith. I hope to return to these issues in a future volume on practical theology—a volume intended to complete the "trilogy" initiated by *BRO* by addressing the more fully concrete concerns of practical theology.

105. Most of them, in fact, struggle implicitly or explicitly against the privatization of religion analyzed in chap. 1 of this work. Few of them seem to relate that privatization to the marginalization of art: Metz's use of Benjamin here and his use of "narrative theology" being one exception to the more general rule.

106. I take this correct demand for empirical social-scientific evidence to be the chief objection of Andrew Greeley to many theological uses of social science (see n. 43). This objection seems to me entirely sound, assuming (with Greeley) that the empirical social scientist also allows for theory (including *in principle,* therefore, "critical theory" like a theory of systematically distorted communication or a theory of communicative competence). For examples of American empirical and theoretical social science in conversation with theology, see the essays by William McCready, Pastora San Juan Cafferty, Bruno Manno and Teresa Sullivan in *Toward Vatican III: The Work That Needs to Be Done,* ed. David Tracy with Hans Küng and Johann B. Metz (New York: Seabury, 1979).

107. Christian ideology critique is intrinsic to any recognition of the defamiliarizing, delegitimating, demythologizing and deideologizing character of the prophetic and mystical strands in both Judaism and Christianity. For more on this, see chap. 5.

108. One obvious issue that fundamental theology should pose for practical theologies (especially liberation theologies) employing the "God acting in history" paradigm is that of the correct way to speak that language. Otherwise, liberation theologies may be repeating the same difficulties exposed by Langdon Gilkey in the earlier biblical theology of G. Ernest Wright et al.: see Langdon Gilkey, "Cosmology, Ontology, and the Travail of Biblical Language," *JR* 41 (1961), 194–205. For some distinct, constructive responses to that question, see Langdon Gilkey, *Reaping the Whirlwind* [14], pp. 239–318; Schubert Ogden, "What Sense Does It Make to Say 'God Acts in *History*'?" in *The Reality of God* [I/100], pp. 164–88; and David Mason, "Can We Speculate on How God Acts?,"

JR (1977) 16–33. For two biblical studies on the "privileged" character of the oppressed, see Norman Gottwald, *The Tribes of Yahweh* (Maryknoll: Orbis, 1979); and Richard Cassidy, *Jesus, Politics and Society: A Study of Luke's Gospel* (Maryknoll: Orbis, 1978).

109. This is especially true of the political theologians' retrieval of apocalyptic (Metz) and the left-wing of the Reformation (Moltmann) as well as the liberation theologians' retrieval of the Exodus motif and the "privileged" status of the oppressed in the prophetic traditions. For an example of the latter, see James Cone, *A Black Theology of Liberation* (Philadelphia: Lippincott, 1970). Philosophically, it might be added, the left-wing Hegelians are the philosophical tradition most often employed by Metz and Moltmann in their political theologies and, either explicitly or implicitly, in the liberation theologies.

110. It seems fair to observe that in all four of these figures Europeanism was the crucial component of Christendom, as stated with the fewest qualifications in Belloc's famous statement: "Europe is the faith and the faith is Europe."

111. For two careful defenses of "liberal Christianity" against these now familiar charges, see George Rupp, *Culture-Protestantism* [I/101]; and William R. Hutchinson, *The Modernist Impulse in American Protestantism* (Cambridge: Harvard Univ. Press, 1976). The fact is that the political and liberation theologians are as much heirs of that admittedly ambiguous liberal and modernist tradition as their more "individualist" predecessors, the existentialist neo-orthodox theologians, were. The historical relationship is nicely stated in Wilhelm Pauck's comment: "Neo-orthodoxy is not orthodoxy but the self-criticism of the liberal tradition." Methodologically, as I have suggested here, practical theologies continue to need the correctives of fundamental theology as much as the latter needs sublation into the praxis concreteness of practical theology. Thought implies action; action already includes thought.

112. See Roger Haight, "Mission" [I/94].

113. For further consideration of these factors in both political and liberation theologies, see chap. 9. In the present chapter, the major theological proviso demanding publicness remains the doctrine of God present in all three theological disciplines. Indeed, the "theistic proviso" (to thus name it) impels the eschatological proviso and the "God acting for the oppressed" provisos of political and liberation theologies, respectively.

114. This would especially be the case if, as suggested above, one reflected upon this matter in terms of the following complementary emphases in each discipline: (1) Fundamental theology: the transcendental—the true related to the religious or holy; the discipline—metaphysics; the major mode of conversation—argument or dialectic. (2) Systematic theology: the transcendental—the beautiful (and *as* true) related to the religious or holy; the disciplines—poetics and rhetoric; the major mode of conversation—interpretation as conversation with the religious classics. (3) Practical theology: the transcendental—the good (and *as* true) related to the religious or holy; the disciplines—ethics and politics related to a transforming faith praxis; the major mode of conversation—Christian ideology critique or conflict (the negative moment) and some positive proposal of a future ideal situation articulated in ethical-political-theological ways. This proposal for the possibility in principle of complementariness, if successful, would validate a general analogical pluralism on the spectrum abstract-concrete as distinct from an eclecticism or a univocal monism. It would not solve the inevitable conflicts and disputes emerging over the results of particular issues in each discipline (e.g., consider how all three disciplines would provide distinct interpretations for the theological concept "the reign of God"). Those further disputes must themselves employ both

the theological necessities of any form of theology (see above on God and church-world and chaps. 6 and 7 on Jesus Christ) and the idea of conversation for a community of inquirers whose first task is to find the most appropriate mode of conversation (dialectics, etc.) for the particular issues at issue in any dispute.

115. The charge against "exclusivist" understandings of Christianity will be raised again in the analysis of christology and grace in Part II.

116. See chap. 8 for a fuller analysis of this spectrum.

117. As noted before, I hope to return to a fuller treatment of practical theology in a future book: At which time, an attempt *to do* practical theology (analogous to Part II of *BRO* and Part II of this work) would be forthcoming. At which time, of course, I may also find that the present observations are inadequate even from the present viewpoint of fundamental theology. The future—more exactly, the conversation—will tell.

Chapter 3

The Classic

i. Introduction: Systematic Theology as Hermeneutical

Like all forms of theology, systematic theology possesses a kind of normative status. Yet the notion of theology as a normative discipline involves some ambiguities. In the minds of many both within and outside theology, the phrase seems to indicate an authoritarian or dogmatic stance. In those forms of theology where authority is effectively a matter of obedience to an external norm rather than an acceptance based on a risk and a personal recognition of the authority of a living religious tradition, the charge is well taken. Indeed, it is interesting to note that when the notion "authority"[1] shifts from a truth disclosed to mind and heart to an external norm for the obedient will, the theologian, in effect, can only repeat the shop-worn conclusions of the tradition. Rarely, if ever, can the theologian also interpret, mediate, translate the meaning and truth of the tradition itself. Eventually, the notion of authority collapses into authoritarianism, dogma becomes the occasion not for original dogmatic theology but for extrinsic dogmatism and doxic thinking in the spirit of Eric Voegelin's "dogmatocracy."[2] Eventually, the central, classical symbols and doctrines of the tradition become mere "fundamentals" to be externally accepted and endlessly repeated.

On this reading, authoritarian, dogmatist, fundamentalist theologies are ideologies, not systematic theologies. The difference between conservative Protestant evangelical theologies and fundamentalist theologies,[3] the difference between the traditionalism of Archbishop Lefevbre's movement and the profound respect for tradition in Hans Urs von Balthasar is a difference become a chasm. Indeed, fundamentalist and authoritarian theologies, properly considered, are not theologies at all.

Nor is this the case merely because such theologies will not take account of contemporary experience. More basically, these theologies are finally not interpretations of the tradition itself. They are but simple repetitions.[4] The heart of any hermeneutical position is the recognition that all interpretation is a mediation of past and present, a translation carried on within the effective history of a tradition to retrieve its sometimes strange, sometimes familiar meanings. But the traditionalist's use of tradition betrays the enriching, even liberating notion of tradition.[5] It is naive to assume that a thinker is so autonomous as to be no longer affected by the effects and influences of that tradition in our very language, a presence carrying us along by providing our initial prejudgments and often unconscious presuppositions as to the nature of reality. It is equally naive, and equally destructive of systematic theology's hermeneutical task, to assume with the traditionalist and fundamentalist that so autonomous in one's heteronomous obedience is the theologian that one can be faithful to the tradition to which one belongs by repeating its *tradita* rather than critically translating its *traditio*.

The systematic theologian, on the contrary, must operate in a manner more faithful to the actual finitude and historicity of every thinker in any cultural tradition. Indeed, the surest mark of contemporary systematic theology is precisely a profound acceptance of finitude and historicity. The Enlightenment "prejudice against prejudgments" is discountenanced by systematic theologians not because it is inconvenient but because it is implausible. Any attempt at an autonomy so pure that it is unaffected by the tradition in which we, willingly or unwillingly, stand is the final form of the general privatization which plagues our culture. If the terms "socialization" and "acculturation" mean anything, if "finitude" and "historicity" are other than empty abstractions, then one must restore a nonauthoritarian notion of authority and norm as well as a nontraditionalist notion of tradition to their legitimate place in all human reflection. As I will suggest below, we are thus required to develop a nonclassicist notion of the classic.

Otherwise, the alternatives seem bleak. We may embrace the increasing privatization of the autonomous self on a positivist model. Then the only move beyond the self seems to be by expansion of techniques for scientific and social control. We may run for security to the increasingly heteronomous privatization in which once proud and enriching traditions harden into ideologies and once daring interpreters of the tradition become bureaucratic personalities. Or systematic theologians may continue to risk an intellectual life by interpreting a religious tradition. Their task, like that of their counterparts in the arts, in philosophy, even in science, involves a risk worth taking.

They realize that as a matter of fact we are always already in a particular history; that the route to liberation from the negative realities of a tradition is not to declare the existence of an autonomy that is literally unreal but to enter into a disciplined and responsive conversation with the subject matter—the responses and, above all, the fundamental questions—of the tradition. In this pluralistic present, in this moment of history where practically all traditions have become porous, a concentration on the subject matter of the classical texts, events, images, persons and symbols seems one hope for a move forward into publicness.

The individual thinker may also recognize that hermeneutical understanding can be understood on the model of authentic conversation. Yet what is authentic conversation as distinct from idle chatter, mere debate, gossip or nonnegotiable confrontation?[6] As the classical model for conversation in the Western tradition, the Platonic dialogue, makes clear, real conversation occurs only when the individual conversation partners move past self-consciousness and self-aggrandizement into joint reflection upon the subject matter of the conversation.[7] The back-and-forth movement of all genuine conversation (an ability to listen, to reflect, to correct, to speak to the point—the ability, in sum, to allow the question to take over) is an experience which all reflective persons have felt. Authentic conversation is a relatively rare experience, even for Socrates! Yet when conversation actually occurs—in a chance meeting, a discussion with friends and colleagues, a particular seminar session—it is unmistakable.

When one reflects upon the meaning of that experienced reality of conversation, as does Hans-Georg Gadamer in his careful analysis,[8] one recognizes certain signal realities. Real conversation occurs only when the participants allow the question, the subject matter, to assume primacy. It occurs only when our usual fears about our own self-image die: whether that fear is expressed in either arrogance or scrupulosity matters little. That fear dies only because we are carried along, and sometimes away, by the subject matter itself into the rare event or happening named "thinking" and "understanding."[9] For understanding *happens;* it *occurs* not as the pure result of personal achievement but in the back-and-forth movement of the conversation itself.

This experience of understanding, moreover, occurs in linguistic form: We do not, in fact, experience some purely nonlinguistic "understanding" and then use language as a tool or instrument for its expression. Rather, from the beginning to the end of our journey to understand we find ourselves in a particular linguistic tradition (primarily our native language) which carries with it certain specifiable ways of viewing the world, certain "forms of life" which we did not invent but find ourselves, critically but really, within. The word "hermeneutical" best describes this realized experience of understanding in conversation. For every event of understanding, in order to produce a new interpretation, mediates between our past experience and the understanding embodied in our linguistic tradition and the present event of understanding occasioned by a fidelity to the logic of the question in the back-and-forth movement of the conversation. We constantly mediate, translate, from our past understanding to our present one. We consistently find that understanding *happens* in precisely this deeply subjective yet intersubjective, shareable, public, indeed historical movement of authentic conversation. So much is this the case that we find ourselves obliged to use such transsubjective language as "understanding happens," "the act of understanding," the "event" of understanding.

If the event of understanding in conversation is allowed to play the paradigmatic role for all true understanding (including, therefore, the reading of a text, the reflections of the solitary thinker, the witnessing of the work of art, the understanding of the questions and responses of the classical events, texts, images, symbols and persons in a particular religious tradition), then we may also recognize one liberating truth: All authentic reflection, all reflection where the subject matter and not the subject determines the questioning, has a properly hermeneutical character.

This move to the normative paradigm of conversation is not a move to a transhistorical claim. In fact, the very opposite is the case. A recognition that the event of understanding in authentic conversation is a model for all understanding is in fact an admission, not a denial, of the radically finite and historical character of all understanding.[10] All understanding is mediational in the sense of happening now as I face the question mediated from the past and projected with hope to the future. I am not in fact leaving history when I interpret a tradition. Rather I am entering that history with a deep consciousness of it. I am willing to accept the risk that the subject matter of this particular text articulates a question worth asking and a response worth considering. When the text is a classic, I am also recognizing that its "excess of meaning" both demands constant interpretation and bears a certain kind of timelessness—namely the timeliness of a classic expression radically rooted in its own historical time and calling to my own historicity.[11] That is, the classical text is not in some timeless moment which needs mere repetition. Rather its kind of timelessness as permanent timeliness is the only one proper to any expression of the finite, temporal, historical beings we are. The classic text's real disclosure is its claim to attention on the ground that an event of understanding proper to finite human beings has here found expression. The classic text's fate is that only its constant reinterpretation by later finite, historical, temporal beings who will risk asking its questions and listening, critically and tactfully, to its responses can actualize the event of understanding beyond its present fixation in a text.[12] Every classic lives as a classic only if it finds readers willing to be provoked by its claim to attention.

These later interpreters will come with their own questions, their own history—including the history of the effects of those very classic texts, events, images, persons, symbols.[13] Their new questions will open anew the subject matter of the text by venturing to interpret its questions and responses. In that manner only will they understand it. If the text is a genuinely classic one, my present horizon of understanding should always be provoked, challenged, transformed. In encountering a classic we are compelled to believe, in Dorothy Van Ghent's apt phrase, "that something else might be the case."[14] I will understand not merely something that was of interest back then, as a period piece, whose use, although valid then, is now spent. Rather I will grasp something of genuine interest here and now, in this time and place. I will then recognize that all interpretation of classical texts heightens my consciousness of my own finitude, my own radically historical reality. I can never repeat the classics to understand them. I must interpret them. Only then, as Kierkegaard insisted, do I really "repeat" them.

But who is this "I" that finds itself needing interpretation rather than contemplative reconstruction? The "I" is none other than the human being who knows the self as, in fact, what Heidegger called a "thrown projection."[15] As "thrown" into this world—this language, this history, this tradition—my understanding is situated by a past which inevitably involves me in the "effective history" of an ambiguous heritage of funded meanings.[16] My understanding must appropriate these meanings as possibilities for the future which I project.[17] My present situation is always one where I possess a finite, temporal horizon within which all that I encounter—persons, texts, images, events, symbols—have their initial meaning for me. To stay in that horizon by refusing the risk of interpretation of the classics of the tradition—in the manner of authoritarian theologies of mere repetition and reconstruction—is to hand myself and my tradition over to the dustbin of history. It is to insist, in effect, that the properly human task and hope is not understanding but certitude; that so obvious, so familiar are the responses that the fundamental questions constituting the responses need not be struggled with; that my present horizon is so clear and distinct that no effort of interpretation is required for it to be relocated by the classics of the tradition; that so eternal is the tradition that I, too, somehow partake in its atemporality—now in the increasingly brittle form of an ahistorical certitude.

The reverse side of the same kind of move away from finitude and historicity, away from interpretation of a classical tradition with all its attendant risks, may be found in the desire to declare autonomy by fiat. Then all the authority and normativity of any classical tradition is declared heteronomy. All recognition of our actual situation as one of real finitude and real historicity may be dismissed as abstract, metaphysical talk. All the meditative understanding of the classical traditions may be relegated to the leisure time of troublesome humanists unable to cope with the rigors of hard-minded, technical reason.

One should not conceive the insistence upon the centrality of hermeneutics as some proposal for a *via media,* usually only an *aurea mediocritas,* between the options of "authoritarianism" and "positivism." The fact is that an insistence upon the hermeneutical understanding of philosophy and theology is not a search for that "middle ground" beloved by "moderates" but an articulation of the only ground upon which any one of us stand: the ground of real finitude and radical historicity in all hermeneutical understanding. Consider, for example, how Aristotle's understanding of knowledge by phronesis in the *Ethics* and *Politics* or his insistence upon the truth of poetry are being retrieved by contemporary thinkers to help articulate the kind of knowledge genuinely available to finite, historical thinkers.[18] Consider the contrary: Aristotle's scientific ideal as postulated in the *Posterior Analytics,*[19] as that ideal was distorted into an ideal of Cartesian certitude via clarity and distinctness by much of ahistorical Christian "orthodox" theology, aids no one but the nonhermeneutical neo-Scholastic manualist in the present situation. The former realities are always being retrieved in new interpretations. The latter are spent. They can be repeated in the manuals. They cannot be retrieved.

All contemporary systematic theology can be understood as fundamentally hermeneutical. This position implies that systematic theologians, by definition, will understand themselves as radically finite and historical thinkers who have risked a trust in a particular religious tradition. They seek, therefore, to retrieve, interpret, translate, mediate the resources—the questions and answers, form and content, the subject matter—of the classic events of understanding of those fundamental religious questions embedded in the classic events, images, persons, rituals, texts and symbols of a tradition. Insofar as their retrievals of the classics are controlled by the subject matter; insofar as they possess a tact, a common (as communal) sense in a genuinely critical manner;[20] insofar as contemporary systematic theologians interpret the tradition in the full sense outlined below rather than simply repeating or dismissing it—then they too can be recognized as performing a fully public function appropriate to this time and place.

Nor does this proposal lack contemporary examples. One need note only such obvious examples as the hermeneutical import of Karl Barth's commentary on Romans[21] or Karl Rahner's retrievals of Aquinas to note this hermeneutical self-understanding in practice. In fact, all those systematic theologies which bear the most promise for being candidates for contemporary Christian systematic classics are profoundly hermeneutical enterprises: Barth's retrieval of Calvin; Lonergan and Rahner of Aquinas; Reinhold Niebuhr of Augustine; H. Richard Niebuhr of Jonathan Edwards; Paul Tillich and Rudolf Bultmann of Luther; all systematic theologians of some primary set of meanings in the scriptures.

All the obvious candidates for contemporary Christian classics in systematic theology are in fact hermeneutical theologies. Each is characterized by a recognition of finitude and historicity that does not occasion the related failure of nerve of either authoritarianism or positivism. Each disowns a model of either pure autonomy or heteronomy. Each develops some appropriately theological model of theonomy[22] (usually correlated to a psychological model of self-transcendence). Each undertakes a retrieval of the tradition both to interpret it and to be interpreted by it. Each disowns any extrinsicism as inappropriate to both the historical situation and the internal demands of theology. Each enters the conversation of the Christian tradition, attempts to understand it critically, interprets it and moves on.

We must also recognize that both text and reader are never static realities but realities-in-process demanding the interaction of genuine conversation to actualize the questions and responses (the subject matter). The principal identity which both text or reader possess is the identity-in-difference of ever new and ongoing interpretation. Every classic text, moreover, comes to any reader through the history of its effects (conscious and unconscious, enriching and ambiguous, emancipatory and distorted) upon the present horizon of the reader. The text can become a classic for the reader only if the reader is willing to allow that present horizon to be vexed, provoked, challenged by the claim to attention of the text itself. The provocation to present complacency often comes through the form itself (e.g., a genre) for only through a specific form is the subject matter produced *as* a provocation to think these questions anew.

In ages where the individual theologian unquestionably belonged to the tradition, with little sense of historical distance from the classical origins of the tradition, with no sense of the brokenness and ambiguity of every tradition and one's own inevitably ambivalent relationship to it, with an assumption that the cultural pluralism of traditions may be met by describing one's own culture as civilization and others as barbarism, regression or distortion,[23] the hermeneutical character of systematic theology was unlikely to be a primary focus. In a pluralistic and historically conscious age, however, the seeming strangeness and foreignness of the past embedded in our classic texts is likely to jar any present complacency into some recognition of historical distance.

We are tempted, I suspect, to alleviate the pain of this disorientation by assuming that the past is irrevocably strange and has no more than spectator interest for us now. In a more sophisticated version of this option, we may well decide that the real meaning of a text may be uncovered by a deciphering, via some new method or technique (for example, by psychological empathy), the mind of the author, the social circumstances, the life-world of the text, or the reception of the text by its original addressees.[24] Then the meaning of the text becomes an object for our insatiable curiosity as to the strange possibilities of the human spirit. The text itself has simply nothing to say to us any longer, for its questions and answers, its subject matter, are now merely historical curiosities. The text is simply a clue to the mind of the author or to a particular social and historical situation. And neither of these realities, we assume, has any more to say to us than the text which articulates them. Philosophical reflection thereby becomes the history of philosophical opinions. Historical theology quickly becomes the history of theological ideas. Meanwhile, we are left with our cherished, if formal and increasingly private, autonomy unchallenged, unprovoked, untransformed by the effort and risk of entering into a conversation with the text. For conversation will demand that movement back and forth between discovery and concealment, respectful awe and critical freedom, suspicion and recovery that characterizes the dialectic of authentically critical understanding.

Yet sometimes, when moved by the thoughts, feelings and actions we sense in the great works of our culture, we realize, however dimly, with William Faulkner that "the past is not really dead; it is not even past." A union of our autonomy and historical consciousness is sufficient to decipher the insignificant, the obvious, the mere vestiges, the period pieces of the past. But only a consciousness like Faulkner's can free us to recognize that the very language we speak involves us in the history of the effects and influences of this particular culture and calls us to interpret its presence among us in a new act of understanding.

As Schleiermacher insisted,[25] our present pluralistic, historically conscious and ambivalent attitude to the traditions within which we stand leads us to be wary above all of misunderstanding. Therefore, we correctly insist upon the need for the controls of historical criticism, social-scientific methods or ideology critique for all our classics.[26] Yet if we think of the problem of hermeneutical understanding as solely or even primarily a problem of avoiding misunderstanding, we are likely to trap ourselves in that halfway house between autonomy and heteronomy which is the understanding of interpretation as only the exercise of those objective, critical controls provided by historical and social-scientific methods. If we concentrate only on those methods of explanation, we will fail to recognize the understanding of a common subject matter in the fundamental questions posed to our common humanity and lurking beneath all our misunderstandings. We may then recognize the truth of Nietzsche's passionate and prophetic outburst in *The Uses and Abuses of History* against our timid, nervous, resentful, historicist refusal to evaluate—more exactly, our refusal to allow the subject matter of the classical texts, events, images, symbols and persons in the tradition to interpret us.

This alienation of ourselves from bringing into consciousness the reality of history embodied in our language and the forms of life disclosed by that language may pretend to an objectivity of purely scientific control.[27] Yet those pretenses are long since unmasked. Just as Freud unmasked the unconscious motivations, compulsions and distortions informing all conscious and rational behavior, so too we now all find fantastic the pretensions to pure objectivity of some Victorian historicists. We have exposed and discarded the myth of progress informing their presumed objectivity. But have we really exposed yet the myth of our own all too certain and technically controlled autonomy? Insofar as we dare not ask the fundamental questions that these strange texts articulate, insofar as we dare not allow ourselves even to consider, much less evaluate their and our responses to those questions, we have not freed ourselves from the myth of progress in its clearest contemporary form: the myth of a pure autonomy achieved solely through a mastery of technical controls upon all allowable meaning. Finally, all is opinion, all thinking is doxic thinking, all philosophy is the history of those opinions, all art the history of changing tastes, all religion the history of curious psyches and shifting social patterns, all history at best gossip. All indeed is ultimately a tale told by an idiot, signifying nothing. With thinking, art, religion and action itself driven from the public forum, each of us may now retire into the sheltered privacy of a pure autonomy and hope that the social engineers will treat us kindly.

When Karl Barth in his *Römerbrief* threw his "bomb into the playground of the theologians," when Karl Rahner upset the clear and untroubled certainties of the neo-Scholastics with his daring retrieval of the forgotten in the excess of meaning in the texts of Thomas Aquinas, they performed a genuinely hermeneutical task. Neither rejected the necessity of some control on interpretation by historical methods. Each did insist that only when the subject matter becomes a question for the interpreter does real understanding of the text of Romans or the *Summa* begin. When Rudolf Bultmann launched his demythologizing program he did not design it principally to alleviate difficulties with Christianity for the modern mind.[28] Rather he correctly insisted that the subject matter of the New Testament itself demanded and performed demythologizing as the necessary moment of negation in its genuinely hermeneutical interpretation of that existence proclaimed in the kerygma. Only when enterprises like those occur does contemporary systematic theology as interpretation of the tradition actually happen. When it does, I believe, every intelligent reader knows the difference: We are suddenly confronted with a challenge to our ordinary mode of thinking; we are surprised by the sudden, event-like disclosure of the genuinely new; we are startled into thinking that "something else may be the case." When that realized experience is not fully determined by the needs and exigencies of the present moment and is backed by the winnowing process of time and the critical appreciation of the wider community of capable readers, we recognize that we may be in the presence of a classic.

An understanding of all authentic understanding as a hermeneutical event, therefore, seems an appropriate way to interpret the nature of the task of the systematic theologian. To grasp the full significance of hermeneutical understanding for systematic theology, however, demands further attention to the normative reality which drives all humanistic, including theological, enterprises forward: the existence of classics confronting, surprising, shocking and transforming us all.

ii. The Normative Role of the Classics: Realized Experience

We may start our reflections from a fact of every culture: Classics exist. To agree with this, one need not limit the candidates for classical status by the elitist criteria of the classicist. Indeed where the all too normative mentality of a purely classical culture reigns, the route to T. S. Eliot's insistence that even Shakespeare does not measure up to these restrictive standards seems inevitable.[29] In a historically conscious culture, however, the fact of cultural pluralism is recognized and affirmed. In American culture, for example, one of the achievements of the cultural movements of the sixties was to challenge earlier formulations of distinction between "high" and "low" culture.[30] Then the candidates for classical status expand: in jazz and the spirituals, in films, popular music and "popular" (not "low") culture.

The notion of a classic is not confined to classicist norms.[31] Rather, the experience of the classic remains a permanent feature of any human being's cultural experience. Indeed, even radical thinkers like Michel Foucault who would eliminate the usual classics (Kant, Hegel, Aristotle) will uncover new candidates (De Tracy, Cuvier) to fill the vacuum left by their genealogical suspicions.[32] Even the countercultural movements are ever in search of new normative expressions to replace the elitist candidates of "establishment" culture.[33] As one moves through neoclassical criteria for the classic in the eighteenth century, through Romantic theories of the classic in the early nineteenth century, to sociologically informed criteria like Sainte-Beuve's in the late nineteenth century, through despairing early-twentieth-century definitions like Eliot's to more recent criteria, open to both cultural pluralism and a pluralism of criteria (like that of Frank Kermode),[34] to the debasement of the very notion "classic" into a synonym for its opposite—the latest cultural fad or celebrity—one reality in the strange and complex history of the word "classic" endures. We all find ourselves compelled both to recognize and on occasion to articulate our reasons for the recognition[35] that certain expressions of the human spirit so disclose a compelling truth about our lives that we cannot deny them some kind of normative status. Thus do we name these expressions, and these alone, "classics." Thus do we recognize, whether we name it so or not, a normative element in our cultural experience, experienced as a realized truth.

Yet what does it mean to find a normative element in cultural experience? My thesis is that what we mean in naming certain texts, events, images, rituals, symbols[36] and persons "classics" is that here we recognize nothing less than the disclosure of a reality we cannot but name truth. With Whitehead, here we find something valuable, something "important"; some disclosure of reality in a moment that must be called one of "recognition" which surprises, provokes, challenges, shocks and eventually transforms us; an experience that upsets conventional opinions and expands the sense of the possible; indeed a realized experience of that which is essential, that which endures. The presence of classics in every culture is undeniable. Their memory haunts us. Their actual effects in our lives endure and await ever new appropriations, constantly new interpretations. Their existence may be trusted to time, to the generations of capable readers and inquirers who will check our enthusiasms and ensure the emergence of some communal sense of the importance of certain texts, images, persons, events, symbols.

So obvious a truth of our cultural lives seems to be widely ignored; at least any claim to truth in the classic is quietly but effectively disowned. Indeed in ordinary language[37] the word "classic" is often used, and therefore just as often either means the province of the "classicist" or serves as a synonym for the latest sensation. Any normative claim to knowledge, any suggestion of truth for the classic is often shunned as that higher form of both category confusion and bad taste dear to the elitist. Yet here we cannot simply trust ordinary language and its possibly debased use by the wider society. Whenever the technoeconomic realm controls the list of candidates for the meaning of what will count as shareable, as public, as knowledge, as truth, then the entire realm of culture—and all the candidates for classic status—must either be levelled to the conventional masked as the ordinary, or retreat into the privacy of some overcrowded reservation of the spirit. We already know what alone will count as truth in the public realm: the methodically controlled results of the technical realm in all its forms. The rest is taste, or emotion, or "art."

And art, finally, becomes a matter of the private vision of the artist: The spontaneous genius[38] of the great Romantics has become the artistic "celebrity" of today. Indeed, Byron's grand imagery for the artistic process—"the volcano which must erupt to prevent an earthquake"—now becomes the aerial photographs of spent volcanos and pleasant, if idyosyncratic, reservations. In a post-Freudian popular culture, the carefully nuanced analyses of Freud's *Leonardo* are forgotten in a rush to remember how neurosis is the the key to private meaning of all artists and thereby of all art. In a post-Marxist culture, the respect and care of Marx and Trotsky for the integrity and relative autonomy of art can be quickly forgotten in the "reductionist" analyses of "vulgar Marxist" criticism serving as appropriate critical analogues to the posters of Soviet "socialist realism." In a post-Christian culture, the beleagured "Christian" critic can occasionally risk forays off the churchly reservation to find "Christ symbols" and "Last Suppers" as the secret "message" in modern works of art. Meanwhile, the relative but real autonomy of the work of art, respected by all the great Marxist, Freudian and theological critics who honor the existence of classics, is destroyed by private ideologies employing psychological, sociological or theological forms of reductionism.

In that kind of unhappy situation it is perhaps not so strange that aesthetic theories can sometimes join ordinary-language understandings of the reality of art as mere personal preferences, private tastes. The discussion ends where it might begin: with one of the few Latin phrases still common parlance in all Western languages: *de gustibus non est disputandum.*

Yet do either those aesthetic theories grounded in "taste," or ordinary-language understandings of the nondisputability of "taste," really fit our actual experience of any work of art? When in the presence of any classic work of art, we do not, in fact, experience ourselves as an autonomous subject possessing certain tastes for certain qualities confronting the expression of someone else's taste, some easily controlled qualities hidden in the work by the artistic "genius." Instead the authentic experience of art is quite the opposite: We find ourselves "caught up" in its world, we are shocked, surprised, challenged by its startling beauty *and* its recognizable truth, its instinct for the essential. In the actual experience of art we do not experience the artist *behind* the work of art. Rather we recognize the truth of the work's disclosure of a world of reality transforming, if only for a moment, ourselves: our lives, our sense for possibilities and actuality, our destiny.

When we ignore the actual experience of art by imposing alien aesthetic theories of taste upon it,[39] we are tempted to misinterpret the experience as a purely, indeed, merely "aesthetic" one. In a manner analogous to our attempted alienation of ourselves and our own effective history into the realm of historicist privacy masked as autonomy, we may deny that the work of art has anything to do with what we name knowledge, truth, reality.[40] In an earlier and more homogeneous culture, training, education and cultivation were designed to aid everyone to experience the tested communal sense of the disclosive and transformative power and truth of the work of art. Now we seem too often content to cultivate a new form of alienation, the aesthetic sensibility. What is the popular understanding of an aesthetic sensibility but the controlled cultivation of an autonomous subject's taste for qualities in objects that exist in their own brittle autonomy over against that same subject? For publicness and truth, the autonomous subject will look elsewhere: to those forms of thinking guaranteed as scientific and technical. We still possess a common, if not a communal sense. But what is common sense now? It is something very like what Bernard Lonergan describes as a "common-sense eclecticism": "For opinions are legion; theories rise, glow, fascinate, and vanish; but sound judgment remains. And what is sound judgment? It is to bow to the necessary, to accept the certain, merely to entertain the probable, to distrust the doubtful, to denounce the impossible, and to believe what Science says."[41]

We may modify the theory of taste somewhat by considering the genuine work of art a production of genius. We may, with Kant, even consider the genius the "favorite" of nature who unconsciously speaks nature's truths. Romantic tributes to the artist as "genius" and their attendant criteria of spontaneity and intensity of feeling are not adequate to the claims to truth of the work of art.[42] For nature's claims in a technological age bent on the control of nature seem more and more remote; even an ecological conscience can often seem the private whim, the *noblesse oblige,* of a latter-day technological aristocracy. Rather the "genius" is envisioned no longer as the Romantic exemplar of nature's truths. Now the genius becomes merely another human curiosity, the peacock of the human species, whose private self seems more exotic and more interesting, but no less private than any other.

Nor will a modern emphasis upon spontaneity and feeling really help. For eighteenth-century understandings of "sentiment" have yielded to twentieth-century popular understandings of "sentimentality." And Romantic notions of intense and spontaneous feelings embedded in the classic poetry of Wordsworth, Shelley, Keats and Byron and the classic and complex theories of Coleridge have yielded to twentieth-century popular notions of feelings as purely private and of spontaneity as a purely individual quality.[43] Who today considers feeling an expression of nature itself, much less an expression of the whole of that overflowing reality first envisioned by Plotinus and articulated anew by Coleridge and Schelling? The work of art, sometimes even for the understanding of the artist, becomes simply the self-expression of a particularly complex, probably alienated, certainly idiosyncratic private self. The work of art, sometimes understood as possessing its own absolute autonomy by some formalist critics, is kept at a distance from our own cherished autonomy. It is always interesting, sometimes even fascinating. For art always provides new qualities to appreciate, new methods to understand how it works its fascination and, in Kierkegaard's sense of the aesthetic, new possibilities for our interesting Don Juan sensitivities to explore. But art does not provide an encounter with anything we can call truth about ourselves or reality. Art, too, is finally private.

Yet it remains worth inquiring whether this familiar, indeed popular understanding of "aesthetic" experience accords with our actual experience of any authentic work of art.[44] In fact it does not. Rather, as Hans-Georg Gadamer among others insists, the actual experience of the work of art can be called a realized experience of an event of truth.[45] More exactly, when I experience any classic work of art, I do not experience myself as an autonomous subject aesthetically appreciating the good qualities of an aesthetic object set over against me. Indeed, when I reflect after the experience upon the experience itself, shorn of prior theories of "aesthetics,"[46] I find that my subjectivity is never in control of the experience, nor is the work of art actually experienced as an object with certain qualities over against me. Rather the work of art encounters me with the surprise, impact, even shock of reality itself. In experiencing art, I recognize a truth I somehow know but know I did not really know except through the experience of recognition of the essential compelled by the work of art. I am transformed by its truth when I return to the everyday, to the whole of what I ordinarily call reality, and discover new affinities, new sensibilities for the everyday.

I do not experience a subject over against an object with my subjective consciousness in complete control. Rather I experience myself caught up in a relationship with the work of art in such manner that I transcend my everyday self-consciousness and my usual desires for control. In experiencing that actual internal relationship (no longer the external relationships of theories about the aesthetic subject or aesthetic object), I experience the impact of a realized experience, an event character of truth as a glimpse into the essential that is the real. I find I must employ words like "recognize" to describe that impact. Such actual self-transcendence, I also recognize, is not my own achievement. It happens, it occurs, I am "caught up in" the disclosure of the work. I am in the presence of a truth of recognition: recognition of what is important, essential, real beyond distractions, diversions, conventional opinions, idle talk, control and use of objects, techniques of distancing myself and manipulating others, the realm of publicness where only the lowest common denominator will count.[47]

I find myself in another realm of authentic publicness, a realm where "only the paradigmatic is the real." If I will not sentimentalize and thereby privatize that experience by destroying its authentic claim to publicness by some such strategy as some forms of "art for art's sake," I will allow myself to experience the event to the point of a suspension of my usual disbelief. Later, perhaps in the "tranquility" of that "recollection" which characterizes much reflection, I may consider how that disclosure relates to my vision of the world. Are real affinities present? Is a confrontation, even destruction, of my present world demanded? Is a strange confirmation, even "a consolation without a cause," present? Is a recognition that "something else may be the case" at work?

Do I wish to discover how this work manages to work its power of disclosure through its form? I may study the best formalist and objective critics. Do I wish to know more about the workings of the artistic process? I may study the Romantic, the Freudian or the Marxist critics. Do I wish to know more about the effects of art upon the audience? I may study the pragmatic critics. Do I wish to know more about the vision of reality disclosed in front of, not behind this work? I may study the hermeneutical critics. The codes and structures in the work and their analogies to other codes and structures? I may study the semiotic and structuralist critics. The strange experience of incompleteness, even of disillusionment with all determinate meanings? I may study the deconstructionists.

The need for a critical pluralism of methods of understanding and explaining that original experience of the work of art—a need recently analyzed by Wayne Booth in his development of criteria of the relative adequacy of vitality, justice and, above all, critical understanding—seems a clear need to this reader of literary criticism.[48] The *only* methods disallowed should be those which disown the original experience of art and replace it with some other kind of experience. Every classic contains its own plurality and encourages a pluralism of readings. The possibilities of the formulation of what Booth names a "monism" towards understanding the experience of art are as multiple, as Abrams and Gunn remind us,[49] as the emphases upon any one of the four elements basic to the total situation of any work of art: the artist who creates the work (expressive theories and methods, often Romantic); the work itself (objective theories and methods, often formalist); the world the work creates or reveals (mimetic theories ranging from Aristotle to hermeneutical understandings of the creative power of mimesis in Gadamer and Ricoeur); and the audience the work affects (pragmatic theories from Philip Sidney to forms of Marxist analysis like that of Lukacs). All these methods, as we shall see below, really do aid an appropriation of the experience of art. Yet it remains the realized experience which must serve as the first word and the final criterion of relative adequacy in any attempt at both understanding and explanation. For only a realized experience and its disclosure of some recognition of the event-character of truth in the work of art will finally count for each as evidence.[50] Only classic works of art, whatever their period, whatever their culture, can be counted on to allow, indeed to compel, that kind of experience and that kind of paradigmatic recognition.

In entering into an experience of a genuine work of art we risk entering a "game" where truth is at stake: the truth of the recognition of our actuality and possibility.[51] To choose the phenomenon of the "game" to understand the experience of art, as Gadamer does, or to understand the experience of language itself, as Wittgenstein does, is a risky choice. What can seem less serious, more private, more the product of subjectivity than the game? Yet an understanding of the actual experience of playing a game yields surprising results. When I enter a game, if I insist upon my self-consciousness to control every move, I am not in fact playing the game. Rather I am playing some curious game of my own where self-consciousness is the sole rule, while any vulnerability and any ability to transcend myself are the forbidden moves in the only role or game I am willing to play.[52]

Pure subjectivity can account for an inability to play, a refusal to act, an impossibility of ever entering any game other than one's own self-designated role, the narcissist game where one is sole actor and sole spectator. But pure subjectivity cannot account for the actual experience of playing any game. Rather self-awareness and self-centeredness are lost in the game. In playing, I lose myself in the play. I do not passively lose myself. In fact, I actively gain another self by allowing myself fully to enter the game. Thus do I allow myself to be played by the game. I move into the "rules" of the game, into the back-and-forth movement, the experienced internal relationships of the game itself. The game becomes not an object over against a self-conscious subject but an experienced relational and releasing mode of being in the world distinct from the ordinary, nonplayful one. In every game, I enter the world where I play so fully that finally the game plays me.

This loss of self-consciousness common to all games becomes the first reality to note when one enters the serious "game" of encountering a genuine work of art. There the same kind of loss of subjectivity is present. Yet now the "stakes" are higher. For in encountering the genuine work of art, in risking playing that game, the minor transformation of the self occasioned in all play becomes a major transformation into structure. Indeed, the spectator is now demanded as an essential part of the play. In allowing ourselves to experience art we are transformed, however briefly, into the mode of being of the work of art where we experience the challenge, often the shock, of a reality greater than the everyday self, a reality of the paradigmatic power of the essential that transforms us.[53] Here the back-and-forth movement of every game becomes the buoyant dialectic of true freedom: surprise, release, confrontation, shock, often reverential awe, always transformation. In our actual experience of the work of art, we move into the back-and-forth rhythms of the work: from its discovery and disclosure to a sensed recognition of the essential beyond the everyday; from its hiddenness to our sensed rootedness; from its disclosure and concealment of truth to our realized experience of a transformative truth, at once revealing and concealing.

The experience of art belies familiar notions of aesthetic distanciation as clearly as the actual experience of the game belies the notion of all those who cannot play because they will not let go of the controls required by their nervous self-consciousness. When we exit from most games, we are refreshed. When we leave a realized experience of entering the game of an authentic work of art (a game, unlike others, where the spectator is needed for the play to occur) we are transformed. There we have witnessed ourselves caught up in a disclosure of the event-character of truth itself,[54] experienced as a recognition of an often unwelcome truth about ourselves and the world. We can control, manipulate, deny the truth of art. We can refuse to play. More subtly, we can turn the whole experience into yet another experience of my "aesthetic" self-consciousness and its limitless taste for the control of all truth.

Yet when anyone of us is caught unawares by a genuine work of art, we find ourselves in the grip of an event, a happening, a disclosure, a claim to truth which we cannot deny and can only eliminate by our later controlled reflection: it was only a play, merely the private expression of a private self, a new quality, an illusion, magic, unreal. But in the experience of art we lose our usual self-consciousness and finally encounter a rooted self—a self transformed into both new possibility and the actuality of rootedness by its willingness to play and be played by that transforming disclosure.

In that sense, the experience of art is not peculiar, private, unreal. Rather, art is public in meaning as paradigmatic of what happens to us in spirit and in truth. When a work of art so captures a paradigmatic experience of that event of truth, it becomes in that moment normative. Its memory enters as a catalyst into all our other memories and, now subtly, now compellingly, transforms our perceptions of the real. It becomes a classic: always retrievable, always in need of appreciative appropriation and critical evaluation, always disclosive and transformative with its truth of importance, always open to new application and thereby new interpretation. That science reaches truth—the truths of verification and falsification—only an obscurantist would deny. That the work of art discloses an event not merely of taste, genius or beauty, but truth—only a philistine, even an "aesthetic" one, will finally deny.[55] We can, to repeat, refuse to enter into the game of the work of art where the usual subject-object relationship of both ordinary experience and science is broken—where a realized experience of the relationship itself, the back-and-forth movement of the event of disclosure and concealment, actually happens. We can refuse to enter the game of conversation where the subject matter produced through the form, not the formless ego, controls the questioning and the responding. We *can* make all these refusals. Yet somehow the classics endure as provocations awaiting the risk of reading: to challenge our complacency, to break our conventions, to compel and concentrate our attention, to lure us out of a privacy masked as autonomy into a public realm where what is important and essential is no longer denied. Whenever we actually experience even one classic work of art we are liberated from privateness into the genuine publicness of a disclosure of truth. It seems foolish, therefore, to develop theories of aesthetics which effectively deny the truth-character of the experience of art as a realized experience of the essential. It seems fatal to hand over the classics to the levelling power of a technical reason disguised as publicness, to consign them to the privacy of a merely entertaining, tasteful, interesting aesthetic realm of temporary refreshment. Instead we need, I believe, a rehabilitation of the notions of the normative, the authoritative—in a word, the classical—now freed from the private domain of elitist classicists and welcomed again as the communal and public heritage of our common human experience of the truth of the work of art.

iii. The Interpretation of the Classics and the Pluralism of Readings

If, even once, a person has experienced a text, a gesture, an image, an event, a person with the force of the recognition: "This is important! This does make and will demand a difference!" then one has experienced a candidate for classic status. If one's own experience has been verified by other readers, especially by the community of capable readers over the centuries, the reflective judgment should prove that much more secure. If the experience is verified at a later period of life, when a new but related understanding of the same classic occurs with the same force of revelatory power, then, once again, a reflective judgment upon the realized experience of this text, event, gesture, image, symbol, person—this structured expression of the human spirit—is rendered yet more plausible, still more relatively adequate. Most of us can recall, for example, recalling a novel, poem or essay that had great impact on our lives. Years later we reread it. If it is a candidate for classic status, it will still have that power. Now however, it will bear a new interpretation for our later, either more mature or less authentic lives. Yet the text will still compel and concentrate our attention with the same kind of power of recognition of an essential truth about ourselves and our lives. If it no longer has that power, no longer compels recognition, then we are better off with our memories. We will be thankful for its former contribution yet we will read it now, if at all, only as a helpful, nostalgic reminder of what life was like back then, not what life means now.

Most of us can also recall another distinct but analogous experience. Think of a text that history has elevated to that cultural eminence expressed in the ordinary use of the word "classic." We read the text unmoved, unresponsive, cold. We may rightly have learned to trust our responses.[56] Do we wish therefore to enter into the lists to dispute this text's pretensions to classic status? Thus does that grand contemporary game, half serious, half fun, of listing "overrated" and "underrated" works ensue. If we are prudent persons in the Aristotelian, not the modern sense, however, we shall unfold our banners of denunciation with some appropriate tentativeness. At the very least, we will be willing to listen to that wider community of inquirers and readers who have found and find this text a classic. We will listen to them and then return to our dialogue with the subject matter of this "formed" text. After that second exposure, we may still decide that the community of inquirers in this instance has been mistaken; that this text is at best a period piece whose exposure as pure sentimentality, sheer obscurantism or rank self-indulgence is long overdue. At that point, tentativeness must cease. For in those instances where a matter of importance is at stake—and the assignment of the status "classic" to any text is a matter of singular importance—then we must insist. But where tentativeness ceases, listening never does. The wider community of readers, living and dead, must continue to be heard as all return to the struggle of finding some appropriate response (from some initial sense of import to a formed judgment) to this possibly classic text.

How can we explain these experiences? Let us use the word "explain" here with care. The hermeneutical tradition which most informs my own approach has been suspicious of the word "explanation" because of its overtones of methodical, technical control.[57] We may and do experience an event of understanding, but can we, more radically should we, wish to explain it? Insofar as the event of any realized experience of any classical text is indeed both initially and ultimately an event of understanding whereby we are caught up in the serious game of the truth of existence played by the classic, this caveat against technique, method or explanation is entirely appropriate. When we also consider that some of our explanatory games—some aesthetic theories or strictly historicist methods, for example—end by contradicting our actual experience and understanding of the truth of the work of art and the reality of tradition, we should be as wary of explanation as Gadamer insists.

If we can so explain, for example, the codes in all our myths, all our stories, our entire culture as just that without remainder—codes with no messages—through methods of explaining with no understanding of our rootedness in this effective history and its disclosure of some essential truth about existence, we seem to be in the presence of a new mode of explanation designed to alienate us still further from our actual experience of history, art, religion, thought and the event of understanding in each. Yet when these analyses are in the hands of a real master—a Lévi-Strauss, a Foucault, a Barthes—we instinctively recognize that these semiotic and structuralist explanations of codes, deep and surface structures, enrich our understanding of the text by developing that understanding further, by challenging our former complacent understanding, by compelling us to think again, by suggesting analogies that provoke our attention and expose our sloth. This is the case even when a particular reader disowns the sometimes imperialist claims of these methods while still finding their readings of the texts illuminating and transformative of one's own reading of the pluralistic reality in every classic text and every prospective interpreter. Indeed, as semiotic and structuralist methods continue to prove their worth by their development in scope, refinement and application and by sheer dazzling critical performances like those of Roland Barthes, there seems little point to nervous humanists' denials of their contributions to the entire hermeneutical enterprise.

It may well be true that Lévi-Strauss' structuralist methods are sometimes entangled with the bleak beauty of a despairing structuralist ideology, that Foucault's genealogical method is often entwined with a bitter polemic against any form of humanism, that Barthes' semiotic method sometimes seems inseparable from a deliberate, if vitalizing, critical perverseness, that Derrida's deconstructionist methods seem to need the aid of *some* determinate meanings as they spill us and all our classic texts into his vitalizing abyss of indeterminacy. Yet all these ideologies possess, after all, their own truth: a suspicion of the illusions, the alienation, often the death and slackness of all self-congratulatory humanisms. Moreover, the ideologies are not intrinsic to the methods of structuralist, semiotic or deconstructionist explanations. The methods—as methods of explanation—stand on their own either to develop and expand our original understanding or to confront and challenge it at the root.

In sum, understanding and explanation are not enemies but uneasy, wary allies. To reject explanation in favor of some often vague and impressionistic notion of "pure understanding," of *Verstehen,* seems pointless in any valid defense of the priority of understanding. Rather one may accept a formulation like Paul Ricoeur's wherein understanding "envelops" the entire process of interpretation, whereas explanation "develops" the initial understanding and illuminates the final understanding of appropriation.[58] Formalist, structuralist, semiotic and deconstructionist methods, on this reading, are enrichments, not denials, of the hermeneutical process. They provide various, often conflicting explanations of the codes and structures of the immanent senses of the text. Or alternatively, with Jacques Derrida, they provide deconstructive explanations of the nondeterminate sense of every text. Thereby do they develop, challenge, correct, refine, complicate and confront[59] the reader's understanding of both the sense *and,* through that sense, the hermeneutical referent in front of the text.

Yet before speaking further of the need for a critical pluralism of readings disclosed by the dialectic of understanding-explanation-understanding, a final word of summary clarification on the nature of the interpreter of any classic text seems in order. The position defended here emphasizes, above all, the *reception* by the reader of the classic text. But before the reader of this text decides that here we have, at best, another instance of the "affective fallacy"[60] or even another plea for the wholesale violation of the text[61] by the reader, the exact character of the interpreter as receptive subject needs further clarification.

In summary form,[62] the interpreter possesses certain distinct characteristics.[63] First, the interpreter of the classic comes to any reading of the text as a subject with a certain preunderstanding of the subject matter of the text; certain personal questions, opinions, responses, expectations, even desires, fears and hopes are present in that preunderstanding. And yet this preunderstanding, although deeply personal and individual, is never merely personal and never simply static. More exactly, the preunderstanding of the subject is itself informed, both negatively and positively, by the history of the effects and influences of the culture—including the history of the effects, influences and interpretations of this classic text in the culture.

The subject of the interpreter, in short, is always a social subject. As related to the other selves in the tradition, the subject is intrinsically intersubjective. As formed by the community and as responsible to the wider community of inquirers and readers, the subject is communal. As involved in this tradition,[64] this culture—above all in any native language which embodies and carries the history of the effects and interpretations of the tradition—the subject is radically and irretrievably historical in the exact sense of historicity. Every present moment is, in fact, formed by both the memories of the tradition and the hopes, desires, critical demands for transformation for the future. The notion of the present moment as pure instant, an ever-receding image, is as mistaken as the allied notion of a pure—isolated, purely autonomous—subject.

The subject as interpreter may despise the tradition as a deadening force, a bourgeois humanist hoax, an obscurantist fraud, a poisonous creature of *ressentiment*. But the interpreter must still interpret that tradition in the hope, and with the ethical demand, of exposing its fraudulence, suspecting its claims, denouncing its injustice. No one—no one, that is, who uses a language which is itself the chief product and central carrier of the tradition—escapes the reality of tradition. Only Aristotle's god or a beast is a really solitary self. The rest of us are radically finite and social selves embedded in this language, this culture, this history. When we approach any classic, that tradition lives consciously or unconsciously in us as much as our own more personal histories—our own more individual questions, opinions, desires, fears, hopes—live in every act of interpretation. Why then bother to approach the classics? Because therein lies the one finite hope of liberation to the essential.

The interpreter, as finite historical subject, approaches a classic. Then the second moment of interpretation begins. If the classic is a classic, to repeat, another force comes into play. That force is the claim to attention, a vexing, a provocation exerted on the subject by the classic text. The subject may not know why or how that claim exercises its power—those are tasks for later reflection and more informed readings. But that the claim to attention is present—that something like what we have called a realized experience, ranging from a haunting sense of resonance and import to a shock of recognition, that sheer event-like thatness—is what cannot be denied. My *doxai* are suddenly confronted with a *paradoxon* demanding attention. My finite status as this historical subject is now confronted with the classic and its claim upon me: a claim that transcends any context from my preunderstanding that I try to impose upon it, a claim that can shock me with the insight into my finitude as finitude, a claim that will interpret me even as I struggle to interpret it. I cannot control the experience, however practiced I am in techniques of manipulation. It happens, it demands, it provokes.[65] In fact, the high claims often made for poetic experience may be viewed as paradigmatic of the kind of realized experience exerted by every classic on every sensitive, intelligent human being. I may, upon further reflection, end by rejecting that claim.

And yet at the moment of the original encounter I am forced, often unwillingly, into a suspension of my usual disbelief. I experience a release from my usual controls, a liberation from my most cherished opinions by the sheer power of the claim now forced upon my attention by the classic itself.

Sometimes a false, an unnatural timidity in asserting my own rights to this paradigmatic experience may keep me from allowing any status other than a purely private one to these experiences. More often, a correct and natural sense of suspicion upon what may be a purely private enthusiasm demands further reflection. As a responsibly social self, the interpreter does want to observe what the wider community of inquirers has to say about their experience of this possible candidate for classic status. As a consciously historical self, the interpreter wants to render explicit the history of this classic's effects, influences and interpretations as well as the history—partly traditional, partly personal—of the interpreter's own preunderstanding of the tradition. Yet the interpreter will not want to do this with the kind of self-consciousness that in effect retreats upon the personal, social, communal and historical preunderstanding of the finite self and upon the original experience of the classic and its provocative claim to attention.[66]

The interpreter in a third step of interpretation will consider the phenomenon of the game in an attempt to grasp the kind of dynamic actually at work in that experience. In a related move, the interpreter will employ some model of dialogue to indicate the appropriate kind of response to the realized experience of the classic. For the phenomenon of dialogue will demand that the interpreter concentrate, above all, on the subject matter of the text: the questions, responses, hints, resonances, feelings—the "world"[67] disclosed in front of the text through the text's form. The dialogue will demand that the interpreter enter into the back-and-forth movement of that disclosure in the dialectics of a self-transcending freedom released by the text upon a finite, historical, dialogical reader and received by the text from a now dialoguing reader.

This same model of dialogue will also encourage the reader to enter into the fourth step of interpretation: the larger conversation of the entire community of inquirers. In the actual praxis of authentic dialogue, interpreters recognize that in every act of interpretation, they are also applying the disclosure of the text to some preunderstanding of the tradition. The interpreter may also recognize resonances in other readers to that self-understanding. As a single interpreter, for example, I may recognize the challenge to my present preunderstanding of a text of Ignatius Loyola which Roland Barthes' vitalizing reading now allows—even when I do not accept Barthes' reading of this text as the most relatively adequate one.[68] I may recognize, as a second example, the challenge to my preunderstanding which T. S. Eliot's readings of Shelley, Milton or Vergil provide—

even when I do not finally accept his rejection of Shelley, his ambivalence towards Milton, his astonishing awe in front of Vergil.[69] In all these experiences, I know that my own preunderstanding of the relevant tradition for these texts (here the Western Christian tradition) is identical to neither Barthes' radical suspicion of it nor to Eliot's famous royalist, Anglo-Catholic, classicist, high-church hymn to it. Yet their interpretations of these texts at once challenge mine and, by that challenge, they inevitably transform, however subtly, my own interpretations of the same texts.

The larger dialogue with the entire community of capable readers is a major need for any claim to relative adequacy in interpretation. In fact, there exists a pluralism of reading traditions whose major point of difference, as we noted above, may be located on what major focus (the reader, the work, the world or the artist) is chosen to concentrate the interpreter's attention. There is also a pluralism within each tradition[70] of reading based on the plurality in text and reader alike. The position defended in this work, for example, principally relates to the tradition which focusses upon the reader's response or the reception of the work. And yet there are real and often conflicting differences even within this single pragmatic (or praxis) tradition of reading.

For example, the emphasis of this theory of interpretation upon the reader's response is analogous to but not identical with the emphasis upon the reader in the free-play (not the dialogical) model of Roland Barthes,[71] much less the "bottomless chessboard," radically deconstructionist free-play model of Jacques Derrida and J. Hillis Miller.[72] And neither their free-play model nor this model of the play of dialogue is identical to the emphasis upon the response of the reader in the tradition of Horace or Philip Sidney and the classical pragmatic debates on instruction or pleasure, much less to any search for the response of the original audience.[73] Yet every reader will recognize that all these diverse models with their common focus upon the reader's response do bear real family resemblances within the "pragmatic" (as praxis) tradition of criticism. And yet a question must be raised here. Can any theory of interpretation focussed on the reader's response really do justice to the readings disclosed by alternative traditions of reading with their different focusses: those traditions focussed on the artist, the structure of the text, or the world disclosed by the text?

The choice of the ethical word "justice" here is not inappropriate. As Wayne Booth has argued in his development of criteria of "relative adequacy" to defend a critical plurality of readings, "justice" to alternative readings and alternative traditions of reading is incumbent upon all readers in any genuine community of inquiry. This demand for justice is aligned by Booth to two other criteria: first, a defense of the kind of vitality that practices new and fresh readings (hence he defends *some* productive "violations" of the text); and second, a demand, above all, for articulated critical understandings.[74] Together these three criteria seem to provide criteria of relative adequacy for a responsibly pluralistic community of readers. Booth's criteria, note, do not remove inevitable, indeed necessary, conflicts. They do provide empirical tests for the presence or absence of the ideal of dialogue and do challenge any form of critical monism.

The question, therefore, recurs: Can the dialogue model with its focus upon the reception of the text by the reader do justice to alternative traditions of readings and their distinct focusses? We have already seen the general response to this demand for justice. Insofar as one accepts the expansion of the original dialogue model from one of pure understanding to the dialectical model of understanding-explanation-understanding, justice can occur. For there any originary and enveloping understanding is internally open to every development, challenge, confirmation or transformation of that originary understanding by every legitimate method of explanation (e.g., formalist, structuralist, semiotic, deconstructionist, etc.) as the interpreter heads through a pluralism of readings to some informed understanding of the text. This same general response provides a second line of defense against the charges of injustice, partiality and provincialism for this "response of the reader" focus. Insofar as the dialogue model expanded (even explained!) as the model of understanding-explanation-understanding functions justly, that model is open to learning from formalist, structuralist, semiotic and deconstructionist explanations of how the text produces its "sense." The real debate of hermeneutics with these positions need not be with their methods but with any ahistorical claims for the method. That debate can also focus upon either the material element of the value judgments or the cultural tradition (in the broad sense, the ideologies) which seem to inform the claims.

Indeed the conflict of interpretations of the tradition informing *all* methods often becomes explicit only later in analyses of the world, the vision disclosed by the text. Yet that conflict is, in fact, operative implicitly in all methods of interpretation and explanation throughout the entire process of interpretation—a process which, as praxis, always includes some kind of application to the situation insofar as the reader recognizes this as a genuine *possibility*.

Or the debate may focus upon whether the sense of the text in the structures and signs, or even in the endless abyss of indeterminacy, does or does not also disclose a referent, a world. On the present model, it is important to recall, the referent of the text will be a referent *in front of* the text, not behind it (as in many forms of "psychological" or "sociological" criticism). Insofar as that latter claim holds, it follows that the "world" of the text (alternatively the vision of reality, the form of life disclosed by the text) is also countenanced, indeed demanded, by this model of reading. If the general principle holds, then the referent will exist in front of the text even for those self-referential texts whose very referent is *to the sense*.

Since the referent of the text, moreover, is to a *possible* way of being in the world, a vision of reality, a form of life, it becomes important to render explicit the conflict of interpretations that was already operative in *all* the methods of interpretation and explanation. For from the initial focus upon reception by the reader, we have moved from an originary *understanding* evoked by the actuality of the claim to attention of the text: first understood in some initial sense of import, then explicable through all those methods of reading concentrating on the structures or forms of the sense of the text and, through those journeys of explanation, understood anew as a referent, i.e., as a *possible* mode of being in the world, now disclosed to the reader for appropriation or rejection. At this point (but only, *pace* Yvor Winters, at this point) does the *further* ethical task of adjudicating this conflict of possible worlds, forms of life, visions of the whole become a central need for another community of inquiry—the ethical and, at the limit, the religious communities of inquiry.[75]

To understand all is not, after all, to excuse all—as any reader of Céline's novels or any viewer of Riefenstahl's films can testify. This additional ethical task of discrimination and adjudication of conflicting views is necessary. It is, however, a distinct task from the ethical tasks of attention to the interpreter's original experience and understanding of the claim exerted by the classic as a genuine possibility for existence, of attention to the text (its structures and forms) demanded by formalist analyses of the text, of attention to the world of the text as a possible one for existence and, finally, of attention, in justice, to a responsible pluralism of readings. The task of discriminating and adjudicating possible worlds impels the interpreter, therefore, into further conversation with ethicians, philosophers and theologians. That same conversation is always already operative in every great critic, even if emphasized only in the grand "moralists" of the Western critical tradition from Plato to Dr. Johnson, Matthew Arnold, Leo Tolstoy and, in our own time, F. R. Leavis.

It is not the case, of course, that only the moralist critics have this agenda of adjudicating the conflict of interpretations on the vision of the work or the tradition. The heady free play involved in Barthes' provocative "violations" of the text, for example, also involves an ethical component influenced by both his negation of the deadening "hoax" of bourgeois humanism and his demand for liberation from that stultifying ethic. Thus will Barthes liberate us to the pleasures of the text and release us from the "repleteness" of traditional images, metaphors and analogies of presence and fullness into the joys of absence. Marxist,[76] Freudian and theological critics of the classics often concentrate much of their critical energy on this common ethical task of discrimination and adjudication of conflicting worldviews, yet without sacrificing the relative autonomy of the text. In the exemplary case of Walter Benjamin,[77] for example, his profound moral passion is not purchased at the price of denying the realized experience of the classic that initiated his journey of interpretation nor the intratextual needs demanded by the forms producing the relative autonomy of the text.

The present theory of interpretation, therefore, with its model of dialogue focussed primarily upon the response of the reader to the classic, does allow for, indeed encourages, a responsible pluralism of readings based on a recognition of the plurality in text and reader alike. In principle, the theory can enter into conversation, albeit conversation inevitably marked by conflict among alternative traditions of reading with their different focusses. The same model, once expanded into Ricoeur's model of understanding-explanation-understanding, will take its own account of the sense of the work (its structures, forms and signs) and, through that sense, the world or vision disclosed as the referent in front of the work. Even the author need not be lost—not, of course, on this theory, as the author *behind* the work (the author reconstructed in biographies), but the author as implied author[78] *in* the work and in the vision of reality disclosed by the entire *oeuvre* of a particular author.

This focus upon the reception of the classic by the reader, therefore, inevitably concentrates attention upon the reader's original experience of the classic rather than upon the production of the classic itself. Yet the broad lines of the interpreter's task sketched above may possibly throw some light on the analogous task of the production of the classic itself.

iv. The Production of the Classic: A Thought Experiment

The concept of the production of the work of art, even more than its interpretation, is an "essentially contested concept."[79] So much is this the case that a word of caution to the reader (and the author) seems appropriate first. I make no pretenses to resolving here the conflict on that essentially contested concept. Rather I will make some suggestions towards its possible resolution by engaging in a relatively simple, straightforward but perhaps suggestive thought experiment. The question is this: What light, if any, does the earlier analysis of the interpretation of the classic throw upon the production of the classic? My hunch is that the processes are analogous. This section will attempt to warrant that hunch partially by developing what may prove a suggestive analogy.

No more than the interpreter of the classic is the original artist a solitary self.[80] The artist, too, is a particular self with a particular history in a particular culture. The artist, too, is a finite, social, historical self employing a language that carries the entire history of the effects and influence of the tradition. And yet the artist, in engaging in the production of the work of art, does have a peculiar, even a privileged place. But wherein lies that peculiarity? One need not minimize the productive power in the artist by means of classicist notions of the artist as a mirror to nature, nor exaggerate it with Romantic notions of the artist as the genius, as nature's darling within and by whom nature itself spontaneously "overflows." Nor need one demand that the artist become a martyr to the work and lose all individuality, as in Eliot's strangely Romantic, anti-Romantic portrait of the artist as martyred to the work, in order to note the truth of Eliot's basic contention: It is the work, not the artist, which must receive the attention of the interpreter.[81] And yet we may legitimately wish to understand not only our own receptive experience and understanding of the work of art and its implied author but also the distinct question of the production of the work itself and its implied classic person, the artist.[82]

The artist, the thinker, the hero, the saint—who are they, finally, but the finite self radicalized and intensified? The difference between the artist and the rest of us is one of intense degree, not one of kind. The difference is one where the journey of intensification—a journey which most of us fear yet desire, shun yet demand—is really undertaken. The journey into particularity in all its finitude and all its striving for the infinite[83] in this particular history in all its effects, personal and cultural, will with the artist be radically embraced. The insistence upon undertaking the journey of intensification into particularity, if aligned with the luck of talent, the discipline of craftsmanship, and the gift of imagination, will yield the possibility of the production of a classic.

The surest sign of the artist is not a striking originality in the sense of novelty and is never a self unembodied in a finite tradition—even if a despised tradition. The purely solitary self is not a human being. It is not even really the God of Jews and Christians who, *pace* Sartre, *is* an artist.[84] The sign of the artist may well be a willingness to undergo the journey of intensification into particularity to the point where an originating sense for the fundamental questions and feelings that impel us all, and a rare response in thought and feeling to those questions, is experienced—and often experienced as some kind of gift, come "unawares."[85] Then the experience—in Henry James' typically exact expression—is "rendered"[86] through all the strategies of semblance of the productive, creative imagination into the actuality of the work of art. Some process like this, I believe, may account for the production of the work of art in a manner that is analogous to the actual *receptive* experience and interpretation of the work of art.[87] Indeed, some realized experience of art seems the surest clue to any entry into the more difficult question of the production of the work of art. For a realized experience of the claim to attention exerted by the classic provides the surest clue, as the nearest analogue, to the very production of the classic itself. To warrant this belief, let us observe how the realities uncovered above in anyone's receptive experience and interpretation of a classic seem isomorphic with the same realities intensified and perhaps sublated in the original production of the same classic.

The moment named "intensification" is, in fact, fundamentally a moment of experience and understanding. More exactly, a person gives oneself over to, is caught up in, the most serious game of all, the game that Eric Voegelin, recalling Socrates and Jesus, calls the game of "the truth of existence." The self can no longer keep at arm's length from life. I am haunted by the thought that I have not lived, I have not entered, I have not allowed myself to be caught up in the self-transcendence of the "game" of life. The self of the artist lets go of the distancing stance of the everyday and enters the subject matter of those fundamental questions. Timidity is no longer possible. A courage to allow oneself to be played and thereby to play this game of the truth of existence must replace the fears and the opinions of the everyday. The artist does not know where the journey will lead; one must wager and risk. The artist will be likely to wager, at least initially, on some classic path.

Yet the path eventually taken cannot be laid out in advance. The personal route of intensification remains unpredictable. Each returns with different reports. Those who return with a report whose expression allows some recognition of an essential aspect[88] of our existence—its fatedness, its challenge, its finitude, its horrors, its possibility, its joy—are those the rest of us cannot but listen to if we too are willing to play the game. They are the artists, the heroes, the saints, the thinkers. Our experience of their expression of that event of recognition in a text, a symbol, a style of life, even a single gesture, leads the rest of us to believe that the intensification process is worth the risk. For at the end of the entire process of interpretation is an understanding that *is* recognized as a belonging to, a participation in and a distancing from some essential aspect of the whole now experienced as disclosure and concealment—come "unawares," as event, even as gift. That understanding which some Eastern traditions choose to name "enlightenment" occurs to envelop all other understandings, to transform all other opinions and explanations with something essential. By means of the artist's journey of intensification into some essential subject matter we recognize that now we can grasp certain essential truths which, as Kierkegaard in his journey knew, touch human existence by their immediacy and irreplaceability.

And yet every journey of intensification needs expression.[89] The hero, the artist, the thinker, the saint: each must express that understanding and that experience in a life, an action, a symbol, an image, a gesture, a text. Each must, therefore, risk the final moment of intensification and understanding: the moment of distanciation of the self from itself in order to express, to render, to produce, a communicable, shareable, public meaning. The artist risks alienation from the original experience. And yet one must thus risk anew and set out on this second journey of intensification.

The notion of distanciation[90] on the side of production is analogous to the notion "explanation" on the side of reception and interpretation.[91] The distancing of the self from its experience, especially its intense and paradigmatic experiences, can, like explanation, prove alienating and reductive, just as the initial shock of the realized experience and understanding in the interpretation of the classic can resist any explanations which deny this experience by alienating us from it and reducing it to something else.

In understanding the actual experience of the work of art, for example, surely Gadamer is correct to decry "the beclouded distance in which the cultured bourgeois consciousness enjoyed its cultural possessions." Yet is it the case that all distanciation is by its very nature alienating, destructive of experience and understanding, as Gadamer and, behind him, Heidegger often seem to imply? Our earlier reflections on interpretation have already suggested that this is not necessarily the case. Rather, the interpretation theory of Paul Ricoeur, as we saw above, can here provide an important corrective to the Heidegger-Gadamer tradition by allowing for a dialectic of understanding-explanation-understanding without abandoning the central insistence of the hermeneutical tradition on the enveloping priority of understanding in the process of interpretation.[92]

Distanciation is not always "imposed on" a situation of radical belonging to and participation in reality. In fact some distanciation is essential for any expression and thereby the very production and preservation of meaning in the work. In all discourse, after all, there is already a distanciation of the noematic, ideal, atemporal meaning (the said) from the noetic, actual, temporal event of discourse itself (the saying). Moreover, the polysemy of the individual word and the ambiguity of individual sentences is further complicated on the level of the text by a plurivocity that arises from the very nature of the text as a structured work.[93] Just as the meaning of a sentence cannot be grasped simply by knowing the meaning of individual words, so too the text is not merely a collection of sentences. Change a sentence or any sequence of sentences in this text, and you change the meaning of the text.

The classical text exploits both these factors through the strategy usually named "genre." Most of us believe, for example, that the meaning of a poem is not finally paraphrasable in a series of propositions that claim to say the same thing. Nor is the meaning simply reducible to the mind of the author so that, if only the author were present, he or she could tell us its meaning in clearer, more straightforward, more literal terms. Who would care to claim that *Hamlet* means such banalities as "life is difficult, often impossible" or that the social and political conditions in medieval Denmark or in Shakespeare's London tended to be extreme? May not these absurdly philistine positions suggest the *reductio ad absurdum* of any refusal on the side of interpretation to find the meaning of the text in the text itself?

The text is a structured whole. The meaning (as sense and referent) is produced in and by the work at work in the text. Even the most intense experience and understanding must find expression, must be rendered through some appropriate strategy of discourse (usually by some genre). Any text (especially, but not only, the written text)[94] fixes or codifies the meaning and thereby allows that meaning to escape the confines of the author's intention, the original addressee's reception or the original sociohistorical locus of the text. Thereby the meaning endures for interpretation. A necessary condition for the preservation of that meaning (including a meaning with both excess and permanence as in the classic) is a distancing from the author, from the original situation and from the original audience.[95] As a work, the text is made on a first level by the semantic and syntactical rules of production. We know we understand and can speak a foreign language, for example, when we know not merely words or memorized grammatical rules but, as Wittgenstein observed, when we know "how to go on."

Works of literature, paradigmatically classics, exploit two further steps of this production process. The most usual generic word for the productive process of art is "imagination." Yet to introduce that word—with its history of the effects of Romantic, anti-Romantic, technological and popular disputes on "fancy" and the "imagination"—risk resolving the original difficulty by compounding it threefold. For many theories of the imagination have been hampered by notions of both image and the imagination as merely reproductive of some absent meaning.[96] Thus do these theories tend to encourage reflection in the direction of some mere reproduction of a literal meaning, rather than in the direction of the production of meaning itself. So linked, indeed, are most notions of "image" to an impoverished notion of perception, wherein image is simply a weak or absent or vague substitute for "real" sensation, that the emergence of a theory of the productive imagination for the production of meaning in a text aids both an understanding of the receptive experience of a classic text and the production of that text by the imagination. Hence, imagination needs to be related not primarily to perception, but to language. More exactly, imagination *is* the correlative intensification power which produces in language the meaning which the work expresses. A classic text is produced only when imagination at work, in a work, impels, drives, frees the creator to express the meaning—both the sense and the referent—of the work in the work.

When thus at work in the work, the notion of productive imagination may clarify two further aspects beyond the semantic and syntactical levels of the work in the production of a structured whole. The first aspect we have already seen under the term "genre."[97] As Kierkegaard's extraordinary sensitivity to genre makes clear, and as any experience of any classic example of any genre can clarify for any reader, genre is not, in spite of its usual use by most biblical exegetes, merely a classificatory device. Genre does not merely classify any more than the power or impetus behind it, the imagination, merely reproduces. Genre produces the meaning of the text. Genre accomplishes this not by remaining in the participatory understanding of the original experience. Rather, the ability to employ a genre distances the author from that original experience into an expression of its meaning by way of a production of a structured whole, a work, which allows the meaning to become shareable by provoking expectations and questions in the reader and, as classic, even enduring, excessive and demanding of constant interpretation and application, even by the author.

Nor is the author now lost. Rather, the final aspect of the productive process, style,[98] comes into play. For style conveys the author's presence not in terms of the original authorial presence but rather as "the implied author." In action, we express our character basically through our style. Those classic persons—the artists, thinkers, heroes, saints—who have forced themselves upon our imagination have produced their work by producing—discovering, recovering, rendering—a distinctive, unmistakable style in the sense perhaps meant by Oscar Wilde when he remarked that he put his talent into his work, his genius into his life.

Just as all written discourse expresses the original gap of distanciation between the saying and the said (event and meaning) so too all literature exploits this same strategy of participation-distanciation via the several strategies of composing a work generically: semantics, syntax, genre, style. The classical work—that work experienced with some recognition of the essential, the permanent, and its surplus of meaning, its never-exhausted need for new interpretation—is simply the uncommon product of this common strategy of distanciation via expression. The artist knows that we dare not allow timidity in entering the "game" of expressing a truth of existence. Here we must enter, play and be played until we have experienced and recognized where and how we belong, where and how we participate in the fundamental questions and responses to life itself. The artist knows that we cannot allow timidity in expressing that understanding. We must feed the imagination; we must be alert to the possible presence of some disclosure; we must recover, discover, invent, create a genre and a style, a personal voice, to render, to express the meaning of that intensified experience of something essential. In both moments the artist allows the intensification process, the demand for real self-transcendence. In the first moment, the artist is not satisfied with any closure of the first intensification process into the fundamental questions by way of particularity until some recognition occurs. In the second, the artist will not be content with any closure of the second intensification process of distanciation, with any implausibly "inexpressible" experience. Rather the artist will dare to render that experience through all the nonalienating strategies of distanciation provided by the imaginative production—genre, style, structure, voice—until that meaning is shareable and thus public. We, the readers, will either recognize or disown that authentic publicness.

And as that final note reminds us, the basic interest of this work remains less on a proposal for the phenomenology of the production of the classic than on the realized experience of reception and interpretation of the classical expressions of the human spirit in a nonalienating, nonprivatizing, shareable, public manner. We have witnessed in this chapter some examples (authentic conversation, thinking, art, history, classic texts, classic persons) where self-transcendence is demanded in order to understand. When we deliver ourselves over to the subject matter produced through form in a classic text, we discover what is other than and beyond ourselves. In the final moments of all interpretation, beyond but through explanation into some appropriated understanding, we discover ourselves as a finite part, as participatory in, belonging to yet distanced from some essential aspect of the whole. In the paradigmatic expressions of the human spirit—in those texts, events, persons, actions, images, rituals, symbols which bear within them a classic as authoritative status, we find in our experienced recognition of their claim to attention the presence of what we cannot but name "truth." The truth we find there may not be adequately expressible in the propositions of objective consciousness.[99] Yet that truth as at once a disclosure and a concealment of what, at our best and most self-transcending in interpreting the classics, we cannot but name "reality." In some matters, only the paradigmatic *is* the real.

Insofar as the arguments of this chapter are plausible, therefore, they yield one crucial insight: The classics cannot be confined to either neoclassicist norms, Romantic enthusiasms or, above all, to the discreet charm of bourgeois or technological privatization. The classics must be freed, as Nietzsche observed, to become our educators in the realities which as noble and true are public.

> But how can we find ourselves again? How can man know himself? . . . The youthful soul should look back on life with the question: What have you truly loved up to now, what has drawn your soul aloft, what has mastered it and at the same time blessed it? Set up these things . . . before you and perhaps they will give you . . . the fundamental law of your own true self . . . for your real nature lies not buried deep within you but immeasurably high above you. . . . There are other means of finding oneself, . . . but I know of none better than to think of one's educators. (*Schopenhauer as Educator*)

v. Conclusion: Systematic Theology as Hermeneutical Revisited

The systematic theologian is the interpreter of religious classics.[100] Like every interpreter of every classic, the theologian will enter the risk of interpretation with the same basic moments: First, the theologian already possesses some preunderstanding of the fundamental questions of religion, some personal opinions and responses on religion, some relationship, conscious and unconscious, believing or skeptical, towards the religious tradition (itself plural and changing) whose history of effects, influences and interpretations is carried by the language employed in all theological discourse. Second, the theologian experiences some exposure to the claim exerted by these religious classics, an exposure that will ordinarily involve some inchoate or radical faith experienced as either some resonance to or even some shock of recognition into a radical gift and demand disclosed in the power exerted by this classic.[101] Third, the theologian as interpreter will initiate some movement of dialogue with the subject matter, the fundamental questions and responses of the classic religious texts, events, persons, symbols. Like all true dialogues, the theological dialogue will be marked by the buoyancy of both critical freedom and real appreciation in the face of the claim of the classic and its exertion of an unmistakable *fascinans et tremendum* power.[102]

The theological dialogue will expand to include explicit reflection on the history of the influences, effects and interpretations—the tradition—of this classic event, text, symbol, person. The dialogue should be enlarged in a fourth moment to include the conversation of all the major hermeneutics of both retrieval and suspicion of the claim of the tradition recognized as plural (as both enriching and distorting), all the major methods of explanation which promise and deliver their own contribution to the critical quest to interpret the realized experience, the recognition of some sense of giftedness and demand exerted by this claim upon the systematic theologian.

Insofar as the systematic theologian performs that hermeneutical task well, insofar as these religious classics are classics and this tradition is a classical tradition, the theologian, like all interpreters, contributes to the common good, to the realm of authentic publicness.

In fundamental theology or in the "apologetic" side of systematic theology itself, the theologian must provide public evidence and argument in the ordinary senses of argument for any personal belief. No one simply announces "my beliefs" and then expects a public hearing in the usual sense of reasoned discourse appealing to any intelligent, reasonable and responsible person. However, systematic theology by definition has a distinctive task appealing to a distinct but related sense of publicness. Systematic theology intends to provide an interpretation, a retrieval (including a retrieval through critique and suspicion) and always, therefore, a new application of a *particular* religious tradition's self-understanding for the current horizon of the community. In Christian systematics, that self-understanding is itself further grounded in the *particular* events and persons of Jewish and Christian history: decisively grounded, for the Christian, in God's own self-manifestation as my God in this classic event and person, Jesus Christ.

How, then, are persons other than Christians to recognize this discourse as public? If it need not be public, then what, on inner-Christian grounds, is one to make of the Christian claim that the truth about God and ourselves is manifested by God in Jesus Christ? Is Christianity finally no more than a set of personal preferences and beliefs making no more claim to either publicness or universality than the Elks Club? If systematic theology does not address itself to the wider public, then how will systematic theologians help to stop the retreat of personal religious experience and communal religious traditions alike into the realm of the merely private, the realm of personal preference where *de gustibus non est disputandum?* Yet if the systematic theologian allows the public claims of Christian faith to be decided simply by public argument in the first and usual sense, a different dilemma occurs. What has happened to the event of giftedness which is the central claim and disclosure of the Christian classic? What has happened to the radical particularity of the relationship of that gift's disclosure to the particular events of God's action in ancient Israel, in Jesus of Nazareth, in the history of the Christian church?

This dilemma is real but not, I have become convinced, as fatal as it at first seems for systematic theology. For as this chapter has tried to show, besides the usual concept of a public expression there remain other candidates for publicness in the culture: the classics. Although radically particular in origin and expression, the classics are public in our second sense:[103] grounded in some realized experience of a claim to attention, unfolding as cognitively disclosive of both meaning and truth and ethically transformative of personal, social and historical life. This disclosure and transformation occurs in all classics even though the ordinary forms of public argument are not employed in them to warrant that disclosive and transformative power. Yet who can deny any classic's claim to a real, even sometimes a paradigmatic, public status? It is counterintuitive to suppose that Dante's *Divine Comedy* is disclosive and transformative only for a fourteenth-century Florentine; that James Joyce's *Ulysses* is disclosive and transformative only for someone who may have personally experienced Dublin on Bloomsday. It is similarly counterintuitive to suppose that such candidates for theological classic status like Karl Barth's *Church Dogmatics* and Karl Rahner's *Theological Investigations* are disclosive and transformative only for a person committed to either the Swiss Reformed tradition or the German (indeed Swabian) Catholic tradition. There is, in fact, some truth in Barth's typically extravagant and nicely provocative statement, "The best apologetics is a good dogmatics."

That truth can be reinterpreted in accordance with the argument of this chapter: Whenever any systematic theologian produces *a* classic interpretation of a particular classic religious tradition (as both Barth and Rahner have), then that new expression should be accorded a public status in the culture. No less than any classic interpretation of any classic, the theological classics are not merely "private" to the individual or to the particular tradition. Their authentically public status should be honored and discussed as recognizable candidates for authentic publicness.

Every classic, after all, is a text, event, image, person or symbol which unites particularity of origin and expression with a disclosure of meaning and truth available, in principle, to all human beings. Is it mere happenstance that those theologies which show the most promise of achieving classic status (Karl Barth, Rudolf Bultmann, Bernard Lonergan, H. Richard and Reinhold Niebuhr, Karl Rahner, Paul Tillich—to name only the generation of the "giants") all employ some explicit model of Christian self-transcendence implying what we earlier named some form of a journey of intensification. Indeed, the extraordinary, the classic analyses of the "stages of existence" (the aesthetic, ethical and religiousness "a" and "b") of Søren Kierkegaard may serve as the clearest illustration in modernity of a Christian thinker employing what may be renamed an "intensification" argument.[104] What, after all, is the point of Kierkegaard's development of his brilliant dialectics[105] if not to lead the self of the reader to share his intensified "journey within" in its full Christian radicality—from the glittering possibilities of the "aesthetic" in Don Juan, "the seducer," and the "pathologically reflective" intellectual and their intensified negation via ennui, through the stern ethical fortitude of Judge William and his intensified negation via despair, to the "pagan" religion of finitude and its negation via tragedy, to the "final" Christian shock of recognition (into God's radical otherness and our sin) in facing the claim of the "absolute paradox" that God became *this* man Jesus.

Indeed, Kierkegaard's classic achievement of dialectical intensification may also serve as an illustration of the second need in every classic: the intensification of distanciation that any intensified and radicalized experience of the self needs to render, to express, its meaning in shareable, public form via genre and style. When that general need becomes personal necessity, some appropriate form of expression—a text, a gesture, a work of art, a style of life—is eventually found to render in semblance and thereby to re-present that possible mode of being in the world as a shareable, public one. In Kierkegaard's case, this recognition of the need for genre and style can also be witnessed with unusual clarity: Kierkegaard's use of pseudonyms for the *indirect* communication of his experience; his insistence, for example, that music is the genre needed to express the aesthetic mode of being in the world of Don Juan, whereas the genre of the diary can best express the distinct and more intensified aesthetic mode of the "seducer."[106] Kierkegaard employs story, parable, edifying discourse, irony, dialectical argument, proclamation; each genre is weighed to find the appropriate one to render the meaning and experience of the self as a self in some particular stage along its journey of intensification to "authentic Christian self-transcendence."

When we read any classic (and Kierkegaard has the advantage of being at once a literary and a religious classic) we find that our present horizon is always provoked, sometimes confronted, always transformed by the power exerted by that classic's claim. Then we find that reasoned arguments alone in their obvious and correct senses—the senses of those forms of public discourse best represented in fundamental theology—are no longer sufficient to account for this realized experience, this shareable, public claim.[107] We need, demand, seek more. The "more" may be found in the disclosive and transformative power of that second candidate for "publicness": the classic text, event, image, person, symbol. Intuitively, most of us know that no classic can be reduced to mere privacy. In terms of argument, we can recognize the reasons for this correct intuition only after some explicit arguments, like those provided in this analysis of the public status of the classic, are put forward for the critical study of the wider community of inquirers. These accounts may be judged by that community as a relatively inadequate accounting for this common intuition. And yet, the intuition grounded in a cultural matter of fact will survive. For any reader's realized experience of any classic will suggest the singular truth theologians have too long ignored: Any person's intensification of particularity via a struggle with the fundamental questions of existence in a particular tradition, if that struggle is somehow united to the logos of appropriate expression, will yield a form of authentically shareable, public discourse. That discourse will exert its claims as a candidate for classic status waiting to complement, confront or transform all our more usual candidates for publicness. That discourse, when focussed on the religious classics, will be named systematic theology.

Our analysis has led us, therefore, to respect the public status of all classics, including the religious classics, as *cultural* classics bearing a recognizably public meaning. The analysis has not yet yielded, however, any understanding of the differentia "religious." In one sense, of course, this theory of interpretation for all classics has yielded the existence of a religious *dimension* to the interpreter's task. For insofar as interpreters recognize the claim exerted by the classic, they recognize as well that we are not the masters of any classic; they interpret us as much as we interpret them. We are, in short, really finite. We recognize ourselves ever anew as radically finite in every actual risk and struggle with the claims exerted by every classic.

It is also true, as M. H. Abrams and Justus George Lawler[108] have shown, that there also exist remarkable resonances, even profound continuities, between many of the major literary and religious classical expressions in the culture.[109] For example, consider the dominance of the metaphor "overflow" in the classic philosophy of Plotinus, the classic theology of Bonaventure, the classic spirituality of Francis, the classic poetry of the great Romantics. Yet that still suggestive metaphor is only one compelling example of the many resonances and continuities among all the classics—literary, philosophical and religious—in the culture.

And yet even this genuinely religious dimension of finitude intrinsic to every authentic interpreter's task, even the profound resonances among the religious and artistic classics of our culture, do not resolve the issue of the difference intrinsic to the word religious. We are left, then, with a further question: What is a religious classic?

Notes

1. For studies of authority, see: in sociology, Robert Nisbet, *The Twilight of Authority* (New York: Oxford Univ. Press, 1975); in philosophy, Hannah Arendt, "What Is Authority?" in *Between Past and Future* [I/17]; Stanley Benn, "Authority," in *The Encyclopedia of Philosophy,* I, 215–18; in theology: in liberal Protestantism, Schubert Ogden, "The Authority of Scripture for Theology," *Interpretation* 30, 243–61; idem, "Sources of Religious Authority in Liberal Protestantism," *JAAR* (1976), 403–17; in Catholic theology, Yves Congar, "The Historical Development of Authority in the Church: Points for Christian Reflection," in *Problems of Authority,* ed. J. M. Todd (Baltimore: Helicon, 1962), pp. 119–55; Bernard Lonergan, "Dialectic of Authority," *Boston College Studies in Philosophy,* II (1974), 23–30; Joseph Komonchak, "Theological Reflections on Teaching Authority in the Church" (unpublished). For an informative historical analysis of different models of authority, see J. M. Cameron, *Images of Authority* (London: Burns and Oates, 1966). I would like to express my thanks for the critical reading and discussion of this chapter to my colleagues on the Committee on the Analysis of Ideas and Methods and to Mr. Werner Jeanrond.

2. Eric Voegelin, inter alia, *The Ecumenic Age* (Baton Rouge: Louisiana Univ. Press, 1974), pp. 159–71.

3. For a study of fundamentalism, see James Barr, *Fundamentalism* (Philadelphia: Westminster, 1978).

4. "Repetition" itself can become a classic mode of interpretation; recall, for example, the contrast between Freud's notion of obsessive compulsive repetition and the distinct, creative notions of repetition as interpretation in Kierkegaard, Proust and Eliade.

5. This notion is rooted in the Enlightenment itself: recall the negative meaning of "tradition" in Jefferson et al. For a critique of the Enlightenment here, see Hans-Georg Gadamer, *Truth and Method* [II/59], pp. 244–53.

6. On idle chatter (*Gerede*), see Martin Heidegger, *Being and Time* (London: SCM, 1962), pp. 211–14.

7. For an example of this analysis, see Hans-Georg Gadamer, *Dialogue and Dialectic: Eight Hermeneutical Studies on Plato* (New Haven: Yale Univ. Press, 1980).

8. *Truth and Method* [II/59], pp. 325–41. Readers of Gadamer will note that I have not emphasized aspects of his fuller position: (1) that the temporal distance between text and interpreter forces the interpreter to recognize his or her historicity, i.e., one's own pre-understanding (or pre-judice) as constituted by effective history (tradition); (2) that the claim exerted by the text on the interpreter frees the

interpreter to enter into conversation with the text in an actual dialectic of questioning (hence, as we shall see below, Gadamer's appeal to the analogy of the "to and fro" movement of the game); (3) that the interpreter's aim, therefore, is to "fuse horizons"—namely, the horizon of the text and one's present horizon—in an interpretation which, by recognizing one's own historicity, will inevitably be a new interpretation. In short, "It is enough to say that we understand in a different way if we understand at all" (p. 264). My reason for not developing these Gadamerian theses in the text is not to register implicit disagreement. Rather the reason is simply to allow for my own emphasis on the preunderstanding and the claim elicited by the text and the need to allow the subject matter (a subject matter produced through the form) to take over. The emphasis on the subject matter does assume the dialectic of questioning and the "buoyancy and freedom of the interpreter" in the "game" of interpretation between text and interpreter. My own disagreement with Gadamer's position is not with these claims, but with his understandable but strained polemic against all "method." My second major difficulty with Gadamer's position is with some of his formulations for the necessary moment of "application" in interpretation. He correctly interprets the role of application for the judge or the preacher (pp. 289–305). Yet Gadamer sometimes claims that these special cases are representative of the role of application in all interpretation. Yet that is not the case: neither legal decisions nor preaching are paradigmatic for the kind of application that is indeed involved in all interpretation. The theologian's interpretation, for example, is distinct from the preacher's in terms of the *kind* of application needed for interpretation. The theologian, in principle, need show only that the world of meaning and truth is a genuinely *possible* one for human beings (and thus "applicable" to the human situation). The preacher needs to do more: concretely to apply it now *in order to interpret it*. In sum, "application" is needed for interpretation but not the fully concrete kind of application needed by either a judge interpreting the law or a preacher interpreting the scriptures. Thus my appeal below to Ricoeur's more adequate paradigm (which, in fact, builds on Gadamer for its first and crucial moment) of "understanding-explanation-understanding." For Ricoeur's own reflections on Gadamer, see "The Hermeneutical Function of Distanciation," *Philosophy Today* 17, esp. pp. 128–29.

To summarize: in the present work, the term "subject matter" means the common subject matter expressed through the form in the text which provokes the questions for the preunderstanding of the interpreter. It is *not* a synonym for "the text." Both text and reader, moreover, are not static but process realities: the identity of each is an identity-in-difference. The major "difference" occurs when a genuine conversation occurs between text and interpreter. Then the classic becomes a classic provoking a genuine (as different) interpretation. And the reader becomes a genuine reader of the classic provoked into a new self-understanding. These constantly shifting horizons of both text and reader in conversation head toward some new "fusion of horizons" (in Gadamer's justly famous phrase)—a fusion of the horizons (in my language) of the identity-in-difference of the text and the identity-in-difference of the reader into a new identity-in-difference: an interpretation that will recognize itself as "understanding differently" insofar as it understands at all.

9. The key to the employment of conversation or dialogue as the focal meaning for these other, not obviously conversational realities lies in the logic of question and response allowing the subject matter to assume primacy. To employ this focal meaning is to think analogically, not reductionistically.

10. See *Being and Time* [6], pp. 383–401.

11. *Truth and Method* [II/59], pp. 253–58.

12. Note, moreover, how every genuine interpretation will be a new interpretation. The converse, of course, does not follow: namely, that every new interpretation will be a genuine one. For this problem, we need criteria of relative adequacy for interpretations: see sec. iii of this chapter. Gadamer's own "criteria" (my expression, not his)—*Bildung, sensus communis,* judgment, taste, tact—may be found in *Truth and Method,* pp. 10–39. For further reflections of Gadamer on interpretation theory, see his *Essays in Philosophical Hermeneutics* (Berkeley: Univ. of California Press, 1976) and the introduction by David Linge. Note, moreover, on interpretation as "new," Gadamer's discussion of how application is intrinsic, not extrinsic to interpretation (esp. pp. 274–305). As noted before, interpretation (as always involving *intelligere, explicare* and *applicare*) involves application and may, therefore, also be understood as always involving praxis and some form of transformation. A separation rather than distinction of disclosure-transformation (and thereby of systematic-practical theologies) could prove fatal to both enterprises. Hermeneutics (systematics) would become purely formalist, with "techniques" of application later added to render practical theology not praxis-determined but practice-determined as occurs, unfortunately, in some understandings of "pastoral theology."

13. Note the crucial role of "effective history" in Gadamer's interpretation theory: *Truth and Method,* pp. 305–45.

14. Quoted in Giles Gunn, *The Interpretation of Otherness: Literature, Religion and the American Imagination* (New York: Oxford Univ. Press, 1979), p. 83.

15. *Being and Time,* pp. 349–83; and *Truth and Method,* pp. 225–41.

16. My own emphasis on the "ambiguity" of that heritage is different in emphasis, though not in substance, from Gadamer's position. For his reply to the frequent charge that his rehabilitation of "tradition" disallows a critique of tradition, see his response to Jürgen Habermas in *Hermeneutik und Ideologiekritik* [II/102]. My own position is that Gadamer's response is substantially appropriate yet still insufficiently sensitive to the radical ambiguity of all traditions including the possibility of "systematically distorted communication" in every tradition. Therefore Gadamer is insufficiently sensitive to the occasional need (personally and societally) for the kinds of ideology critique provided by the great hermeneutes of suspicion, Freud, Marx and Nietzsche. Sometimes we need theory in order to interpret. To speak more theologically: without the defamiliarizing and deideologizing power of the prophetic, eschatological and even utopian visions of the ancient Jews and Christians (as retrieved, for example, philosophically by Ernst Bloch and theologically by the liberation and political theologians), envisionments of a radically new future (as *adventum* and *promissio,* not *futurum* and *telos*) become close to impossible. In that situation, even Gadamer's masterful retrieval of the classical humanist tradition from the Greeks through Heidegger is in danger of becoming an unconsciously retrospective Utopia. Heidegger's radical critique, destruction and retrieval of the tradition is moderated in Gadamer's less suspicious and more balanced use of Heidegger's ontological analysis of understanding to retrieve the classical humanist tradition. For Heidegger here, see Werner Marx, *Heidegger and the Tradition* (Evanston: Northwestern Univ. Press, 1971).

17. The word "projection" is used in the ontological sense of Heidegger's analysis, not in the more familiar psychological senses of Feuerbach and Freud.

18. Examples of the former (on phronesis): *Truth and Method* [II/59], pp. 278–89; Bernard Lonergan, *Method in Theology* [I/10], p. 41. Examples of the latter (on poetics): Paul Ricoeur, *The Rule of Metaphor* (Toronto: Univ. of Toronto

Press) pp. 9–44; Elder Olsen and Richard McKeon in *Aristotle's Poetics and English Literature: A Collection of Critical Essays,* ed. Elder Olsen (Chicago: Univ. of Chicago, 1965), pp. 175–92, 201–36.

19. See Bernard Lonergan, "Aquinas Today: Tradition and Innovation" [I/54].

20. *Truth and Method,* pp. 10–39. Note also how Enlightenment thinkers (including Hume) could assume common as *communal* sense even when attacking "tradition": e.g., see Garry Will's interpretation of Jefferson's relationship to the "common sense" Scottish school in *Inventing America: Jefferson's Declaration of Independence* [I/29]. The classic Enlightenment philosophical defense of common sense as communal may be found in Kant's *Critique of Judgment* (New York: Hafner, 1957), pp. 135–38. Kant's defense of "communal sense" provides some check on his famous formalism; only "some" check, as communal sense is related by Kant to the a priori judgment of taste.

21. On Barth's hermeneutical significance see the essay by James Robinson in *The New Hermeneutic,* ed. John Cobb and James Robinson (New York: Harper & Row, 1964), pp. 1–78.

22. The expression "theonomy" (as distinct from "autonomy" and "heteronomy") is Paul Tillich's: for example, see *Systematic Theology* [II/25], I, 147–50. For a good study of the relative adequacy of various psychological models of self-transcendence, see Don Browning, *Generative Man:* (Philadelphia: Westminster, 1973).

23. See Bernard Lonergan on the distinction between "classical" and "historical" consciousness: "Dimensions of Meaning," in *Collection,* ed. F. E. Crowe (New York: Herder and Herder, 1967), pp. 252–66.

24. For an expression of this difficulty, see Paul Ricoeur, *Interpretation Theory* (Fort Worth: Texas Christian Univ. Press, 1976), esp. pp. 25–44. My own understanding of the significance of Ricoeur here may be found in *BRO*, pp. 72–79.

25. Friedrich Schleiermacher, *Hermeneutics: The Handwritten Manuscripts,* ed. Heinz Kimmerle (Missoula: Scholars Press, 1977), trans. James Duke and Jack Forstman. For a summary history of the development of hermeneutics from Schleiermacher to Gadamer, see Richard Palmer, *Hermeneutics: Interpretation Theory in Schleiermacher, Dilthey, Heidegger and Gadamer* (Evanston, Northwestern Univ. Press, 1969).

26. For my own understanding of the place of these methods in theology, see the Introduction to Part II.

27. Note how Gadamer's understanding of interpretation as mediation does not involve his position in the same kind of radical pluralism of "language games" and "forms of life" as Wittgenstein's analogous position: for an analysis here, see David Linge's introduction to *Essays in Philosophical Hermeneutics* [12], pp. xxxiii–xl, and Gadamer's own reflections, pp. 173–77.

28. The still popular misunderstanding of Bultmann's demythologizing program as occasioned only by his concern for contemporary relevance as distinct from his properly hermeneutical concern for the demythologizing demanded by the New Testament itself is refuted by a reading of his actual hermeneutical performance in dealing with Paul and John in his classic *The Theology of the New Testament* [II/6].

29. See T. S. Eliot, "What Is a Classic?" in *Selected Prose of T. S. Eliot,* ed. Frank Kermode (New York: Harcourt Brace Jovanovich, 1975), pp. 115–32. Note Eliot's hierarchical distinctions: the "greatness" of "the great Europeans" (like Shakespeare), the "classical" style (like Pope), the "maturity" of the "perfect classic" (Vergil). See also "Dante" in *Selected Essays of T. S. Eliot* (New York: Harcourt, Brace and World), pp. 199–241.

30. See Morris Dickstein, *Gates of Eden: American Culture in the Sixties: An Intellectual History* (New York: Basic, 1977), for a recent analysis of the collapse of elitist criteria. For three different examples of antielitist manifestoes of the Sixties, see Norman O. Brown, *Love's Body* (New York: Random, 1966); Susan Sontag, *Against Interpretation* (New York: Farrar, Straus, 1966); and Theodore Roszak, *The Making of a Counter-Culture* (New York: Doubleday 1969).

31. A fact recognized in a distinct way by Eliot himself in his distinction between "the classical writers" (Racine, Pope et al.) and the "classics" (Vergil and Dante). A cultural fact intensified by the collapse in the 1960s of former "high-culture" charters like Eliot's own, or in France by the emergence of the "new criticism," or in the United States by the difference between Lionel Trilling's modernist canon and the more "democratic" canon of his former student, Morris Dickstein. For a helpful account of the French development (centered around the Raymond Picard-Roland Barthes controversy in 1964), see Serge Doubrovsky, *The New Criticism in France* (Chicago: Univ. of Chicago, 1973). For a more recent counterattack on the post-Sixties' radical criticism, see Gerald Graff, *Literature Against Itself: Literary Ideas in Modern Society* (Chicago: Univ. of Chicago, 1929).

32. Michel Foucault, *The Order of Things: An Archaeology of the Human Sciences* (New York: Vintage, 1973), esp. pp. 78–120 (De Tracy) and pp. 263–80 (Cuvier). Influential here is the genealogical method of suspicion inspired, for Foucault, by Nietzsche; see Michel Foucault, *Language, Counter-Memory, Practice,* ed. Donald Bouchard (Ithaca: Cornell Univ. Press, 1977), pp. 139–65. The significance of the "New Nietzsche" in France and the United States is crucial here; see *The New Nietzsche,* ed. D. Allison (New York: Delta, 1977).

33. For some candidates, see Theodore Roszak, *The Making of A Counter-Culture* [30].

34. Frank Kermode, *The Classic* (New York: Viking, 1975), esp. pp. 1–45. Kermode's analysis is intended as a direct response to T. S. Eliot's classicist (*imperium*), more restrictive criteria. An extremely useful selection of critical texts (several, like Schiller and Sainte-Beuve, on criteria for the classic) may be found in W. J. Bate, ed., *Criticism: The Major Texts* (New York: Harcourt Brace Jovanovich, 1970). An informative study of six different meanings that the word "classic" (or "classical") have occasioned may be found in the article "Classicism," in *Princeton Encyclopedia of Poetry and Poetics,* ed. Alex Preminger (Princeton: Princeton Univ. Press, 1965), pp. 136–41. A fine study of the development of the analogous notion of "masterpiece" in the visual arts may be found in Walter Cohn, *Masterpieces: Chapters on the History of an Idea* (Princeton: Princeton Univ. Press, 1979).

35. The choice of a word like "recognition" has been central in Western aesthetics since Plato's doctrine of *anamnesis* in *Phaedrus*. Here the word refers to the sense of the important and essential which takes one away from the everyday to re-cognize what we forget in the everyday, even though in one sense (the sense of our basic humanity) we always knew—the essential truths about human existence: finitude, death, joy, peace, etc. For a helpful survey of aesthetic theory, see Monroe C. Beardsley, *Aesthetics from Classical Greece to the Present* (Alabama: Univ. of Alabama Press, 1966). For an informative survey of the use of aesthetic theory in practical criticism, see Hazard Adams, *The Interests of Criticism: An Introduction to Literary Theory* (New York: Harcourt, Brace and World, 1969).

36. I employ the word "symbol" as the more general term that allows for the full range of possibilities. This general use of "symbol" in aesthetic theory may be found especially in the neo-Platonic tradition beginning with Plotinus and in the

Romantic and German Idealist traditions. What art "symbolizes" ranges from the cosmic harmony of Plotinus through the disputes on the nature and hierarchical ranking of art as re-presentation (in relationship to religion and philosophy) in the different views of Hegel, Schelling and Schopenhauer to Susanne Langer's understanding of art as symbol of "feeling." The most influential notion of "symbol" in modernity remains Kant's notion of those re-presentations in which imagination "binds up" or concentrates so many ideas that they "arouse more thought than can be expressed in a concept determined by words." Clearly this conception of symbol as re-presentation remains operative in philosophical works like Paul Ricoeur's *Symbolism of Evil* [I/47] as well as in formalist accounts of the priority of poetry and symbol over prose and "paraphrase." For the clearest example in literary criticism, note the authoritative use of Kant's position throughout the influential work of Rene Wellek, *Theory of Literature* (New York: Harcourt, 1949). It remains somewhat remarkable that modern theologians, who have paid such close attention to Kant's first two critiques, have paid such relatively little attention to the *Critique of Judgment*. Equally influential on modern notions of symbol is Goethe's famous distinction between allegory and symbol: "It makes a great difference whether the poet starts with a universal idea and then looks for suitable particulars, or beholds the universal *in* the particular. The former method produces allegory, where the particular has status merely as an instance, an example of the universal. The latter, by contrast, is what reveals poetry in its true nature: it speaks forth a particular without independently thinking of or referring to a universal, but in grasping the particular in its living character it implicitly apprehends the universal along with it" (*Conversations with Eckermann*, entry dated October 29, 1823).

37. Ordinary language analysis, although clearly fruitful, too rarely allows for the recognition that (1) common-sense language in our age is itself influenced by theory; (2) ordinary language can become debased by the manipulative techniques of modern media technology and by systematic distortions (ideologies). The word "classic" is a key example of both phenomena. In its ordinary use "classic" often means either the elitist preserve of the classicist or the instant "classic" film, record or book of modern consumerism. So much is this the case that I have been tempted to abandon the word to its present unhappy fate(s) and use another (e.g., the paradigmatic, the authoritative, the normative). Yet none of the alternatives captures as well as the word "classic" (once freed from its bondage to classicists and consumerists alike) the sense of the essential and permanent along with the sense of the constant need for new interpretations. For a good example of a classical scholar who is not a "classicist" toward his classic materials, see William Arrowsmith's commentaries on the ancient Greek tragedies.

38. Although the concept "genius" is often identified with the Romantics, analogues for the concept exist as far back as Plato (or, more exactly, one aspect of Plato's complex and shifting theories on art). In the *Apology* and in *Ion*, Plato affirms the nonrationality of the poetic "genius" while in *Phaedrus* the "genius" or "madness" of the poet is regarded as inspired and "above" reason. The classic modern philosophical account of "genius" is Kant's *Critique of Judgment* [20], pp. 150–64.

39. The key word is "alien" theories of aesthetics, i.e., those based on the assumption that taste is merely private. In contrast, recall Kant's defense of the *judgment* of taste in the *Critique of Judgment*. Kant's position, in my opinion, need not have led to the "subjectivization of aesthetic theory" which Gadamer charges to the Kantian legacy (*Truth and Method* [II/59], pp. 39–73). Admitedly, the formalism of the Kantian approach and Kant's relatively impoverished notion of

experience (i.e., relative to Gadamer's notion of "realized experience") can lead to a "subject over against an object model" for aesthetics. I remain unpersuaded, however, that Kant's own position (as distinct from the "history of its effects" in neo-Kantian aesthetic theory) inevitably leads to those difficulties. Indeed, the explanatory power of Kant's critique aided the emergence of needed formalist theories (e.g., Wellek) and still bears retrieval as one moment of "explanation" of the autonomy of the work of art.

40. Note how Gadamer relates both these issues in *Truth and Method*: the First Part on the question of truth in art (pp. 5–150) leading to the Second Part on the "extension" of that question to the historical sciences (pp. 151–341).

41. *Insight* [I/28], p. 417.

42. For a study of Romantic theories, see M. H. Abrams, *The Mirror and the Lamp* (New York: Oxford Univ. Press, 1953).

43. The "popular" notions would have been assigned by Coleridge to "fancy," not to "imagination": see R. L. Brett, *Fancy and Imagination* (London: Methuen, 1969), pp. 31–54. For a good study of the relevance of Coleridge to modern theology, see Stephen Happel, "The Function of Imagination in Religious Discourse: An Historical Critical Study of the Theological Development of Samuel Taylor Coleridge" (Ph.D. diss., Louvain, 1977).

44. For a good expression of the "actual experience" of culture, see Josef Pieper, *Leisure, the Basis of Culture* (New York: NAL, 1964).

45. *Truth and Method* [II/59], pp. 73–91.

46. Ibid., pp. 80–91.

47. The recognition of the need for shareability and publicness is, once again, classically represented in Kant's *Critique of Judgment*. For an analysis of the "art for art's sake" movement, see Beardsley, *Aesthetics* [35], pp. 284–90. For a fascinating study of the notion of an "avant-garde," see Renato Poggioli, *The Theory of the Avant-Garde* [I/42].

48. Wayne Booth, *Critical Understanding: The Powers and Limits of Pluralism* (Chicago: Univ. of Chicago Press, 1979), esp. pp. 219–35 (for criteria). Note the generic character of Booth's criteria which allow, therefore, for a real pluralism; at the same time, the criteria also disallow eclecticism. Booth's argument for his own critical pluralism, in contrast to the hidden "monisms" in the claims to pluralism in three critics he greatly respects (R. S. Crane, pp. 37–99; M. H. Abrams, pp. 139–97; and Kenneth Burke, pp. 99–139), provides a good example of these criteria in operation. Contrast, for example, the easy eclecticism which marks the informative but practically criteria-less work of Grant Webster, *The Republic of Letters: A History of Postwar American Literary Opinion* (Baltimore: John Hopkins Univ. Press, 1979). Webster's appeal to T. S. Kuhn's "paradigm-shift" position seems to become Webster's own relativist shifting "charters" in historical periods—all, it seems, is "taste" (see especially pp. 3–47). For an example of the difference between criteriological pluralism and eclecticism in performance, compare Booth's analysis of Kenneth Burke (pp. 99–139) with Webster's (pp. 172–76).

49. M. H. Abrams, *The Mirror and the Lamp* [42], pp. 3–26; Giles Gunn, *The Interpretation of Otherness* [14], pp. 58–91.

50. Here the ground-breaking work of Martin Heidegger (upon whom Gadamer partly depends) is crucial: see *Poetry, Language, Thought* (New York: Harper & Row, 1971), especially the influential essay "The Origin of the Work of Art," pp. 15–89. On Heidegger here, see *Martin Heidegger and the Question of Literature: Toward a Postmodern Literary Hermeneutics*, ed. William V. Spanos (Bloomington: Indiana Univ. Press, 1980); Hans-Georg Gadamer, *Hegel, Hölder-*

lin, Heidegger (Karlsruhe: Badenia Verlag, 1971); Albert Hofstadter, *Truth and Art* (New York: Columbia Univ. Press, 1965); David A. White, *Heidegger and the Language of Poetry* (Lincoln: Univ. of Nebraska Press, 1978).

51. *Truth and Method,* pp. 91–119. It is also relevant to note that in art, as distinct from other "games," the spectator is necessary to the play.

52. The studies of Erving Goffmann and his use of the "game" analogue employ this other notion of the "game" (either the game of the narcissist self or games forced upon us by modern society) in contrast to the ontological analysis of game in Gadamer. For a classic study of "game" that bears its own ambiguous history of effects, see Schiller's *Letters on the Aesthetic Education of Man* (London: Routledge and Kegan Paul, 1954). The classic modern study of the ludic character of human existence remains Johan Huizinga, *Homo Ludens* (Boston: Beacon, 1955). It is important to note that in my analysis I emphasize the attitude of the players. An attitude, as Gadamer correctly insists, is ontologically dependent upon the phenomenon of the *game* itself. It is that reality that determines the attitude of the players, not vice versa.

53. There seem remarkable analogies here to John Dewey's notion of art as an experience of consummation, i.e., as experience both in interaction with and transformative of the environment, in *Art as Experience* (New York: Capricorn, 1958).

54. See Martin Heidegger, "The Origin of the Work of Art" [50]. Note, also, Heidegger's fascinating if perplexing concept of the "conflict" of "earth" and "world" in this event (pp. 42–50).

55. This insistence on the priority of art over philosophy is classically portrayed in Schopenhauer contra Hegel and in Nietzsche's portrait of the Apollonian-Dionisiac integrity of the Greek tragedies before the onslaught of "Socratic inquiry" and "theoretical man." For Nietzsche, see *The Birth of Tragedy* and *The Case of Wagner* (New York: Vintage, 1966). For Schopenhauer, see "The Metaphysics of Music," in *The World as Will and Representation,* II (New York: Dover, 1966), 247–57.

56. The example of Nietzsche here is especially instructive. Much of his work could be read as a sustained argument with himself on which works deserve what we here call classic status: his love of Goethe and Spinoza, his hatred for Paul and Luther, his ambivalence toward Socrates and Jesus; his early reflections on the "hero, the artist, the thinker and the saint" (here the classic persons) and his later elimination of the "saint" from the list of those involved in the self-overcoming of both Romantic "decadence" and Jewish-Christian *ressentiment*.

57. The original contrast, set in the context of Dilthey's analysis of the distinction between *Naturwissenschaften* and *Geisteswissenschaften,* is between *Verstehen* (understanding) and *Erklären* (explanation). On Dilthey's enterprise, see Matthew Lamb, *History, Method and Theology* [I/61], pp. 282–357. This original contrast is intensified in the modern period with Heidegger's contrast between "calculative" and "meditative" thinking. These traditions recur in Gadamer's own analysis, not only in his interpretation of Dilthey (*Truth and Method,* pp. 192–214) but even in the title of the work which could just as well read "Truth or Method."

58. Paul Ricoeur, *Interpretation Theory* [24], pp. 71–89. In the discussion of Ricoeur in the text, readers of Ricoeur will note that I exclude his analysis (following E. D. Hirsch) of "the initial guess" and the process of "validation" (which is, as Ricoeur calls it, a logic of probabilities, not a verification). I exclude this moment for four reasons: (1) a positing of the guess for validation is not necessary but already sufficiently accounted for by the logic of questioning internal to the

model of conversation; (2) the introduction of Hirsch's notion of "validation" seems to me to obscure rather than clarify Ricoeur's position, given his fundamental agreement with Gadamer (and against Hirsch) on the nature of interpretation theory; (3) one can allow (contra Gadamer) for explanatory methods without the "validation process" of the guess by means of Ricoeur's own move of showing how these methods develop the *enveloping* understanding as well as by my own suggestion (step 5) of an expansion of the conversation to the wider community of capable readers; (4) Ricoeur's own developed notion of a text (see below) already allows for his post-Gadamer moves. In brief form, see Ricoeur's analysis of the three moments of "distanciation" in a text, in "The Hermeneutical Function of Distanciation," *Philosophy Today* 17, pp. 129–41. See also his clear and systematic statement of the issue in "Explanation and Understanding: On Some Remarkable Connections Among the Theory of the Text, Theory of Action, and Theory of History," in *The Philosophy of Paul Ricoeur: An Anthology of His Work,* ed. Charles E. Reagan and David Stewart (Boston: Beacon, 1978).

59. The reader will note that I shift Ricoeur's language from "develop" to the more expansive "challenge, correct, refine, complicate and confront." "Develop" seems to me to account for many possibilities (e.g., formalist, structuralist and semiotic methods can *develop* the original understanding by their diverse explanation of the "sense" of the text and through the sense to the referent). However, often the claims of these methods (and not only the "ideologies" sometimes behind them) cannot be accounted for by the word "develop." This is the case especially when these methods challenge or confront the priority of understanding in all hermeneutical methods or the possibility of the emergence of any referent through the sense. Ricoeur is clearly aware of these challenges and argues his case (e.g., in relationship to semiotics via the semantics of the sentence) not only on ideological but also on methodological grounds. Still his choice of the word "develop" (despite its nice resonance with the "envelop" of understanding) tends to mute the challenge. Thereby does the choice of "develop" alone also seem to lessen the power of Ricoeur's own creative development of the Heidegger-Gadamer tradition with the wider conversation (and thereby critical pluralism of readings) rendered available by the paradigm "understanding-explanation-understanding." For these reasons, I have changed Ricoeur's language while maintaining his paradigm—a paradigm, note, open to the general criteria developed by Wayne Booth. For Booth even some deconstructionist readings or some "violations" of the text are "vitalizing" and can therefore be encompassed in the pluralist community of critical readers. On the criterion of "vitality," see Wayne Booth, *Critical Understanding* [48], pp. 220–23; on "violations," pp. 244–59.

60. W. K. Wimsatt and Monroe Beardsley, "The Affective Fallacy," in *The Verbal Icon: Studies in the Meaning of Poetry* (Lexington: Univ. of Kentucky Press, 1954). This volume also includes Wimsatt's famous "The Intentional Fallacy." The central point of the "the affective fallacy" is to disallow "impressionism" and "relativism." The latter can occur since an emphasis on response risks confusing the poem with its reader's impressionistic responses and thereby risks losing the poem itself in the reader's response. Similarly, "the intentional fallacy" (i.e., interpretation focussed on the author's intentions) risks losing the poem in the author. The dangers of "the affective fallacy" are real. Yet if the paradigm "understanding-explanation-understanding" is taken seriously and if criteria of relative adequacy to establish a genuine pluralism of capable readings are employed, neither impressionism nor relativism are likely to follow. Neither Gadamer nor Ricoeur ignore structural or formal problems (of the sense of

the text). Both of them are also clearly against the notion of the author's meaning as the key to interpretation. In the European tradition they do not speak of the "intentional fallacy" but refer to the same phenomenon by their rejection of the notions of "psychological empathy" and "divinization" in the Romantic hermeneutics of Schleiermacher and Dilthey. Both also deny E. D. Hirsch's creative (Husserlian) but still flawed reintroduction of the "intention of the author" as the key to interpretation. For the latter, see E. D. Hirsch, *Validity in Interpretation* (New Haven: Yale Univ. Press, 1967). The problem of "the affective fallacy" is often formulated in Anglo-American criticism under the rubric of "the problem of belief": for Ricoeur's contribution to that discussion, see Mary Gerhart, *The Question of Belief in Literary Criticism: An Introduction to the Hermeneutical Theory of Paul Ricoeur* (Stuttgart: Verlag Hans-Dieter Heinz, 1979). For an analysis of the developments on the notion of the "text" in Ricoeur's work, see David Pellauer, "The Significance of the Text in Paul Ricoeur's Hermeneutical Theory," in *Studies in the Philosophy of Paul Ricoeur,* ed. Charles E. Reagan (Athens: Ohio Univ. Press, 1979).

61. For the most influential (and engaging) argument for "violation," see Roland Barthes, *The Pleasure of the Text* (New York: Hill and Wang, 1973).

62. An alternative "summary" may be found in David Couzens Hoy's interpretation and use of Gadamer's interpretation theory in *The Critical Circle: Literature and History in Contemporary Hermeneutics* (Berkeley: Univ. of California Press, 1978), pp. 41–73. Hoy's analyses of the French theorists (Barthes, Derrida and Ricoeur) are far less satisfactory (pp. 73–84, 141–46).

63. For the implications for theological hermeneutics of this schema, see the Introduction to Part II of this work.

64. The emphasis here, of course, is on an interpretation of the classics of one's own tradition. The model of interpretation as conversation could be employed, however, for the interpretations of other cultures as well, as it is implicitly in Clifford Geertz and other cultural anthropologists (see *The Interpretation of Cultures* [I/18]). For a nonhermeneutical, structuralist interpretation of the cultural anthropologist's role, the major example is, of course, Lévi-Strauss. For a deconstructionist-like interpretation of that role, see the fascinating study by Edward Said, *Orientalism* (New York: Pantheon, 1978). Cultural anthropologist James Boon has provided an important analysis of the French literary sources as distinct from the structuralist explanatory method behind Lévi-Strauss's work in *Symbolism to Structuralism: Lévi-Strauss in a Literary Tradition* (Oxford: Blackwell, 1972) as well as an interesting study of Western interpretations of Balinese culture in *The Anthropological Romance of Bali, 1597–1972* (Cambridge: Cambridge Univ. Press, 1977). It is perhaps not too much to claim that the work of cultural anthropologists (the paradigmatic instance, along with historians of religion, of interpretation of other cultures) discloses the same kind of spectrum of options ("objective functionalism," "hermeneutic," "structuralism," "semiotics" and even "deconstructionism"). Cultural anthropology also includes the same possibilities of employing the model of conversation expanded to the model of "understanding-explanation-understanding" along with the development of context-dependent criteria of relative adequacy for a critical pluralism of readings (here readings as interpretations of cultures other than one's own). The example of the cultural anthropologist becomes especially critical for historians of religion and for those theologians engaged in the necessary task of real conversation with non-Western religious traditions. For some further suggestions on the latter, see chap. 11.

65. For an excellent illustration of this recognition, see Martin Heidegger's

reflections *On Time and Being* (New York: Harper & Row, 1972), pp. 1–25, on the "giving" in "It gives Time" and "It gives Being."

66. Recall Jean Paul Sartre's comment in his autobiography, *The Words* (New York: Braziller, 1964), that his relatives could always believe long enough to enjoy a toccata by Bach!

67. On the notion "the world," see Paul Ricoeur, *Interpretation Theory* [24], pp. 36–77; Hans-Georg Gadamer, *Truth and Method,* pp. 397–414.

68. See Roland Barthes, *Sade, Fourier, Loyola* (New York: Hill and Wang, 1976), pp. 38–76. By way of unusual contrast, see Karl Rahner and Paul Imhof, *Ignatius of Loyola* (London: Collins, 1979).

69. See *Selected Prose of T. S. Eliot* [29], pp. 258–77 (on Milton) and pp. 115–32 (on Vergil); on Shelley, see the essay "Shelley and Keats" in T. S. Eliot, *The Use of Poetry and the Use of Criticism* (London: Faber and Faber, 1933).

70. Note, for example, the pluralism within the American "formalist" school: the emphasis on "paradox," "tension," "ambiguity" and "metaphor" in the "contextual" meaning of the words among the New Critics as distinct from the emphasis on the formal categories of "plot, character and genre" of R. S. Crane and the neo-Aristotelians. For the New Critics, see, inter alia, Cleanth Brooks, *The Well Wrought Urn: Studies in the Structure of Poetry* (New York: Reynal and Hitchcock, 1949); John Crowe Ransom, *The New Criticism* (New York: New Directions, 1941); Murray Krieger, *The New Apologists for Poetry* (Minneapolis: Univ. of Minnesota Press, 1956); and the influential text of Cleanth Brooks and Robert Penn Warren, *Understanding Poetry* (New York: Holt, 1938). For Crane, see *The Languages of Criticism and the Structure of Poetry* (Toronto: Univ. of Toronto Press, 1953). Note also the wide spectrum of positions in two recent anthologies of "poststructuralist" and "deconstructionist" criticism: *Textual Strategies: Perspectives in Post-Structuralist Criticism,* ed. Josue V. Harari (Ithaca: Cornell Univ. Press, 1979); and *Deconstruction and Criticism* by Bloom-de Man-Derrida-Hartman-Miller (New York: Seabury, 1979). For the "earlier" period, see *The Structuralist Controversy,* ed. Richard Macksey and Eugenio Donato (Baltimore: Johns Hopkins Univ. Press, 1972).

71. Roland Barthes, *The Pleasure of the Text* [61]. For one response from the hermeneutical side, see Matei Calinescu, "Hermeneutics or Poetics," *JR* (1979), 1–18.

72. For examples, see *Deconstruction and Criticism* [70]: Jacques Derrida, pp. 75–177; J. Hillis Miller, pp. 217–55.

73. See M. H. Abrams, *The Mirror and the Lamp* [42], pp. 14–21; William K. Wimsatt and Cleanth Brooks, *Literary Criticism: A Short History* (New York: Vintage, 1967), pp. 77–97. Valuable studies on the reader and reception are available in Wolfgang Iser, *The Act of Reading: A Theory of Aesthetic Response* (Baltimore: Johns Hopkins Univ. Press, 1978), and in the work of the reception-critic Hans Robert Jauss.

74. *Critical Understanding* [48], pp. 223–28, 235–37.

75. A point recognized in theological hermeneutics by Schleiermacher with his distinction of the "hermeneutical" and the "ethical." There is, of course, an ethical task to literary criticism itself, but this should not be confused with rendering ethical judgments on the vision or world of the work as part of the interpretation of the work. The latter seems to me to be the usual practice of Yvor Winters, e.g., *In Defense of Reason* (Denver: Swallow, 1947). Ethical judgments seem far more hermeneutically appropriate *after* the interpretation of the "world" of the work as a *possible*-mode-of-being-in-the-world: see Paul Ricoeur, *Interpretation Theory* [24], pp. 82–88. The relationship of religious and ethical inquiry in terms of

"limit-questions" may be found in Stephen Toulmin, *An Examination of the Place of Reason in Ethics* (Cambridge: Cambridge Univ. Press, 1961), pp. 202–22.

76. For studies of Marxist literary criticism, see Frederic Jameson, *Marxism and Form* (Princeton: Princeton Univ. Press, 1978); Raymond Williams, *Marxism and Literature* (New York: Oxford Univ. Press, 1977); Terry Eagleton, *Criticism and Ideology: A Study in Marxist Literary Theory* (Atlantic Highland: Humanities Press, 1976). For a good anthology of classic Marxist studies, see Ernst Bloch et al. (Georg Lukacs, Bertolt Brecht, Walter Benjamin, Theodor Adorno), *Aesthetics and Politics* (Atlantic Highlands: Humanities Press, 1977).

77. See especially *Illuminations* (New York: Schocken, 1969); note also the insightful introduction by Hannah Arendt (pp. 1–59).

78. Wayne Booth, *The Rhetoric of Fiction* (Chicago: Univ. of Chicago Press, 1961), pp. 71–76 and 211–21; see also his later reflections on the "author" in *Critical Understanding* [48], pp. 268–77. For a radically different account, see Michel Foucault, "What Is an Author?" in *Textual Strategies* [70], pp. 141–61.

79. The expression is W. B. Gallie's as employed by Wayne Booth in *Critical Understanding*, pp. 211–15.

80. For two different accounts of the relationship of the artist and the tradition, see T. S. Eliot's influential essay "Tradition and the Individual Talent," in *Selected Essays* [29], pp. 3–12; and Harold Bloom, *The Anxiety of Influence* (New York: Oxford Univ. Press, 1973). The debate on the role of "tradition" from Eliot to the deconstructionists and Bloom's kabbalistic method bears some similarities to the philosophical debate between Gadamer and Habermas and to the theological debate on christology outlined in the Introduction to Part II and in chap. 7. For the moment my concern is simply to note that "tradition" inevitably plays some constitutive role (even if the interpreter either holds that tradition should be negated [as do Foucault and Barthes] or interprets tradition in Oedipal and kabbalistic ways [as does Bloom]). The reality of "tradition" no more exclusively belongs to traditionalists than does the reality of "the classic" exclusively belong to classicists.

Tradition is inevitably present through the language we use: a recognition of that presence can also occasion a recognition that every tradition is both pluralistic and ambiguous (i.e., enriching, liberating and distorting). The fact that every tradition is ambiguous need not become the occasion to reject the reality of tradition as enriching. Rather the need is to find modes of interpretation that can retrieve the genuine meaning and truth of the tradition ("hermeneutics of retrieval") as well as modes of interpretation that can uncover the errors and distortions in the tradition ("hermeneutics of critique and suspicion"). Gadamer, for example, is correct to insist that there is no escape from the reality of the history of the effects of the tradition in our language and thereby in our understanding. He is also, in my judgment, correct to be suspicious of any claims that we can ever be fully conscious of those effects (as in Hegel's claim to "absolute knowledge") or that critical reflection can ever fully escape from the history of the effects of tradition (as in objectivist notions of theory). Interpretation, properly understood, does involve critical reflection by the interpreter from the beginning of the provocation to that reflection by the text itself until the final (and critical) fusion of horizons. Nevertheless, Gadamer does not seem sufficiently conscious of the systematic distortions that are also present in every tradition. To uncover those distortions we do need, as Habermas correctly insists, critical theory (i.e., theory which is reflexive and possesses an emancipatory thrust like Freudian psychoanalysis and ideology critique). Whether we also need a "theory of communicative competence" (as Habermas' later work insists) to provide de jure rules for our de facto ability to dialogue and find consensus seems to me far more debatable.

81. For Eliot's doctrine of the "impersonality" of the poet, see, inter alia, "Tradition and Individual Talent" [80], pp. 6–7.

82. Note that my principal interest in the "artist" here is as an instance of the classic person, an instance analogous to the other classic persons: the hero, the thinker, the saint. On the latter, see n. 56 on Nietzsche and his criteria of "self-overcoming." For the ambiguities of the notion of the "hero," see Eric Bentley, *A Century of Hero-Worship* (Boston: Beacon, 1957). On the "saint," see William James' discussion in *Varieties of Religious Experience* (New York: Collier, 1961), pp. 211–299. For an analysis of how James' criteria for the "strenuous life" allowed him to call the saint "the strenuous life" par excellence, see Don Browning, *Pluralism and Personality* (Cranbury, N.J.: Bucknell Univ. Press, 1980). For theological criteria, see the discussion of Dietrich Bonhoeffer as "witness" and "martyr" in Eberhard Bethge, *Bonhoeffer: Exile and Martyr* (New York: Seabury, 1975), pp. 11–26, 155–67. In contemporary theology, Hans Urs von Balthasar has provided penetrating analyses of the relevance of reflection on the phenomenon of the saint; inter alia, see *A Theological Anthropology* (New York: Sheed & Ward, 1967), pp. 252–58 (on Thérèse of Lisieux). In history of religions, a ground-breaking reinterpretation of late classical ambiguity concentrating on the shift of power from "sacred things" to "sacred persons" (saints, martyrs, prophets and monks) may be found in Peter Brown, *The Making of Late Antiquity* (Cambridge: Harvard Univ. Press, 1978). In religious philosophy, see the reflective analyses of the models for soldier, sage and saint via the models of will, intellect and desire in Robert C. Neville, *Soldier, Sage, Saint* (New York: Fordham Univ. Press, 1978).

83. For a cultural anthropologist's view of the importance of "particularity" over "universal features" for understanding our common humanity, see Clifford Geertz, "The Impact of the Concept of Culture on the Concept of Man" [I/18]. For a classic expression of the opposite "neoclassical" view, recall Dr. Johnson's famous praise of Shakespeare for his "generality" and "universality," not his particularity, as well as Johnson's insistence that the poet "does not number the streaks of the tulip" (*Rasselas*). The debate on the need for particularity in modern literary criticism is widespread. For one instance, note the emphasis on "regionalism" among the agrarian critics. For an example of the latter, see Allen Tate, *On the Limits of Poetry: Selected Essays, 1928–48* (New York: Swallow, 1948). For a continuation in modern literary criticism of the Goethean tradition of finding the universal in the particular symbol (n. 36) as well as of the Hegelian search for the "concrete universal," see W. K. Wimsatt, "The Concrete Universal," in *The Verbal Icon* [60].

84. See Sartre's critique of Mauriac, "Francois Mauriac and Freedom," in Jean Paul Sartre, *Literary and Philosophical Essays* (New York: Collier, 1962), pp. 24–25.

85. For a philosophical interpretation of the "happening" and "event" character of art, recall Martin Heidegger's thesis that the work of art is dependent upon its creator but the creator is also dependent on the work; thus the "origin" of the work of art is art: see "The Origin of the Work of Art" [50].

86. See Henry James, *The Art of the Novel* (New York: Scribner, 1962), for the famous prefaces to the novels of the "Master" where he shares his "indirect" approach and the art of rendering his novels.

87. The emphasis upon the ontological "event" character of the work of art, influenced by Heidegger and Gadamer, distinguishes this kind of aesthetic theory from the "expressive" theory of Croce and the neo-Kantian developments of

Ernst Cassirer and Susanne Langer. The arguments for the former may be found in the works of Heidegger and Gadamer already cited.

88. For the importance of the phrase "some essential aspect" of the whole in contrast to a "self-manifestation of the whole by the power of the whole," note the discussion in the next chapter on the explicitly religious classic.

89. For a phenomenological study employing a form of "intensification principle" for a "hierarchy of values," see Max Scheler, "The Forms, Modes, and Kinds of Love and Hatred," in *The Nature of Sympathy* (Hamden: Archon, 1970), pp. 169–74.

90. For the positive meaning of "distanciation," see Paul Ricoeur, *Interpretation Theory* [24], pp. 43–44; idem, "The Hermeneutical Function of Distanciation" [8].

91. The suggestion is my own as a possible analogue on the side of production.

92. It is important to note that Ricoeur's position, in my judgment, is a corrective of, not replacement for, the priority of understanding in the post-Romantic, ontological hermeneutical tradition of Heidegger and Gadamer. For Ricoeur, as much as for Heidegger and Gadamer, "understanding" remains prior by "enveloping" the entire process of interpretation from the original receptive moment of understanding to the final moment of understanding as "appropriation." Ricoeur's position here is clearly developed in *Interpretation Theory* from the level of "event and meaning," and word and sentence, through "speaking and writing" to the "work" of a text via composition, genre and style. In sum, Ricoeur develops his analysis from the level of the polysemy of the word through the ambiguity of the sentence to the plurivocity of the text as a structured work (the structure governed by the rules of production, genre and style). It is somewhat unfortunate that this small and valuable collection on Ricoeur's theory of interpretation does not also include the essay "The Hermeneutical Function of Distanciation," since this essay is the clearest indication of Ricoeur's critical relationship to Gadamer. For two helpful studies of Ricoeur's complex development, see Don Ihde, *Hermeneutic Phenomenology: The Philosophy of Paul Ricoeur* (Evanston: Northwestern Univ. Press, 1971); and Patrick L. Bourgeois, *Extension of Ricoeur's Hermeneutics* (The Hague: Martinus Nijhoff, 1975). Ihde emphasizes the consistency of Ricoeur's development as a phenomenologist; Bourgeois emphasizes the presence of hermeneutical interests throughout Ricoeur's work.

93. *Interpretation Theory,* pp. 1–25.

94. For discussion of the priority of "writing" over "speaking," see the debates surrounding Jacques Derrida's *Of Grammatology* (Baltimore: John Hopkins Univ. Press, 1977). My present text does not address that question but rather the question of the codification of meaning in written texts—and elsewhere. For an example of the latter, see Paul Ricoeur, "The Model of the Text: Meaningful Action Considered as a Text," *New Literary History* 5/1 (1972). For Ricoeur on writing, see *Interpretation Theory,* pp. 25–44.

95. This is not, of course, to disown these enterprises (biography, sociohistorical criticism, audience criticism) as distinct enterprises but simply to note that they *are* distinct from the interpretation of the text. One need not accept the "explication du texte" methods of the formalist critics or their model of the "ideal reader" to accept the truth of their corrective. That corrective is reformulated in the hermeneutical tradition as the moment of "explanation" on the side of interpretation and the moment of "distanciation" on the side of production. The hermeneutical tradition's ability to incorporate a formalist (or a structuralist or a semiotic) moment as necessary without abandoning the priority of reception is the

principal reason for my claim for the greater relative adequacy of the hermeneutical model. Moreover, I continue to believe that this model (and its attendant criteria) allows for a critical pluralism (not eclecticism) of readings which is open to the kind of general criteria for capable readings developed by Wayne Booth. If one criterion of relative adequacy is comprehensiveness and another the ability to allow for a principled critical pluralism of readings, then the claim for this model seems warranted. The further and necessary discussion would have to be with the more strictly philosophical claims of Derrida, de Man and others.

96. See Paul Ricoeur's analysis of the positions of Aristotle, Spinoza, Ryle, Sartre and others in his lectures on imagination (unpublished as yet to my knowledge), especially "From Picture to Fiction" and "The Bible and the Imagination." In theology, see, on the theoretical side, Ray Hart, *Unfinished Man and the Imagination* (New York: Seabury, 1974); and, on the performative side, Julian Hartt, *Theological Method and Imagination* (New York: Seabury, 1977). The persuasiveness of Ricoeur's position on the imagination, for myself, is the fact that his position is both post-Romantic and postpositivist. More exactly: (1) Imagination, for Ricoeur, is a *rule-governed* form of invention (alternatively, is a norm-governed productivity). This disallows any purely Romantic understanding. (2) Imagination is also the *power* of giving form to human experience. This position allows Ricoeur to retrieve *mimesis* as creative redescription and to develop the notion of fiction as a redescription of reality challenging everyday descriptions and thereby challenging earlier notions of image and representation (Ryle, Sartre, Aristotle, Spinoza, et al.). In keeping with his general program of a philosophical mediation of antinomies (best expressed in his development of the interpretative process as understanding-explanation-understanding), Ricoeur demands both an explanatory account of the "rule-governed" nature of imagination and an understanding of the imagination's redescriptive *power* of giving forms (and thereby he holds to the indispensability of form to meaning). Ricoeur's position on the imagination (like his related positions on more particular examples like symbol, metaphor and narrative, and his basic position on interpretation theory itself as demanding both understanding and explanation) can join the Romantic insistence on the "fullness" of poetic language and the creative power of imagination without succumbing to Romantic dichotomies. Those dichotomies are best seen in Romantic attacks on any notion of the "rule-governed" character of imaginative production and attacks on the fruitfulness of explanatory (e.g., structuralist and semiotic) methods for the study of either the general principles of composition, genre and style or such specific genres as narrative.

97. Paul Ricoeur, "The Hermeneutical Function of Distanciation," pp. 135–36. Note also the neo-Aristotelian critics "genre analysis": for examples of the latter, see R. S. Crane, ed., *Critics and Criticism* (Chicago: Univ. of Chicago, 1952). For a brief summary of some classical discussion, see "Genre," in *Princeton Encyclopedia of Poetry and Poetics* [34], pp. 307–9. For a representative anthology of the different contemporary approaches to genre analysis, see *Theories of Literary Genre*, ed. Joseph P. Strelka (University Park: Pennsylvania State Univ. Press, 1978). Ricoeur's own notion of genre is influenced by Noam Chomsky's notion of genre as a set of generating rules for encoding and decoding a text. To date Ricoeur has provided particular analyses of the genres "parable" and "narrative" (for references, see chap. 6). For a recent use of the theories of genre of Ricoeur, Todorov and others for "genre study," see Mary Gerhart, "Generic Studies: Their Renewed Importance in Religious and Literary Criticism," *JAAR* (1977), 309–27. For examples of the striking differences in genre analysis in the present conflict of interpretations among literary critics, compare Northrop Frye, *The*

Anatomy of Criticism (Princeton: Princeton Univ. Press, 1957), with Paul Hernadi, *Beyond Genre: New Directions in Literary Classification* (Ithaca: Cornell Univ. Press, 1972).

98. Paul Ricoeur, *Interpretation Theory,* pp. 80–88. For an informative historical study of the changing judgments on the notion of "style," see "Style," in *Princeton Encyclopedia of Poetry and Poetics* [34], pp. 814–17. Ricoeur's concept of style as that which renders a work "individual" should not be confused with Romantic notions of "self-expression." Ricoeur has not, to my knowledge, developed his concept of "style" technically, but I assume it would bear the same post-Romantic understanding he accords "imagination" and "genre" (as suggested by his phrase, "renders the work individual") as distinct from Romantic notions of "self-expression" or classical (Horace, Longinus) moral notions of the relationship of style and the person or neoclassical rhetorical notions of style as "ornament."

99. In religious studies, this problem can be compounded by the failure to investigate concrete religious images as distinct from ideas (sometimes named "doctrines") about those images. For correctives of this tendency, see Mircea Eliade, *Images and Symbols* (New York: Sheed and Ward, 1969); Paul Ricoeur, *The Symbolism of Evil* [I/47]; Mary Douglas, *Purity and Danger* (London: Routledge and Kegan Paul, 1966); and Victor Turner, *The Ritual Process* (Chicago: Aldine, 1969); idem, *Dramas, Fields and Metaphors: Symbolic Action in Human Society* (Ithaca: Cornell Univ. Press, 1974).

100. See the discussion in chap. 6 on the use of literary criticism for biblical studies.

101. See especially Martin Heidegger on truth as *a-lêtheia*; inter alia, see "On the Essence of Truth," *Basic Writings* [II/52].

102. The latter expression, derived from Rudolf Otto's *The Idea of the Holy* (Oxford: Oxford Univ. Press, 1971), is discussed further in the next chapter's interpretation of the distinctiveness of the religious classic.

103. This definition of the classic, with its emphasis on particularity-publicness via distanciation, is from the point of view of the *production* of the classic. From the point of view of the *interpretation* of the classic, the key is the realized experience elicited by the claim to the point where publicness, permanence and excess of meaning are present as the dominant characteristics of a classic. What relates the two distinct analyses as genuine analogues is the similar note of publicness distinctly expressed in each. To continue the analogy, from the viewpoint of interpretation we could also use intensification language: viz., the intensification in the realized experience of the classic is related to the "distanciation" provided by methods of explanation of the sense of the text (for interpretation) as the intensification of a realized particularity is related to the "distanciation" demanded for expression (for production).

104. It is perhaps also noteworthy that the most fruitful recent Kierkegaard scholarship concentrates on the kind of hermeneutical and literary critical analyses suggested here. For example, see Mark Taylor, *Kierkegaard's Pseudonymous Authorship* (Princeton: Princeton Univ. Press, 1975); and Stephen Crites, "Master of Irony Demystified: Josiah Thompson's *Kierkegaard,*" *JR* (1975), 235–47; idem, "Pseudonymous Authorship as Art and as Act," in *Kierkegaard: A Collection of Critical Essays,* ed. Josiah Thompson (New York: Doubleday, 1972). In Kierkegaard himself, see especially *Philosophical Fragments* [II/23], *Concluding Unscientific Postscript* [II/23], *Either-Or,* 2 vols. (Princeton: Princeton Univ. Press, 1971), *Stages on Life's Way* (New York: Schocken, 1967), *The Concept of Dread* (Princeton: Princeton Univ. Press, 1970), and *The Point of View for My Work as an Author: A Report to History* (New York: Harper, 1962).

105. Kierkegaard's famous attack on "Hegel" may be viewed not as an attack on dialectics (Kierkegaard is, in fact, a brilliant dialectician, especially in the *Fragments* and *Postscript*), but on the claims of Hegelian dialectic as the *Aufhebung* of religion. In brief, Kierkegaard's dialectic is a Christian theological form of a negative dialectic in direct conflict with the sublation claims of Hegelian positive dialectic. For more on this issue, see the discussion in chap. 10, sec. i.

106. One of the most revelatory exercises in understanding actual performative criteria of judgment for genres in aesthetic theory is to note the standards operative in according different places in a hierarchical arrangement to the major art forms. Contrast Kierkegaard on music (as an expression of possibility without the actuality of decision), for example, with Augustine (for whom music is a "higher" art than painting since it participates less in the sensible); or Hegel's hierarchy of the art forms from the "symbolic" (architecture) through the "classical" (sculpture) to the "romantic" (painting-music-poetry and in that order)—the whole hierarchy determined by the criteria of Hegel's own phenomenology of Spirit; or Schopenhauer, for whom music is the highest art precisely as the singular expression (i.e., the direct representation) of the Will itself. The Romantic preference for the comparison of poetry to music in contrast to the neoclassical preference for the comparison of poetry to painting under the Horatian dictum "ut pictura poesis" is also revelatory of the same kind of debate. For the Romantic-neoclassical struggle, see M. H. Abrams, *The Mirror and the Lamp* [42]. For an influential formalist text on these matters, see W. K. Wimsatt and Cleanth Brooks, *Literary Criticism* [73], pp. 339–63. It is interesting to note that the analogy to music occurs even in such different contemporary anti-Romantic thinkers as Gadamer (who appeals to music as expressive of both vagueness and significance) and Lévi-Strauss (in his statement that to think mythologically is to think musically since music "unites the contrary attributes of being both intelligible and untranslatable").

107. See Paul Ricoeur, *The Rule of Metaphor* [18], for both a critical survey of the major theorists of metaphor and a constructive philosophical account of the "truth-status" of metaphor. The earlier formalists' defense of the priority of poetry (in spite of their often polemical tone under the banner of "the heresy of paraphrase") remains relevant to this discussion of a second and more concrete form of publicness in the classic symbols. Note also how the further criteria of the New Critics (such as ambiguity, paradox, tension, a sense of the tragic) are employed to show both the relative adequacy of various poetic expressions and the greater adequacy of poetic expression itself over prose. One need not accept these particular criteria to accept the need to develop criteria of relative adequacy to account for *both* claims. In a similar manner, in theology one need not accept the particular theological criteria of the major neo-orthodox theologians of that same period. In fact, the criteria of the neo-orthodox theologians (especially ambiguity, paradox, tension and a sense for the tragic, the negative and the conflictual) are remarkably similar to the criteria of the "New Critics" of the same cultural period. The present work, to repeat, defends (1) the general model of interpretation as conversation, (2) the paradigm of understanding-explanation-understanding and (3) general criteria for a critical pluralism. All three moves allow for the continued use (but *not* the exclusive or monistic use) of the earlier New Critics. As we shall try to show in Part II of this work, the actual candidates for classic status in both the Christian tradition and the present post-1960s' situation are wider than earlier New Critical or theological neo-orthodox particular criteria allowed. And yet, within the contemporary pluralism of both literary criticism and theology, the genuine achievements of both the New Critics and the neo-orthodox theologians should function as valued conversation partners far more than many contemporary literary critics and theologians seem willing to

allow. Within that wider contemporary conversation, moreover, a general heuristic statement on the full arc of interpretation and of a responsible pluralism for the community of inquirers seems in order. By way of a summary statement of the "steps" of interpretation for the classic, therefore, the following are those defended throughout this work:

(1) The interpreter enters with some *preunderstanding* of the subject matter.

(2) The interpreter notes a *claim to serious attention* elicited by the classic text as some kind of realized experience of meaning and truth.

(3) The interpreter enters into the logic of questioning in relationship to that subject matter expressed in the text. The to-and-fro movement of that questioning suggests, first, the model of the *game* and, second, the specific model of *conversation* to grasp the dialectic of respect and freedom elicited by the conversation of interpreter and text in relationship *to the subject matter* formed in the text.

(4) The recognition that the subject matter is expressed in the structured form of a *text* frees the interpreter to expand the model of conversation to a model for the whole process of interpretation as one of understanding-explanation-understanding. In short, conversation need not suggest interpretation as truth *or* method (Gadamer) but truth *and* method (Ricoeur). The principal methods involved will be *explanatory* methods on the structure and sense in the text that produce via the distanciation of expression a referent as the world-in-front-of-the-text awaiting understanding.

(5) Every one of the first four steps already suggests a critical pluralism for interpretation: a pluralism related to distinct preunderstandings; a pluralism related to the richness and plurality of the subject matter formed into a text and the attendant realized experience elicited in the pluralistic consciousness of the reader by the classic; a pluralism related to the dialectic of question and response in the conversation; a pluralism related to explanatory methods (formalist, structuralist, semiotic, deconstructionist, etc.) used to explain the sense of the text and its production of meaning; a pluralism of ethical methods for appropriating the final understanding. Each form of pluralism here remains context-dependent; each is also often dependent on other more general issues—e.g., the debates between semiotics and hermeneutics on the sentence, the philosophical debates between deconstructionist and other positions on determinate or indeterminate meanings. Each form of pluralism is also expressible in terms of general criteria like Booth's (justice, vitalization and critical understanding) as the *conversation* continues.

108. M. H. Abrams, *Natural Supernaturalism: Tradition and Revolution in Romantic Literature* (New York: Norton, 1971); and Justus George Lawler, *Celestial Pantomime: Poetic Structures of Transcendence* (New Haven: Yale Univ. Press, 1979).

109. The relevance of the discipline ordinarily called "religion and literature" is obvious here. Besides the work of Gunn and Scott already cited, the following representative collections are noteworthy: *Religion and Modern Literature: Essays in Theory and Criticism,* ed. G. B. Tennyson and Edward Ericson (Grand Rapids: Eerdmans, 1975); *Literature and Religion,* ed. Giles Gunn (New York: Harper & Row, 1971); *The New Orpheus,* ed. Nathan Scott (New York: Sheed and Ward, 1964); "Literature and Religion: The Convergence of Approaches," *JAAR* Supplement (June, 1979); Amos N. Wilder, *Theopoetic: Theology and the Religious Imagination* (Philadelphia: Fortress, 1976). A recent survey of the field, too often marred by polemical opinions and quick dismissals, yet genuinely informative, may be found in Vernon Ruland, *Horizons of Criticism: An Assessment of Religious-Literary Options* (Chicago, ALA, 1975). For a judicious survey of the field, see S. Bruce Kaufmann, "Charting a Sea-Change: On the Relationships of

Religion and Literature to Theology," *JR* (1978), 405–28. For an account of religion and literature as a discipline, see Anthony C. Yu, "Religion and Literature," *Criterion* (1974), 22–24. Some uses of structuralism and phenomenology in the discipline are discussed in Robert Detweiler, *Story, Sign, and Self: Phenomenology and Structuralism as Literary Critical Methods* (Philadelphia: Fortress, 1978); see also Detweiler's review essay of representative work entitled "Recent Religion and Literature Scholarship," *RSR* (1978), 107–17. A clear statement of the relevance of literary criticism within theology as hermeneutical is Sallie McFague, "Theology's Encounter with Literature," *Commonweal* (1978), 405–14.

Chapter 4

Interpreting the Religious Classic

i. The Conversation and Conflict of Interpretations of Religion[1]

The classics, with their two notes of permanence and excess of meaning, always demand interpretation, never mere repetition nor simplistic rejection. The interpreter must risk being caught up in, even being played by, the questions and answers—the subject matter—of the classic. Where either the subject matter or the attitude expressed in the form is minor the result will prove refreshing, delightful, a stimulation to a needed *joie de vivre,* as in the existence of treasured minor classics like the works of Max Beerbohm or Noel Coward. Where both form and subject matter are major—where the truth of existence if engaged, indeed at stake—the risk is greater, and the result will prove not refreshing but transformative. To enter the world of a major classic the interpreter must be prepared to be caught up in the back-and-forth movement of disclosure and concealment of a truth about life itself, to be carried along by the intensification process of the mode of being in the world disclosed by the text. To risk interpretation of all classics is to enter a possibility of a realized dialectical experience of belonging to and distanciation from what cannot but be called reality in its irreplaceability and its demands.

The philosophical thinker, even one like Heidegger engaged in a destruction-retrieval of a philosophical tradition, is finally an interpreter risking the possibility that the fundamental questions of the tradition will come alive again. All cultural critics are most faithful to their ownmost task when they become interpreters with all the risks, no longer aesthetically distancing themselves from the reality of the world disclosed but daring to be caught up in the creative risk of an interpretation: of events, as in Burckhardt's classic interpretation of the Renaissance; of persons, as in Boswell's life of Johnson; of texts, as in Bultmann's interpretation of the New Testament; of images, symbols and rituals, as in Eliade's classic interpretations of the dialectic of the sacred and the profane. Like Eliade's model of the historian of religion as creative hermeneute,[2] the systematic theologian is nothing more nor less than an interpreter of the religious classics of a culture. Theologians must risk interpretation of the meaning and truth of these classic texts, events, persons and images whose world discloses the reality of religion, whose effective history forms the horizon of our own efforts to understand and appropriate, to retrieve and criticize the reality of the religious dimension of the culture. To risk an interpretation of the religious classics of the culture is, in its manner, to risk entering the most dangerous conversation of all. For there the most serious questions on the meaning of existence as participating in, yet distanced, sometimes even estranged from, the reality of the whole are posed. There, as Eliade reminds his colleagues, one must employ the full rigor of scholarship without allowing philosophical or artistic "timidity" in the risk of a creative interpretation.[3]

As the aesthetic sensibility effectively distances itself from any claim to truth in the work of art, so too our own contemporary, often religiously unmusical sensibilities may keep at a distance any claim to truth disclosed in the classic religious texts, events, images, rituals, symbols and persons. Then we become the cultured among the despisers of religion—yet without the explosive Romanticism of Schleiermacher's own contemporaries, but with the lowered temperatures, the reduced expectations and sometimes the pathos of a religious philistinism masked as a purely objective cultural sensibility. For some it is no longer that religious questions cannot be answered. They cannot even be articulated. We may reject Comte's progressivism as arrogant, even fantastic, but many intellectuals do not reject his assumption that religion belongs to a primitive, outgrown moment of culture. And so—in a curious cultural expression of the dictum that ontogeny recapitulates phylogeny—we assume without further questioning that religious questions at best belong to our childhood memories, now nostalgic, now traumatic.

Yet what if the authority of religion is not the authoritarianism in our impacted memories of "religion" but the authority of those authentic, indeed inevitable fundamental questions about the meaning of the whole codified in the questions and responses of classical religious texts, events, images, symbols, rituals and persons? What if we have trapped ourselves into a religious philistinism that mirrors the "aesthetic sensibility" of the bourgeois critic unable to allow any claim to truth in the work of art? What if we have allowed the obscurantism and authoritarianism of so many official religious institutions and spokespersons for "religion" to so engage our attention and enrage our spirit that we cannot even formulate a question about religion, much less risk interpreting a religious classic? Should we cease reflection upon the reality and dignity of the vocation of politics because of the indignities and unreality of so many politicians? Should we not risk reading (i.e., interpreting) the meaning and truth of the realm of the truly public, the "polis" in the classic interpretations of

Hannah Arendt, as more likely to introduce us to the authentic reality of the political?[4] To risk reading good systematic theology is exactly the same kind of risk: a wager that on the other side of the necessary rejection of all authoritarianisms may lie authoritative expressions of religion, that on the other side of our distancing of ourselves from any public claims to truth in art and religion may lie the reality and the risk of authentic interpretation.

The stakes in a willingness to interpret religious classics are higher even than the stakes in interpreting art, science, morality and politics. For every major religion has functioned in a profoundly ambiguous manner. Its effective history[5] includes a world-sustaining power than can and has merely blessed the status quo, and a world-creating power that has not only released powerful forces for the good, but savage, even demonic realities in history. The sickening account of religious fanaticism become world-historical slaughter has plagued every culture. It still plagues the contemporary world. Is it possible for a Catholic to read an account of the Saint Bartholomew's Day massacre and not be tempted to reject a tradition whose leader could sing a *Te Deum* in Saint Peter's to celebrate that betrayal of the central vision of Catholicism? Is it possible for a Protestant to read the story of Cromwell's savage destruction of Irish Catholics and not want to part company with the religiously empowered self-righteousness endorsing that disgrace? Is it possible for any Christian, after the Holocaust, to read the anti-Jewish statements in the entire tradition from the New Testament forward and not be tempted to have nothing further to do with so seemingly resentful a tradition?[6] The demonic possibilities of all religions seem so engrained in them that no one with the slightest historical knowledge need look far—even in our time—to find sufficient evidence to reject religion.

The risk of interpreting so ambiguous a phenomenon as religion is so great that there seems little wonder that many persons refuse to risk entering any real interpretation of that phenomenon. It is not, after all, only the ambiguity of the reality of religion in our history—with its world-sustaining, world-creating, world-destroying creative and demonic possibilities—that leads one to hesitate entering that conversation. On intellectual grounds as well, the prospective interpreter of religion faces a pervasive conflict of interpretations on the meaning of religion in the wider culture. The sanguine Enlightenment assignment of all "positive religions" to error has been intensified in the modern period into the contemporary, far more radical charge of "illusion" and "projection" in Feuerbach, Marx, Nietzsche and Freud. The locus of religion in human experience has been debated from earlier accounts of "natural religion" through the alternative accounts of Schleiermacher, Otto, Tillich, Wach, Eliade, von Hügel, Dupré and other hermeneutes of a retrieval of the positive meanings and truth of religion. To read Weber, Durkheim, Marx,

Troeltsch and their successors on the sociological reality of religion, or Freud and Jung and their successors on the psychological reality of religion, is to enter a conflict of interpretations of religion from which there can often seem no honorable exit.[7] Within Christian theology itself a hermeneutics of suspicion has been cast upon the very notion "religion" by the articulation of a Christian nonreligious "faith" in Barth, Brunner, Bonhoeffer and Moltmann to call into theological question any analysis of Christianity as a "religion."[8]

The modern conflict of interpretations on religion has made it clear that it is not really possible to provide *one* definition for the essence of religion.[9] Earlier proposals for that definition in the "normative" disciplines, theology and philosophy, can now be seen as so determined by the Western monotheistic religious traditions as often not to be applicable to other traditions.[10] Earlier anthropological proposals for understanding the origin of religion in evolutionary terms (E. B. Tylor, James Frazer) have been seen to rest on an unacceptable evolutionary modern Western model often unconsciously employing the genetic fallacy and bearing at least as much speculation on "origins" (on "animism," "totemism," "mana" and "tabu") as any ever engaged in by Hegel.[11] Earlier accounts of the nature of religion in the modern discipline of the history of religions[12] (Max Müller, Nathan Søderblom, Wilhelm Schmidt, Friedrich Heiler) have expressed, in some of their evaluative formulations, Christian theological origins. Earlier accounts of religion in the social sciences like that of Branislow Malinowski have been shown by later functional (not functionalist) analysts of religion to rest on too narrow a notion of symbol and sometimes too one-way a functional account of the relationships between Malinowski's religion and "common sense."[13] To state these negative conclusions in the debate over religion is not, of course, equivalent to stating that these masterful, often classic interpretations of religion do not still merit, even demand study by every prospective interpreter.[14] It is to state that the conflict of interpretations on religion—a conflict faithful to the enormous complexity and variety of the religions—should make any interpreter wary in proposing any universal definition of religion.

The cultural anthropologists, social scientists, psychologists and historians of religion have demonstrated that religion functions in very diverse, often contradictory ways in individuals, societies and whole cultures. Those functions must be described by the appropriate discipline or method before any evaluations occur. The further risk that the theologian, or the philosopher, or any full-fledged interpreter of the religious phenomenon or the creative hermeneute of religion in any discipline takes is to assume or argue for the position that, however diverse the functions of religion, religion is *also* analyzable in substantive terms. More exactly (and more in keeping with the argument of this book), the questions which religion addresses are the fundamental existential questions of the meaning and truth of individual, communal and historical existence as related to, indeed as both participating in and distanced from, what is sensed as the whole of reality.

This "substantive" position on religion in fact needs explicit philosophical and theological warrants, yet finds initial support in the ordinary use of language. In common-sense discourse we do distinguish "religious" concerns from moral, scientific, aesthetic and political ones. Ordinarily a religious concern, as Van Harvey suggests, involves a perspective expressing a dominating interest in certain universal and elemental features of human existence as those features bear on the human desire for liberation and authentic existence.[15] Substantively, what counts as religious in ordinary language is what expresses that dominating interest. Functionally, religion plays several overlapping, even sometimes contradictory roles in an individual, a society, a culture. Both substantively and functionally, religion is profoundly ambiguous: alive with creative possibilities for the true, the good, the beautiful and the holy; alive as well with demonic possibilities for error, thoughtlessness, obscurantism, mystification, illusion, evil and those "beyond-good-and-evil" possibilities of the genuinely demonic. Religious experience and language, therefore, seem even on common-sense terms an ambiguous limit-experience with an intrinsically dialectical character.[16]

The fuller meaning of this latter description of religion demands, I believe, the kind of substantive analyses provided by the normative disciplines of philosophy and theology. Yet even these "normative" disciplines cannot claim to provide a universal definition of "religion" which, in keeping with classicist notions of definition, will apply to all cases of religion and only to cases of religion.[17] Nor is this philosophical and theological present de facto inability to produce a universal definition caused only by the conflict of interpretations on religion noted above. The emergence of that conflict into clearer contemporary theological consciousness, to be sure, has occasioned a hesitancy among most philosophers and theologians to claim a universal definition of religion with the surety of Schleiermacher, Hegel, Feuerbach or even Tillich. The increasing sophistication of empirical and theoretical-functional, especially social-scientific,[18] analyses of religion have correctly warranted a greater modesty on the part of all philosophers and theologians attempting to define so various, so complex and elusive, so seemingly contradictory a functional reality in human lives, societies and cultures as religion. Moreover, the sense of cultural boundedness, even parochialism, now shared by many Western thinkers (by theologians, it seems, far more than by philosophers)[19] have led most "normative" thinkers to recognize the prevalent Jewish and Christian presuppositions of even our best Western classical definitions of "religion" to date. That same sense informs the present theological recognition of a responsibility to what Eliade names a future planetary culture where the classical religious traditions of the East and the archaic religions will not be studied in an appendix on the "other religions" in Christian systematics, but will enter into the self-understanding of the Christian religion from beginning to the end.[20] In that light, the present scholarly dialogue among historians of religion and theologians, although clearly in its initial stages, seems just as clearly a major demand of both the present and the future for serious Christian systematic theology. And that dialogue in turn warrants the accelerating belief among many scholars of religion that only a multidisciplinary and collaborative approach to the religious phenomenon can hope for any degree of relative adequacy.

All these reasons are warrants for the present theological hesitancy to attempt a single definition of religion. Yet the principal substantive cause for that hesitancy, I believe, is the theological recognition that whatever else it is, religion is not just another cultural perspective alongside morality, art, science, economics and politics. From a functional viewpoint, of course, "religion" is precisely that: one more perspective to be studied in unravelling the complexity of an individual, a society, a culture. As such religion, like any phenomenon, must be studied by the appropriate discipline. And yet, in its own self-understanding, a religious perspective claims to speak not of a part but of the whole; without the sense of that reality of the whole, I believe, there is no "religion."[21] There will be morality, art, science, politics, economics, each of which locate a central part or dimension of our reality as personal, social, political and cultural human beings. A religious perspective, on the contrary, articulates some sense of the whole; it must inform, transform, even sometimes form the rest of our cultural lives with that sense or it loses its properly religious character.[22] Then religion becomes, in fact, a synonym for morality, art, science or politics.

In terms of classical disciplines, two continue to seem particularly appropriate for analyzing the claims to meaning and truth of the religions: philosophy and theology. Philosophy here includes not merely explicitly philosophical reflection on "religion" (as in Wittgenstein or Whitehead), but also the implicit or explicit philosophical dimension of "functional" analyses of religion (as in those aspects of Freud, Jung, Marx, Weber, Durkheim).

In its most explicit and deliberate moments, a philosophical analysis of religion often involves an explicitly metaphysical account of the general and abstract features of the reality of the whole disclosed in the phenomenon of religion and explicated and adjudicated in an explicit metaphysics (as in Hartshorne).[23] This explicitly metaphysical or transcendental moment, *if* united to an adequate phenomenological description of "religion," yields, from the theological viewpoint, the reality of a "fundamental theology."

From the viewpoint of fundamental theology, certain essential characteristics of religion can be explicated even when a universal definition of religion is neither attempted nor countenanced. Chief among them is the recognition of a limit-character to all religious experience and language.[24] Since fundamental theology is chiefly concerned, in its phenomenological moment, with our *common* human experience and, in its transcendental or metaphysical moment, with the abstract, general, universal and necessary features of that common experience, the main emphasis in these normative analyses of religion will be upon some "religious dimension" to our ordinary experience. A common characteristic of analyses in fundamental theology, therefore, will be the insistence that the religious dimension of our experience and language is first disclosed as a *limit-to* dimension: a dimension present in the "limit-questions" of scientific inquiry and moral striving, and in those experiences (either negative, like anxiety as distinct from fear, or positive, like fundamental trust, wonder and loyalty as distinct from trust in and fidelity to a particular cause) disclosive of the "limit-situation" which is the human situation.

In that sense, the analyses of fundamental theology can be viewed, in the present perspective, as analyses which also warrant the authentic inquirer of the religious classics to enter the conversation where those fundamental questions of the meaning of existence are at stake; where a religious dimension to existence is disclosed in the very positing of those seemingly unanswerable questions demanded by the analysis of the limit-questions to science and morality and evoked in the limit-experiences recognized most clearly in the "boundary-situations" (death, guilt, trust, love, order).

The philosophical analyses of fundamental theology, therefore, free the inquirer to study the possible meanings of such recognized "situational" limit-experiences as finitude, contingency, mortality, alienation or oppression and thereby to explicate, indeed to state, the character of that reality as a limit-to our existence. In that explicit stating of a limit-to, the inquirer may also be able to disclose or show the existence of a reality here named a "limit-of" (alternatively horizon-to our ground-of). In its metaphysical or transcendental form, the analysis can also *partly* state the character of that reality of the *limit-of*. This is the case, in the Western tradition, when the metaphysical reality of God as the one necessary existent grounding all reality is explicated as *the referent* of just such limit-experiences of a religious dimension to our lives.[25] When the philosophers of religion or fundamental theologians claim that this analysis can *partly* state that reality, they mean that strictly metaphysical analysis always and only claims to provide the abstract, general, universal and necessary features of reality, including the reality of God as the sole strictly necessary reality.

Even the claim of dipolar theism, for example (most clearly set forth in the work of Charles Hartshorne), is not a claim to state, much less determine God's concrete manifestations in the religions. The claim is a quite different one: to state *that* the reality of God is strictly necessary and *that* the meaning of a coherent concept for theism must include both the abstract (essential) characteristics of the divine reality (e.g., absoluteness) and the concrete characteristics of the same reality (e.g., supreme relativity). That position argues for the strict necessity of the reality of God to account for our *common* human experience by explicating the abstract, general, universal and necessary features of a coherent concept for the divine reality (including the necessity for both abstract and concrete "poles"). Such public arguments are what fundamental theology, with a phenomenological and transcendental formulation, attempts to affirm, explicate and thereby warrant for the reality of that religious dimension disclosed as the referent, the ground-to, horizon-to, "limit-of" in any explicit stating of the transcendental conditions of the possibility of any religious-as-*limit-to* experiences and questions.

For those thinkers whose philosophical judgments disallow a strictly transcendental or metaphysical moment in fundamental theology, of course, only a phenomenological moment is countenanced as yielding any real results. Then, with the Wittgensteinians, the inquirer may hold that we can state a limit-to but only "display," "show" or "disclose" any "limit-of" or horizon-to reality, including the referent of that reality, God. This familiar, complex philosophical debate (between, for example, Thomists and Hartshornians on the one side and Wittgensteinians and probably most phenomenologists on the other) was classically formulated in the modern period in Hegel's formulation against Kant that the ability to state a limit means, if one reflects upon it, that the thinker is, in some manner, already beyond the limit stated.

My brief comments here, however, are meant to indicate only the nature of the debate on what I call stating a limit-to and showing and *partly* stating the reality of a limit-of in fundamental theology proper. For present purposes, the most important feature to note is that even those, like myself, who argue the so-called "hard" (i.e., the metaphysical or transcendental) line on this central issue for fundamental theology, claim no more (and, admittedly, no less) than an ability to partly state—more exactly, to metaphysically state—the abstract, general, universal and necessary features of the reality of God as the one necessary existent which can account for the reality of a limit-of, ground-to, horizon-to the whole disclosed in earlier phenomenological accounts. Other fundamental theologians, especially most linguistic analysts and phenomenologists, will advance the "softer" claim that a "limit-of" reality may be displayed, disclosed or shown but cannot in principle be stated.

At that point, most parties to this important debate within fundamental theology and philosophy of religion will urge that in order to experience, understand and explicate the fully concrete reality of this horizon-to, ground-of, limit-of the ordinary, the inquirer must be attentive to the concrete religious experiences and expressions both disclosed and stated in particular concrete religions.[26] For example, this position is stated with some clarity in the logic of Karl Rahner's influential position.[27] For Rahner, the philosopher of religion can provide persuasive philosophical arguments for the necessary existence of an absolute mystery as ultimate horizon to all thinking and living. If that argument holds, then Rahner is correct to insist that the human being, now understood as always already within that horizon of ultimate mystery, can be redescribed, in his now famous phrase, as a hearer of a *possible* revelation from this horizon, i.e., a self-manifestation by the power of ultimate mystery itself.

In the actual experience of that self-manifestation of God in Jesus Christ, the Christian believer *now,* according to Rahner, recognizes that the concrete revelation is a pure gift or grace from the incomprehensible God of Love. Then the believer "recognizes" that all reality is graced by that gift: that all reality partakes in a "transcendental" revelation disclosed in the categorial revelation of God's own self-manifestation in Jesus Christ; that revelation, as "transcendental," is always already present in this concretely graced world; that revelation as "categorial" is present in the gratuity of God's self-manifestation in the events of "salvation history," decisively present, for Rahner, in the event of the manifestation of who God is and who we are in Jesus Christ.[28]

Whatever the internal complexity of Rahner's philosophical traditions here, and whatever the difficulties of some of Rahner's formulations within those traditions,[29] the logic of his position seems a sound one. We are always already in the presence of absolute mystery—a position defended in "philosophy of religion." We are, therefore, in fact hearers of a *possible* revelation or self-manifestation from the freedom of the absolute mystery—a position explicated in "formal fundamental theology."[30] But for the Christian, that revelation (as self-manifestation of God) has in fact occurred in the free and decisive event called Jesus Christ—a position explicated in systematic theology. Hence we now, on the basis of that decisive revelation, know that all reality is graced—a position explicated in a systematic theology with a transcendental cast and now allowed to affect the philosopher turned fundamental theologian.[31] One need not commend the details of Rahner's position in order to see it as a clear example of how the move from fundamental to systematic theology is logically always a move from the abstract, general, universal, necessary features of a "religious dimension" in all reality to the particular, concrete reality of an "explicit religion."

In my own non-Rahnerian language this means that even in their "hard" formulations, the claims of fundamental theology are, in fact, "soft" ones.[32] They are not claims—except, perhaps, among the strict rationalism of right-wing Hegelians or Cartesian neo-Scholastics—to render the particular, concrete, explicit religion redundant by bringing it before the judgment seat of "metaphysics."[33] On the contrary, the fundamental theologian both warrants the existence of a religious dimension and thereby warrants a further willingness to enter into the conversation of the religions, to pay attention to the claims in their classic expressions, even to risk being caught up in the reality of a classic religious tradition. If fundamental theologians perform their task well, then they also show how systematic theology is in fact a reasonable, responsible, human risk. If one's experience of art, history or thinking has already alerted one to the authoritative status of the claims to truth in any classic expression, then the willingness to risk an interpretation of a classic religious tradition, the willingness to become a systematic as distinct from a fundamental theologian, becomes that much more responsible a wager.

For who is the systematic theologian except the finite, historical, risk-taking interpreter of the religious classics of a classic tradition? Yet what is a religious classic? On present terms, a religious classic may be viewed as an event of disclosure, expressive of the "limit-of," "horizon-to," "ground-to" side of "religion." Like all classics, religious classics will involve a claim to meaning and truth as one event of disclosure and concealment of the reality of lived existence. Unlike the classics of art, morality, science and politics, explicitly religious classic expressions will involve a claim to truth as the event of a disclosure-concealment of the whole of reality *by the power of the whole*—as, in some sense, a radical and finally gracious mystery.[34] That event will be some manifestation in some concrete expression of the reality of the whole in all explicitly religious expression. Its truth must resonate to those limit-to experiences disclosive of a religious dimension to existence.[35] Its disclosive power will, of course, prove partly dependent upon an antecedent willingness to enter the conversation of religious questions where our existence as authentic or inauthentic must inevitably be at stake.

Because religious classics are experienced as *from* the power of the whole, moreover, they will involve, as Clifford Geertz observes, an "aura of factuality," and thereby an authority that is distinctive to *religious* classics.[36] Indeed, that sense of authority, as a sense of coming (as gift, as not my achievement) from the power of the whole, pervades a religious classic to such an extent that there ethos and worldview are inextricably intertwined. For in the actual moment of response to a religious classic, religious persons are convinced that their values, their style of life, their ethos are in fact grounded in the inherent structure of reality itself. In that response to a religious classic, religious persons seem to sense that there exists an unbreakable inner connection between the way one ought to live and the way things really are. In the actual experience of the religious classic—a realized experience of response and recognition, as in the experience of all classics—the respondent suspends the usual disbeliefs and is liberated to believe that here the power of the whole discloses itself; to believe that this event discloses that how we ought to live is grounded in reality itself.

The interpreter may of course, in a later reflective, distancing moment, question that original religious experience and reinterpret it as some "as-if" experience produced by the human imagination. But in the moment of encounter-response itself, the moment Christians call "faith," there is no "imagine-reality-as-if-it-were-this-way" experience. There is, rather, the realized experience of a recognition as that response of trust called faith to the reality of the whole disclosed in the religious classic:[37] a reality experienced as liberating one to trust that how we ought to live and how things in reality are, are finally one.[38] This faith is a response of both trust and command: trust that this indissoluble union of ethos and reality is the case and a command to live accordingly. In that sense, all religious faith elicited by religious classics resonates, as Alfred North Whitehead observed, with our deepest yearnings: "The difference is that religion is the longing of the spirit that the facts of existence should find their justification in the nature of existence."[39] It is for that reason as well, as Whitehead also observed, that "the final principle of religion is that there is a wisdom in the nature of things."[40]

The disclosive power of any classic religious expression will, of course, prove partly dependent upon the specific form that the fundamental questions take in my particular situation.[41] The focus of the religious fundamental questions may be finitude, as for many in the patristic period, or, more radically, mortality, as for Ernest Becker and many others in our own period;[42] it may prove a recognition of radical personal estrangement or sinfulness, as for Luther and Kierkegaard;[43] it may prove a need for some principle of order to the universe of scientific inquiry or moral striving, as for Aquinas, Kant or Whitehead;[44] it may prove an experience of the uncanny as meaninglessness or absurdity, or no-thingness, as for Tillich or Camus;[45] it may prove a recognition of fundamental trust and wonder in the very meaningfulness of existence, as for Marcel or Ogden;[46] it may prove a recognition of a profound loyalty to and responsibility for the whole beyond our particular loyalties, as for Royce or H. Richard Niebuhr;[47] it may prove an inchoate sense of the reality of "something more," as for William James;[48] it may prove a transcendent sense of justice, as for Simone Weil or Reinhold Niebuhr;[49] it may prove a sense of profound personal and societal alienation or oppression, as in Gutierrez, Cone, Segundo, Ruether, Moltmann and Metz;[50] it may prove a sense of a love which knows no restrictions, as in Lonergan or Scheler.[51] The major situational focus of my limit-to experience and thereby its disclosure of some limit-of reality will partly determine which images, symbols, myths and conceptual frameworks will be employed in systematic theology to explicate the limit-of reality. In Part Two of this work I will attempt to explicate more fully some of these situational moments in our contemporary theological situation. For the moment, however, my concern is simply to articulate some initial understanding of the limit-of character of religion: an understanding, moreover, which may in principle resonate with any one of these situational limit-to experiences. The hypothesis is twofold. First, a defining characteristic of the situational "religious dimension of common experience and language" is the "limit-to" character of the experience itself, whatever its particular existential focus. Second, a defining characteristic of any explicit religion—more exactly any classic religious expression—is a limit-of character bearing the status of event-gift-manifestation of and from the whole, and experienced as giving the respondent wholeness. That limit-of character, moreover, radicalizes the intensification process in all classic expressions to the point where some dialectical account of the experience and expression of this event-manifestation is ordinarily needed.[52]

There seems to be certain existential conditions to any reflective person's willingness to enter the conversation of interpreting the religious classics. Some sense of a basic trust and confidence in the very worthwhileness of existence is experienced in the very willingness to go on living. But any experience always involves some understanding. This experience includes an understanding that eventually issues forth into the fundamental questions on the meaning of existence in the whole and some personal search for wholeness.[53] That search impels a willingness to enter the conversation, the back-and-forth movement of authentic fundamental religious questions and answers expressed in classic religious texts, events, images and persons. Both that experience of basic confidence and its self-understanding as basic faith, however, will be threatened by the profound negativities that any sensitive, intelligent human being experiences in personal, societal or cultural life. The experience of a "once-born" healthy-minded religious life undoubtedly happens, as William James documents and as our own contemporary puzzled response to the still existing once-born, untroubled ones among us also shows.[54] Yet for most of us most of the time, I suspect, the threats to that basic confidence and faith are at least as real and often more powerful than the experience of basic confidence itself. We really do doubt that there exists an inner connection between how we believe we ought to live and how reality itself is constituted. We really do fear that religion may be, as Santayana observed, a "splendid error." We really do want, with James, the right to believe.[55] And yet we fear, with Clifford, that we may not possess that right.[56] Even those who do finally resonate to the extraordinary yes of a Molly Bloom, or the triumphal graced yes "forged in the smithy of a thousand no's" of a Karl Barth or a Karl Rahner, also recognize the truth of Melville's dictum: "Say no with thunder, for all who say yes, lie."[57]

The presence of the negative is central to most religious experiences and expressions: surely central to any experience available in this contemporary situation.[58]

It is difficult, for example, for any contemporary person not to despise Augustine's more than occasional bullying tactics towards Pelagius and Julian of Eclanum.[59] But it is equally difficult not to recognize that Augustine's dialectical, even tortured vision is more true to our actual experience of the dialectical nature of time and history. We may find frightening the profound realism in the later Michelangelo or the breaking of all forms to see reality in Cezanne and van Gogh. Yet we cannot deny that their firmer disclosure of the truth of the fascinating and frightening complexity of actual lived existence resonates more deeply to our actual experience of life than does the untroubled world disclosed in art resonant with the beauty and created goodness of finitude as in Raphael or Renoir.[60] We have learned in this century, perhaps too well, the need we have, as Joseph Conrad saw, to submit ourselves to the destructive element.

We may, for example, especially if we are Catholic in our fundamental religious sensibilities, turn with some reluctance from Rubens to Rembrandt. But, we find, turn we must, even if we ultimately return to a now chastened Rubens. We may turn for needed refreshment and delight to such minor classics as say, Nancy Mitford's charming evocations of life at the Versailles of Louis XIV and Louis XV. Yet even in allowing ourselves to be thus bewitched in the reading, we are unable to forget the always palpable reality of the life beyond and the destiny awaiting that civilized, charmed, fated garden. We in the North Atlantic community may not wish to face the realities beyond both our civilization and our cherished alienations in the experiences of oppression articulated in the various theologies of liberation or the reality of horror forced upon our consciousness by a Solzhenitsyn. Yet we cannot avoid the fear, quietly but relentlessly becoming an anxiety, that without facing that reality we may now be Versailles.

Many in our culture may envy the "first naivete" of their former religious selves but most of us know that, save as nostalgia, it is no longer possible.[61] Not only reflection but life itself has smashed it beyond repair. The options now become: resigned stoic resignation, life as usual with occasional sentimental journeys, outright cynicism, a strict morality of duty and obligation, a tragic vision of existence or a willingness to wager entering the conversation—the questions and the answers—present in the religious classics. The possibilities for a once-born entry into that conversation, like the options for a first naivete itself, seem spent to most contemporary thinkers. The only experience that we are likely to find of the whole will prove not merely a partial but inevitably a broken one. We have learned too much, we hope, to allow any new God of the gaps to enter, unannounced and unwelcome. We have experienced too much of the threats in this blood-drenched century to enter the conversation of the religious classics without an experience that is itself an inevitably dialectical one of hope and fear.

But above all, we cannot enter the conversation with the religious classics with the false distancing of the aesthetic sensibility. For then, as we discovered in our earlier understanding of the truth-disclosure of the work of art, we do not really enter at all. We must enter that conversation, if at all, critically but really: with a recognition that here the truth of existence itself as related to and distanced from the whole may now be at stake.

The religious classics, we know, may prove to be illusions and projections of our own infantile needs or social conditions or insatiable will to power. Then we must move elsewhere—with the integrity and courage of Freud, Nietzsche or Marx.[62] But we cannot honestly discount the possibility that religion may prove genuinely disclosive of a reality that cannot be denied. Hence we must join the conversation of the religions without holding back. We must listen with both respect and critical freedom, attempt to express what we have experienced and understood—however partial, however flawed—then move on. We must risk a systematic theology.

ii. The Religious Classic

If we allow the experience of any classical work of art to provide some guidelines for an entry into the conversation of the religious classics, then we find certain rubrics worth noting once again.[63] The interpreter of the religious classic, like the interpreter of all classics, enters with some preunderstanding of those questions and responses named "religious." As an individual with a particular temperament, effective history, needs, hopes, desires and fears, the interpreter enters with some personal preunderstanding of what religion is. One's personal temperament (in William James' sense) and tradition, along with the major situational focus for the fundamental questions of existence, provide the primary focus of that preunderstanding. Yet no individual interpreter, as we saw above, lives as a sheer individualist. Rather each lives in some relationship—either unconscious or conscious, trusting or rejecting—of the history of the effects, influences and interpretations of the religious dimension of a culture. For some, a particular church tradition may have principally formed that history. For others, some minor or major secularization of a religious tradition—as with the Romantics and their secular successors—may prove the principal carrier of the tradition. Some particular method of interpretation that the interpreter has learned to trust may prove the foremost carrier of the tradition itself as the tradition enters, via the method, into one's preunderstanding of "religious" issues.[64]

More usually, some combination of these distinct, sometimes conflicting, sometimes complementary carriers of the tradition will emerge to help form the interpreter's initial preunderstanding of religious questions and responses. Especially when the reality of the tradition is united to some powerful personal sense of the limit-situations to the everyday, or the limit-questions to science, art and morality, the preunderstanding of the prospective interpreter of the religious classics is likely to prove more fully alert—intelligent, sensitive, open, critical, responsive—to the possibilities for existence disclosed in the religious classics.[65] Nothing so concentrates the mind, Doctor Johnson once observed, as the thought that one is to be hanged in the morning. Analogously, nothing so concentrates the attention of the prospective interpreter of the religious classics as a powerful sense of some focussed situational experience of a fundamental question for existence—death, trust, anxiety, wonder, loyalty to a cause greater than self, radical contingency, meaninglessness, wonder, joy, love.

With some preunderstanding of religion (due to some preunderstanding of those fundamental questions) and with some experience (either negative, positive or ambivalent) of a particular religious tradition and its diverse carriers, every interpreter approaches the religious classic—now trusting, even eager, now wary, skeptical, suspicious. At this juncture, rather than describing the whole spectrum of conflicting interpretations of the religious classics, I will now attempt to articulate one major, indeed classic approach—an approach that I have found to be the most adequate one. I cannot fully defend that adequacy here. Indeed this entire book can only partially warrant it. For the moment, therefore, let us formulate the belief as a proposal for the appropriate preunderstanding for an interpreter of religion, not as an already warranted conclusion but as an "if-then" proposition still in search of its warrants.

The approach is this: If one is guided by a sense for those fundamental questions, if guided as well by that great modern tradition of interpretation of the *sui generis* character of religion ranging from Schleiermacher through James, Otto, Søderblom, von Hügel, van der Leeuw, Scheler, Wach, Eliade and Tillich,[66] the interpreter is likely to find relative adequacy in the kind of interpretations of the appropriate responses to the religious classics described in different, sometimes conflicting ways by these great modern phenomenologists of the *sui generis* character of religions. For example, despite the difficulties, even occasional bizarreness, of Rudolph Otto's neo-Kantian schematisms and his demand for a religious "a priori," the kind of experience of "the holy" which Otto classically delineated is still a fitting description of the kind of realized experience (to employ my own language) that a genuine religious classic often does elicit.

More exactly, the kind of claim to attention that a religious classic, *as religious,* provokes is a claim that discloses to the interpreter some realized experience bearing some sense of recognition into the objectively awe-some reality of the otherness of the whole as radical mystery. The genuinely religious person (James' "mystics" and "saints"),[67] it seems, do experience that reality of mystery as the reality of the holy bearing overwhelming and life-transformative force.

From many phenomenonological (i.e., descriptive) accounts of that experience, the same sense—now usually in more muted, more mediated-as-interpretative tones—is available to the prospective interpreter of the religious classic.[68] For the religious classic elicits in the interpreter, by the very power of its ownmost claim to attention, a heightened awareness of the reality of what Otto named the "numinous."[69] The interpreter is unlikely to be struck dumb with the kind of amazement familiar to the classic religious persons, the saints, prophets and mystics. And yet the interpreter cannot but sense in any religious classic the force of the claim by a power not one's own. Anxiety in any particular preunderstanding of the fundamental questions may yield, however momentarily, to an awe, or, at the limit, a dread disclosed in that *tremendum* claim. Wonder and the trust in any preunderstanding may yield to the enticing, evocative, even seductive *fascinans* power in that same reality. Yet what seems most likely to account for these experiences of anxiety, wonder and trust becoming their intensified (as explicitly religious) analogues—awe and dread (for anxiety), love and ecstasy (for wonder and trust)—save the claim evoked by the religious classic itself?

In a manner analogous to that of any later dismissal of the realized experience of the work of art, we may upon reflection become skeptical and suspicious of the original experience of the religious classic. We may even have good reasons for that later suspicion. It is, for example, difficult in a post-Freudian age to take William James' relatively innocent account of the "unconscious" at face value. Yet does a difficulty with James' theory of the unconscious (a theory proposed to explain a religious experience that was first described phenomenologically) allow us to call into question his original phenomenological description of religion? In any conflict of interpretations one primary criterion of relative adequacy endures: whether the experience being interpreted is itself acknowledged and described as it appears to consciousness. Most of us have relatively little interest in theories of music formulated by the tone-deaf, or theories of painting formulated by the color-blind. Most of us, as the previous chapter suggested, possess relatively little interest in aesthetic theories which discount the actual experience of the work of art.

Some interpreters of religion make the directly analogous suggestion that what we need above all in any adequate interpretation of religion is a phenomenology of the religious experience *as* religious. An interpreter need accept neither Schleiermacher's Romantic, indeed sometimes effusive language, nor James' own "over-beliefs," nor Otto's schematism, his analysis of the "irrational," nor his faculty-of-divination language, nor von Hügel's particular understanding of mysticism, nor Søderblom's or van der Leeuw's classification systems, nor Wach's Romantic hermeneutic and metaphysical "decision," nor Scheler's "nonformalist" claims, nor Tillich's formulation of religion as "ultimate concern," nor Eliade's particular formulation of the dialectic of the sacred and the profane to see and accept what unites these otherwise diverse, often even conflicting interpretations of the religious phenomenon: the insistence that the first responsibility of the interpreter of religion is to describe the experience itself as it appears to consciousness. The description, itself necessarily an interpretation, must attempt to develop interpretative categories that fit the realized experience ranging from a sense of resonance to a full-fledged shock of recognition. Some realized experience is the response of the religious person to the religious classic and is often the initial response of the phenomenological interpreter of the religious classic to the same, now mediated, event of disclosure.

Since I have not found persuasive reasons to deny this seemingly obvious but widely challenged insistence posed by the phenomenological interpreters of the *sui generis* character of religion, I will in the remainder of this chapter align myself with that tradition and attempt an interpretation of the religious classic. If one desires the warrants for that alignment, I can only recall that they are the same kind of warrants as those provided for interpreting the work of art: to begin with some description of the realized experience of art or religion; to allow the focus upon the response to provide the central clue for understanding the object or work being responded to, followed by methods of explanation for the modes of expression internal to that work and the vision of reality disclosed by and in that work.[70] Any attempt at *relative* adequacy to an interpretation of the reality of art or religion would seem to demand some kind of phenomenological, hermeneutical approach. Moreover, if the fuller model for hermeneutics described above is also allowed (the model not of *Verstehen* alone but of the dialectics of understanding-explanation-understanding), then the further conversation with all legitimate methods of explanation—methods that correctly develop the understanding or even confront or challenge it—should also be encouraged in the process of interpretation.

But if those methods of explanation are finally reductionist ones (for example, Malinowski's functionalist method as distinct from Geertz's functional one), then one will, of course, still be likely to learn something of real importance (e.g., the functional interactions of religion and society in Malinowski). And yet these methods will also be likely to be described as relatively inadequate—because unable or unwilling to account for the *sui generis* character of the initial religious response—by claiming that religion is "nothing but" a product of society, neurosis, that its "origins" are exclusively in animism, totemism, magic, etc.[71] To state this position is, of course, not to warrant it. For that, only the multidisciplinary conversation among competing and conflicting hermeneutics of retrieval and hermeneutics of suspicion would prove sufficient. Yet to state the position may at least serve the function of clarifying the kind of positive warrants entailed: the warrants that any claim to relative adequacy must provide some initial description of the religious phenomenon that is hermeneutically appropriate to a realized experience of the phenomenon under investigation.

On those grounds, the tradition of the phenomenological interpretation of the *sui generis* character of religion, from Schleiermacher through Eliade, seems the clearest candidate among competing traditions of interpretation for relative adequacy. The more speculative elements in that tradition of retrieval (like the analogous speculative elements in the "origins" of religion in "totemism" in the distinct positions of Durkheim and Freud) are easy enough to spot and thereby to bracket. What warrants that tradition of interpretation, however, is not its more speculative moments (like Otto's schematism of James' search for origins in the unconscious). Rather its major warrants lie in its insistence that the first moment of interpretation of religion should be a phenomenological one appropriate to the *sui generis* character of an explicitly religious response. From that response, as from the response to art, all else follows. To understand and explain that response, all methods, all readings, all conflicts of interpretation should be geared.

With that tradition of interpretation of the *sui generis* character of religion, therefore, we enter the conversation with the religious classics at great risk. For we may find that our present mode of being in the world is disclosed as either inauthentic, spent, finished—or disclosed as confirmed beyond any hope for confirmation; we may find some manifestation of another style or ethos of living bearing the redescriptive power[72] of a manifestation that this is what reality itself in its sheer actuality is, along with the prescriptive force of a demand that our present mode of living be changed. We may also recognize that if this particular religious classic is genuinely a classic then we should free ourselves to experience the dialectic of the classic: the dialectic of respect and critical freedom that allow us to be caught up in the dialectic of the fundamental questions and answers, the subject matter of the classic itself. We should allow for the possibility that an *event* of truth as both disclosure and concealment may happen.[73]

No more than in experiencing the genuine work of art should we become merely passive. But we do need minimally to move beyond the enslaving self-consciousness of those who cannot play any game, enter any conversation, allow any disclosure into the critical freedom and receptivity of the real conversation partner, the authentic player, the responsible self. On the side of critical freedom, we must, of course, remain open to the possibility that we will discover that this conversation is really misnamed. For religion may prove a classic expression, but not really of some limit-of reality. Rather religion may prove to be a classic expression of morality (as with Braithwaite) or of cosmology (as with Huxley) or of poetry (as with Santayana).[74] We must remain open to the possibility that the conversations of the religions are not merely risky, but fatal, poisonous. Then we must leave this sick and resentful game and enter—with Freud, Nietzsche, Marx, Feuerbach—into another classic conversation with alternative, postreligious visions of a promised wholeness and the whole.[75] Yet we must also be open to the possibility that the conversation elicited by the religious classics is, on the other side of both critique and suspicion, a public conversation open to all responsible thinkers: a conversation with classics whose event-like character may liberate the interpreter for and to the whole and to a wholeness which cannot be achieved. Yet religion can be experienced, received and understood as event, gift, even what Christians name grace.

It might also be noted that even if the religious character of the classical religious expressions is denied, the event character of true disclosure and concealment implied in its classical status will yet endure—as Santayana articulated in his cryptic dictum that "poetry is religion that supervenes upon life; religion is poetry that intervenes in life"[76] and as any secular person can and ordinarily does experience, with or without the aid of Henry Adams, in experiencing the event of Chartres.

However, if the experience of the religious classic is what it claims for itself—a genuine manifestation of the whole from the reality of that whole itself—then we may surmise that every religious classic will bear the essential characteristic of all genuinely religious experiences as limit-experiences. The religious classic, if really religious, will at the very least disclose a limit-to experience distinguishing religion from morality, science, art and politics. The religious classics of a living religious tradition will also disclose an event of manifestation by the whole of a limit-of, ground-to, horizon-to experience—in sum, an authoritative-because-classic expression of the whole that promises a wholeness to life. The testimony to some dialectical experience of the whole expressed in the religious classics will not prove available *as* religious to either the heteronomous or the narrowly autonomous consciousness, i.e., to all who refuse to enter and be caught up in and played by the conversation, the game of the religious classic itself. To either the autonomous or the heteronomous self, another game is going forward, one wherein the religious classics are simply out there, external to and under the rule of my subjectivity. That subjectivity and its present worldview and that alone will determine whether I extrinsically will accept, in heteronomous obedience to authoritarian norms—or extrinsically reject, in autonomous obedience to the norms of a finally technical reason—any claims to truth in the religious classic. In what Tillich named a theonomous consciousness in a person, a society or a culture, however, another possibility beyond heteronomy and autonomy occurs: the risk of interpreting the world of the religious classic and studying its claims to a truth of an event-like manifestation of the whole—that event of self-manifestation by the power of the whole which Christians and Jews name "revelation."

As with the experience of all classics, by entering the world of the religious classic, the interpreter enters an intensification process that promises and promotes experiences of both participation in reality and distancing from reality. Unlike the experience of nonreligious classics, in the religious classics this common intensification process is itself intensified to the point of a transgression of the usual limits of both participation and nonparticipation in the whole.[77] Beyond even the intensification process of all limit-to experiences, the religious classic expresses the power of a manifestation of a "limit-of" experience, an experience of a self-manifesting power, an eruption of both radical participation and nonparticipation in the whole.

Authentic religious experience, on the testimony of those all consider clearly religious, seems to be some experience of the whole that is sensed as the self-manifestation of an undeniable power not one's own and is articulated not in the language of certainty and clarity but of scandal and mystery. The religious person does not claim a new control upon reality but speaks of losing former controls and experiencing, not merely affirming, a liberation into a realm of ultimate incomprehensibility and real, fascinating and frightening mystery. When religious persons speak the language of revelation, they mean that something has happened to them that they cannot count as their own achievement. Rather they find themselves compelled to honor that realized experience as an eruption of a power become self-manifestation from and by the whole in which, by which, and to which they live.[78] They employ language like "liberation," "emancipation," "wholeness," "salvation" to articulate the conviction elicited and empowered by that experience itself. That conviction, that faith, takes many forms: ethos and worldview are radically united; wholeness in life has come not as personal achievement but as gift from the whole;[79] above all, how one ought to live is ultimately grounded in what reality itself is.

In the religious intensification of the common experience disclosed in all major classics religious persons often describe themselves as being caught up in and by the power of this manifestation to the point where they both radically participate in the whole while yet, with equal radicality, are distanced from the whole. Religious awe in the face of mystery involves both real anxiety, sometimes even dread, and the real fascination of love and ecstasy. The "mystics" and "saints" do not speak as if the experience they describe were merely a limit-to experience, nor even one adequately captured by some limit-language like that of "limit-of," "horizon-to," "ground-to." Rather they ordinarily employ an irretrievably dialectical language to express the character of their experience of this limit-of.[80] The language of John of the Cross, for example, is both disclosive and dialectical in the poetry while seeming contorted, forced, broken, almost useless in the Scholastic conceptual language employed in some of his commentaries on the experience. The poetic language seems appropriately disclosive of the kind of intensely religious dialectical experience he describes; the intellectualist Scholastic language of his tradition seems to break apart every time he attempts to articulate the mystical experience through it.[81] The testimony of the genuinely religious is that this manifestation, this revelation, does not disclose the certainty of a clarity and a control but the reality of a power at once *tremendum et fascinans*. The event of revelation does not seem to disclose only our radical participation in the whole. The event conceals that participation with equal radicality—precisely as a participation in a realized experience of the whole as radical mystery both disclosing and concealing itself. The reality of mystery is, after all, experienced and understood as mystery only on the other side of the breakdown of the clarity of the everyday.

For such dialectical experience, dialectical speech like silence may prove the only relatively adequate form of expression. The tributes to silence by mystics in all traditions might well lead the rest of us to distrust all our attempts to translate their dialectical experience of participation-nonparticipation, clarity-obscurity, comprehensibility-incomprehensibility, disclosure-concealment of the whole.[82] Silence may indeed be the final and most adequate mode of speech for religion. And yet silence is possible as silence only to a speaker. The mere existence of religious classics should alert any interpreter that, whatever else these strange expressions are, they are, precisely as expressions—whether in the texts of the mystics and the theologians, the styles of life of the saints and witnesses, the imagery of the icons, the founding symbols of the tradition, the events of religious history—all finally discourse.[83] We must interpret them.

A further clue to the genuinely religious character of all religious classics as expression may be found in the analogies of the religious classic to other classics, more exactly to the positive and negative functions of distanciation involved in all classic expressions.[84] Insofar as we strive to communicate through expression the meaning of any experience, we always distance the said from the saying, the noema from the event of noesis. Through the levels of the word to the sentence, the paragraph, the genre of the work as a whole and the style of authorial presence in the *oeuvre,* the same positive function of distanciation for producing a communicable meaning through an appropriate expression occurs. Where the originating experience is real but minor, the form will ordinarily prove fully adequate to express the meaning, as in the existence of those "minor classics" distinct from both period pieces and major classics. Where the original experience of participation and alienation in reality is major, the form—both the genre and the style—will be relatively adequate for the expression of the meaning· partly tentative, partly a matter of design, partly a matter of accidents and fate become destiny in the masterpiece. With the major classics, the form somehow works to the point where the expression assures both the permanence of the meaning and allows a fullness, even an excess of meaning that is always in need of reinterpretation, even by the author.

If the religious experience of participation-nonparticipation in the whole is as radical as I have claimed for the intensified (as both limit-to and limit-of) and the thereby intrinsically dialectical experience of an event grounding all religious expression, then it follows that the process of distanciation common to all classics will also be intensified in the case of classic religious expressions. Since expression occurs, the same positive role of distanciation occurs; even the silence of the mystic is an expression of a meaning produced by a speaker. Since the originating experience whose meaning is expressed via distanciation in classic religious texts is also the result of an intensification process into a particular route that the subject both engages in and lets happen, since that religious experience is the radical one of both participation-nonparticipation in the whole's manifestation of itself, the religious expression (by means of genre and style in texts and images, by means of style in lives, ritual and events) will always prove at best only relatively adequate to the experience of a gifted, graced self caught up in a power not its own.

In principle, classic expressions other than the religious may find some adequate form: in minor classics with relative ease; in major classics with varying degrees of tentativeness, unsteadiness, accident, flaws, unsurety. In principle, the religious classic expression cannot find an adequate form. For the whole experienced as radical mystery is experienced as giving itself in the religious response. The whole, in manifesting itself, is also experienced as freeing the real self of the respondent to its true freedom: a freedom where the self's new ethos is experienced as grounded in reality itself—a reality both disclosed and concealed as the whole by the power of the whole. Any religious experience of participation-nonparticipation in that whole remains a dialectical one incapable in principle of full adequacy: a principle expressed even in the best finite, dialectical religious forms. The giftedness of the event of manifestation can be evoked or elicited for others through the production of relatively adequate forms. Yet the reality granting that sense of giftedness can never be expressed adequately. Since the respondent's sense of radical mystery points to but does not encompass the reality of the whole, the sense of mystery will include experiential elements of both a *fascinans* and a *tremendum* character. That sense of mystery reexperienced as event from the whole will take the respondent beyond all alternative realized experiences of the classic works of art, beyond the good and evil realities of ethics, and beyond the powers of expression possible to any finite human being caught up in a disclosure of the infinite by the infinite.

The intensification process involved in the experience of participation-nonparticipation in the whole seems to force the genuinely religious person to an experience of awe beyond anxiety, an experience of radical reverence beyond wonder, an experience of fascination, even terror, beyond both trust and alienation. That same process elicits its dialectical opposite: a radicalized sense of existential estrangement in the light of the event-ful, gifted presence of real mystery. So too the same kind of intensification process occurs on the side of expression for the religious classic to impel all modes of religious expression—classic texts, persons, images, rituals, myths, symbols, events. Yet the process disallows any idolatrous suggestion that any of these expressions is adequate to the event itself. As symbols, religious symbols do participate in that reality to which they point.[85] As intrinsically inadequate symbols, religious symbols bear their own internal demand that idolatry be disallowed and their own internal hints that they too must finally be broken to allow the event to occur.

An adequate religious expression seems, therefore, impossible.[86] We are left with a search for what at first sight sounds disappointing: a search for relatively adequate forms of religious expression. We are left, in sum, with the religious classics—where the form expresses both the necessity and the reality of a human response to a reality that cannot finally be adequately expressed. In the religious classics more clearly even than in any other classics, the interpreter will note that the expression itself must be as dialectical as the originating experience. At best religious expression can hope for relative adequacy. Even Bernini in his classic "Saint Teresa in Ecstasy" would claim no more. More to the point, perhaps, Teresa herself in her classic writings claims far less. The relativity of religious expressions must always be open to new negations as novel forms are discovered and new religious experiences occur. Its relativity must be open above all to the negations needed when the form tries to replace both the experience and the reality whose meaning the form serves only to disclose.[87] In every religious tradition, forms evolve, break, disappear, reappear as the dialectics of religious expression enters the dialectics of a religious tradition. Consider, for example, the history of religious art. As one example, the Baroque, in its greatest expressions in Rubens or Bernini, astonishingly works as *religious* art and works largely by means of negations and shock to evoke wonder and affirmation. In lesser hands, the intrinsically dialectical character of the strangely exalted yet self-negating religious and artistic Baroque confidence lives no more. Then one finds merely the dazzling virtuosity of form attempting to live on its own, ripped from its religious roots and trying to redress that loss through the ever more ingenious, undialectical experiments of Rococo virtuosi.

To enter the conversation of the religious classics through real interpretation, therefore, is to enter a disclosure of a world of meaning and truth offering no certainty but promising some realized experience of the whole by the power of the whole. That world affords no technically controlled comprehensibility yet it does release the self to the uncontrollable incomprehensibility of an experience of radical mystery.

The mystery elicits, even empowers the religious self to believe that how we ought to live (for the Jew and Christian, with compassion, in justice and in love, in righteousness) is grounded in the fundamental nature of reality itself. That mystery evokes a sense of freedom[88] that is at the same time a gift; a command to live that empowers even as it commands. That mystery begins to be sensed in the wonder, anxiety and fundamental trust of our earlier experiences of a religious dimension to all reality. That sense of mystery is intensified as it transforms the self's initial experiences of wonder, anxiety and trust by a response to the stark otherness of the religious reality disclosed in the religious classic. For the religious person, wonder, anxiety and trust yield in the religious experience to awe, sometimes even rapture and dread, the sense of giftedness disclosed by pointing to the enveloping, self-manifesting whole in which we live and move and have our being. That same sense of radical giftedness both fascinates and frightens as it shocks and transforms the self to believe what one dare not otherwise believe: that reality is finally gracious, that the deepest longings of our minds and hearts for wholeness in ourselves, with others, with history and nature, is the case—the case granted as gift by the whole; the case expressed with relative adequacy determined by the intrinsic inadequacy of every classic religious expression. The appeal of any religious classic is a nonviolent appeal to our minds, hearts and imaginations, and through them to our will.[89] Its authoritative status is not, therefore, the violent appeal to obedience demanded by authoritarians in all religious traditions. These latter, in fact, have lost the sense of the only authoritative, nonviolent appeal that any religious classic or any religious tradition faithful to its ownmost vision can possess. For religious authoritarians replace the nonviolent appeal of the authoritative religious classics with their own distortions of those realities into ideological demands forced upon a heteronomous will. The damage done to the cause of the religious classics by authoritarian distortions and their seeming capture of the religious classics as their property is incalculable. Fortunately, the religious classics themselves can be counted on always to challenge those distortions at the root.[90]

Nor will the world of the explicitly religious classics domesticate the earlier common human experiences of a religious-as-limit-to dimension to the everyday so that it becomes the false security of one more ideology or worldview. Rather interpretation of the world of the religious classics can actually intensify that limit-to experience by liberating it from its troubled confines through some experience of the limit-of reality: a disclosure of an event of manifestation of the whole by the power of the whole. The religious classic will demand of all those caught up in the interpretation of its world that its religious subject matter—its fundamental questions and responses upon my present relationship to the whole—be openly addressed. To allow for the world of the religious classics is in the end to allow for a world of meaning and truth disclosing the truth of the paradigmatic, the classical, the extraordinary. Every religious classic expresses an event of a "limit-of" reality that has the full force of a power finally liberating us from ourselves, summoning us to and by a power not our own.

If this proposal for an understanding of religious classics is plausible, then it follows, for theologians, that we both can and must move from an analysis of the limit-to experiences proper to fundamental theology and risk an interpretation of the reality of a limit-of disclosure in the explicitly religious classics of our own tradition. In that move to systematic theology we may also find that limit-language must yield, as a relatively adequate language for a religious dimension to our lives, to the intrinsically dialectical language of systematic theology: a language appropriate to the originating religious experience of the event—an event eliciting the dialectical experiences of fascination, trust, fear and awe, an event disclosing and concealing our radical belonging to and estrangement from the whole. It remains to be seen what major forms of dialectical expression the religious consciousness employs and what distinct, conflicting, even contradictory worlds of meaning and truth are disclosed in the religious classics through the risk-ridden interpretations of systematic theologies.

Notes

1. The ideal remains the hermeneutic ideal of conversation; the reality, as we shall see, is radically conflictual. Conflict, however, has a second meaning beyond the empirical reality: namely, the inevitable conflicts that emerge in genuine conversation as the dialectic of question and answer elicited by fidelity to the subject matter takes over. If the conversation ideal is not allowed, one will find conflict as mere controversy and polemics; if conversation is allowed, conflict will recur but under the control of subject matter. Conflict as controversy is an expression of the will to mastery and power that disallows conversation and control by the subject matter. Hermeneutics challenges exactly this will to mastery and control present in mere controversy by its challenge to every participant to enter a conversation where the subject matter is allowed primacy. The stakes for this choice in approaching the phenomenon of religion, as we shall see, are high indeed. This

hermeneutical commitment has impelled me to note especially the hermeneutical phenomenologists of the *sui generis* character of religion from Schleiermacher through Eliade (see text below).

2. See especially Mircea Eliade, *The Quest* (Chicago: Univ. of Chicago Press, 1969), pp. 1–12. It is also interesting to note how Eliade's interpretation of the sacred employs language that resonates with the Heidegger-Gadamer language of the "event of truth" (in the work of art) as both "disclosure" and "concealment"; for Eliade, this sacred is understood as "the dialectic of the sacred" since the sacred both "manifests" and "withdraws" or "remains hidden": inter alia, see *Patterns in Comparative Religion* (London: Sheed & Ward, 1958), esp. pp. 1–38; and *The Sacred and the Profane: The Nature of Religion* (New York: Harper, 1961), passim, esp. pp. 20–65.

3. Mircea Eliade, *The Quest,* pp. 4–11.

4. See especially, Hannah Arendt, *The Human Condition* and *On Revolution* [I/17].

5. As in the former discussion, readers may note that I accept the insistence of Gadamer on the presence of effective history through tradition for any preunderstanding. Yet I also emphasize more than Gadamer does (with his concentration on the Greek and German humanist traditions) the radical ambiguity of *any* tradition (including the humanist and surely including *any* religious tradition). For example, even a religion like that favored culture of many Western intellectuals, the remarkably rich aesthetic-religious world of Balinese culture, bears its own ambiguities: see James Boon, *The Anthropological Romance of Bali* [III/64]; or Clifford Geertz, "Deep Play: Notes on the Balinese Cockfight," in *Myth, Symbol and Culture* [I/18], pp. 1–39. The expressions "world-sustaining," "world-creating," "world-destroying" are my interpretations of the analyses of religion and "world construction" and "world maintenance" in Peter Berger, *The Sacred Canopy* [I/1], pp. 3–29 and 81–105 (on alienation).

6. See *Auschwitz: Beginning of a New Era?*, ed. Eva Fleischner (New York: KTAV, 1977). For a good summary of the New Testament difficulties, see Samuel Sandmel, *Anti-Semitism in the New Testament* (Philadelphia: Fortress, 1978). As Sandmel himself observes (p. xxi), anti-Semitism (as distinct from anti-Judaism) is not the correct (as anachronistic) label for the difficulties in the New Testament, yet those scriptural statements (especially in John) did help to occasion the bloody, frightening history of later Christian anti-Semitism. For an example of the ambiguity of a tradition, note the book on largely German biblical scholarship by Charlotte Klein, *Anti-Judaism in Christian Theology* (Philadelphia: Fortress, 1978). The magisterial work of George Foote Moore in an earlier era aided some Anglo-American scholars to avoid following German exegetes in some of their caricatures of the Judaism contemporary to Jesus and Paul.

7. Besides the well-known *loci classici* in the individual thinkers, the following secondary sources are helpful: James Collins, *The Emergence of Philosophy of Religion* (New Haven: Yale Univ. Press, 1967); Louis Dupré, *The Other Dimension: A Search for the Meaning of Religious Attitudes* (New York: Doubleday, 1972); idem, *A Dubious Heritage* (New York: Paulist, 1977); Michael Banton, ed., *Anthropological Approaches to the Study of Religion* (New York: Praeger, 1966); Ninian Smart, *The Religious Experience of Mankind* (New York: Scribner, 1969); Roland Robertson, *The Sociological Interpretation of Religion* [I/77]; Gregory Baum, *Religion and Alienation* [I/1]; John Bowker, *The Sense of God: Sociological, Anthropological and Psychological Approaches to the Origin of the Sense of God* (Oxford: Clarendon, 1973); idem, *The Religious Imagination and the Sense of God* (Oxford: Clarendon, 1978); and Frederick Ferré, *Basic Modern Philosophy of*

Religion (New York: Scribner, 1967). Vol. 15 of *The New Encyclopedia Britannica* (15th ed., 1974) contains several helpful articles by different experts on the relevant questions and disciplines in religion; see especially the articles by Charles Adams ("Classification of Religions"), Ninian Smart ("Study of Religion") and Frederick Streng ("Sacred or Holy"). The survey in Eric J. Sharpe, *Comparative Religion: A History* (London: Duckworth, 1975) is also informative on the history of the discipline usually called "history of religions" in North America. A recent attempt to employ the method of the Institute for Philosophical Research to show logical types of "concepts" of religion is John Edward Sullivan, *Ideas of Religion: A Prolegomenon to the Philosophy of Religion* (Washington: Univ. Press of America, 1979). For a helpful historical account of Western definitions of religion up to the early nineteenth century, see Michel Despland, *La Religion en Occident* (Montreal: Fides, 1979).

8. See especially Karl Barth, *Church Dogmatics,* I/2, "The Revelation of God as the Abolition of Religion," pp. 280–303; Emil Brunner, *Die Mystik und das Wort* (Tübingen: J. C. B. Mohr, 1924); Dietrich Bonhoeffer, *Letters and Papers from Prison* (London: Fontana, 1965), pp. 91–96; and Jürgen Moltmann, *Theology of Hope* (New York: Harper & Row, 1967), pp. 95–100, 311–25. Insofar as this neo-orthodox tradition from Barth through Moltmann makes the following two points, I agree with the critique: (1) no abstract religious a priori can account for the concrete *event*-character of Christian faith (and thereby its particularity as response to an event); (2) religions *can* be exercises in "self-salvation" and as such fall under the Christian (and Jewish and Islamic) suspicion of "idolatry." The first point is in agreement with the general methodological position of this work; the second with sound inner-theological (and, it seems to me, inner-religious) criteria—or even cultural criteria cognizant of the "ambiguity" of religion. Obviously Barth et al. wish to state far more than these two claims (and far more than I, at least, can agree to), but that "more" is dependent on inner-Christian theological discussions addressed in Part II of this work. For an equally vigorous (and exclusivist) anathematizing of Barth's anathema on religion from the "other" side, see *La Foi Prophétique et le Sacré,* ed. Henry Corbin et al. (Paris: Berg, 1977).

9. For a good example of the kind of difficulty that one discipline has in attempting "definitions of religion," see Roland Robertson, *The Sociological Interpretation of Religion* [I/77], pp. 34–51. For an example of the legal problems in defining religion (for the U.S. Supreme Court), note the analysis of Martin Marty, "North America: The Empirical Understanding of Religion and Theology," in Mircea Eliade and David Tracy, eds., *What Is Religion? An Enquiry for Christian Theology* (= *Concilium* 136; New York: Seabury, 1980). It is not special pleading, I trust, to observe that for Christian theologians this volume of the journal *Concilium* contains several informative and constructive articles: among them, on theology, John Cobb and Paul Knitter; on sociology, Gregory Baum; on cultural anthropology, Victor Turner; on history of religions, Lawrence Sullivan; and on problems particular to theology practiced in different religious cultural settings: the articles on Latin American debates over "popular religion" (Segundo Galilea), on North American "empirical" understandings (Martin Marty), on French discussions of a "religionless culture" (Jacques Audinet) and on German discussions of the "mystico-political" (Matthew Lamb). The volume is directed to Christian theological questions on religion.

10. This would apply not only to Schleiermacher, Hegel and Tillich but to most Western theologians and philosophers—including the present author who is aware of the Christian preunderstanding operative in this present discussion. Although

the analysis in this chapter does not employ explicitly theistic language for the religious phenomenon, for example, it does still employ language (namely, the manifestation of the whole by the power of the whole) clearly influenced (not, I hope, determined) by Christian theological discussions of revelation as "the self-manifestation of God." A word of caution should be noted here: my attempt in this chapter is *not* to provide a single definition of "religion" (an attempt for which I do not have the scholarly competence in non-Western and archaic religions). The present attempt is analogous to the attempt in the fundamental theology of *BRO* to claim that "limit-to" language is a defining characteristic (*not* essential definition) for "religious dimension" language. The present attempt is to try to show that, in continuity with the understanding of the interpretation of classics and in harmony with the "hermeneutical" tradition of interpretation of the *sui generis* character of religion (or religious classics), a *defining characteristic* of an explicit religion (as distinct from a "religious dimension") is its "limit-of" or "ground-to" character, further specified as "some concrete manifestation of the whole by the power of the whole." In sum, I recognize that the latter description of a defining characteristic of religion is influenced by my own Western philosophical and theological preunderstanding. My hope is that it is not so determined by that Western preunderstanding as to prove useful only for interpreting Western religious classics. But that hope can only be validated or invalidated by the future conversation incumbent upon all Western thinkers with alternative traditions (both with the religious traditions themselves and with the scholarly traditions—especially cultural anthropology and history of religions—interpreting those traditions). A final note: Since I have not been persuaded by the arguments against the use of the word "religion" by either Wilfred Cantwell Smith (who basically substitutes the word "faith") or John Cobb (who employs the word "way" as more relatively adequate than "religion"), I continue to use the more familiar expression "religion." Smith's and Cobb's alternative formulations, however, raise important issues for the wider conversation for all scholars (especially the issue of how the conversation might become a conversation determined by the subject matter, not by Western definitions) that are worth noting. See Wilfred Cantwell Smith, *The Meaning and End of Religion* (New York: NAL, 1966), pp. 47–49; John Cobb, "Is Christianity a Religion?" in *Concilium* 136 [9].

11. Inter alia, see the article "Religion, Study of" in the *New Encyclopedia Britannica;* and the relevant discussions in Michael Banton, ed., *Anthropological Approaches to Religion* [7].

12. For representative examples of the disputes on methods of interpretation in history of religions, see Mircea Eliade and Joseph M. Kitagawa, eds., *The History of Religions: Essays in Methodology* (Chicago: Univ. of Chicago Press, 1969); Lawrence E. Sullivan, "History of Religions: The Shape of an Art," in *Concilium* 136 [9].

13. Bronislaw Malinowski, *Magic, Science and Religion and Other Essays* (New York: Doubleday, 1955). It might be more accurate to state that Malinowski's understanding of religion is almost exclusively "practical"; his functionalist method, as applied to religion, I believe, is more representative of a "practical" preunderstanding of religion than it is of the "evolutionary-schema" preunderstandings of his predecessors Tylor and Frazer. Indeed this "practical" understanding of religion has roots in the Western tradition as well: not only, in modernity, in some Kantian and neo-Kantian understandings but among the ancient Greeks and Romans. Recall, for example, Plato's understanding of religion as "justice to the gods" or Cicero's "civic" religion as justice and "binding" a society together. Recall, as well, how Cicero believed that if the Epicurean rejec-

tion of divine benevolence and beneficence were accepted, "religion" would be destroyed since no practical benefits to humans would any longer exist (see Cicero, *On the Nature of the Gods,* Book 1, 40–44).

14. A singular instance here is Emile Durkheim, whose classic sociological interpretation, *The Elementary Forms of the Religious Life* (London: Allen and Unwin, 1915), continues to inspire not only strictly functionalist accounts of the role of religion for order and stability in society but creative reinterpretations uniting functional and substantive understandings of religion like Robert Bellah's notion of "civil religion" and Peter Berger's notion of "the sacred canopy." On the functional-substantive distinction, see the forthright article by Peter Berger, "Some Second Thoughts on Substantive Versus Functional Definitions of Religion," *Journal for the Scientific Study of Religion* 13 (1974), 125–33. Note also how Bellah unites both "functional" and "substantive" (largely Tillichian) concerns in his concept of "symbolic realism," in *Beyond Belief* (New York: Harper, 1970), 237–57.

15. See *The Historian and the Believer* [II/32], p. 261.

16. For a philosophical analysis of the dialectical nature of religious experience and language, see Louis Dupré, *The Other Dimension* [7], pp. 1–20. For Dupré's later shift away from the category of the "sacred" as the primary category of transcendence, see *Transcendent Selfhood* (New York: Seabury, 1976), pp. 18–31. Dupré's major mode of analysis remains, however, dialectical: see, for example, the analysis of alienation and redemption in *Transcendent Selfhood,* pp. 66–79.

17. For the classicist understanding of "definition," see Bernard Lonergan, *Method in Theology* [I/10], p. 82.

18. More explicitly still, within the social sciences, especially the discipline of cultural anthropology. For an example of the creative use of cultural anthropology within history of religions, see Jonathan Z. Smith, *Map Is Not Territory* [I/28], especially the last four methodological essays.

19. An exception to this generalization on philosophy may be found among ethicists: see David Little and Sumner Twiss, *Comparative Religious Ethics: A New Method* (New York: Harper & Row, 1978).

20. For a recent theological challenge to that understanding of "the other religions," see Wolfhart Pannenberg, *Theology and the Philosophy of Science* [I/51]. It is no disparagement of this important work to observe that, even here, the explicitly Christian-theological understanding of religion seems to dominate. For an analysis of the problem of the "other religions" among Catholic theologians, see Paul Knitter, "Christianity as Religion: True and Absolute? A Roman Catholic Perspective," in *Concilium* 136 [9]. For a typological approach to the theological issues, see George Rupp, *Beyond Existentialism and Zen* (New York: Oxford Univ. Press, 1979), pp. 27–72.

21. Note Pannenberg's analogous formulation in *Theology,* pp. 311–14. To speak of "the reality of the whole" is not by definition to fall into a nondialectical understanding of religion (as suggested, for example, by Theodor Adorno's maxim "the whole is the untrue"). Any right-wing Hegelian claim to totality is open to exactly that charge. Yet the present understanding does not fall prey to that difficulty for the following reasons: (1) the insistence on the need for particularity and for an event-character; (2) the recognition that both the experience of that event (as disclosing-concealing [Heidegger] or manifesting-withdrawing [Eliade]) and the language for the event are properly described as dialectical and thereby only relatively adequate to the limit-to and limit-of nature of the religious experiences and expressions. These central factors in the present position will be discussed in the text and may serve to warrant my belief that the present definition's use of the language of the "whole" does not merit suspicion as another right-wing

Hegelian formulation nor is it identical to what might be called Pannenberg's own proleptic-Hegelian understanding of "religion" in his discussion of the "sense of the whole," principally in relationship to "God" as the "all determining reality."

22. It is perhaps clarifying to recall here that in the earlier discussion of "the classic," I employed the language of the disclosure-concealment in art of "*some essential* aspect of the whole"; the differentia of the religious classic can be described as some "self-manifestation (and concealment) of the whole by the power of the whole." All major classics may bear a limit-to "religious dimension" as manifesting some essential aspect of the whole or some essential human response to that aspect (e.g., fundamental trust in response to an experience of wonder and finitude). Religious classics bear the further "limit-of" claim to attention that here the whole has manifested itself. When the latter claim has been experienced, a candidate for religious classic status is present. Then, with Schleiermacher, an interpreter may possibly sense not only wonder and fundamental trust but even "a feeling of dependence," or a sense of "piety" and, for the Christian, a sense of sin and grace. Such seems to be the claim exerted by the religious classic: a claim recognized in the distinct interpretations of its fuller reality in the great tradition of the interpretation of the *sui generis* nature of religion from Schleiermacher through Otto, Wach, von Hügel, Tillich and Eliade. The closest analogue to this claim of the "religious classic" in aesthetic theories are the reflections on "the sublime" in Shaftesbury, Burke and Kant.

23. For a defense of this option (as well as references to the relevant thinkers), see *BRO*, pp. 146–72. For an analogous analysis on "signals of transcendence," see Peter Berger, *A Rumor of Angels* (New York: Doubleday, 1969).

24. Ibid., pp. 91–120, for discussion and references.

25. Note that the analysis of God as "referent" is confined to a metaphysical analysis of the religious dimension of our *common* human experience. Although this is obviously relevant to the later conversation (in systematics) among theistic and nontheistic religions, it does not prejudge that later conversation. For examples of the philosophical conversation (largely, but not exclusively, Western), see Charles Hartshorne and William Reese, ed., *Philosophers Speak of God* (Chicago: Univ. of Chicago Press, 1953).

26. The logic of the position is important to note. Fundamental theology involves a phenomenological and a transcendental moment: the phenomenology of the "religious dimension" and the appropriateness of "religion" to our *common* human experience and a transcendental analysis of the reality of God as the necessary referent for that experience. Systematic theology involves a phenomenological moment that bears an explicitly hermeneutical nature: the hermeneutic phenomenology of an explicit religion (and, therefore, to those *un*common or paradigmatic religious experiences expressed in the religious classics); the transcendental moment must relate the conditions of possibility of these uncommon experiences to the necessary, abstract conditions of possibility established in the earlier metaphysical as transcendental conditions of possibility of our *common* human experience. Fundamental theology has, therefore, a necessary but abstract and corrective (not constitutive) role to play in relationship to the fuller concreteness, the paradigmatic experience expressed in the religious classics and interpreted in systematic theologies. *Ordinarily* the systematic theologian as interpreter will be a believer in the religious classic being interpreted: at least in the minimal sense of one who has experienced some resonance with the claim to attention of that classic and the resonance of that claim with the limit-questions of existence; or in the maximal sense, with the response called faith—itself a shock of recognition freely experienced by the theologian and experienced as given (gift) by the event expressed in the classic.

27. For a study of Rahner, see Anne Carr, *The Theological Method of Karl Rahner* (Missoula: Scholars Press, 1977). For the basic texts in Rahner, see *A Rahner Reader*, ed. Gerald McCool (New York: Crossroad, 1976). For the clearest and most systematic expression by Rahner of his own position, see *Foundations of Christian Faith: An Introduction to the Idea of Christianity* (New York: Crossroad, 1978), pp. 24–176. A clear and systematic study of Rahner's position (based on the structure of *Foundations*) may be found in the essays in Leo O'Donovan, ed., *A World of Grace: An Introduction to the Themes and Foundations of Karl Rahner's Theology* (New York: Crossroad, 1980).

28. Karl Rahner, *Foundations*, pp. 153–62. See also his use of a "transcendental" and a "categorial" christology, pp. 206–28.

29. For myself, the major difficulties are these: (1) His concept of the "self-luminosity" of being via consciousness—a concept Rahner has never abandoned despite his later enriching and widening notion of experience from cognitive to "historical" to "mystagogical" experience. This Thomist notion of self-luminosity seems in need of further reflection to relate it to the more enriched concept of experience in Rahner's later work. This is perhaps simply to say that Rahner's developed notion of experience and his own Heideggerian method of hermeneutical "retrieval" seems to imply a more Heideggerian position (disclosure-concealment) than the Thomist one (self-luminosity) that *Spirit in the World* endorses. (2) Rahner's fear of "ontologism" and his correct insistence on "gratuity" seem to keep him from seeing the implications of his own philosophical position in *Spirit in the World* and *Hearers of the Word:* namely, that, as a philosophically mediated *immediacy,* the dynamism of human intentionality "always already" relates us *directly* to the only God there is, the God of Love. As *love* God *is* always already directly related to us and we to God. We can make this claim, in sum, *not only* after categorial revelation discloses this always-already reality but through the very transcendental reflection that Rahner's philosophy of religion develops. This does not deny the utter gratuity of God's love as love (as Uncreated Grace for Rahner). It simply recognizes that the same God we know decisively as my God now in "categorial revelation" we know as well in transcendental reflections upon God as the God of Love who, as Love, is *directly* experienced in the very dynamism of the human spirit to Ultimate Mystery as Gracious. I agree that we may (and should) call this "transcendental *revelation*" only after systematic theological reflection upon the classics of "categorial revelation" (namely, the event of Jesus Christ). But we may also (and should) call this same reality the God of Love understood as gracious mystery disclosed through transcendental reflection as the condition of possibility of our fundamental trust in existence and *directly* experienced in that common human experience. (3) Rahner's notion of "formal fundamental theology," therefore, needs some revision: of course, any preunderstanding is influenced by a response to "categorial revelation." Still the transcendental thinker can (and, for Rahner, clearly should) provide strictly philosophical (and, therefore, abstract) reflections on our *common* human experience. In sum, what Rahner distinguishes as "philosophy of religion" and "formal fundamental theology" I believe is more appropriately described as simply "fundamental theology" on the model presented above—a model which this note suggests may be more in keeping with the basic logic of Rahner's own position. For a good analysis of the mystagogical element present in Rahner's work, see James J. Bacik, *Apologetics and the Eclipse of Mystery: Mystagogy according to Karl Rahner* (Notre Dame: Univ. of Notre Dame Press, 1979).

30. Note the cautions on this latter position in n. 29—the basic logic of Rahner's position, I repeat, even if my criticisms are accepted, remains a sound one calling, however, for the kind of substantive and terminological changes suggested above.

31. On the limited but real role for the "transcendental moment" in systematic theology (i.e., as corrective rather than constitutive as it is in fundamental theology) I find Rahner's position exactly right.

32. An observation made by Van Harvey (employing Karl Barth's distinction between "hard" and "soft" apologetics) on my own position in *BRO*. Harvey was correct to employ this distinction. Yet I fail to see how it responds to the real issue: whether metaphysical or transcendental analysis (whether described as "hard" or "soft") does or does not warrant its claims. Harvey's own skepticism on metaphysics as a discipline accomplishing its modest but real claims (as in Hartshorne) seems more a cultural observation than a philosophically argued position. For Harvey's distinction, see "The Pathos of Liberal Theology," *JR* (1976), 385–86.

33. Note Hans Küng's similar criticisms of strictly rationalist positions in *Existiert Gott?* (Munich: Piper, 1978), pp. 119–55 (E. T. *Does God Exist?* [New York: Doubleday, 1980]).

34. Theological readers will note the parallelism of this expression to the theological understanding of "revelation" as "self-manifestation of God" in theology from Hegel through Rahner.

35. The truth "resonates" to our common human experience (especially the limit-experiences, questions and situations common to the human situation). The transcendental results of fundamental theology are also relevant here: namely, to provide abstract concepts either to correct incoherent systematic understandings of the event or to develop coherent concepts. The principal example here is the concept "God" which, once metaphysically formulated, does *not* exhaust but may be needed to *correct* or *develop* necessary metaphysical presuppositions of religious symbols (expressive of an event of God's self-manifestation) like the "reign of God" or "the hidden and revealed God."

36. Clifford Geertz, *The Interpretation of Cultures* [I/18], pp. 109–19.

37. Note that this claim is directly parallel to the earlier claim for the classic work of art. The "aesthetic sensibility" may also take over (and destroy) the response to the religious classic. In a consumer culture where "religion" can often become another "private" consumer good suitable for some "tastes" but "distasteful" to others, this inevitably occurs. The claims to truth in both art and religion, I believe, stand or fall together. As art becomes more marginalized and religion privatized, they are both in constant danger of destruction. The delegitimating powers of negation in art and religion toward the culture become merely more enticing, exciting consumer goods to an extent which even Kierkegaard's prophetic rage against the "aesthetic sensibility" did not foresee.

38. This is perhaps especially the case in authentic ritual, as Victor Turner's illuminating categories of "communitas" and "liminality" show: see *The Ritual Process* [III/99], pp. 94–166.

39. Alfred North Whitehead, *Religion in the Making* (New York: Meridian, 1966), p. 83.

40. Ibid., pp. 137–38; note also his analysis of religion as "world-loyalty" (p. 57). This recognition should undo the "God of the Gaps" problem of Bonhoeffer and others. Even as Pascal (often unjustly cited as "gambling" on God because of his profound existential recognition of human "misery") is clearly *not* an advocate of the philosophy of misery become the misery of philosophy! For a recent and helpful psychological study of Pascal, see Brian Mahan, "Toward Fire and Light: The Faith of Blaise Pascal," in *Trajectories of Faith,* ed. James Fowler and Robin Lovin (Nashville: Abingdon, 1980), pp. 92–119.

41. For the theological concept "situation," see chap. 8, sec. i.

42. Ernest Becker, *The Denial of Death* (New York: Free Press, 1973).

43. Martin Luther, *Bondage of the Will* (New York: Revell, 1957); Søren Kierkegaard, *Fear and Trembling* and *The Concept of Dread* [III/104].

44. Recall how a revision of the argument from order was Whitehead's own major approach to the philosophical question of God. The concern, even "rage," for order in Aquinas and Kant is more a concern for an architectonic to their thought (and, therefore, to reality). All three of these "classic" thinkers' concern for order should be distinguished from the kind of Deist period pieces and "arguments from design" demolished by Hume.

45. Paul Tillich, *Systematic Theology* [II/25], II, 19–29; *Albert Camus: The Essential Writings,* ed. with Interpretive Essays by Robert E. Meagher (New York: Harper & Row, 1978).

46. Gabriel Marcel, *Homo Viator* (Chicago: Regnery, 1952); Schubert Ogden, *The Reality of God* [I/100], pp. 21–43.

47. Josiah Royce, *The Philosophy of Loyalty* and *The Problem of Christianity* [I/82]; H. Richard Niebuhr, *Radical Monotheism and Western Culture* (New York: Harper, 1960), esp. pp. 16–38.

48. William James, *Varieties of Religious Experience* [III/82], pp. 59–78.

49. On Simone Weil's remarkable thirst for justice, see Simone Pétrement, *Simone Weil,* (New York: Pantheon, 1976); Reinhold Niebuhr, *The Nature and Destiny of Man* [II/24], pp. 265–301.

50. Gustavo Gutierrez, *A Theology of Liberation* (Maryknoll: Orbis, 1973); James Cone, *God of the Oppressed* (New York: Seabury, 1975); Juan Luis Segundo, *The Liberation of Theology* [I/74]; Rosemary Radford Ruether, *New Woman, New Earth* (New York: Seabury, 1975); Jürgen Moltmann, *The Crucified God* (New York: Harper & Row, 1974); Johann Baptist Metz, *Faith in History and Society* [II/35].

51. Bernard Lonergan, *Method in Theology* [I/10], pp. 104–5; Max Scheler, *The Nature of Sympathy* [III/89], pp. 147–213.

52. See especially Mircea Eliade, *The Sacred and the Profane* [2]; Louis Dupré, *The Other Dimension* [7]. Dupré's basic position on the need for mediation and the dialectical character of religion (along with his constant and sophisticated philosophical retrievals of the mystical traditions) merit careful study from all scholars of religions. For the relationship of Thomas J. J. Altizer's radically dialectical understanding of religion to Eliade's work, see Thomas J. J. Altizer, *Mircea Eliade and the Dialectic of the Sacred* (Philadelphia: Westminster, 1968); idem, "Mircea Eliade and the Death of God," *Cross Currents* (1979), 257–68. Altizer's interpretation of Eliade is, in my judgment, a profound Christian theological meditation on Eliade rather than a strict interpretation of his work: a meditation that unites Eliade more with the radical negative dialectics of Blake and Nietzsche (and Altizer) than with the dialectic of "manifestation" of Eliade himself. The third volume of Eliade's trilogy should disclose how his own reflections on the "deus otiosus" and the sacred dialectically manifested *in* the contemporary profane actually relate to positions like Altizer's dialectical and Christian theological vision of the death of God. For myself, in Christian theological terms Eliade's work may also (not only!) be read as an expression of the "cosmic Christianity" emphasis of Eastern Christianity (recall Eliade on the incarnation as "theophany" and the role of ritual and image [icon?] along with the dominant manifestation orientation of his work). Even if my hypothesis on Eliade is correct, however, it would disclose only one aspect of the multifaceted interpretation of religion of this modern master of retrieval of manifestations—and master of suspicion with regard to the "banalization" of the sacred and the nonrecognizability of "miracle" in contemporary urbanized, historized Western Christianity and Judaism.

53. The "search" metaphor for religion is creatively employed in the work of Michael Novak, *Ascent of the Mountain, Flight of the Dove* (New York: Harper & Row, 1971); and John Dunne, *Reasons of the Heart* (New York: Macmillan, 1978).

54. William James, *Varieties* [48], pp. 78–114. Recall the contemporary controversy over Benjamin Franklin (the "once-born" man par excellence): his defenders vs. his "sick-soul" opponents like D. H. Lawrence and Georg Lukacs. One of the most attractive qualities of James' little classic is the extraordinary generosity which his own "sick-soul" nature accorded the "once-born" and the "healthy-minded." Christian theology would have been remarkably different if Augustine, the Christian sick-soul par excellence, could have had a more Jamesian response to Pelagius and Julian of Eclanum!

55. William James, *The Will to Believe and Other Essays* (New York: Dover, 1956). James later admitted that much confusion and controversy could have been averted if he had given his famous essay the more accurate title "The Right to Believe."

56. See the discussion of Clifford in Van Harvey's "The Ethics of Belief Reconsidered" [II/32].

57. Quoted in Leslie Fiedler, *No! In Thunder: Essays on Myth and Literature* (Boston: Beacon, 1960).

58. For a defense of this statement, see the discussion of "the uncanny" in chap. 8. Perhaps the major material difference of the position on religion defended in this book in contrast to *BRO* is the greater importance accorded the negations in human experience here.

59. See the fascinating account in Peter Brown, *Augustine of Hippo* (Berkeley: Univ. of California Press, 1969).

60. Recall the formalist criteria of greater adequacy to a poetic work by its ability to incorporate complexity, tension, paradox, ambiguity and "the tragic sense of life."

61. For the concepts "first" and "second naiveté," see Paul Ricoeur, *Symbolism of Evil* [I/47], pp. 347–57.

62. For a major consideration of Freud on religion, see Paul Ricoeur, *Freud and Philosophy* (New Haven: Yale Univ. Press, 1970), esp. pp. 524–53. The "totalization" phenomenon in the interpretation of religion in Freud's *Future of an Illusion* or in Marx's famous comment on the "opium of the people" or in Nietzsche's analysis of Christianity's *ressentiment* and its status as a "Platonism for the masses" are at least as striking as any theological "totalization" procedure. Their brilliant "suspicions" of religion remain, however, the major postmodern classical hermeneutic of suspicion of religion (just as the *sui generis* tradition remains the major postmodern hermeneutic of retrieval). Both traditions present classic alternatives for all contemporary students of religion to address—surely, at least, any student cognizant of the radical ambiguity of the religious phenomenon in individuals, societies and cultures. For further discussion of these great postmodern masters of suspicion, see chap. 8.

63. See chap. 3, n. 107.

64. For the relevance of this for the Christian theological study of christology, see the Introduction to Part II and chap. 7.

65. Joachim Wach, among hermeneutes of religion, was especially concerned with the issue of the interpreter's "preparation" for the study. Although my own account relates to the post-Wach (i.e., post-"Romantic") tradition on interpretation of Gadamer and Ricoeur, Wach's contributions remain an invaluable source of insight on the major questions involved in an interpretation of religion. For two studies of Wach's contributions here, see J. M. Kitagawa, "Verstehen and Er-

lösung," *History of Religions* XI (1971); and Charles Wood, *Theory and Religious Understanding: A Critique of the Hermeneutics of Joachim Wach* (Missoula: Scholars Press, 1977). Wach's own major contributions include *Das Verstehen: Grundzüge einer Geschichte der hermeneutischen Theorie im 19. Jahrhundert,* 3 vols. (Tübingen: J. C. B. Mohr, 1926–33); *The Comparative Study of Religions* (New York: Columbia Univ. Press, 1958); *Types of Religious Experience: Christian and Non-Christian* (Chicago: Univ. of Chicago Press, 1951). The last volume contains particularly valuable studies (for this analysis) of "the classical" in religion (see esp. pp. 48–61).

66. *Loci classici:* Friedrich Schleiermacher, *On Religion: Speeches to Its Cultured Despisers* (New York: Harper, 1965); Rudolph Otto, *The Idea of the Holy* (New York: Oxford Univ. Press, 1958); William James, *Varieties of Religious Experience* [48]; Friedrich von Hügel, *The Mystical Element in Religion,* 2 vols. (London: Dent, 1961); Gerardus van der Leeuw, *Religion in Essence and Development* (New York: Harper & Row, 1979); idem, *Sacred and Profane Beauty: The Holy in Art* (Nashville: Abingdon, 1963); Max Scheler, *On the Eternal in Man* (Hamden: Shoe String, 1972); Mircea Eliade, *Patterns in Comparative Religion* [2]; idem, *The Myth of the Eternal Return* (Princeton: Princeton Univ. Press, 1954); idem, *A History of Religious Ideas,* Vol. I, *From the Stone Age to the Eleusinian Mysteries* (Chicago: Univ. of Chicago Press, 1978); Vol. II, *From Gautama Buddha to the Triumph of Christianity* (forthcoming—these last two works are important for demonstrating the "historical" side of Eliade's earlier "morphological" work, the latter especially in *Patterns*); Paul Tillich, *What Is Religion?* (New York: Harper & Row, 1969); idem, *Theology of Culture* (New York: Galaxy, 1959), pp. 3–53; idem, *The Protestant Era* (Chicago: Univ. of Chicago Press, 1948), esp. pp. 55–115, and *Ultimate Concern: Tillich in Dialogue,* ed. D. Mackenzie Brown (New York: Harper, 1965).

Certain similarities stand out among all these thinkers, in spite of their real differences in both method and conclusions, to allow them to be called a "tradition" of interpretation: (1) In their distinct ways, all are concerned to interpret the *sui generis* character of the religious phenomenon. All explicitly reject "reductionism," not a priori but as a result of their a posteriori studies of religion. (2) All may be considered (in the broad sense) hermeneutical phenomenologists of religion. Although only Scheler is a "strict" phenomenologist and only Wach provides extensive reflections on hermeneutics, all these thinkers *in fact* perform their interpretative task in basic agreement with the first four steps of interpretation outlined in chap. 3. Otto, van der Leeuw and Eliade have in fact named themselves "phenomenologists" (in the "soft," non-Husserlian sense—i.e., as providing descriptive not evaluative interpretations). I do not find anything intrinsic to this tradition of interpretation of religion, moreover, that would disallow the expansion of the interpretative process to the paradigm of Ricoeur (understanding-explanation-understanding). (3) Most of these thinkers provide explicit and often more than occasional (especially Schleiermacher, Eliade, Otto, von der Leeuw and Tillich) reflections on the similarities between the experience of the work of art and the experience of religion. (James, who ordinarily relates religion to morality, is the exception here.) These similarities may warrant my suggestion that these thinkers, for all their diversity, display sufficient family resemblances to be considered candidates for inclusion in what might be called the modern tradition of retrieval of the *sui generis* nature of religion. For myself, moreover, the hermeneutical character of their enterprise, their earned a posteriori insistence upon the *sui generis* character of religion, their insistence on the need to interpret the classic religious *expressions* and their sensitivity to the often little noted analogies (by religionists and theologians) between the experience of the classic work of art and the religious classics warrant my belief that anyone who accepts the earlier analyses of this work (on the interpretation of classics) will not find it strange that in this section of the work I should turn principally to these modern masters of retrieval of the religious classics as religious and as classics. For two helpful surveys of modern interpretations of religion, see John Macquarrie, *Twentieth Century Religious Thought* (London: SCM, 1963); and Jean J. Waardenburg, *Classical Approaches to the Study of Religion,* 2 vols. (The Hague: Mouton, 1973-74) Vol. I includes an anthology of representative writings of major figures; Vol. II is an invaluable bibliography. A helpful pedagogically oriented work is Frederick Streng, Charles Lloyd, Jr., and Jay Allen, *Ways of Being Religious: Readings for a New Approach to Religion* (Englewood Cliffs: Prentice-Hall, 1973). For an argument that in social science Simmel (via the notion of "piety"), Weber (via the notion of "charisma") and Troeltsch (via the notion of "mysticism") bear striking resemblances to what I here name the hermeneutic tradition on the *sui generis* character of religion, see William R. Garrett, "Troublesome Transcendence: The Supernatural in the Study of Religion," *Sociological Analysis* (1974), 167–81. An argument against many uses by religionists of the category of "reductionism" may be found in the important methodological reflections of Hans Penner; inter alia, see Hans Penner and Edward Yonan, "Is a Science of Religion Possible?" *JR* (1972), 107–34; and Hans Penner, "The Fall and Rise of Methodology: A Retrospective Review," *RSR* (1976), 11–17. It might be observed that Penner's consistent argument for explanatory methods and his allied suspicion of the appeals to *Verstehen* are on target for Romantic hermeneutical formulations but not for the post-Romantic hermeneutical tradition employed here. The present hermeneutical position reformulates (and, I believe, can retrieve) the intent and genuine hermeneutical achievement of the *Verstehen* tradition without falling into Romantic formulations and without disallowing explanatory methods (like Penner's) in the fuller arc of the hermeneutic process. At the same time, the five steps outlined for the present hermeneutical position (in chap. 3) are far more in harmony with the intent and accomplishments of the hermeneutical tradition on religion than with the explanation-oriented claims of Penner—hence my appeal to that tradition despite its occasional methodological misformulations of its own hermeneutical findings. I hope to return to this question, in more strictly methodological terms, in future work on the relationship between religious studies and theology.

67. *Varieties,* pp. 299–337 (on mystics) and pp. 211–99 (on saints).

68. The classic interpreters of the religious classics sometimes produce interpretations that communicate to the reader their own religious resonance just as their natural analogues, the classic literary critics (Johnson, Dryden, Arnold, Eliot et al.), often produce interpretations that are themselves works of art. Note, for example, the aesthetic and religious claims to attention elicited by Schleiermacher's *On Religion* or Eliade's *The Myth of the Eternal Return* [66].

69. Rudolph Otto, *The Idea of the Holy* [66], esp. pp. 5–41.

70. In the interpretation of religion, as much as in the interpretation of art, explanatory methods like structuralist methods, semiotic methods and formalist methods can play the same role of explaining the "sense" of the myths and symbols and thereby "developing" or even challenging our enveloping "understanding" of religion. For two examples here, see the discussion of the influential work of George Dumezil in C. Scott Littleton, *The New Comparative Mythology* (Berkeley: Univ. of California Press, 1973); and the structuralist study of myth of Claude Lévi-Strauss: inter alia, see *Myth and Meaning* (New York: Schocken, 1977). For a critique of the nonhermeneutical character of some purely "empiri-

cal'' and ''factual'' studies in ''history of religions,'' see Charles Wood, *Theory and Religious Understanding* [65]. For examples of recent work on the hermeneutical character of history of religions, see the efforts of such younger historians of religion as Charles Wood and James Buchanan and their efforts to make the hermeneutical discussion central again to the discipline of history of religions. I may note that if historians of religion could accept the expansion of the post-Romantic tradition of interpretation by Ricoeur into the paradigm of ''understanding-explanation-understanding,'' there need be no fear of a ''Romantic'' rejection of formalist, structuralist and semiotic methods.

71. The major problem with the hermeneutics of suspicion of religion is its tendency (not an inevitability) to produce a totalizing and reductionist account of religion: for example, all religion is explained by its ''origins'' in animism, totemism, magic etc., or *all* religion is nothing else but morality, bad science, poetic metaphysics or art. If Freud and Dewey, for example, had consistently allowed the same relative autonomy to religion that they allowed to art, they would have undone their own occasionally reductionist accounts (religion as ''illusion'' or the ''origins'' of religion in totemism in Freud; religions as ''supernaturalism'' and ''mystification'' in Dewey) as distinct from the nonreductionist accounts in Freud's *Civilization and Its Discontents* (surely not consolatory and surely still correctly suspicious but not reductionist) or in Dewey's *Art as Experience* on the ''religious dimension.'' (See here William M. Shea, ''Qualitative Wholes: Aesthetic and Religious Experience in the Work of John Dewey,'' *JR* [1980], 32–51). If the first step of the interpreter of religion is to be attentive to the claim elicited by the religious classic, as the first step of the interpreter of art is to be attentive to the claim elicited by the work of art, then the masters of suspicion should themselves be somewhat suspect as interpreters of religion. Just as surely, though, the major strength and the invaluable contribution of these ''suspicions'' is in their genuinely hermeneutical ability to discern and interpret the real negativities (even demonic ones, as Tillich insisted) that *are* also present in the ambiguous actuality of the religious phenomenon. Nietzsche, Freud, Marx and Dewey remain, in sum, masterful interpreters of those real and actualized negativities. Yet by ''totalizing'' that real insight and interpretation into such language as ''all religion is X,'' they unwittingly commit the same kind of ''nothing but'' error of the most innocent theologian of retrieval—classically satirized in Henry Fielding's marvelous character, Parson Twackum: ''When I mention religion I mean the Christian religion; and not only the Christian religion, and not only the Protestant religion, but the Church of England. And when I mention honor, I mean that mode of Divine grace which is not only consistent with, but dependent upon this religion; and is consistent with and dependent upon no other'' (quoted in Sidney E. Mead, *The Nation with the Soul of a Church* [I/29], p. 8).

In brief, the very ambiguity of the religious phenomenon suggests the need for both hermeneutics of retrieval and hermeneutics of suspicion in the conversation elicited by the religious classics—classics which, far more than the classics of art, are concretized and often institutionalized in concretely ambiguous religious traditions.

72. For the creative vs. redescriptive (not mere imitative) nature of ''mimesis,'' see Paul Ricoeur, *The Rule of Metaphor* (Toronto: Univ. of Toronto Press, 1977), pp. 37–43.

73. This is especially emphasized in Mircea Eliade's language of an event of manifestation that impels the dialectic of the sacred and the profane: see *The Sacred and the Profane* [2]. I suspect that a major part of the reason for Heidegger's influence on contemporary theology may be found in the resonance which his

event of disclosure-concealment language elicits among the "religiously musical." For a brief survey of that influence, see John Williams, *Martin Heidegger's Philosophy of Religion* (*SR* Supplements, 1972), pp. 1–86. For an informative interpretation of Heidegger's early unpublished lectures on phenomenology of religion, see Thomas Sheehan, "Heidegger's 'Introduction to the Phenomenology of Religion,' 1920–21," *The Personalist* (1979), 312–24.

74. See R. B. Braithwaite, *An Empiricist's View of the Nature of Religious Belief* (London: Cambridge Univ. Press, 1955); Julian Huxley, *Religion Without Revelation* (New York: Harper, 1957); George Santayana, *Interpretations of Poetry and Religion* (New York: Harper, 1957). For an analytical analysis of critiques of religion, see Kai Nielsen, *Contemporary Critiques of Religion* (New York: Herder & Herder, 1971).

75. Note George Steiner's acute observation on how Freud, Marx, Nietzsche and Heidegger can *function* in the wider secular culture as "post-theologians," performing the same role of interpretation of the fundamental questions for secular culture that theologians perform for religious traditions: George Steiner, *Martin Heidegger* (New York: Viking, 1978), pp. 156–7. The reservations on the notion "the whole" are relevant here. Otherwise the "post-theological" religious sense of Theodor Adorno's dictum "the whole is the untrue" would be relevant. The systematic theological discussion in Part II on the inner reality of the always-already, not-yet in the Christian self-understanding is also relevant (see chaps. 6, 8 and 9).

76. George Santayana, *Interpretations* [74], p. v. A careful study here is Nathan A. Scott, Jr., "Santayana's Poetics of Belief," *Boundary* (1979), 199–224.

77. For the notion of the transgression present in religious language, see Paul Ricoeur, in *Semeia* 4, ed. John Dominic Crossan (Missoula: Scholars Press, 1975), pp. 107–45.

78. On the concept of revelation as "self-manifestation" of God, see Karl Rahner, *Foundations* [IV/27], pp. 117–26 (on "self-communication" of God). A major contemporary critic of that tradition is Wolfhart Pannenberg with his notion of "indirect revelation through historical events," in *Revelation as History,* ed. W. Pannenberg (New York: Macmillan, 1968), pp. 123–59. For analyses of the expressions of revelation (and implicitly of classic religious expressions), see H. Richard Niebuhr, *The Meaning of Revelation* [II/61]; and Paul Ricoeur, "Toward a Hermeneutic of the Idea of Revelation," *Harvard Theological Review* (1977), 1–37.

79. As we shall see in Part II, wholeness is never an accomplished fact but takes the form of an always-already, not-yet reality; the doctrines of eschatology and the doctrines of justification-sanctification are especially pertinent here. The notes of "disclosure-concealment" and "manifestation-withdrawal" in the present discussion set the context for those later systematic theological discussions.

80. See Louis Dupré, *The Other Dimension* [7], esp. pp. 484–547; idem, *Transcendent Selfhood* [16], pp. 92–105.

81. For an excellent phenomenological study of John of the Cross, see Georges Morel, *Le sens de l'existence selon S. Jean de la Croix,* 3 vols. (Paris: Aubier, 1960). For sensitive linguistic analyses of how conceptual language can play the same disclosive role, see David Burrell, *Exercises in Religious Understanding* (Notre Dame: Univ. of Notre Dame Press, 1974), esp. pp. 80–141, on the language of Thomas Aquinas.

82. For one example, see Josef Pieper, *The Silence of Saint Thomas* (Chicago: Regnery, 1957).

83. The analysis of "expression" highlights the need to expand the original

Heidegger-Gadamer theory of interpretation into Ricoeur's model which demands a moment of explanation of the *sense* of the text produced *as* expression in the work by the work and, thereby, allows a certain limited priority to the phenomenon of the text and to the limited but real use of formalist, structuralist, etc. methods of "explication du texte." Note, moreover, the differences of this theory of expression from earlier Romantic "expressive" theories or from the "expressive" theory of Benedetto Croce and the expression of "feeling" position of Susanne Langer.

84. It might be noted that the discussion of the "religious classic" has shifted from the earlier discussion of the reception of the classic to the present one of the production of the classic. My comments here are obviously dependent on the "thought experiment" for that production suggested in chap. 3, sec. iv. Note also the similar criteria for religious classics developed in Joachim Wach, esp. *Types of Religious Experience* [65], pp. 48–61, and his analysis of classic "types" of religious authority (founder, prophet, saint, seer, etc.) in *Sociology of Religion* (Chicago: Univ. of Chicago Press, 1957), pp. 331–74.

85. Recall Paul Tillich's analysis of symbols and their participatory character: inter alia, see *Systematic Theology* [II/25], I, 238–47.

86. The central exception to this principle for Christianity is, of course, the event of Jesus Christ as self-manifestation of God. For the discussion of this decisive "beyond relative adequacy" paradox, see chaps. 6 and 7.

87. In Christian theology this occurs principally when a particular relatively adequate expression of response to the Christ event assumes the place of the event itself, as in biblicism or dogmatism as distinct from original (as hermeneutical) biblical theology or doctrinal theology. By way of contrast, Karl Rahner's hermeneutical "retrieval" of the existential disclosure and transformation realities in the classic Catholic doctrines, for example, always includes the properly hermeneutical move of a "reductio ad mysterium." Indeed, Schleiermacher's interpretation of the classic Protestant confessions assumes the same hermeneutical recognition.

88. For an excellent theological account of the freedom evoked and commanded by Christian faith, see Schubert Ogden, *Faith and Freedom* (Nashville: Abingdon, 1979), pp. 41–67.

89. See Paul Ricoeur in "Toward a Hermeneutic of the Idea of Revelation" [28].

90. In Christianity, as we shall see in Part II, the "dangerous and subversive memory of Jesus plays this role for the church." Inter alia, see Hans Küng, *On Being a Christian* [I/96], pp. 119–26.

Chapter 5

The Religious Classic

Manifestation and Proclamation

i. The Realized Experience of Truth in Religious Classics

The experience of the religious classic is fundamentally the same as that of any classic. Indeed, the classical expressions of any major religion can be experienced as an event, a happening of a religious truth not personally achieved or achievable. Although the various limit-situations intrinsic to the human condition may show us our affinity with the reality disclosed in the religious classics, neither those limit-to experiences nor reflection upon them in metaphysics can produce the kind of revelation present in any concrete religion.

The capacity to experience revelation—religious disclosure by the whole—is, however, aided by an antecedent willingness to reflect upon the disclosive reality of "limit-situations." Indeed, the greatest aid provided by those "limit-to" experiences is that their resonance with the concrete manifestations of all "limit-of" experiences in the concrete religions may free the prospective interpreter to enter that conversation on their (and, ultimately, our) own terms—terms proper to a truth recognized as manifestation.[1]

For anyone who has ever experienced even once the power of disclosure present in and by a classical religious expression, this argument is probably unnecessary save, perhaps, to aid its memory to return to consciousness from its haven in the unconscious and its temporary abode in dreams and in all the secular substitutes for the classical religions in our culture.[2] For anyone who has considered the claims of a classical religious testimony, a willingness to enter the conversation of the religious classics can become an urgency. In the case of the religious *participant,* there is truth in Mircea Eliade's insistence that, after an authentic experience of the sacred, the participant cannot but feel and believe, at least at the moment and in memory, that "only the paradigmatic is the real."[3] Indeed, the paradigmatic character of all classical religious expressions evokes a psychological recognition of its event-like character.

In the case of the *interpreter* of the claims of a classic religious testimony, a distinct but related acknowledgment occurs: One cannot keep this claim forever at a distance. For this claim comes as a disclosure that frees the self from its ordinary attempt to distance itself from any claims that cannot be controlled as objects over against its own subjectivity. Rather the interpreter of religious classics may admit that this classic testimony bears a claim to truth. That claim is, more exactly, a nonviolent appeal to the instinct of the human spirit for some relationship to the whole. If this sense of recognition perdures, we may also agree with William James' insistence that a study of religion should include a study of its "most intense" testimonies (for James, the mystics and saints). On present terms, we can reformulate the Jamesian insight as follows: The interpreter of the religious classic can address their claims by letting go of both earlier models of autonomy and heteronomy. With that initial insight interpreters will allow themselves to become caught up in the fundamental questions and responses which these paradigmatic testimonies address and often transform. Like the interpretation of any classic, the interpretation of the religious classic demands a minimal respect for the actuality of a classic and thereby for the actuality of a serious claim to an event of truth which many become recognizable again.

Serious interpretation also demands a critical spirit that will not abandon its own classical journey on behalf of the human spirit. This journey of real critique—impelled by the two major strands of our Western culture, the Jewish prophetic tradition and the Greek philosophical quest for critical knowledge—remains a part of any contemporary Western religious spirit. Critique comes to the religious spirit in many forms, ordinarily as that "crisis" of critical reflection named "modern doubt" or contemporary "suspicion." As crisis, reflection becomes an essential negative *and* positive moment throughout the entire process.[4] For the Christian consciousness, the moment of critical freedom in the act of being caught up in the disclosure of faith is intrinsic to the kind of radical receptivity which authentic faith evokes and demands. A second mediated immediacy—a second naivete on the other side of critical interpretation—may be possible for the contemporary intellectual in relationship to any religious tradition. A first naivete is at best unlikely, at worst an understandable nostalgia for a lost innocence uneasily cloaking a possible intellectual failure of nerve and a religious failure to recognize the radical demands of faith itself. Contemporary interpreters of the religious classics will want to unravel how the paradigmatic religious expression of the "limit-of" resonates to the limit-situations disclosive of our fundamental questions, needs and desires. They will want their systematic theologies to resonate to the critical demands of their fundamental theologies.

In any case, the truth of the insistence that on the question of religious classics "the paradigmatic is the real" should be acknowledged. The first type of response to the religious classics is represented by one's first, usually childhood, experience of authentic wonder at the power of religion or by one's respect for the "archaic ontology"[5] in certain cultures and the religious practices of the East, by one's ungrudging reverence for classically religious persons,[6] the mystics, prophets, sages and saints in all traditions, by the symbols erupting in one's dreams, by the caught-up character of one's commitment to—indeed one's "religious" fervor in—a cause of social justice, by the fascination despite oneself that a particular ritual, a great religious work of art, the integrity and peace which a person of sturdy faith often elicit.[7] All these experiences can provoke in even the most determinedly secularist consciousness a sense of recognition, however critical or suspicious, of the kind of reality disclosed in any religious classic. Indeed, on the testimony of the undeniably religious, a fidelity to the truth disclosed in a particular religious tradition is often challenged from within (as in Job, Amos, Paul, Luther or Loyola, Teresa, John of the Cross, Calvin or Wesley). Yet that challenge seems to transform an original easier confidence and the original experience of dryness, doubt, even terror into a firmer recognition that here "the paradigmatic is the real."

The second type of response to the religious classics is represented by the systematic theologian and many modern interpreters of the retrieval of the religious phenomenon. Even here there exists an analogous acceptance of the dictum that "the paradigmatic is the real." Whenever the crucial break with the model of an autonomous or heteronomous subject over against an object occurs, real interpretation occurs. When technical rationality reigns, no recognition of the event-character of truth can occur. Any interpreter of the religious classics must early decide whether to impose some standards of technical rationality upon all classical expressions or risk exposing oneself to another mode of rationality: a mode proper to the thing itself as it discloses itself to consciousness. We cannot, in fact, verify or disprove the claims of classical religious expressions through empiricist methods.[8] We cannot adequately adjudicate the world disclosed by Dante's *Divina Commedia* simply by bringing Dante's traditional metaphysics before the judgment seat of a more adequate contemporary metaphysics.[9] As we argued in the case of all artistic classics, the classic by definition incarnates a notion of truth that is neither mere adequation nor correspondence, neither verification nor falsification. Rather truth here becomes a manifestation that lets whatever shows itself to be in its showing and its hiddenness.

Unless we are to claim that religious classics, and religious classics alone, are not to be interpreted in the sense proper to any classic, then we cannot but affirm that here too the paradigmatic is the real. Every classic is a sign, a testimony scattered in the cultural world, calling for a reader who will render an interpretation faithful to the testimony itself. One mode of interpretation is the form called systematic theology. Some systematic theologians (Karl Barth is a ready example) will, in effect, claim that *only* their paradigmatic is the real. Then interpretation quickly shifts to the first model and sometimes to an exegesis of the classical scriptural texts that is in fact an eisegesis. Most systematic theologians, however, are usually both critical and receptive interpreters of the classics of their tradition. As systematic theologians—i.e., as creative interpreters—they will hold that "the paradigmatic is indeed real" with all the full-fledged reality of an event of disclosure;[10] the classical is true with the truth of a recognition of an authentic manifestation. The existence of fundamental theology (or the apologetic side of systematic theology) will cause these interpreters to hesitate to use the dangerous (as exclusivist) word "only." For every "limit-of" religious revelation should resonate to the "limit-to" questions and situation in our lives. This remains true even when the revelation transforms not merely the answers but also the questions of every limit-situation.

For most modern interpreters of religion this "crisis" of reflection has occurred. It cannot, even on classical or paradigmatic grounds, be abandoned. For the critical reflection of the Western religious spirit is itself a part of the classical Western religious journey. It is true that the "dialectic" of the eighteenth-century Enlightenment has given rise to a cultural configuration of profound ambiguity:[11] the positive side is clear enough; the negative reveals a merely technical, a narrowly autonomous reason set over against an equally frightening (as merely technical) heteronomous, traditionalist reason. Both Enlightenment models of rationality and traditionalist models of heteronomy tend to destroy our ability to interpret the claims of the classics by interpreting all claims through the restrictive lenses of techniques developed by autonomous and heteronomous interpreters. This dark side of both the Enlightenment and the religious traditions—a side exposed by the critiques of Marxist and conservative alike—is not, however, their fuller reality. That reality remains an ambiguous mixture of gain and loss.

For that same Enlightenment remains a real enlightenment not only for its presently ignored (because taken for granted) positive accomplishments in asserting civil liberties but also for its fidelity to the Western religious insistence on the necessity of critique in the interpretation of all religious classics.[12] The roots of that insistence are, to be sure, partly in the first "enlightenment," that of the classical Greek and Hellenistic philosophers' critical reflections on the myths of ancient gods.[13] Yet those roots are also grounded in the classical texts and testimonies of the Jewish and Christian traditions: in the anguished and self-critical searchings of the prophets, the brilliance and nonheteronomous reflections of a way of life of the Torah, in the critical search of the sages of the Wisdom literature for manifestation of God's truth in the limit-situations of our lives—classically, in the profound mode of recognition of the book of Job where cosmos and ethos unite in the pathos of suffering grounded in faith and hope. The same insistence upon critique may be found in the Christian tradition, not only in Paul Tillich's insistence that contemporary faith always involves doubt, or in Luther's "freedom of the Christian," or in the "apologetic" thrust of the medieval discussions of "faith and reason" or in the patristic logos theologies. Ultimately, the power of critique is grounded for the Christian in the New Testament itself, as Rudolf Bultmann's insistence upon the demythologizing performed by the kerygma throughout the New Testament itself reveals with classical interpretative force. The moment of critical reflection in the Christian and Jewish religious journeys must remain a classic moment in their religious consciousness. Even the rediscovery of the truth of the paradigmatic cannot eliminate that critical moment without betraying the paradigmatic power of the journey itself.

It seems unnecessary, therefore, for any Christian systematic theologian to face the religious classics with the rubric "only the paradigmatic is the real." Yet if the loss of that "only"becomes the occasion to lose the claim and power of the paradigmatic, then the decisive character of religious truth as manifestation of the whole may collapse into the general cultural configuration where all the classics are relegated to a fatal privateness.[14] But if a heightened sensitivity to our actual realized experience of the event-character of the classics can take hold again in the culture, then the interpretations of the religious classics will continue on their own critical and fully public terms.

A realized experience of any religious classic, therefore, will bear the main characteristics of our common experience of any major classic. Moreover, the subject matter of the religious classic—some manifestation of the meaning and truth of the whole by the whole—demands an expression analogous to the expressions in a major, not a minor, classic. The form of the religious classic, as we saw above, sometimes but rarely attains the sureness of form of the major artistic classics. Indeed, the uniqueness of the subject matter of religion—an expression of the whole believed to be, because experienced as, a manifestation of the whole by the power of that whole, not ourselves—also occasions the uniqueness of all expressions of genuinely religious classics.

Let us assume that a prospective interpreter of a particular religious classic senses there the kind of realized experience that he or she has already experienced with other classics. Let us also assume that the interpreter, although cognizant of the various critiques of religion and especially of the major contemporary hermeneutics of suspicion, cannot deny that the experience of a religious classic is a realized experience bearing some sense of recognition of what can be named reality and truth. The only way to disallow this experience is to retreat to a now-disowned aesthetic distancing from its claim to attention. Does it not follow that, although the interpreter will continue to honor critique and suspicion on both inner-religious and extra-religious grounds, the interpreter will still risk an interpretation of retrieval?

For, in that fidelity to experience itself which is one of the hallmarks of a critical mind, the interpreter of the religious classic may disown false distancing. Critical reflection upon the experience will be disclosed as a crisis within experience itself.[15] But the concrete ground must always be in the concrete, the realized experience of a truth that promises to transform all prior experience and understanding. The only ground to religious expression, if indeed religion is a manifestation of the whole, is that concrete universal recognized as the claim to an event of truth expressed in a particular concrete religion. The ground is not some abstract universal developed by the powers of critical reflection. Fundamental theology's metaphysical reflections do provide a real, logically necessary and critical warrant for the claims to truth of religion by the development of an abstract universal which is not a false distancing. But only systematic theology's fidelity to the truth of interpretation can provide a sufficient warrant for the concrete universal manifested in the concrete religious classic.[16] Critical fidelity to experience means fidelity to the concrete; fidelity to the concrete means, logically, fidelity to the sufficient and, in and through that decisive sufficiency, to the necessary and necessarily abstract metaphysical conditions of possibility. Fundamental theology warrants the claims to truth of the religious dimension to existence on ordinary public grounds; systematic theology as interpretation warrants the claims to truth of *a concrete religion* on those kinds of authentically public grounds appropriate to the kind of disclosive publicness expressed in all classics.

This is the case, moreover, for radically experiential reasons: The realized experience of the truth-character of the religious classic is an experience of its purely given character, its status as an event, a happening manifested *to* my experience, neither determined by nor produced by my subjectivity. Insofar as I honor experience itself, I may accord this experience the status of a claim to truth as the manifestation of a "letting-be-seen" of what is, as it shows itself to experience.

Is it not also the case that one of the hallmarks of a contemporary mind—i.e., a mind that has appropriated the distinctive and liberating characteristic of our postmodern period—is a recognition of the profound ambiguity at the heart of Enlightenment modernity? That ambiguity can be most clearly seen in its negative moment under the rubric of the "illusions" of self-consciousness: more exactly, the Cartesian and Enlightenment dream of the control of all reality through the autonomous and self-regulating techniques of a pure and immediate consciousness. If the horrors of a technology in danger of becoming a technocracy and the full-scale retreat of all claims to truth in art, history, ethics, metaphysics and religion into the realm of the private have not alerted a contemporary mind to the fatal dangers of this illusion, then the arguments advanced by thinkers as diverse as Nietzsche, Kierkegaard, Freud, Marx and Heidegger should.

For whatever their distinct, indeed often mutually exclusive[17] claims on "religion," these contemporary "masters of suspicion" have so exposed the illusions of Enlightenment consciousness that one cannot but wonder how the fundamentalist worshipers of a merely technical reason can continue in their untroubled manner. What control can be hoped for from a purely autonomous, an immediate private self-consciousness, if no such reality exists? What use is it to try to reject the insight which common sense and contemporary critical reflection alike honor: that the "I think, therefore I am" motif grounding this drive for technical control is an empty and hollow truth built on quicksand?[18] For the concrete self is always mediated by the ideas, actions, works, images, texts, institutions and monuments that objectify our experience.[19] What gain can be found in positing an immediate self-consciousness whose illusions a Freud (through the reality and unrecognized motivations of the unconscious), a Marx (through the reality and unrecognized motivations of socioeconomic forces), a Nietzsche (through the reality of the unrecognized motivation of a will to power empowering our cultural accomplishments) have long since exposed? What gain is there in casting aside the classical expressions of the culture when they, and they alone, bespeak a full-fledged, concrete, paradigmatic truth which cuts through our conscious controls? That concrete truth liberates our unconscious needs by respecting the concrete actuality of a cultured self. That self finds itself by risking an interpretation of the classic signs and testimonies to a power greater than the self scattered in its midst: signs to a reality to which the self finds it ultimately belongs.

Any contemporary person who has experienced both the event-character of a realized experience of a religious classic as well as the necessity of critical reflection grounded in the classics themselves may engage in some form of a "hermeneutics of retrieval." If that same interpreter finds intelligible my proposal for the production of meaning via expression in the classic, then he or she is also likely to reflect further on the similarities and differences between religious classics and other classics.

The major similarity is structural: Any classic will produce its meaning through the related strategies of intensification of particularity and intensification of distanciation in expression. The first journey of intensification into one's own particularity will ordinarily free the person (or community) from the limitations of self-consciousness into a sense of a real participation in, a belonging to, a wider and deeper reality than the self or the community. That experience of intensification, like all experience, must involve some understanding and some expression. When the struggle for expression—the second, self-distancing journey of intensification—finds its appropriate genre, style and form, then the self is positively distanced from the original experience in order to express the meaning of that experience. Then a person can communicate the disclosive meaning to others who may not now share it, but can share its meaning through experiencing the now-rendered expression. In a minor classic, the very character of the subject matter (as "fanciful," "playful") will lessen the need for intensification and aid the finding of a form which is usually fully adequate to the subject matter. In a major classic, the character of the subject matter (as the meaning of some essential aspect of existence) will intensify the need for the self's intensification into a liberation to and by a reality greater than the self. In the cases of any major classic, the search for an adequate form of expression is difficult, indeed well-nigh impossible.

In the greatest classics (a Shakespeare, a Dante, a Tolstoy, a Michelangelo, a Mozart, a Beethoven, a Homer, a Sappho) the triumph of form is always unsteady, always partly flawed, partly accidental. And yet with a secret lost even to the author, the work works. Accident becomes destiny, the flaws themselves can contribute to the greater whole, the very unsteadiness of the form can steady it and free it to express the ambiguous and complex actuality of a lived existence of participation and nonparticipation in a reality greater than the self. The form does express, can communicate a world disclosive of a radical sense of both participation and nonparticipation in the incomprehensible mystery that is our existence, the mystery which we can now feel, not merely affirm. That meaning cannot be stated with the same adequacy outside the form. It can be, because it is, stated through the form: *Ab esse ad posse valet illatio.* Neither we nor the author can adequately explain either the experience of the classic or its production. Yet we know that we do experience it as a realized experience of a claim to truth. And we can make proposals like those above to try to understand its structure and its power. We can, above all, remain faithful to its insatiable need for interpretation.

In the religious classics, the subject matter, as yet more intense, complex and ambiguous (as a manifestation not of some essential aspect of the whole but of the whole itself by the power of the whole), cannot but take over the entire process more intensively yet. Indeed the surest clue to the reign of the subject matter by the religious classic can be witnessed by the relative inadequacy of any religious form for communicating its meaning. The intrinsic unsteadiness of the major classic becomes the sheer dialectical tension of the religious classic. Why should this surprise us? If, in fact, our realized experience of the religious classic is a recognition of the event-character of a true manifestation of the whole, how can we expect a fully adequate form, genre or style to express *that?* Mark's gospel is not a literary classic. It is a religious one. Even those works (some of the Psalms, Job, Jeremiah, Paul's hymn to love, parts of John's gospel, the prose of Augustine, Pascal, Newman, Kierkegaard, the poetry of Dante, John of the Cross, Milton, Donne or Eliot) which are acknowledged as both literary and religious classics are not, under the same rules of production, identically both at the same time. On purely literary grounds, Milton's Satan is far more successful than Milton's God; and yet, contra Blake and Empson, this is not the final clue to the religious vision of *Paradise Lost*.

For the authentically religious impetus is one where the intensification process is itself abandoned into a letting go of one's own efforts at intensity. One lets go because one has experienced some disclosure of the whole which cannot be denied as from the whole. One is actually, finally related to the whole because one participates in, belongs to, is caught up in some disclosure of that whole. That disclosure is simply given, recognized, accepted. The self acknowledges a power not one's own while also recognizing that this radical "belonging-to" posits itself as gift only by implying its contrary.

That experience of not belonging takes several ever more intense forms. It is first experienced as a renewed sense of one's essential creatureliness—a sense of fundamental trust expanding to a sense of "absolute dependence" upon the whole.[20] Then, through its own intensification process, the experience of not belonging comes as a radical, judging and healing sense of an actual estrangement from the defamiliarizing and transformative powers of the whole. And that experience engenders, on the other side of both finitude and estrangement, some release into the radical and gracious mystery at the heart of human existence.[21]

That final gift has its own dialectical character. The gift posits itself by implying its other: a demand to express that experience and its meaning and truth in a form—a text, an image, a gesture, above all, a style of life. The demand to express, to render, to communicate sets in motion the distanciation process whereby the self distances itself from its own self-consciousness and finds the proper genre for some expression of that meaning and truth. Where that form is found, where that demand is met, the gifted, enabling, transformative and disclosing-concealing character of the subject matter itself will also be communicated—now as the world referred to by the text and speaking to the heart, the imagination, the mind and, through them, to the will. Yet even that communication will prove at best relatively adequate. In principle, its inadequacy is dependent, above all, on the nature of the subject matter. For the experience is itself experienced as given, as a disclosure and concealment from the side of the whole, not of some essential aspect of the whole but of the whole itself. Even the demand to communicate is experienced as enabled and empowered by the whole.[22] The meaning and truth communicated is expressed in a form—whether a text, an image, a ritual, a symbol, a life—which, as itself not the whole, cannot adequately express the whole. And yet the form of the religious classic, as empowered and enabled by the original journey of intensification-become-releasement of radical participation and nonparticipation in the whole, does express that meaning in the only way the form can: with an adequacy relative to who we are and what this subject matter is.

Both the expression and the experience of a religious "limit-of" disclosure and concealment of and by the whole remains, therefore, intrinsically dialectical throughout the entire process. The demands of the journey of intensification into the fundamental questions of the meaning of existence imply their opposite: a letting-go, a being-caught-up-in, a radical belonging-to some disclosure of the whole by the whole. And the very radicality of that belonging-to the whole posits itself by implying its opposite: I as a self recognize that I am absolutely dependent upon the whole, recognize myself as in actuality profoundly ambiguous in all my experience, my understanding, my ability and willingness to live by and in the radical mystery which envelops and empowers me.[23] As the dialectic intensifies, this recognition of the disclosure of radical mystery posits itself as disclosure by implying its opposite: The mystery is also concealed from me by and in its disclosure as mystery. The revelation is also a revelation of hiddenness; the flooding, white light of its comprehensibility frees me to recognize the dark impenetrable incomprehensibility of both the whole and myself in the whole. In a moment of appropriation of that self-recognition, I may also recognize that the gift posits itself as gift by implying a command: a command to communicate by incarnating that reality in a word, a symbol, an image, a ritual, a gesture, a life. And that command, when attended to, posits itself by implying through its very expression that the command is not a mere duty or obligation,[24] but an enabled, empowered, elicited, gifted expression of the whole. The intrinsic inadequacy of any classical expression of a disclosure-concealment of and from the whole implies its genuine adequacy for us. Our earlier limit-language, forged to express the meaning of the limit-to experiences of the religious dimension of our lives, now yields to the dialectical language of explicitly religious expression.[25] What major forms that dialectical expression may find may now be interpreted.

ii. Classical Forms of Religious Expression: Manifestation and Proclamation

Any classical religious expression will bear an event-character in its paradigmatic claims to truth and reality. If that note of event, happening, occurrence is missing, all the familiar caricatures of authentic religion occur: fundamentalism, authoritarianism, fanaticism, period-piece religiosity, hardened ideology, personal projections for security, nostalgic sentimentality. If that event-character is maintained, however, both religious persons and the interpreters of religion will honor the complex and liberating truth that "the paradigmatic is the real."

The power of the event of disclosure—a power driven by the subject matter of the whole manifesting itself—will demand a dialectical expression faithful to the radically dialectical character of the experience. On the hypothesis of the production of any classical expression proposed above, the two main dialectical moments—an existential intensification of particularity, expressing itself through distanciation in a shareable form—will operate dialectically at every moment in the process. A final proposal, however, for religious expressions remains to be made: When the dialectic of intensification of particularity releasing itself to a radical sense of participation predominates, the religious expression will be named "manifestation"; when the dialectic of intensification of particularity releasing itself to a sense of radical nonparticipation dominates, the religious expression will be named "proclamation."[26] This dominant (not exclusive) experience, either manifestation or proclamation, may prove a more helpful clue to the central distinctions of religious expressions than some other usual alternatives for schemas of classification of religious expressions. In Christian theology, the alternatives are ordinarily formulated under the rubrics "sacrament" and "word": the emphasis upon sacrament distinctive of Catholic and Orthodox Christianity and the emphasis upon word distinctive of Protestant Christianity.[27] In the wider context of the history of religions, the alternatives are variously formulated often by the contrast between two ideal types: religions with a mystical-priestly-metaphysical-aesthetic emphasis and those religions with a prophetic-ethical-historical emphasis.[28]

In any actualized major religion, of course, the ideal type employed to describe the religion often shatters in the presence of the actual complexity of the religious tradition itself. In the Hebrew scriptures, for example, there exist genres expressive of both mystical and prophetic strains: The narrative discourse upon the founding events of Israel relates naturally to the prophetic and prescriptive discourse (both of which are ethically and historically oriented); the philosophical discourse of the Wisdom literature relates far more readily to the aesthetic and mystical hymnic discourse of the Psalms. In terms of classical religious persons, the same kind of distinction holds: prophets and heroes on one side of the emphasis; priests, mystics and sages on the other. In any particular religion (here the major Western religions of Judaism, Christianity and Islam are the clearest examples), interpreters still debate the dominant strain in the religion. Can anyone doubt that a major issue between Gershom Scholem and Leo Baeck is the interpretation of the relative weight to be accorded the ethical-historical and the mystical trajectories in Judaism? Is not that same conflict of interpretation present in Christian self-understanding when we consider the ethical-political emphasis of Reinhold Niebuhr in contrast to the metaphysical-mystical emphasis of the later Paul Tillich; the conflict between the ethical-political emphasis of Johann Baptist Metz and the metaphysical-mystical emphasis of Karl Rahner; the lived conflict in the Christian community between the styles of Christian living proposed by "charismatic" Christians as distinct from those for whom a religious passion for social justice functions as the paradigmatic expression of Christianity? In Islam, the continuing debate over the relative importance of Sufism is striking for its revelation of the same kind of conflict of interpretation.[29]

To many Eastern religious eyes, it seems, the entire Western religious tradition seems so involved in the trajectory of ethics, with its emphasis upon the individual and history, that the Western religious sense (i.e., its mystical or metaphysical power) can seem muted, even broken. Yet a study of any actual Western religion shows that a nondialectical understanding of Western religions proves shortsighted. To Western religious eyes, the great Eastern religions as well as the archaic and "primitive" religions can sometimes seem so mystically and metaphysically oriented that the Western interpreter wonders and, if tempted by Western arrogance, actually suggests that the classic Eastern traditions fail at ethical, political-historical and thereby *religious* responsibility.[30] Yet a closer look at any Eastern religion—not only Confucianism and Buddhism but even the prime "suspect," Hinduism—soon dispels that nondialectical, too familiar Western misunderstanding.

That there remain major differences of emphasis (even major and irreducible conflicts of focal meaning)[31] among and even within the religions is clear. That any religion is really *only* mystical-metaphysical or *only* ethical-political seems an illusion produced by some partial vision of the complexity of the whole. One way of unravelling some of that complexity is to shift the analysis away from the theological language of word-sacrament, and away from the history-of-religions language of prophetic-mystical or natural-historical, and away from philosophical language of ethical-aesthetic, in order to analyze the kind of preverbal and verbal expressions of what Paul Ricoeur has named the realities of manifestation and proclamation in any particular religion.[32]

This new distinction does not claim to provide a radically new way of viewing the reality of religious expressions. Rather the choice of this rubric among the various candidates for classification schemata is based on three factors: first, the generality allows for a distinction between prelinguistic and linguistic expressions of religion and thereby frees one from a Western emphasis upon the verbal—an emphasis that can lead to a too intellectualist understanding of the religious phenomenon; second, the dynamics, more exactly the dialectics, peculiar to each emphasis seem to match the dialectics already analyzed for religious expression in general; third, the distinction is a central one for understanding the complexity, even the conflicts, in that Christian self-understanding which is at the center of this work's attention.

The distinction between manifestation and proclamation, therefore, will provide the main rubric for the present thought experiment. The very positing of either manifestation or proclamation, I will suggest, implies its genuine other in the Christian consciousness. Each needs the other. The particular dialectic peculiar to either manifestation or proclamation does clarify the emphasis on either participation or nonparticipation to a degree of radicality where each is tempted to exclusivity—and yet that exclusivity must be resisted. To test these proposals in relationship to Christian religious self-understanding, let us first examine religious expression as manifestation. In the extraordinary, indeed classic hermeneutics of religion by Mircea Eliade one may see this understanding of religious expression as manifestation at its clearest, and in many ways its most radical.[33] Indeed, the radicality of Eliade's understanding of religion is the result of the neglected (by Western interpreters) power of religion as manifestation. Eliade has articulated that power in his remarkable *oeuvre* uniting scholarship, philosophy, art and religious passion.[34] In fact, Eliade's classic achievement—still too little appreciated by most Western theologians—paradoxically serves a prophetic religious role to challenge the dominant prophetic, ethical, historical trajectory of Western religion in favor of its grounds in the power of manifestation. The first fact that strikes any Western Christian theologian about Eliade's proposal for understanding *how* religious expression occurs through the hierophanies, theophanies, archetypes, rituals, myths and symbols delineated in his work is that here the verbal, as the power of word addressing us, does not play the dominant role.[35] Rather the "archaic" ontology articulated by Eliade becomes the focal meaning for understanding religion as an eruption of power of some manifestation of the whole now experienced as the sacred cosmos.[36] The manifestation occurs preverbally: in a space and a time separated from ordinary space and historical time; the ordinary now becomes the "profane"; the extraordinary becomes the sacred because of the power saturating the manifestation of this rock, this tree, this ritual, this cosmogonic myth only to intensify that becoming into the sacred time of origins, the sacred spaces of some manifestation of the sacred cosmos.

By entering the ritual, by retelling the myth, even by creatively reinterpreting the symbol, we escape from the "nightmare" of history and even the "terror" of ordinary time. We finally enter true time, the time of the repetition of the actions of the whole at origin of the cosmos.[37] *In illo tempore,* the power from the whole was first disclosed as sacred. That power discloses itself to those participating in its manifestations by entering into the true time—the time of repetition of the origins of the cosmos. Only by entering the separated and saturated realm of the sacred through the rituals, symbols and myths that repeat that time of cosmic origins can we impoverished and parochial Western moderns be freed from the banalities and illusions of the profane: from ordinary time and space, indeed from history itself. For only by entering into the originally non-linguistic manifestations of the power of the sacred in the ritual, the symbol, the festival, the myth, can we participate in, belong to, a realm disclosed on the other side of the ordinary: a realm which has manifested itself as sacred, which exposes the ordinary as profane, a realm which at the same time chooses *any* ordinary reality—this rock, this tree, this city, this mountain, this rite—as the medium for the saturated power of the sacred—the "center of the world," the sacred mountain, the cosmic tree, the rites of initiation, the rituals which free us by their repetitions to enter the sacred time of the origins of the cosmos.[38]

We can experience the realm of the sacred only by a willingness to enter into that purely given, that sheer event of manifestation. In Eliade's work, one finds a radical negation with a vengeance: a real separation from the ordinary—even ordinary ethical and the historical senses—now become the profane. Yet if that separation occurs, we can and we will—in the ritual, myth or symbol disclosing the *true* time of the repetition of the archetypes—find a new orientation in, a radical participation in and belonging-to what we have lost by our immersion in history and time: the cosmos, the whole, now experienced in its saturating power as the sacred. We find ourself saturated with a power that is sheerly given—but given *only* in the manifestations, the hierophanies and theophanies of the sacred. We become empowered beyond the good and evil of ethics. We realize that both history and time are "terrors" that yield no final meaning. We seek "no more souvenirs" from the ordinary.[39] We recognize the truth that "*only* the paradigmatic is the real." And we find the paradigmatic, not in the illusions of ordinary time and history, not even in the recovered time of Proust, but in the ahistorical, atemporal time of repetition in the myths, rituals, symbols and images of the true time of the origins of the cosmos. In that time of the sacred, we find ourselves with a language of all-inclusive correspondences between our now real-as-repetitive actions in the rituals, myths and symbols as they repeat the reality and power of the time of origins. The whole, a "limit-of" reality, has manifested itself in the great hierophanies of all the religions. We have lost their power through our betrayal of the sacred into the banalities become the terror of history, and by our inability to recognize the presence of miracle in nature itself. We find this reality of manifestation really alive in the West, if at all, only in rural cultures; in urban settings, only in the vague remnants of the cosmic in the liturgies of an ethical and historical Judaism and Christianity, only in the troubled archetypal dreams of the night, in the ecstasy of sexual expression, in the disturbing underflow of our unconscious, in the desperation of our fascination with fantasy, astrology, alchemy, science fiction[40] and the "East" we insist on calling "mysterious" and the archaic cultures we insist on labelling "primitive," in the move by many of the most modernist secular artists—Faulkner, Joyce, Eliot, Pound, Picasso, Stravinsky—away from the banalities and terrors of our history and its conquest of nature into a search, via an art destructive of all traditional historical forms, for some ahistorical, atemporal myth which may yet save us.

More than any contemporary Western thinker, Eliade has articulated—through his extraordinary scholarship, his constructive ontology, his religious passion and his art—what the reality of a participation in the whole as the sacred might be: a participation familiar, I believe, in ordinarily more muted tones to be sure, to any genuinely religious experience and expression, including the modern Christian. His dialectic of the sacred and the profane is a radical dialectic of separation from profane reality *because* of the ontologically prior manifestation of the sacred itself in this rock, tree, myth, ritual, mountain, image, symbol. Eliade's doctrine of the *coincidentia oppositorum,* his insistence that all myths—even the eschatological ones of Judaism and Christianity—are finally cosmogonic myths of origins, his scathing judgments upon Western cultural "parochialism" and even Western madness in expecting ultimate meaning from time and history, his doctrine of the *deus otiosus,* his insistence upon our need for a global "new humanism," his belief that even Judaism and Christianity are grounded in the cosmogonic where end will be origin,[41] his preference for Goethe over Hegel, his love for the early Renaissance search for a primordial revelation, his belief that Indian religious practices and philosophy and the archaic practices of the despised "primitives" best reveal that search, his affinity for the Platonic doctrine of forms and Jung's delineation of the archetypes of the unconscious (now become Eliade's own doctrine of the historical archetypes), his seldom expressed but active envisionment of the cosmic, ritual, iconic character of authentic Christianity, his choice (again like Eastern Christianity's) of word as manifesting logos over word as proclamatory power of address, his implicit belief in the divinization reality in that logos and thereby in the human spirit: all these realities lead Eliade to posit, on the other side of the religious person's separation from the profane, the presence and power of radical participation in the whole, the cosmos, the true time of repetition revealed in the archetypes, the models, the paradigms in the rituals, symbols, myths of religious participation and in the creative interpretations of *all* religious expressions.

No single Western thinker seems as able to disclose this radical sense of belonging to, participating in, even saturation by the power of the cosmos, of the whole, as a sacred power as well as Eliade.[42] Few thinkers, moreover, seem as able to challenge our Western prejudices in favor of the centrality of ethics and history, and even more radically in favor of the centrality of the proclamatory word and time as future-oriented, for ultimate religious meaning. From a Christian theological perspective, moreover, no contemporary thinker seems as able to challenge our usual Western Augustinian assumptions as does Eliade with his extraordinary retrieval of the genius of Eastern Christianity: a theology oriented to and from not history and ethos, but the cosmos and aesthetics; a style of religious practice oriented not so much by the word of scripture as by the manifestations of the sacred in image, icon, ritual, logos and cosmological theologies; a way of being Christian that both demands radical separation from the ordinary via the rituals and myths of the repetition of the origins of the cosmos and allows real participation in the manifestations of the sacred available to our "divinized" humanity. That any interpreter of Christianity could argue that this way of being religious—indeed, as suggested above, this way of being Christian—lacks the "obedience" of faith to the kinds of desacralization commanded by the ethical, prophetic, historical "core" of Judaism and Christianity is an authentic concern. Yet that concern is valid, I suggest, only on the other side of a recognition *and* acceptance on inner-Christian grounds of that sense of radical belonging to and participation in the whole which Eliade's work articulates with modern and classical force.

And yet another religious dialectic has occurred in the West which Eliade's emphasis upon manifestation alone sometimes tends to obscure:[43] those religious expressions where the power of a word of proclamation from God in an address to an ambiguous self occurs as the paradigmatic disclosure of religious reality. The first clue to why the paradigmatic role of proclamation is not present in Eliade is his crucial emphasis upon the radical sense of participation in the sacred cosmos. Manifestation's dialectic of the sacred and the profane both discloses and elicits that sense of participation. And yet the nature of that dialectic as a dialectic of the sacred and the profane suggests that the experience of the sacred as a real power that saturates our sense of radical belonging to the whole posits itself by implying its opposite. The individual's feeling of essential dependence upon the whole in which the self now participates dialectically implies the individual's nonidentity with the whole and thereby the presence of a finite individual self. The self's memory of its actual "profane" estrangement from that participating power may posit itself by implying that even the participation in the moment of saturation is a participation not merely of a finite but of an estranged individual self. The very radicality of that participation discloses the equally real nonparticipation of this finite and estranged, emergent and uneasy conscience in the essentially good, existentially estranged, participating-nonparticipating, ambiguous self of a finite, historical individual.[44]

In the context of these dialectical recognitions implied by Eliade's own dialectic of the sacred and the profane, therefore, a word of proclamation may be addressed to the self. For Jews, Christians and Muslims, that word is itself a, and ultimately *the,* paradigmatic event of disclosure of and concealment from the whole now experienced by a finite individual self living the reality of a graced history and time;[45] a word of defamiliarizing proclamation now experienced by the self as the transcendent, unnameable Other which has now disclosed itself in word as like a *who*: the *self* of God, the radically monotheistic, the jealous and loving God.[46] This God speaks a word of proclamation whereby and wherein the whole discloses itself in a new manifestation as the presence of a personal, gracious, acting, judging, proclaiming God. This God acts in the word-events of ordinary history and time.[47] This God proclaims paradigmatic words and deeds which shatter our usual sense of participation. That word discloses the existence of a participating-nonparticipating, ethically and politically responsible self: responsible to conscience and to others, responsible for this world and this history, responsible to the words and deeds of this God. That word comes not only as logos to reconfirm our radical participation in the cosmos of our divinization by the sacred. This prophetic word comes also as stark proclamation, as kerygma,[48] to disconfirm any complacency in participation, to shatter any illusions that this culture, this priesthood, this land, this ritual is enough, to defamiliarize us with ourselves and with nature, to decode our encoded myths, to inflict its passionate negations upon all our pretensions, to suspect even our nostalgic longings for the sacred cosmos, to expose all idols of the self as projections of ourselves and our mad ambitions, to expose all culture as contingent, even arbitrary, all philosophic wisdom as foolishness, to demand disillusionment as the precondition of insight;[49] to make us recognize that Judaism and Christianity disclose a radical world-affirmation only because they have first undergone a radical, decentering experience of world-negation in the kerygmatic, proclamatory word of address of prophetic religion.

If that paradigmatic word of address does occur, then the existential complexity of the actual self as both participating and not participating in the reality of the whole now disclosed as God also happens. That same self is caught up in the saturated, paradigmatic power of a proclamation by God. The self finds that the response to that proclamation by the self and the people to whom the self belongs is that radical paradigmatic response of trust and obedience called faith. That faith will enter its own process of distanciation to express its experience of a self participating and not participating in the whole and in the community addressed by radical faith. Prophetic faith's primary expression will prove to be a faith in the power of the word addressed to it, a faith empowered by the paradigmatic manifestation of God in the word and freed to express a liberated hope in ordinary history and in ordinary time, freed to dare to express itself in historical action, not only repetition, liberated to love the other, the ordinary, the "neighbor," freed to enter history and the cosmos, freed to hope in a future as *adventum* and *promissio*; freed to believe in an end not identical with, nor even foreseeable in, our paradisical, participatory origins.[50]

The emphasis upon the proclaimed word in Judaism and Christianity will occasion expressions in words via different genres—narrative, prophecy, hymn, prescriptions, proverb, parable[51]—expressions produced by the impulse to witness to, by reexpressing *that* the event happens and what the paradigmatic proclamation means for the individual and communal conscience in historical life.[52] And these normative words, these scriptures, will themselves be continually reinterpreted, applied and preached by the individuals and communities empowered by a word of proclamation. These scriptures will aid the expression in deed of the freedom of the self—a freedom for society, for history and for a new future which that paradigmatic word promises as pure gift from God and real command to the self to act in history for justice.

Recognition of the self's dialectical participation and nonparticipation in the light and by the power of the proclaimed word implies the need for witnessing to that power in expressions of word and deed: expression in what was formerly considered the "profane" yet now recognized, in the hearing of the word, as the realm of faith-ful action named the "secular."[53] All expression involves some distanciation: The expression of this religious paradigmatic experience of the shattering, disclosive, eschatological power of the proclaimed word demands some distancing from the original and compelling sense of a saturated participation in the whole. The kerygmatic word will, in short, demand some kind of distancing ordinarily named the desacralization of the cosmic and nature religions familiar to the prophetic character of both Judaism and Christianity.[54] For the very power of the proclaimed word—a word addressed by God to both a community and a self, a word of address shattering their security and their idols—demands that the major expression of one's *religious* experience now be found in fidelity through word and deed in this time and this history to the God who gives that word as enabling command. In giving the address of command to the faithful one, God empowers the individual and the community to listen, to obey, to act—to express the word of freedom anew. That same emphasis upon expression in "ordinary" time and history, now become the realm of the secular, that religious experience of world-affirmation on the other side of kerygmatic world-negation, implies the need to express ever anew what that kerygmatic word of power is and means. The proclaimed word implies the need to search for means of codifying that word through the normative texts called scripture and through all the forms of response produced by the creative imagination of the believers.[55]

The religious expressions of manifestation need not be lost in this paradigm of proclamation. Without them there is no place for the word to be heard and perform its shattering and affirmative tasks. Yet just as surely manifestation no longer bears the dominant role, the focal meaning it once did.[56] For another and distinctive paradigmatic religious experience has now occurred: the experience of a word proclaimed from the whole now disclosed as God—a word which discloses the reality of the whole as itself a self, in some sense, while it yet conceals that same reality.[57] For the God disclosed in this proclamatory revelation cannot be appropriately named even by those who most participate in the power communicated by the addressing word and its supporting manifestation. That same proclaimed word discloses as well the reality of the self as both essentially good and actually participating in the whole, and yet as also radically estranged from the whole: a self comprehensible to itself only in the incomprehensibility of the word proclaimed to and about both itself and the whole.[58] The language of radical participation in the religions of manifestation will now seem extravagant, sometimes even idolatrous. The rejection of the ordinary as the separated profane will now, in the proclamation of the word about the extraordinariness of the ordinary as the central expression of God's word and action, will now itself be rejected in favor of a classical, paradigmatic religious ethics of the secular. All claims to radical participation will be suspect by this new religious hermeneutics of suspicion upon the "nature religions" as "idolatry," "magic," "superstition," "blasphemy"—new *religious* words of proclamation. The realities once considered merely profane—time, history, the individual as individual—now become saturated with the religious meaning and truth proclaimed in the word's call to obedience, action and freedom. The religious dialectic of the manifestation of the sacred and the profane becomes the dialectic of the kerygmatic word and the secular. For the secular now emerges not as the realm of nonreligion but the realm where the power of word must be constantly expressed in new action for justice and radical neighbor-love, the realm of faithful historical religious meaning.

The affirmation of the secular in contemporary Jewish and Christian theology, therefore, is not properly understood as some collapse of Christianity and Judaism in the face of contemporary secularism. Rather a secular Christianity and a secular Judaism are, in fact, faithful to the paradigmatic eruption of a proclaimed and addressing word-event which founds these traditions and drives them on as their religious focal meaning. *Some* desacralization of the claims of participation via manifestation must occur whenever this kind of world-shattering and world-affirming paradigmatic religious experience of proclamation happens.[59] For the very proclamation which affirms time and history and demands expression in and for ordinary time and history frees Jews and Christians in and for the world. When the paradigmatic religious power of that word has become a nostalgic echo, a presupposition that is no longer an impulse, then the great danger of a merely secularist Judaism, a merely secularist Christianity, a finally secularist culture emerges.[60] Yet the classic religious movements of Reform Judaism and Liberal Christianity have become classic religious events releasing the Jew and the Christian for the world in fidelity to the world-affirmation released by the world-negation of the proclaimed word. That same fidelity to that same word was actualized anew in Christian history in that classic religious event called *the* Reformation in its response to the graced freedom of the Christian before God's Word in Jesus Christ: a freedom which enabled and commanded *all* Christians to live in and for the "world."[61] Where the paradigmatic power of that word saturates the religious consciousness with its power, then the negation of all over-claims to participation, the religious negation of the forces of "magic," "superstition," "legalism" and "ritualism" will burst upon any complacent resting in any religion of manifestation, any non-dialectical solace in a too easy humanism or any hardened priestcraft.

Yet where the dialectical relationship of word to its originating manifestation still holds, preaching will become not just ethical application but religious sacrament.[62] Preaching as sacrament will join the sacraments of baptism and eucharist to assure that the manifestation now transformed by the proclaimed word lives. Where dialectics of the affirmation of the secular still lives through and in its releasement by the paradigmatic, negating power of the word, then the reformation-transformation of the church in and often by the world will continue—as in Schleiermacher's, or Harnack's, or Maurice's insistence that Liberal Christianity in all its forms is impelled and enabled to its responsibility for the world not by the world itself but by the word affirming that world. The ordinary is now recognized as extraordinary by being affirmed not as profane but as secular; the "world," as in *Gaudium et Spes* of the Second Vatican Council, is truly affirmed without being canonized; the world's real ambiguity—its possibilities for both good and evil—is recognized on religious grounds. The new time of a real future, not only a repetition of origins, is genuinely hoped for by hearing the promises in that word. Where that relationship between world and word is broken, where only the dim echoes of that paradigmatic proclamation are heard, then Liberal Christianity loses its religious vitality. It loses its religious dialectic of the world and the secular and becomes another decent, ethical vision living in, by and for a world which sets its agenda and writes the words for its decent, ethical, but ultimately irreligious tunes. The liberal churches are always in danger of losing their paradigmatic religious dialectic and becoming only psychological counseling centers or resources for societal causes.[63] And yet the fidelity of the liberal churches to the world empowered by their listening to the Christian word of proclamation compels them, as it must, to aid all authentic causes of personal wholeness and societal justice. Only when that word has lost its paradigmatic power of world-affirmation through world-negation does it become difficult to see how the cause is any longer religious.

Where Christians remain faithful to that paradigmatic experience of a word of proclamation in and for the world, they are freed in and for the secular—as were the prophets and reformers before them. Yet the world is not affirmed here undialectically (as John's gospel reminds us). The world's reality is an ambiguous and a religiously dialectical one: the significance and goodness of history, the estrangement and sin in self and society, the ultimate incomprehensibility of self, society and history, the hope for a really new future, the radical affirmation of world that is released by radical world-negation. The authentic righteousness of one who has heard that word and lives that dialectic produces those classic persons named reformers and prophets in each generation who will be heard because they have first been addressed by that shattering and releasing proclamatory word. There are abundant resources in the word itself, as Karl Barth, Dietrich Bonhoeffer or Jürgen Moltmann remind us over and over, to keep that righteousness from becoming its undialectical opposite: the self-righteousness of those evangelical Christians who forget that they live *simul iustus et peccator* in and for the world, by the power of the *sola gratia, sola fides* of the word disclosed and proclaimed in the cross and resurrection of Jesus Christ. So alive to the paradigmatic power of that word can some Christians become, so afraid of any claim to radical participation, any language of "divinization," any reality of *eros,* any "point of contact" between the utterly transcendent, the hidden and revealed God who proclaims that liberating word[64] that they, like Dietrich Bonhoeffer, are tempted to want to remove all manifestation from this paradigmatically word-centered Christianity, remove all mysticism, all metaphysics and finally all "religion" itself from the stark and obedient faith of a "religionless" secular Christianity come of age and living in and for the world.[65]

With the same kind of radicality as Eliade, Barth and Bonhoeffer will also insist: "*Only* the paradigmatic is the real." Yet their paradigm of the proclaimed word will drive them into a direct confrontation with the equally radical "only" of Eliade through its dialectic in and for the world, in and for time and history. For Eliade, manifestation discloses not an entry into the secular but an escape from the terror, the nightmare, the banality, the latent nihilism of ordinary time and history. Not the profane, not the secular will save us; *only* an entry into the religion of manifestation, the worlds of sacred space and the repetitions of sacred time can do that. Eliade's work serves in the contemporary period as a classic expression of the power of religion as manifestation releasing its dialectic of the sacred and the profane and its passionately religious sense of radical participation in the cosmos through the saturating repetitions of myth, ritual and symbol. His is a recognizably iconic consciousness. In an analogous manner Barth and Bonhoeffer, with their distinct and sometimes conflicting positions,[66] represent two contemporary classic expressions of Christian faith as a faith living by the power of the proclaimed word releasing its dialectic of the word and the secular and its suspicion of "religious participation" and repetition.

Yet must that proclamatory word's dialectic really lead us to the impasse, indeed the abyss, which Barth and Bonhoeffer demand? What of all those religious persons, including Christians, who cannot accept the crucial "only" insisted upon by either Eliade on the one side or Barth and Bonhoeffer on the other? These Christians may, to be sure, simply be those who have never experienced the power and force of any paradigmatic religious expression. Then, in either honesty or confusion, they may reduce both "religion" and "faith" to ethics or aesthetics or metaphysics. Yet these same persons may know that Christianity does not live by means of any "only." Christianity lives in and by the paradigmatic power of both manifestation and proclamation.[67] The manifestation-power in Christianity is present in the tradition from its origins to the present. It is true that for the Christian all manifestations are themselves confronted, defamiliarized, challenged and transformed, yet never eliminated, by the power of the proclaimed word. The dialectic of the Christian religion is one in which the word does negate any claim to a mode of participation which logically approaches identity or existentially relaxes into complacency—a dialectic which, in fidelity to the word, must radically negate all idolatries, yet a dialectic which implies, includes and demands genuine manifestation. As Christianity transforms the manifestations of nature by the power of that word into Christian sacrament, Christianity forbids the expressed words even of the scriptures or the expressed actions even of its best ethical and political reflections to divorce themselves undialectically from the encompassing manifestations of God's power in nature. Christianity embraces nature in and through its doctrines of creation—transformed, to be sure, in the light of the doctrines of redemption and future eschatology. Indeed Christianity celebrates nature in and through its doctrine of incarnation as theophanous manifestation—understood, to be sure, only in the light of a shattering, defamiliarizing cross and a transformative resurrection. Even the radical Pauline doctrine of justification by grace through faith will receive, in the later Pauline tradition of Colossians and Ephesians, a transformation by and in the manifesting reality of the cosmos.

Whenever any Christian word loses its roots in real manifestation, it can continue for a time—even a long time—to live by the power of the Word. Yet an exclusively word-centered Christianity is always in danger of becoming either fanatical or, more likely today, arid, cerebral and abstract.[68] Nor is this insight lost upon the theologians of the word. What Karl Barth snatches away through his attacks on religion and mysticism he replaces through his doctrine of creation—or risks letting nature and the body be untouched by the God proclaimed in the Word. A genuinely Christian theology of ecology must be one that from the very beginning roots history in nature.[69] Otherwise no amount of righteous, anthropocentric indignation over our rape of nature and no amount of theological exposition of our tasks as stewards of creation will repair that rupture at the core of the reflection. For no amount of Christian ethical reflection ungrounded in a Christian sense of manifestation can respond to Eliade's disturbing inquiry: Does the Christian any longer really *feel* the world as God's creation?

Manifestation is always the enveloping presupposition of the emergence and, at the limit, the eruption of the defamiliarizing word of proclamation.[70] The prelinguistic always precedes and envelops even as it is transformed by the linguistic power of proclamation. Kerygma ultimately joins logos. Word becomes sacrament. Manifestation envelops every word from beginning to end, even as it allows itself to be transformed by the shattering paradigmatic power of the proclaimed word. But manifestation returns, thus transformed, to reunite even the secular, the historical, the temporal, the self with the whole disclosed in nature and the cosmos. A Christianity without a sense of radical participation in the whole—that sense which Schleiermacher named "the feeling of absolute dependence," which others name a fundamental trust in the very worthwhileness of existence—is a Christianity that has lost its roots in the human experience of God's manifesting and revealing presence in all creation, in body, in nature, in spirit, not only in history. From a historical viewpoint, Christianity is a religion which includes both a prophetic-ethical-historical defamiliarizing focus and power and a mystical-metaphysical-aesthetic transformed and transformative enveloping ground. Must every Christian theologian finally choose some single *only* to interpret Christianity? Is there not a wisdom implicit in the complexity of a symbol system which resonates with the complexity of human experience itself to demand both manifestation and proclamation? Is not the whole symbol system grounded in the radical Christian faith that Jesus Christ is both the decisive word and the decisive manifestation of God and ourselves? The real journey of the Christian religion—in fidelity to its decisive, paradigmatic Christic recognition of both God and humankind—must demand that both manifestation and proclamation prevail in the contemporary Christian consciousness. Christianity's necessary moves into the secularity of time and history cannot be at the expense of nature. Christianity's fidelity to its own paradigmatic proclamation can only posit itself by implying a real fidelity to an enveloping manifestation.

The emergence, even eruption, of the power of the proclaimed word is profoundly new in its decisive disclosure of a religious reality which releases history, time and the secular for religious significance. And yet that deeply defamiliarizing power is itself rooted in the enveloping cosmic manifestations. Like the alienation techniques in the plays of Brecht, that word forces us to face the radical contingency and arbitrariness of all our complacent hopes in an already achieved participation. The novelty of the proclaimed word—indeed its decisive novelty for the Jewish and Christian religious spirits—is that the paradigmatic power informing its logos transforms the former world of the profane into the now religiously charged world of ethics and history. The word radically negates the profane as profane. Thereby, but only thereby, does the word desacralize and defamiliarize the cosmos. The kerygmatic word's dialectical powers of negation are irreversible towards the profane. But they are transformative and defamiliarizing only, not simply negative towards the sacred cosmos itself. The sacred time of origins (*Urzeit*) is reformulated and transformed as the proclaimed and promised time of the end-time, hoped for as really new. That restatement frees the time-in-between, the ordinary time of history and action, to be the time in which the future, the really new, the advent has already occurred proleptically in Jesus Christ, yet has also not yet occurred but will yet occur through that promissory, proclaiming Word.

To speak Christian eschatological language is to speak a language where the religious power of the whole has entered time and history in the decisive proclamation of this particular word and event, where that power has freed the "profane" to become the "secular" and has liberated the present *and* the future from the exclusive hold of the sacred time of past origins by empowering history and ethical action with religious power. That Christian religious dialectic continues to occur in the empowering of Christians to enter the struggle of history and time, to search for, work for, think for the *new* of a future which is an empowered *adventum* and a hoped-for, paradigmatic *promissio* in the always-already, not-yet reality of the present.

Yet even the Christian negation of the profane by the secular, the past-present-future of actual historical time does not negate the sacred cosmos. Indeed, at every major moment in the trajectory of the proclamatory dialectic of Christian faith and secularity, the cosmos is decisively re-presented under and with the liberating and paradigmatic power of a decisive word which is always-already, not-yet a manifestation. Consider for example the sacramental vision of Catholic Christianity: Nature and the secular become sacrament in their transformation-sublation by the word, the "prime sacrament" and decisive manifestation or representation named Jesus Christ. There can be no negation of the cosmos or nature. Indeed a sacrament is nothing other than a decisive re-presentation of both the events of proclaimed history and the manifestations of the sacred cosmos. In baptism, the water re-presents not only the Christian's dying to self and rising in Christ Jesus, not only the Christian's entry into the Exodus events which constitute God's history, but also our and history's own entry into the waters of chaos—the chaos where all form disappears, yet the chaos which gives life and allows cosmos.

Where the kerygmatic power of the word in sacrament is lost, the distinctively Christian paradigmatic power of proclamation is soon spent and sacrament becomes magic, aesthetics or even mechanics. Yet the opposite danger is equally debilitating to Christianity. If the cosmic and symbolic reality is disallowed, if the paradigmatic power of real manifestation is allowed to slip away quietly under the defamiliarizing blows of the paradigmatic power of the proclaimed word, then the deepest needs of our hearts and imagination are themselves discarded and Christianity eventually retreats into a righteous rigorism of duty and obligation.[71] We are in nature. We are embodied. However ethical our consciences, however committed to time and history our spirits, we rob ourselves and history of their roots when we dare to strip away the power of religious manifestation. It has always puzzled me, I confess, to read some neoorthodox Protestant commentators on Catholicism (or, for that matter, on Schleiermacher) who announce, with sadness to be sure, that Catholicism, although partly Christian, is also partly "pagan." For myself, this "pagan" Catholic insight into the need for manifestation transformed by word is Catholic Christianity's strength, not its weakness.[72] For the religious experience of the Christian, transformed through the proclaimed word, transforms but never destroys its roots, its grounds and its envelopment in the reality of the manifestation of the sacred. And by those means a Christian sense of religious participation in and correspondence to the entire cosmos is expressed in the classic rituals, symbols and myths of our "pagan"—and our Jewish and Christian—ancestors.

Nor need one appeal only to the reality of sacrament in Christian life to see the importance of manifestation for the Christian religion. The proclaimed word itself, decisively focussing the Christian sacramental environment of all reality, is itself expressed in *its* classical expression, the scriptures, in transformative, not negative, relationships to nature.[73] The narratives of the Exodus resonate not only to the realities of the covenant but also to the drama of a sacred universe where victory occurs over the powers of chaos. The proverbs do not speak simply to the mind and will but to the heart and the imagination, to the great rituals of initiation where "narrow is the gate and straight the path." The parables resonate through their use of ordinary characters (shepherds, herdsmen, farmers) to the great symbolic cycle of nature itself. The resurrection, incarnation and cross are symbols disclosing God's acts not only in time and in history but in the cosmos itself—as in the New Testament accounts of "transfiguration."

By this insistence upon the need for the enveloping power of manifestation in Christianity, it is not my intent to mitigate the profound iconoclasm upon the claims of the cosmic in Judaism and Christianity—in present terms, the recognition that their paradigmatic religious power comes from a focus upon the proclaimed word. Yet contemporary Christians do need to see again that we must find not only proclamatory word but word rooted in, even while defamiliarizing to and transformative of, the manifestations of the sacred in the cosmos. The "profane" may be no more. The secular has been disclosed as religiously significant. A real desacralization has occurred and will continue to occur under the religious impact of that word. And yet the sacred cosmos and its manifestations live. These manifestations still encompass us, now transformed into the power of the narratives of scriptures resonating to the deepest instincts of heart and mind, now reexpressed in the transformative power of the Christian word-sacrament. To restore the power of manifestation to the Christian religion—on the other side of and through the paradigmatic power of its word—is a struggle which probably only a seriously, indeed radically ecumenical Christianity will allow. By themselves, Protestant, Orthodox and Catholic Christianity seem trapped in historically hardened emphases: unable alone to restore the power of both proclamation and manifestation in a manner that does not seem some uneasy compromise. Yet there is neither place nor time for compromise on fundamental religious issues—at least on so central an issue, as the next chapter will attempt to document. For this demand for both manifestation and proclamation is incumbent upon all Christians who recognize the reality of Jesus Christ as the Christian classic, i.e., as the decisive re-presentation in both word and manifestation of our God and our humanity. Thus will christocentric Christians recognize that the paradigmatic Christ event discloses the religious power of both manifestation and proclamation. A dialectical sense, not a juxtapositional one nor any relaxed compromise, is present in the entire Christian symbol system to bespeak this need: word and sacrament; the transcendence and immanence of God; operative and cooperative grace; creation and eschatology; prophet-reformer and mystic-sage-priest; incarnation and cross-resurrection; nature-grace and grace-sin; aesthetics and ethics; nature and history; the centering, encoding myth and the decoding, decentering kerygma; epiphany and historical event; analogy and negative dialectics; metaphor and metonymy; ontic event and ontological structure; world-negation and, through that negation, a real release to world-affirmation. What is this always-present "and" in the Christian consciousness? It is, I believe, none other than the radically dialectical, transformative, always-already, not-yet "and" rooted in the classic event and person of Jesus Christ as true word *and* decisive manifestation.[74] Thus is the Christian ethos rooted in the dialectics of an enveloping always-already manifestation constantly transformed by a defamiliarizing, often shattering, not-yet proclamation. And both Christian manifestation and proclamation are ultimately rooted in that God whose radical otherness in freedom posits itself to us as the radical immanence of an all-pervasive, defamiliarizing, shattering, enveloping love in cosmos, in history, in the self.

Notes

1. Recall the Heidegger-Gadamer position: manifestation includes both disclosure and concealment (Heidegger); analogously, in religious classics manifestation also includes withdrawal (Eliade).

2. See Mircea Eliade, *Myths, Dreams and Mysteries: The Encounter between Contemporary Faiths and Archaic Realities* (New York: Harper, 1960). The work of Carl Jung is also important here: for Jung himself, see especially *The Collected Works*, Vol. 9, pt. 1, *The Archetypes and the Collective Unconscious* (New York: Pantheon, 1959), and Vol. 11, *Psychology and Religion* (New York: Pantheon, 1963); and his autobiography, *Memories, Dreams, Reflections* (New York: Random, 1961). For a helpful and balanced study of Jung's understanding of religion and modernity and his own role in both, see Peter Homans, *Jung in Context: Modernity and the Making of Psychology* (Chicago: Univ. of Chicago Press, 1979). For two studies of Jung for contemporary theology and religious studies, see Clifford Brown, "The Theological Significance of C. G. Jung's Hermeneutic" (forthcoming in AAR series); and Robert Doran, "Psychic Conversion," *Thomist* (1977), 200–36. Although some articles have been addressed to the issue, there is a need for a full-scale study of the similarities and differences between the positions of Jung and Eliade on the "archetypes," etc.

3. The theme of the "paradigmatic" reality of the sacred (and the allied notions of "participation," "saturation," "eruption" and the time of "repetition" as the "true time") is a constant in Eliade's interpretation of the sacred. Inter alia, see *The Sacred and the Profane* [IV/2], pp. 95–113, 20–29; *The Myth of Eternal Return* [IV/66], pp. 17–21 (on "repetition"), pp. 21–34 (on models and archetypes).

4. For an interesting study of the biblical influence here, see Herbert Schneidau, *Sacred Discontent: The Bible and Western Tradition* [II/10], where the biblical "prophetic" spirit is contrasted to the mythical.

5. For an interpretation of the role of the "archaic ontology" in Eliade's work, see Guilford Dudley, III, *Religion on Trial: Mircea Eliade and His Critics* (Philadelphia: Temple Univ. Press, 1977), esp. pp. 84–119; for important cautions to Dudley's interpretation, see the review of J. M. Kitagawa in *JR* (1979), 362–64; for a careful and critically creative (especially on chaos) study of Eliade's notions of "sacred space" and "sacred time," see Jonathan Z. Smith, "The Wobbling Pivot," *JR* (1972), 134–50; for a phenomenological study of Eliade, see Douglas Allen, *Structure and Creativity in Religion: Hermeneutics in Mircea Eliade's Phenomenology* (The Hague: Mouton, 1978).

6. For a recent comparative study of such "classic" religious persons, see Robert Neville, *Soldier, Sage, Saint* [III/82]; see also Joachim Wach in *Sociology of Religion* [IV/84], pp. 331–74.

7. The novels of Tolstoy, Bernanos and, more recently, Solzhenitsyn are particularly disclosive of this possibility.

8. The complaint is against empiricist, not empirical, methods. For analyses of the distinct, often conflicting philosophical and theological usages of "experience," see Bernard Meland, "The Empirical Tradition in Theology at Chicago," and Schubert Ogden, "Present Prospects for Empirical Theology," in *The Future of Empirical Theology* (Chicago: Univ. of Chicago Press, 1969), pp. 65–89 and 1–65. It might be noted that, in the Anglo-American empirical (not empiricist) tradition, Meland's work represents the major example of the employment of the art-religion analogy: for his most recent work, see *Fallible Forms and Symbols* (Philadelphia: Fortress, 1976). For an illuminating study of the aesthetic dimension in the American tradition of religious thought, see William Clebsch, *American Religious Thought: A History* (Chicago: Univ. of Chicago Press, 1973).

9. Recall here the cautions of T. S. Eliot in his essay on "Dante" [III/29].

10. Recall, on the methodological side, the use here of the schema: abstract-concrete (chap. 2, nn. 32 and 44).

11. Theodor Adorno and Max Horkheimer in *The Dialectic of Enlightenment* [I/106].

12. A reality sometimes forgotten by liberation and political theologians and their secular analogues in their critiques of Western society. For an analysis of this situation on the secular side (principally in relationship to Marcuse's critique), see Gary Thom, *Bringing the Left Back Home: A Critique of American Social Criticism* (New Haven: Yale Univ. Press, 1973), esp. pp. 45–119.

13. Inter alia, see Bruno Snell, *The Discovery of the Mind* (New York: Harper, 1960).

14. For myself, the recognition of the Christian paradigmatic reality as paradigmatic is at the heart of Karl Barth's hermeneutical achievement. Barth's formulation of the "only," even on inner-Christian theological grounds, is at the heart of his theological difficulty with "analogy," "points of contact," etc., and of my own difficulties with Barth's position.

15. This will be warranted as well by the fact that the ambiguous reality of the religious classic will also disclose the truth realities manifested in the interpretations of suspicion. Yet even without that ambiguity, the prophetic strains in both Judaism and Christianity (with this recognition of the not-yet in every concrete manifestation of the always-already) will demand it.

16. The "sufficiency" here is also relative to the abstract necessity of fundamental theology. Systematic theology's own emphasis upon "disclosure" needs the further concreteness of practical theology's praxis emphasis upon transformation. Every disclosure does involve a transformation, yet the latter needs its own fuller explication as practical theology for concretely sufficient warrants: for the issues here, see chap. 2, sec. iii.

17. The critiques of the great masters of suspicion become "mutually exclusive" only when there occurs a totalization of the claims in their interpretations. Otherwise their interpretations could, in principle, find some complementarity, as suggested, for example, by the efforts to incorporate Freud by the "revisionary Marxists" (Marcuse, Fromm, Habermas); the efforts to incorporate Jewish and Christian eschatological and utopian (Bloch) or kabbalistic (Benjamin) or Jewish negative theology (Adorno, Horkheimer, Benjamin) in various programs of revisionary Marxist analysis; or the attempt by Sartre to relate existentialist and Marxist resources; or the recent French politically left-wing incorporation of the "genealogical method" of Nietzsche (DeLeuze, Foucault). Although I have cited here only revisionary Marxist resources, the same revisionary journey exists among Freudians (see Paul Robinson, *The Freudian Left* [New York: Harper, 1969]) and among Nietzscheans (recall the distinction between the "old," i.e., "existentialist," Nietzsche and the "new Nietzsche" of Derrida, de Man et al.) and among Jewish and Christian theologians (see chap. 9). In every case, the tradition of interpretation (whether Marxian, Freudian, Nietzschean or Jewish-Christian) becomes "revisionary." In theological terms, any contemporary systematic theological option that recognizes that creative interpretation always involves new interpretation with intrinsic application to one's own situation and that the prophetic character of Judaism and Christianity demands these defamiliarizing, critical and suspicious moves as well will prove "revisionary." The alternative is nonhermeneutical, nonprophetic simplistic repetition (fundamentalism, traditionalism, dogmatism) which renders the tradition no longer operative as effective history. For in all traditionalism or dogmatism, the tradition no longer appeals to the mind, heart and imagination with its classic and thereby authoritative claims

to religious manifestation. Rather traditionalism tries to impose its authoritarian norms as threats upon an obedient will. The reign of technocracy with its insistence on mastery through technique appeals to both secularists and religionists whose rejection of the need for interpretation masks the will-to-power and force impelling their antirevisionary declarations.

18. Recall, for example, the discussion of the model of aesthetics as "realized experience" and intrinsically relational, not the Cartesian subject over against an object of the alternative model for "objectivity."

19. An insight mediated not only through modern social science but with classic philosophical power throughout Hegel's *Phenomenology of Spirit* (Oxford: Clarendon, 1977). See the informed commentary on Hegel here in Hans-Georg Gadamer, "Hegel's Dialectic of Self-Consciousness," in *Hegel's Dialectic: Five Hermeneutical Studies* (New Haven: Yale Univ. Press, 1976), pp. 54—74.

20. The expression is, of course, Schleiermacher's. Yet note in contemporary theology how theologians who have appropriated the paradigmatic resources of the Reformed tradition (from Calvin through Schleiermacher and Barth)—the "piety" grounded in a living sense of the sovereignty of God—can move (as does Schleiermacher) from the language of "fundamental trust" to the language of real and radical dependence on God. For a recent example, see James Gustafson's use of this language in *Ethics in a Theological Perspective* [II/69].

21. Recall the structure of Tillich's systematics (from essence to existence to life; from finitude to estrangement to ambiguity) and his fidelity (especially on "estrangement") to the retrieval of his own Lutheran heritage by means of Kierkegaard's dialectic. Note Karl Rahner's movement from "transcendental" revelation and christology to categorial revelation and christology where the original sense of mystery and incomprehensibility experienced as existing always-already in the presence of Absolute Mystery is not eliminated but intensified after the "recognition" of categorial revelation, which, for Rahner, will be yet more intensified in the "Beatific Vision." To see how Rahner holds that his insistence on radical mystery and ever greater incomprehensibility is found in Thomas Aquinas, see Karl Rahner, "Thomas Aquinas on the Incomprehensibility of God," in *Celebrating the Medieval Heritage* [I/54], S107–S126.

22. Note that even on the side of fundamental theological arguments for the existence of God, this sense for the whole is crucial: recall Charles Hartshorne's acute observation that the argument may begin with thinking through the implications of the insight "I am not the whole."

23. Recall Kierkegaard's analysis of the comic dilemma of the philosopher who builds a castle of speculation while living in a hut next door!

24. A position expressed in the American philosophical and theological traditions by the development of an "ethics of appreciation" relating ethics and aesthetics, classically expressed in the Puritan tradition by the extraordinary aesthetic theology of Jonathan Edwards: see Roland Delattre, *Beauty and Sensibility in the Thought of Jonathan Edwards* (New York: Columbia Univ. Press, 1960).

25. *BRO*, esp. pp. 91–120; for an excellent study of Kant on religion, emphasizing the historical (rather than formalist) character of Kant on religion, see Michel Despland, *Kant on History and Religion* (Montreal: McGill-Queen's Univ. Press, 1974).

26. This paradigm is developed in Paul Ricoeur's suggestive article "Manifestation and Proclamation," *The Journal of the Blaisdell Institute* 12 (Winter 1978). Readers of Ricoeur's article will note that in my use of his paradigm, I change the analysis considerably (on both manifestation and proclamation) in my own readings, partly the same, partly different, of these two classic possibilities of classic religious expression. For myself, Ricoeur's emphasis is classically Reformed. I

suspect he might find mine classically Catholic. A recent study emphasizing what is here named a "manifestation" orientation in the scriptures in the analysis of Old Testament and New Testament "epiphanies" and the dialectic of glory and name is Samuel Terrien, *The Elusive Presence: Toward a New Biblical Theology* (San Francisco: Harper & Row, 1978). A creative if somewhat overexcited use of literary criticism on the whole Bible, which includes an attempt to show the intrinsic relationships between cosmogonic and covenantal myths, is Leonard J. Thompson, *Introducing Biblical Literature* (Englewood Cliffs: Prentice-Hall, 1978). A distinct set of categories for "religious expressions" is developed in the important study by Joachim Wach of "expressions of religious experience" in thought, action and "fellowship": *The Comparative Study of Religions* [IV/65], pp. 59–146.

27. See chap. 9 for theological examples here. In art ciriticism the same distinction is often operative, as in T. S. Eliot's well-known distinction between Milton's imagery of hearing and Dante's imagery of vision. In painting note the distinction between Rembrandt's use of light emanating from the word and from "within" the introspective conscience of the Reformed believer as distinct from early Renaissance uses (like Correggio's) of light in Nativity scenes. In the latter the light comes from the child in the manager and manifests the nonintrospective but blessed faces of the bystanders, especially the figure of Mary. I have suggested elsewhere that just as a hermeneutical theologian like Gerhard Ebeling can interpret the Reformation as a "Word-Event," in a similar manner a Catholic hermeneutical theologian could interpret the Catholic Reformation as an "Image-Event." My own belief is that the religious classics of Catholicism in the Tridentine and immediately post-Tridentine period are less likely to be found in the explicitly theological works of the period than in the works of art and the use of imagery in spirituality (recall Loyola's innovations here and Trent's decree on images) and in the manifestative power of the classic persons, the extraordinary saints and mystics of the sixteenth and seventeenth centuries. The Catholic theologians of the period, although impressive as commentators on Scholasticism and developers of it (Cajetan, John of St. Thomas, Bellarmine, Suarez) seem far less expressive of the religious manifestation orientation of Catholic Christianity than are the clearly classic saints and artists of that period.

In Jewish theologies these two strains are united in extraordinarily creative ways, especially in Franz Rosenzweig, Abraham Heschel and Martin Buber. The retrieval of the mystical strain in Judaism through the scholarship of Gershom Scholem may be considered one of the major achievements in contemporary religious studies and theology. (For Scholem, see *Major Trends in Jewish Mysticism* [New York: Schocken, 1961]; and *On Jews and Judaism in Crisis,* ed. Werner Dannhauser [New York: Schocken, 1976]. For a helpful study of Scholem, see David Biale, *Gershom Scholem, Kabbalah and Counter-History* [Cambridge: Harvard Univ. Press, 1979].) The same creative tensions in Western Christian theologies (usually formulated as Catholic-Protestant) may be found in Jewish theologies in the conversation between prophetic-ethical orientations like the distinct ones of Leo Baeck, Manfred Vogel, Eugene Borowitz and Emil Fackenheim and those with a mystical orientation like Arthur Green's. Other contemporary Jewish theologians (for example, Arthur Cohen) seem more in harmony with the Rosenzweig-Buber-Heschel emphasis on the need for both strands of the Jewish tradition (now supported, as well, by the scholarship of kabbalistic mysticism of Scholem, Green and others). Besides the usual theological gains from any genuine conversation between two classic religious traditions, the contemporary Jewish-Christian dialogue has much to teach Christian theologians on how to retrieve both manifestation and proclamation orientations in their own tradition. Indeed, it is hard to name a major Christian theologian of the "age of the giants" (Tillich, with his "Protestant Principle and Catholic Substance," being the major exception) who united manifestation and proclamation in the manner of Rosenzweig, Buber and Heschel. The Jewish religious and theological sense for a "way of life" (see especially the many scholarly works of Jacob Neusner on the "Mishnaic way"), the Jewish sense for the centrality of narrative in theology (especially Buber in his theology and Eli Wiesel and Arthur Cohen in their "theological" novels) and the Jewish theological attempt to retrieve the whole biblical and postbiblical manifestation and proclamation orientations bear rich resources for both Jewish and Christian theological reflection. I hope, in the future, when more cognizant of the Jewish theological traditions in their fuller complexity, to be able to make some more constructive suggestions for the Jewish-Christian theological conversation along these lines.

For some works from which I have learned what little I have grasped of the rich complexity of the religious and theological Jewish heritage, see Martin Buber, *Two Types of Faith* (New York: Harper, 1961), *The Prophetic Faith* (New York: Harper, 1960), *I and Thou,* and *Between Man and Man* [I/5]; Franz Rosenzweig, *The Star of Redemption* (Boston: Beacon, 1971); Abraham Heschel, *God in Search of Man* (New York: Meridian, 1959), and "The Mystical Element in Judaism," in *The Jews: Their History, Culture, and Religion,* ed. Louis Finkelstein (New York: Harper, 1949), pp. 602–23; Manfred Vogel's penetrating reviews on major aspects of Judaism in *The Journal of Religion,* and his "The Significance of the Category of Worship in Judaism" (forthcoming); Eugene Borowitz, *A New Jewish Theology in the Making* (Philadelphia: Westminster, 1968); Emil Fackenheim, *God's Presence in History* (New York: Harper, 1970), *Encounters Between Judaism and Modern Philosophy* (New York: Basic, 1973), and *The Jewish Return into History* (New York: Schocken, 1978); Jacob Neusner, inter alia, *History and Torah: Essays on Jewish Learning* (New York: Schocken, 1969). Neusner's continuing monumental study of Mishnah-Tosefta (with special reference to the Order of Purities) has put all religious scholars in his debt. His ability to render his scholarly conclusions available as well in more popular form should help to dispel continuing Christian theological ignorance of the fuller complexity of the postbiblical Jewish tradition. For Neusner's own theological reflections, see "The Tasks of Theology in Judaism: A Humanistic Program," *JR* (1979), 71–87. For a good example of Neusner's interpretation of the heritage of Rabbinic Judaism, see *Between Time and Eternity: The Essentials of Judaism* (Encino: Dickensen, 1975).

See also Elie Wiesel, *Night* (New York: Pyramid, 1961), and *The Gates of the Forest* (New York: Holt, Rinehart, and Winston, 1966); Arthur A. Cohen, theology: *The Natural and the Supernatural Jew* [II/65], *The Myth of the Judaeo-Christian Tradition* (New York: Schocken, 1969), *The Tremendum: A Theological Interpretation of the Holocaust* (New York: Crossroad, 1981); novels: *A Hero in His Time* (New York: Random House, 1976), and *In the Days of Simon Stern* (New York: Random, 1973). I would also like to express my thanks to such younger Jewish scholars as Chaim Lipskar (especially on Rosenzweig), Steven Kepnes (especially on Buber), David Blumenthal (on medieval Jewish theology) and Steven Katz (on contemporary thought) who have aided me in understanding the remarkable fecundity of contemporary Jewish religious thought.

28. For example, see Joachim Wach, *Sociology of Religion* [IV/84], esp. pp. 331–74.

29. For example, see Annemarie Schimmel, *Mystical Dimensions of Islam* (Chapel Hill: Univ. of North Carolina, 1975).

30. This tradition is at least as old as Hegel. For a discussion of Hegel on the

Christian religion and other religions, see Emil Fackenheim, *The Religious Dimension in Hegel's Thought* (Bloomington: Indiana Univ. Press, 1967); and James Yerkes, *The Christology of Hegel* (Missoula: AAR, 1978).

31. Within Christian theology, see the discussion in chap. 6.

32. "Manifestation and Proclamation" [26]—one may note how the emphasis on "preverbal" and "verbal" provides a more generalized way of recognizing this.

33. For Eliade, besides the works already cited [IV/2, IV/66], see *Yoga: Immortality and Freedom* (Princeton: Princeton Univ. Press, 1958); *Shamanism: Archaic Techniques of Ecstasy* (New York: Pantheon, 1964). For Eliade's methodology, see especially *Patterns in Comparative Religion* [IV/2] for the structural or phenomenological moment; his work in progress, *A History of Religious Ideas* [IV/66], for the creative "historical" reinterpretations of that morphology in different crises (e.g., the discovery of agriculture and the "rebirth" fertility cults); also "Methodological Remarks in the Study of Religious Symbolism," in Mircea Eliade and J. M. Kitagawa, eds., *The History of Religions: Essays in Methodology* [IV/12]; and the methodological observations in the Foreword to *Shamanism*, pp. xi–xxiii, on the relationship of "historical" and "morphological" considerations. For the heart of Eliade's constructive ontology of "the dialectic of the sacred and the profane," see especially *The Myth of the Eternal Return* [IV/66] and *The Sacred and the Profane* [IV/2]. For books on Eliade, see Douglas Allen, *Structure and Creativity in Religion* [5]; Thomas J. J. Altizer, *Mircea Eliade and the Dialectic of the Sacred* [IV/52]; and Guilford Dudley, III, *Religion on Trial, Mircea Eliade and His Critics* [5]. For an excellent anthology of critical tributes and bibliography, see *L'Herne: Mircea Eliade*, ed. Constantin Tacou (Paris: l'Herne, 1977). See also Seymour Cain, "Mircea Eliade: Attitudes toward History," *RSR* (1980), 13–17; Paul Ricoeur, "Review Article on Vol. I of Histoire," *RSR* (1976), 1–4; Jonathan Z. Smith, "The Wobbling Pivot" [5].

34. Besides Eliade's scholarly works cited above, note his work as a writer of novellas and novels; see especially his remarkable novel, *The Forbidden Forest* (Notre Dame: Notre Dame Univ. Press, 1978). For analysis, see Matei Calisnescu, "Imagination and Meaning: Aesthetic Attitudes and Ideas in Mircea Eliade's Thought," *JR*, 57:1977.

35. For interpretations of the hierarchy of significance from kratophanies to hierophanies to theophanies, see *Patterns*, pp. 26–29; *The Sacred and the Profane*, pp. 11ff.

36. The expression "archaic" does not refer only to archaic religions but to the presence of those realities in the higher religions as well and especially to the phenomena of shamanism and yoga. Moreover, for Eliade, the Platonic ontology of the "forms" is itself an expression of this archaic ontology; see *The Myth of the Eternal Return*, pp. 34–35.

37. Note, as illustrative, "Magic and the Prestige of Origins," in *Myth and Reality* (New York: Harper, 1963), pp. 21–39. His novel *The Forbidden Forest* discloses this possible mode of being-in-the-world with singular power.

38. See *Patterns* for the morphologies of all these classic images.

39. Note the English title of Eliade's "fragments" from his journal: *No Souvenirs: Journal, 1957–1969* (New York: Harper & Row, 1977).

40. See Mircea Eliade, *Occultism, Witchcraft and Cultural Fashions* (Chicago: Univ. of Chicago Press, 1976), esp. pp. 1–18, 47–69.

41. Eliade's interpretations of Judaism and Christianity receive several expressions. This is only one of them. For the most recent interpretations, see the appropriate sections in *The History of Religious Ideas*, Vols. I and II. There is need, I believe, for a full-scale study of Eliade's complex interpretation of Judaism

and Christianity, dealing with his notions of the modern distortions of both traditions into the "banalities" of some Western beliefs in salvation-through-history, the possibly cosmogonic character of Jewish and Christian eschatological myths, his Kierkegaardian interpretations of Abrahamic "faith," the concept of a "second fall" into history, the Christian "theophany" in the incarnation and his more recent, less morphological, more historical interpretations of both traditions in his *History of Religious Ideas*. I have emphasized some of the themes in his more morphological interpretations of Judaism and Christianity but do not claim that these themes define his fuller interpretation of both traditions. Indeed, that fuller interpretation now seems more available as the "historical" analysis of his present work, *The History of Religious Ideas,* can be related to his earlier and provocative morphological interpretations of Judaism and Christianity in the light of the general rubric announced in Vol. I of the *History*: "For continuous reading reveals above all the *fundamental unity* of religious phenomena and at the same time the inexhaustible *newness* of their expressions" (p. xv, emphasis his). Vol. III, moreover, promises to provide Eliade's own interpretation of the "desacralization" of the modern Western world: namely, "the complete camouflage of the 'sacred' "—more precisely, its identification with the "profane" as the "sole, but important, religious creation of the modern Western world" (I, xvi). My present interest is a more limited one: to suggest how Eliade's work shows the presence of "manifestation" in both Judaism and Christianity. In fact, Eliade's hermeneutics makes that power startlingly clear even as his often radical critique of the present "banalization" of that manifestation power in contemporary Judaism and Christianity proves disturbing to any contemporary Christian or Jew. This is the case even for those interpreters who hold to the proclamation orientation, and especially for those who believe (as I do) that both traditions need to include both proclamation and manifestation. On the latter, Eliade's work is a classic interpretation in modernity. Moreover, even Eliade's notion of the end as the restoration of the beginning also possesses Eastern Christian warrants—classically in Origen.

42. What might be called the profound Platonic (or neo-Platonic Renaissance strain) in Eliade's thought is clearest in his frequent appeals to "participation" language and is intensified and radicalized by his equally frequent appeal to "saturation" language.

43. The qualifications cited in n. 41 are the reason for the phrase "tends to obscure."

44. Recall, once again, the structure of Paul Tillich's dialectic as worked out in his *Systematic Theology* [II/25]. The collaboration of Tillich and Eliade in seminars perhaps partly accounts for Tillich's remarkable "final" lecture, "The Significance of the History of Religions for the Systematic Theologian," and Eliade's typically generous tribute, "Paul Tillich and the History of Religions," pp. 31–39. Both appear in *The Future of Religions,* ed. Jerald Brauer (New York: Harper & Row, 1966).

45. It is important to note that the word of proclamation is a word *event*—the fact *that* it happens is what counts, as Bultmann consistently insisted. The "words" (including the scriptural words) employed by the communities responding in faith to that event express a response to the event—the response (as faith) itself experienced as given by the event. For a classic statement by Bultmann on the power of the proclaimed word as preached, see Rudolf Bultmann, "The Concept of the Word of God in the New Testament," in *Faith and Understanding* (New York: Harper & Row, 1969). For the relevance of this for christology, see chaps. 6 and 7. For a more Catholic theological approach to "word," see Frederick Crowe, *Theology of the Christian Word* (New York: Paulist, 1978). It is

interesting to note that Gadamer provides a manifestation-oriented interpretation of ancient Greek religion but accords the Christian religion a purely proclamation interpretation. See, for example, his article "Religious and Poetical Speaking" (delivered at AAR, 1978; to be published in the Boston University series on religious thought).

46. H. Richard Niebuhr, *Radical Monotheism in Western Culture* [IV/47], esp. pp. 24–49. Note also George Steiner's acute observations in *In Bluebeard's Castle: Some Notes towards the Redefinition of Culture* (New Haven: Yale Univ. Press, 1971), pp. 36–43. A recent psychological critique of this "radically monotheistic" self may be found in James Hillman, *Re-visioning Psychology* (New York: Harper & Row, 1975), esp. pp. 61–67; for Hillman's own proposal for "soul" and a "pluralistic" consciousness, see esp. pp. 167–230. Distinct theological proposals analogous to Hillman's psychological ones have been made by David L. Miller in *The New Polytheism* (New York: Harper & Row, 1974); William C. Shepherd, "On the Concept of 'Being Wrong Religiously,' " *JAAR* (1974), 61–81; Lonnie D. Kliever, "Polysymbolism and Modern Religiosity," *JR* (1979), 169–95. Whether these creative proposals are (in the terms of the present discussion of criteria of relative adequacy for pluralism) pluralistic as distinct from creatively eclectic remains a question for me. Perhaps some of these "pluralistic" new options for theology are best read as post-Christian theological retrievals of ancient "paganism" for our contemporary pluralistic situation. However, as Lonnie Kliever observes (ibid., 175–81), even Miller's proposal is not lacking in traces of "monotheism." As one might also observe, Shepherd's proposal seems to insist upon disowning *any* public criteria for religious realities while Kliever himself basically appeals for criteria to a "cultural sense" and then to T. S. Kuhn's "paradigm shifts," Ernest Gellner's notion of "ironic cultures" and Hans Vaihinger's philosophy of the "as-if." In sum, in present terms these proposals seem more creatively eclectic than genuinely pluralistic. For a good analysis of some of the epistemological issues at stake in some uses of Gellner's position on "ironic cultures," see Charley Hardwick, "Ironic Culture and Polysymbolic Religiosity," *Theologische Zeitschrift* (1977), 283–93.

47. The expression "word events" is intended to indicate the need for both. For an analysis relating the "word" emphasis in Bultmann to phenomenological, transcendental and Catholic theological understandings of "word" and "sacrament," see Charles Winquist, *The Communion of Possibility* (Chicago: New Horizons, 1975), esp. pp. 18–48.

48. An insight central to the neo-orthodox, Reformed theologians, especially Barth, Bultmann and Gogarten. For representative examples, see James M. Robinson, ed., *The Beginnings of Dialectic Theology* (Richmond: John Knox, 1968). For further discussion of this retrieval of kerygma or proclamation as word of address in contemporary theology, see chap. 9, sec. ii.

49. For a cultural analysis of this phenomenon, see Herbert Schneidau, *Sacred Discontent* [II/10].

50. Recall the retrieval of the eschatological sense of the future as the genuinely new in the philosophy of Ernst Bloch (*A Philosophy of the Future* [New York: Herder & Herder, 1970]) and the theology of *promissio* and *adventum* of Jürgen Moltmann (*The Theology of Hope* [IV/8]).

51. See chap. 6 for discussion and references.

52. Note how theologies of the kerygmatic word can take either an individualist or a political cast, each empowered by the proclamation's disclosure *that* it happens. For the first, see especially Rudolf Bultmann's powerful retrieval of the power of the kerygma (see chap. 9); for the second, note Dorothee Soelle, *Political Theology* (Philadelphia: Fortress, 1974).

53. See Friedrich Gogarten, *The Reality of Faith* (Philadelphia: Westminster, 1959); Dietrich Bonhoeffer, *Letters and Papers From Prison* [IV/8], pp. 108–13; Harvey Cox, *Secular City* (New York: Macmillan, 1965). Note also the crucial distinction between "secularity" and "secularism" in the responses to Peter Berger of Langdon Gilkey, Schubert Ogden and David Tracy in *TS* (1978), 486–508.

54. Note how Norman Gottwald (*The Tribes of Yahweh* [II/108]) shifts this familiar perspective on Israelite religion into a political context whereby premonarchical Israel's experience of the event of Yahweh's word elicited their efforts to attempt an egalitarian communitarianism against the "imperialistic" centralizations of the societies surrounding them. Note, as well, the scholarly critiques of an overemphasis on the "Israelite vs. Canaanite" contrast in the work of such different scholars as Gosta Ahlstrom and Frank Moore Cross: e.g., Frank Moore Cross, *Canaanite Myth and Hebrew Epic: Essays in the History of the Religion of Israel* (Cambridge: Harvard Univ. Press, 1973). A similar critique is made from the viewpoint of history of religions by Jonathan Z. Smith, "Earth and Gods," in *Map* [I/28], pp. 105–28.

55. Note the debate surrounding the "canonical criticism" of Brevard Childs. See, especially, Brevard Childs, *Introduction to the Old Testament as Scripture* (Philadelphia: Fortress, 1979).

56. In Christian theology, note how Friedrich Schleiermacher is a theologian of the word while still maintaining a clear manifestation orientation (see the defense of Schleiermacher here against the word-centered critique of Emil Brunner in B. A. Gerrish, *Tradition and the Modern World* [II/36], pp. 22–48).

In Catholic theologies (especially liturgical theologies) note how the post-Vatican II retrieval of a word-centeredness for a proper theological understanding of the sacraments does not efface the manifestation orientation of sacramental theologies. For example, see Edward Schillebeeckx, *Christ the Sacrament of the Encounter with God* (New York: Sheed and Ward, 1963); more recently, Stephen Happel, "Sacrament: Symbol of Conversion" (forthcoming in Lonergan Festschrift [Marquette, 1981]); and George S. Worgol, Jr., *From Magic to Metaphor: A Validation of the Christian Sacraments* (New York: Paulist, 1980); and in Lutheran theology, Robert Jenson, *Visible Words: The Interpretation and Practice of Christian Sacraments* (Philadelphia: Fortress, 1978). The attacks of Barth, Brunner and Bultmann on mysticism (despite their legitimate protests against some forms of Christian mysticism as too far removed from the word and as veering toward claims to self-salvation) can in this context be recognized as dangerous impoverishments of the manifestation reality of Christianity.

57. The use of the expression "in some sense" and elsewhere in this text the phrase "like a who" is indicative of the analogical, not univocal nature of Christian theological language for God as a "person"; inter alia, see *A Personal God?*, ed. Edward Schillebeeckx and Bas von Iersel (=*Concilium* 103; New York: Seabury, 1977); and Hans Küng, *Existiert Gott?* [IV/33], pp. 690–726.

58. Note how a basically manifestation-oriented theology like that of Karl Rahner will employ "comprehensible-incomprehensible" language to express the same *kind* of insight expressed through the language of the "hidden-revealed God" in proclamation-oriented theologies like those of Calvin and Luther. On the latter, see B. A. Gerrish, "To The Unknown God: Luther and Calvin on the Hiddenness of God," *JR* (1973), 263–93. For Rahner, see "Thomas Aquinas on the Incomprehensibility of God" [21]. In the "theologia crucis" tradition, moreover, one may note the daring speculative theology of Eberhard Jüngel on the "present-absent God" revealed in the Word of the Cross: *Gott als Geheimnis der Welt* (Tübingen: Mohr Siebeck, 1977), esp. pp. 135–38.

59. Note the discussion in chap. 2 of the coaffirmation of church and world in

the affirmation of God. The present discussion provides, I trust, further warrants for my earlier preference for the model of church as "sacrament of Christ and eschatological sacrament of world" and shows how, on inner-theological grounds, the relationship church-world must be a dialectical one.

60. Note the powerful criticisms of contemporary "anthropocentric" positions in James Gustafson's *Ethics in a Theological Perspective* [II/69].

61. The classic expression remains Luther's "The Freedom of a Christian," in *Three Treatises* (Philadelphia: Fortress, 1960), pp. 261–316.

62. I am indebted to B. A. Gerrish for this insight into a central religious and theological innovation performed by the Reformers for all Western Christianity.

63. I trust it is clear that this criticism is directed only at the *abuses* of "pastoral counseling" or "social justice ministries": the realities addressed in both, on inner-theological and prophetic religious grounds, are constitutive for Christianity. They are necessary, but necessarily grounded as well in their theological roots.

64. For a classic modern expression of this anti-*eros* tradition, see Anders Nygren, *Eros and Agape* (New York: Harper & Row, 1969). The Lutheran tradition seems especially prone to these kind of dichotomies: for two inner-Lutheran correctives here, however, see Joseph Sittler, *Essays on Nature and Grace* (Philadelphia, Fortress, 1972); and Jaroslav Pelikan's eloquent account of Eastern Christianity (including its notion of "divinization") in *The Spirit of Eastern Christendom (600–1700)* (Chicago: Univ. of Chicago Press, 1974). The "point of contact" language is, of course, Karl Barth's in his famous *No!* to Emil Brunner, in *Natural Theology* (London: Centenary Press, 1946).

65. Dietrich Bonhoeffer, *Letters and Papers* [IV/8], pp. 108–111.

66. Recall Bonhoeffer's charging Barth with "revelational positivism" (ibid., p. 92).

67. The fuller warrants for this position must await the analyses of Part II, especially chaps. 6 and 9.

68. See Paul Ricoeur, "Manifestation and Proclamation" [26].

69. Note how process theologies (with their manifestation orientations) have a readier route to a theology of ecology than most theologies of the word: inter alia, see John Cobb, *Is It Too Late? A Theology of Ecology* (Milwaukee: Bruce, 1971).

70. Ricoeur, "Manifestation and Proclamation."

71. A charge often made with some justice about the Puritans—whose historical destruction of images do not recommend them, to be sure, to contemporary sensibilities. Yet as recent scholarship has made clear, the Puritans possessed their own aesthetic and sometimes, as in Jonathan Edwards, a fundamentally aesthetic-religious approach of extraordinary scope and depth. For representative studies here, see Sacvan Bercovitch, ed., *The American Puritan Imagination: Essays in Revaluation* (Cambridge: Cambridge Univ. Press, 1974).

72. Note here the postliberation retrieval of the manifestative power of "popular religion" among Spanish and Latin American Catholic theologians: e.g., Segundo Galilea in *Concilium* 136 [IV/9]; for a good analysis of the ambiguity of popular religion, see Harvey Cox, *The Seduction of the Spirit: The Use and Misuse of People's Religion* (New York: Simon and Schuster, 1973). A generalization seems in order here. The temptations (not an inevitability) of manifestation-oriented positions are withdrawal from the world (as "profane" in the *fuga mundi* and *contemptus mundi* traditions of spirituality) and fatalism (as in some expressions of "popular religion"). The temptations (again not an inevitability) of proclamation-oriented positions are self-righteousness and moralistic rigorism choking the manifestation powers of the religion itself. The Catholic tradition of

Marian piety is a good example of a tradition of piety that, in its historical manifestations, discloses both these temptations and the authentic possibilities of uniting both manifestation and proclamation realities into a believable Christian spirituality: inter alia, for the manifestation orientation, see Andrew Greeley, *The Mary Myth* (New York: Seabury, 1977); for the proclamation orientation, see Raymond Brown et al., *Mary in the New Testament: A Collaborative Assessment by Protestant and Roman Catholic Scholars* (Philadelphia: Fortress and New York: Paulist, 1978). The work of Harvey Cox may be read as an example of an original proclamation-emphasis theology (*The Secular City*) that later appropriated manifestation orientations, for example, in *The Feast of Fools* (Cambridge: Harvard Univ. Press, 1969) and *Turning East* (New York: Simon and Schuster, 1977), without losing its own theological center of gravity in a proclamation-affirmed world and the struggle for justice. A disclosive example of a modern Christian spirituality and theology grounded in both manifestation and proclamation may be found in Sebastian Moore, *The Crucified Jesus Is No Stranger* (New York: Seabury, 1978).

73. For the following, see "Manifestation and Proclamation" [26], and note how this article widens (and, for me, deepens) the earlier exclusively proclamation orientation of Ricoeur's analysis in *Semeia* [IV/77] of the language of the proverbs, parables and eschatological sayings. Perhaps it is worth observing that the same dialectic could be applied to Ricoeur's earlier *Symbolism of Evil,* not to remove its central proclamation orientation but to relate dialectically Ricoeur's "Pauline itinerary" (actually Paul of Romans, Augustine and Calvin) to the *manifestation* realities in the same myths and symbols of evil. I recognize that my own Catholic preunderstanding is operative in these remarks—and, indeed, in my interpretation of Ricoeur's own manifestation-proclamation paradigm. The kairos of a contemporary ecumenical Christian theology calls all theologians to expand their preunderstandings in order to appropriate what works like Eliade's in history of religions and Ricoeur's in philosophy of religion can allow all to see: the need for both manifestation and proclamation in any Christian theology.

74. For theological discussion of this always-already, not-yet paradigm, see the extensive discussions in Part II.

Part II

INTERPRETING THE CHRISTIAN CLASSIC

Introduction to Part II

A Methodological Preface

The logic of the methodological argument of Part One of this work now needs application to a distinctively Christian systematic theology. Insofar as the claim for the classic holds, there is a second candidate for publicness besides the usual ones: the classic text, image, event, symbol, person. Insofar as the claim for the distinctiveness of the religious classic holds, religious classics should also be accorded a public status in the wider culture. Insofar as the more inner-theological argument of chapter 2 holds, the theocentric character of theology demands some kind of publicness for every theological discipline (fundamental, systematic and practical). In that same chapter, I also argued that the coaffirmation of church and world allows for the recognition of the social realities (church, society, academy) as specifications of church and world. Hence there are three distinct principal referents or publics for the distinct kinds of publicness achieved by each theological discipline. Insofar as systematic theologies are principally related to the church, they are candidates for a kind of publicness like the distinctively public character of all classics: expressions from a *particular* tradition that have found the right mode of expression to become public for all intelligent, reasonable and responsible persons. If systematic theologies are interpretations of the religious classics of a particular tradition, the next question can become more sharply formulated as follows: What are the classic texts, events, symbols, images, events, persons in a tradition?

In the Christian tradition, as we shall see, there are several candidates for classic status. Yet on inner-Christian grounds there is one classic event and person which normatively judges and informs all other Christian classics, and which also serves as the classic Christian focus for understanding God, self, others, society, history, nature and the whole Christianly: the event and person of Jesus Christ.[1] Yet where amid the myriad possible expressions (in symbol, image, doctrine, praxis) for that event can one find its classic expression? Such is the problem posed for any distinctively Christian theology. Such is the reason for the many traditional and contemporary christologies. Such is the problem to which we now turn.

There seems little reason to doubt that, in terms of criteria for any classic expression of the human spirit or in terms of criteria for any religious classic, the Christ event merits serious consideration.[2] One need not be a believer in that event to accord the Christ symbol a major role in Western and other cultures: That symbol clearly functions as *at least* a cultural classic. One need not be a believer in Christianity to accord it (and thereby its central, paradigmatic, classic event) authentically religious status: a manifestation from the whole by the power of the whole.[3] But if the prospective interpreter is also a Christian believer (i.e., one for whom that event has happened and does happen) or even if the prospective interpreter is interested in knowing what Christians believe *in*, there is no way to avoid the concerns traditionally named christology. For christology is the attempt to respond through some interpretation to that event in one's own situation.[4] Hence the structure of Part Two of this work: first an interpretation of the event of Jesus Christ (chapters 6 and 7); second, an interpretation of the religious dimension of our own situation (chapter 8); finally, an interpretation of certain major theological responses to that event in the situation (chapter 9), followed by a personal systematic theological response (chapters 10 and 11).

If we allow the interpretation of the religious classic to provide the first major guideline for an analysis of the Christ event, one fact becomes clear: The interpreter should allow for the recognition of the character of the Christ event as an event from the whole and by the power of the whole. In Christian theological terms, this means that the interpretation of the Christ event as religious event must be interpreted primarily from the side of the event itself (from the whole and by the power of the whole).[5] More exactly, the Christian interpreter of this classic event recognizes *in some present experience* of the event—more precisely, in the claim disclosed in that event (paradigmatically in experiencing the event in manifestation and proclamation) as an event *from God* and by God's power. To speak religiously and theologically of the Christ event is ultimately to speak of an event from God. To note that the event is more accurately named the event of *Jesus Christ* is also to note the intrinsic connection of every present experience of the event to the person Jesus of Nazareth. Who is this Jesus? He is the Jesus remembered by the tradition which mediates the event in the present through word, sacrament and action; the Jesus remembered as the Christ, the presence among us of God's own self.[6]

The expression "the event of Jesus Christ" means for the Christian tradition, therefore, that we recognize Jesus in the Christ event as the person in whom God's own self is decisively re-presented as the gift and command of love.[7] The always-already reality of a graced world is made present again decisively, paradigmatically, classically *as event* in Jesus Christ. The event, as re-presentative of the reality always already present to us as human beings, is present again as the decisive *that* it happens. The event as command is also present as the not-yet-actualized reality internal for each person and for all history responding to that one decisive event of God.[8]

Given the complexity, conflicts and confusions of contemporary christology, this general position on the central meaning of the event of Jesus Christ and thereby of the confession that Jesus is the Christ needs further analysis: first, to clarify this interpretation as a relatively adequate interpretation of the event; second, to see where the present interpretation is distinct from alternative ones. As a first step in that clarification, let us recall the major steps for the interpretation of any classic and how they relate to any systematic theologian's interpretation of the event of Jesus Christ.

As in the interpretation of any religious classic, the key for the interpretation of the event of Jesus Christ must be the claim exerted in the present by that event as the claim *that* it happens now. When that claim is recognized religiously as from God, then the response called faith—a response to the claim and recognized as given by the event itself, a response to the claim above all *that* it happens—is the appropriate response. The preunderstanding the interpreter brings to the interpretation surely conditions but does not determine that response. The form of expression for that event for any particular person (classically proclamation, manifestation, action) also conditions but does not determine the response. That response called faith is itself recognized in experiencing the event as given in the fact that the event happens now as both gift and command. As in the interpretation of any classic, the focus must be primarily on the claim exerted by the classic if the realized experience of the classic is not to evaporate into some other kind of experience. As in the interpretation of every religious classic *as* religious, the claim exerted by the classic will be recognized as from the whole and by the power of the whole. As in the interpretation of every radically monotheistic religious tradition, the claim will be further recognized as from God. The Christ event, in sum, is re-presentative of the same "that-it-happens-now" event from the whole disclosed in every religious classic.

Yet the Christ event is also the event of *Jesus* Christ. In so recognizing it, the Christian also recognizes the intrinsic relation of the event to the person Jesus of Nazareth. In so recognizing and naming the Christ event as the event of Jesus Christ, Christians also affirm *that* the event itself is mediated to them principally through the tradition, community and church which remembers this Jesus and keeps alive his dangerous memory.[9] Why that memory is kept alive in the event is a question primarily for the tradition and community mediating it to answer.[10] And that response has not been wanting: From the implicit christology of the tradition's earliest witness in the Jesus-kerygma of the New Testament, through the mixtures of Jesus-kerygma and Christ-kerygma in the synoptics, through the Christ-kerygma of John and Paul and the christological affirmations of Nicaea and Chalcedon,[11] to most contemporary christologies (whether "from below" or "from above"), the same basic response has been given by the tradition. The Christ event is represented as the event of *Jesus* Christ because the tradition itself has witnessed that this man Jesus *is* the Christ, this Jesus Christ is God's own self present among us—decisively present in Jesus himself, mediately present through word, sacrament, action in every later classic Christian expression where the Christ event happens.

Who is this Jesus?[12] As John Knox observed with the clarity needed, this Jesus is none other than the one remembered by the church from the earliest apostolic tradition to the present. The Jesus we know is the Jesus remembered by the church. How do we know this Jesus religiously? We know him in our response to the event of Jesus Christ: an event which exerts its claim on us as an event from God happening now and an event which mediates to us the tradition's own memory of this Jesus as the Christ present in every experience of the Christ event. If we are to know Jesus as he was and is, we must know him through the mediation of the whole tradition as witness to him and immediately as we have ourselves experienced him either individually or communally in our experience of the Christ event as from God and happening now.[13]

As the prospective theological interpreter moves from a personal response-oriented position to the Christ event as the event of Jesus Christ, the interpreter moves as well into the whole community of Christian theological interpretations of that event. If guided by the same rubrics as those enunciated throughout this work, the interpreter will now be interested principally in entering the conversation of the classics of the tradition:[14] those symbols, images, doctrines, actions which the tradition itself recognizes as its ownmost classic self-understanding of Jesus Christ. If the interpreter fundamentally trusts the tradition mediating the event and does so because of a personal and communal present experience of the event mediated through the tradition, she/he will wish to take into account all the classic christological images, symbols, doctrines, witnesses and actions of the entire tradition. The interpreter will also note that the tradition's own criteria for its fidelity to the event of Jesus Christ is the later tradition's fidelity to the original apostolic witness to the event. Then the original apostolic witness will prove a major internal corrective employed by theologians to understand both developments and distortions in the tradition.

In sum, the theologian as interpreter moves from a personal response that the Christ event happens now and a personal recognition of the intrinsic, mediating role of the tradition which remembers this Jesus as the Christ present anew as the tradition re-presents this event in word, sacrament and action. The theologian enters, therefore, into a conversation with the tradition with a fundamental trust in the classic expressions of the tradition. Yet the theologian knows as well that the tradition is also ambiguous: fundamentally to be trusted yet ever in need of self-reform, self-correction, self-clarification.[15] The theologian knows, too, this reality primarily from the tradition itself: The Christian tradition, from New Testament kerygmatic demythologizing and deideologizing, to conciliar self-correction and self-clarification to the need for constant reformation as graced and sinful church, is a tradition which lives *as tradition* by ever-new interpretations, ever-new reformations, ever-renewed fidelity to the apostolic witness which originated and sustains the tradition. Christians believe *in* Jesus Christ *with* the apostles as witnesses to Jesus Christ and thereby in the tradition which mediates that belief in Jesus Christ *with* and *through* the apostolic witness.[16] A central sign of the tradition's fidelity to that witness, and thereby to its own religious as prophetic reality, is the tradition's own self-reformation. Theologians, therefore, fundamentally trust in the tradition for the sake of the tradition. They join others in the whole church community to attempt that fidelity through both participatory and critical new interpretations of the tradition including, when warranted, proposed correctives of the tradition itself. The whole church community decides in the long run whether these new interpretations and proposed correctives are faithful to the tradition's own call to constant self-reformation in its fidelity to its witness.[17]

How might such correctives occur as disciplined, collegial correctives for the community? As we shall see below three general methods (historical-critical, literary-critical, social-scientific) have proved themselves good *public* means for the community of inquiry called theology to employ.[18] Theologians employ these methods either to *develop* their enveloping understanding of the tradition through methodical explanation or to argue publicly for the need to correct the tradition at appropriate points. Part of the reigning confusion that exists in contemporary christological discussions within the enriching pluralism of contemporary new interpretations and correctives, I believe, is occasioned by a confusion on the exact status of these methods.

To state my own position: The tradition is the major constitutive *mediating* reality of the event of Jesus Christ. For the immediate personal response to the Christ event becomes a communal response as soon as the Christ event is recognized as the event of *Jesus* Christ—the Jesus remembered as the Christ by the tradition and its fidelity to the original apostolic witness.[19] To correct the underdevelopments, confusions and distortions also mediated in and through the tradition, theologians employ these three methods of explanation as major correctives of the constitutive, mediating tradition. The personal response to the event immediately and the whole tradition mediately constitute and thereby envelop all theological understandings of the event. The methods of explanation serve as public, shareable, collegial ways by means of which the community of theologians either develops or corrects the tradition for the sake of the tradition and in terms of the tradition's own call to constant self-reformation. But to fail to distinguish those constitutive-enveloping and corrective-developing roles in theological interpretation, like the analogous failure to distinguish the roles of understanding-explanation-understanding in general interpretation theory, is to risk confusion.

That risk is increased when a second confusion occurs: the failure in much contemporary christology to distinguish criteria of appropriateness to the tradition from criteria of intelligibility (the latter either as criteria of the internal coherence or incoherence of the tradition's own present self-understanding or criteria of lack of intelligibility as some failure in existential meaningfulness or truth). Where these criteria are distinguished, both developments of traditional understanding and internal and relatively external correctives of the tradition become possible. Where these two distinct sets of issues and thereby criteria are not distinguished, confusion inevitably occurs.

To be specific: Each of the three methods may be employed to articulate problems of appropriateness or problems of intelligibility. It is crucial to be clear on which problem is principally at issue in the particular employment of any method. Although we shall see more on each method in the next two chapters, some brief methodological comments may orient the reader to the substantive discussions to come. Historical-critical methods are employed primarily to establish the *appropriateness* of a particular interpretation to the tradition. In the present work, those methods are principally needed for the reconstruction of the classical texts of the tradition, especially those texts that are, by the tradition's own internal criteria, authoritative for the tradition: namely, the scriptural texts and more specifically still, the primary apostolic witnesses reconstructed from the scriptures by historical method. Such methods are sometimes also employed to establish criteria of intelligibility for a twentieth-century person who wants historical evidence on historical-critical grounds for intelligibility.

The "historical Jesus" controversy[20] is merely the central example of how these two different problems can become confused. This is the case whenever problems with intelligibility (e.g., I, as a historically conscious person, wish to know what historians on strictly historical grounds can tell me about the "historical Jesus") become confused with problems of appropriateness. Consider, for example, the frequent claim that the "norm" or "standard" for the tradition is "the historical Jesus." Yet on the tradition's own terms this is *not* the case. That norm on the tradition's own internal grounds is the apostolic witness *to* Jesus—the actual Jesus remembered by the community and proclaimed as the Christ. Hence it follows that historical-critical methods may be employed for the entire witness, especially the earliest apostolic witness.[21] The "historical Jesus" is *at best* a relatively external and secondary criterion of appropriateness for certain necessary assumptions or presuppositions of that witness to Jesus.

The "problem" of the "historical Jesus" is actually, for some, more a problem of intelligibility than a problem of appropriateness and should be formulated as such.[22] For others (like the present author), who do not believe that "the historical Jesus" (i.e., the Jesus retrievable through modern historical-critical methods), as distinct from "the Jesus witnessed to by the apostolic witness," can prove an appropriate standard or norm for the tradition (*that* norm is the apostolic witness),[23] the relevance for theological interpretation of the "historical Jesus" question is a different one: namely, as a contemporary theological way to keep alive and reformulate the "dangerous" or "subversive" memory of Jesus for the present community in fidelity to the original Jesus-kerygma and Christ-kerygma of the scriptural communities. The theological use of the historical Jesus actually *functions* in contemporary christologies as a continuation of the early apostolic witness and thereby does *in fact* maintain appropriateness to the tradition's own internal criteria.[24] Yet the claims for the "historical Jesus" as "norm" or "standard" are mistaken as claims of normative appropriateness to the tradition itself. To summarize: The relevant Jesus for theology is the actual Jesus in the event of Jesus Christ—the Jesus remembered by the tradition and community as re-presentative of God's own presence among us and as mediated to individuals and community in all the classic words, sacraments and actions expressing the Christ event in the present community, in conformity with the original apostolic witness.

Literary-critical methods may be employed for the same two tasks of appropriateness and intelligibility. Basically, they are used to show claims to relative adequacy on hermeneutical grounds for the different classic expressions of the Christian tradition. For example, we will use these methods in the next chapter to explore the possibility of the greater adequacy *as expression* of the distinct New Testament uses of proclamation, narrative, symbol and reflective thought (as the most relatively adequate paradigm) along with apocalyptic and doctrine as distinctive corrective genres. The attempt will be to show degrees of lesser or greater adequacy of distinct *forms of expression* of the scriptural witness and thereby criteria of relative adequacy for contemporary expression appropriate to the full range of the scriptural witness.[25]

Sometimes these methods are also employed as, in effect, criteria of understandability as in discussions of "The Bible as Literature," the "Christ symbol" as a cultural classic, or some versions of theology as "story" or "theologies of culture." All such attempts at understandability are entirely relevant enterprises but distinguishable from systematic theological interpretations of the event of Jesus Christ as that event is expressed as a *religious* classic in responses of the scriptural communities in distinct genres. In the latter case, as in chapter 6, the main aim is to develop aesthetic and theological criteria of appropriateness to the classic forms of expression in the New Testament (and, in principle, to the whole classic tradition).

Social-scientific methods can also be employed for either appropriateness or intelligibility. Sometimes they serve as part of (or replacements for) the historical-critical reconstruction of the original witness. At other times, especially in those employing some form of ideology critique, they serve as clarifications of the deideologizing faith praxis expressed in classic christological expressions (and thereby as theological criteria of appropriateness). At other times, methods of modern ideology critique are in fact employed as criteria of intelligibility: either to challenge the tradition (e.g., as patriarchal) or to insist that, in spite of its patriarchal expressions, the tradition is retrievable as understandable in nonideological terms.[26]

In sum, these three methods serve either as developments or correctives of the tradition. In terms of appropriateness, these methods serve either to develop more adequate interpretations of the tradition in terms appropriate to the tradition or to correct or even confront the tradition's present self-understanding by means of the authoritative expressions of the tradition itself (e.g., through historical-critical reconstructions of the original apostolic witness, literary-critical interpretations of the greater adequacy of certain forms of expressions over other forms, praxis-oriented reinterpretations of the deideologizing and demythologizing internal to the tradition's own authoritative faith-praxis). In terms of intelligibility, these methods may be employed to develop new interpretations for a new situation or to challenge traditional interpretations as no longer intelligible in a new situation (e.g., as the emergence of evolutionary theory challenged a literal reading of Genesis, as the emergence of historical consciousness challenged the reading of the gospels as "biographies" of Jesus, as the emergence of process metaphysics challenged some traditional theological understandings of Christ).

To provide these kinds of developments and correctives—some relatively more internal (namely, those related to appropriateness), some relatively more external (namely, those related to understandability)—is an essential task for the tradition itself on the tradition's own nonmythological, nonideological, self-reformatory, defamiliarizing prophetic and eschatological religious grounds. In that task theologians serve the whole community by means of their proposals for new interpretations: developments, correctives, challenges of the tradition for the sake of the tradition. Theologians[27] provide these corrective and developmental truths through their employment of these public methods which in turn are developments and correctives of the encompassing understanding constituted by some present response to the Christ event become the communal response to the event of Jesus Christ mediated through the constitutive tradition. Theologians perform their task best, on these criteria, when they provide new interpretations appropriate to the tradition and intelligible for the situation. The first of these tasks is an interpretation appropriate to the tradition. It remains our task in the next chapter to employ the literary-critical and hermeneutical criteria of Part One of this work to see what relatively adequate forms of expression might be found in the fuller range of genres employed in the authoritative witness of the New Testament.[28]

Our present more methodological reflections are intended only to outline where those literary-critical and hermeneutical methods fit into the larger enterprise of interpreting the Christian classic, the event of Jesus Christ. Within that context, these methods may serve primarily to develop criteria of appropriateness to the fuller range of the scriptural religious witness, and secondarily as criteria of understandability of those expressions as religious classics retrievable in and for our contemporary situation. Those criteria can provide, I believe, both developmental and corrective possibilities for the tradition. What those possibilities might be we must now analyze.

Notes

1. There are other candidates for the "Christian classic": e.g., the doctrine of the Spirit, the doctrine of God, the doctrine of the human, the doctrine of the church. Although responsible arguments can be made for each of these options (e.g., "Spirit" in Quaker and some Eastern Orthodox theologies, "God and/or the human" in some Unitarian Universalist theologies, "church" in some Roman Catholic and Anglican theologies or in Josiah Royce), still I believe the doctrine of Christ remains the major candidate for *the* Christian classic. My reasons are that (1) in fact, the Christ has been the major candidate from the New Testament forward; and that (2) in principle, the other candidates can be fully understood on Christian terms only by rendering explicit their relationship to the Christ event, e.g., the Spirit as the Spirit of Christ, the Christian understanding of both the divine and the human as fully understood only in the context of the Christ event, the church understood as the sacrament of Christ and thereby as eschatological sacrament of world and principal mediator of the event of Jesus Christ. To claim christocentrism is not necessarily to opt, as we shall see below, for an exclusivist christology nor for a christomonism (nor, as H. Richard Niebuhr nicely labelled it, for a "Unitarianism of the Second Person"). For a powerful critique of some forms of "christomonism" (as "christocentrisms") from Scotus forward, see Eugene TeSelle, *Christ in Context* (Philadelphia: Fortress, 1975). The lack of development, for example, of "objective" doctrines of the Spirit in most Western Christian christocentric or, better, christomorphic theologies (including this one!) is an obvious flaw. All the major symbols must be interpreted in a full systematic theology, especially one as central as the doctrine of the Spirit. And yet systematic interpretation needs some central focal meaning—one appropriate to the distinctive particularity of Christianity—and so, for myself, the only relatively adequate focal meaning for the Christian classic (as one faithful to Christian particularity and open to all the other major symbols) remains the event of Jesus Christ.

A final clarification of the present project: fundamental theology (as in *BRO*) starts with the logic of the question of religion, then the question of God, then the reasonableness of the Christ event as decisively representative of the event of God's love as here now. Systematic theology, on the contrary, starts with the concreteness of the event of Jesus Christ and expands through interpretations of that event to understand God and the human, church and world, etc. in the light of that focal meaning. For an example of the latter enterprise, see chap. 10, sec. ii.

2. See Theodore Ziolkowski, *Fictional Transfigurations of Jesus* (Princeton: Princeton Univ. Press, 1972); and John Cobb's creative theological use of the work of André Malraux in *Christ in a Pluralistic Culture* (Philadelphia: Westminster, 1975), pp. 31–43.

3. I assume here primarily the conversation among religions where a religious believer in another tradition can recognize the genuinely religious character of the Christian belief in Jesus Christ even without sharing that belief in Christ (and, of course, the reverse should be true of the Christian). For an example, see Franz Rosenzweig, *The Star of Redemption* [V/27], esp. pp. 336–79.

4. The notion of "situation" is analogous to the praxis notion of application in general hermeneutical theory and cannot, therefore, be considered merely external, even if language like "relatively external" is appropriate for purposes of clarification.

5. As this note indicates, I am suspicious of some uses of the "christology from above, christology from below" distinction. Insofar as this distinction intends to clarify the actual development of New Testament christologies, or insofar as it intends to emphasize the real humanity of Jesus and thereby demythologize popular misunderstandings of some uses of "preexistence" language, etc., it serves an appropriately hermeneutical function. But insofar as this distinction is employed (as in Pannenberg's *Jesus–God and Man* [II/27], pp. 33–37) to suggest that the correct theological procedure is to reconstruct historically the humanity of Jesus on historical-critical grounds and then account for the reasonableness (for Pannenberg, through his historical analysis of the resurrection accounts) of the claim for divinity, the distinction is not *theologically* correct. What we find even in the earliest apostolic witness of the Jesus-kerygma are *witnesses to* the event of Jesus Christ happening now and in that sense "christologies from above." If the interpreter wishes to engage in the distinct historical enterprise of seeing how those witnesses stand up to the accounts of "the historical Jesus" as the latter is reconstructed through historical-critical methods, then a legitimate historical, but not necessarily theological, enterprise is going forward. Theologically, the primary relationship is to the event—and that means, as in the case of *any* religious classic so here for the Christian classic of the event of Jesus Christ, to a religious event: hence a "christology from above" (even if the latter is a "low" christology).

6. See John Knox, "The Church Is Christ's Body," *Religion in Life* 27, 54–62; idem, *The Early Church and the Coming Great Church* (New York: Abingdon, 1955), esp. pp. 44–45; Schubert Ogden, "The Authority of Scripture for Theology" [III/1]; idem, "The Point of Christology," *JR* (1975), 375–95; and note Van Harvey's notion of "memory-image" in *The Historian and the Believer* [II/32], pp. 268–81, as well as his later reflections and partial corrections in "A Christology for Barabbases," *Perkins Journal of Theology* (1976), esp. pp. 9–13.

7. See *BRO*, chap. 9.

8. As we shall see below, the preferable formulation here is the "always-already, not-yet" event—the not-yet is present even in the notion of the Christ as the *suffering* Messiah: an important theological reality that heightens the sense of the not-yet (as all real suffering does); see especially Edward Schillebeeckx's phenomenology of the intractable negation always present in suffering: *Jesus: An Experiment in Christology* (New York: Crossroad, 1979), pp. 612–26, and

throughout his brilliant second volume, *Christ: The Experience of Jesus as Lord* (New York: Crossroad, 1980).

This recognition of suffering and the suffering Messiah leads to a heightened recognition of *our* not-yet state—personally, societally and historically—and the not-yet reality of Messianic times and, in that sense, to a heightened recognition of the cross, suffering and rejection in christology. For one view of the implications for christology of that recognition of the not-yet, see Rosemary Radford Ruether, *Faith and Fratricide: The Theological Roots of Anti-Semitism* (New York: Seabury, 1974), pp. 246–51. For a helpful survey here, see Michael B. McGarry, *Christology After Auschwitz* (New York: Paulist, 1977). If one holds to a social understanding of all reality, then (as in process concepts) the notion of "suffering" (as both affecting and being affected) is also applicable analogously to God's own self in relationship to the world.

9. Note that the prior discussion of the complex preunderstanding of the theological interpreter of the Christ event expressed in some classical form assumes the previously mentioned first three general hermeneutical steps for the interpretation of any classic (summarily: preunderstanding, realized experience, dialogue model). The relevance of the last two steps (the use of explanatory methods and a pluralism of readings) is discussed below. In the case of the interpretation of the Christian classic as the event of Jesus Christ, there occurs a heightened recognition of the role of tradition in *all* hermeneutical preunderstanding: namely, that here the primary mediator will be the tradition which *remembers* this Jesus as the Christ.

10. Again, as in the general hermeneutical case, this tradition is retrieved as a classic tradition for the interpreter only through a realized experience of the event. Then tradition (and the classics it mediates) does not merely function as unacknowledged horizon of preunderstanding but is personally appropriated *as* tradition and, in that sense, *becomes* the interpreter's tradition.

11. See the discussions in chaps. 6 and 7 for details here. For the present, see the work of Willi Marxsen on the Jesus-kerygma in critical relationship to Martin Kähler and Rudolf Bultmann on the Christ-kerygma of John and Paul (*Introduction to the New Testament: An Approach to Its Problem* [Philadelphia: Fortress, 1968]).

12. It is imperative to see that Christianity without Jesus is no longer Christianity; the Christ-principle without Jesus is always in danger of captivity to a personal or cultural mood. The Jesus of Christianity is the actual Jesus remembered by the church in the scriptures: the same "dangerous memory" of the same dangerous Jesus is needed now. For myself, that dangerous memory is best seen in the synoptic narratives of the life, ministry, death and resurrection of Jesus. Any christology geared only, for example, to a christology of incarnation or to a Chalcedonian christology alone is ever in danger, despite the clear intent of both incarnational and Chalcedonian christologies, of preventing both the "full humanity" and the dangerous and subversive memory of Jesus (that memory narrated in the confessing narratives of the synoptics) from fulfilling their always necessary role of critique of all christologies. For some similar suggestions, see George Stroup, III, "Chalcedon Revisited," *TT* (1978), 52–65.

13. My general hermeneutical position on "tradition" as primary mediator along with my defense of the fuller scriptural witnesses (chap. 6) may account for a significant difference between this position and one otherwise quite close to it, that of Schubert Ogden. Where Ogden employs the expression "canon within the canon" for the earliest apostolic witness, I employ the expression "the major internal corrective" for the same reality. Perhaps this difference is also partly

accounted for by the distinctively Protestant and Catholic attitudes toward "tradition" operative in a particular theologian's preunderstanding (as suggested in the discussion of Loisy-Harnack-Troeltsch in chap. 7). I do not doubt the presence of my own "Catholic" preunderstanding of tradition here, but it is not the major point at issue. On general hermeneutical grounds, the present experience of the event of Jesus Christ (an event mediated through the tradition) can and does allow any theological interpreter (Catholic or Protestant) to *begin* with a fundamental trust in the mediating tradition and its several modes of expression and then to note correctives appropriate to the tradition on the tradition's own terms: the major but not sole corrective will then be the "earliest apostolic witness" in fidelity to the tradition's own norm of apostolicity. For Ogden's careful position, see especially "The Authority of Scripture for Theology" [III/1]. The historical work of Robert Grant on the diverse criteria actually operative in the early church's formation of the canon is relevant here: see, inter alia, *The Formation of the New Testament* (London: Hutchinson, 1965).

14. The word "principally" is important to note: for the initial but not sole relevant community of inquiry here will be the community of systematic theologians interpreting the classics of the tradition. The concerns of fundamental theologians (emphasizing criteria of understandability) remain as relevant as ever. Moreover, as we shall see, the concerns of interpreters using explanatory methods to develop, correct or challenge the enveloping understanding mediated by the tradition become (in step 4 of the hermeneutical process) an entirely relevant community of inquiry.

15. Hans Küng's notion of "the indefectibility of the church in spite of errors" is directly relevant here: see Hans Küng, *Infallible? An Inquiry* [I/96], pp. 81–24.

16. The theological relevance of the norm of "apostolicity" to the "material" norm (the Christ event) as the *source* of authority in discussions of the canon is obvious here: see Hans von Campenhausen, *The Formation of the Christian Bible* (Philadelphia: Fortress, 1972); Robert Grant, *The Formation of the New Testament* [13]; Willi Marxsen, *The New Testament as the Church's Book* (Philadelphia: Fortress, 1972); and Schubert Ogden, "The Authority of Scripture for Theology" [III/1], 250–54. My own position, as noted earlier, accords more with Grant's historical and theological judgments than it does with von Campenhausen's.

17. The presupposition of these reflections, as of the entire book, is the ecumenical one of the church as the entire Christian church. The debates within any particular church tradition range from the debates in my own Roman Catholic communion on "infallibility" to Southern Baptist debates on "inerrancy." Insofar as any church takes the fuller reality of the entire Christian church with *theological* seriousness (and not merely ecumenical friendliness), this generalized discussion is relevant to the particular discussions within particular church traditions. On internal Catholic grounds, the famous shift in language from "is" to "subsists in" in the schema on the church at Vatican II logically suggests that this generalized move is also appropriately Catholic.

18. In general hermeneutical terms, these methods are explanatory methods that develop, correct or challenge our enveloping tradition-mediated understanding. I take for granted that philosophical methods can also serve both as "criteria of appropriateness" principally to *develop* our understanding (recall Rahner's interpretation of Chalcedon or Chalcedon's own use of postbiblical philosophical language) and as "criteria of intelligibility" (recall Piet Schoonenberg's use of process categories to challenge traditional interpretations of Chalcedon and to present a more intelligible one: *The Christ* [New York: Herder and Herder, 1971]).

19. The word "decisively" here indicates the heightened consciousness of the tradition's mediating role for the memory of Jesus in interpreting the event of Jesus Christ as analogous to the role of tradition in the interpretation of every classic.

20. Amidst the extensive literature see, as representative, James M. Robinson, *A New Quest of the Historical Jesus* (Naperville: Allenson, 1959); and Leander Keck, *A Future for the Historical Jesus* (Nashville: Abingdon, 1971). Several contemporary christologies discussed below give some form of normative status to the "historical Jesus" (definable as the actual Jesus who lived *insofar as he is known or knowable today by way of empirical-historical methods*). This is not identical to the *actual Jesus who lived,* which every christology must affirm. The question is not *that the actual Jesus who lived* be affirmed but *how*—through the memory of the tradition (and the necessary correctives of that tradition by different methods) or through historical-critical reconstruction of the "historical Jesus." My own option is clearly for the first.

21. I agree with the insistence of Schubert Ogden that a search (like that of Willi Marxsen) for the historical-critical reconstruction of the earliest apostolic witness to Jesus would be a genuinely "new quest." On the "new quest" itself, see Van Harvey and Schubert Ogden, "How New Is the New Quest of the Historical Jesus?" in *The Historical Jesus and the Kerygmatic Christ: Essays on the New Quest of the Historical Jesus,* ed. Carl Braaten and Roy Harrisville (Nashville: Abingdon, 1964), pp. 197–242; more recently (on Marxsen's own ambiguities), see Schubert Ogden, "Christology and the Historical Jesus" (unpublished lecture).

22. For clarity on this issue, see Van Harvey, "A Christology for Barabbases" [6].

23. I state this for properly theological reasons: i.e., the Christian faith, as Ogden correctly insists, is a faith *in* Jesus Christ *with* the authoritative witnesses to that faith, the apostolic witnesses. What those witnesses witness to is their faith *in* the event of Jesus Christ. Of course they *assume* (as do I) that their understanding of Jesus is faithful to the actual Jesus who lived. To test their memory against the results of historical-critical inquiry on "the historical Jesus" is an entirely defensible if difficult (because of the sources as testimony) exercise in historical inquiry. But that quest is not *theologically* necessary to the Christian affirmation of Jesus Christ. To understand the Jesuanic theology better (see Norman Perrin, *Rediscovering the Teachings of Jesus* [London: SCM, 1967]) does enrich our understanding of one expression of *Christian* faith. The historically reconstructed Jesuanic theology does not "ground" Christian faith. The tradition from the earliest apostolic witness to Jesus to the present community's memory of Jesus grounds that faith. In this sense (though not in other ways, especially on "tradition"), I concur with that insistence of the Kähler-Bultmann tradition rather than with the post-Bultmannian "new quest" of Käsemann, Ebeling, Fuchs, Robinson et al., or the "historical Jesus" orientation of such works as Joachim Jeremias' *New Testament Theology: The Preaching of Jesus* (London: SCM, 1971), or the many recent christologies where work like that of the "new quest" is employed to "ground" a "christology from below." Further discussion of this central issue follows in the next two chapters.

24. The "historical Jesus" is often reformulated as the "dangerous and subversive memory of Jesus" (and, therefore, in fact as the Jesus-kerygma of the apostolic witnesses more than as "the historical Jesus"). For example, see the different and at times confusing uses of this "dangerous memory" (as both "Jesus-kerygma" and "historical Jesus") in the christologies of Leonardo Boff, *Jesus Christ Liberator* (Maryknoll: Orbis, 1978); Jon Sobrino, *Christology at the*

Crossroads (Maryknoll: Orbis, 1978); and Hans Küng, *On Being a Christian* [I/96], esp. pp. 119–26, 145–66.

25. The earlier hermeneutical discussion (chap. 3) argued for the nondisposability of "forms of expression." For one analysis of this in the use in the synoptics of metaphor, hyperbole, repetitive patterns, etc., see Robert C. Tannehill, *The Sword of His Mouth* (Philadelphia: Fortress, 1975). Hence we need a hermeneutical theory which allows explanatory methods to develop our original understanding by showing (e.g., through the process of distanciation) how the understanding of the original witnesses became shareable *by being expressed* in forms of expression of various degrees of adequacy. If (as the next chapter attempts) one can claim a degree of relative adequacy for one hermeneutical-literary critical analysis of the major forms of expression in the scriptures, then one has also provided another *internal* corrective to the tradition by providing a scriptural model of relative adequacy among forms of expression that is applicable to later forms of expression. In that sense, the use of Ricoeur's reformulation of the Heidegger-Gadamer hermeneutical tradition into understanding-explanation-understanding (on the side of interpretation) and expression via distanciation (on the side of production) allows for a new set of criteria (namely, criteria on expression in texts, genre, style, etc.) alongside the "effective history" of the tradition itself (Gadamer). If successful, this enterprise would provide further warrants for an interpreter's basic trust in the whole tradition by showing how later forms of expression are grounded in the biblical and apostolic witness. The historical-critical correlate of this enterprise would be to show the continuity from the Jesus-kerygma of the earliest apostolic witness (reconstructed by form critics like Marxsen from Q and the early Markan narratives) to the mixtures of the Jesus-kerygma and the Christ-kerygma of the synoptics (reconstructed by redaction critics like Perrin and Conzelmann), to the Christ-kerygma of John and Paul (Bultmann) and "early Catholicism" (Käsemann) and, in principle, to the Christ-kerygma of Nicaea and Chalcedon (Grillmeier and Lonergan) and forward. Relative adequacy here need not make claims (like Bultmann) that John and Paul represent "the high point" (indeed "the canon within the canon") while the rest either "leads to" John and Paul (the synoptics) or "falls off" from them ("early Catholicism"), nor claims (like Grillmeier) that since there is a continuous line of "development" from the New Testament to Chalcedon, Chalcedon as the "high point" (and implicit canon "outside" the canon) is to be employed retrospectively on the scriptures. Rather the claim to relative adequacy would be that there exist substantial reasons to trust *basic* continuity (including that genuine continuity as change) while demanding the use of criteria internal to the tradition itself (e.g., the authority of the "apostles" and the source of authority for the apostles, the event of Jesus Christ) to "test" all christologies. The latter kind of enterprise would be the theological and historical-critical correlate to the present theological exercise in literary criticism and hermeneutics.

26. For a clear analysis of how *theological* praxis criteria for christology as faith-praxis criteria function as criteria of appropriateness to the tradition's own faith praxis, see Johann Baptist Metz, *Faith in History and Society* [II/35], pp. 49–88. For an analysis of the deideologizing internal to Christian faith as praxis (and analogous to the demythologizing internal to that same faith as praxis), see Schubert Ogden, *Faith and Freedom* [IV/88], pp. 43–65. The argument of Christian liberation theologians, feminist theologians and black theologians is effectively that Christian faith itself as praxis demands an ideology critique (a Christian ideology critique) of Christian (and other) forms of ideological expression, including, therefore, the patriarchical, anti-Jewish, proauthority (Romans 13) expres-

sions of the scriptures and Christendom's own sometimes racist, sexist, anti-Semitic, antioppressed record of non-faith-praxis over the centuries. These arguments as theological arguments are based on criteria of appropriateness to the deideologizing nature of faith praxis itself in the scriptures. They are not simply "imported" from "outside" to undo the tradition. They are, to be sure, often first learned "outside" the Christian church: often in various secular liberation movements. Once employed theologically, however, the theologian employs these criteria as criteria *appropriate* to the demands of the praxis of faith itself (as in Cone, Gutierrez, Ruether and Elizabeth Schüssler Fiorenza).

27. The point is not, of course, that only theologians do so. Every Christian, paradigmatically every authentic Christian movement, does so effectively. Consider, for example, the fact that the impact of Francis of Assisi probably still remains a greater impetus for the church's self-reform than does the classic Franciscan theological self-understanding of Bonaventure; closer to home, Dorothy Day will probably have a greater impact for American Christian self-reform than any living American theologian.

28. The latter assumes the five steps of the general hermeneutical process and then tries to see the enrichment provided by a genuine *pluralism* of expression (and, therefore, a pluralism of readings) for Christian self-understanding in its own classic text, the New Testament.

Chapter 6

The Christian Classic I

The Event and Person of Jesus Christ

i. The Event and the Text: Jesus Christ Witnessed to in the Scriptures

Every classic is the result of a particular journey of intensification and distanciation. Every religious classic recognizes itself not as its own but as a gift and command from and by the power of the whole. For the Jewish, Christian and Islamic traditions, this experience of the whole is an experience of a who: a loving and jealous, living, acting, covenanting God, a God who discloses who God is, who we are, what history and nature, reality itself ultimately are. For the Christian community from the New Testament communities to the present there is one single expression from God proclaimed to be, manifested and represented in a myriad of symbols, images, genres, concepts, doctrines as God's own self-manifestation and thereby—only thereby—as beyond all relative adequacy: the decisive event named Jesus Christ. For the Christian the present experience of the spirit of the Risen Lord who is the crucified Jesus of Nazareth *is* the Christian religious classic event. That event impels a whole host of relatively adequate religious expressions in the attempt to confess, proclaim and manifest its truth as public, indeed universal. The original and normative responses to the Christ event are those expressions of the earliest communities codified in the texts named the New Testament. For Christians, these texts, along with the Hebrew Scriptures (now become for Christians the Old Testament), become not just more texts, more expressions, but scripture.[1]

The scriptures serve not as the object of the community's worship, save in bibliolatry, but as the normative, more relatively adequate expressions of the community's past and present experience of the Risen Lord, the crucified one, Jesus Christ. The event which is proclaimed and confessed in a startling diversity of genres, images, symbols, styles of life and events in those classic texts is the event of the act of God in this Jesus as Christ and Lord. The reality of that event is experienced in the present Christian community when these texts and what they disclose become proclamation and sacrament. The present meanings of that present event must always find their inspiration and their correctives in these written texts, these classic religious expressions, these scriptures, above all in the original apostolic witness in the scriptures. But even these texts are recognized by Christians as themselves only relatively adequate expressions of the Christ event itself. Yet so foundational are these texts that the scriptures, as expressions of the apostolic witness, serve as normative for Christian self-understanding.[2]

These scriptures are themselves only a relatively adequate expression of the earliest Christian community's experience of the Risen One as Jesus.[3] They remain open to new experiences—new questions, new and sometimes more adequate responses for later generations who experience the same event in ever different situations.[4] Yet throughout the Christian tradition these scriptures will serve as finally normative: as that set of inspirations, controls and correctives upon all later expressions, all later classical texts, persons, images, symbols, doctrines, events that claim appropriateness to the classic witnesses to that event.

Save for those later Christian communities who forget that the scriptures themselves are the church's book,[5] these texts do not disallow new experiences, new expressions, new events as the community mediates the meaning of these texts to us in tradition. And yet the scriptures remain primary—provoking, challenging, eliciting, demanding, transforming all later answers and questions of Christians as they experience in their situation that same event in fidelity to the original apostolic witness to Jesus Christ.

Although Christianity is not strictly a religion of the book but of an event and a person, still that event is normatively codified in the texts named scripture.[6] To these texts Christians turn to understand their own present experience of that event. The classic event for the Christian is the religious event of God's self-manifestation in the person Jesus the Christ: an event that happened, happens and will happen. The classic person for the Christian is none other than this same Jesus of Nazareth, proclaimed and manifested as the Crucified and Risen One who is Lord. The classic images for the Christian are those related to that event and that person: the dialectics of the symbols of cross-resurrection-incarnation. The classic texts remain the scriptures of the New Testament as the original witnesses to the event. There we find the event, the person, the story and the images of the Christian classic codified in a diversity of genres, symbols, concepts, images, doctrines, each expressing with some degree of adequacy the meaning and truth of that decisive event. We must bring our own limit-questions and our own partial, tentative, broken experiences of the whole, our own present experience of the Christ event—that it happens *now* in word, sacrament and action—to these texts. We must risk, as we do with all classic texts, an interpretation of their meaning. For here, as in all religious classics, the truth of one's existence may be at stake; here a disclosure and concealment from and by the power of the whole may be present; here a power not our own, a series of questions and responses not of our own making may be present. Once we recognize the possible presence of that reality, we can no longer distance ourselves from the risk of interpretation. We must allow ourselves to enter with both critical freedom and a real participation grounded in the to-and-fro movement of the conversation initiated by these classic texts.

Yet how can we take this risk of interpretation? Where is the entry or the key? As soon as we read these texts we find only one clear unity: the confession that the self-manifestation of God has occurred, does occur, will occur in the event of this crucified and risen Jesus Christ.[7] Yet that unity seems soon to dissipate as the interpreter faces the wide diversity of relatively adequate and inadequate expressions for this single event: from confessions and proclamations, through narratives, hymns, letters, apocalypses, symbols, images, doctrines, ethical teachings, proverbs, parables, sayings about Jesus, sayings and actions attributed to Jesus; from titles and designations confessing this Jesus as prophet, son of David, son of man, son of God, Lord, God;[8] from the Jesus kerygma of the original apostolic tradition, through the mixture of Jesus kerygma and Christ kerygma in the synoptics, to the Christ kerygma of John and Paul; from statements in several genres indicating that the event has already happened, to statements that it is happening now, to statements that it will happen;[9] from language like the explosive tensions of Paul's logic of superabundance to the lowered expectations and human, all-too-human expectations of James; from the tensive symbols and meditative releasements of John to the seeming anticlimax of the clear doctrines and controlled institutions of "emergent Catholicism"; from the apocalyptic tensions of Mark 13 and the Book of Revelation to the imaged and hieratic rituals of Hebrews; from the proclamations of the reign of God by Jesus to the proclamation by the community that this Jesus is Christ and Lord: The proclaimer has become the proclaimed.

Nor is any prospective interpreter, remembering that the scriptures were and are the church's book, wrong to look first to the present experience of the Christ event in the Christian church. Indeed, from the experience of response in the present, the Christian theological journey of interpretation begins.[10] And yet no interpreter seeking a single expression for that event will find any easy consolation by looking, as one must, to the present reality of the Christian church. For there one finds by several names the actual operation of several canons within the canon.[11] Many theologians will insist, in effect, that proclamation and proclamation alone may serve as the interpretative key to the scriptures. Yet which proclamation? Justification by grace through faith of the Epistle to the Romans and its disclosures to Luther, to Bultmann, to Käsemann? The historically reconstructed apostolic witness of Marxsen and Ogden? The prophetic tradition of justice for the oppressed of Soelle, Cone, Ruether, Miranda? The eschatologically realized kerygma of C. H. Dodd? The proclamation of the reign of God by Jesus himself of Jeremias and Manson? The crucified one of Moltmann and Sobrino? The "advocate" of Küng? The eschatological prophet of Schillebeeckx?

Other contemporary theologians will insist that the key is, in effect, what we have earlier named manifestation. Then we find Eastern Orthodox Christians appealing first to the imagery and symbolism of personal and cosmic glorification and mysticism in John and to the realities of Spirit, tradition and the *imago dei*. For some, even Paul did not really possess the "introspective conscience" of Augustine and Luther but takes some form of manifestation.[12] We find Teilhard de Chardin rushing to Colossians and Ephesians to disclose the scriptural backings for his daring vision of the cosmos. We see a Rahner moving in and out of scripture via his retrieval of doctrines, yet basically resting for his scriptural defense in the emergence of doctrine in "early Catholicism" and the manifestation power in the doctrines and symbols of John and the later logos tradition in Nicaea and Chalcedon.[13] We find a John Cobb or a Van Harvey appealing to that same logos tradition yet in very different ways.[14]

Still others will find the singular clue to all interpretation in the narrative structure of the gospels.[15] Yet which narratives? The narrative patterns disclosing God's agency in Barth or the "realistic" narrative approaches of Auerbach and Frei?[16] The narratives of the parables of Jesus and their shock to the ordinary in McFague, Crossan, Via, Funk?[17] The story of Jesus himself as the control on all other materials in Perrin?[18] The narrative memory of the suffering of the oppressed in the apocalyptic texts in Metz?[19]

Nor is there anything to be gained by simply closing the door to further proposals for "a canon within the canon" by declaring, in effect, that the scripture is, after all, the church's book. We need, therefore no further discussion of actual New Testament "diversity." Is not the Christian church precisely that: the *Christian* church embracing not one church tradition but all that are grounded in the confession that Jesus Christ is Lord? Moreover, diversity returns in yet another form when the interpreter asks: Where is the New Testament church itself?[20] In the apocalyptic sects? The charismatic communities? The disciplined order of emergent Catholicism? The earliest apostolic witness? The testimony of which particular classic prophets, sages, mystics, priests codified in the various texts of the New Testament? Where shall we go for some exclusive view of the classic events, texts, persons and images of the New Testament? To the event and person, the dominant images and thought about Jesus Christ, to be sure, but by what route? Through what other classic New Testament person: The expectancy of the Baptist? The heroic stature of Luke's Paul? The extraordinariness of the ordinary disclosed in the nonheroic bridge-builder Peter? The rigor of James? The courage of Luke's Mary? Through which images? Resurrection alone, cross alone, incarnation alone? Through which founding events? The classic events of the ministry of Jesus narrated in the synoptics,[21] the epoch-making event for the early Jewish Christian communities of the desecration of the temple at Jerusalem; the expectancy of that event which did not come, the parousia; or other epoch-making events of the New Testament, the persecutions, the Gentile mission, or, as seems right and unifying, the events of the passion and resurrection confessed in again diverse ways throughout the New Testament and confessed anew in distinct and sometimes conflicting narratives in the gospels?[22]

That there is real diversity in the New Testament should be clear to any reader of the text. That such diversity is enriching to all should be clear to any contemporary Christian who has actually experienced the event known as ecumenism. For the experience of an authentically Christian ecumenical consciousness discloses that the diverse ways of being Christian represented in different church traditions is also grounded in the New Testament and enriches all those who will allow it: at least, by exposing the limitations of our own way; at best by allowing us to appropriate in relationship to our own particular tradition its ownmost drive to the fuller reality of Christian life and tradition.[23]

Moreover, when one considers what may be named a situational analysis of the fundamental questions which focus any religious search, and thereby any entry into the conversation of interpretation with the classical texts, again an experience of authentic diversity occurs. Whether we name this horizon of our preunderstanding,[24] these questions of the fundamental meaning of life and of the whole, by the more experiential term "situation," by more traditional expressions like "discerning the signs of the times" or "the movement of the Spirit," matters little for present purposes. However named, the reality of the focus of my present discernment of those fundamental questions which are properly religious questions provides the initial horizon by means of which anyone actually enters the interpretative process of these texts. Our questions may, indeed in good interpretations of classic religious texts they will, be themselves transformed by the event. Still these questions do serve as an initial horizon to focus our concerns and our probing, do heighten our sensitivities to certain meanings disclosed by the text and do deaden our perceptions to others. Any personal horizon, moreover, is itself formed not only by the interpreter's personal history but by the tradition mediating the Christ event to the contemporary interpreter. A particular tradition, too, forms and transforms both the questions and the responses in any individual interpreter's horizon.

Is it really so surprising, for example, that the same New Testament work, Luke-Acts, can seem disclosive in such different ways to Liberal Protestant Christians, to pentecostal and charismatic Christians, to mainline Catholic Christians and to those prophetically oriented Christians concerned with social justice? Apocalyptic will seem sheer mythology to one generation of existentialist theologians addressing the question of meaninglessness in the modern situation. The same tradition of apocalyptic will seem a disclosure of prophetic political responsibility to a later generation.[25] What is "only" political to one horizon may seem radically religious to another: and then the prophetic, the apocalyptic, the categories of the "new" and the "future" of history, not only historicity, will highlight the genuinely religious possibilities of the political in ways that a more "private" concern with the meaning of individual death tend to disown.[26] If the interpreter's fundamental experience of Christian life has been through some experience of real manifestation—of community, mysticism, ritual, sacrament, art, even metaphysics—then certain texts (John, Colossians and Ephesians, Hebrews and, to a lesser but real extent, the Pastoral Epistles) will seem immediately and authentically disclosive, as in christologies from Hegel to Rahner. For these horizons even the apocalyptic and prophetic texts may take the character of sheer manifestation, as in Eliade's appeal to the apocalyptic imagery of the Book of Revelation's disclosure that "time shall be no more." If the interpreter's fundamental experience of the Christian life, or life itself, has been through an experience of the genuine event-character of word, the shattering power of proclamation, then there are sure to be appeals to the Paul of Romans and to the kerygmatic elements in all the synoptics, especially Mark.[27]

Nor is a situational analysis adequately described as a search for some "only"—some one, exclusive focus for the fundamental religious questions. Even the most authentic solitary one facing the reality of death as one's own, the reality of personal guilt, the actuality of the constant temptation of the self to flee from itself by means of the thousand strategies of inauthenticity, must one day see that the realities of societal oppression and the terrifying consequences of structural injustice cry out to the genuinely religious conscience of every solitary one. These realities demand that the prophetic, the apocalyptic texts be interpreted as speaking to both the individual and to the struggle for justice in history. Even the most committed fighter against oppression and for real and lasting justice in the commanding and conflictual light of the "impossible possibility" of love must also see that loneliness, death, illness, anxiety, repression, personal guilt and interpersonal fears are genuine, fundamental realities and demand religious responses: the kind of responses found in Romans by a Luther and a Bultmann; found in John for a Bonaventure, a Schleiermacher, a Rahner. And both the solitary one and the prophetic activist against structural injustice and oppression must also note that the experiences of fundamental trust and loyalty are equally real and demand religious response; that the realities of peace and silence, the actuality of nature and its powers and disclosures may and should also focus our religious questions: as they do in John, in Colossians, in Ephesians and in Hebrews.

Each theologian comes to these classical scriptural texts with some personal "discrimen,"[28] some horizon of fundamental questions and experiences, some focussed situation, some attempt to be alert to the possible promptings of what Christians name the "Spirit," or "discerning the signs of the times," or, more simply, an honest and searching intuition for the fundamental questions of life itself and the responses disclosed in the Christ event.

Each Christian interpreter responds to the event-character—*that* it happens—of the event of Jesus Christ represented in word, sacrament and action. Each joins the community of Christian interpreters of that event. Each theologian recognizes the need to take seriously the classic interpretations of the event of the whole tradition that mediates the Christ event and the dangerous memory of Jesus to us. Each theologian attempts to understand the classic expressions of that event from the Jesus kerygma of the earliest witness through the full range of expressions for the event in the New Testament to the present. Each ends an interpretation, if fortunate, with the horizons of questions and concerns enlarged, often even transformed. Yet each theologian also ends with some "working canon," some guiding rubric, some "rule of thumb," some final horizonal discrimen which seems relatively adequate to the initial religious, situational questions and their transformation by the Christ event of God's own self-manifestation disclosed with varying degrees of relative adequacy in the texts Christians call their scriptures.[29]

The reality of diversity must be affirmed as fact in the New Testament, in the entire Christian tradition, in the contemporary Christian community, in the diverse life journeys and discernments in the contemporary situation. The reality of pluralism is a value: a value to enrich each by impelling new journeys into both particularity and ecumenicity—a journey into a particular personal and traditional way whose very vulnerability and self-exposure to other ways of being Christian promises to transform all; a journey where, for the Christian, each and all will be transformed together in witnessing to the proclamation and manifestation of the event of Jesus Christ.

Each theologian has, in fact, some "working canon" for both the situation and the message to serve as an ordering principle for all theology, including christology. How can any of us claim any more than a relative adequacy for any particular rubric? One way—a way taken here—is to render as explicit as possible some criteria of relative adequacy for the interpretation of the New Testament and see where they may lead. For the present work, the criteria may be stated, in brief form, as follows.

First, insofar as we are dealing with classical texts, the interpreter should be open to the genuine risk of all authentic interpretation: a possible realized experience of a disclosure of existential truth. The interpreter must allow her/his preunderstanding to operate in relationship to that strictly existential subject matter. The interpreter must disallow any aesthetic distancing from the claim to attention as a nonviolent appeal which such texts *may* disclose. As with all authentic conversation, critical freedom and receptivity are equally important in allowing the subject matter to take over in the back and forth movement between text and interpreter. In a non-Romantic sense, I must be prepared to allow the text to interpret me: my questions and my answers to the meaning of existence by its articulation of its own questions and responses. There need be no fear of all "methods" of explanation (historical-critical, literary, social-scientific, structuralist, semiotic, etc.) insofar as they function to develop, correct, or even confront our enveloping and developing understanding of the subject matter disclosed by the text as mediated by the whole tradition.

Second, if these texts are more adequately described as religious classic expressions than as classics of literature, then the peculiarities of religious classics must also become operative. The preunderstanding needed by the interpreter will include the preunderstanding of the strictly existential question (whatever its more particular focus) of the ultimate meaningfulness and truth of my existence as encompassed somehow in the reality of the whole. As religious classics, the claim will be a nonviolent appeal that here is an expression of an event of truth from the side of and by the power of the whole of reality itself. If Jewish, Christian or Islamic, the texts will witness to a faith that the whole is like a who, involved in a self-manifestation in the event or events to which these texts bear witness.

Nor do these principles common to the interpretation of all classics and intensified in the case of religious classics mean that as interpreter I am now robbed of my freedom. This is especially the case for those religious texts whose claim to a self-disclosure by God includes a disclosure of a free, responsible self, a self radically dependent upon the encompassing reality of God, yet at the same time radically disclosed as gifted to be a free self, commanded and enabled to personal responsibility. The dialectic of freedom and receptivity characteristic of all authentic conversation demands the highest use of a critical freedom by the empowered, enabled, elicited self in the conversation with the God disclosed in the event expressed in these texts.

Methods of explanation to develop, correct, confront my understanding of the sense and referent of these texts (historical-critical, literary-critical, social-scientific, structuralist, semiotic methods, etc.) are thereby crucial to understanding how the world of ultimate meaning disclosed *by* the text is produced with relative adequacy *in* the text. In more familiar theological terms, deideologizing and demythologizing are demanded not only by the critical freedom of the interpreter as conversation partner but also by the interpreter's receptivity toward the dialectic internal to the texts themselves. As Bultmann shows with classic sureness, the christological texts demand and perform a demythologizing as a constant reinterpretation of the ultimate existential, religious significance of the eschatological event witnessed to and in the texts themselves.[30]

The same hermeneutical impetus frees and commands the interpreter to note the particular situational focus of one's preunderstanding: to note, above all, its grounding in both a personal life-history and a particular church tradition, its relative adequacy or inadequacy to the disclosure of the full range of questions and responses in both the scriptures and the contemporary situation.

The interpreter of texts should attempt, therefore, to note that the wide spectrum of a more particular focus for these all-pervasive ultimate questions (finitude, mortality, forgiveness, trust, anxiety, oppression, alienation, loyalty, etc.) suggests a complex understanding of the self of the interpreter: a self who is a free and responsible individual, who recognizes the intrinsic relations of that event of individuality to a particular tradition and society, to other selves (interpersonal), to the *structural* realities of society, culture, politics and history; a self whose very selfhood is concretely actual only by the partial determination by, partial freedom from, these encompassing structures; a self internally related to the reality of the cosmos which encompasses all selves, structures and history; and, above all, a self internally related to the reality of the whole now both disclosed and concealed as like a who—a living, empowering and commanding reality, a judging, healing, loving God. Whatever the more particular focus for the driving power of the existential questions are for any single interpreter of these texts, the fuller realities of the social self must be kept in view. Otherwise the disclosures of a particular text (e.g., a prophetic christology) may be misinterpreted as speaking only to the "single one" in solitariness as one faces personal anxiety, loneliness, death, the dizziness of freedom and terror of finitude. Similarly, christological texts which do speak fundamentally to the "single one" (e.g., Paul's Romans) may be brushed aside too quickly as individualist, "introspective," even "bourgeois,"[31] as holding no real interest for the social self related to the structures of emancipation and alienation, liberation and oppression in society and history, nor to the self internally related to the manifestations of an encompassing, a threatened and threatening nature. Relative adequacy to the situation[32] means, after all, what it states: an adequacy appropriate to the complexities of any self, at once individual, historical, social and natural, struggling with the disclosures of a series of yet more complex texts.

The only relatively adequate theological preunderstanding for these religious texts is one which takes seriously my responsibility as a self to all reality: other persons, society, history, cosmos; to the disclosure that it happens in the event itself; to the tradition and community which mediates that event and thereby to the tradition's own internal criteria (apostolicity) for witnesses to the event; to all persons—especially, for the Christian gospel, the outcasts, the forgotten ones, the suffering, the poor, the oppressed.[33] Each is saved only in relationship to all. The concrete is the particular, yet the concrete is not only the particular—my experience, my friends, my community, my tradition. The concrete is the all reached through the particular: all the living and the dead, especially the suffering. If theologians can no longer take seriously these christological texts, especially the prophetic and apocalyptic texts and the symbols, cross and resurrection, which disclose this intrinsic relationship of each to all the living and the dead, above all to the outcasts of all history and every society, perhaps it is because theologians cannot take seriously these "others." Yet then, by Christian and all standards of human decency, we cannot finally take seriously even our precious, protected, private self.

On the level of preunderstanding, therefore, the concrete means both the journey of intensification into the limit-situations (both positive and negative) of my own particularity in a particular life-history and the event-character of the Christ event mediated through a particular tradition and the journey of intensified self-exposure by a never-ending expansion of active concern for all others—especially for those caught in the individual, historical and structural Procrustean bed of oppression, including those who have died and whose memory and hope these texts will not allow to be forgotten. The concrete preunderstanding of every theological interpreter of christology, whatever the urgency of a more particular focus, must strive for the fully concrete—for the all—when confronted in the classical christological texts by the concrete universal of God's self-manifestation in this Crucified and Risen Lord, Jesus the Christ.

The full spectrum of expressions for religious classics must also be allowed their role in any attempt at relative adequacy. At the very least, the full reality of both manifestation and proclamation—of both hearing and seeing, both image and word—must be present. Otherwise, some truncation of the fully disclosive power of these religious classics will be unconsciously endorsed. Proclamation does not eliminate genuine manifestation; manifestation does not ground itself for the Jew or Christian in separation from proclamation. The full range of classic religious expressions must be allowed: prophets, mystics, sages, priests, saints; events of personal disclosure, historical disclosure, disclosure in and of nature; words in various genres—proclamation, narrative, proverb, theological reflection, hymn, ethics, law, confession, symbol, doctrine; images that disclose both the reality and pain of the negative (cross) and symbols which disclose the transformation by the positive (resurrection, incarnation); symbols disclosive of present reality ("realized eschatology"), symbols disclosive of the promised and proleptic reality of a really new future for all history and nature.

From the viewpoint of the theological interpreter, therefore, the full range of concerns in the "situation" must be controlled by some focussed, existential, fundamental religious question into the ultimate meaning of our existence as internally related to an encompassing whole. So too, the full range of secondary classic possibilities in the New Testament texts—of other persons (Paul, Peter, James, Mary); other events (the fall of Jerusalem, the persecutions, the crises of the Gentile mission, the delay of the parousia), all the christological titles (Son of David, Son of God, Servant of God, Lord, Son of Man, Savior, Word of God, Image of God, King) must be controlled by the disclosure of the event of God's ever-present self-manifestation in and through Jesus Christ. For that event is what lives now and is witnessed to in all the classic forms of New Testament witness—preliterary, literary, persons, events, images, titles—codified to different degrees of relative adequacy in these classical Christian texts, these scriptures.

If that kind of existential religious question is brought to a conversation with these texts, if the event-character of the happening of God's self-manifestation in Jesus Christ grounding the witness explicated in these texts is allowed to take hold as the subject matter of these texts, then the sense become a shock of recognition, which for the Christian is called radical "faith," may occur. Whenever faith does occur, and whenever faith finds its own modes of self-expression—in the reflective language of classic systematic theology, in the authentic syle of life of real discipleship, in the imagery, ritual and symbols of artistic and religious self-expression—that same sense of recognition may be articulated with new and sometimes classic force.

In that sense, certain later persons become recognized as paradigmatic persons who witness to a life like that disclosed in Jesus Christ—witnesses, disciples, saints. Certain later events bear their own paradigmatic force—the christocentric word-event of the Protestant Reformation in the theologies of Luther and Calvin; the christocentric image-event of the Catholic Reformation in the art of Raphael, Michelangelo, Bernini and the Spiritual Exercises of Ignatius Loyola. Certain later images of the Christ begin to bear their own paradigmatic power—a Grünewald for Barth, a Chagall for Moltmann, a Rouault for Maritain, an iconic Christ for Solzhenitsyn, an Indian cross for Gutierrez, a tragic apocalyptic visionary for Schweitzer, the creative transformation of the explicit Christ into the implicit and pluralistic ones of modern art for André Malraux and John Cobb. When we look down the famous "well of history" to search for the real Jesus we may, it is true, see only the reflection of our own face (the good liberal Jesus, the revolutionary Jesus, the priestly Jesus, the monastic Jesus, etc.).[34] Yet as all later classic christological reinterpretations of the event of Jesus Christ remind us, we may also see, from the dual focus of our real situational religious fundamental questions and the text's own disclosure of the event of God's self-manifestation in the Jesus Christ remembered by the whole tradition—we may yet see, dimly but really, the real Jesus in this Christ.

Yet we can only hope to see the reality of that event with clarity by also turning from the present experience of the event to the classic, paradigmatic and normative witnesses to the event in the New Testament. There, especially in the Jesus-kerygma of the original witness, we find the first, the authoritative and dangerous memories of Jesus of the first communities. Those memories function as both confirmatory and dangerous as they provoke, elicit, challenge, confront, disclose and transform all later, including present, experiences of the Christ event for the Christian. The scriptures for the Christian are their classic religious expression: a series of relatively adequate witnesses to and memories of an event of God's own self-manifestation where full adequacy, no longer relative, decisively happened, happens and will happen. That event continues in the present of the community and the tradition to interpret Christian experience. That event and its relationship to the dangerous memory of Jesus demands that Christian theologians attempt to hear and see it anew with the risk of new theological interpretations of the classic normative expressions of the event itself in the New Testament.

ii. The Classic Expressions of the New Testament: A Proposal

The basic systematic theological criteria of relative adequacy for a "working canon," therefore, may be described as twofold: an interpretation whose understanding honors in practice the kind of fundamental existential religious questions these texts address, and an interpretation which recognizes that the fundamental disclosure of the text—the world in front of, not behind, all these texts—is the world of a religious event: an event of disclosure and concealment from and by the power of the whole. Both criteria honor the paradigm of authentic conversation demanded for all interpretation of the subject matter disclosed by any classic religious text.

Yet the movement from some preunderstanding to an initial understanding and some later appropriation of the world of the text moves through several possible moments of explanation. Chief among those methods of explanation in the modern period are three: historical-critical methods, social-scientific methods and literary-critical methods. If the earlier arguments on the two principal criteria for interpreting religious texts hold true, then any purely reductive method of explanation (whether social-scientific, historical-critical, literary-critical, structuralist, semiotic, etc.) cannot, in principle, fully interpret the subject matter of these texts. Each and all these methods do interpret the functional character of any religious phenomenon as *also* a cultural, historical, social phenomenon. Each and all these methods will also contribute, often in major ways, to theological interpretation by providing explanations that can and do develop, challenge or even confront a theological interpreter's original understanding of the text. For example, historical-critical methods allow for a reconstruction of the present text into a text either of Jesus (Jeremias' reconstruction of the parabolic texts into the texts of the parables *of Jesus*),[35] or for the reconstruction of the text by way of form criticism into the individual units of the tradition recodified in the present text, or the reconstruction of the text by way of redaction criticism as expressive of the personal theological vision of the implied author of the text, the redactor (as in Marxsen and Perrin on Mark or Conzelmann on Luke).[36]

Insofar as these now familiar historical-critical, especially form-critical and redaction-critical methods, work well, they provide the prospective interpreter with a reconstructed text (the parables of Jesus, the earliest confessions of the apostolic witnesses, the original structure of the Gospel of John, the theological vision informing Mark, Luke, Matthew). They also provide important, indeed irreplaceable analyses of the functional (especially the social-scientific and historical) realities of this religion in its contemporary setting.[37]

Yet insofar as it is also true that all classic religious expressions are not only functional realities but also substantive ones—more exactly classic religious texts are also *sui generis* disclosures to an existential questioner of some event of real disclosure from the whole and by the whole—then these methods of explanation can develop, challenge, even confront theological interpretations. But these methods cannot simply displace an enveloping act of properly religious understanding as an understanding in real conversation with a classic religious expression and its disclosure of the event. Hence, Bultmann, a classic example of both historical-critical and theological interpretation in the modern period, employed not only history-of-religions methods and form-critical methods but also used these explanations to provide either a reconstructed text for new theological interpretation (as in his reconstruction of the gospel of John) or a reconstruction of the present text by way of form-critical analysis of the original units of tradition in our present snyoptic texts (as in his *History of the Synoptic Tradition*), or a history-of-religions-oriented, functional analysis of Christian origins (as in his *Primitive Christianity*).[38] All these analyses freed Bultmann as a theologian to risk an existential-religious, theological interpretation of these now reconstructed texts (as in his interpretation of the theology of John in his classic work *The Theology of the New Testament*).[39]

For Bultmann, as also a theological interpreter, always risked an interpretation of the existential religious meaning of the "scandalous," eschatological kerygmatic event-happening-act of God in Jesus Christ attested to in all these reconstructed texts. For Bultmann, his earlier methods—form criticism, history-of-religions methods, historical-critical methods—served to develop, correct, confront later and contemporary theological interpretations of the text. Yet these methods never finally transformed that existential religious and theological understanding into some purely functional reality. In Bultmann's own language, both our contemporary situation and the text itself demand that the interpreter demythologize; both our contemporary experience of the Christ event in the proclamation of the kerygma and the text itself as a religious, kerygmatic text demand that we do not dekerygmatize the eschatological event of Jesus Christ.[40]

In a similar manner, Norman Perrin, after employing form-critical, redaction-critical and literary-critical methods, also insisted that these explanatory methods develop, correct and challenge theological understanding but not replace it: we also need a religious existential, a theological understanding of the world-event disclosed by these texts.[41] Robert Grant employs a historical-critical method to write *An Historical Introduction to the New Testament* of exemplary clarity and then employs social-scientific methods to explain the social reality of early Christianity, only to remind his readers that these studies and these methods develop, correct, challenge theological interpretations but do not replace them.[42] Where fuller enterprises like these occur, the dialectic of preunderstanding and explanation-understanding occurs to various degrees of relative adequacy: relative to the clarity of the original and initial preunderstanding and the understanding of the existential questions; relative to the suitability and careful application of the method or methods of explanation; relative to the ability to interpret the world of religious meaning disclosed in front of these texts (whether the Jesuanic texts like the parables disclosing the "reign of God" or the Christian texts disclosing the event of God in Jesus Christ); relative to an ability to rearticulate that meaning in accordance with a relatively adequate situational focus (whether Bultmannian existentialist analyses implicitly expanding to social-political religious concerns, or liberation- or political-theology analyses implicitly contracting to the concerns of the solitary individual facing anxiety, repression, guilt, and death).

If the present concern with interpreting the New Testament were exclusively with the functional reality of religion (an entirely appropriate concern), then an interpreter need employ only some method of explanation united to some model of social-scientific or historical-critical inquiry. To be sure, the complexities of the exact relationships between explanation and understanding in any of the social sciences or in history is exacting enough to demand the attention of any lifetime of inquiry. Yet if the prospective interpreter of the New Testament texts also seeks some understanding of the religious (as "substantive," more exactly, existential) meaning of the text, another dialectic of interpretation must also be employed. Then all appropriate methods of explanation should be used to develop, correct, challenge one's understanding of the text, while both initially and ultimately some enveloping existential religious-theological understanding of the *sui generis* religious world disclosed in front of the text remains the major goal of all religious-theological interpretation.

In the latter case, methods of explanation must be tested for their relative adequacy for an appropriately existential understanding of the world of the text. There seem no good reasons to doubt that all the methods mentioned above do develop and often correct and challenge a theological understanding of the text; especially historical-critical methods (and their correlates in social-scientific analyses) have shown their ability to aid, develop, correct theological understanding. They do so principally but not solely through their ability to reconstruct the existing scriptural texts into texts more likely to represent the languages of confession, proclamation and narration of the early Christian communities and redactors.

Even those interpreters like myself who turn to explicitly literary-critical methods to develop the understanding of the meaning of these texts must acknowledge one crucial fact: Usually only after the historical-critical reconstruction of the texts through form criticism and redaction criticism can the methods of literary criticism play a distinct and productive explanatory role in elucidating the sense of the text. On this understanding, one criterion for the relative adequacy of any use of literary-critical methods on these texts is whether that use pays attention to the earlier results of historical-critical reconstructive methods. The text of Mark, for example, has been shown to contain far more textual integrity than most form critics or even earlier redaction critics usually admitted. The redactor of Mark was not merely a collector of earlier units of tradition. Rather, as Norman Perrin, Norman Petersen and, more recently, Frank Kermode show, the Markan redactor was, in a limited but real sense, the creative, implied author of the defamilarizing, puzzling narrative of Mark.[43] Literary-critical approaches to the text of Mark are in fact genuinely disclosive of the sense and, through that sense, the religious world or referent of the strange, secretive and deceptively chaotic and "simple" text of Mark's gospel.[44] When those methods of literary criticism are employed with clear consciousness of the results of earlier form and redaction criticism, the results for theological interpretation can be startling and disclosive: as in Perrin's analysis of Mark as an apocalyptic drama, as in Petersen's analysis of the intrinsic poetics of Mark's narrative, as in Kermode's analysis of the deconstructive genesis of secrecy through and in the narrative of Mark.

In general terms, literary-critical methods (which include, as we saw in chapter 3 their own pluralism of methods and readings)[45] develop, challenge, correct theological understandings of the text by explaining the "sense" of the text in its structure, its form and its creative productivity of the referent: the world of religious and imaginative meaning disclosed by and through the sense of the text. Indeed, once a productive, not merely classificatory or taxonomic nature of genre itself is employed (as, by and large, it is not by more traditional, historical-critical exegetes), then literary-critical analyses of the productive character of the different genres employed in the scriptural texts develop, correct, refine, challenge all understandings of the world as referent from the productive power of the generic senses and structures in the text itself. Hans Frei's recent bold and erudite call for a rediscovery of the "realistic," "history-like" force of the biblical narrative by means of a rediscovery of the nature and necessity of narrative itself in the scriptures may be viewed,[46] on this reading, as one example of the task awaiting theological interpretations informed by literary-critical analyses of the historically reconstructed texts of the New Testament. These New Testament texts are religious classics: responses of both faith and imagination to the classic event of Jesus Christ. If the power of that response and the world it discloses are to be noted, then literary-critical analyses of the immanent structures of the text and their intrinsic relationships to the world in front of the text need far more study than most exegetes or most theologians have yet allowed.[47] An emphasis upon the productive, not taxonomic, role of genre is one step forward now employed by many New Testament interpreters.

In the terms of the criteria explicated earlier in this book—criteria of intensification of both particularity and distanciation whereby the productive role of genre, and impelling it, the productive power of the imagination itself—literary-critical methods can play a central role in the theological understanding of the New Testament. On those terms, it seems obvious that literary-critical methods of explanation of the production of the sense and referent of the text will also serve as partial but real criteria of relative adequacy for the religious and sometimes also literary classics of the New Testament.

By those criteria the present proposal for understanding the religious worlds disclosed by the New Testament texts is not determined exclusively by historical-critical methods. By the use of historical-critical methods, many theologians have interpreted the New Testament in several ways. Some theologians, for example, search for the *earliest* expression in the New Testament, as the canon within the canon, the "gospel" within the scriptures, to judge all later canonical and postcanonical developments. Sometimes this search occurs as another expression of the genetic fallacy: the search for the origin, the earliest expression as by definition the best. More often, this search for a canon within the canon is occasioned by a reformatory Christian religious and theological sense faithful to the tradition's own criterion of apostolicity. A present sense of the ambiguity, including the confusions, errors and distortions in the present tradition, along with a recognition of the tradition's (including the scriptural tradition's) authoritative criterion of apostolicity, impels the theologian to search for some more original norm: first in the scriptures and then, within the scriptures, for the earliest apostolic witness—the Jesus-kerygma historically reconstructed from the text.[48]

Other alternative positions also appeal to historical-critical methods. Some search for some developmental schema that is intended to show on historical grounds either how the last expression (e.g., "emergent Catholicism") is, in effect, the *telos* of the whole "development" (and, thereby, implicitly provides a doctrinal "canon within the canon" leading to later developments like Nicaea and Chalcedon)[49] or how the same last expression is the first (or the second or the third) clue to "where and how it all went wrong."[50]

If, however, the interpreter judges diversity to be a value not a hindrance, then he or she is likely to find the reality of New Testament diversity (from the historically reconstructed original apostolic witness through emergent Catholicism) a blessing, not a curse. If one finds the list of criteria of relative adequacy summarized above plausible, then the theological interpreter is also likely to turn to this actual diversity and try to uncover by a literary-critical method informed by the model of the religious classic a relative adequacy in the whole complex of genres disclosed in the historically reconstructed texts. Then one may find not *the* sole norm but one plausible route for uncovering "a working canon" appropriate to the actual diversity of the classic Christian self-understanding in the scriptures and the whole Christian tradition in its fidelity to the authority of apostolicity and the primary criterion of the event of Jesus Christ as source of all authority.

If the interpreter also notes, within the variety of genres, the unity of the grounding religious event of God's self-manifestation in Jesus Christ as expressed in the Jesus-kerygma of the original witnesses and as reexpressed in the mixture of Jesus-kerygma and Christ-kerygma in the synoptics and the Christ-kerygma of Paul, John and "early Catholicism," then the following proposals may seem at least initially plausible. Let us assume that some major genres of the New Testament are as follows: apocalyptic, proclamation-confession, gospel (especially narrative), symbols-images, reflective theology and doctrine. Within that complex, a further proposal for relative adequacy seems to emerge: The basic unity and diversity of the New Testament expressions may be found not only in the earliest witnesses but in the later witnesses as well through the genres of proclamation-confession to narrative to symbol to reflective thought. The genres "apocalyptic" and the "doctrines" of early Catholicism may be employed as correctives upon this basic complex. Such is the proposal. Let us now examine its elements individually to see if the schema does provide some relative adequacy for a theological interpretation of forms of expression in the texts. In that examination, we will first study two "corrective" genres, apocalyptic and doctrine, before turning to the analysis of the basic compound: proclamation-narrative-symbol-thought.

iii. The Correctives: Apocalyptic and the Doctrines of Early Catholicism

The designation of apocalyptic as a *corrective* genre signalized by principles of intensification and negations need not indicate that this genre is less than a central one for the New Testament.[51] Indeed, apocalyptic serves, in various forms, as a major contextual presupposition of the intertestamental period and of the New Testament itself.[52] Apocalyptic is the genre evoked in times of crisis (for example, in persecution or in facing the destruction of Jerusalem), in recognizing rejection and conflict in history; the genre most frequently employed to articulate the sense of expectancy for the parousia; the genre providing a major context for Jesus' own proclamation of the reign of God and for the important christological title "Son of Man."[53]

By any criteria, therefore, apocalyptic is a central New Testament genre. Whether apocalyptic demands demythologizing into eschatology with Bultmann and Dodd, or compels recognition as "the mother of all Christian theology" with Käsemann, or invites rehabilitation and retrieval through the distinct strategies and interpretations of apocalyptic in the "political theologies" of Metz and Moltmann, the theology of "universal history" of Pannenberg[54] or the prophetic protest and sense for the struggle for historical justice sensed in apocalyptic by the liberation theologians, apocalyptic remains a central New Testament genre. Apocalyptic challenges all present Christian interpretations as starkly as Weiss' earlier rediscovery of apocalyptic first challenged Ritschlians' liberal domestications of the reign of God.[55] I will not presume here to resolve the intense historical-critical debates on the characteristics of New Testament apocalyptic. Rather I will abstract merely one central factor: apocalyptic's challenge and reminder of the explosive intensification and negations needed within all other genres; as a challenge, for example, to any purely "private" understanding of the Christian event by forcing a recognition of the genuinely public, the political and historical character of all Christian self-understanding; as a challenge to all the privileged to remember the privileged status of the oppressed, the poor, the suffering in the scriptures; as a challenge to all the living not to forget the true hope disclosed in these texts of a future from God for all the dead; as a challenge to all wisdom and all principles of order to remember the reality of the pathos of active suffering untransformable by all thought ordering cosmos and ethos; as a challenge to each to remember all; as a challenge to face the reality of the really new, the *novum,* and the future breaking in and confronting every present, exploding every complacency; as a challenge of the sheer intensity of the "pain of the negative" in the cross needed as an intrinsic moment in any adequate theology of incarnation or any present-oriented theology of resurrection; as a challenge to remember the eschatological "not-yet" in every incarnational "always-already" and even every "but-even-now" resurrectional transformation; in sum, apocalyptic may be viewed as a major context and a signal key to the intensification principle itself in all New Testament expressions. Apocalyptic seems better observed in fidelity to the New Testament by allowing its contextual and pervasive role to act not as a central genre but as a central corrective to all other genres through its challenge of intensification, its disclosure of the pain and seriousness of the negative, its challenge towards any claims to more than relative adequacy in the realities of the *novum* and the future in the event of Jesus Christ.

On this reading, apocalyptic is not adequately described as simply the "context" for the New Testament or as merely one of its major genres. Rather apocalyptic pervades the entire Testament: sometimes explosively, in Mark 13, 1 Thessalonians and the Book of Revelation; sometimes transformatively, as the context of Jesus' proclamation of the reign of God in the parables and the ministry narrated in the synoptics; sometimes as disclosive of the cross, as in Mark's Son of Man christology or Paul's theology of the cross; at still other times dimly, as in 2 Peter's somewhat routine yet real reminder of the presence of apocalyptic hopes in the world of "early Catholicism."

If the presence of a principle of intensification which negates all complacency and all claims to adequacy signalizes a major characteristic and contribution of apocalyptic, then the phenomenon known as "early Catholicism" and its major genre of doctrinal confessions discloses an entirely different world.[56] Here the tension seems relaxed, though not spent; the sects, the charismatic communities, have become an ordered institution of the "great church"; the act of proclamation and its disclosure of the sheer "that it happens now" has largely yielded to the content of its confession; the tensions of the narratives of the passion-resurrection, the shock of the proverbs, parables and eschatological sayings of Jesus, the tensive character of the symbols resurrection-cross-incarnation are transformed not into stenosymbols, but into the specificity, explicitness and measured clarity of the genre "doctrine."[57] The tensive logic of superabundance of Paul's theological language yields to the more relaxed analogical language of the Pastoral Epistles.

And yet any fair analysis of the world disclosed by these doctrinal texts of early Catholicism shows that here too the event of God's self-manifestation in Jesus Christ is indeed mediated to the more ordinary reality of the everyday situation in which Christians must also live. Those who despise the ordinary do not do so on inner-Christian grounds. For part of the Christian gospel's disclosure is the "extraordinariness of the ordinary"[58] disclosed on the other side of the extraordinary. This reality may be witnessed with clarity (especially in Luke's gospel) in the table fellowship of Jesus,[59] his appeal in his parables and proverbs to everyday reality, his love of the everyday in contrast to the Baptist—a contrast that earned Jesus' rejection by some as a "glutton and drunkard." That same honoring of the everyday may be found in new forms in the phenomenon of early Catholicism.

That respect is at the heart of the world of early Catholicism and its preferred carriers of meaning to the everyday: through doctrine rendering certain clear, explicit and in that sense ordinary meanings rather than the world of the extraordinary disclosed in tensive symbols; through an ordered institution rather than sect or charismatic community; through analogies which assume and employ but rarely disclose the tensions of the negative within their measured tones, their drive to harmony, even their willingness to compromise on nonessentials in order to clarify and explicate the essentials into doctrines. In one sense these mediating realities—doctrine, analogy, institution—are ordinary, not extraordinary. Yet what they mediate is none other than the same extraordinary *event* of God's self-manifestation in Jesus Christ to and for the ordinary: that the event also happens in the everyday, the stable, the measured, the ordered, the nontensive, nonchaotic world of the ordinary. The worlds disclosed by the texts of early Catholicism may lack the full-fledged and paradigmatic tension of the other New Testament writings. Yet they also serve who only stand and wait in the everyday. They also disclose that same event to and for the everyday by rendering explicit some essential truths into the clarity of doctrine.

Those who feel free to despise these realities should reflect on the crucial difference between the ordinary as "run-of-the-mill" and the ordinary as itself extraordinary and so disclosed by the extraordinary event. So the ordinary seemed, by the gospel accounts (especially Luke), to Jesus. So the ordinary seemed to the world of early Catholicism and its favored genre of confessional doctrines. So the ordinary seems to any Christian consciousness that realizes that the extraordinary event of Jesus Christ discloses that all is grace, that the event happens everywhere, that we can clarify certain essential moments in the event as shared truths or doctrines.

If one grants this interpretation of the genre "doctrine" in early Catholicism, then one may also grant two further conclusions from my present proposal. First, the realities of the world of early Catholicism—

including the classical realities of institution, doctrine, mediation—are genuinely Christian and New Testament disclosures of the same event of Jesus Christ and merit the respect of all who honor that reality. Second, the loss of intensity in these texts—the relaxation, though not elimination, of both the profound negations in the Pauline theology of the cross and the profound affirmations in the Johannine theology of exaltation, the relative loss in doctrine of the tensive character of symbol by its transformation into the more modest, clearer and, in its manner, necessary reality of doctrine, the relative downplaying in doctrine of the apocalyptic and prophetic and their eschatological urgency of the future happening which confronts the present, the relative inability of doctrines to maintain the same kind of tensive character of the narratives of the synoptics—all these losses signal that the confessions and doctrines of early Catholicism are not the primary place to locate the most relatively adequate expression of the New Testament event.[60] Like apocalyptic, though in an exactly opposite sense, doctrine plays a corrective rather than a central constitutive role in the New Testament.

Both these major genres—apocalyptic and the doctrines of early Catholicism—may best serve their roles in a contemporary interpretation of the actual diversity of the New Testament not as *the* truth but as the truth of important correctives. Apocalyptic serves constantly as the corrective of any slackening of eschatological intensity for real history, for the *novum* and the future, any relaxing of the power of the negative and the not-yet in all other genres. Early Catholicism serves as the corrective of any temptation to shirk the ordinary, including the ordinary and necessary human need to find some clarity and explicitness for certain central shared beliefs as doctrines to allow for the human need to find order in thought and some structure in community. The doctrines remind us that every *act* of proclamation involves a content that can be explicated to mediate that event, that every *fides qua* does involve a *fides quae*. The confessions and doctrines remind us as well that sheer intensity without any principles of ordering can lead eventually to a self-destructive chaos, that all immediacy must eventually find some mediation, that the witness of symbol does give rise to the clarifying thought of the doctrines, that the extraordinary, if it is to live, must return to the ordinary and, in that very return, disclose the extraordinariness of the ordinary itself. As correctives, both apocalyptic and doctrine aid every contemporary theological search for a relatively adequate expression of New Testament understanding of Jesus Christ. However, for greater relative adequacy we must turn to a complex of genres that do maintain both intensity and order, both immediacy and mediation, both act and content, both the negative and the positive. In sum, we must turn to the principal proposal of this chapter: that the surest clue to the New Testament world and the event it discloses may be found in the complex of genres named proclamation-narrative-symbol-thought.

iv. Proclamation as Event and Content

As we noted in the preceding chapter, proclamation is a classic religious expression.[61] For the Christian, proclamation is experienced paradigmatically as kerygmatic address: a word of address bearing a stark and disconcerting shock of recognition for the self; a word of address with the claim of a nonviolent appeal to listen and receive its gift and demand; a questioning, provocative, promising and liberating word that the event happens now; a judging, forgiving word.[62] The proper Christian response to this word is called faith: a new self-understanding elicited by the proclamation and eliciting both freedom and a sense of dependence, forgiveness and sin, radical acceptance of the gift and command to the hearer disclosed in the kerygmatic word of address.

The constitutive character of that word as kerygmatic proclamation has led many European interpreters to employ the language of "word-event" to articulate its force.[63] It has led many Anglo-American interpreters to employ the more modest but analogous language of "self-involving performative utterances" in order to locate the kerygma's constitutive and redescriptive-prescriptive power on the language map.[64] Proclamation appeals primarily to a sense of hearing, not vision—as Luther recognized in his insistence that we "must put our eyes in our ears" as well as in his radical innovation whereby preaching itself was recognized as sacrament.

Proclamation as a religious expression is fundamentally act and event and, as event, content. Bultmann's existential recognition of the active character of the kerygmatic word as eschatological event—the recognition *that* it happens—confronting all present self-understanding also becomes Bultmann's attempts to retrieve through an existential interpretation appropriate to its event-character, the nonmythological, theological content of the kerygma. In reading the earliest kerygmatic confessions of the synoptics or in reconstructing them into a still-earlier oral apostolic witness, or in reinterpreting them into contemporary theological language, the interpreter cannot but note that the kerygma is a language of response and witness to a founding event recognized and confessed as the decisive event of the self-disclosure of God. The confessional content of the kerygma is understood *as content,* as confession, only if it is first understood as proclamation-event.[65] Only by recognizing "that it happens" does what happens become disclosed.

The kerygmatic confessions witness to the event itself: texts expressive of a particular community's confession that, in its experience of the Risen Lord who is the Crucified One, the Jesus of Nazareth who lived and preached among us, the decisive event happens now. The *lex credendi* is, from the very beginning, a *lex orandi.* The gift of the spirit of that Lord to the present is also a promise for the future and a disclosure of the true meaning of the past. In the present experience of the proclamation, Christian communities recognize, with Bultmann, that "every moment is the eschatological moment; you must awaken it.''[66] The content of the kerygma is the content constituted by the genre witness or response to an event disclosed in a particular situation.[67] The event is witnessed to, in the proclamation, as giving and commanding a new responding self-understanding by the event's decisive disclosure of the startling nearness of the God of Jesus Christ, to the community, to history and cosmos, to past, present and future. The event of the proclaimed word is experienced as present and is acknowledged in the response of faith of both individual and community to the reality of the presence of the spirit of the Risen Lord in the community from the earliest Jesus-kerygma to the Christ-kerygma of John, Paul and early Catholicism.

Acknowledgment of that word is the response of faith issuing in authentic discipleship and occasioning new confessions in particular situations, new preaching of the same present event. When the *orthopraxis* of discipleship is authentic, the *orthodoxy* of the confessions ring true. In the kerygma, saying the truth does demand doing the truth: more exactly, allowing the event-as-truth to be heard, acknowledged, lived. The route from the acknowledgement in life and preaching of the word-event of God's self-disclosure in Jesus Christ to stating what that event, act, happening of God means in this particular situation is the route to the content of the kerygmatic confessions. The same route expands to include the confessional, kerygmatic element in all other New Testament genres—teaching, ethical exhortation, apologetic, polemics, narratives, hymns, letters, proverbs, doctrines, theological reflections. Yet the New Testament route starts and ends in confession, response, witness, kerygmatic act of proclamation.[68] The narratives of the gospels are confessing narratives written from "faith to faith." Even the cross is not merely recounted as historical event by Paul but confessed as eschatological event. The "ethical teachings" of the New Testament receive their theological center of gravity from the kerygmatic witness to the Christ event that impels them.[69] The later, more content-oriented confessions of "early Catholicism" witness to the explosive impact of the originating *event* of proclamation.

The candidates for the earliest content of the kerygma are several in modern New Testament scholarship: C. H. Dodd's ground-breaking plea for its unified character in *The Apostolic Preaching and Its Development*;[70] Bultmann's disclosure of its many routes through his use of form criticism in *The History of The Synoptic Tradition* and his theological interpretation of the existential- and event-character of the Christ-kerygma in John and Paul in his *Theology of the New Testament;* the redaction critic's reconstruction of the mixture of Jesus-kerygma and Christ-kerygma in the synoptics;[71] the event-character of primal language in the Jesuanic discourse and the claims for a "new hermeneutic" in Fuchs, Ebeling, Funk and Robinson; and the really "new hermeneutic," the reconstructions of the Jesus-kerygma of the original apostolic witness of Marxsen and others.[72] The general diversity of the New Testament now becomes a diversity of *kerygmata*: different responses, witnesses, confessions, proclamations to the same event. The differences of the responses are largely occasioned by the difference in particular situations: distinct focusses for formulating the fundamental, existential, religious questions in distinct cultural, social, historical situations. A myriad of forms appears in the New Testament as the different communities and traditions respond in their situation to that event:[73] "Son of God," for example, will mean different, even conflicting, realities for a Jew or a Gentile; "Son of Man" will mean little if anything to a Gentile but a great deal to any Jew who has appropriated that aspect of the prophetic and the apocalyptic traditions; "Messiah" will bear one meaning for the Jew who recalls Isaiah 53, yet another for others and very little to a Gentile; "Lord" will shift meanings with cultural contexts.

In understanding these kerygmatic titles or designations for Jesus, the explanatory methods of historical-critical and social-scientific analysis are obviously crucial. Indeed these methods have proved their fruitfulness in the works of Hahn and Fuller.[74] In this particular instance of the more general case of all interpretation, these explanatory methods *develop* one's understanding of the kerygma. They do not replace it by reducing it to the particular situation behind the text. In my own terms, these methods show how a particular situation allows for a particular focus to the fundamental religious questions and thereby a particular response to the religious event of disclosure. As in all journeys into particularity, these responses may achieve classic status: some, like the logos tradition, clearly have; others, like the Son of Man christologies, seem retrievable today only by a major effort of interpretation; others, like the pneuma christologies, seem to have flourished among some Jewish Christians only to lead a checkered, conflictual history thereafter, only to resurface again as live options in modern spirit christologies like Walter Kasper's;[75] more than most, the titles "Christ" and "Lord" have shown a remarkable resilience in different cultural situations as different confessional responses emerged throughout Christian history. We cannot fully understand these "titles" unless we explain the meaning they bear in the original cultural situation. And yet any explanation cannot replace the further effort of understanding and appropriating their existential-religious significance for any questioning human being who is open to hearing a word-event of disclosure in all the titles.

We need, therefore, some such criteria as those defended here: an analysis of the kinds of preunderstanding of the fundamental questions which constitute religious questions in any situation; an analysis of the subject matter of these confessions as primarily the event of proclamatory disclosure proper to its religious, here Christian, character; a recognition that when that event encounters a particular situational focus, the response will prove particular yet, if successful as an expression of a Christian response to that event, may well prove classic and thereby ever retrievable through new interpretations; a recognition that on the grounds of the material criterion of apostolicity in the tradition itself, the primary content criterion should be the Jesus-kerygma of the original apostolic witness; a further recognition that the genres employed in particular contexts for the titles by the later redactors can also be judged on literary-critical and hermeneutical grounds in terms of their relative adequacies as forms of expression for the event of Jesus Christ—as here in the study of certain major genres within which the Jesus-kerygma, the mixtures of Jesus-kerygma and Christ-kerygma and the Christ-kerygma occur.

The fundamental unity of the various confessions is twofold: the material unity of the event itself as event and the formal unity of the pattern "particular situation–event–particular response." Yet it is also appropriate to see whether there is some unity of content in the unifying event compelling all these kerygmata. That unity also exists.[76] The diverse New Testament kerygmata from the original apostolic witness of the Jesus-kerygma to the Christ-kerygma of John and Paul confess that the *present* reality of Jesus as the exalted one (as *Kyrios,* Risen Lord, Son of Man, Son of God, Messiah-Christ, etc.) is experienced *now* as the decisive disclosure of who God is and who we are. The same New Testament kerygmata insist that this same presently experienced reality of the exalted one is none other than Jesus of Nazareth who preached, lived, ministered, was crucified and raised by God. There occurs first the proclamation of the risen, exalted Jesus present now: a proclamation which, as provocative word of address, calls for the response of faith, for acceptance of and commitment to none other than the Jesus proclaimed as Christ and Lord. That proclamation discloses, as gift to the present, the realities of presence and promise: the realities of Spirit, "forgiveness," "salvation," "life," union with the Risen One—all grounded in the trust evoked by the event towards the past of Jesus, the present of the Lord to the community, and the future of the world in the exalted one. The kerygmata do not confess the faith *of* Jesus but faith *in* Jesus:[77] the Jesus who was, is and will be Son of Man, Christ, Son of God, Lord. Indeed, there exist good exegetical warrants for the insistence of James D. G. Dunn that "the bedrock of the Christian faith confessed in the New Testament writings, is the unity between the earthly Jesus and the exalted one who is somehow involved in or part of our encounter with God in the here and now."[78] And this unity of an abstract sort seems itself in harmony with the Jesus-kerygma of the original witness and thereby with the tradition's own internal criterion of apostolicity.

These present formulations of the content-unity of the New Testament confessions are, of course, abstractions from the concrete written and preliterary particular confessions of the New Testament itself. Like all abstractions, these formulations enrich our understanding by clarifying and specifying some unity amidst the rich diversity of concrete situational New Testament confessions. Like all abstractions as well, these formulations also impoverish the understanding by not allowing the particular focusses of situation and response to play their concrete and enriching roles. Still, such abstractions do serve to aid the interpreter in acknowledging a real content-unity grounded in the unity of the event witnessed to from the original apostolic witness through early Catholicism. This encourages later interpreters to interpret the particular New Testament confessions with both these factors in mind: the criterion of the original apostolic witness of the historically reconstructed Jesus-kerygma and the further criterion of the unity of content of all the later scriptural witnesses that maintain basic continuity with, even as they develop to greater and lesser degrees of adequacy, the original Jesus-kerygma to the Christ-kerygmata of John, Paul and "emergent Catholicism." With such general and necessary rubrics, later interpreters will attempt new interpretations-responses in relationship to their own particular situations as their questions and expectations are transformed by the same unifying content and the same act of the originating decisive event of proclamation in their present experience of the event happening now. New confessions of personal and communal faith-response are always needed to allow the response to the event to be as disclosive and transformative in the present as "Messiah" was to some Palestinian Jewish Christians, as "Son of God" was to some Hellenistic Jewish Christians, as "Lord" was to some Gentile Christians, as "Logos" was to the Johannine communities.

Yet any reinterpretation for a new contemporary proclamation of that event should also note that there do exist principles for the content, however abstract, in the New Testament itself. Above all, any christological reinterpretation must note that the disclosive reality in a present experience of the Christ event (the experience as mediated principally through the tradition judging itself by the original apostolic and wider scriptural traditions of witness) should provide the central theological clue to new interpretations of the event. A present experience of the event of proclamation, in turn, should and will be checked, confirmed, refined, developed, corrected or even confronted by the basic unity of content in the New Testament kerygmata. The dialectic of present experience and past paradigmatic expression—the dialectic internal to the central affirmations referring to both the person Jesus remembered by the community and the present event of Christ in Jesus Christ—is the dialectic present in the New Testament and the present to guide Christian theological interpretations of the classic Christian event, the event of God's self-manifestation in Jesus Christ.

Proclamation, therefore, exists primarily as word-event from God, secondarily as word of preaching and response by the community and therefore also as word of content in this Jesus as the Exalted One present now in word, sacrament and community, this Jesus Christ the Lord. Proclamation is both act and content. As that genre involving a word of address with a nonviolent, yet provocative, enabling appeal, proclamation is a fundamental genre for the entire New Testament. Proclamation, in fact, is the transformative presupposition of all further genres. The narratives will be proclaiming narratives telling the story of the ministry, life, words, actions, passion and resurrection of this Jesus now confessed as the Christ. The later symbols of transformative manifestation (incarnation and the "signs" of John, the infancy narratives of Luke and Matthew, the nature miracles of the synoptics, the cosmic encompassments of Colossians and Ephesians, the hieratic imagery and ritual of Hebrews, the tensive apocalyptic imagery of Revelation)[79] will, one and all, be understandable only in relationship to their presupposition of the fundamental New Testament proclamation-as-manifestation of Jesus Christ. The stories of who Jesus was, the apocalyptic symbols disclosive of what reality will be for all: All are grounded in the event of a word proclaimed and witnessed to in the earliest genre of the New Testament, proclamation.

The other genres are also needed for relative adequacy. Without them proclamation is ever in danger of becoming either merely abstract content or violent and authoritarian act of address. The narratives are needed to allow the interpreter to understand the kind of life proclaimed as commanded of us. The symbols and images are needed to relate us more fully to the transformative realities of manifestation and to the manifesting event-quality of proclamation itself. Theological reflection is needed to clarify the kind of conceptual language appropriate for a reflective response to this encompassing word-event of real address from God to humankind. Yet if we lose the reality of proclamation, we stand in jeopardy of losing a primary relationship to the event-character of the Christian religious classic, the blunt fact "that it happens" (proclamation as act). If we ignore proclamation we are also in danger of losing the content witnessed to by the earliest apostolic witness and the entire scriptural witness and thus in danger of forgetting that we believe *in* Jesus not on our own but *with* the apostles (proclamation as content).

That event, first disclosed as proclamation and witnessed to in the diverse kerygmata is present in every other genre of the New Testament. Without the actuality of proclamation, the narratives lose their character as confessing narratives and become disclosive but nonkerygmatic stories or quarries for historical reconstruction. Without proclamation, the symbols (cross-resurrection-incarnation) lose their tensive religious reality and become occasions for other kinds of reflection: aesthetic, ethical, historical, metaphysical. Without proclamation, the theologies of John and Paul lose their reality as confessional theologies and become philosophies of religion. Without a sense of the religious event-character of proclamation, the New Testament itself ceases to be a religious classic open to properly theological interpretation and lives on in memory, if at all, as literature.[80] Only with a sense of the religious-event reality named proclamation is the New Testament recognized anew as the Christian classic text, the scripture.

v. Narrative in the Gospels

It is not necessary to decide between proclamation and narrative as *the* primary (too often synonymous with sole or exclusive) New Testament genre. The New Testament includes and demands both. So, it would seem, does human experience.[81] There is something intrinsic in experience which demands narrative. In part, I suspect, narrative alone provides us with some fuller way to order and unify our actual lived experience with its tensions and surprises, its reversals and triumphs, its experience through memory of a past and, through anticipation and hope, of a future in the tensed unity of the ever-vanishing now of the present and its possibly illusory sense of sequence. The stories persons tell disclose their character. The story each person *is* discloses a human possibility that otherwise might go unremarked. The classic stories disclose the meaning of a life lived in the grip of a classic possibility: real tension and struggle, the lived actuality of hope, tragedy, resignation, fulfillment, justice, love. The particular focus of the fundamental questions in the situation often receive far more disclosure from some classic story than from other modes of reflection: the story of how a single human being lived and faced death, as distinct from philosophical reflections upon mortality; a classic story disclosing *hybris* and *nemesis,* as distinct from ethical reflections upon finitude; a classic story disclosing the reality of a Utopian world, as distinct from sociological reflections upon ideologies and utopias.

If stories employed to focus the fundamental questions in the situation are intended only to provide persuasive arguments for some formulation of these questions, then the narratives are, of course, disposable, once we "get" the idea. Then we turn, for example, to Aristotle's *Rhetoric* and compare the persuasive power of these "arguments" with those of a more demonstrative dialectical sort. Yet if the narrative bears its own classic power, Aristotle's *Rhetoric* and its descendants will not prove sufficient. We must turn instead, with Aristotle, to the *Poetics*[82] and its insistence that, for certain expressions, form and matter are indissoluble, that the disclosive and transformative power and meaning of the story are grasped only in and through the narrative itself.

So it seemed in our earlier account of a realized experience of the event-character of the disclosure of truth in and through the form of any classic work of literature. So it also seems we should approach the event-character disclosed in the narratives of the Christian gospel. For the religious event first proclaimed in a confronting and empowering word of address is also recounted in a disclosive and transformative narrative of deliverance. The gospels share the prejudice of life for narrative as a key to lived experience. They share the assumption common to humankind that life itself has the character of a story. The gospels emerge from a response to the event of proclamation that Jesus the crucified Messiah is risen and vindicated by God, only to submerge themselves in the story of this Jesus, the proclaimer of God's reign in word and deed, the crucified and risen one, now experienced and confessed by the community as present to it as the Christ. Where proclamation confronts us directly with its word of address and its powerful appeal to respond to the nearness of God disclosed in the event of Jesus Christ, the gospels prefer to tell the story of this Jesus and allow that narrative's disclosive power to work its event-ful disclosure and transformation of the same truth. The gospels remain, of course, confessed and confessing narratives. And yet they are confessing narratives whose classic religious power is not separable from the narrative form itself. In them the event of proclamation comes to expression as narrative.

The genre "gospel" is a complex genre whose exact nature is still debated.[83] At the least the gospel is a complex structure containing several narratives: the form-critical "miniature gospels" of individual sayings about Jesus or attributed to him which make visible grace and deliverance through typical episodes and anecdotes (victories over Satan, confrontations with those who will not "hear," expressions of self-sacrificial suffering and love);[84] the "parables" interpreted by literary and hermeneutical thinkers as the paradigmatic Jesuanic disclosure of what the "reign of God" is like—it is like what happens in these unsettling and jarring stories where metaphorical disclosure takes narrative form;[85] the narratives of the deeds of Jesus in his ministry—deeds which express in action the coming of God's reign proclaimed in word, his deeds, above all, for the lowly, the poor, the outcast, the oppressed; the strange and convention-shattering narratives of his "table fellowship" with "tax-collecters and sinners," his overturning of the money-changers in the temple, the cry of the respectable that this man is a "glutton and a drunkard," a despiser of the sabbath and tradition, a flouter of decency and social convention, a false and deceptive spirit set loose upon an unsuspecting "rabble."[86] Above all, there remain the key narratives in the gospels, the passion narratives. Martin Kähler no doubt exaggerated the matter when he uttered his famous statement on the Gospel of Mark that the gospel is "a passion narrative with an extended introduction."[87] Yet whatever the exegetical exaggeration in Kähler's words, they bear a mark of existential truth. For in the passion narratives, if anywhere, the heart of the Christian story about Jesus, the main plot, must still be found.[88] What is the nature of a story which in confessing a community's faith in Jesus Christ, the crucified and risen one, chooses to tell the story of the rejection and crucifixion of this Jesus, the proclaimer of the reign of God, now himself proclaimed as Jesus Christ among us?

The passion narratives are set in the context of the proclamation of the presence of God to the community in their experience of the spirit of Christ in the Crucified and Risen One. The story is set, as well, in the context of the larger story of deliverance of the covenanted people, Israel, in the texts now named, by Christians, the "Old Testament."[89] It is not only that a reader cannot understand the concepts—covenant, deliverance, law and prophecy, suffering messiah and apocalyptic hope, promise and fulfillment, wisdom and confession—of the New Testament without the enveloping context of the Old. The story of Jesus confessed and narrated in the gospels find its basic presuppositions, its larger context, in the story of promise and fulfillment, covenant and creation, the chosenness by the God of Israel and Israel's deliverance, in the texts of confession and narrative, law and prophecy, hymn, wisdom and apocalyptic, the realities of both manifestation and proclamation, in the Old Testament.

Whereas in the Old Testament the narrative ranges over the long history of an entire people, the people Israel, in the New Testament the entire weight of the story of deliverance is concentrated upon a single individual, Jesus of Nazareth. Here is a narrative of the ministry and deeds, words, actions, passion and resurrection of a single man who focusses the entire plot of the story and discloses the meaning of all the subplots. Jesus' character in the narrative illuminates all the other characters—the Baptist, Peter, James, Mary, Herod, Pilate and all others. The event of Jesus' death and resurrection discloses the meaning to the Christian community of later events, some recounted, some presupposed in the story of Jesus: the fall of Jerusalem and the desecration of the Temple in 70 A.C.E.; the imminence and the delay of the parousia; the meaning of the Gentile mission and the mission to the people Israel; the suffering, even persecution of the community. Jesus' experienced reality as the Crucified and Risen One now discloses the fuller meaning of his proclamation of the reign of God, his deeds and words of judging, healing reality, his fate of rejection and crucifixion and his ultimate vindication by God in resurrection.

The present reality of the Christ to the community frees Mark to develop a narrative which is like an apocalyptic drama where this Jesus is the apocalyptic Son of Man whose Messianic secret discloses the necessity for a suffering Messiah.[90] The experience of the present reality of Jesus Christ frees Luke and Matthew to develop narratives of this Jesus which serve as distinct "foundation myths" for the later community experiencing and witnessing to his present reality among them.[91] The presence of the narrative form allows even John to prevent his profound theological meditations, his imagery and symbols, from escaping from their intrinsic connection to the person Jesus remembered and confessed as the Logos through a confessing narrative. Luke and Matthew will develop "infancy narratives" disclosive of the manifestation power of the proclaimed and experienced Crucified and Risen One.[92] The form of the passion narrative allows the fundamental symbols of deliverance, both cross *and* resurrection, to play their disclosive and transformative roles by means of a narrative of the passion, death and resurrection of one person, Jesus of Nazareth.[93]

The narratives find different ways to unfold the character of Jesus in the plot of the story.[94] Jesus' strength-in-weakness, his active and redemptive suffering and love are disclosed in the narratives: from the incognito character of the suffering Son of Man in Mark, through the more open yet still reticent visibility of Jesus in Luke and Matthew, to the sheer manifestation in the "lifting up" of the cross of Jesus' heroic stature in John. The authority of the man Jesus in these narratives is startling, both like and unlike that of the prophets:[95] the reign of God is not only proclaimed in parable, proverb and eschatological saying on his own authority but is narrated as happening even now in his deeds;[96] his willingness to flout both social convention and sabbath law where *he* sees fit; his prophetic insistence upon openness to the poor, the oppressed, the sick, the outcast; his signs of manifestation to faith—his exorcisms, cures, miracles; his prayer of intimacy to the Father as "Abba"; his actions like a prophet, yet one who assumes an unprophet-like authority of his own grounded in a shocking intimacy with God.[97]

In these narratives, that reign of God is now recognized as not coercive power but as the sovereignity of *agapic,* other-regarding love from God to all.[98] In the actual Jesus remembered by the community, that agapic love becomes compassion and forgiveness to all who recognize that they need and can accept it—all, especially the outcasts of the "world." That same love can become sheer confrontation and aggressive conflict towards the secure, the self-righteous, the "safe" and respectable ones.

The authority of this remembered Jesus in both his preaching and his deeds is the authority of one who witnesses that the final power is gracious, that the final power *is* love. The narratives insist that a life lived in fidelity to that power is a life like that cruciform life of freedom, conflict, suffering, love, peace, authority confessed as lived by Jesus of Nazareth. Our expectations of God's power are shattered by the preaching of the life and words of Jesus. They are transformed into a recognition that God's power, the ultimate power at work in the universe, is none other than love. Our expectations of life—for happiness, security, comfort, success, justification—shatter against that preaching and that defamiliarizing life: a life lived in fidelity to the agapic power of God, a life meeting rejection and crucifixion from the powers of this world, a life receiving vindication from the final power of God. The community's memory of Jesus remains a dangerous memory endangering it yet.

When we approach these confessing narratives *as narratives,* therefore, with the aid of literary-critical methods, we can begin to sense their fuller religious and existential significance. We sense that significance by studying the dangerous memory of Jesus in the form that best reveals it: the narratives disclosing a person, a life, and thereby disclosing through the narrative form what a human life can be.[99]

These gospel narratives, moreover, maintain the same tensive character of the founding symbols, cross and resurrection, of the original proclamation and of the earlier and the later theologies. The narratives maintain that tension through their frequent strategies of surprise and shock in the intensification procedures of proverb, parable and eschatological saying; in their portrayal of the shocking and authoritative fitness of this Jesus in an anger which is compassion, a weakness which is strength, a love which is judgment. The order of the different narratives return again and again to redisclose its meaning through its form, even in the moments of surprise. The sheer mode of repetition of the same sort of thing over and over again recalls at once the inevitability of the foreseen outcome and the release from chaos by the return to the order of cosmos of true origins with the God of Israel, the covenant and the deliverance, the creation and the end.[100]

These proclamatory narratives, moreover, end in the transformation of the event of resurrection of Jesus—the event of vindication of Jesus by God disclosing the true significance of the cross,[101] while cross and resurrection together show the significance of the whole ministry of deed and word.[102] And still the reader cannot avoid noticing that these narratives do not really seem to end—especially in the parousia-orientation of Mark.[103] Even in Luke-Acts the story goes on into an open future whose reality has already been disclosed proleptically. A tension pervades these narratives between some fulfillment of the eschatological reign of God in the ministry, passion and resurrection of Jesus and the as yet unfulfilled hope for the end time and for all, the living and the dead, in that reign of the Coming God. Above all the negative symbols disclose this not-yet character of the narrative: a story which ends in the incredible paradoxical triumph of cross and resurrection and begins in that ending its movement to history and the cosmos.

The concentration of these gospel narratives upon the single person and proclamation of Jesus in the narratives, and upon the proclamation of Jesus Christ by the whole confessing narrative, concentrates the attention of any individual reader, as such a narrative of a single life must, upon that reader's own individuality as authentic or inauthentic. And yet, the constant presence of the not-yet throughout the gospel narratives reminds the sensitive reader[104] not to transform the radical importance of individual decision into the myopic concern of individualism—even for salvation. The not-yet of the eschatological reign of God proclaimed by Jesus, the not-yet of the future transformation proclaimed in the narrator's confession of Jesus Christ and in the narrative's strange non-end suggest to the Christian that no *one* is fully, concretely saved without a relationship to all; that no Christian can turn this call to radical personal decision and to real and authentic individuality into a compulsive concern with myself and my salvation, into the false security of an already present salvation. The *no* of that not-yet, like the yes of the command to love the neighbor, is a no to all that: an enabling to real, active concern with all others, indeed with all the living and the dead—especially the "privileged" ones of the Christian gospel and the ancient prophets, the unprivileged, the poor, the outcasts, the repressed, the tax-collectors and sinners, the oppressed. Only when that "all" comes will the total hope and radical promise of these narratives be fulfilled. Only then can the story end.[105]

In the time in-between, for the Christian our time, this story and its plot of this Jesus who taught, ministered, was crucified and then raised by God, this Jesus Christ the Lord whom this community experiences and proclaims will be the dangerous, subversive story by means of which Christians try to focus and live out the individual stories of their lives. For a life of Christian discipleship means the opposite of any relaxed security in the reality of what has already happened in Jesus. Rather discipleship is a vision as witness to a life like the life disclosed in this strange story—the life of this Jesus now proclaimed as the crucified and risen one, now confessed, with Paul, as he in whom we live. The prophets and apocalyptic-minded among us are likely to resonate to one temporary end of the story of the crucified one: the frightening, shattering, not-yet cry of Jesus in Matthew and Mark, "My God, my God, why have you forsaken me?" The more "ordinary" Christian—a type which the gospel also honors and to whom it demands that attention must be paid—is more likely to overhear the trusting words of Luke's crucified Jesus, "Father, into your hands I commend my spirit." The contemplatives and mystics and all those who honor the religious manifestations of cosmos from chaos are more likely to turn to the words of John's exalted-as-crucified one, "It is accomplished."

Yet whatever classical route of spirituality any individual Christian takes in trying to live a life like the life of Jesus of Nazareth narrated in the gospels, no one can forget that the story must finally be remembered in its entirety: as a narrative of real negation and real exaltation, of real suffering and active love, as a proclamation and manifestation of the Crucified and Risen One who lived, lives and will live, as an unsettling, disorienting narrative which discloses the judging, healing truth that the final power with which we all must deal is neither the coercive power of this world nor our own tortured memories but the power of that pure, unbounded, compassionate, judging love which *is* the final reality, who *is* God. The Christian story has not ended and will not end until all the living and the dead are touched—how we know not. That story discloses the tense reality of both a real always-already presence and an equally real not-yet. That narrative of Jesus discloses the individual as individual and as related to all.[106] The dangerous gospel story of Jesus of Nazareth disallows *any* assumption that the reality of not-yet is not as real as the always-already presence of God in creation, covenant and Jesus Christ. That story informs and ultimately forms the lived dialectic of an authentically Christian existence into an individual story that is unpredictable through its memory of this dangerous and subversive Jesus of Nazareth.

vi. Symbol and Reflective Thought: The Theologies of Paul and John

Throughout these reflections on New Testament genres the event-character of God's self-manifestation through Jesus Christ is what most needs theological attention. Otherwise both the fundamental religious questions in our situation and the event of disclosure itself in these classic religious expressions will be ignored and eventually displaced by other concerns. The proclamation's questioning, provocative, confronting, healing word of address discloses another possibility of self-understanding recognized in the encounter with the Christ event—as the power *that* it happens. The proclaiming narratives disclose what an authentic life can be by narrating who this Jesus was, the Crucified and Risen One, the one who lived among us, preached God's reign, and acted with the authority of one free from the usual compulsions and illusions, free to love the concrete neighbor in the hard, real sense of a judging, aggressive, compassionate, healing love.

The New Testament and the later Christian tradition also turn to certain tensive symbols and images to disclose the fuller manifestation and power of the proclaimed *that* and the narrative *who* and *what*. Classic among those symbols are three: cross, resurrection and incarnation. Each decisively discloses some major aspects of the event of God's self-manifestation in Jesus Christ. All three form a dialectical unit to reveal the fuller range and meaning of that event. The cross discloses the power, pain, seriousness and scandal of the negative: the conflict, destruction, contradiction, the suffering of love which is the actuality of life. The cross discloses God's power as a love appearing as weakness to the powers of the world. It discloses the rejection incumbent upon the preaching and ministry of Jesus. The cross resonates as well to the great themes of all religious classics: the death of the present self as the way to new life; the stupidity and obtuseness of human beings when confronted by goodness and courage.[107] The cross discloses to the Christian the suffering love of God's own self by its intensified focus on that love as the ultimate, binding, internal relationship of the divine and the human.

The resurrection vindicates, confirms, and transforms that journey in and through its negations of the negations of a suffering love. The resurrection of Jesus by God grounds our hope in a real future for all the living and the dead where pain shall be no more. It discloses the enabling power of that reality as here even now: indeed as the reality that is always already here if we would but note it—the reality of incarnation. Incarnation[108] discloses the reality of the only God there is as here now, as here always, as here in past, present and future, through the decisive self-manifestation of that same God in the cross-resurrection of Jesus Christ. Incarnation fulfills its liberating function only in intrinsic relationship to cross and resurrection. Cross and resurrection live together or not at all. The heart of the Christian symbol system is none other than the unbreakable dialectic of cross-resurrection-incarnation disclosing through its own internal tensions the fuller meanings of the event of Jesus Christ.

These symbols, related to both proclamation and narration, also give rise to thought. More exactly, the symbols give rise to the response of that critical reflective thought named theology. Just as the kerygmatic proclamation is expressed in the responding witness of reflective thought in the earliest confessions, just as the narratives tell their story within the framework of the story of Israel in the Old Testament and the theological frameworks provided by the individual redactors, so too these symbols give rise to thought, to theology. The symbols may lead some theologians to respond through a liturgical theology of the risen and crucified one, imaged as high priest in the heavenly sanctuary of Hebrews. They may lead yet other theologians to articulate a theology of the apocalyptic judge of the living and the dead, as the negator of the lies, delusions, compulsions, oppressions and terror of history itself in the Book of Revelation. Yet before those theologies occurred, and before the more stable, measured, ordered doctrinal and pastoral theologies of the Pastoral Epistles emerged, two major theologies exploded into the thought-world of the New Testament: the tensive dialectical theology of Paul and the meditative thinking of John.

In Paul and John we find theology in its ownmost role. For there we find responses to the power of that event which are responses of modes of thinking at once critically reflective and genuinely participatory. For some persons even their most intense religious experience is so involved in their experience of thinking that the two can barely be distinguished and can never be separated. So it was for Paul and John. For the theologian, after all (and surely John and Paul are *the* theologians of the New Testament),[109] the experience of thinking is so intrinsic to life itself that every experience must also be experienced as thinking and every thought bears all the signs of a lived experience. The power of the event of God's self-disclosure proclaimed in word, manifested in the experience of the Spirit to the Christian community through its sacraments and liturgy, related anew in the confessing narratives of Jesus' ministry, becomes concentrated as well into the reality of religious tensive symbols: the unrelieved tension of the dialectical juxtaposition of cross-resurrection in Paul's proclamatory theology of the Crucified and Risen One ("we preach Jesus Christ and him crucified"), and the transformative manifestation of the cross itself as exaltation-glorification and ultimately radical incarnation, sheer manifestation, in John's theology of the Logos ("and we have seen his glory").

No interpreter need claim of Paul that he possessed a less than "robust" conscience in order to see that the strength of both his faith and his thinking had to find expression in a pattern of thought that was dialectical through and through: a dialectic which hurls the reader about and destroys any escape from facing the contradiction, and at the same time the giftedness, of the shattering reality of the cross of Jesus Christ. Whether "justification by grace through faith" is or is not at the heart of Paul's theology is an important but for the moment a secondary question.[110] It is enough to know that a dialectical theology of justification is present in Paul and is coherent with the dominant strain of his language and thought: a dialectic which, in facing the stark reality of the cross, moves back and forth through dialectical intensity after intensity to the release of recognition of the Crucified as the Risen One, only to return again to face and express anew in yet more intensified dialectical language the thought that cannot be thought through—that the Crucified One is the One who is Risen.

Through every strategy of authentic dialectical thinking, Paul's logic of superabundance[111]—his language of "so much more," "not yet," "as though not"—impels the reader to recognize the undeniable negations in every human existence by seeing them exposed in the light of the unthinkable thought, the cross: the conflicts, delusions, compulsions in every human heart, the conflicts and contradictions in the Christian community, in history, in the cosmos itself, the sin which ravages all. And yet for Paul all the negations are themselves negated in the "so much more" disclosed in the scandal of the cross of the Risen One. That cross ravages sin even now while not yet fully conquering it. Paul will not let loose his grip upon the cross, that burning symbol-event of unrelieved tension and contradiction.

Paul's theology forces the reader again and again to face the "scandal," the "folly" of the cross of Christ: an event where all our lies, fears, anxieties, compulsions, illusions and distortions, our thousand strategies to justify ourselves are decentered and defamiliarized as they are brought to recognize the power of God on the cross as seeming weakness, suffering, forgiveness. Paul's texts will not let loose his grip on his exposure of both our pathetic and our heroic-tragic attempts at self-justification. At the same time the Pauline texts disclose and conceal the reality of a new self in Christ enabled, empowered, commanded, freed to become a transformed self who is even now caught up in that power and lives even now through that gift: a self who must die to all else with the logic of "as though not"; a self who must live even now to that gift and power with the ever-repeated acknowledgement of a radical faith of trustful obedience in the "so much more"; a self involved in the dialectic of a constant decentering self-recognition of the never-ending "not-yet" in every "even now." For Paul, only the shock of recognition evoked by the scandal of the cross reveals the actuality of the "even now" and the reality of the "not yet." The tension, the decentering, defamiliarizing scandal disclosed in that revelation of cross must always be intensified. Only then will the actual individual, *simul iustus et peccator,* recognize its intensified experience of the reality of the power of the gift of the cross as enabling and commanding a faith which works through love. For Paul, all is gift. Yet gift is power and command; gift is the cross. The authentic response of thought to that power, that gift, that contradiction is to find some expression of thought appropriate to the dialectical reality it dares to interpret. Thought itself must learn to express those negations, that tension, that contradiction, that release. In Paul's theology—and here Luther's instincts for the heart of the matter were sure—we find a mode of thinking, a theology, which is finally freed from the usual compulsions to affirm *my* achievements, *my* success, *my* self-justification, and thereby released into the capacity to face the stark, conflictual, contradictory reality of the cross at the heart of reality: the cross as commanding power, enabling gift, amazing grace.[112]

Where Paul proclaims Jesus Christ and him crucified through all the linguistic strategies of a genuinely dialectical thinking, John moves to a form of more meditative thought appropriate to his emphasis on the manifestation of the Logos.[113] In John even the symbol "cross" is so united to the symbols of glorification (exaltation-incarnation) that cross itself now becomes the disclosure of that glorification. In John, the "lifting up" of Jesus upon the cross is both prefigured in John's story of the ministry as the "Book of Signs" (chapters 1–12), only later to be figured forth in the story of the passion and resurrection in the "Book of Glory" (chapters 13–20) to manifest the cross itself as glory.[114] The negative remains the authentic way of humiliation-exaltation. But now the negative negates itself in its manifestation of God's glory in Jesus Christ. That glory shines forth in the "overture" of the prologue and moves on to the "sacred oratorio" of the gospel.[115] The narrative as oratorio unfolds through the "signs" of the miracles and the great discourses interpreting them. The narrative climaxes in the exaltation of the lifting up of the humiliated strong one whose glory, the glory of God, is now fully manifest in exaltation, whose risen, exalted glory manifests, incarnates the very glory and grace of God.

In John thought itself has found a mode of meditative, manifestory expression for this reality of unfolding, encompassing exaltation. The shock of beauty in that glory manifests the need for a meditative, a contemplative mode of thought—a mode common to both the contemplative mystical traditions of releasement and the more ordinary, everyday experiences of the giftedness of God and life itself. That sense of giftedness may, perhaps, be best expressed in icon or in hymn—as in the great overture of the prologue. Yet that same sense, John knows, may also be expressed in the mode of an authentically meditative thought which finds even narrative an occasion for manifestation, even cross an expression of glory. The route to realize that glory is a religious journey that learns to let go through a humiliation which is not weakness but the very strength of the glory of God as love. Love's strength, for John, lies in its ability to let go; to sacrifice itself for the other; to let go into a manifestation of the love of Jesus Christ—the love disclosing God's own self as Love and disclosing the gift of a new self-understanding as a self in love without restriction.

In the theologies of both Paul and John, all is grace. Yet in Paul grace is disclosed as the *power* of the proclaimed word of the cross to confront and expose the radical negativities of each and all—all who are "without excuse," all. In John the grace is disclosed as the gift of manifestation, the glory, of the Word who is Love. That gift will be rejected by many, as Jesus is rejected in the Book of Signs. And yet the gift may also be accepted and re-presented in a life of humiliation-exaltation, a life that manifests that released love. The meditative character of John's thought discloses a kind of thinking that comes upon any thinker as a releasement in the very letting go,[116] as a power not our own, a gift not achieved. The kind of theological thinking most appropriate to John's theology is that kind of meditative reflection upon and in symbols, images, signs which the poet and the mystic know. Here even the narrative itself becomes manifestation in becoming like a sacred oratorio. Even the harsh negative reality of the cross becomes a manifestation of glory and grace. Even the stark contrasts pervading the gospel (light-darkness; truth-falsehood; life-death; faith-unfaith) become contrapuntal themes manifesting the fuller sacramental reality of bread, water, wine, the fuller contemplative meaning in the great discourses, the pervasive, haunting, falling and rising melody of humiliation-exaltation in the entire narrative to produce the ultimate harmony of the oratorio where the cross itself is the lifting up which reveals the release of glory. Throughout John's gospel the reader may listen, as one listens not to words but to music, to a sense of the pure giftedness of love as complete self-giving.[117] And as the reader listens, one also seems to see, as the music yields to an icon of a love that becomes some ultimate manifestation of who God is and who we are called and enabled to be.[118] The theology of John—meditative, contemplative, manifestation-orientated, love-intoxicated—is the kind of thinking of releasement that provides its own "scandal" and its own "folly"—the kind of folly which fools, clowns, mystics, artists and lovers understand.

It is not, however, the case that we find in Paul only the reality of proclamation and in John only the reality of manifestation. John's manifestation is one grounded in the Word, Paul's proclamation finds its ground and its final releasement in his manifestations of what it means to live "in Christ." The texts of the later Pauline "school"—especially Ephesians and Colossians—expand that manifestation power of living "in Christ" to the whole cosmos, a cosmos groaning to be set free.[119] John's manifestations in signs and symbols retain, it is true, only a muted futural not-yet note, in the context of their overwhelmingly realized manifesting character. And yet that strange and provocative product of the Johannine school, the Book of Revelation, employs its own set of jarring manifesting symbols, signs, images disclosing the presence of a shocking, even an apocalyptically intensified manifestation of the reality of the not-yet in the heart of the later Johannine tradition.

Both Paul and John, moreover, provide their own strategies to assure that their thought remains response—critical and reverential response, but finally response to, not replacement of, the event of God's self-manifestation in Jesus Christ.[120] For all their thought and all the symbols—cross, resurrection, incarnation—which impel their thinking are grounded in a response of faith to the event and person of Jesus Christ. Paul's dominant proclamation-orientation leads him to rest content with the pure *that* of Jesus with little concern for the what of Jesus' life and ministry in favor of the eschatological reality of cross and resurrection. And yet Paul's eventlike "that" as the that-it-happens-now grounds his theology and his proclamation in none other than the same Jesus of Nazareth, just as surely as do the narratives of the ministry in the synoptics.

John's dominant manifestation orientation empowering his "high" christology leads him to reexpress the narrative of Jesus' ministry into a series of signs of his glory in a life of humiliation-exaltation of the Logos who is Jesus Christ. John's narrative becomes not so much a story as a verbal icon or a listening through music. Yet John remains grounded in that story and in that person. Unlike the Gnostics, John will not free himself from the fact or even the story of Jesus. John will not allow any opening to the thought that the manifestation of the Word has not become flesh. More than his most natural "ancestors" in the scriptures—the authors of the Wisdom literature of the Old Testament—John finds the manifestations of wisdom itself in the confessing story of this one man: the story which becomes a sign, the proclamation which becomes manifestation, the cross and resurrection-exaltation which become radical incarnation. "In the beginning was the Word and the Word was with God and the Word was God" (John 1:1).

Notes

1. See David Kelsey, *The Uses of Scripture in Recent Theology* (Philadelphia: Fortress, 1975), esp. pp. 14–32, 158–218.

2. For examples in major Protestant theologians of how the scriptures have functioned as "authority," see David Kelsey, ibid., esp. pp. 139–218.

3. For an account of the pluralism of those expressions in the New Testament: see James D. G. Dunn, *Unity and Diversity in the New Testament* (Philadelphia: Westminster, 1977), for a historical-critical account; for an account employing the resources of literary criticism along with historical criticism, see Norman Perrin, *The New Testament: An Introduction* (New York: Harcourt Brace Jovanovich, 1974); for a theological orientation, see Willi Marxsen, *Introduction to the New Testament* [Pt. II Intro./11]. For historical surveys of New Testament criticism, see W. G. Kümmel, *The New Testament: The History of the Investigation of Its Problems* (Nashville: Abingdon, 1972); Stephen Neill, *The Interpretation of the New Testament, 1861–1961* (London: Oxford Univ. Press, 1964); for an account of some concepts employed for New Testament theologies, see Hendrikus Boers, *What Is New Testament Theology?* (Philadelphia: Fortress, 1979); and James Robinson, "The Future of New Testament Theology," *RSR,* 2:1 (1976), 17–23.

4. For analyses of the development of the new interpretations provided by Nicaea and Chalcedon, see Bernard Lonergan, *The Way to Nicaea* (Philadelphia: Westminster, 1977); Aloys Grillmeier, *Christ in Christian Tradition,* Vol. 1, *From the Apostolic Age to Chalcedon* (Atlanta: John Knox, 1975); and Jaroslav Pelikan, *The Emergence of the Catholic Tradition (100–600)* (Chicago: Univ. of Chicago, 1971). For a history-of-religions analysis of the function of christologies in distinct historical and cultural situations, see William Clebsch, *Christianity in European History* (New York: Oxford Univ. Press, 1979). For the nineteenth-century Hegelian tradition, see George Rupp, *Christologies and Cultures* [I/101], pp. 85–161. For a theological analysis of the ethical orientations provided by christologies, see James Gustafson, *Christ and the Moral Life* (New York: Harper & Row, 1968). For an insightful development of ideal types for the understanding of Christ (as "normative," "exclusivist" and "constitutive") see Peter Schineller, "Christ and Church: A Spectrum of Views," *TS* (1976), 545–67.

5. For an analysis of this common insistence, see Willi Marxsen, *The New Testament as the Church's Book* [Pt. II Intro./16].

6. The contrast between Judaism and Christianity on the one side and Islam on the other is striking here. From the Jewish and Christian perspective, the Bible is the authoritative expression of the faith—community in response to the source of authority, the event of God in covenant with the people Israel and in Jesus Christ. In Islam the event *is* the book. The *Quran* (recital) *is* the revelation. Any interpretations of the Quran are, therefore, strictly secondary commentaries on the revelation. Interpretations of the Bible by Jews and Christians are more properly interpretations in the full sense enunciated in chap. 3. Even the key index of

interpretation, namely, translation, is operative here: for the Jewish and Christian communities translations (which are, by definition, interpretations) are crucially important. For the Islamic community, translations of the Quran are secondary to the recital of the original. On Islam, see Fazlur Rahman, *Islam* (Chicago: Univ. of Chicago, 1980); Clifford Geertz, *Islam Observed* (Chicago: Univ. of Chicago, 1968); Marshall Hodgson, *The Venture of Islam,* 3 vols. (Chicago: Univ. of Chicago, 1974). The variety of Islamic traditions and culture is documented in these works to show how a "religion of the book" gives rise, in its own distinct terms, to a remarkable pluralism. In a curious historical irony, Christian fundamentalist doctrines of "inerrancy" seem more faithful to Islamic principles of interpretation than to either Jewish or Christian ones.

7. My reformulation of the thesis of "unity amidst diversity" in James Dunn, *Unity and Diversity in the New Testament* [3], esp. pp. 51–52—a valuable study occasionally marred by some historically improbable reports of the "religious experience" of Jesus and Paul, and by a somewhat curious disparagement of "early Catholicism."

8. On "titles," see Ferdinand Hahn, *The Titles of Jesus in Christology* (London: Lutterworth, 1965); Reginald Fuller, *The Foundations of New Testament Christology* (New York: Scribner, 1965).

9. For a survey of the debates on "realized," "futurist" and "in process of realization" eschatologies, see Norman Perrin, *The Kingdom of God in the Teaching of Jesus* (Philadelphia: Westminster, 1963).

10. This principle is in keeping with the principles for interpretation set forth in chap. 3: a "response" must be both personal and mediated as preunderstanding by the tradition; the tradition is then appropriated *as* tradition and the principles internal to the tradition (namely, the authorities of the apostolic, biblical and conciliar witnesses and the source of authority in the event of Jesus Christ) become operative in a properly *theological* interpretation.

11. For a contemporary example, recall the debate between Hans Küng and Ernst Käsemann; see Hans Küng, "'Early Catholicism' in the New Testament as a Problem in Controversial Theology," in *The Council in Action: Theological Reflections on the Second Vatican Council* (New York: Sheed and Ward, 1963), pp. 233–93; Ernst Käsemann, "The Canon of the New Testament and the Unity of the Church," in *Essays on New Testament Themes* (London: SCM, 1964), pp. 95–107.

12. See Krister Stendahl, "The Apostle Paul and the Introspective Conscience of the West," in *Paul Among Jews and Gentiles* (Philadelphia: Fortress, 1972), pp. 78–92.

13. This is true of Rahner's earlier christological work, yet qualified by his emphasis on the resurrection and greater attention to exegesis in Karl Rahner and Wilhelm Thüsing, *A New Christology* (New York: Crossroad, 1980), and especially in *Foundations of Christian Faith.*

14. John Cobb, *Christ in a Pluralistic Age* [Pt. II Intro./2], pp. 31–97; Van Harvey, *The Historian and the Believer* [II/32], pp. 288–89.

15. See David Kelsey, *The Uses of Scripture* [1], pp. 32–56.

16. For references in Barth, see the discussion in Kelsey [1]; see also Hans Frei, *The Eclipse of Biblical Narrative* (New Haven: Yale Univ. Press, 1974), for the important notion of the "realistic" (in the sense of nineteenth-century realistic novels), "history-like" character of biblical narratives; for Frei's own use of this for christology, see *The Identity of Jesus Christ* (Philadelphia: Fortress, 1975); see also Erich Auerbach, *Mimesis* (New York: Doubleday, 1953), on the realistic and everyday character of biblical narrative, esp. pp. 35–43 for the famous analysis of the "realistic" (and antiheroic) character of the gospel accounts of Peter's denial.

17. Sallie McFague TeSelle, *Speaking in Parables* (Philadelphia: Fortress, 1975); John Dominic Crossan, *In Parables* (New York: Harper & Row, 1973); Robert W. Funk, *Language, Hermeneutic, and Word of God* (New York: Harper & Row, 1966); Dan O. Via, *The Parables* (Philadelphia: Fortress, 1967). For some later work, see John Dominic Crossan, *Cliffs of Fall: Paradox and Polyvalence in the Parables of Jesus* (New York: Seabury, 1980); Robert Funk, *Jesus as Precursor* (Philadelphia: Fortress, 1975).

18. Norman Perrin, "Jesus and the Theology of the New Testament," forthcoming in special Perrin memorial issue of *JR*.

19. Johann Baptist Metz, *Faith in History and Society* [II/35], pp. 205–19.

20. For an informed summary and discussion of recent scholarship, see Richard McBrien, *Catholicism* [I/89], pp. 565–603; Paul Minear, *Images of the Church in the New Testament* (Philadelphia: Westminster, 1960); Eduard Schweizer, *Church Order in the New Testament* (London: SCM, 1961); Myles M. Bourke, "Reflections on Church Order in the New Testament," *Catholic Biblical Quarterly* 30 (1968), 493–511; Raymond Brown, "The Unity and Diversity in New Testament Ecclesiology," in *New Testament Essays* (London: Chapman, 1965), pp. 36–47; Ernst Käsemann, "Unity and Multiplicity in the New Testament Doctrine of the Church," in *New Testament Questions of Today* (London: SCM, 1969), chap. 13.

21. The most impressive recent attempt is Edward Schillebeeckx in *Jesus: An Experiment in Christology* [Pt. II Intro./8], esp. pp. 105–272. Schillebeeckx's more nuanced position on the "historical Jesus" (pp. 62–77) is perhaps occasioned by his explicit use throughout this magisterial work in both exegesis and theology of sociocritical and faith-praxis criteria along with more familiar historical-critical methods. The result, for this reader, is that the "historical Jesus" is in fact employed as a "dangerous memory" (i.e., principally as a Jesus-kerygma from "Q"), a memory informed at least as much by Schillebeeckx's own theological use of sociocritical and faith-praxis criteria as by his use of historical-critical results on the "historical Jesus."

22. For the importance of these "classic events," see Norman Perrin, *The New Testament* [3], pp. 39–65.

23. See, for example, James Robinson and Helmut Koester, *Trajectories through Early Christianity* (Philadelphia: Fortress, 1961); Stephen Neill, *Jesus Through Many Eyes: Introduction to the Theology of the New Testament* (London: Lutterworth, 1976); John Macquarrie, *Christian Unity and Christian Diversity* (London: SCM, 1975); Howard Clark Kee, *Jesus in History: An Approach to the Study of the Gospels* (New York: Harcourt Brace Jovanovich, 1977); Patrick Henry, *New Directions in New Testament Study* (Philadelphia: Westminster, 1979).

24. Recall the earlier (chap. 3) discussion of the role of preunderstanding in interpretation.

25. Johann Baptist Metz, *Faith in History and Society* [II/35], esp. pp. 169–84.

26. For the relationship to Bultmann's "individualism," see Dorothee Soelle, *Political Theology* [V/52]; for the "religious dimension" of politics itself, see Langdon Gilkey, *Reaping the Whirlwind* [II/2], pp. 3–117.

27. The trajectory from Paul to Mark is most familiar in the Bultmannian tradition: e.g., in Norman Perrin, "Towards the Interpretation of the Gospel of Mark," in *Christology and a Modern Pilgrimage: A Discussion with Norman Perrin*, ed. H. D. Betz (Claremont: New Testament Colloquium, 1971), pp. 1–78; and in Willi Marxsen's shift from the Christ-kerygma of Bultmann's Paul to the Jesus-kerygma of the original witnesses (i.e., Q and the earliest stratum of Mark): inter alia, *Mark the Evangelist* (Nashville: Abingdon, 1969). A helpful survey of recent Markan scholarship from Bultmann and Dibelius through redaction critics Marxsen and

Perrin to more recent developments is Jack Dean Kingsbury, "The Gospel of Mark in Recent Research," *RSR* (1979), 101–7. See also the challenge to the priority of "Mark" and "Q" in the work of William Farmer: inter alia, *The Synoptic Problem: A Critical Analysis* (Dillsboro: Western North Carolina Press, 1976). Although it is clear that I follow those exegetes who hold to the priority of Mark and Q, the work of Farmer (and others) to restore the "Griesbach hypothesis" reminds us all that there is still no completely satisfactory solution to the synoptic problem. The majority consensus on Mark and Q remains, however, the option followed here.

28. Kelsey, *The Uses of Scripture* [1], esp. pp. 160–69; Kelsey's notion of "discrimen" is basically analogous to my earlier hermeneutical use of the concept of a horizon of preunderstanding with which the interpreter enters into conversation with the fundamental questions and responses (the "subject matter") of the text.

29. The use of the expressions "working canon" and "criteria of relative adequacy" are intended to indicate an abandonment of a search for "a canon within the canon" in favor of the full diversity of the New Testament witness—which, as both diverse and unified, can accord to the Jesus-kerygma of the earliest apostolic witness the primary role of checking, but not of replacing or controlling, the mixtures of Jesus-kerygma and Christ-kerygma in the synoptics and the Christ-kerygma of John, Paul and emergent Catholicism. *All* are witnesses. All meet the need for diverse and unified expressions of the Christ event. All intend (and, are, therefore, open to testing for) continuity with the earliest Jesus-kerygma. Yet to concentrate *only* on the latter (as the expression "canon within the canon" seems to suggest) risks losing the enriching diversity of the whole scriptural (and, in principle, postscriptural) witness and thereby risks losing the full reality of "tradition" for the contemporary theological horizon. Hence my use of the term "a working canon" and my attempted development of criteria of relative adequacy for diverse forms of expression of the kerygma. This principle becomes especially important for incorporating the narratives of Jesus into the contemporary ecclesial and christological consciousness. A relatively adequate contemporary christology demands, on this reading, a fidelity to the whole range of expressions: both the Jesus-kerygma and the confessing narratives on the ministry, message and fate of Jesus; both cross-resurrection and incarnation; both symbol and doctrine. Nor does this suggest that the genuine diversity of New Testament expressions for christology becomes a criteria-less pluralism. Rather, as the New Testament itself suggests, there is real diversity yet real limits as well—as the rejection in the New Testament of Ebionites, Docetists and Gnostics witness. Hence, one need not fear a "rubber ruler" by abandoning a single "canon within the canon" in favor of a working canon faithful to the pluralism and limits of the original apostolic witness and to the whole range of witnessing forms of expression in the New Testament.

30. For the classic statements here, see Rudolf Bultmann, *Jesus Christ and Mythology* (New York: Scribner, 1958); and for the classic use, idem, *Theology of the New Testament* [II/6].

31. For an example of exegesis sensitive to the prophetic-social but insensitive to alternative interpretations emphasizing the dilemmas of the solitary individual, see José Miranda, *The Bible and Marx* (Maryknoll: Orbis, 1977).

32. See the fuller discussion in chap. 8.

33. A point emphasized in political and liberation theologies; the latter, especially, attempt to read the gospel "through the eyes of the oppressed." Claims for a "hermeneutical privilege" here, however, seem confused: the real privileged status of the oppressed in the gospel is not equivalent to a *hermeneutical* privilege of interpretation. The "liberation hermeneutics" are needed in the wider conver-

sation of *all* interpreters—as fellow conversation partners with the text addressed *to all.*

34. See here the fine analysis of Hans Küng in "Which Christ?" in *On Being a Christian* [I/96], pp. 126–45.

35. Joachim Jeremias, *The Parables of Jesus* (New York: Scribner, 1963). Note how later exegetes like Norman Perrin will use literary-critical criteria on the historically reconstructed parables (as parables *of* Jesus): e.g., "The Parables of Jesus as Parables, as Metaphors and as Aesthetic Objects," *JR* 50 (1970), 340–46. By way of contrast, see the nonhistorically reconstructed text study of Louis Marin in "Essai d'analyse structurale d'un récit-parabole: Matthieu 13, 1–23," *Etudes Théologiques et Réligieuses* 46 (1971), 35–74.

36. Marxsen and Perrin [27]; Hans Conzelmann, *The Theology of St. Luke* (New York: Harper & Row, 1960).

37. For two examples of the use of social-scientific theories, see Gerd Theissen, *Sociology of Early Palestinian Christianity* (Philadelphia: Fortress, 1977); and John Gager, *Kingdom and Community: The Social World of Early Christianity* (Englewood Cliffs: Prentice-Hall, 1975). For an example of the use of historical methods, not sociological theories, to establish "social facts," see Robert Grant, *Early Christianity and Society* (New York: Harper & Row, 1977). One of the most ambitious and promising projects in recent American scholarship is the attempt to understand the "social world" of early Christianity: for a careful review of the literature, problems, relevant distinctions and possibilities, see Jonathan Z. Smith, "The Social Description of Early Christianity," *RSR* (1975), 19–25.

38. For Bultmann, besides the works already cited, see "Is Exegesis without Presuppositions Possible?" in *Existence and Faith* [II/10], pp. 289–97; "The Problem of Hermeneutics" in *Essays, Philosophical and Theological* (New York: Macmillan, 1955), pp. 234–62; *The Gospel of John: A Commentary* (Oxford: Blackwell, 1971); *The History of the Synoptic Tradition* (New York: Harper & Row, 1968); *Primitive Christianity in Its Contemporary Setting* (New York: Meridian, 1956).

39. *Theology of the New Testament,* II, 33–95.

40. For interpretations of Bultmann here, see Schubert Ogden, *Christ Without Myth* (New York: Harper & Row, 1961); and Norman Perrin, *The Promise of Bultmann* (Philadelphia: Lippincott, 1969).

41. Introduction, pp. 17–39.

42. Robert M. Grant, *A Historical Introduction to the New Testament* (London: Collins, 1963); *Early Christianity and Society* [37]. Grant's masterful clarity and scholarly exactness may also be noted in: *The Bible in the Church: A Short History of Interpretation* (New York: Macmillan, 1948); *Gnosticism and Early Christianity* (New York: Harper, 1966); *The Formation of the New Testament* [Pt. II Intro./16].

43. Norman Perrin, "Towards the Interpretation of the Gospel of Mark" [27]; Norman Petersen, *Literary Criticism for New Testament Critics* (Philadelphia: Fortress, 1978), pp. 49–81; Frank Kermode, *The Genesis of Secrecy: On the Interpretation of Narrative* (Cambridge: Harvard Univ. Press, 1979).

44. Kermode's analysis of "secrecy" in the Markan narratives is notably helpful here.

45. See chap. 3, sec. iii.

46. Hans Frei, *The Eclipse of Biblical Narrative* [16]. The recent work on narrative (including narrative in the biblical texts) of Paul Ricoeur is relevant here. Before the publication of his forthcoming book on the issues of narrative theory, see his article from the Chicago "narrative conference" (1979) published in *Critical Inquiry*. The papers from this conference (including papers by Jacques Derrida, Frank Kermode, Hayden White, Nelson Goodman, Roy Schafer and

several others) are a valuable source for many of the major participants in the present debates on narrative theory: see *Critical Inquiry* 7 (Autumn, 1980).

47. See William A. Beardslee, *Literary Criticism of the New Testament* (Philadelphia: Fortress, 1970); and Amos Wilder, *The Language of the Gospel: Early Christian Rhetoric* (New York: Harper & Row, 1964).

48. See the discussions of Marxsen and Ogden cited above [Pt. II Intro./16].

49. Even the extraordinary accomplishment of Aloys Grillmeier, *Christ in Christian Tradition* [3], is occasionally marred by the employment of what seems to be a "telos" developmental paradigm sometimes used retrospectively to schematize New Testament developments. The failure of Jean Galot to understand the New Testament-based christologies of Hans Küng and Edward Schillebeeckx among others (including the present author) may be occasioned by this difficulty. Galot employs an authoritative source (Chalcedon) anachronistically to judge contemporary christological discussion employing the results of scriptural scholarship and analyses of the contemporary situation: see Jean Galot, *Cristo contestato: Le cristologie non Calcedoniane e la fede cristologica* (Florence: Libreria Editrice Fiorentina, 1979). In Galot's case (unlike Grillmeier's) the polemical debating spirit and use of neo-Scholastic inference rather than contemporary interpretation do not encourage a reader to believe that here one may find an interpretation modelled on conversation rather than on mere controversy. For Galot, it seems, any theologian who does not follow his christological method ends up explicitly or implicitly "abandoning" (i.e., by neo-Scholastic inference) the affirmation of the divinity of Christ, the Trinity and full redemption (pp. 91–96). Such "interpretations" are what occur when interpretation on the model of conversation is "abandoned" for an ahistorical model of neo-Scholastic controversy.

50. Recall Käsemann's interpretation of "early Catholicism" in "An Apologia for Primitive Christian Eschatology," in *Essays on New Testament Themes* [11], chap. 8; and his later theological reflections on the phenomenon in "Paul and Early Catholicism," in *New Testament Questions of Today* [20]. The post-Bultmannian tradition on this particular theological issue is rarely genuinely *post*-Bultmannian.

51. For a valuable historical-critical analysis of the genre of apocalyptic, see John Collins, *Apocalyptic As Genre* (Missoula: Semeia, 1978). For relevant New Testament historical-critical work, see Ernst Käsemann, "The Beginnings of Christian Theology" and "On the Subject of Primitive Christian Apocalyptic," in *New Testament Questions of Today,* chaps. 4 and 5; Klaus Koch, *The Rediscovery of Apocalyptic* (London: SCM, 1972); Robert Funk, ed., *Apocalypticism* (New York: Herder & Herder, 1969); D. S. Russell, *The Method and Message of Jewish Apocalyptic* (London: SCM, 1964). For distinct theological accounts, see Jürgen Moltmann, *Theology of Hope* [IV/8]; Wolfhart Pannenberg, *Revelation as History* [IV/78]; and Johann Baptist Metz, *Faith in History and Society* [II/35]. For relevant literary-critical analyses, see Amos Wilder, *The Language of the Gospel* [47], pp. 118–28; idem, "The Rhetoric of Ancient and Modern Apocalyptic," *Interpretation* 25 (1971), 436–53; William Beardslee, *Literary Criticism of the New Testament* [47], pp. 53–63. For an excellent historical study of apocalypticism, see the introduction (pp. 1–37) by Bernard McGinn in *Visions of the End: Apocalyptic Traditions in the Middle Ages* (New York: Columbia Univ. Press, 1979). Readers may note that my present analysis makes no claims to resolving the extraordinary complexity of historical-critical debates on the nature of apocalyptic (and its relationships to the genres prophecy, wisdom, etc.). My limited focus is on the *language* operative in the "apocalyptic" language of the New Testament: viz., the presence of negations and the not-yet embedded in that language usage as hermeneutically retrievable whatever the outcome of the important historical-critical

debates on the role(s) and kinds of apocalyptic in the New Testament period. In that sense, my analysis is a theological hermeneutics more in harmony with the interpretation of Metz and Moltmann than with the analyses of either Bultmann or Pannenberg.

52. See especially the work of Käsemann cited in n. 51.

53. Perrin, *The New Testament* [3], esp. pp. 65–87 on apocalyptic; pp. 42–51 and passim on "Son of Man."

54. The conflicts among contemporary theological uses of "apocalyptic" bear commentary: Bultmann demythologized "apocalyptic" into an existentialist theological eschatology (for one example of the latter see *History and Eschatology* [Edinburgh: Edinburgh Univ. Press, 1957]. In the post-von Rad and the post-Käsemann exegetical situation, many different theological retrievals of "apocalyptic" have been attempted. In the contemporary context, the works of Pannenberg, Moltmann and Metz [51] are notable. However, the conflict of interpretation among these three theologians remains sharp: all three employ apocalyptic to deindividualize the eschatological understandings of earlier theology (especially Bultmann); yet Moltmann and Metz develop a basically left-wing Hegelian interpretation of apocalyptic to show the not-yet, the radical nonidentity of reason and rationality that apocalyptic discloses, in direct contrast to Pannenberg for whom apocalyptic seems both "reasonable" and, as proleptic of the end, far more positive. Readers will notice that my own theological use of the genre of apocalyptic agrees far more with those of Metz and Moltmann in its emphasis on the negations of present reality in apocalyptic genres and with all three on the nonindividualized (i.e., the sense of history) and nonmythological retrievability of apocalyptic.

55. The *locus classicus* here, which despite its inevitably dated biblical scholarship still retains its theological force, is Albert Schweitzer, *The Quest of the Historical Jesus* (New York: Macmillan, 1964).

56. For some of the relevant exegetical literature here, see the work of Ernst Käsemann [50]; Hans Küng, *Structures of the Church* (London: Burns and Oates, 1965), pp. 135–51; J. H. Elliott, "A Catholic Gospel: Reflections on 'Early Catholicism' in the New Testament," *The Catholic Biblical Quarterly* 31 (1969), 213–33. I emphasize in my interpretation the notion of "doctrine" as a genre (or the *content* of the kerygmatic confessions in "early Catholicism"). For the other side of the phenonemon (viz., the social reality of "institution"), see Ernst Troeltsch, *The Social Teaching of the Christian Churches* (London: Allen & Unwin, 1931), pp. 89–200.

57. An appreciation of "doctrine" as a genre seems to suffer from one of two mutually exclusive difficulties. The first difficulty is an overestimation of "doctrine"—a familiar position which seems to hold that doctrine's "explicitness" and "clarity" renders unnecessary any further concern with the concrete symbolic language upon which "doctrine" reflects. This overestimation is sometimes united to a philosophical notion of "concept" whereby (as in Hegel) *Begriff* fully sublates *Vorstellung*. The same kind of overestimation is more often related to the dogmatic linguistic presupposition that the clarity of "doctrine" adequately paraphrases (rather than interprets important aspects of) the originating religious symbolic and metaphorical language—a position in dogmatic theologies analogous to the use of the "heresy of paraphrase" in literary criticism. The second difficulty is the exact opposite: the assumption that "doctrine" is either an abstract, spent or impoverished genre (compared to the concreteness of symbolic and poetic expression), or the assumption that a community does not need any explicitness or clarity to express its shared judgments on matters of belief. Doctrine *is* an abstrac-

tion from the concreteness of symbolic, metaphoric, poetic language. Yet this abstraction, like all abstractions, can be enriching by producing some needed explicitness and clarity for the community's self-understanding. At the same time, doctrines, as abstract, are relatively less adequate as expression than the originating metaphorical or symbolic language. This insight suggests why those contemporary christologies which begin with the scriptural rather than the conciliar statements are not only correct on the inner-theological grounds of the normative role of scripture but correct on hermeneutical grounds as well. The scriptural expressions (other than doctrinal or confessional expressions) are relatively more adequate *as expressions* to the event of Jesus Christ itself. A recognition of the greater adequacy of symbol over doctrine, however, should not occasion the rejection of other modes of expression (including the doctrinal) by turning into a monism of "symbol": see, for example, the cautionary critique of exaggerated claims for "symbol" in Michael Buckley, "On Being a Symbol: An Appraisal of Karl Rahner," *TS* (1979), 453–74. There is a need for more work on doctrine as a genre along the lines suggested above. In the meantime, the genre "doctrine" exists not only in the New Testament itself—as a crucial "corrective" genre to refine, formulate, clarify, explicate certain central beliefs of the Christian community from the Jesus-kerygma through the "doctrines" of early Catholicism. For a Catholic theological analysis of the relationships betwen kerygma and doctrine, see Karl Rahner and Karl Lehmann, *Kerygma and Dogma* (New York: Herder & Herder, 1969).

58. For the contemporary theological discussion, see chap. 9, sec. ii.

59. For a good analysis of that reality, see Edward Schillebeeckx, *Jesus* [Pt. II Intro./8], pp. 200–229.

60. Yet one cannot but note how doctrine can be retrieved in extraordinarily disclosive and transformative ways. Note, for example, the theology of Karl Rahner—a fact appreciated by J. B. Metz (who prefers the genre "narrative") in his fitting tribute to Rahner's hermeneutical accomplishment (*Faith in History and Society* [II/35], pp. 219–29).

61. Note chap. 4, sec. iii.

62. See Rudolf Bultmann: inter alia, *Theology of the New Testament* [II/6], I, 238–41, 307–8; and *Jesus Christ and Mythology* [30]. As a genre, proclamation expresses the sheer power or force of a word of address that confronts the reader with a defamiliarizing demand. The Reformed model of the "sermon" has been especially influential in Bultmannian and post-Bultmannian circles.

63. Inter alia, see Gerhard Ebeling, *Theology and Proclamation* (Philadelphia: Fortress, 1966); Robert Funk, *Language, Hermeneutic and Word of God* [17].

64. David Kelsey, *The Uses of Scripture* [1], pp. 56–88; Donald Evans, *The Logic of Self-Involvement* (London: SCM, 1963).

65. The emphasis here, supported by the New Testament use of kerygma for preaching, is on the performative force of the word of address: the contrary to that of the genre "doctrine" or "confession" (or kerygmata as confessions) in our former discussion. In literary-critical terms, kerygma as preaching appeals to the power of a confrontational word of address (analogous, for example, to the effects of Brecht's alienation techniques or German expressionist painting and literature, which bear, in fact, startling literary resemblances to the Bultmannian language for kerygmatic address or the language of address in Barth's *Romans*). Doctrine appeals to the need for the clarification and explication of content and the mediation of the event to and in the ordinary (analogous, for example, to "realist" literature rather than to the literature of extremity, or analogous to "realist" or even impressionist as distinct from expressionist painting).

66. *History and Eschatology* [54], p. 155.

67. Arrived at methodologically through form-critical method. For the latter, see Edgar V. McKnight, *What Is Form Criticism?* (Philadelphia: Fortress, 1969).

68. It is the recognition that the entire New Testament is a record of witness to the event that renders "the quest for the historical Jesus" difficult (not impossible) on general historical-critical grounds. As mentioned earlier, it is the same theological recognition of the authoritative role of the apostolic-biblical witnesses to the Christ event for the whole tradition that renders that "quest" theologically inappropriate.

69. For an example, see Victor Furnish, *The Love Command in the New Testament* (Nashville: Abingdon, 1972).

70. London: Hodder & Stoughton, 1936. Dodd's emphasis is, of course, on the content of "the kerygma"; he also emphasizes narration over kerygma (unlike Bultmann).

71. On redaction criticism, see Norman Perrin, *What Is Redaction Criticism?* (Philadelphia: Fortress, 1969). For example, see the work of Perrin on Mark [27] or Conzelmann on Luke [36].

72. See references on the "new hermeneutic" cited above and Paul J. Achtemeier, *An Introduction to the New Hermeneutic* (Philadelphia: Westminster, 1969).

73. Inter alia, see here Perrin, *The New Testament* [3], pp. 39–61; James Dunn, *Unity and Diversity* [3], pp. 33–52; Reginald Fuller, *The Foundations of New Testament Christology* [8].

74. The references to Hahn and Fuller are cited above [8].

75. Walter Kasper, *Jesus the Christ* (New York: Paulist, 1976).

76. See James Dunn, *Unity and Diversity* [3], esp. pp. 11–32.

77. By way of contrast, see the representative use of the "faith of Jesus" in James Mackey, *Jesus the Man and the Myth* (New York: Paulist, 1979), esp. pp. 159–71. Mackey's powerful and clarifying work here is weakened by his attempt to build a theological case on the weakest historical link of all—a historical-critical retrieval of the "faith of Jesus." Yet his case is made with such clarity that it is a better candidate for this familiar position than less clear statements of the same kind of position (e.g., Jon Sobrino). Mackey's major concerns in this book and his prior one (*The Problems of Religious Faith* [Dublin: Helicon, 1972], esp. pp. 111–213) seem to deal more with problems of understandability for contemporary historically conscious persons than with problems of appropriateness to the scriptures. Those concerns are, to be sure, real. Yet to render them through the weakest link of all (the "faith of Jesus" as distinct from the more usual "message, ministry and fate of Jesus") is strange. For an example of a thinker who shares Mackey's concern for understandability (under the rubric of an "ethics of belief") without getting trapped in theologically inappropriate and historically unlikely searches for "the faith of Jesus," see Van Harvey, *The Historian and the Believer* [II/32], and "Christology for Barabbases" [Pt. II Intro./6]. The theological point is that we are asked by Christianity to have faith *in* Jesus, not in so unpromising a phenomenon as the historically reconstructed "faith *of* Jesus."

78. Dunn, *Unity* [3], p. 57.

79. On the function of the "signs" in John, see Raymond Brown's encyclopedic scholarly commentary, *The Gospel According to John,* I (New York: Doubleday, 1966); idem, for a brilliant exegetical retrieval of the theologies of the infancy narratives in *The Birth of the Messiah* (New York: Doubleday, 1977); on Colossians, see C. F. D. Moule in *Peake's Commentary on the Bible* (London: Thomas Nelson & Sons, 1962), pp. 990–95; on Hebrews, see Myles M. Bourke in *The*

Jerome Biblical Commentary (Englewood Cliffs: Prentice-Hall, 1968), pp. 381–402; on the Book of Revelation, see Dunn, *Unity*, pp. 331–34.

80. See the discussion of "the Bible as Literature" in Amos Wilder, *The Language of the Gospel* [47], pp. xii–xxi.

81. For an influential study here, see the essay by Stephen Crites, "The Narrative Quality of Experience," *JAAR* (1971), 290–307. An important bibliographical survey of the different uses of narrative in theology may be found in George Stroup, III, "A Bibliographical Critique," *TT* (1975), 133–44. See also, R. Scholes and R. Kellogg, *The Nature of Narrative* (New York: Oxford Univ. Press, 1966). For a formalist analysis of the resonances between narrative structural elements (character, plot, tone, etc.) and religious concerns (otherness, wholeness, etc.) see Wesley Kort, *Narrative Elements and Religious Meanings* (Philadelphia: Fortress, 1975). As the reader will note, I do not develop narrative theory here but simply employ some basic notions on narrative for the limited purposes of the present analysis. The recent explosion of interest in narrative as a genre in both literary criticism and theology promises to make this the most fruitful genre study for New Testament concerns. In fact, all the conflicts we noted in chap. 3 among literary critics over explanatory methods for genre analysis return in force in the study of narrative. Note, for example, the hermeneutics of suspicion of narrative in the deconstructionist-like essay of Hayden White; the hermeneutical retrieval of narrative with an accounting of semiotic and structuralist methods in the forthcoming book of Paul Ricoeur; the "genesis of secrecy" embedded in certain classic narratives in Frank Kermode's creative analysis of Mark's gospel, Joyce and Conrad; the claims (influenced by Auerbach) for the resonances between the history-like narratives of the gospels and the realistic novel tradition in Hans Frei; and the more traditional understanding of narrative in William Beardslee (all works cited above). I mention these important developments to remind the reader that the exercise of this section on narrative as a genre in the New Testament at best merely initiates the kind of far more complex analysis of narrative indicated above—forms of analysis clearly vigorous in the present conflict of interpretation over narrative theory.

For a more ambitious interpretation of narrative, several further questions would have to be asked. Among those questions are the following: (1) What is the relationship between semiotic and structuralist accounts of narrative (like Roland Barthes') and more traditionally hermeneutical enterprises (here Ricoeur's work on narrative theory employing his paradigm of interpretation as understanding-explanation-understanding is vital)? (2) What are the claims for understanding the relationship of narrative and experience (here the debates between positions like Stephen Crites' and those like Frank Kermode's are central)? Philosophically, the question of narrative ontological understandings of temporality is involved in this issue. (3) Is narrative in our postmodern situation a "reactionary" form that imposes order upon a chaos we refuse to face—the so-called "inenarrability" question? See, for example, the essay of Hayden White or the essay on Samuel Beckett's "anti-narratives" by Ted Estess ("The Inenarrable Contraption: Reflections on the Metaphor of Story," *JAAR* [1974], 415–34) and the reply by Dale Cannon ("Ruminations on the Claim of Inenarrability," *JAAR* [1975], 560–85). A central work here is Frank Kermode, *The Sense of an Ending: Studies in the Theory of Fiction* (London: Oxford Univ. Press, 1967). Also relevant here (although not mentioned in the prior debates) is the use of narrative for explicitly antireactionary, indeed emancipatory purposes as in the criticism of Walter Benjamin, the philosophy of Ernst Bloch and the theology of Johann Baptist Metz. For the latter thinkers, narratives of the memory of suffering and apocalyptic narratives break or "interrupt" both bourgeois "evolutionary" and traditionalist notions of time and order. (4) What are the relationships between fictional and historical narratives? Included in this concern (as in the different positions of Paul Ricoeur and Hayden White) are the first three issues plus the issue of the "narrative" structure of history itself (e.g., Danto and Mink vs. Hempel). The same kind of issue emerges in theological discussions (e.g., in the debates on Hans Frei's interpretation of the history-like realistic character of the biblical narratives, modelled on the nineteenth-century "realistic" novel). (5) Within analyses of biblical uses of narrative, moreover, the general problems listed above are joined by some further problems specific to biblical interpretation. Among those questions are the following: (a) What claims are made for narrative as a biblical genre? Is it a central but not exclusive genre? (This work holds this position by relating narrative to other New Testament genres.) Or is narrative *the* paradigmatic genre needed for Christian (or Jewish) biblical self-understanding? (This seems to be the claim of Frei, Stroup and, for different reasons, Metz.) (b) What is the role of narrative in the biblical texts? Answers here range from the claim that narrative functions "to form personal or communal identity" (Frei and perhaps Barth) to claims that narrative texts disclose a world of meaning in front of these religious narrative texts (Ricoeur, Wilder, Beardslee and this work). (c) *Which* narratives demand the primary attention in the New Testament? Many interpreters (e.g., Via, Funk, Crossan) claim the parables must. Others (as here) insist that the parabolic narratives are important but should also be seen in the context of the larger structural narratives of the gospels (especially the passion narratives for relative adequacy for Christian theological interpretation). Indeed, when a concern for those larger structures is absent, it seems that the invaluable literary-critical analyses of the Jesuanic parables either can veer in the direction of "historical Jesus" research (as in the earlier work on parables of Crossan and Funk) or can become creative occasions for developing theological options (as in the later work on parables of Crossan and Funk). These latter options, to be sure, are valuable contributions to contemporary pluralism by developing notions of Jesus as "precursor" (Funk) or by showing the remarkable polyvalence of the Jesuanic parabolic discourse and its analogies to such postmodern parables as Kafka's and Borges' (Crossan). Still, for a contemporary theological hermeneutic appropriate to the full New Testament witness, the parables (and their remarkable polyvalence) cannot function as an implicit "canon within the canon" for contemporary Christian theological discourse any more than earlier candidates for that role can. In short, narrative is clearly a central genre for the New Testament yet not the exclusive genre; a fortiori one particular kind of narrative within the gospel narrative (viz., the Jesuanic parables), however important and disclosive, should be honored but should not be accorded an implicitly canonical role for contemporary theological discourse.

The present use of narrative, to repeat, does not pretend to answer these "further questions" on narrative with adequacy. It does claim to show how some basic notions of narrative (e.g., character, plot, temporal actions) do demonstrate the disclosive power of New Testament narrative. Further discussions of narrative in general and of narrative in biblical literature, for myself, await further work in both narrative theory and in biblical narrative. For the moment, the present text simply employs a traditional understanding of narrative as congruent with the kinds of narratives actually present in the New Testament texts: narratives not "imposed" upon experience but disclosive of a religious-as-limit world of experience. These gospel narratives redescribe individual and communal human possibilities, disorient the everyday and re-present an event of divine self-manifestation in such manner that a reader of the gospels may re-cognize through the narrative form an essential religious possibility (viz., a life-at-the-limits like Jesus' own) as the world-in-front-of these narrative texts.

I also wish to express my thanks to two younger scholars presently completing theses on questions of narrative for theology: Steven Kepnes for his creative interpretations of the use of narrative in Jewish theology and Patrick Keifert for his study of the conflict of interpretations over the function of narrative in Mark's gospel.

82. In fact, of course, the turn to Aristotle here cannot be only to the *Poetics* since the latter basically considers only the mimetic form of *techne*. Sections of his other works (especially *The Nicomachean Ethics* and *Metaphysics*) are relevant for Aristotle's fuller position.

83. See Norman Perrin, "The Literary Gattung 'Gospel'—Some Observations," *Expository Times* 82 (1970), 4–7.

84. See William Beardslee, *Literary Criticism of the New Testament* [47], pp. 14–29.

85. For references, see n. 17. For the notions of parable as metaphor in narrative form, see Paul Ricoeur, *Semeia 4* [IV/77]; David Tracy, "Metaphor and Religion: The Test Case of Religious Texts," in *On Metaphor,* ed. Sheldon Sacks (Chicago: Univ. of Chicago Press, 1979), pp. 89–105. The parable discussion is undoubtedly the major instance to date of the use of different literary-critical methods to study New Testament use of genres, ranging from the earlier general hermeneutical (and proclamation-oriented) analyses of Robert Funk to Ricoeur's hermeneutical use of his theories of metaphor and narrative, to Via's structuralist analysis, Marin's semiotic analysis and, in his recent work, Crossan's deconstructionist analysis (see references in n. 17 for the earlier work; for examples of Crossan's more recent work, see also *The Dark Interval* [Niles: Argus, 1975] and *Raid on the Articulate* [New York: Harper & Row, 1976]).

The parable discussion (since the earlier historical-critical work of Dodd and Jeremias) is also usually cited as the central evidence for the language of the Jesuanic discourse. Note, for example, how Perrin's earlier historical-critical work in *Rediscovering the Teaching of Jesus* [Pt. II Intro./23] is complemented by his later analysis on literary-critical and hermeneutical grounds of the "tensive" (as distinct from "steno") character of the Jesuanic use of the kingdom of God language (*Jesus and the Language of the Kingdom* [Philadelphia: Fortress, 1978]). One need not employ recent parable research, however, only to engage in the quest for the "historical Jesus." Indeed, on the position defended throughout this work, the latter exercise is far less theologically relevant than the analysis of the parabolic language as the classic Jesuanic (and, among the redactors, Christian) discourse disclosing the disorienting claim to attention of this religious mode-of-being-in-the-world and releasing the dangerous memory of Jesus. The very success of the kinds of analysis mentioned above (along with the relationships of much parable research to the "new quest") have occasioned some exaggerated theological claims for the paradigmatic Jesuanic discourse of the parables. Still, the fruitfulness of parable research deserves serious attention from all theologians (whatever their other theological positions on the "new quest") as an example of the results of hermeneutical and literary-critical analyses on the New Testament use of a productive genre that keeps the defamiliarizing memory of Jesus alive today. That linguistic focus provides the basic interest, for example, in the theology of Eberhard Jüngel, *Paulus und Jesus* (Tübingen: Mohr, 1967). For a good account and use of recent parable research (along with a defense of some uses of "allegory") see also Mary Ann Tolbert, *Perspectives on the Parables: An Approach to Multiple Interpretations* (Philadelphia: Fortress, 1979).

86. These realities are articulated with clarity and massive historical-critical scholarship in Edward Schillebeeckx' *Jesus* [Pt. II Intro./8], esp. pp. 179–272. Those theologians, like myself, who disagree with the relative priority Schillebeeckx accords a form of the "new quest," can still applaud his extraordinary (and creative—especially in the use of Q materials) exegetical accomplishment while suggesting that literary-critical methods also be employed on those historically reconstructed narratives to show their disclosive and transformative power *as* religious narratives (see n. 21 for my reasons why Schillebeeckx's praxis criteria in his use of historical-critical methods seems to render his form of the "new quest" less problematic than some other ones). Schillebeeckx's second volume, *Christ* [Pt. II Intro./8], does employ some literary-critical methods with originality to disclose the meanings of salvation in the New Testament.

87. Kähler's famous remark, which is not applicable to Luke or Matthew, seems exaggerated even in relationship to Mark: see Norman Perrin, *The New Testament* [3], esp. p. 148. For an exegesis of the trial narrative in Mark, see John Donahue, *Are You the Christ? The Trial Narrative in the Gospel of Mark* (Missoula: SBL Series, 1973); and for individual studies, see *The Passion in Mark,* ed. Werner Kelber (Philadelphia: Fortress, 1976). An extensive use of literary criticism (as distinct from redaction criticism) may be found in Donald Juel, *Messiah and Temple: The Trial of Jesus in the Gospel of Mark* (Missoula: Scholars Press, 1977).

88. This seems confirmed by the role Perrin assigns the "passion story" in the "apocalyptic drama" (*New Testament,* pp. 146–48) and by Perrin's own assignment of the central role in the synoptics to the "story of Jesus." For the latter, see "Jesus in the Theology of the New Testament," ibid.

89. Recall the use of proclamation and narrative motifs in Gerhard von Rad, *Old Testament Theology,* 2 vols. (New York: Harper & Row, 1962, 1965). An informative study of von Rad for theologians is James L. Crenshaw, *Gerhard von Rad* (Waco: Word, 1978).

90. Perrin, *New Testament,* pp. 143–69; for the "secrecy" motif, see Frank Kermode, *The Genesis of Secrecy* [43], for a fascinating literary-critical analysis.

91. See Perrin, ibid., pp. 169–221. One need not accept Perrin's creative use of the "foundation myth" language to note the shift *in the narratives* of Luke and Matthew from the parousia-future (and "secret") narrative structure of Mark to the more past-oriented, order-producing narratives of Luke and Matthew (see Beardslee [47], pp. 18–29, for some suggestive comments here; and Petersen [43], pp. 49–81, on another proposal for the narrative structure in Mark). A recent and illuminating historical-critical exegesis of Matthew may be found in John Meier, *The Vision of Matthew: Christ, Church and Morality in the First Gospel* (New York: Paulist, 1979). A powerful defense of the kerygmatic character of Luke (vs. Conzelmann and others) is Richard Dillon, *From Eye-Witnesses to Ministers of the Word: Tradition and Composition in Luke 24* (Rome: Biblical Institute, 1978).

92. Raymond Brown, *The Birth of the Messiah* [79]. Brown's massive exegetical achievement awaits a complementary literary-critical analysis of the narrative structure *as narrative* in the theologies of the infancy narratives retrieved by Brown. Brown's own use of "narrative" is largely historical-critical and taxonomic yet open to the kind of analysis of narrative as productive genre suggested here.

93. This suggestion would also be applicable in principle to the preresurrection christology of Q and to what might be called Schillebeeckx's delineation of a "narrative of rejection" in the ministry of Jesus. That rejection narrative could be fruitfully employed as a narrative disclosive of the central negations present in the later christologies of the Suffering Messiah.

94. The use of neo-Aristotelian literary-critical analysis of "plot" and "charac-

ter'' in the New Testament narratives could also prove fruitful here. Recall, as well, Erich Auerbach's analysis of the ''realistic'' character of these biblical narratives and their use of ''lowly'' characters (like Peter) in contrast to the ''heroic'' and aristocratic characters of the Greek tragedians (*Mimesis* [16], esp. pp. 20–43).

95. The present appeal to the ''authority'' of Jesus is an appeal to the authority of the Jesus portrayed in these *confessing* narratives as distinct from the ''new quest''-like apologetic use of this motif: for the latter, inter alia, see Günther Bornkamm, *Jesus of Nazareth* (New York: Harper & Row, 1960), pp. 159, 179; for some theological-apologetic uses along the latter line, see John Cobb, *Christ in a Pluralistic Age* [Pt. II Intro./2] pp. 133–35.

96. For a fine analysis of the ''but even now'' motif, see Hans Küng, *On Being a Christian* [I/96], pp. 220–26. To recall a comment made earlier on Schillebeeckx's christology: even a theologian like myself who disagrees on theological grounds with the role accorded ''the historical Jesus'' by Küng, can applaud, as I do, his brilliant analysis of the confrontational nature of the Jesus confessed in these narratives. In Küng's christology the ''dangerous and subversive memory of Jesus'' (for me, therefore, the Jesus-kerygma; for Küng, the ''gospel'' *and* the ''historical Jesus'') comes alive anew to challenge any complacent christology. Küng's own observations on ''narrative'' (pp. 416–19) seem largely confined to proper warnings of not allowing ''narrative theologies'' to make exaggerated claims in theology. His own exegetical analysis is on historical-critical grounds (and related to the ''consensus'' of exegetes). Yet his ''consensus'' results could, in principle, accord historically reconstructed narratives of the message and ministry of Jesus open to narrative analysis like the literary-critical analyses of the historically reconstructed ''parables of Jesus.''

97. If we approach these narratives with the aid of modern historical-critical methods we can *also* know with a certain degree of historical probability some facts about the ''historical Jesus'': Jesus was baptized by John the Baptist; he ministered in Galilee; he preferred the rejected ones of his society; he was himself rejected and crucified. Above all, we can know the basic outline and forms of his teaching as a proclamation of the reign of God in proverb, eschatological saying and parable. In the most ''historically reliable'' memory-image of the earliest communities of this Jesus, moreover, we can recognize how his actions are viewed as symbolic, paradigmatic expressions of his teaching of the reign of God as present even now in those actions; how both actions and preaching seemed to possess an extraordinary ability to force a religious crisis on those with whom he came in contact. Jesus' sense of personal ''authority'' came through to his contemporaries as a confrontation to a decision of faith in God and God's reign: a decision that could not be postponed but must be accepted or rejected now (adapted from Van Harvey, *The Historian and the Believer* [II/32], pp. 265–75).

Yet I must repeat here the cautionary remarks of the earlier methodological reflections: although we *can* know ''the historical Jesus'' to some degree of historical probability through historical-critical methods, it is *not* ''the historical Jesus'' but the actual Jesus remembered by the community and confessed in these narratives about Jesus which must bear the theological weight. *Only* the latter is fully ''appropriate'' to that witness on the tradition's own criteria. The Jesus we know in the Christ event is the Jesus remembered and confessed by the original community of witnesses: the Jesus *confessed* in proclamation, narrative, symbol and reflective thought. For the opposite position, see Leander Keck, *A Future for the Historical Jesus* [Pt. II. Intro./20]; or Joachim Jeremias, *New Testament Theology: The Proclamation of Jesus* [Pt. II Intro./23]. I take the position defended in this work to be in fundamental continuity with the positions of Martin Kähler (*The So-Called Historical Jesus and the Historic, Biblical Christ* [Philadelphia: Fortress, 1964]), Rudolf Bultmann and Schubert Ogden. My other differences with these positions I have already mentioned: viz., my theological reluctance to employ "canon within the canon" language (whether Kähler and Bultmann's Christ-kerygma or Marxsen and Ogden's Jesus-kerygma) as distinct from calling the Jesus-kerygma the primary witness within the *whole* tradition of witnesses. Moreover, I am in fact less skeptical than Ogden seems to be on the historical-critical results of inquiries like Perrin's and Bornkamm's. Yet whatever the relevance of these differences, the main theological point is other: viz., it is not the "historical Jesus" but the confessed, witnessed Jesus that is theologically relevant. The familiar theological charges of "docetism" to positions like this (e.g., Käsemann on Bultmann) are frankly confused and confusing; no one is denying the actuality of Jesus or the intrinsic relevance of Jesus for Christian faith. Indeed, quite the contrary: what is being denied is the assumption that this theological faith claim is to be adjudicated by *historical-critical inquiry* into "the historical Jesus"!

98. See Günther Bornkamm, *Jesus of Nazareth* [95], pp. 109–17.

99. The use of praxis criteria for christology by Metz, *Faith in History and Society* [II/35], are relevant here. In present terms: criteria emphasizing personal, social and historical *transformation* via these narratives are related intrinsically to the *disclosive* realities manifested by these narratives *as narratives*. Metz's suggestive use of narrative via transformation praxis criteria needs complementing by literary-critical and hermeneutical analyses of narrative as disclosive.

100. See Beardslee, *Literary Criticism of the New Testament* [47], pp. 14–29.

101. The interpretation of resurrection by Langdon Gilkey, Hans Küng and Edward Schillebeeckx are especially helpful here: for Küng, *On Being a Christian* [I/96], pp. 343–411; for Schillebeeckx, *Jesus* [Pt. II Intro./8], pp. 320–90, 516–45, 640–50; for Gilkey, *Message and Existence* [I/100], pp. 178–94. Earlier Bultmannian, so-called "subjective" interpretations of "resurrection"—as in effect an event for the disciples revealing the significance of the cross but not an event for Jesus ("objective" interpretations)—seem to me spent on both exegetical and theological grounds (see the arguments in Gilkey, Küng and Schillebeeckx to this effect). Yet that does not mean a return (even a revisionary return like the sophisticated one of Pannenberg) to earlier purely "apologetic" concerns with "proving" the resurrection of Jesus. Rather a recognition of the "objective" resurrection of Jesus belongs more to the more properly theological interpretations of the biblical resurrection narratives like the distinct but analogous interpretations of Gilkey, Küng and Schillebeeckx. In their different ways, each of these theologians maintains that the event of resurrection is an event of God vindicating Jesus, not only an expression of the "Easter faith" of the disciples. (Schillebeeckx's analysis of the phenomenon of "conversion" is especially suggestive in showing both "objective" and "subjective" characteristics of the resurrection of Jesus.)

102. Schillebeeckx's use of the rejection motif in the ministry is especially suggestive here: see *Jesus*, pp. 36–69.

103. See Beardslee, *Literary Criticism*, pp. 18–29.

104. The reference to the "sensitive reader" is intended to recall the literary-critical criteria of formalist critics like Cleanth Brooks and their relevance for an interpretation of the "negations" and "not-yet" realities in the gospel narratives (especially Mark): the criteria are "tension, paradox, ambiguity, complexity, a sense of the negative in existence"; criteria similar, for example, to Schillebeeckx's analysis of "suffering," in *Jesus*, pp. 612–26, and in *Christ*, passim.

105. See John Macquarrie, *Christian Hope* (New York: Seabury, 1978), esp. pp. 106–30.

106. For the Christian tradition, the focal meaning of its radical challenge is the neighbor, not as with the ancient Greeks the "friend." See Victor Furnish, *The Love-Command in the New Testament* [69]. Nietzsche's critique of the Christian love of neighbor (e.g., Zarathustra: "I preach the friend, not the neighbor") assumes that neighbor-love must come from weakness and *ressentiment*. In the New Testament the evidence is the opposite: the love portrayed as that of Jesus in these confessing narratives comes from strength, not weakness—a fact confirmed by Nietzsche's own ambivalence toward "Jesus." (For an analysis of that ambivalence, see Walter Kaufmann, *Nietzsche: Philosopher, Psychologist, Anti-Christ* [Princeton: Princeton Univ. Press, 1974], pp. 337–91.) The theological significance of Nietzsche's critique of neighbor-love and his retrieval of the aristocratic-heroic Greek understanding of friendship-love are disclosive of Nietzsche's extraordinary sense for the heart of the matter in the Christian "transvaluation of all values"—a transvaluation that does provide a new ideal of humanity, and when distorted does deserve Nietzsche's devastating exposure of the weakness and *ressentiment* which can masquerade as neighbor-love in bourgeois Christendom.

107. Van Harvey, *The Historian and the Believer* [II/32], pp. 273–74; Jürgen Moltmann, *The Crucified God,* [IV/50] esp. pp. 32–82.

108. Note the present debate on "incarnation" in *The Myth of God Incarnate,* ed. John Hick (London: SCM, 1977); *The Truth of God Incarnate,* ed. Michael Green (London: Hodder & Stoughton, 1977); *The Debate Continued: Incarnation and Myth,* ed. Michael Gouldner (Grand Rapids: Eerdmans, 1980). The third volume is especially helpful in clarifying the issues. This is obviously not the place to attempt a full response to all the issues, save to observe that "incarnation" in christology can have a nonmythological meaning not dependent on popular misconceptions of "a god descending in the livery of a man" language. One can share the theologically necessary and forthright demythologizing concerns of Maurice Wiles even while not sharing his conclusions on this particular symbol. In sum: for myself, aside from its more general use (as roughly equivalent to a "sacramental" view of reality), the symbol "incarnation" also has a properly christological use. The incarnation is a symbol employed *in relationship to cross and resurrection* to reexpress their meaning: viz., that for Christian faith Jesus Christ is the decisive re-presentation of God; that Christians believe that in this one man Jesus, God's own self is present amongst us. I repeat, however, my previous cautionary comment: a purely incarnational christology not only runs the risk of rendering the death and resurrection secondary but also tends to downplay the actuality of Jesus as that actuality is confessed and narrated in the synoptic accounts of the ministry, message and fate of Jesus. When the latter occurs, Christianity is always in danger of becoming mere Christendom, an incarnational theology is in danger of becoming the mythology Wiles fears and exposes, and the Chalcedonian balance and restraint is in danger of sliding into the "God-in-the-livery-of-a-man" myth of "neo-Chalcedonianism." For the more general theological use of "incarnation," see the discussion of the "extraordinariness of the ordinary" in chap. 9, sec. ii.

109. See Rudolf Bultmann, *Theology of the New Testament* [II/6], II.

110. For a good analysis of Paul that takes this perspective, see Günther Bornkamm, *Paul* (New York: Harper & Row, 1971). For an alternative interpretation, see Krister Stendahl, *Paul Among Jews and Gentiles* (Philadelphia: Fortress, 1976), esp. pp. 1–97; and Ernst Käsemann's critique of Stendahl and Stendahl's response in *Perspectives on Paul* (Philadelphia: Fortress, 1971), pp. 60–78, 129–33. My own reading of Paul is more continuous with the position represented by

Bornkamm, Käsemann and others than with the reading by Stendahl, even though the latter's critique of any "introspective" reading of Paul has much to recommend it (especially its firm discrediting of all Christian theological caricatures of Jewish "legalism"). Still the truth of Stendahl's interpretation seems to me more the truth of a corrective than a full exposition of the *dialectical* reality *in* Paul's very use of language. For an excellent anthology of some classic interpretations of Paul, see *The Writings of St. Paul,* ed. Wayne Meeks (New York: Norton, 1972). For another important corrective to any interpretation of Paul that caricatures the Judaism contemporary with Paul as "legalism," see E. P. Sanders, *Paul and Palestinian Judaism: A Comparison of Patterns of Religion* (Philadelphia: Fortress, 1977). My own preference for the more "Bultmannian" interpretation tradition here is focussed on the character of the Pauline language as "dialectical." It does not depend on the results of the debate on the place of "justification through faith" in Pauline theology—and surely not on those parodies of the Rabbinic Judaism contemporary with Paul that too often have accompanied the German Christian exegetical tradition.

111. See Paul Ricoeur, *Semeia* 4 [IV/77], pp. 37–107; and Eberhard Jüngel, *Paulus und Jesus* [85].

112. A tradition of Pauline thought retrieved in political theological terms resonant with the "negative dialectics" of the early Frankfurt School: in Jürgen Moltmann, *The Crucified God* [IV/50], esp. pp. 325–29.

113. On John, see James Robinson, "The Johannine Trajectory," in James Robinson and Helmut Koester, *Trajectories through Early Christianity* [23], pp. 232–68; C. H. Dodd, *Interpretation of the Fourth Gospel* (Cambridge, Cambridge Univ. Press, 1953); and especially Raymond Brown, *The Gospel According to John* [79]. The latter encyclopedic volumes have informed my reading of the structure of John's gospel. My interpretation in terms of the hermeneutical categories of "meditative thinking" (Heidegger) and "manifestation" are in accord with the categories developed earlier in this book. Perhaps these hermeneutical categories receive some exegetical backing as a possible reformulation of C. H. Dodd's famous paradigm for John: a pattern of action which leads to dialogue, dialogue which leads to monologue (or, as I prefer, to self-manifestation). For the important question of the "sacramental" character of John's thought, see Raymond Brown, "The Johannine Sacramentory" and "The Eucharist and Baptism in John," in *New Testament Essays* (Milwaukee: Bruce, 1965).

114. For the categories "Book of Signs" and "Book of Glory," see Brown, *The Gospel According to John,* I, cxxxiii–cxlv.

115. See the suggestive reflections of Amos Wilder, *The Language of the Gospel* [47], pp. 30–31. For analyses of the christological hymns in the New Testament, see J. T. Sanders, *The New Testament Christological Hymns* (New York: Cambridge Univ. Press, 1971); and Reginald Fuller, *Foundations* [8], pp. 203–27.

116. For a creative theological use of Heidegger, see John Macquarrie, *Principles of Christian Theology* (London: SCM, 1966), pp. 111–61.

117. In contemporary poetry, the *Four Quartets* of T. S. Eliot are representative of this "Johannine" (and Anglican) tradition, in contrast to the more negation-oriented (and, in that limited sense, more Pauline) character of Eliot's *The Waste-Land.* Both are collected in *The Complete Poems and Plays of T. S. Eliot* (New York: Harcourt, Brace, 1952). In my analysis of the "contrasts" in John, I have eliminated his anti-Judaic strain—a strain which, in my judgment, should be eliminated as unworthy of the text and revolting in its historical consequences.

118. In art history compare the manifestation orientation of the Byzantine tradi-

tion of icons with the stark, Pauline reality of Grünewald's crucifixion for two classic expressions of these distinct Christian sensibilities. In theology, note how the more manifestation-oriented theologians (e.g., Schleiermacher, Lonergan, Rahner, Maurice) appeal frequently to John whereas the more proclamation-oriented theologians (e.g., Luther, Barth, Bultmann, Moltmann) appeal more often to Paul. Some contemporary manifestation-oriented thinkers (especially those concerned with the relationship of Christianity to the other world religions) have developed christologies related to the genre of wisdom literature: for a good review of this option, see Robert J. Schreiter, "The Anonymous Christian and Christology," *Occasional Bulletin of Missionary Research* (1978), 2–12. A helpful anthology of representative scholarship on the wisdom tradition may be found in James L. Crenshaw, ed., *Studies in Ancient Israelite Wisdom* (New York: KTAV, 1976). It seems clear that the genre "wisdom" will become a major one for theological retrievals of biblical possibilities.

119. Notice how a manifestation-oriented thinker like Teilhard de Chardin will appeal intuitively to Ephesians and Colossians while generally avoiding Romans, while a proclamation orientation like Jürgen Moltmann's will interpret Ephesians and Colossians (and thereby "nature") only after first establishing a Pauline political theology of the cross.

120. For the critical moment in both theologies, see Bultmann's analysis of the demythologizing moment internal to both theologies, in *Theology of the New Testament* I, 314–30 (on Paul); II, 70–92 (on John).

Chapter 7
The Christian Classic II

The Search for a Contemporary Christology

i. Retrospect: The Forms of the Whole and the Search for Adequacy

Criteria of relative adequacy for an appropriately Christian christology should attempt to be faithful to the range of disclosures in the whole spectrum of principal forms—literary, written and oral, verbal and nonverbal—which the original New Testament responses to the event involve.[1] Above all, any christology in any period must find some way of bringing to expression the event-gift-act-happening character of the event of Jesus Christ in a manner appropriate to both the present community's experience of the event and the content and structure of the New Testament witnesses. No classic religious expression, moreover, speaks from or to a situational vacuum. Hence the interpreter must also struggle to understand the particular focus of the fundamental religious questions impelling each expression and disclosed as part of the world of meaning of each form and genre: not only, for example, in the "titles" attributed to Jesus[2] but in the genres and nonverbal forms which inform and transform the New Testament use of implicit and explicit christological titles. Every enterprise in form criticism, redaction criticism and literary criticism must develop, correct, refine and challenge but not replace a properly theological understanding of the fundamental religious situational questions, the particular responses to the Christ event disclosed in front of all christological (early Palestinian, Judaic-Hellenistic, Gentile, Markan, Lukan, Matthean, Pauline, Johannine, apocalyptic, early Catholic) expressions.

The same recognition of the intrinsic dialectical relationship of situation-event-response should impel every later theological interpreter to focus as clearly as possible on one's own "situation" to allow it to be both disclosive of and transformed by the classic event witnessed to in the original religious Christian classic expressions. As the next chapter will argue, the search for a relatively adequate understanding of our contemporary situation is as difficult as the present quest for criteria of relatively adequate appropriateness to the normative and classic expressions of the scriptures. If, for example, our situation is understood principally in the light of basic trust, wonder and a sense of gracious mystery, we are likely to note particular disclosures in these christological classics and miss others. If our situation is understood principally in the light of the negativities of existence—the pain, conflicts, destruction, contradictions, anxiety and suffering of both individual and society, the decentering of history or nature—we are likely to understand with immediacy certain disclosures of certain christological texts and miss or even dismiss others. Insofar as each theologian is faithful to the particular journey of intensification that is her or his own, insofar as each is attentive to the possibility of another's journey, insofar as all theologians pay heed to the full range of forms in the normative, classic texts witnessing to the classic event of God's act of self-manifestation in Jesus Christ, no one need fear real diversity of expression, ever new interpretations of that event.

Yet the contemporary search for relatively adequate criteria for understanding the christological expressions of the New Testament by interpreting the clues disclosed by its images, symbols and genres has not been without some results. Insofar as the earlier analysis of genres seems accurate, we may conclude that relative adequacy in christology will mean not only fidelity to the earliest witnesses (as it must) but will also mean relative adequacy to the full and diverse range of forms of expression found in the New Testament.[3] Relative adequacy will mean keeping in clear view the "corrective truth" of the genre "doctrine" in the New Testament as the articulation of some clarity and some harmony in the doctrinal-confessional (indeed propositional) christological expressions in the "content" of all kerygmatic expressions and the doctrinal expressions of "emergent Catholicism." This development of the genre doctrine, leading to such later expressions as Nicaea and Chalcedon, has the ability to specify, clarify and order what the beliefs, the "doctrines" implied by this basic belief in the event of God's self-manifestation in Jesus Christ are. Relative adequacy will also mean keeping in view the ever present "corrective truth" of the demand for the intensification of negations: the constant presence of the new, the historical and the future, the not-yet in the apocalyptic forms buried throughout the New Testament, especially in those christologies where the messianic times of the Messiah are both already here and genuinely not yet here. Apocalyptic serves its corrective function as a minefield in store for all christologies, waiting to explode any attempt at complacency, any reach for a too easy or a too private harmony, any claim to perfectionism by apocalyptic's stark disclosure of the not-yet actuality in even the most realized present actuality.

Both corrective genres, doctrine and apocalyptic, are needed to understand the full range of christological expressions. And yet the fuller truth of the New Testament and of contemporary christology lies elsewhere: in the relative adequacy of the related forms of proclamation-narrative-image-symbol and reflective thought. In that interwoven complex of the New Testament, a theologian finds the surest clues to a relatively adequate expression of the event disclosed in all these texts. We need proclamation to hurl at us, often "like a stone," an unsettling, provocative word of address that upsets, shakes, questions us, which both judges and heals by its stark disclosure *that* the event occurs now. We need the narratives to shape the *what* as the story of this Jesus proclaimed as the event-ful that, Jesus Christ, in a manner faithful to our own experience of the storylike character of life itself, with its tensions and surprises, its shocks and achievements, its disclosures of authentic and inauthentic life.

We may find the focus of New Testament disclosures in the confessing narrations of this singular individual: this strange, authoritative Jesus who proclaims God's reign in words that confront our ordinary modes of apprehension, who acts in word and deed with a freedom and a sometimes harsh, sometimes tender love that commands the attention of his contemporaries and of us; this Jesus who consorts with all, especially with the outcast—the privileged ones in his eyes whom the privileged in every age feel free to ignore or to crush with either violence or patronizing contempt; whose story challenged the compulsions and temptations of his contemporaries to domesticate and control God through laws and doctrines as surely as that story challenges the contemporary Christian church's same temptations now; this Jesus who dies disgraced with the death reserved for society's outcasts while "the Pilates die in their beds";[4] this Jesus who is yet raised by God and vindicated as the one who is God's own; who discloses what an authentic life might be to all who hear that story and, in hearing it, join their plot in trusting hope to the non-end of this strange narrative. That non-end discloses that all, in one sense, has already happened. And yet the story does not end.[5] There remains in that non-end to the synoptic narratives of Jesus in the New Testament the not-yet of each individual Christian's never-ending decisions for or against allowing the empowering plot and character of the story to become one's own story, however ordinary our subplot may prove to be (like Luke's Peter), however extraordinary our character may be (like Luke's Paul).

The narratives, in turn, disclose those tensive symbols which focus the meaning and truth of that event and that story in images which disclose and transform anew: cross-resurrection-incarnation. To the self who has already recognized that we find ourselves most surely not through our own achievements but through and in the classic signs and symbols scattered in our world, these symbols—the stark contradictory power of the cross, the transformative hope of the resurrection, the "hint half guessed, the gift half understood'' of incarnation—give rise to authentic reflective thought. In the sustained, indeed unrelieved, dialectical tension of Paul's language, the conflict and contradiction of the cross is hurled at all human attempts at self-sufficiency and thereby breaks through our cherished defenses to disclose its healing, judging, graced scandal. In the meditative releasement of John's theology, the symbols of glorification—the exaltation and incarnation, and even the ''lifting up'' of the cross—allow the reader to sense the ''already'' reality of existence itself as gift, indeed to sense the always-already reality of God's gracious presence in and to each and all, to history and its drives to justice, to nature and its manifestations of power in the decisive manifestation of God's own self in Jesus Christ.

The full complexity of those symbols and those modes of thinking—cross-resurrection-incarnation, dialectics and meditative thought—disclose the reality of an event which is here even now, which has always already been here, which is still not yet here. The dialectic of these symbols is the adverbial dialectic of an always-already which is yet a not-yet. Only when christological thinking functions as a new interpreted response to those symbols, only when the symbols find the identity of who the Crucified and Risen One is in the gospel narratives of Jesus' life and ministry, death and resurrection, only when the narratives themselves function as both story and confession, both manifestation of the symbols and new narrative proclamation of the original act of proclamation—only then does the full actuality of the event of Jesus Christ witnessed to in all these modes of expression occur in relatively adequate theological expression.

Nor does the actual rich diversity of forms in the New Testament grounded in the unifying unity of an event seeking a response of personal faith signal the call to any kind of thoughtless, lazy theological pluralism. Rather the New Testament diversity is impelled by the dynamism of the event itself and its self-expression into the otherness of a wide range of responses to, witnesses to, that event: responses which posit themselves in and by the event by implying their own fulfillment in the next needed form. Proclamation's positing of the bare *that* of the event of Jesus Christ implies the *who* and *what* of the narratives; the surprises, the resolutions, the end and non-end of the narratives imply the need for tensive *symbols* and *images* able to capture in manifestation the clues disclosed by the narrative as the key to their interpretation of the ministry; the irreducible tension of each symbol and the conflict within the whole complex of symbols (cross-resurrection-incarnation) demands the interpretation of critical reflective thought. That thinking as critical theology responds to the symbols in showing that the authentic break, the crisis which is authentic thinking distances itself in its judgment (*krisis*) only by positing at the same time its own primordial participation in the symbols impelling and encompassing its reflection; the symbols-signs-images keep their tensive concentration from becoming "mere" symbols, mere ciphers of transcendence, simply examples of possibility by implying their grounding in the testimony and witness to the concreteness of a single human life—the life and ministry narrated in the gospels; these narratives tell their story in order to confess their faith in the content of the earliest apostolic confessions; the content of those confessions discloses, as proclamatory witness, a word of address which is an event of God's own self-manifestation and a manifestation and proclamation of the Christian's hope, gift, command and promise.

All later theological and doctrinal expressions receive their fundamental appropriateness by showing their fidelity to the classical expressions of the Christian scriptures. Like all other religious classics, the christological expressions of the scriptures claim no more, and no less, than forms of relatively adequate expressions as responses to an originating event of disclosure from God and by the power of God. Yet what the entire complex of these classic religious expressions testify to in all their expressions—in proclamation, narrative, symbol and thought—is the startling faith of the Christian community in one event of full, decisive adequacy: the event of God's self-manifestation through and in Jesus Christ; the event of the decisively true word and manifestation that already happened, that happens now, always happens, that will happen in Jesus Christ, the event of God.

Nor do these present criteria of relative adequacy and their development of one "working canon" for the New Testament seem inappropriate to contemporary discussions of christology. For the search in contemporary christology includes a search for criteria of appropriateness to the distinctive particularity of Christianity. The distinctively Christian is none other than this Jesus confessed by the New Testament as Christ and Lord. Those scriptural confessions show their own diversity—not only in titles but in the forms of expression, both verbal genres and nonverbal symbols which contextualize all titles; forms which disclose a particular situational focus to the fundamental questions and the particularity of the disclosive and transformative power of the same classic event of God's self-and-other-manifestation in Jesus Christ.

When the interpreter allows the particularity of each focus to play its own role of intensification of some particular aspect of the fundamental questions, when the interpreter allows for the diversity of the classical expressions in apocalyptic and doctrine, above all in the full spectrum of proclamation and narrative, in the manifestations of image and symbol and in the responses of critical reflective theology, when the interpreter employs the scripture's own criterion of apostolicity to serve as a focussing clue to show the continuity of all later expressions to the original apostolic witness, then one may find a diversity that does enrich. For here we find a diversity not forced into the demand for a single expression of its faith, nor resigned to the search for an enfeebled lowest common denominator. Rather the New Testament is a diversity whose unity is its ground in the single event of God's self-disclosure in Jesus Christ witnessed to by the early communities; an event demanding response and encouraging and empowering all later Christian responses. The only fully appropriate, fully adequate expression of that event is the event itself—the event of God in Jesus Christ, true word, decisive manifestation.

What we find in the New Testament are the original, classic responses to that event: above all, the original apostolic witnesses who, with varying degrees of relative adequacy, responded to the event of Jesus Christ in a series of expressions, which as a whole and as related to the earliest witness, define the possibilities of relative adequacy for a scripturally based christology. Moreover, the very fidelity of each New Testament classic expression to the particularity of its own situation not merely allows but demands that later Christians be as focussed in and to their own situation. The Christian belief in the reality of the Spirit—so powerful in Eastern Orthodoxy's "objective" doctrines of the Spirit, so explosive in Western "subjective" emphases and charismatic renewals, so central to several early Jewish-Christian pneuma christologies and their fidelity to the Old Testament's (*and* the New's) faith in the reality of the Spirit of Yahweh—impels Christians to search anew for the "signs of the times." There interpreters find those "discerning questions and possible answers" in the situation whereby they rearticulate and allow to live again (as a new expression of spirit christology in and to a new situation)[6] the empowering and discerning event of God's self-disclosure in Jesus Christ. All responses from the New Testament to the present must be as concrete, as decisive and as rooted in their situation as the event which elicits and empowers them. All responses will be *new* interpretations of that scriptural foundation.

In the less charged terms of Whitehead, the Christian event remains "a special occasion" compelling and intelligible in itself, seeking a mode of universal expression proper to its universality and intelligibility. It is little wonder, then, that the logos tradition in christology has set and still largely sets the mainline Christian tradition of philosophically oriented responses to that event: from "John" through Justin, Origen, Augustine and Aquinas to our own period with Rahner, Lonergan, Cobb and Ogden. The logos tradition in christology, it is true, may always be in danger of losing its grasp upon and its being grasped by the decisiveness of the concrete particularity of the event.[7] And yet the logos tradition's fidelity to universality is none other than the recognition impelled by the decisive, concrete event itself that here the only God there is manifests who God always already is. Any logos christology discloses the radicality of a truly graced world and self, the reality of a "transcendental," an "original" revelation, as the always-already—the universal—reality in every human experience, all history, indeed in the cosmos itself *as* that reality is decisively re-presented in the event of God's self-manifestation in Jesus Christ.[8]

Logos christologies disclose a situation where wonder, where fundamental trust in humanity, in history and in the cosmos live: live as the disclosure of the always-already reality of the gracious presence of the God of love disclosed in the history of Israel, disclosed as well in all religions and in all authentic human searches for truth and life, decisively disclosed for the Christian in Jesus Christ. In these christologies rooted in John, in Colossians and Ephesians, in Luke's Paul of the Areopagus speech—the cross and its disclosure of negativity, conflict, contradiction and sin tend to be transformed into the exaltation of a fundamental trust, a wonder at the giftedness of life itself, a radical, universal and finally incomprehensible grace, a pervasive sense of a God of love who is never an "inference" but an always-present reality to each and to all. And yet the not-yet remains active in this always-already reality of logos christologies, this re-presentation of God and self: now as the sheer incomprehensibility of who it is we experience and find faith in; now as the unsettling call to ever-renewed decision to direct our basic faith, our trust and loyalty, away from all the idols of our compulsions, all our usual "gods"—success, security, fame, self-salvation—and place that trust in the God of love, the God whose decisive re-presentation of divine and human reality happened, happens, and will happen in Jesus Christ.

For still other christologies the concreteness and decisiveness of the event of the *cross* of Jesus Christ disclose a different situation and yield a different reading, a distinct interpretation of the situation in which we now live. With roots in the prophetic strain in the Old and New Testaments, with affinities to the apocalyptic and eschatological expressions in the New Testament, with natural affinities to the dialectical language and theology of the cross of Paul, these christologies focus upon the defamiliarizing conflict, contradiction, negativity of the cross.

The always-already reality of the event's disclosure remains present, yet understood in the light of the stark not-yet and the overwhelming revelation of negativity of the cross; Karl Rahner's always-already logos christology can become Hans Küng's dialectic of the "not yet but even now"; Schubert Ogden's decisive representative christology of universal grace can become the stark negativity of Jürgen Moltmann's crucified God.[9] The "situation" for these christologies of the cross will prove open to a profound sense of the negativities existing in our situation: the compulsions, lies, distortions, fears and anxieties of our individual lives; the conflicts, terrors, contradictions and systemic sin of our social and historical lives; the threats and terrors disclosed in nature itself. The decisiveness of the event will prove to be the decisiveness of the cross and its disclosure of the need for reform, refusal, aggression, protest, suspicion, conflict, to and in our not-yet ecclesial and historical-political situations.[10]

In these christologies of the cross—as in Moltmann and Sobrino—our fundamental trust will be directed to and by the hoped-for future, our attention here and now will be less on the always-already character of our graced state, less on the wonder and gift of existence itself, more on the pain, conflict and suffering at the heart of all individual repressions and all social and historical oppressions and alienations. Our sense of the situation will be charged with the prophetic, apocalyptic, eschatological sense of a "great refusal" to the present order of things, an exposure of all the rest as deceptive, a suspicion of all christologies of incarnational and resurrectional presence as in danger of becoming ideologies of control. For any universal cut off from the decisive negativity of the cross and its disclosure of the not-yet in all reality and its promise of a genuine *novum* and a really different future is always in danger of becoming an ideology.[11]

Yet if the paradox of a "distinctively Christian" christology is, as we have claimed, a paradox of an always-already which is yet a not-yet, then the God of love, as 1 John reminds us, is/is not/is like love and we are/are not/are like those who are redeemed.[12] Only the whole of the New Testament expressions will disclose with relative adequacy the whole dialectical meaning of both our situation and the event of Jesus Christ. Only the search for the whole in our contemporary situation—the search for the concrete as the decisively particular journey of each as related to all, the search through the diversity of expressions in Christianity and in the present situation, the search through and in that analogical journey of intensification of both particularity and self-exposure in each one's distinctive particularity to the other through the diversity of classic expressions in the New Testament and from the New Testament to our own contemporary period—can approach relative adequacy. For only that search for an always-already, not-yet whole will free the contemporary Christian spirit for its hermeneutical responsibilities to its classic self-expressions in the New Testament and the whole tradition.

In the meantime, the present search for criteria of relative adequacy for the diversity of New Testament expressions of response to the event of God's self-manifestation in Jesus Christ has, perhaps, not been without some fruit. For if the analysis holds true, then it warrants my trust in the possibilities of an authentically Christian analogical imagination:[13] an imagination which finds and discovers even its own particularity and its truest disclosure of real universality only through an intensified journey into a particularity that is accompanied by a willing self-exposure to the concreteness of the whole: here to the real diversity of particular expressions of particular visions of the situation and particular responses in distinct forms and genres whose authority is the apostolic authority of the original witnesses and whose ground or source of authority is the encompassing (as truly concrete and ultimately inexpressible) *event* of Jesus Christ as God's ownmost self-manifestation.

Each Christian theologian risks a journey of intensification into some particular form—some verbal genre, some nonverbal symbol—of the original New Testament diversity of expression. In remembering that the New Testament is the book of the whole Christian church, each contemporary theologian can also learn to trust his or her own particular confessional church tradition and its lived relationship by and in some New Testament classic expression. If self-exposure is not part of the contemporary Christian journey, however, then the actual diversity of interpretations of our contemporary situation, the diversity in the entire history of the Christian church, and even the diversity in the New Testament itself will be shunted aside as an unwelcome pluralism. Yet if the whole is genuinely disclosed in the actual diversity of forms in the New Testament and the whole tradition, then each journey into a particular New Testament or later form of christology needs its self-exposure to the corrective of the others, above all of the original witnesses and, eventually, of the whole tradition.

The corrective truths of the ordering, harmonizing, clarifying, tradition-oriented doctrines in the content of the kerygmata and in emergent Catholicism and the intensifying, exploding, not-yet future-oriented expressions of apocalyptic need one another if the always-already, not-yet character of christology is to be seen with clarity. Both these expressions, singly and together, inform, challenge and correct, but are themselves transformed, challenged and corrected by the relatively adequate paradigm of the range of expressions in the classical New Testament route from proclamation to narrative to symbol-image and reflective thought.

Each of these classical expressions needs self-exposure to the other: the act-of-proclamation orientation of Bultmann, for example, to the narrative-pattern orientation of Barth and the image-symbol-thought orientations of Tillich and Rahner—and vice versa. Within each classic choice, moreover, the need for self-exposure also seems clear: Dodd's emphasis on proclamation as content needs Bultmann's insistence on proclamation as act. The narratives within the narrative form of the gospels imply and need one another: the "miniature gospels" of the sayings in Q unearthed by form criticism imply the need for the larger theological narrative structures of Mark, Luke, Matthew and John uncovered by redaction criticism and the narrative structures as structurings of meaning uncovered by literary critics—and vice versa. The historical-critical reconstruction of the original Jesus-kerygma can only fulfill their material claims by also opening up to the "working canon" provided by literary-critical retrievals of the existential meaning of the larger narratives of the story of the ministry, the words and deeds, the passion and resurrection of Jesus of Nazareth confessed as the Christ and portrayed in his significance through and in narratives.

Moreover, the confessing narratives of the privileged Jesuanic parables need to be related not only to their "natural" analogues, the proverbs and eschatological sayings of the remembered Jesus, but to the larger confessing narrative of the ministry of Jesus in each gospel, to the passion narratives in all the gospels, and hence to the unusual confessing-narrating genre of gospel itself and, through gospel, to proclamation-symbol and theological reflection in the community's confession of Jesus Christ.

Within the forms of those major symbols and images giving rise to the reflective thought of theological expression (those forms most natural to theologians), moreover, the same need for self-exposure to the really other occurs. The incarnation emphasis of the different logos christologies, from John through Nicaea and Chalcedon through many Anglican, Orthodox, Catholic and Liberal Protestant christological traditions to Maurice, Rahner, Ogden and Cobb in our own period, needs to find further ways to allow the negations and the not-yet of the cross, the hope-and-future orientations of the resurrection to play a greater disclosive role in their profound disclosures of the always-already, the universal re-presentative reality of the event of God in Jesus Christ.

The resurrection emphases of all pneuma christologies, from early Judaic Christianity through many Orthodox christologies to Kasper in our own period, and the distinct resurrection emphasis of proleptic vindication in and for universal history of Pannenberg need to expose themselves further to the stark contradiction of the cross and the negativities—personal, social, political, historical and natural—of our and every situation.

The emphasis upon the cross in christology—whether in the distinct Pauline approaches of Küng and Moltmann or in the prophetic emphases of Sobrino, Miranda, Soelle and most liberation theologians or the recent apocalyptic emphasis of Metz—can profitably expose their not-yet emphasis towards the present, their hope in the not-yet of the eschatological future, their profound sensitivity to the not-yet embedded in the distortions, compulsions, conflicts and contradictions of the contemporary church, society and history to the always-already disclosure of incarnation and its radical openness to secularity, its confident self-exposure to the incarnate creativity and transformative reality of the other "non-Christian" religions.[14]

Each emphasis—upon cross, resurrection, incarnation—needs the other as a self-corrective moment in its own particular journey of intensification, not as a merely external corrective or "reminder" of other aspects of the whole. Each needs a real, internal, self-exposing relationship of its thinking to those "other" symbols deemphasized by its own concentration. And all christologies of symbol-image need to be related to the narratives of the ministry and message, the passion-resurrection of Jesus and to the confessing proclamation of the original apostolic witness in order to prove faithful to the same kind of relative adequacy represented by the New Testament diversity. The journey to the transformative always-already, not-yet reality disclosed in the spectrum of New Testament responses to the event of God's self-manifestation in Jesus Christ is a journey which achieves a real relative adequacy only in intrinsic relationship to the whole spectrum of forms present in the New Testament in continuity with the original apostolic witnesses and their descendants in the whole classic tradition, including the contemporary period. Only then will each partial journey of intensification into the particular find not merely its affinity to its most natural analogue in the expressions of the New Testament but find as well its own self-exposure—in our contemporary situation of necessary self-exposure—to the pluralistic yet unified whole of the New Testament and the later tradition and the broken whole of the contemporary situation.

Unifying and impelling all later responses, grounding all the expressive responses of the New Testament itself, is the witness of the entire Christian tradition beginning and grounded in the original apostolic witness to its faith in the reality of one decisive, one fully adequate event of God's self-manifestation and God's manifestation of ourselves, history and nature: the event Christians name Jesus Christ, true word, decisive manifestation. The route that each theologian follows in responding to that event has many turns; that route will involve some understanding of the situation and the seriousness of the fundamental religious questions focussed in both contemporary and classic terms (finitude, mortality, anxiety, trust and loyalty, wonder, giftedness, alienation, oppression, suffering). That route needs as well an experience, however intense, however everyday, of the reality of the event itself, the reality of the presence of God mediated through and in word and sacrament, community and meditation, tradition and critique, the thought and praxis of the Christian church in the full range of its diverse responses to that event in the several christological traditions of confession, spirituality and community. The particular focus of the question and the particular history of one's ownmost familiar or intense response to the religious and theological reality named the Christian church will unite to lead each individual theologian to her or his own response to that event.[15]

By a communal ecclesial and collegial theological concentration of focus on the whole spectrum of New Testament expressions as related to the original apostolic witness and as providing a framework of relative adequacy for forms of expression of that witness into later witnesses, we may all yet learn from that diversity and that unity. Each theologian can learn much by recalling the New Testament's own journey from the original witness of the Jesus-kerygma through the mixture of the Jesus-kerygma and the Christ-kerygma in the synoptics to the Christ-kerygma of John, Paul and early Catholicism. Each theologian may also recall the possibilities of relatively adequate forms of expression for the event of

Jesus Christ by employing literary-critical and hermeneutical criteria for the whole spectrum of New Testament expressions: here from apocalyptic and doctrines, through proclamations and narratives, to symbols, images and that reflective thought named theology. Even before theologians turn to apocalyptic and doctrine, to proclamation and narrative, they find the tensive symbols of cross-resurrection-incarnation disclosing intrinsic demands upon all interpretations of the Christ event. They find the decisiveness of the event disclosed in all its tension in the cross and that cross's demand for negation, its reminder of the not-yet in the present, its insistence that we face the reality of the others, especially the outcast, the gospel's privileged ones. Theologians may find the symbol of the resurrection revealing that the Crucified One is the Risen One, that Jesus has been accepted and received by God as the surest ground for our hope in the transformation of our compulsions, alienations and oppressions, as the ground of a total hope—for history and nature, for the living and the dead, and their acceptance by the same God of suffering love who raised the crucified Jesus from the dead. Theologians will find the decisiveness of the event disclosed as well in the symbol of incarnation: a symbol which comes after cross and resurrection and moves with them to disclose how decisive that event of God really is—decisive as fully adequate to the re-presentation of the actuality of God's love and the universality of God's grace as always-already here to each, to all, to history and nature.

Theologians try to understand this God through every strategy of genuine theology: through the tradition of the "hidden and revealed God" and its fidelity to the reality of the cross, through the traditions of the triumphant God of mercy and judgment, of promise and fulfillment, and their fidelity to the reality of the resurrection, to the tradition of the God of gracious mystery, of comprehensible-incomprehensible gift and its fidelity to the reality of incarnation. Through all these authentic and diverse strategies of classical Christian theology, theologians find the need always to return to the always-already, not-yet reality of the cross-resurrection-incarnation of Jesus Christ and its decisive disclosure of the nearness and the distance of the God of suffering, self-giving, other-regarding Love. As Schleiermacher observed for us all, the doctrine of God is not "another" doctrine in any systematic theology. Rather God—as doctrine, as symbol, as reality—must pervade all other doctrines[16] just as the event of God's self-manifestation as love in Jesus Christ pervades all the responses of the New Testament: the proclamation of Jesus Christ as Lord by the community, the narratives of the ministry of Jesus disclosing Jesus' own proclamation of the nearness of the reign of God and the nearness of God as "Abba" in his message and deeds; the passion narrative's disclosures of the reality and meaning of self-sacrificial, other-regarding, actively suffering love as the strength-in-weakness, the impossible possibility which is God's own reality and is our ownmost need and command; the symbols of cross-resurrection-incarnation, the dialectical tensions of Paul and the meditative releasements of John—all disclose a self-disclosure by this God as the loving and suffering one whose reality encompasses and commands our lives.

The New Testament from beginning to end confesses that this Jesus of Nazareth is none other than the Christ, the Lord, true and saving word, decisive manifestation of the whole as the "who" named God: the pure, self-giving, self-exposing unbounded Love which is the whole encompassing us, who is the reality meeting us in the event of divine self-manifestation proclaimed and manifested in Jesus Christ.

ii. Some Questions for a Contemporary Christology

At the center of Christianity stands not a timeless truth, nor a principle, nor even a cause, but an event and a person—Jesus of Nazareth experienced and confessed as the Christ. Through the diverse genres, titles, confessions of the New Testament there is the constancy of a confession, constituted by the community's present experience of its Crucified and Risen Lord to this person Jesus of Nazareth. Throughout Christian history, more genres, images, titles, symbols, confessions have emerged in Christian responses to the presence of the Christ and the Spirit in different cultural situations. The constant there is less a material than a formal one of the same pattern: the religious event of disclosure and concealment of God, self and world—the event of Christ and the Spirit—continues to challenge, confront, confirm the questions and expectations of ever-shifting situations and to impel the journey to find new responses to express in new confessions, images, titles, genres who this Jesus Christ is.

The religious event of the experience in the Spirit of the Christ is the constitutive reality mediated through the traditions in all christologies. Yet that event never occurs save in a particular cultural situation and is never expressed save in a particular form of response. Some responses in Christian history, like those of Nicaea and Chalcedon, have achieved classic status in the genre of doctrine for much of the Christian tradition. Other responses have emerged for other individual or communal Christians to express their ownmost understanding of the Christ event in their midst. Still other responses have died or been discarded sometimes quietly, sometimes violently, as no longer disclosive of the reality of that event or no longer faithful to the memory of Jesus. Yet other "secular" responses—as André Malraux and John Cobb have shown—have served as creative transformations of the Christ event into religious and secular art.

In this basic formal pattern grounded in the Christ event and the tradition's dangerous memory of Jesus the contemporary situation is no different from earlier ones. Now, too, Christians find themselves, individually and communally, responding to the religious event of Christ in the Spirit. Now, too, Christians find themselves thankful to the tradition which mediates this event and this memory of Jesus by its own fidelity to the apostolic witness. Now, too, Christians find themselves in particular situations where certain fundamental questions and expectations are highlighted to receive their confrontation, confirmation, transformation in and by the religious event of Jesus Christ. Now, too, that response in a concrete, particular situation to that event will impel a continual series of creative new interpretations in new christologies grounded in the tradition to understand and articulate the meaning of that reality now.

Although the same basic pattern (situation-event-response) remains, the contents of contemporary christologies are likely to bear certain distinctively modern characteristics. We will analyse in the next chapters certain prevailing characteristics of our contemporary situation (chapter 8) and the journeys of Christian responses in that situation (chapter 9). Until those tasks are clarified it is not possible to speak adequately of a contemporary Christian response to the reality of Jesus Christ. However, even now some implications of the journey of the present chapters for addressing the question of a contemporary christology—at least one which intends fundamental appropriateness to the New Testament witness—seem in order here.

For these chapters have risked a personal interpretation of that New Testament witness. I have, through the application of the model of a religious classic to the event and person of Jesus Christ as the Christian classic, attempted to show one way of articulating the religious-theological character of these texts. I have attempted to relate that model of a religious classic to the earlier analyses of the reality of any classic and thus allowed for the appropriateness of a notion of genre as productive of meaning. With that notion of the productive character of genre, an interpreter can turn to a study of the diversity of New Testament genres as the surest clue to how relative adequacy of forms of expression may be achieved.[17] Then it became possible to suggest the relative adequacy of one model (proclamation-narrative-symbol and reflective thought, with apocalyptic and doctrine serving their distinct corrective roles) for understanding the spectrum of relatively adequate forms of expression for the reality of the Christ event as witnessed to in the New Testament. That suggestion, if accurate, warrants my belief that the actual pluralism of the New Testament, like the pluralism of contemporary christologies, is not a regrettable reality but a fundamentally enriching one. There is, for example, no reason in principle to resist either alternative christological interpretations of the logos tradition (like John Cobb's or Karl Rahner's) or to resist alternative non-logos-oriented positions like Walter Kasper's attempt to retrieve the spirit christology of early Jewish Christianity or

Edward Schillebeeckx's retrieval of a parousia christology in the pregospel confessions (especially of the Q community and the eschatological prophet model of an early Palestinian community) or Hans Küng's retrieval of Jesus as advocate.

Where, then, does one resist pluralism if the actual pluralism of contemporary Christianity is not to become a mindless, genial pluralism of "Let a thousand flowers bloom"? If each interpreter recognizes that all christological formulations are, in principle, at best relatively adequate, this negative moment also entails a search for positive criteria of relative adequacy to sort out unacceptance candidates (for example, the monophysite tendencies of much official Christian piety wherein Jesus is imaged as God disguised in the livery of a man, or the unnecessary and finally hopeless search of an earlier Liberal theology for the "religious consciousness," the "psychology," of Jesus, or contemporary attempts to employ "the historical Jesus" as norm or standard of theology, or any exclusivist christology that paradoxically disallows the very inclusiveness disclosed in the Christ event).

The primary material criterion of the New Testament remains the historically reconstructed original apostolic witness and its explication into explicit christologies in the later witnesses. Another set of criteria for these later expressions, I have suggested, can prove to be the kind of literary-critical and hermeneutical analyses of the relative adequacy of different forms of expression and the recognizable relative adequacy of the whole pluralistic spectrum analyzed earlier. When those material criteria are united to the formal criteria elaborated here, one has further warrants for trusting the whole tradition (scriptural and, by implication, postscriptural) as in fundamental fidelity to the original unifying witness and in fidelity to the need of tradition as tradition to achieve ever-new interpretations in new forms of expression for ever-new situations. This search for criteria of relative adequacy also allows one to adjudicate on a collaborative basis the inevitable and necessary conflicts among various christological formulations. On the criteria defended in this work, this much seems clear: Pluralism is not only a fact present throughout Christian history from the New Testament period to today; any pluralism faithful to the original witnesses and to the need for diverse expressions is in principle an enrichment of Christian consciousness.

Pluralism is an enrichment insofar as any particular formulation, on inner-Christian hermeneutical grounds, is at best relatively adequate for interpreting the final inexpressibility of the Christ event, and at best relatively adequate in analyzing the contemporary situation. The final inexpressibility of the event does not disallow, indeed encourages, all faith responses involving a recognition of that giftedness and that inexpressibility as an intrinsic moment in the drive to express anew its meaning for some focussed fundamental question in the complexity of the human situation. The fact that historical criticism is by definition an exercise in "relative adequacy" (alternatively plausibility arguments accumulating to a degree of real probability) does not disallow, indeed encourages, the use of historical criticism to check, refine, develop, correct or confront all christological formulations by comparing them critically with the earliest memory images of the community.

This central hermeneutical principle discloses its own hermeneutics of suspicion upon any and all claims that christology can *only* be expressed in some one manner. The search for the *only* allowable form of expression in the New Testament diversity usually will also develop additional criteria (usually from the changing cultural situation) to allow for its own mode of pluralism. Yet that diversity will also often prove an altogether secondary phenomenon as the one and only norm for all expression (e.g., proclamation or doctrine) returns to "check," adjudicate and reformulate alternative positions.

What are criteria of relative adequacy additional to the ones already outlined for developing a contemporary christology appropriate to what we have seen in the New Testament itself? The further criteria, implicit in the analysis of these chapters, take the following form. First, the heart of the matter remains a concentration on a faith response taking the form of a realized experience of recognition in the religious event, the Christ event in the present. This means that the faith response of an individual Christian to Jesus Christ is at once highly personal and irrevocably communal. Christians experience the Christ event principally in the many mediated forms of the Christian church: paradigmatically in the re-presentation of the event in word and sacrament, in individual and communal prayer, in the struggle for justice and freedom, in the meditations of thought, the disclosive realities of secular and religious art, thought and action. The Jesus Christ Christians know and respond to is the Jesus remembered as Christ and Lord by the Christian church from the earliest apostolic witnesses in the New Testament to the present. The Jesus Christ Christians respond to in that living tradition is their paradigmatic religious event of disclosure and concealment: who God is, who we are and what history and nature will be; *that* reality itself is finally gracious and can be trusted in spite of all; that a life like that confessed as Jesus' own can become the pattern and ethos of all Christian life.

If that kind of faith response to that kind of religious event occurs for an individual, then the Christ event is present. The event occurs as sometimes confirmatory, sometimes confrontational, always transformative of all one's usual questions, expectations, hopes, desires, fears. In the response of authentic faith to the Christ event, the believer trusts in Christ and thereby in the final power, God, whose power is not coercion but love, the believer in Christ trusts in the self and world disclosed as beloved, while commanded to become loving. The response to that event, like any response to the event-character of the disclosure of a work of art, must, of course, be deeply personal. Yet a faith response is never merely individualist. The event is mediated to us in and through the community of the Christian church. We may, for good reasons, feel impelled—sometimes, as with Tolstoy, by one's response to the Christ event itself—to reject that church in its present form. Yet even then we live by its indirect mediation. For the Jesus we experience as the Christ is the Jesus remembered and mediated to us by the church from the earliest New Testament communities to the present.

This dilemma for many Christian believers often becomes intensified in the contemporary period. Indeed, the now-familiar cry "Jesus, yes; the church, no" is no longer confined to the religious intensity of a Tolstoy. In our period one can find intensely religious, even Christian responses to Jesus, even to the Jesus Christ remembered by the church but not to the Jesus Christ ambiguously remembered and actualized in the infuriating, gifted actuality of the existing church. What theologian can deny that each of us can resonate to the denunciations of Tolstoy, the passionate exposure of church compromise and duplicity by Kierkegaard ("Luther had ninety-five theses; I have only one—we are no longer Christians")? The prophets and reformers in every period in church history have exposed the failures—the blatant and indecent, the irreligious and un-Christian failures—of the Christian church in every period of its history, including our own.

The church, as we observed in chapter 1, *is* an ambiguous social reality. Theologically, the church is at once both gift from God, primary mediator of the church-remembered Jesus Christ, and yet "sinful church," frequent betrayer of the very event entrusted to its care. The recognition of the gifted, mediating reality of the church is the vision at the heart of the Christian trust in and reverence for the church as the living tradition, as the beloved community, as the sacrament of Christ and the world. The recognition of the ambiguity of the reality of church, when exposed by the Christ event mediated in the church and the Jesus dangerously remembered by the church, is the vision at the heart of the Christian hermeneutics of suspicion upon traditionalism and "mere" mediation in favor of some new, reformed form of mediated immediacy of the originating event.

In the debate between Harnack and Loisy in the modern period,[18] for example, these different, even seemingly contradictory religious impulses in Western Christianity exploded anew with classic force. In Harnack, the classic reformatory principle is operative: a religious and historical sense of a confused and ambiguous tradition and therefore the journey back to scripture, from scripture back to the gospel, from the gospel about Jesus back to the real, normative "gospel" (for Harnack, the gospel *of* Jesus). In Loisy, the classic Catholic principle is at work: the "fullness" of Christianity is what we seek and de facto live by—that fullness is present to us in the living developmental tradition of the church and its many mediations of its centuries-long remembrance of the Jesus who preached the reign of God and was preached by the church as the Christ.[19] This kind of debate, internal to the Western Christian consciousness, discloses (as Newman observed) another dispute, a dispute not over words but over first principles; here originary existential religious-theological principles. Those principles are still operative as distinct and conflicting principles in contemporary christological debates—no longer confined to the relatively manageable types "Catholic" and "Protestant" but crossing all confessional borders and impelling in all major confessions a strife not first over method but over religious, theological principles that should inform all methods of interpretation. To be sure, no major contemporary christology is content with Harnack's liberal portrait of Jesus' personality and his consoling message, yet the same kind of quest for the "canon within the canon" goes forward. Few major contemporary christologies are content with Loisy's portrait of the "development" of doctrine into present fullness, much less with its more conservative analogues in Newman[20] or the early Tübingen school, yet the same kind of quest—in Kasper, in Rahner, in von Balthasar, in Lonergan—continues.[21]

For myself, it was Ernst Troeltsch who saw most clearly the real issue in the Harnack-Loisy debate and who pointed the way forward.[22] One need not agree with the details of Troeltsch's program to agree[23] with his central insight: It is the tradition of the church that *is* our central mediation to the actual Jesus—the Jesus remembered by the church; it is our present experience of that mediated Christ event which impels our belief in Jesus Christ; it is our task in the present situation to understand that tradition in its fullness and its pluralism historically by developing critical methods to free us from the distortions that are *also* present. For Troeltsch, of course, the major critical tools for that reformatory, critical task are those provided by historical-critical methods. In the present situation, however, that method and other methods are now available to serve the same kind of necessary critical reformatory task towards the enveloping, mediating tradition.

In my own terms, the search for criteria of relative adequacy in christology can be expressed in the following terms. Our primary understanding of the Christ event is fundamentally a present experience—a realized experience of recognition of that event's disclosure of God and ourselves, a recognition in the response named faith. That experience and that response are mediated to us, directly or indirectly, through the tradition—i.e., the whole church as the living tradition re-presenting that Christ event paradigmatically in word and sacrament, remembering as its ownmost critical criterion for discerning its own authenticity or inauthenticity to the event the apostolic witnesses to the dangerous memory of this Jesus now experienced and confessed as the Christ. Insofar as we trust in the present reality of that event, we also trust in its mediation to us via that tradition which is the church. The tradition, moreover, focusses our response as a communal and historical one and challenges every individual response with its centuries-long memory and its fundamental fidelity to the authoritative apostolic witnesses to the event itself.

The church's memory includes all the classic persons—the saints and witnesses to that event, the reformers, mystics, theologians, activists, prophets, sages and the privileged ones of every age: the unprivileged, the outcasts in every period whose memory, often effaced, cannot be forgotten. All the other classic religious persons come to us now in the light of the church's primary apostolic memory of this one person, Jesus of Nazareth. The church's memory includes all the classic symbols, images, rituals, doctrines, traditions which witness to that event and remember that person. Insofar as we accept that tradition, we accept our responsibility to all those classic witnesses to the event and memory of Jesus. Insofar as we accept the challenge of those classics upon our deceptively isolated consciousness now, we become consciously part of the tradition: We explicitly include an ecclesial faith in our primary faith in Jesus Christ. We live in the Christ event in and by the tradition, the community, the church. There is little to be gained and too much to be lost by denying this reality of our history and our historicity. We also learn in the personal response to the Christ event to trust with a basic trust the tradition that mediates the event to us.[24] That trust, like the understanding it entails, envelops all our other understandings of the event itself with its gift to us of all these classic witnesses of the tradition in continuity with the earliest apostolic witnesses.

Other experiences in the present may also free us to develop our understanding of the event and the tradition for our own situation and its new resources into new interpretations. Such "developments" of doctrine, symbol, concepts, frameworks, images, rituals and praxis have occurred throughout the tradition and continue to occur now: as in Karl Rahner's persuasive contemporary defense of Chalcedon's religious existential significance even now and his development of that classic tradition of christology into new conceptualities for the contemporary situation.[25]

Yet the notion of development through new resources in ever-new situations does not account for the fuller reality of the theologian's relations to the tradition. A respect for tradition grounded in the recognition of its mediation to us of the Christ event and the memory of Jesus, its very formation of our capacity to experience that event, does call for a faith in the church. It does not call for, or even allow, the familiar distortions of that faith into ecclesiolatry and traditionalism. The faith response to the Christ event—the primary faith response of the entire tradition—frees the believer for the tradition and for its ever-necessary, ever-present self-reform. The tradition of *ecclesia semper reformanda* is one of the surest signs in the ecclesial tradition itself of the reality of a living tradition. To disown that reformatory impulse at the heart of the tradition is also to disown the church's apostolic memories of the message, actions and fate of Jesus. It is to disallow that subversive and dangerous memory of Jesus in the church.[26] Both tradition and church remain ambiguous realities. We cannot allow for that ambiguity (as Rahner, for example, does allow for it in his concept of the "sinful church")[27] and then announce that we can account for *all* ecclesial expressions as simply "developments."[28] We need the reformatory impulse present in the gospel and the entire tradition to find new ways not merely to develop, but also, when necessary, to challenge, confront, transform the tradition itself for the sake of the tradition's own fidelity to the apostolic witness to Jesus Christ and the fuller forms of expression in the scriptures to that witness.

At this point, I believe, the much-discussed *theological* import of historical-critical methods and all other appropriate methods—especially ideology critique and literary-critical methods—becomes clearer. Theologically viewed, all these methods are expressions of the necessary reformatory impulse at the heart of gospel and the Christian tradition. They are, in their present forms, distinctly modern expressions of that impulse. Yet each method is available not only to "develop" the tradition but also to aid its own reformatory impulses by providing distinct modern and public ways to focus and formulate that religious impulse anew. The import of the historical-critical recovery of the original apostolic witness is to provide a new and legitimate check upon any lack of fidelity to the Jesus remembered by the early church by providing an accurate historical portrait of the authoritative witnesses to the event. The import of various social-scientific methods, especially those that also allow for some possibility of ideology critique, is to provide a new and legitimate check upon the distortions which various expressions of the tradition's memory have occasioned and still do occasion. A Christian theological ideology critique is in fidelity to the deideologizing and demythologizing character of the event itself and the original scriptural witnesses. The import of the kind of literary-critical, hermeneutical approach employed in this work is also to provide a legitimate, reformatory corrective of present ecclesial and societal praxis and thought by means of a renewed sense of the disclosive and transformative need for such genres as proclamation and narrative, such symbols as the reign of God preached by the Jesus narrated in the gospels and the symbols, cross, resurrection, incarnation of Jesus Christ, such modes of liberating models for systematic theology as Paul's dialectical thought or John's meditative style, such liberating principles of intensification and negation as provided in apocalyptic, or principles of necessary clarification as provided in the doctrines of early Catholicism.

The Christ event mediated through the tradition is, in fidelity to that tradition from its apostolic inception to the present, an event that is constituted by its relationship to this one person, Jesus of Nazareth. When historical-critical methods provide a modern and trustworthy way to interpret the earliest apostolic witnesses to the person of Jesus—their confessing memories of his message, actions and fate—more clearly and cleanly (as they do), then the results of those methods also provide a modern, reformatory way to uncover the distortions in the tradition, to challenge its and our thought and life to radical fidelity to the actual, remembered Jesus who is the Christ. When methods of ideology critique are employed upon the tradition's remembrance of Jesus, they provide new correctives of the temptations of the tradition: temptations, for example, to sentimentalize the love in that dangerous memory by removing the conflict present in the love for which Jesus is remembered; temptations to endorse the fatalism that too often accompanies much official Christian preaching to the poor on their need for "suffering" in favor of recognizing that gift of suffering love as empowering all persons, especially the oppressed, to enter the struggle for justice elicited by the hope for all history revealed in the event of Jesus Christ and disclosed in the church's own memory of Jesus' preference for the outcasts of his society; temptations of an earlier existentialist individualism and its inability to recognize the nonmythological universal, historical, future-oriented disclosure of the resurrection—an event of God validating and vindicating Jesus and, through the power of Jesus as the Christ and Risen Lord, proleptic for all.[29]

When methods of hermeneutics and literary criticism are employed, they should free the interpreter to recognize anew that the Christ event is mediated to us in genres disclosive of a world of religious significance: Even the *that* of proclamation may yield to our legitimate need for confessing narratives and their disclosure of the story of a life, the reality of the person remembered and confessed. Greater sensitivity to the disclosure of the meaning of that life through a recognition of that meaning's inseparability from its narrative form frees the theologian to employ the world disclosed by the narrative as a new and critical corrective of all present practice and thought in the tradition. Consider, for example, the liberating effect of recent literary-critical studies of the parables of the remembered Jesus. The interpreter learns, through literary-critical methods, the shock and confrontation to our everyday manner of living disclosed by any reading of the parables which honors their form as intrinsic to their message. We learn through these methods to cease allegorizing, moralizing, historicizing these parables and allow them to confront us with their provocative disclosure of what the reign of God is like. In the parables, the reign of God is not an idea clothed in a dispensable story, not a moral point, not an allegory, not simply another occasion to search for "the historical Jesus." Rather, as parable, in parable, the reign of God is confessed as like what happens *in* these stories. As remembered parable, the message of Jesus continues to confront and challenge every complacency, every attempt to disown and forget the radicality of his challenge to those who "have ears to hear." Literary-critical interpretations of the parables help the modern Christian to see that challenge, to hear it anew by honoring its form and refusing to allow the parable form to become domesticated or replaced by some other traditional, more manageable, less troublesome form.

What does it mean to become a Christian? It means at least this: to trust that, empowered, enabled, gifted and commanded by the Christ event of God, I can because I must attempt to risk a life like that disclosed in these gospel narratives. The gospel narratives of the message, actions and fate of Jesus of Nazareth are the primary story that the Christian learns to trust: to focus, confirm, correct, challenge, confront and transform my present questions, expectations, reflections on life and all my attempts to live a life worthy of the name "human."

Not only may these three methods challenge and correct present and traditional responses to the event of Jesus Christ. Each method also serves to confirm the religious dimension of some fundamental need in the contemporary situation. Thereby can these methods also serve as criteria of intelligibility while functioning in their principal role as criteria of appropriateness to the tradition. A part of modern intellectual liberation, after all, is the modern ethical demand for the knowledge rendered available by historical consciousness. Although that knowledge still seems as traumatic to some Christians as it was for the Victorians, the fact is that most Christian theologians respect that historical consciousness. Some have even argued that the emergence of historical criticism was itself an expression of a fundamentally Christian horizon. Others have suggested, as here, that, theologically considered, historical-critical methods can be one expression of the reformatory impulse intrinsic to Christian consciousness. That method does, after all, promise a liberation from the linked realities of the kind of Cartesian rationalism and proud superstition informing the deceptively religious model of "certainty" in traditionalist and fundamentalist notions of faith, tradition and theology.[30]

Most theologians have abandoned the earlier Liberal quest for the historical Jesus and its historical search for the "psychology of Jesus." Most have recognized that the "psychology of Jesus" is unavailable to modern scholarship. Rather, historical critics can and do find the basic outlines of the original apostolic witness to Jesus. As employed in contemporary christologies, the historical-critical recovery of the original apostolic witness and the memory images of Jesus by the later New Testament communities may serve one principal function: to provide a corrective, sometimes even a principle of confrontation upon all later formulations and practices that claim a basic continuity with the Jesus remembered by the apostolic witnesses.

The use of a sociological imagination as well—especially one that incorporates a moment of ideology critique in its method—also serves to correct, challenge, confront and transform any complacent Christian self-understanding. As employed in the christologies of political and liberation theologians, Christian theological ideology critique informed by a sociological imagination attempts to perform two principal tasks: to show the deideologizing character of the primary Christian self-understanding in the early community's dangerous memories of this conflictual, emancipatory Jesus who is the Christ; to uncover the ideological distortions of that memory that have occurred, do occur and will recur unless checked by a Christian critique of ideologies grounded in the mystical-political reality of the praxis of authentic Christian faith.[31] When systematic distortions occur, as we saw in the earlier discussion of hermeneutics, a moment of ideology critique may be needed to uncover any tradition's temptations to illusion, distortion, ideology. The enveloping reality in theological hermeneutics is the understanding in and of the tradition. The developing, purifying, conflictual, confrontational reality is the mode of understanding through a Christian ideology critique of all christologies provided by the methods of discernment and critique of such praxis-oriented christologies as those of Metz, Moltmann, Sobrino, Cone and Ruether.

The dialectic of the cognitive crisis and the liberation of Christian self-understanding involved in historical consciousness and its fidelity to the Enlightenment now joins the dialectics of the social-ethical crisis of a post-Enlightenment sense of both societal alienation and oppression to allow for the liberation of Christian praxis from ideological distortions and to impel theologians to develop new christologies in and for that situation. These christologies too will be controlled by present responses in the tradition to the event of Jesus Christ—a Christ remembered as the subversive memory of this loving, suffering, aggressive, conflictual Jesus: a Jesus who showed his preference for the outcasts of his society; who promised and preached with authority a real liberation for the self, for history, for the cosmos; who was himself preached as the crucified and risen one vindicated by God and believed in by Christians as the Christ; who is now experienced in this situation as Jesus Christ Liberator.

The focus of both a historical consciousness and a sociological imagination can unite to allow the contemporary theologian to respect as well the productive power of the religious imagination in all the classic genres and in the re-presentative transforming power of disclosure and concealment in the religious event of Jesus Christ.

The use of literary-critical methods for the New Testament, defended in this work, is dependent on the prior use of historical-critical methods for the reconstruction of the scriptural text. These methods challenge the usual historical-critical notion of genre as merely taxonomic in order to show how distinct modes of expression achieve adequacy and why all are needed. If those literary-critical methods are also informed by a notion of the religious classic, they demonstrate their properly theological character. These methods remain open to the kind of Christian ideology critique demanded by political and liberation theologians. These methods do so insofar as they also involve the demythologizing and deideologizing use of a Christian theological hermeneutic grounded in the faith praxis of the tradition's own response to the classic Christian event of Jesus Christ. Although the more hermeneutically oriented approach of most uses of literary criticism does not ordinarily render explicit this moment of ideology critique, the hermeneutical approach is entirely open to any defensible public use of Christian ideology critique towards any systematically distorted expression in the tradition. The secular examples of this reality in Adorno, Horkheimer and especially Benjamin are perhaps the best analogues for the kind of literary criticism that does include a moment of ideology critique while still respecting the relative autonomy of the text. Although it is not explicitly developed here, there are good reasons to believe that recent literary-critical and theological approaches could be developed into a theological hermentutics with an explicit moment of ideology critique.[32]

In the meantime, literary-critical methods should join historical-critical methods and methods of ideology critique (presuming all also include a theological component) to inform the search for an adequate contemporary christology. Literary-critical methods have in fact already done so: from earlier modern christologies of symbol, to christologies of proclamation as word-event, to recent narrative theologies designed to remain faithful to the gospel narratives and thereby to confirm, focus and challenge our ever-wandering, distracted attention by their concentrated and liberating focus upon the person and life recounted in these confessing narratives.

In the dialectic of Christian theological understanding, each theologian in articulating a response to the event of Jesus Christ also encounters the tradition that remembers and mediates its memory of Jesus Christ to us. Each learns to trust fundamentally in the enveloping understanding that the tradition provides. Some also attempt to develop that understanding by reinterpreting it for and in the contemporary situation. Some learn as well to challenge, correct, even confront some traditional self-understandings by means of the methods of historical criticism, the methods of social science, the methods of literary criticism. As theologians move through some personal appropriation and use of those methods, they return to and with the tradition to some new interpretation of the event of Jesus Christ. The communal character of the tradition, when matched by the collegial character of theology, can be trusted to develop and employ implicit or explicit criteria of relative adequacy for resolving the inevitable conflicts to trust in the Spirit released by that Christ event in the church to discern and to guide the church in its fidelity to Jesus Christ. To believe in the indefectibility of the church in the truth of the gospel is to trust the tradition, the church;[33] to discern, in the Spirit and in the long run, the church's communal sense of relative adequacy, its fundamental fidelity to the apostolic witness and need for ever-new interpretations. In the meantime, there exists as a part of that wider process of discernment in the entire church the collegial sense of theologians to formulate and employ criteria of relative adequacy for any interpretation of christology. The criteria developed here are, perhaps, clear enough on the methodological side. On the substantive side, they seem to yield a clear series of religious meanings to the central belief of Christianity in Jesus Christ.

iii. Conclusion: The Belief in Jesus Christ

For the Christian to affirm "I believe in Jesus Christ" is to affirm the reality of God's own self-manifestation in the person Jesus Christ. That event and that person, as we have seen above, are mediated through the church and tradition which re-presents the Christ event paradigmatically in word and sacrament and keeps alive the dangerous memory of this Jesus who is the Christ. For the Christ event affirms its intrinsic relationship to none other than this same Jesus of Nazareth *in* whom the tradition believes and the apostles *with* whom the tradition believes.

Above all, the christological affirmation is a religious-existential one: an affirmation that bears the character of a response. That response of trust in its disclosure of all reality is named faith. To state "I believe *in* Jesus Christ" is to affirm that, in whatever form of mediation I have experienced this event, the event itself as the decisive event of God's self-manifestation in Jesus Christ takes primacy. The event happens as a realized experience of the truth of life bearing its own shock of recognition of who we are and who God is, bearing as well its own defamiliarizing confrontation of our usual performance, even our ordinary expectations and questions by its disclosure that "something else may be the case."

The moment of recognition also occurs as a profound confirmation that our deepest yearnings for wholeness in ourselves, in history, in nature, in the whole are grounded in the structure of reality itself. We may now dare to let go of our other, usual "gods"—success, fame, security, self-justification—by letting go into the final reality with which we all must ultimately deal; the power of that pure, unbounded love who is God, the knowledge that reality itself is finally gracious, that existence—ourselves, history, nature—in spite of all is not absurd.

A moment of confrontation occurs as well through the intrinsic connection of this Christ event to Jesus of Nazareth. His dangerous memory confessed by the tradition mediating the event and, through that mediation, as present now challenges our usual views on what life is, what happiness might be, what history, nature, the whole are. That present experience of the presence of Christ liberates the dangerous, defamiliarizing memories of Jesus as suffering Messiah in the entire tradition and liberates us to a real trust in the future—for oneself, history, nature, for the whole—for all, the living and the dead. The memory of Jesus confronts all sentimentalized notions of love with the intensified extremity of the actual thing in the remembered life of Jesus of Nazareth: compassion and conflict; preference for the outcasts, the poor, the oppressed; love of the enemy; love as hard other-regard that looks to the strength of the kind of love present in Jesus' ministry, expressed in his cross, vindicated by God in his resurrection; love as a freedom for the other that comes as gift and command from the strength of God to disallow the resentful weakness in the too-familiar caricatures of that love as mere "niceness."

In response to the Christ event as God's own self-manifestation the believer dares to trust: to trust in the God who is Love, now re-presented anew in the Christ event; to trust in the gift and command to the self to trust and live in freedom and in love; to trust in the ordinary and its extraordinariness; to trust in history and its struggle for justice, for authentic freedom, for the coming reign of love, for the future as God's own future enabling and commanding us to enter into that struggle in the present; to trust in nature and its manifestations and its yearnings for the whole; to trust *in* Jesus Christ as primal word and sacrament of God's own self.

In the moment of re-cognition enabled by the event of representation, the Christian believer senses that here in the event of Jesus Christ the primal word and manifestation of God and thereby of ourselves, of history, nature, the whole is decisively revealed as an event not of our own making yet confirming our deepest longings for wholeness in the whole.[34]

In the moment of confrontation elicited and commanded by that same event, the believer senses that here a different mode of life is both enabled and commanded: a life at the limits like that proclaimed in word and sacrament, like that symbolized in the indissoluble and dialectical connections of the central symbols, cross-resurrection-incarnation, like that thought through in the dialectical intensifications of Paul and released in the meditative thinking of John, like that intensified to release the great negations, the not-yets in all apocalyptic; like that clarified to manifest the extraordinariness of the ordinary itself in the very ordinariness of the doctrines and mediations of early Catholicism; a life like that expressed with the pulse of life itself in narratives of conflict-compassion-love disclosed in the synoptics narrating the message, ministry and fate of this Jesus of Nazareth who is the Christ.

That kind of life is elicited and commanded in the Christ event disclosing that now possible limit-possibility. That kind of life is now recognized as possible, indeed as always-already possible, to all those who will trust in the God who is Love and whose decisive re-presentation is Jesus Christ.

Yet the very disclosure of that always-already reality is at the same time the disclosure of our not-yet actualization of the reality. In this second disclosure the internal dialectic of Christian existence begins anew. The revealing, self-disclosing, comprehensible, present God who is always-already present to us is at the same time the hidden, concealing, incomprehensible, even sometimes absent God of Christian experience. Jesus Christ as always-already primal word and sacrament is also, as suffering Messiah, as the God who *is* suffering love, disclosive of the not-yet reality of Messianic times, the not-yet actuality alive in suffering and in the memory of all suffering now and then. The engifted, enabled, commanded self recognizes itself as justified yet sinner, freed from the world for the world, freed to freedom, freed to enter the struggle in history for justice while freed at the same time to hope in the future as God's own gift; freed through the paradigmatic, decisive extraordinariness of the Christ event to recognize the extraordinariness of the everyday, the ordinary; freed to trust the tradition mediating that event while at the same time distrusting any claim to more than relative adequacy in all its expressions of that event's meaning, freed to employ all the resources of reason and critique in the unending search for its true meaning—metaphysics, historical-critical method, ideology critique, literary-critical methods, the various Christian and secular hermeneutics of suspicion. For the Christian belief in Jesus Christ as the decisive self-manifestation of God is also the decisive disclosure for Christians of all existence—the self, history, nature, the whole. All are internally related by that engifted and commanded love to the power who is Love. In that dialectic, Christians sense that at last they are freed from the gods of the self's irresistible, relentless drive to self-justification; freed to accept the gift of that acceptance by God for God, for others, for history and nature in Jesus Christ.

If the always-already presence of that love is the final key to reality disclosed in the central symbol of incarnation, then the cross is also always-already present in every attempt to live that love. For the cross can be counted on to disclose our, history's, nature's not-yet actualization, our nonacceptance of that reality, our constant need to understand and accept the suffering inevitable to any person who attempts to live that faith grounded in the hope to be found in the even-now vindication of the life and cross of Jesus of Nazareth and, through him as Jesus Christ, for all and for history itself in resurrection.

To live a life based on a fundamental trust in the power of love as God's own reality and God's own gift and command to human beings bears its own kind of verification. As even a day's attempt to live that kind of life can disclose to any person, any Christian attempting to become a Christian will learn swiftly the harsh truth in the narratives about this Jesus: rejection, conflict, suffering, cross. To follow the path of that kind of life of trusting, other-regarding love is to trust in that vision and accept that fate in a hope embraced for the sake of the hopeless and a faith grounded in his resurrection. The final test of that vision will always be the risk of a life. The final test is the future. In the present, there exists the Christ event to elicit, enable and command that risk by its presencing of the Christian tradition and its dangerous memory of this Jesus who is the Christ. The shock of recognition and confrontation in that event commands Christians to risk a life on that always-already, not-yet vision of what reality ultimately is. For the Christian truly believes in Jesus Christ only by risking the kind of life narrated as Jesus' own. The Christian believes in Jesus Christ as God's ownmost self-manifestation by trusting that the risk is grounded in the nature of reality itself and by living that trust. The Christian believes, with Paul and all the other classic persons of the tradition, the saints and witnesses who actually took that risk, that "all is yours and you are Christ's and Christ is God's." The rest is commentary: necessary and important commentary that takes the form of some personal or communal new response, new interpretation, new praxis to the Christ event in particular situations, but commentary all the same.

What our contemporary situation might disclose and some of the responses contemporary Christian theologians have given to that event will be the search of the remaining chapters. In the meantime, the event of God's self-manifestation in Jesus Christ lives in Christian theology seeking ever-new responses, interpretations, commentaries in and for the situation. Informing and transforming both all those commentaries and the basic pattern of situation-response itself is the event and person of Jesus Christ. To that event and to that person, the final commentary is the risk of a life like that lived by Jesus of Nazareth; the final test is the future; the final confession is that this remembered Jesus is the Christ, the very self-manifestation of God's own self, commanding and empowering a kind of life like Jesus' own; the final disclosure is the paradoxical power of an always-already Love who is the final reality who even now, even here touches our always-already, not-yet humanity.

Notes

1. This implies, of course, the need for historical-critical and social-scientific reconstruction of the present written expressions of the scriptures. The uses of the first in form criticism, especially on the earliest narrative sources in Mark and the sayings source in Q, are well known. The use of the second needs further work, especially in relationship to anthropological studies of *oral* traditions. On the latter, see John Gager, "The Gospels and Jesus: Some Doubts about Method," *JR* 54 (1974), 244–72. The emphasis of the present study on relative adequacy in

forms of expression, to summarize, applies principally to the historical-critically and social-scientifically reconstructed expressions from the early apostolic witness to the confessional doctrines of early Catholicism in the New Testament—in distinction, for example, to that "canonical criticism" which studies the final canonical form.

2. Not to understand the differences between uses of the title "Son of God," for example, is to misinterpret the meaning of those texts. As Andrew Greeley has argued, every title is a narrative. A major study here showing the complexities involved—viz., the fact that earlier distinctions (e.g., Bousset's) between "Jewish" and "Hellenistic" motifs are too rigid for the complex reality of several forms of Hellenized Judaism, including Palestinian Judaism—is Martin Hengel's *Judaism and Hellenism,* 2 vols. (Philadelphia: Fortress, 1974). Hans Dieter Betz's commentary on Galatians is an excellent example of recent recognition of this complexity: *Galatians,* Hermeneia Series (Philadelphia: Fortress, 1977).

3. On the historical-critical side, a similar situation holds: both Ogden and Marxsen, for example, despite their use of "canon within the canon" language for the Jesus-kerygma of the original apostolic witness also hold that the merely "implicit" christology of that witness leads to (implies) the "explicit" christology of the Christ-kerygma of John and Paul. As soon as such language as "implicit" enters, the move to a relative adequacy by means of the whole range of expressions of the scriptural and, in principle, postscriptural traditions ensues. In short, we find "tradition" in the full sense with some primary control accorded the original apostolic witness while other modes of control and correctives (e.g., degrees of explicitness in the doctrines, degrees of tensiveness in the symbols etc.) are *also* needed. In other words, we need a "working canon" appropriate to the full range of expressions.

4. See Van Harvey, *The Historian and the Believer* [II/32], p. 273.

5. The "not-yet" character of the narrative is emphasized in Mark's parousia emphasis. The "already" character is present not only in John but also, in their distinct ways, in Matthew's "New Torah" emphasis and Luke's use of "salvation history" and the "heroic" models of Paul and Peter in Acts in ways parallel to his earlier use of the model of Jesus (as a model of *Christian* piety) in the gospel. For an interesting use of literary-critical categories here (viz., "apocalyptic drama" for Mark and "foundation myths" for Matthew and Luke), see Norman Perrin, *The New Testament* [VI/3], pp. 143–221.

6. Walter Kasper, *Jesus the Christ* [VI/75], esp. pp. 254–59. The most innovative move of Kasper is his retrieval of the tradition of Spirit christology. For a critical comparison of Kasper and Pannenberg here, see Philip Rosato, "Spirit Christology: Ambiguity and Promise," *TS* (1977), 423–50.

7. This is especially the case with the misuse of the Chalcedonian formula in so-called neo-Chalcedonianism whereby the balance of the formula "true God–true man" is lost in a one-sided emphasis upon divinity. Many contemporary revisionary christologies are, in fact, engaged in the fully legitimate enterprise of restoring the Chalcedonian balance; an intention to be honored even when one must sometimes judge the results as another kind of one-sidedness. For examples, see Piet Schoonenberg, *The Christ* [Pt. II Intro./18]; and John A. T. Robinson, *The Human Face of God* (London: SCM, 1973). For an informative account of Dutch Catholic revisionary christologies, see *In Search of The Human Jesus,* ed. Robert North (New York: Corpus, 1971).

8. For examples here: (a) on the notion of revelation, see Karl Rahner, *Foundations* [IV/27], pp. 153–62; idem (with Joseph Ratzinger), *Revelation and Tradition* (New York: Herder and Herder, 1966), pp. 11–24; Schubert Ogden, "On Revela-

tion," in *Our Common Life as Christians: Essays in Honor of Albert C. Outler,* ed. John Deschner et al., (New York: Oxford Univ. Press, 1975), pp. 261–93; (b) on logos, see John Cobb's innovative interpretation of "Christ as the Logos" as the process of "creative transformation" in contemporary secularity and religious pluralism (*Christ in a Pluralistic Age* [Pt. II Intro./2]).

9. Hans Küng, *On Being a Christian* [I/96], esp. pp. 214–26, 396–402; Jürgen Moltmann, *The Crucified God* [IV/50], pp. 254–56 (note how Moltmann here shifts Whitehead's "fellow-sufferer" motif into his own left-Hegelian note of Christ's "God-forsakenness").

10. Jon Sobrino, *Christology at the Crossroads* [Pt. II Intro./24], esp. pp. 179–236; Leonardo Boff, *Jesus Christ Liberator* [Pt. II Intro./24], esp. pp. 63–80.

11. Recall Moltmann's criticism of Pannenberg on the interpretation of apocalyptic in *The Crucified God,* pp. 176–77; and the balanced analysis of Rahner's emphasis on incarnation by Sobrino in *Christology at the Crossroads,* pp. 23–25.

12. See my use of metaphor theory to interpret the Johannine "God is love," in "Metaphor and Religion: The Test-Case of Christian Texts" [VI/85], pp. 100–104.

13. See chap. 10 for one spelling out of the Christian "analogical imagination."

14. For examples of the latter, see John Cobb, *Christ in a Pluralistic Age* [Pt. II Intro./2]; and Paul Knitter in *Concilium* 136 [IV/9].

15. In fact, as mentioned before, my own belief in the disclosive theological power of contemporary christologies that claim they are grounded in "the historical Jesus" (e.g., Cobb, Griffin, Boff, Küng, Sobrino, Schillebeeckx, Ebeling et al.) is that even though that claim does *not* hold (see above) these christologies remain remarkably disclosive theological interpretations of the Jesus-kerygma now experienced as dangerous and subversive in a particular tradition and retrieved for a particular situation. For example: Boff's Franciscan tradition and Sobrino's Ignatian tradition and their joint sense of the oppression in the Latin American situation; Cobb and Griffin's liberal Protestant and process traditions and their sense of secularity and a religiously pluralistic situation; Küng's Evangelical-Catholic tradition and sense of a distorted contemporary ecclesial situation; Schillebeeckx's Dutch Catholic tradition and sense of the power of suffering in our ecclesial and societal situation; Ebeling's firmly Lutheran tradition and Heideggerian sense of the necessary power of Word for our technicized situation. In all these christologies, the dangerous and subversive memory of Jesus lives anew as a disorienting sense of an endangered and challenging situation. That these theologians make that dangerous memory of Jesus live anew as a disclosive-transformative word and manifestation of Jesus Christ *now* is what makes their works new and important christologies—not their theological claims about the role of "the historical Jesus."

16. For a fuller discussion here, see chap. 10, sec. ii.

17. It is worth repeating that a "form of expression" is not a secondary phenomenon in any classic, including the religious classic, especially one bearing a re-presentative expression of an event. In that sense, Paul Tillich's insistence that it is the "picture" of Jesus in the New Testament that counts is on target. In present terms: we need to study the basic forms of expression employed to express the event of Jesus Christ in the New Testament and throughout the tradition. We need to study the relative adequacies and inadequacies of different forms of expression (e.g., doctrine's greater adequacy than symbol in clarifying certain central realities abstractable from the symbol; symbol's greater adequacy than doctrine for expressing the always-already, not-yet character of the event; the greater adequacy provided by the whole spectrum of forms of expression as inter-

nally self-corrective than that provided by any one form alone). For Tillich on the need for the "picture" of Jesus Christ, not the "details" of the "historical Jesus," see *Systematic Theology* [II/25], II, 97–138. For Van Harvey's corrective of Tillich here, compare his later comments in "A Christology for Barabbases" [Pt. II Intro./6] with his analysis in *The Historian and the Believer* [II/32], pp. 147–53. For myself, Tillich's implicit recognition of the importance of "forms of expression" ("picture") and his explicit recognition that it is *not* "the historical Jesus" which determines a christology (a recognition he shared with his mentor Martin Kähler and with the mainline Catholic tradition and with Bultmann, Barth and the Niebuhrs) needs retrieval in the present christological obsession with "grounding" christology in the "historical Jesus," his "faith," "consciousness," etc.

18. The original *loci classici:* Adolf Harnack, *Essence of Christianity* (Magnolia, Ma.: Peter Smith, 1958); and Alfred Loisy, *The Gospel and the Church* (Philadelphia: Fortress, 1976). It should be noted that I employ Harnack and Loisy here as Weberian "ideal types." Thereafter I exaggerate certain typical characteristics and dominant emphases in their work. The fuller complexity and subtlety of both thinkers should be apparent to any reader of the classic works cited. Harnack, after all, is one of the classic interpreters of the entire Christian tradition.

19. This insistence is present in Loisy's work, yet reformulated with greater clarity in Blondel, however poor Blondel's interpretation of Loisy's use of historical-critical method may be (Maurice Blondel, *The Letter on Apologetics, and History and Dogma* [London: Harvill, 1964], esp. pp. 226–87). For a careful study of tradition as *actus tradendi,* see Albert Outler, *The Christian Tradition and the Unity We Seek* (London: Oxford Univ. Press, 1958), esp. pp. 111–13.

20. For a recent careful and critical study of Newman's "hypothesis" of development, see Nicholas Lash, *Newman on Development: The Search for an Explanation in History* (Shepherdstown: Patmos, 1975). For a recent critically appreciative analysis of Newman from a phenomenological and comparativist perspective, see Lee Yearley, *The Ideas of Newman: Christianity and Human Religiosity* (University Park: Pennsylvania State Univ. Press, 1978).

21. Rahner [8]; Kasper [6]; Bernard Lonergan, *De Verbo Incarnato* (Rome: Gregoriana, 1964); Hans Urs von Balthasar, *A Theological Anthropology* [III/82], pp. 275–306. A good study of von Balthasar's complex and creative position (a position which includes extensive use of aesthetic and hermeneutic categories) may be found in Giovanni Marchesi, *La cristologia di Hans Urs von Balthasar: La figura di Gesù Cristo Espressione Visibile di Dio* (Rome: Gregorian Univ. Press, 1977). Kasper's case is, perhaps, the most interesting one on tradition. For myself his christology combines a daring retrieval of a Spirit christology with a notion of tradition which, in fidelity to the earlier "Tübingen tradition" and Kasper's own speculative roots in Schelling's later philosophy, correctly affirms the constitutive role of tradition. And yet Kasper also uses "tradition" too easily and too sweepingly. Kasper's notion of "tradition," like an allied model of "development," does not allow his reader to know how the correctives of the tradition from historical-critical and philosophical methods (which Kasper clearly wants) could operate on other than a personal preferential basis. Perhaps the kind of textbook genre of Kasper's *Jesus the Christ* disallows his spelling out of his methodological criteria for the exact relationship of the constitutive tradition and corrective explanatory methods. For an informative critical analysis of Kasper's presuppositions, see William Loewe, "The Theology of Walter Kasper," *Heythrop Journal* (Winter, 1979). For an informed and affirmative analysis of Kasper's christology, see Gerald O'Collins, *What Are They Saying About Jesus?* (New York: Paulist 1977).

22. See Ernst Troeltsch, "What Does 'Essence of Christianity' Mean?," and "The Significance of the Historical Existence of Jesus for Faith," in Ernst Troeltsch: *Writings on Theology and Religion,* ed. Robert Morgan and Michael Pye (Atlanta: John Knox, 1977), pp. 124–82, 182–208; and B. A. Gerrish, "Jesus, Myth, and History: Troeltsch's Stand in the 'Christ-Myth' debate," *JR* 55 (1975), 13–36. Gerrish's study, besides providing singular clarity on Troeltsch's complex position and several other major positions of that period, also develops a critical constructive alternative that is as relevant to today's contemporary christological debates as to those of Troeltsch's own period. Indeed, one cannot but wish that the contemporary debate were better informed by the earlier one. Moreover, Troeltsch's position on the "essence" and "principle" question remains a masterly methodological analysis of the need for both Harnack's critical enterprise and Loisy's notion of "tradition." This is the case despite Troeltsch's occasional and unfortunate "neo-Protestant" disparagement of (and failure at interpreting) Catholicism (e.g., *Writings,* p. 140).

23. See B. A. Gerrish, ibid., for the clearest critique of Troeltsch's christological program.

24. I take this to be the major theological reason for my own reluctance to employ "canon within the canon" language as distinct from a "working canon" authoritatively grounded in the apostolic witness, authoritatively expanding to the later scriptural and classic conciliar witnesses.

25. Inter alia, see Karl Rahner, "Current Problems of Christology," in *Theological Investigations,* I (Baltimore: Helicon, 1961); *Foundations* [IV/27], pp. 285–305. It is also important to note Rahner's insistence that Chalcedon is a "beginning" not an "end." The possibilities of process categories for the reformulation of the Chalcedonian formulation seems promising, as in the distinct suggestions of John Cobb, David Griffin and Norman Pittenger as well as in Rahner's own process-like categories for his trinitarian theology of the Son (*Foundations,* pp. 219–23). It is possible to affirm this suggestiveness without endorsing the use of the "historical Jesus" tradition in various forms in all these theologies. For example, see David Griffin, *A Process Christology* (Philadelphia: Westminster, 1973), pp. 195–233.

26. This is the principal reason why the church itself in its own christological self-reflection cannot be content with the Christ-principle but always needs the memory of Jesus of the earliest witnesses to allow the Christ to judge the church and tradition now. For a historical and theological analysis of reform in the church, see the magisterial work of Yves Congar, *Vraie et Fausse Reforme dans l'Eglise* (Paris: Éditions du Cerf, 1950).

27. Karl Rahner, "The Sinful Church in the Decrees of Vatican II," *Theological Investigations,* VI (New York: Herder & Herder, 1969), 270–95.

28. For a theological analysis of the notion "development" as employed in principally Catholic theologies, see Jean Walgrave, *Unfolding Revelation* (Philadelphia: Westminster, 1972); and T. M. Schoof, *A Survey of Catholic Theology, 1800–1970* (New York: Paulist, 1970).

29. The theological analyses of resurrection as an event both for the apostolic witnesses *and* for Jesus as received and vindicated by God ("dying into God," Küng; "validated by God," Schillebeeckx; "the sign of God's presence within Jesus' life and destiny," Gilkey) seem far sounder hermeneutics of the biblical witness than alternative analyses. For one alternative analysis, see Willi Marxsen in *The Resurrection of Jesus of Nazareth* (London: SCM Press, 1970). For references, see chap. 6, no. 101. Note, also, how the approaches of Küng, Gilkey and Schillebeeckx are more properly hermeneutical and systematic theological analyses of the resurrection than apologetic in the traditional style. The most sophisticated contemporary apologetic on the "resurrection belief" remains Wolfhart

Pannenberg's in *Jesus–God and Man* [II/27], esp. pp. 53–115. The very fragility of Pannenberg's elaborate argument suggests that the *theological* reality of resurrection is best approached on hermeneutical, systematic theological grounds (i.e., principally criteria of appropriateness to the authoritative witnesses) rather than as an argument developed on historical-critical and philosophical grounds. For myself, the major relevant apologetic (or fundamental theological) issue here is whether (in terms of criteria of understandability) the concept "resurrection" (as Pauline transformation) is intelligible—a point argued soundly by Pannenberg and others on philosophical grounds, even without the further warrants of his elaborate (and shaky) buttressing of that philosophical position through the use of historical-critical methods on the New Testament confessional (and thereby systematic theological) resurrection narratives. Küng, Schillebeeckx and Gilkey, to repeat, basically employ criteria of appropriateness to the biblical witness with secondary criteria of intelligibility to defend the understandability of the theological concept of "resurrection" (as in general, Pauline transformation). I suspect that a major issue between Pannenberg and these other theologians is a methodological difference in the general area of hermeneutical theory and thereby on claims to "objectivity"; for examples of this difference, note Pannenberg's emphasis on "propositional language" for "assertive statements" in his critique of Gadamer ("Hermeneutics and Universal History," in *History and Hermeneutic* [New York: Harper, 1967], esp. pp. 145–46). Note also Pannenberg's formulation of "objectivity" in his defense of Luhmann's systems analysis over Habermas' more hermeneutical position (*Theology and the Philosophy of Science* [I/51], pp. 88–103). Pannenberg's valuable concept of "contextual meaning," in my judgment, complements rather than displaces those "intentionality" theories of meaning (e.g., Lonergan) that Pannenberg criticizes. In sum, the main differences between Pannenberg and my own position here, although they surface anew in approaches to the resurrection faith, are basically differences on the questions of interpretation theory, language and objectivity discussed in chap. 3 as here applied to the question of resurrection.

30. For analyses of the ahistorical character of neo-Scholastic theologies, see T. M. Schoof, *A Survey of Catholic Theology* [27], esp. pp. 146–57; Gerald McCool, *Catholic Theology in the Nineteenth Century* [I/65], pp. 129–215.

31. See Johann Baptist Metz on a praxis christology in *Faith in History and Society* [II/35], pp. 51–58. Metz's work is also a good illustration of the reformatory impulse in the notions "tradition," "memory," "narrative" and "doctrine." Metz's own praxis position is far more impressive than his too-ready charge of "idealism" to the christologies of Küng, Schillebeeckx and Rahner (p. 79).

32. Recall the discussion of "disclosure" criteria and "transformation" criteria in chap. 2. I hope to return to this issue in a future work on practical theology. For the present, some groundwork for that position seems clear. Insofar as every classic disclosure also involves transformation, and insofar as the explicitly Christian disclosure in the event of Jesus Christ involves both demythologizing and deideologizing as intrinsic to the kind of proclamation and manifestation involved in this religious classic, there is no theological reason to disallow the development of faith-praxis criteria related to various ethical and political-praxis criteria (including ideology critique). Thus can the practical theologian explicate degrees of relative adequacy of transformation in the disclosive genre apocalyptic (in contrast to earlier existentialist theologians for whom apocalyptic was purely mythological and thereby neither disclosive nor transformative).

33. See Hans Küng, *Infallible? An Inquiry* [I/96], pp. 185–200; Edward Schillebeeckx, *The Mission of the Church* (New York: Seabury, 1973), pp. 11–20.

34. I understand this position to be in fundamental continuity with the "deci-

sive re-presentative'' christology suggestions I made in *BRO*. The major differences are twofold: first, the sense of the negative and the not-yet is far more emphatic in the present formulations of the always-already, not-yet reality of the event of the suffering Messiah; second, the present systematic theological emphasis on beginning with particularity, with the distinctively Christian in its authoritative apostolic and scriptural witness, allows for a fuller explication of the fuller meaning of the reality of Jesus in the event of *Jesus* Christ than did the distinct logic and questions of fundamental theology. The earlier concern of fundamental theology with intelligibility is here further backed by the systematic theological understanding of the demythologizing and deideologizing internal to the event of Jesus Christ in its classic expressions. In sum: save for the greater emphasis on the negative and the not-yet in relationship to the always-already decisive representative christology of *BRO* (an emphasis that could and should have been present even in that fundamental theology) and the greater explication of the actuality of Jesus made possible by a systematic theological focus, the present christological formulations are continuous with and expansions upon those of that earlier fundamental theology. I continue to be astonished, therefore, by the critique of that earlier position by Avery Dulles (*TS* [1976], p. 314; *The Resilient Church* [New York: Doubleday, 1977], pp. 78–81): a serious misinterpretation apparently based on a reading of *BRO* that believes that to speak ''representative christology'' language and to oppose christological ''grounding in the historical Jesus'' is to eliminate *the actual Jesus who lived and who is confessed as the Christ* by Christianity from the New Testament to the present. Perhaps the more extensive analysis allowed by the systematic theological approach of the present work can eliminate at least that kind of misreading of the ''decisive representative'' christology positions in *both* fundamental theology and, in a more expanded form, in systematic theology.

Chapter 8

The Situation

The Emergence of the Uncanny

i. The Theologian and the Situation

Every theology lives in its own situation. The creative and liberating resources of the tradition provide a horizon of questions which theologians bring to bear upon their interpretations of the situation. In this move, theologians are no different from other cultural critics who bring their own orientations, questions and possible, probable or certain modes of analysis and response to the situation encompassing all. Sometimes, as we have seen, theologians tend to speak of this aspect of the theological task as the role of the "world" in theology, or as an attempt to "discern the signs of the times." "Discernment" seems a correct word: to discern suggests an imagery of tentativeness, groping, risk-bearing alertness, that self-exposure of an authentically spiritual sensitivity to the anxieties and fears, the possibilities of both kairotic moments and demonic threats, the refusal to accept timidity in the risk of uncovering the fundamental religious questions in the situation—questions which the very attempt to formulate, however hesitantly, is always worthwhile.

Yet even "discernment" of the "signs of the times" seems somehow too secure an image for the radical risk of self-exposure to the other that any attempt to analyze the present cultural situation must involve. For no thinker, not least the theologian, dwells in some privileged place from which to view what is happening "out there." Like all those creatures who dwell in, not on the sea, we are all in our culture and our history: affected by it at every moment for good or ill, groping at every moment to understand, to discern how to live a worthwhile life in this place, at this moment. With the prophetic passion of a Jeremiah, an Isaiah, an Amos, theologians may confront and denounce their age. But no one escapes it; nor does the authentic prophet wish to. With the foolhardiness of a truly misplaced concreteness, contemporary persons in every age may announce that the ever-elusive now and the all-encompassing ego are all that really matter.[1] Then, struggling to live not in but on the sea, we drown:

having remembered nothing, hoped for nothing, risked nothing. With the pathos of a Miniver Cheevy we may long for a better, a clearer, a cleaner age but, even if such ever existed, we know it is not ours. The worlds of classical Greece, early Christianity, the medieval, Renaissance and Reformation worlds, the self-confident pre–World War I Europe, "innocent" pre–World War II America: All have classical resources to be retrieved for this later time and place. Yet all are gone and will not, cannot return. We are in this contemporary situation: soon to be yesterday, soon to endure its own inadequate label, soon to receive the judgment and, incredibly enough, possibly even the nostalgia of later generations and ages. We are responsible for retrieving that past in our memories, our tradition and our lives; we are responsible to the future in our hopes, our actions, our promises. If both memory and hope, nostalgia and fantasy are to live at all, they must live as live options in and for the situation encompassing all.[2]

Yet what is the "situation" from a theological perspective?[3] With Tillich, we must remember that an interpretation of the situation is only one of two major tasks for the theologian. An interpretation of the Christ event in dialectical correlation to an interpretation of the situation remains, as we have seen, the primary task of every Christian theologian.[4] Yet, again with Tillich, an analysis of the situation remains a major task incumbent upon all theologians who would allow that event and the tradition mediating it to live anew.[5] To understand the situation we may well turn to social-scientific analyses of the macrostructure affecting us all or to the microstructure of our individual psyches.[6] Both macrostructure and microstructure, to be sure, are indispensable conditioning factors in every cultural analysis. Each must serve a corrective role towards any cultural analysis. Yet, in keeping with the prior understanding of the theologian as interpreter of the religious classics of the culture, we must turn elsewhere for the heart of a properly *theological* analysis of the situation. Then, with Tillich, we turn to the notion of the situation as the "creative interpretations of existence":[7] those interpretations which are carried out in every period of history under all kinds of psychological and sociological conditions. The "situation" is not, of course, independent of these factors but does bear a relative autonomy from those conditions by its employment of the creative, productive power of the imagination impelling every classic cultural expression.[8] Theology as interpretation of the religious classics deals primarily with the cultural expressions to be found in practice as well as theory, not with the conditioning factors as such.

This Tillichian position can be reformulated in keeping with the argument of the present work as a whole. In place of Tillich's more general term, "cultural expressions," let us search for the *classic* interpretations of the contemporary situation. In place of Tillich's basic term for religion, "ultimate concern,"[9] let us search for the particular forms that those worthwhile, fundamental questions on the meaning of existence find in those classics. These present reformulations are not without their own use, since our contemporary situation seems both different from and similar to Tillich's own situation. For unlike the "situation" in Tillich's period, as we shall see below, our situation poses no one *dominant* question. Even the profound sense of meaninglessness, absurdity, the radical threat of nonbeing elicited by Tillich and his existentialist contemporaries[10] as at the heart of his situation may now be viewed as one fundamental *and* permanent question in the present postexistentialist situation. That formulation by Tillich of the question as one of meaninglessness may well have been an appropriate formulation of the driving concerns of the existential classics of early twentieth-century inquirers. Conditioned by the threat to real individuality from the levelling powers of mass society, the classical expressions of creative self-interpretation in that period of "classic modernity" spoke from and to that sense of meaninglessness.[11] From Eliot's *Waste Land* and Camus' *Stranger* to Yeats' "widening gyre," Weber's "iron cage," Sartre's *No Exit,* Bogart's fidelity to a personal code, Hemingway's stoical heroes and heroines, Bergman's God-intoxicated, shattered ministers, the existentialist rediscovery of Kierkegaard, Dostoyevsky and Nietzsche, the "revolt of the masses" of Ortega, Giacommetti's evocative sculptured emaciations, and so many other classics in that brilliant period, including Tillich's own beloved German expressionists—all evoked the bleak and frightening image of an ever more fragmented, more privatizated self;[12] a self struggling for an ever elusive authenticity; a self plagued from the outside by the recent demonic outbursts in history (Nazism, Stalinism, Hiroshima, Auschwitz, Guernica) and the overwhelming societal forces of a levelling technicization; a self plagued within by the frenzied internal conflicts unmasked by psychoanalysis; a self sensing nihilism as lurking both outside and within.

Before these visions of existential genius became reduced to the canned goods and cant words of a consumer self-fulfilling society—"alienation," "absurdity," "the masses," "authenticity"—Tillich saw and spoke for his situation in a brilliant series of theological analyses of the situation. Central to his analysis was his focus upon our fundamental question today as the threat of meaninglessness, of nonbeing itself. Anyone who has since that time become a really "authentic self," an "individual" in Kierkegaard's and Nietzsche's demanding senses; anyone who has since mastered the threats and promises of an accelerating technology, who has understood and appropriated the demonic, if not satanic, nonmeaning of Guernica, Auschwitz and the Gulag, is free to dismiss these early classics of modernity and their disclosure of our still-present plight. The rest of us will recognize the enduring truth of their disclosures, the continuing import of their existential concerns. We honor them best, however, as we honor all classic disclosures of the human situation, by attempting to reformulate their fundamental questions in order to ask their and our questions anew in our own distinct situation.

A distinguishing mark of the contemporary situation is the conflictual pluralism existing on what worthwhile fundamental questions are now to be asked. A distinct dilemma of our time seems to be a sensed inability to ask those questions at all, to be able to watch and listen amidst a Babel of voices for any saving word, any gift of hope, any worthwhile question. Theologians, as intellectuals, live culturally in a post-Christian and post-modern intellectual situation. The explosive hopes and ideals of the Jewish and Christian traditions theologians share in explicit conviction. Yet many of their fellow intellectuals share these hopes, if at all, without even knowing them or wishing to.[13] The seemingly more "human" hopes and ideals of the Enlightenment, the ideals of *aude sapere*,[14] have themselves become ever more fragile, even distorted as the dialectical character of the Enlightenment comes more and more clearly into view for all those intellectuals[15]—including most theologians—who know they live in that heritage. The existentialist cries for an authentic solitary self seem still true in their demands, but increasingly hollow as contemporary intellectuals struggle to recognize their responsibilities to others, with others, as they struggle to aid the emergence of an authentically global consciousness, as they struggle against the homocentrism of the dominant culture exposed in its aggressive domination of nature itself.

As the neoconservative intellectuals[16] never tire of reminding the rest of us, we suffer in the contemporary situation from "overload": How many more responsibilities, how much more guilt, how much more hope for equality, how many more questions can we bear? The myth of progress now seems yet one more curiosity of our Victorian forebears—as dangerous to other peoples, to nature and now to us, their descendents, as their sexual repressions were to themselves. The self-confidence of an earlier liberalism now seems a contemptible contemporary option. Even the well-earned, dusk-ridden, dialectical, restless self-confidence of Hegel seems at once entirely admirable and completely impossible. The triumphs of technology do still provoke wonder—witness the "earthrise" from the moon, the smile of Truffaut in *Close Encounters of the Third Kind*. And yet we know that technology—and the age it defines—is a radically ambiguous phenomenon. Its obvious liberating possibilities occur hand in hand with the negative actualities all around us: privatization, environmental pollution, population explosion, false economic hopes of continual growth and, looming over all as our technological final solution, the threat of nuclear holocaust. Even "pure science" can either prove the last refuge of Western arrogance or a new, ever-new, hope for liberating possibilities: Witness the scientism and positivism of earlier and of much contemporary philosophy of science grounding the curiously untroubled self-satisfaction, even willed innocence, of many scientists in contrast to the recognition of the self-transcendence constitutive of scientific inquiry itself grounding the chastened and liberating formulations of a nature-participatory, a nonspectatorial, a value-concerned, "postmodern" science in the works of Toulmin, Ferré, Lonergan, Polanyi.[17]

The necessary empirical work of social scientists moves forward to allow all some better, empirical vision of the conditioning factors in and upon all analyses of the cultural situation. Yet the situation itself—the creative self-interpretations of what a decent, self-respecting, responsible, worthwhile human life might be, what orientations and options those conditions enhance or threaten, what focus for our fundamental questions of existence those conditions demand: For these concerns, with some notable exceptions among the social scientists, we must turn elsewhere. Yet where? In keeping with the entire argument of this book, to the classic activities of the human spirit—we must turn to those activities of the human spirit willing to risk responsible generalizations beyond the necessary specialties, because willing to ask a worthwhile, necessary, fundamental question. We turn, in sum, to art, religion, philosophy, ethics and cultural criticism. We turn to those disciplines whose only contribution to the wider culture is to ask not further and necessary questions on the conditions (and sometimes causes) of our situation, but questions on the situation itself, on the fundamental questions that situation elicits, provokes, discloses. Here the theologian joins all other cultural critics to ask that kind of question in and to that situation.

There is no doubt that any critic's horizon of preunderstanding for asking those kinds of questions will be formed by the implicit or explicit value orientations, voluntary and involuntary, of a personal life history as well as the unconscious effects and the conscious memories of the classic events, texts, images, symbols, explosive or muted hopes—both utopian and eschatological—in the traditions informing our culture. That kind of preunderstanding forms the initial horizon of every interpreter of the situation: sensitivities to, and convictions on, what is possible or impossible for the human spirit; openness to and listening for a possible *kairos,* a demonic path, a liberating word, a power not one's own. Any cultural critic possesses some combination of all these orientating discernments formed by a preunderstanding both individual and traditional, conditioned by the social, political and economic realities of a particular society. Christian theologians differ from other interpreters only by their decision to focus their value orientations in explicit dependence upon and with an explicit new interpretation of that complex phenomenon we all too easily believe we grasp when we utter that disclosive word ever in danger of becoming an empty label, "Christianity." The theologian's own interpretation of the Christ event and the complex tradition mediating it, to be sure, is also conditioned by and partly determined by the same "macro" and "micro" conditions, the same cultural situation which encompasses all.[18] Above all, the theologian's horizon of interpretation is formed by some personal response in the present situation to the Christ event that is the driving, constituting power of Christianity as a lived experience. Yet that event occurs to the individual theologian in a particular situation. The situation, for the theologian, is itself partly conditioned by economic, social, political forces, partly interpreted by the event and the tradition mediating the event and partly the key to interpreting the event itself. A mutually critical correlation occurs in any individual theology between the theologian's interpretation of the event and the tradition in the particular situation and the theologian's interpretation of the situation by means of the event. The actuality of that situational focus cannot be missed in any historically conscious interpretation of the classics of theology itself. Was Augustine's journey uninfluenced by the cultural crises and social-economic conditions of late classical antiquity? Was Barth's *Romans* uninfluenced by the general cultural collapse of European self-confidence in 1918? Are Jacques Ellul's denunciations of modern technology as "satanic" occasioned only by his appeals to the Bible?

Thus does the wider culture have the right to turn to the artists, philosophers, critics and theologians as cultural critics who aid in the understanding of the situation; to help us to ask in our own time those worthwhile, perennial questions which we must ask if we are to lead a human life, to formulate some response—a less mean metaphor, a better, more honest symbol, a striking, even terrifying image, a concept which has not lost the power of negation,[19] an affirmation which is neither cheap nor forced, an expression of faith in a revelatory gift, a happening, a breakthrough not our own. The necessary correctives provided by the social sciences, the inevitable presence of the conditioning factors upon all creative interpretations of the situation, the yet more inevitable demands in each person's experience of life itself can all be depended upon to challenge, confront, enhance, refine or transform the claims to recognizable truth in any classic interpretation of the situation. In the meantime, some thinkers must attempt an explicit interpretation. They take that risk on behalf of all who would move beyond the conditioning of a consumerist banalization of all life. They take that risk by attempting to respond to the questions present in any life worthy of the name human: the fundamental questions present in the orienting thought, images, rituals and symbols accompanying any life worth the effort of living.

Yet the task of discerning the very presence of situational analyses in the contemporary world remains an uneasy one. For many of the philosophers have declared such questions meaningless or, at best, unaskable, and have retreated into the monastic cells of ever-finer analyses of ever more manageable questions. Many of the artists have retreated as well into a self-proclaimed incorruptibility, into the overcrowded margins of the culture, only to find their art later co-opted by the society. Yet now the art is castrated of its power for any real negation of the present.[20] It has become yet another pleasant, eccentric distraction adorning the "affirmative culture" which the artist despised only long enough to misunderstand its fierce and deadly power. Many of the theologians have fled as well: some into the less pressing demands upon the human spirit where the visions of other theologians can be reduced to curiosities and labels, where the risk of asking the questions which constitute religions and theologies can be replaced by the less arduous, more respectable task of asking about the curious questions which other people seem to ask. Others have fled into that genuine growth industry, the building of new, proudly marginalized citadels, new intellectual ghettoes, where the house theologian, lacking as yet the powers of a full ayatullah, must be content to fire denunciations upon "modernity" in all its forms over the walls of the citadel before returning to the purity of one's "unworldly," "churchly" concerns.

And yet, as these final chapters hope to document, there have been many in our time—artists, critics, philosophers and theologians—who have tried to ask those worthwhile situational questions for us all and whose efforts will live as part of the horizon of all. By participating in their conversation we take part in the ongoing conversation of the classics of our culture and begin to understand again how to ask a worthwhile question, how to be attentive to a response which commands attention. Even if the bleakest prospects of some of the best cultural critics are true (Marcuse's painting of a one-dimensional, affirmative society, Arendt's analysis of the banality of modern evil, Steiner's image of the collapse of language, Kermode's articulation of the loss of a "sense of an ending," Habermas's reluctant vision of a systematically distorted communication situation), still one may, with them, join in the perennial conversation which they and others continue.[21] Each joins that conversation in the responsible hope that we must remain faithful to the emancipatory interests in all critical reason, the negations of the errors, illusions and delusions that infest us, and the genuine releasements provided in all real thinking; the power in all great art to unmask and negate present distortions, to project a future of real hope and honorable ideals; the liberating energies in all classic religions to disclose the reality, however hidden, even in its very absence, of a power that can be recognized as not one's own.

ii. The Dialectic of the Classics of the Contemporary Situation

Whether the interpretations of the situation be viewed in terms of "radical pluralism" in the Anglo-American style or as a seemingly insoluble conflict of interpretations in the European fashion, one fact remains clear:

There is no one central interpretation around which all interpretations focus.[22] There is no longer one, single fundamental question that all ask. There are several. For some, even the realities of dialogue and conversation must be challenged in this systematically distorted communication situation.[23] For others, all traditions of fundamental affirmations—Christian, Romantic, Enlightenment, liberal-democratic, humanism in all its forms—seem a rallying center.[24] For yet others, humanism itself seems now a new form of bad faith, a too-easy affirmation masking the slack feelings, the willful innocence and rank illusions and distortions in the contemporary self, society and history. The extraordinary self-confidence of early modernity—classically expressed in the *Logic* of Hegel—has yielded to a contemporary contempt for the *Logic* and a pillaging of the negations in the *Phenomenology*. The absolute standpoint is no more. And yet the dialectic continues as contemporary interpreters move through and in the *fascinans et tremendum* power of the negative in the illuminated Piranesi-like ruins of the *Phenomenology* with its imagery of incessant unrest, vibrating movements of doubt, distortion, contradiction, conflict. The dusk of Minerva has yielded to a night which still awaits some dawn; the circle to the spiral; the waterfall of all logocentric neo-Platonic emanations—emanations still rushing forward in Hegel—to the whirlpool of Nietzsche's deconstructions.

If there are any right-wing Hegelians left, their silence is their most remarkable trait. We seem left instead with unsteady, making-do alliances of various constellations of the fragmented middle and ever more forceful articulations of the power of the negative in an expansive left wing.[25] The left-wing Hegelians of the nineteenth century—Feuerbach, Bauer, Stirner, Marx and, in the wider sense, Kierkegaard, the later Schelling and Nietzsche—seem yet alive in ever-new modes to smash any new icon daring to move beyond the boundaries of the nonidentity of the rational and the actual.

As Hegel once set the basic terms of the early modern cultural debate on the situation, so today Nietzsche, Marx and Freud set many of the basic terms of the postmodern situation. They remain our clearest, steadiest postmodern classics. Their classical force is, above all, at first a relentlessly negative one: They have robbed us of the last illusion of the Enlightenment—the illusion that if we are autonomously conscious and rational we need fear no further illusions. The self-confidence of autonomous, rational, objective Enlightenment consciousness has yielded its own dialectic of both liberation and despair. The myth of progress was merely the first illusion to fall. It was quickly followed by a three-pronged and interconflictual attack of Marx, Nietzsche and Freud upon the pretensions of conscious rationality itself: All the expressions of consciousness possess not only their manifest meanings but conceal and distort a series of latent, overdetermined meanings that demand new modes of analysis.

For Marx the "superstructure" in all cultural products both manifests and conceals, expresses and distorts, the conditioning, sometimes even causal, socioeconomic-materialist structures at its base.[26] In blatant cases, that superstructure expresses nothing other than the ideology as false consciousness of the dominant classes—now the bourgeoisie. In those cases, the language of "determination" is fully appropriate. Yet the analysis must not be confined to the blatant cases, the "period pieces" of a culture. For in all cases, cultural expressions are at best only relatively autonomous from the socioeconomic structures of the "base." Culture always expresses, even if unintentionally, the conflicts and contradictions, the distortions and bad conscience, of the society which gave it birth. For the classics in the culture, the more tentative languages of "condition" and "correspondence" seem more appropriate to most Marxist critics—and to Marx himself. In every case, however, we must remain suspicious of all the self-interpretations of the age, including their classics. No element in the total process of the whole can be isolated and given a significance unaffected by the realities at the base. To pretend they do is to risk "idealism" and "culturalism" masking their own hierarchical ideology and distorting even their liberating promises.[27]

Only when we understand history as process, humanity as social, as always a result of its own labor, can we understand the profoundly alienating reifications of the socioeconomic base hidden and awaiting unmasking in all "culture." Only then can we uncover—beyond the fetishism of facts endorsing the status quo and the idealism of philosophers and humanist critics—the actual conflicts of society reflected in all cultural expressions. The Marxist hermeneutics of suspicion ordinarily demands a central role for the concept "class" to unmask the pretensions to objectivity of empiricist ideologies and the pretensions to humaneness in humanist culture. For some Marxist critics, this unmasking of the class realities in the dominant aristocratic and bourgeois cultures will be accompanied by a search in cultural expressions for the reality of the liberating agent of humanity—the proletariat and its many successors.[28] For others, even the classics of feudal and bourgeois cultures will include their own unintentional negations of the dominant power; their own, sometimes unconscious, betrayal of their own class through the integrity of the artistic imagination and its powers of negation.[29] But whether "determined," "conditioned" or "correspondent to" the material productive base, *no* cultural self-interpretation can any longer be trusted to provide its own meaning. All are now under suspicion. All the classics—even the "happy childhood" classics of Marx's own beloved ancient Greeks—include the illusions and distortions, are disclosive of the conflicts within their societies and sometimes of their societies, the Utopian possibilities for liberation awaiting the properly suspicious interpretation.

Whatever illusions might have remained after so radical a challenge to our culture as Marx provided, Freud supplied through his hermeneutic of suspicion.[30] Consciousness was soon uncovered as wounded at its core: the phenomena central to the analytic situation—resistance, transference, repetition—signal the distortions and compulsions, the infrapersonal conflicts and traumas, the presence not merely of a preconscious but of a structural and content-filled conditioning and perhaps determining consciousness itself. The "mixed discourse" of Freudian analysis, as Ricoeur has shown, is a discourse necessary to uncover the mixed, indeed dialectical, reality of repression and reflection, the unconscious and the conscious, causal distortion and creative autonomy in all the overdetermined symbols of the unconscious.[31] The 'I" of Enlightenment, Romantic and all humanist thought has been and remains to some extent a thing. Freud's language of force ("energy," drive," "repression"—all the famous mechanistic metaphors) must now be seen as necessary to understanding any language of "meaning." Every teleology will now demand an archaeology.[32]

The method, the technique of psychoanalysis, as Habermas has argued,[33] also poses a serious threat to the very possibility of the ideal of communication via dialogue and conversation in the Western tradition. In analysis we do not find two conscious and reflective dialogue partners searching in a conversation for truth. We find an "analysand" and an "analyst." We find one partner (the analyst) employing techniques dependent on a theory of causal explanation to uncover the latent meanings in the symptomatic expressions of the other, the analysand (obsessive thoughts, repetition compulsions, hysterical body symptoms). The analyst must perform that task not through a model of conversation between free subjects but by means of manipulative techniques (free association, uncovering of resistance, insistence upon repetition of the originating trauma, if necessary, even through techniques of intensification like privation).[34] All these theoretically informed techniques are designed to lead to *the* analytic experience of transference. There can be no quick humanist recourse after Freud to suggesting that the "higher," value-laden, reflective, cultural possibilities of dialogue and conversation are necessarily adequate to interpreting every situation.[35] Rather interpreters of the situation must now face the fact that some of our discourse may be systematically distorted by the infrapersonal conflicts unmasked by Freud and his successors just as Marxian analysis has taught us that some of our cultural discourse may be so systematically distorted by structural societal conflicts and contradictions at the base that it functions as, and therefore is, nothing less than an ideology.[36] Here interpretation needs the aid of theory to allow for interpretation itself.

Where Marx and Freud relentlessly exposed the distortions in our conscious, cultural "products" by relating them to the conditions (and sometimes causes) of the infrapersonal and infrasocietal conflicts, contradictions, illusions, delusions and distortions unmasked by their theories, Nietzsche opened another attack on the dominant culture and its pretensions to enlightened, autonomous self-consciousness. With an arsenal of explosive, unmasking aphorisms, with an insistence upon the metaphorical truth of the will to power driving all our "higher" states of reflection, with Dionysiac laughter and dancing on the grave of our cultural illusions, with an insistent and radical perspectivism beyond the half-hearted attempts of all liberal humanism, with a wrenching of all ordering principles to expose the chaos, the no-thing which is their nonground, with an exposure of the *ressentiment* which may define our "nobler" instincts of self-sacrifice and egalitarianism, with a denunciation of the half-awake, timid, lazy, self-indulgent tone of much humanism, with a genealogical hermeneutics of suspicion upon all moral and religious codes, with a recall of the reality of body over spirit proleptic of Freud's later rehabilitation of eros, pleasure and sexuality, with an insistence upon wit and self-overcoming, upon laughter and dance not in spite of, but because of the good news that God is dead and we have killed him, Nietzsche performed his art, his magic, his explosive, radical hermeneutics of suspicion upon the entire Western cultural heritage.[37] Amidst the deadly fireworks of his exposure of humanist illusions, Nietzsche provides a quiet aside: "We are in the phase of the modesty of consciousness." And so, no doubt, we are. For where now, after these three postmodern classic masters of suspicion have exposed the pretensions, the distortions, the illusions, the conflicts in reflective consciousness, where now are our humanist and Enlightenment hopes in autonomous, rational consciousness? The postmodern mind begins to fear, with Nietzsche in *The Dawn,* "that all our so-called consciousness is a more or less fantastic commentary on an unknown, perhaps unknowable, but felt text."

More traditional humanists and theologians often seem to sit by and hope it will all go away, as did those neo-Platonic philosophers in late antiquity witnessing the "vulgarity," the "morbidness," the "sickness" of Augustine's demand that we face the dialectical bondage of our distorted and disoriented wills. Yet no less than the permanent achievements of Enlightenment—the demand for emancipatory reason and freedom from the bonds of oppressive and mystifying traditions, the belief in critical reason and civilized discourse, the need for authentic tolerance of differences and real cultural, political and civic pluralism—will the permanent achievements of postmodern secular consciousness disappear.

Freud, Marx and Nietzsche have served in Western culture as classic postmodern prophets, proclaimers of the unsettling evangel of the loss of our former innocence and self-confidence, proclaimers of the reality of the power of the negative to unmask illusion, conflict, contradiction, distortion, compulsion in our individual, societal and cultural lives. Yet the stories that each master of suspicion has unleashed—stories with us yet—bear their own dialectical tale. It is not, after all, only the Enlightenment which yielded a story which seemed to have no central plot: a belief in critical reason united with a reduction of authentic concepts to mere formulae; an empowering of authentic scientific inquiry united to a destructive manipulation and domination of nature and a self-destructive manipulation via technology and instrumental reason of humankind itself; a development of a genuinely historical consciousness along with an all too easy pluralism, a fearful but unwilling relativism, a repressive tolerance, an undemanding humanism, a political achievement of individual liberties and the common good of a democratic ideal united to unexamined economic ties: capitalist systems masking their inequities under the banners of democracy and individual liberty, state socialist systems hiding their unjustices under the banners of equality and its "necessary" demands.

The stories let loose by the proclamations of Marx, Freud and Nietzsche on the illusions of reflective consciousness have not been without their own dialectics. It is absurd to blame Marx for the horrors of Stalinism. Yet it is equally absurd not to recognize that lurking in Marx's own mixed dialectical discourse—at once Utopian and humanist, scientific and quasireligious, critical and closed, modern and postmodern—lurk all the frightening possibilities in the history of empowered Marxist systems in our century. It is dishonest not to honor Freud's insistence on bringing sexual repression to the light of analysis, not to honor his liberating demand for the release of the full reality of pleasure, sexuality, eros, self-fulfillment, not to respect his refusal of consolation.[38] Yet was not Freud's own mixed discourse partly responsible for its own collapse into the partial truths of the post-Freudian journeys in our psychological culture: on the one hand, the partial discourse of an easy, humanist, self-fulfilling psychology completely at home in a self-regarding consumer culture; on the other hand, the "scientific," mechanical and naturalistic discourse of the technologists of behavior awaiting their cue to save us? It is absurd—or, as Nietzsche himself would have said, it is indecent—to call Nietzsche to task for the obtuse misinterpretations of his thought by self-proclaimed "supermen" and "Aryans" and for the vulgar stupidity of arrogant cults of aristocratic pretensions of some of his unwelcome followers. Yet Nietzsche's own mixed discourse, once freed from his integrity and intelligence, yielded its own dialectics: where the will to power loses its metaphorical and thus its real truth, it can become a cover for the idolization of a Cesare Borgia; where his call to life-affirming "self-overcoming" loses his force and his intelligence it can become merely the posturings of arrogance and brutality; where Nietzsche's critical and passionate admiration for the classical triumphs of reason in Goethe and the Enlightenment is quietly forgotten, his thought can become merely another expression of a tired, Romantic, ambiguous, too easily assimilated "existentialist" posture; where his life-affirming "yes" to the self-same is forgotten, the truth of the eternal recurrence can become merely another disputed cosmological doctrine; where his extraordinary combination of gaiety and seriousness is split asunder, his complex understandings of Socrates and Jesus, Hegel and Spinoza, of tragedy, laughter and dance, of dialectics and critical passion, can become new masks for new forms of *ressentiment* against all the classic images, texts, symbols and witnesses of our and his heritage.

Each classic expression of the human spirit seems inevitably to produce its own dialectic into a story at once liberating and manipulative, healing and murderous, even *fascinans et tremendum*. Every product of civilization, as Walter Benjamin reminds us, is at the same time a product of barbarism.[39] Classical Greece and Judaism, Christianity, the Renaissance, Reformation and Counter-Reformation, the scientific revolution and the Enlightenment—and now the postmodernity of Marx, Freud and Nietzsche which promised and promise to free us at last of illusions: All have set in motion dialectics of liberation and domination, genuine conversation and systematically distorted communication, freedom and alienation, critical and instrumental reason. And so we find ourselves in a situation, still confused, struggling for some final liberation that is always deferred. We are left where we began: with a partiality for critical reason and its emancipatory interests, a belief in conversation and dialogue with all the classics of our heritage, and a hope that remains given to us only for the sake of the hopeless.[40] The real task for all is to find ways to unite in critical conversation *all* the forces left in the culture who share a belief in critical reason, in dialogue, in hope itself.

We find ourselves in this postmodern journey of the spirit moving from the fundamentally ahistorical and emancipatory dialectic of the Enlightenment through the liberating dialectic of the historical consciousness of the age of liberalism to the recent rehabilitation of the historicality of our beings and the genuine, nonauthoritarian authority of authentic tradition, i.e., of all classics. We now seem to find ourselves in a situation where all the traditions and all the classics have become porous, where there is no "windowless monad," no language game where anyone can find refuge from the conflict of the radically pluralistic present. The necessity for all the interpreters of the classics in the situation to expose themselves as themselves to the genuinely other, the need to discern when and how a systematically distorted communication moment is upon us, where dialogue and conversation are possible—or, if not now possible, how they can be rendered possible again—the need to reformulate fundamental questions that are worth our asking in this pluralistic, conflictual, often chaotic present. All these imperatives are now upon all those—secular and religious, artist, philosopher, critic, social scientist, theologian—who will enter the conversation of the classics amidst the shouts and Muzak of the period pieces of a consumer society and with renewed, if desperate, willingness attempt to converse.

iii. The Self-Exposure of the Classics to and in the Situation: The Ideal of Dialogue

The Enlightenment and its release of a dialectic of both emancipation and alienation was part of the epoch-making event of Western, even global consciousness named the seventeenth-century scientific revolution. As Herbert Butterfield correctly insists, even the Renaissance and the Reformation, classic events for our culture, seem like family quarrels compared to the new way of viewing reality—in Butterfield's British phrase, the new "thinking cap"—that the scientific revolution bequeathed us.[41] When that calm was shattered by the sometimes frightening technological achievements of science, other metaphors begin to emerge to define our present state: the "iron cage" of Weber, the "one-dimensional society" of Marcuse, the "air-conditioned nightmare" of Henry Miller, the triumph of "instrumental rationality" of existentialists and revisionary Marxists alike. Less graphic, perhaps, but in the long run both more liberating and more frightening, is Heidegger's insistence that technology and its attendant technical reason have become the very framework (*Gestell*) of our time. What is this framework that envelops us?[42]

For Heidegger himself, the framework is none other than a monstrous provocation of nature whereby we rob ancient *techne* of its true vocation, its classical intrinsic relationships to nature (*physis*) and to *poesis*.[43] Now *techne* becomes the product of the will to domination, power and control. Soon a dominative *techne* arrives as the very framework of what will count as thought: a power on its own, leveling all culture; annihilating all at-home-ness in the cosmos, uprooting all other questions in favor of those questions under its control: producing a planetary thought-world where instrumental reason, and it alone, will pass as thought.[44] As Nietzsche predicted, nihilism becomes our fate. Knowledge is now mastery through technique. Truth is an expression of a subject controlling and being controlled by a technical object held at a distance. Nature will now, as Francis Bacon insisted, be "put to the rack to compel her to answer our questions." The object cannot think. The subject will not. We began as technical agents of our willful destiny. We seem to end as technicized spectators at our own execution.

For Heidegger, even Nietzsche is an expression of the long Western journey of domination begun with Plato and Aristotle, reinstated in modern form with Descartes and Hegel, consummated in Husserl's noble and fated attempt to produce a presuppositionless, apodictic, rigorous science marked by control and certainty.[45] For Heidegger, this journey is the journey of the forgetfulness of the question of Being, the "onto-theological" journey of two worlds—the real and the other, the true and the false—ending in the self-sufficient modern subject's distance from and mastery of the object, the journey where all the gods have fled, yet "only a god can save us now."[46] Heidegger's critique of modernity seems a profound reflection on the last words of Nietzsche's *Genealogy of Morals:* "Mankind will will the void, rather than be void of will." The only hope Heidegger will offer, it seems, in this time "in between" is the need to turn to the last custodians and watchers of that question, the poets and the thinkers.[47] They alone, for Heidegger, give us questions worthy of our participatory response, by their releasement into primal language, their letting be of the world in its fullness. They alone, for Heidegger, can release us from the rack where the modern *aude sapere* of modern science has become the *parendo vincere* of modern technology as our ownmost *Gestell*.

Thus does Heidegger join the earlier masters of suspicion upon our situation. Thus does he join such unlikely comrades as revisionary Marxists, even the dismissed "existentialists" who have "misunderstood" his thought by refusing to hear the only question he wanted to ask—the question of Being. Thus will Heidegger himself be reinterpreted by antihumanists who playfully, joyfully, gaily dance and sing over the corpse of anthropocentric humanism and a metaphysics of presence.

Surely we must attend to Heidegger's critique of the crisis—a critique whose violent yet controlled energy in both expression and thought bears classic force. We must attend above all to his demands for the claims to truth in art and meditative thinking, to their promise of a possible releasement that will free us again to participate in nature, to let go of our will to dominate, manipulate, control, to let Being—and beings—be, to ask a fundamental question. Heidegger's contributions—for me, his classic contributions—cannot be gainsaid by easy misinterpretations of his thought as existentialist. And yet there are important caveats to Heidegger's critiques of science and technology: Scientific inquiry does not necessitate dominance, mastery, control; it bears within itself its own immanent norms of critical, emancipatory self-transcendence opening it to values, ethics, art, religion, to the fundamental questions. Like so many thinkers in the European tradition of reflection on science (indeed, such otherwise diverse thinkers as Marcuse, Gadamer, Sartre and Ellul), Heidegger seems unwilling to notice that the very performance of the scientist is not characterized by domination but by an intellectual self-transcendence even when the official philosophers of scientism and positivism disallow that reality in their theories. The European tradition of reflection on science often fails to see that scientific inquiry—hypotheses, explanations, verification and falsification procedures—are not marked fundamentally by the will to mastery and control but by the emancipatory interests of all authentically critical reason.[48] They cannot seem to view either the ecological movement or ecological theory as other than penitential movements masking utilitarian motives. Rather, these movements are fundamentally signs of the emergence of a postmodern science wherein *techne*'s relationship to nature is once again participatory, not dominative, and where our false images of ourselves as spectators may be replaced by the kind of participatory, responsive relationship that both classical *techne* and modern critics of science and technology demand.

So bleak is the usual European picture of technology as our "fate," our "framework," our "cage" that the authentic ambiguity in both science and technology is in danger of being lost to view: its liberation of disease and ignorance, its enhancement of communication and its performative fidelity to emancipatory inquiry. One need not embrace either the energetic Utopian enthusiasm of Buckminster Fuller or the frightening forthrightness of B. F. Skinner and other technologists of behavior to be willing to grant that humanists should honor science along with art, philosophy and religion. For science, contra Heidegger, is a genuine expression of both emancipation and authentic thinking. Our technological framework is a destiny fraught with danger, not a necessary fate. Theory and explanation exist to develop, challenge, correct, confront our enveloping understanding, not to serve as its unnatural enemy.[49] Empirical thought need not become empiricism. Science need not become scientism. Technology need not prove technocracy.

And yet, even after all these largely Anglo-American caveats are entered, we too sense that the negative realities in our present technologically and scientifically oriented situation bear more reality than humankind may be able to bear. Many of us recognize from any everyday contemporary experience of life that truth is too often a coverword for conquest, manipulation, domination, the rape of nature and humankind alike; that every radical critique—every classic work of art, thought, prophetic religion, every true movement for liberation (the sexual revolution, the struggles against racism, sexism, classism, economic exploitation) is in constant danger of absorption and co-optation by the societal whole as some new thrill, some new distraction for an insatiable consumer appetite;[50] that the technologists of behavior are in the wings waiting for the pathetic humanist play to end so that the final bureaucracy may be established; that the no to power of Nietzsche, Kierkegaard, Freud, Marx, Solzhenitsyn and many others may be heard only long enough to be mistaken for an echo of those bogus affirmations demanded by business as usual; that the *nihil* in our nihilism will probably not be faced and lived through but will first be ignored and then hunted down; that Descartes' mask of *parendo vincere* is slipping to expose our willful journey and our disoriented wills. Even the imagery and language of art may become as battered and dispersed as our wills: an art honestly unable to repeat the grand affirmations of our Romantic forebears, unwilling to risk a statement of the whole in a time of fragments, refusing a statement to the whole society in a time of forced marginalization, righteously incapable of making art "easier" for all to understand lest that very attempt at communication only prove the final betrayal of art to the levelling forces, the gray-on-gray contours, in our fragmented technological present.

Intellectuals in all traditions often find themselves, as William Barrett suggests, living Kafka's prophetic parable of "The Great Wall of China."[51] Once we knew, or, at least we think we knew, why we were building that wall. Yet now we stand in our own little groups—some like-minded Christians and Jews here, Marxists there, Freudians, liberals, deconstructionists, structuralists, conservatives some miles away; scientists, artists, philosophers, theologians; all keep building, but somehow the point of it all now seems lost to view; the center is not in contact any longer; the center, one hears, has become horizon.

iv. Orientations, Options, Faiths: The Uncanny

The classic works of postmodernity serve, as George Steiner reminds us, as after-theologies, post-theologies.[52] This is not merely to state, as Steiner and many before him have, the obvious quasireligious and quasitheological elements in the thought of the masters of suspicion: the messianic-prophetic and eschatological strains in Marx; the stoic, even Augustinian, pessimism on the human being in Freud; the deliberately post-Christian doctrines of the will to power, the "overman" and the "eternal recurrence" in Nietzsche; the tonalities of Augustine, Luther, Pascal and Kierkegaard in the analysis of *Da-sein* in the early Heidegger; the unmistakably pietist, even mystical strains in his later "releasement" where thinking becomes thanking. More fundamentally, one may note that the tonalities of these works disclose a post-Jewish and post-Christian expression of genuine religious and theological import. All four classic masters on the contemporary situation, it is important to note, appeal back to the classical myths and symbols of the ancient Greeks and Persians, not the ancient Jews and Christians: Oedipus, Prometheus, Dionysus, Zarathustra, the "gods."

The images and symbols, the thought and myths of ancient Greece, have become for many intellectuals in our secular postmodern spirit a golden age of origins. Yet we know that however powerful contemporary retrievals of the disclosive and transformative myths of classical Greece in these post-theologians (retrievals directly comparable to the retrievals of classical Judaism and Christianity in the theologians), we are all engaged in radical reinterpretations, translations, from a pre-Enlightenment, a prescientific and pretechnological age to our own radically different situation. Like the best Jewish and Christian theologians of our era, these post-theologians are engaged in interpretations that include a series of negations of present alienation, oppression, repression as well as often desperate, brilliant, healing retrievals of an alternative *mythos* for the technological situation—a non-Jewish, non-Christian, nonscientific ethos disclosed to the post-theologians among the ancients, paradigmatically among the Greeks.

Yet even these post-theological retrievals of an alternative symbol system do not occur without the memory, half-effaced yet still powerful as an undertow, half-forgotten but jarred by involuntary memories of the Jewish and Christian myths, symbols and ethos. The prophetic strain in Marx explodes into the explicit retrieval of the power of apocalyptic messianism, eschatology, and Utopia in Ernst Bloch and in the dangerous memory of the suffering of the oppressed in Walter Benjamin.[53] The ancient Jewish refusal to name God, the refusal to provide images for the future inform the demand for a purely negative dialectic towards the present in Adorno and Horkheimer.[54] The kabbalistic tradition retrieved by Gershom Scholem returns to complicate almost beyond recognition the mysteries in any single text in the brilliant cultural criticism of Benjamin and Bloom.[55] That destructive force towards ancient pagan self-confidence named Augustine comes to provide the familiar tone, the attunement, the form of the sturdy pessimism in Freud and Heidegger. The figure of Moses, once transformed by Michelangelo into the image of a self-confident Renaissance, is retransformed by Freud into a daring conquistador of the spirit alive to the uncanniness of our homeless moment: However "Egyptian" Freud's theory, the spirit of Freud's Moses remains profoundly Jewish.[56] And where Freud hesitated, Jung advanced:[57] to strike a demand for the retrieval of all the religious symbols of East and West, to demand that the archetypes return to consciousness again to help heal our fragmentation, our not-at-homeness.

Heidegger may repeat, correctly and over and over again, that he is *not* a theologian, that he has nothing to state for or against Christian theology.[58] Yet even his Greeks come to us with evangelical tones, even his "mystical" utterances bear a familiar pietist ring of unexpected grace, even his and Hölderlin's "gods" cannot seem to loose themselves of the eclipse of God. His theological interpreters—Bultmann, Rahner, Ebeling, Fuchs, Ott—sense this, embrace his method of retrieval, yet move on to retrieve the other classics, the Jewish and Christian classics, that he ignores.

With Nietzsche, the secret, along with Kant's, Fichte's and Hegel's, is released: "The Protestant minister is the grandfather of German philosophy." From the stern, serious, strenuous Protestant tones from Kant through Nietzsche's chief existentialist successor, Karl Jaspers, to the

Jewish and French tonalities of laughter and dance, of antigravity in Nietzsche's chief deconstructionist and antiexistentialist successor, Jacques Derrida, the liberating, often shocking music of the classical Jewish and Christian symbols rejoin the harmonies of ancient Greece and Persia to provide new postmodern, post-Jewish, post-Christian, post-theologies for many secular intellectuals. The role that theology once played for the wider secular culture—a role which, since the Enlightenment, seems ever more unwelcome and seemingly unnecessary—was once provided by the Romantics' secularization of the Christian redemption scheme.[59] In our situation, however, when even the Romantic affirmations through negations seem impossible to many, the power of the purely negative returns in the great post-theologies of our period.[60] The dismantling and demystifying interpretations of all "positive" religion by the Enlightenment thinkers, the explosive demands for genius, creativity and individuality in the Romantics have yielded to the Muzak religion of a bogusly affirmative culture for some and to the classic negative critiques of religion by the postmodern masters of suspicion.

For how long will secular intellectuals remember only the slogans of the masters of suspicion in religion and not their courageous risk? Religion as the "opium of the people," projection, *ressentiment* have often become not the powerful critiques on religion of Marx, Freud and Nietzsche but the conventional secularist wisdom repeated with a dogmatic secularist self-assurance that could be the envy of any Christian fundamentalist.[61] How often will accepted masters of interpretation of the accepted secular masters—a Bloch, a Benjamin, a Jung, a Jaspers, an Erikson—have to rediscover the fuller complexity, the liberating resources in that ambiguous phenomenon, religion, before explicit and sophisticated retrievals—post-theological if necessary, theological if possible—of the resources in religion for the situation are rendered available to the secular culture?

In a sense, it matters very little, as long as the post-theologians themselves are really listened to—as Walter Benjamin understood with clarity:

> A puppet in Turkish attire and with a hookah in its mouth sat before a chessboard placed on a large table. . . . Actually, a little hunchback who was an expert chess player sat inside and guided the puppet's hand by means of strings. One can imagine a philosophical counterpart to this device. The puppet called "historical materialism" is to win all the time. It can easily be a match for anyone if it enlists the services of theology, which today, as we know, is wizened and has to keep out of sight.[62]

What is our fundamental question today? Where is the situation we seek: nowhere, no one place; everywhere, every place we live. As the secular traditions set loose by the postmodern classics show us, the experience of the uncanny awaits us everywhere in the situation.[63] Our very homelessness provokes an evocation of that not-at-homeness which is one, perhaps the most familiar, kind of experience in our situation.

For some interpreters of the situation, this experience of the uncanny will focus upon the not-yet of some future, some Utopia, some apocalypse, some sense of an ending released to empower our negations of present alienation and oppression, retrieved to shatter our human, all too human affirmations and to disclose the always-already reality of the uncanny in our midst.[64] As we retrieve the reality of the uncanny in the Utopian visions and the apocalyptic movements of our cultural heritage, as we experience the empowerment of that experience in the daydreams of the present for a better future and the great movements of real praxis for concrete liberation in our time, as we allow memory to work its liberating function and recall the dangerous memories of the traditions of suffering in our heritage, as we embrace the power of the negative in all great art and all prophetic religion, we release ourselves to the empowerment of an experience of the uncanny. In that experience, the force of the not-yet unmasks our present bondage and, in that very unmasking, discloses an always-already hope: a hope sheerly there—given, we know not how, or by what or by whom, given as gift, as threat, as promise in an ineradicable, always-already power that we acknowledge as given to us only for the sake of the hopeless.

For other interpreters of the situation, this experience of the uncanny will emerge as the not-yet of our homelessness in history and nature evoking the astonishing always-already reality of a sheer wonder in existence itself. As we reflect upon the reality of our ordinary, everyday lives—the wanderings, meandering, detours, conflicts, contradictions, preconscious and conscious feelings and thoughts, loyalties and hatreds, ideals and practices, voluntary and involuntary memories, pleasures and fears, all jumbled together in a confusing stream whose shore seems nowhere, all chaos where every thread of order seems to stand but for a moment—we may recognize with Joyce or Buber, with Proust or the Tao, the uncanny extraordinariness of the ordinary itself. Witness the paradigmatic postmodern journey of Joyce: the deliberate and extraordinary no of the artist in youth frees the exile to move on inexorably to the uncanniness of the extraordinary-ordinary yes of the wisdom of the body, of eros and sexuality, of pleasure and desire in the ordinary-extraordinary Molly Bloom, only to end in the confusing, rushing, releasing uncanniness of ordinary language and the dreams of the night in the river-run, here comes everybody, liffey that is our individual, familial, communal, universal, waking and dreaming lives in the everyday.

Nor do conservative interpreters of the situation miss the uncanniness of our moment, however differently they may interpret its causes. Indeed, as we reflect, with the authentic conservative, on the *no*-longer of the presence of the liberating classics of our heritage, the no-longer of real community and nonauthoritarian authority, the no-longer recognizability of mystery, enchantment and origins, the no-longer classical recognition of limits destroyed by our Promethean wills and our Protean consciousness, the no-longer of a conversation which should not have been broken, we all experience the reality of our homelessness in the situation and the presence of the uncanny in that sensed reality of the "no-longer."[65] As the conservative thinkers attempt to retrieve some fragments to shore up against our ruin, as they lash out against the iron cage of disenchantment that encircles us, they do so with the dual recognition that the no-longer of our present pain, confusion and disorientation releases us to an always-already sense of the giftedness of existence itself, even "the hint half guessed, the gift half understood."[66] In the relentless waves of negativity towards modernity of the true conservative, the brilliant bitterness of Evelyn Waugh, the classically serene dismissals of the modern by Leo Strauss, the authentically humanist, the quiet, civilized, firm no to all that of a Hans-Georg Gadamer and a Hannah Arendt, we may recognize the presence of an always-already undertow of the sensed presence of some gift, some participation beyond all homelessness and absence in a history that is also a heritage, a fate which can become again a destiny, a culture which can release us, through its very negations, to the gift and wonder of a grounding at-home-ness in the wonder of the gift of historical existence itself.

Nor will the scientific humanists miss analogous experiences of the presence of the uncanny in their journeys. For as they move with the modern spirit of scientific inquiry beyond the theories of positivism and scientism to the postmodern participatory science actualized in ecology and grounded in the self-transcending, self-structuring immanence of the pure, detached, disinterested desire to know, they recognize with J. B. S. Haldane the uncanniness of their own discovery. "Nature is not only stranger than we imagine; it is stranger than we can possibly imagine."[67] As we check our disoriented and dominating wills, as we throw aside our ladders and try, at last, to "look, not think," we begin to sense, with Wittgenstein, the uncanny truth "that the world is, is the mystical."[68] In our present wintry mood where the myth of entropy has replaced the vacuum left by our embarrassment at the collapse of the myth of progress,[69] we sense that science and technology, beyond their long imprisonment in positivist dismissals of value issues as purely "emotional," "private" or "personal preferential," have resurfaced those issues in the scientific community. We begin to believe that, perhaps after all, the global consciousness set loose by science and technology may yet yield to the dawn of an interdependence of a truly human technology for the planet earth. Prometheus, Faust and Proteus, Oedipus and Narcissus, have played their uncanny roles. It is time in science for new uncanny myths.[70]

As that global consciousness which Western science, Western technology and Western imperialism have engendered returns home to the West, the unnerving and possibly emancipatory resources of the other cultural and religious traditions finally begin to play their own uncanny role upon Western consciousness. As Wittgenstein sharply insisted, as Whitehead with his urbane suggestion of the importance of the vague over the clear more modestly suggested, as William James with his generous sanity democratically and pluralistically hurried to embrace, as Heidegger with his strange combination of violent, energetic speech forcing us to release ourselves and our language to the uncanny nonviolence and dignity present in van Gogh's painting of a peasant's shoes, as Rothko and Newman imaged for us as the sacred void, as those masters of the retrieval of the hidden, despised resources in our own traditions, Jung, Eliade and Scholem, repeat over and over again, the routes of negation in all the spiritual traditions await our entry to work their uncanny releasements upon us from the terrors of our own history. To pass through the sacred void of our own moment disallows any easy, clever, "canny" refusal of the route of the *nihil* in our uncanny nihilism. And yet, like the great spiritual traditions of the East, like the apophatic theologies, the hermetic and mystical traditions in the West itself, we may now learn to drop earlier dismissals of "mysticism" and allow its uncanny negations to release us. It *may* be possible. In the meantime, we can at least try to learn to listen again, to wait, and in the paradox internal to our strange dilemma, to *try* to let be; to try to care and not to care. For some, the full uncanniness of the mystical traditions has, it would seem, already exploded. They, perhaps, have already sensed that "all will be well and all manner of things will be well." For most of us, we must be content to allow our present negations of our former negations of "all that" suffice, as we catch a glimpse—no more, but no less—of the astonishing always-already reality that there is anything at all: "That the world is *is* the mystical."

For still other interpreters, there is another route to the uncanny. For there is today in every text, every image, every act of interpretation, indeed every act, no origin, no center, no end, no correct, no right, not even a determinate meaning.[71] There is, rather, the incessant play of signs in the labyrinth, the web, the whirlpool which *is* every classic of our culture. We will embrace the always-already absence uncannily present-absent in every realm of order that is not yet disclosive of the chaos that is always about to be. A deconstructionist negative dialectic—a negation beyond the gravity of humanist seriousness and the dominating will to order in our usual deceptions—will "deconstruct" all "meanings" and unravel the thread of every confining web of order. We will do so in order to experience the joyful, life-affirming, self-overcoming vertigo of the underlying, nongrounding nothingness which is the uncanny we should seek and must learn to love. We will free ourselves, with Roland Barthes,[72] from the revolting "repleteness" of our traditional symbols of plenitude in order to experience the pleasures of the text with our own contributions of new signs. We will replace all the existing, boring, scattered signs in our culture and find joy in that absence. We will cure ourselves of the deadly boredom which our bourgeois-humanist search for certitude has imposed upon us by disclosing the indeterminacy of every determinate meaning, the always-already, about-to-be, uncanny absence lurking in every present and past meaning.

We will learn to overcome our needs for the anthropocentrism of historical consciousness, our entrapment in an *episteme* which should be allowed to die. We will fashion, with Foucault[73] and Deleuze, an antigenetic, antihistorical, antihumanist Nietzschean genealogical method which will break all codes—family, state, humanist culture—using the very codes first discovered by Saussure in a manner which Saussure or even Lévi-Strauss dared not imagine. The codes will now become weapons to cure our need for presence, for reference, for history, for reason itself.

The game of humanist conversation with the world disclosed by the text will now become, with Derrida,[74] the free play of our own putting into motion of another chain of signs to deconstruct the sealed echo chamber of the text; an uncannily endless play of newly generated signifiers to set into motion the incessant play of signification that goes on within the seeming immobility of these writings, these black marks on white paper. We will joyously trace and erase the always-already present-absent "traces" of the difference in these sounds and signs as their differentiability from all other signs. These self-effacing traces of difference will free us to defer indefinitely any determinate present meaning which we formerly and vainly pursued. We will experience the uncanny moment wherein order becomes chaos, determinacy becomes indeterminacy, differing becomes deferring, difference becomes differ*a*nce. The always-already presence of this nonpresence—emanating from no voice, intended by no one, referring to no-thing, careening in the void—will disclose the vitalizing always-already, about-to-be, uncanny moment releasing us from the power of the metaphysics of presence to the joyful affirmations of that Dionysian laughter and Apollonian dance which is the free play beyond the too serious play of all earlier conversations. Through such moves will the deconstructionists find their own experience of the uncanny in the contemporary situation.

For still other interpreters of the situation, there are no texts, no traditions, no symbols, no images, no methods of interpretation or deconstruction which can be allowed to stand in the presence of the overwhelming absence of all meaning exposed by those events in our century which are satanic explosions of anti-Spirit. These events challenge all interpretations by paradigmatically expressing a repressed truth in our situation: the Holocaust, the Gulag, Hiroshima.[75] These events—classical negative events[76] seeking for an always inadequate classical text—become the final caesura to our fated journey of domination.[77] The task of interpretation becomes to try to face the nameless horror they disclose in order to allow their *tremendum* power to call into question all traditions. We must learn to wait, to tell the story,[78] to give voice to those who have no voice, to face the nonidentity of our actuality to reason, to spirit, to reality, to despise as obscene any easy grasp for meaning in such meaninglessness. We must not allow these paradigmatic events to fixate our attention but to free our spirits for hope and action. We must discern the affirmations still left to us in the songs and stories of the enslaved black, the humanity in the death camps, the massive, unspeakable suffering, the struggle for minimal survival of the countless voiceless, wretched ones of the earth everywhere. We pray now because *they* saw fit and see fit to pray. We accept the uncanny gift of hope in survival itself they give us because we know that we clutch that hope only for the sake of the hopeless. We will tell their story because it must not be forgotten. We seek the releasement of their stories' dangerous and uncanny memories upon our all-too-canny illusions of rationality and humanity.

The journeys to and from the experience of the uncanny in the contemporary situation are as diverse, often as conflicting, as the classical paradigms chosen to focus our ever-wandering, homeless, exiled attention. The elective affinities between representative contemporary theologies and these secular post-theologies await our attention in the remaining chapters. In the meantime, this much amidst the pluralism, the conflict of interpretations, and, perhaps, the cultural chaos expanding as rapidly as the desert itself expands each year on this planet seems clear. We must keep alive the sense of the uncanny—the postreligious, religious sense of our situation. We must fight against all temptations to canniness—to those bogus affirmations, those principles of domination, those slack feelings which tempt us beyond mere error and even illusion to the final distortions of indecency.

The self-respect of each demands the intensified focussing upon one's own focal meaning, one's own paradigmatic experience and expression of the uncanny. If the self is not to scatter itself into the void of sheer fascination at our pluralistic possibilities, then the *tremendum* power of the always-already, not-yet uncanniness of our homelessness—with ourselves, others, history, society, nature—must first be lived through and only then reflected upon. My own paradigm, my own focal meaning, as I shall try to express it in the remainder of this book, is an explicitly Christian formulation I call an analogical imagination.[79] And yet if *any* paradigm, *any* focal meaning becomes a journey of intensification into its own particularity without the constant self-exposure to the other, that paradigm will finally lose its focus and force and scatter itself amidst the clutter of the present by a self-imposed deafness and blindness to the reality we all face. Each focal meaning, each journey of intensification into the particular, each post-theological and theological expression of the uncanny can become a particular focus for a vision of the really concrete which is always the whole. Each interpreter can, because each does throw out an expanding series of somehow ordered relationships to hear and learn from the other. We understand one another, if at all, only through analogies. Each recognizes that any attempt to reduce the authentic otherness of another's focus to one's own with our common habits of domination only seems to destroy us all, only increases the leveling power of the all-too-common denominators making no one at home. Conflict is our actuality. Conversation is our hope. Where that actuality is systematically distorted, conversation must yield for the moment to the techniques of liberation and suspicion classically expressed in Freud, Marx, Nietzsche and Heidegger. Where that conversation is possible—on the other side of all techniques of explanation and suspicion—lies the hope of understanding in the continuing conversation of the classics of the culture, including the postmodern classics disclosing the uncanniness in the contemporary situation.

In the meantime there may be some way to formulate our common hope and our uncommon experiences of the uncanny into the rubric of an analogical imagination. Then the journey of intensification into the particularity of each focal meaning will be encouraged, the reality and power of the negative will be demanded, the search for some order—a code, a story, a vision, an image, a dance, a life—will be enhanced, the demand imposed upon all to hear one another, to allow all our paradigms, all our traditions, all our classics expose themselves *as* themselves in all their intense and focussed particularity to the other as other will occur. This journey too—the journey of an emerging analogical imagination in our culture—has its own experiences of the uncanniness of and in our situation. That journey finds that those fundamental questions we must ask because they command our attention by their very worthwhileness are focussed no longer in any one place. The questions, like ourselves, are both no-where, no single place, no longer, yet everywhere. The questions are everywhere, above all through the somewhere of each one's focussed particularity into one classic tradition of interpretation. At the same time, and as the uncanny peculiarity of the contemporary situation, the questions are focussed through the no in our common no-where, our sensed no-longer, not-yet at-home-ness in this time and place given to us.

Any affirmation that will come to any of us will be likely to come in and through the power of facing that no.[80] And yet we sometimes sense—in authentic conversation, in real explanation, in art, in story, in thinking, in laughter, in image, in love, in action for a cause greater than the self, in religion—that we may yet be coming home. We know that we may not be able to answer those questions and yet we respond. In the uncanny sense of a reassurance in the unknown depth of the self and the unknowable depth of history and nature alike, we begin to recognize in all the classics some always-already affirmation in and through their very negations. We recognize that uncanny affirmation only because we finally sense some reality, vague yet important, which we cannot name but which is, we sense, not of our own making. We recognize that reality when we recognize the disclosive and transformative power in every classic of our post-modern situation. We recognize it because it is there in the first place. For that uncanny affirmation has always-already been there in the not-yet and the no-longer of our not-at-home-ness in this contemporary situation.

Notes

1. For examples of this reality in the contemporary period, see Christopher Lasch, *The Culture of Narcissism* [I/7]; and Philip Rieff, *The Triumph of the Therapeutic* [I/7].

2. For the notion of "living, forced and momentous" options in the fundamental questions of existence, see William James, *The Will to Believe* [IV/55], pp. 3–11.

3. See Paul Tillich, *Systematic Theology* [II/25], I, 3–8. For the important Tillichian notion of "kairos" as distinct from "chronos," see *The Protestant Era* (Chicago: Univ. of Chicago, 1948) pp. 32–55. For examples of Tillich's own analysis of culture, see *Theology of Culture* [IV/66], pp. 53–159. For an analysis of Tillich's development of his position, see James Luther Adams, *Paul Tillich's Philosophy of Culture, Science and Religion* (New York: Schocken, 1970). For contemporary examples of analyses of Tillich here and of Tillichian scholarship, see *Kairos and Logos: Studies in the Roots and Implications of Tillich's Theology*, ed. John Carey (Cambridge: North American Paul Tillich Society, 1978). For Catholic theological critical appreciation of Tillich, see *Paul Tillich and Catholic Thought*, ed. Thomas O'Meara and Cletus Wessels (Dubuque: Priory Press, 1964). Two theologians of contemporary culture who continue the Tillichian tradition are Langdon Gilkey and Nathan A. Scott. Besides Adams' book, the most helpful and rigorous analysis of the dialectical character of Tillich's thought may be found in Robert Scharlemann, *Reflection and Doubt in the Thought of Paul Tillich* (New Haven: Yale Univ. Press, 1969).

4. Recall the earlier discussions (chap. 2) of the need for "mutually critical correlations" between these two "sources" in all three disciplines of theology. I employ the phrase "dialectical" here to indicate this two-way (mutually critical) correlation process.

5. As noted in chap. 3, insofar as every interpretation is a new interpretation (and involves "application" as an internal moment of the interpretation process), any theological interpretation of the event and the mediating tradition also involves application to the contemporary situation. As noted in chaps. 6 and 7, the Christian classic event also involves demythologizing and deideologizing moments as intrinsic to the demands of the event itself. The warrants for this claim are, therefore, twofold: from general interpretation theory and from the inner-theological warrant of the nature of the event interpreted in Christian theology. In fundamental theology this same point can be made in reference to "*common* human experience" as a "source" for theological reflection (see *BRO*, pp. 44–46, and my difference from Tillich here, p. 57, no. 12). In ecclesiology, insofar as one

accepts the model of church as eschatological sacrament of world, the "world" enters intrinsically into the theological interpretative task.

6. Note, for example, the emphasis upon social-scientific descriptions of the situation (Bell, Berger, Greeley, Lasch et al.) in chap. 1.

7. Paul Tillich, *Systematic Theology* [II/25], I, 4.

8. Contrast here the analyses of Frederic Jameson, *Marxism and Form* [III/76]; and Terry Eagleton, *Marxism and Literary Criticism* (London: Methuen, 1976). For an even more striking contrast, compare the shift away from autonomy language in the recent "strict-observance" British Marxist approach of Lesley Johnson (*The Cultural Critics: From Matthew Arnold to Raymond Williams* [London: Rutledge and Kegan Paul, 1975], esp. pp. 1–18, 199–209) with both Williams' own earlier Marxian-like emphasis upon relative autonomy (*Culture and Society* [I/50], esp. pp. 265–339) and his explicitly Marxist emphasis upon relative autonomy in his more recent work (*Marxism and Literature* [III/76]).

9. See Paul Tillich, *Systematic Theology,* I, 8–28.

10. Ibid., pp. 163–68; II, 19–29.

11. Recall, as well, the criteria of the formalist critics of that same period ("complexity, paradox, ambiguity, a sense of the tragic") and the use of analogous theological criteria (ordinarily related to a model of the shattering, judging, healing, defamiliarizing power of the "word") in the great dialectical neo-orthodox theologians of the same period.

12. In literary and cultural criticism, recall the influence concentration of Lionel Trilling's criticism in the same period on the "adversary culture" of the modern artist and intellectual vis-à-vis the wider, leveling society: inter alia, see *The Opposing Self* (New York: Viking, 1955) and *Beyond Culture: Essays in Literature and Learning* (New York: Viking, 1956).

13. A fascinating case here on the nonbelieving retrieval of this heritage on morals may be found in the work of George Orwell. A recent and important defense in terms of modern analytic philosophy of the need to recover this tradition of morals from Judaism and Christianity at the heart of modern Western secular morality may be found in Alan Donagan, *The Theory of Morality* (Chicago: Univ. of Chicago Press, 1978). I avoid the more familiar expression the "Judaeo-Christian" tradition because of the persuasive arguments against this notion in Arthur Cohen, *The Myth of the Judaeo-Christian Tradition* [V/27].

14. Classically formulated by Kant in "What Is Enlightenment?" in Lewis W. Beck, ed. *Critique of Practical Reason and Other Writings in Moral Philosophy* (Chicago: Univ. of Chicago Press, 1949), pp. 286–92. An excellent interpretation of the positive achievement of the Enlightenment is Peter Gay, *The Enlightenment: An Interpretation* (New York: Vintage, 1968).

15. See Max Horkheimer and Theodor Adorno, *Dialectic of Enlightenment* [I/106].

16. See Peter Steinfels, *The Neo-Conservatives* [I/16].

17. See Bernard Lonergan, *Insight* [I/28]; Michael Polanyi, *Personal Knowledge* (Chicago: Univ. of Chicago Press, 1958); idem, *The Tacit Dimension* (New York: Doubleday, 1967). Frederick Ferré employs the phrase "post-modern science" explicitly in a forthcoming article entitled "Religious World-Modelling and Post-Modern Science," as does Stephen Toulmin (here influenced by Ferré) in his forthcoming book, including his Nuveen lectures on natural theology and cosmology. Lonergan and Polanyi, without employing the expression, provide analogous analyses of the same kind of postpositivist understanding of scientific inquiry.

18. For an example here, see the analysis of "society" in chap. 1, sec. ii.

19. For an analysis here, see Max Horkheimer, "Traditional and Critical Theory," in *Critical Theory* [I/27], pp. 188–244.

20. On the power of negation in all great art, even ideologically "conservative" work, see Herbert Marcuse, *The Aesthetic Dimension* [I/43].

21. See Herbert Marcuse, *One-Dimensional Man* (Boston: Beacon, 1964); Hannah Arendt, *Eichmann in Jerusalem: A Report on the Banality of Evil* (New York: Viking, 1963); George Steiner, *Language and Silence* (New York: Atheneum, 1972), esp. pp. 3–171; idem, *In Bluebeard's Castle* [V/46]; Frank Kermode, *The Sense of an Ending* [VI/81]; Jürgen Habermas, "On Systematically Distorted Communication," *Inquiry* 13 (1970), 205–18.

22. I employ the concept "pluralism" in the Anglo-American mode in this work. For the notion "conflict of interpretations," see Paul Ricoeur, *Freud and Philosophy* [IV/62], pp. 20–37. The notion "pluralism" need indicate neither a "repressive tolerance" (Marcuse) nor a "bourgeois complacency" (de Beauvoir). True pluralism develops criteria of relative adequacy (and is, thus, distinct from its caricature: an easy, relaxed eclecticism). Pluralism demands conversation and expects conflict. European commentators (including theologians) seem unable to note the radicality of the Anglo-American notion of pluralism which they often mistake for an anticonflictual, "one-dimensional" eclecticism just as they mistake the Anglo-American notion of "experiential" for "empiricist." For one Anglo-American response to one form of this familiar Continental charge, see Alasdair MacIntyre, *Herbert Marcuse: An Exposition and a Polemic* (New York: Viking, 1970), pp. 69–99. For a defense of the tradition of pluralism, see Wayne Booth, *Critical Understanding* [II/48].

23. See the debate of Jürgen Habermas and Hans-Georg Gadamer in *Hermeneutik und Ideologiekritik* [II/102].

24. For one example here, note the exchange between Wayne Booth, M. H. Abrams and J. Hillis Miller on the Romantic affirmations, in *Critical Inquiry* (1977), 407–49.

25. For the notion of the "fragmented middle," see Emil Fackenheim, *The Religious Dimension in Hegel's Philosophy* [V/30], pp. 223–42. For the influence of Hegel after the collapse of the Hegelian claim, see the balanced account in Charles Taylor, *Hegel* (Cambridge: Cambridge Univ. Press, 1975), pp. 537–72. For the "left-wing," many accounts are available—among them, see Karl Löwith, *From Hegel to Nietzsche: The Revolution in Nineteenth-Century Thought* (New York: Holt, Rinehart and Winston, 1964), esp. pp. 65–137. For more recent scholarship, see the review article by James Massey, "Reappraising the Young Hegelians," *JR* (1973), 499–504.

26. Amidst the vast literature on Marx, two helpful studies are David McLellan, *The Thought of Karl Marx, An Introduction* (New York: Harper, 1971); Sholomo Avinieri, *The Social and Political Thought of Karl Marx* (Cambridge: Cambridge Univ. Press, 1968). On Marxism see the important works on the "varieties" of Marxism of Kolakowski, Avinieri and Gouldner [II/92].

27. For Marxist conflictual formulations of this debate, see the work of Lesley Johnson and Raymond Williams [8]. A good example of careful Marxian analysis may be found in Frederic Jameson, *Marxism and Form* [III/76]. The classic "masters" and their debates (Bloch, Lukacs, Brecht, Benjamin, Adorno) may be found in the important collection *Aesthetics and Politics* [II/76].

28. See Jameson's fair treatment of the many shifts in the career of George Lukacs, ibid., pp. 160–206.

29. Herbert Marcuse, *The Aesthetic Dimension* [20].

30. See especially Paul Ricoeur, *Freud* [IV/62]; Philip Rieff, *Freud: The Mind of*

the Moralist (New York: Viking, 1959). For a good discussion of the significance of the work of Ricoeur, Don Browning and Peter Homans on Freud for religious studies and theology, see Walter Lowe's review article in *RSR* (1978), 246–54.

31. Paul Ricoeur, *Freud,* pp. 59–159.

32. Ibid., pp. 459–94.

33. See especially, *Knowledge and Human Interests* [I/24], pp. 217 ff. The attempt of the early "Frankfurt School" (Adorno, Horkheimer, Fromm, Marcuse) to relate Freudian theory to their own revisionary Marxist work is continued in Habermas' work and represents a major contemporary attempt to relate critically these two often contradictory (and sometimes mutually vilifying) traditions of suspicion. For two accounts, see Martin Jay, *The Dialectical Imagination* [II/96], pp. 86–113; and Paul Robinson, *The Freudian Left* [V/17] (on Marcuse). The best known example probably remains Herbert Marcuse, *Eros and Civilization* (Boston: Beacon, 1968).

34. This model has been challenged implicitly by some psychoanalysts in favor of a model of two joint authors of a single narrative: see Roy Schafer, "Narration in the Psychoanalytic Dialogue," in *Critical Inquiry* 7 (Autumn 1980).

35. See Walter Lowe's critique of many theological uses of "third-force" psychology [30].

36. For the Marxist concept of ideology, see the recent study by Martin Seliger, *The Marxist Conception of Ideology* [II/99].

37. This interpretation of Nietzsche is obviously related to the interpretation of the so-called "New Nietzsche" in contrast to the earlier "existentialist" Nietzsche. For representative examples of the new interpretation, see *The New Nietzsche* [III/32]; *Nietzsche aujourd' hui* (Paris: Univ. Generale d'Éditions, 1973); Jacques Derrida, *Spurs, Nietzsche's Styles* (Chicago: Univ. of Chicago, 1978), pp. 34–146; idem, "White Mythology," *New Literary History* (1974), 5–74. For representative examples of the "older" interpretation, see Walter Kaufmann, *Nietzsche* [VI/106]; Karl Jaspers, *Nietzsche and Christianity* (Chicago: Regnery, 1961); idem, *Nietzsche: An Introduction to His Philosophical Activity* (Chicago: Regnery, 1966). Influential on the newer interpretation (especially for Derrida) has been Martin Heidegger, *Nietzsche* (Pfullinger: Neske, 1961)—in English the section "The Will to Power as Art" is published as Vol. 1 (New York: Harper & Row, 1979).

38. On the latter, see especially *Civilization and Its Discontents* (New York: Norton, 1962).

39. Walter Benjamin, "Theses on the Philosophy of History," in *Illuminations* [III/77], p. 256.

40. Walter Benjamin, quoted in Marcuse, *One-Dimensional Man* [21], p. 257.

41. Herbert Butterfield, *The Origins of Modern Science, 1300–1800* (New York: Free Press, 1965), p. 7.

42. See Martin Heidegger, "The Question Concerning Technology," in *Basic Writings* [II/52], pp. 287–317. Two recent studies of the cultural significance of Heidegger's analysis are William Barrett, *The Illusion of Technique* (New York: Doubleday, 1978), esp. pp. 109–229; and George Steiner, *Martin Heidegger* [IV/75].

43. See Heidegger, "The Question Concerning Technology," esp. pp. 300–304.

44. For an application of Heidegger's reflections here to contemporary American culture, see Barrett, *Illusion,* esp. pp. 176–201.

45. Heidegger, *Nietzsche,* Vol. 1, *The Will to Power as Art* [37], esp. pp. 1–37; and *The End of Philosophy* (New York: Harper & Row, 1973) (includes the "destruction" of metaphysics in Heidegger's Nietzsche study).

46. Note the influence of Heidegger's critique of humanism in current French thought: see especially "Letter on Humanism," in *Basic Writings,* pp. 189–243.

47. For examples, see the excellent representative collection: Martin Heidegger, *Poetry, Language, Thought* (New York: Harper & Row, 1971), esp. "The Thinker as Poet" (pp. 1–15) and ". . . Poetically Man Dwells . . ." (pp. 211–28); and *What Is Called Thinking?* (New York: Harper & Row, 1972).

48. An exception in the European tradition here is Jürgen Habermas: inter alia, see *Knowledge and Human Interests* [I/24] and *Communication and the Evolution of Society* (Boston: Beacon, 1979). For a clear analysis of Habermas, see Thomas McCarthy, *The Critical Theory of Jürgen Habermas* (Cambridge: M.I.T. Press, 1978). In the Anglo-American tradition, note the works cited in n. 17.

49. Recall the relevance here of the earlier discussion (chap. 3) of Gadamer and Ricoeur on interpretation theory.

50. Note here the Frankfurt Institute's studies of "mass culture" and "affirmative culture": for a good summary, see Martin Jay, *The Dialectical Imagination* [II/96], pp. 173–218.

51. I owe this suggestion to William Barrett, *The Illusion of Technique* [42], p. 122. The original parable may be found in Franz Kafka, *The Basic Kafka* (New York: Pocket, 1979), pp. 66–80.

52. George Steiner, *Martin Heidegger* [IV/75], pp. 156–57; idem, *In Bluebeard's Castle* [V/46], esp. pp. 27–57. Steiner's analysis of Heidegger is particularly strong on Heidegger's cultural significance and his "later" thought on poetry, language and technology; his analysis of *Being and Time* provides a more existentialist interpretation than Heidegger's text seems to allow.

53. Ernst Bloch: inter alia, see *Man on His Own* (New York: Herder and Herder, 1970); Walter Benjamin, esp. *Illuminations* [III/77], esp. pp. 253–65.

54. For relevant discussions of the Jewish background, see Jay, *The Dialectical Imagination* [II/96], pp. 41–85; and Susan Buck-Morss, *The Origin of Negative Dialectics* [II/96], pp. 5–6, 48–49.

55. The Scholem-Benjamin relationship is discussed in Jay, pp. 178–200. On Bloom, see Harold Bloom, *Kabbalah and Criticism* (New York: Seabury, 1975). On Scholem, see David Biale, *Gershom Scholem: Kabbalah and Counter-History* [V/27], including the discussion of Benjamin, esp. pp. 103–08, 196–98. Scholem's work represents a paradigmatic example in modern religious scholarship of the return of forms of interpretation largely rejected since the Enlightenment and the rise of historical consciousness. In all fields and traditions, in fact, one may now speak of a growing interest in allegorical, esoteric, mystical and even gnostic modes of interpretation.

56. Sigmund Freud, *Moses and Monotheism* (New York: Knopf, 1939); idem, "The Moses of Michelangelo," in *Freud, Standard Edition,* Vol. 13 (London: Hogarth, 1952), pp. 211–26.

57. For the Freud-Jung relationship, see one of the classic exchanges of letters in our period: *The Freud-Jung Letters,* ed. William McGuire (Princeton: Princeton Univ. Press, 1974). For Jung, see especially *The Archetypes and the Collective Unconscious* [V/2].

58. See Martin Heidegger, "Phenomenology and Theology," in *The Piety of Thinking,* trans. and commentary by James Hart and John Maraldo (Bloomington: Indiana Univ. Press, 1976).

59. See M. H. Abrams, *Natural Supernaturalism* [III/108].

60. For a suggestive study of the role of the negative in the contemporary period (especially in the novel), see Marie Janus Kurrik, *Literature and Negation*

(New York: Columbia Univ. Press, 1979), esp. pp. 82–206 (on the novel), and the interesting contrasts of negations in "modernism" (pp. 206–37). I am also thankful to Robert Jones for his analysis of "negation" in contemporary poetry and the novel. For a sensitive study of some dilemmas of the self disclosed in modern literature, see Enrico Garzilli, *Circles Without Center: Paths to the Discovery and Creation of Self in Modern Literature* (Cambridge: Harvard Univ. Press, 1972). For a clear and systematic phenomenological study of "absence" in thinking and being, see Robert Sokolowski, *Presence and Absence: A Philosophical Investigation of Language and Being* (Bloomington: Indiana Univ. Press, 1978).

61. For the *loci classici,* see the valuable collection *Marx-Engels on Religion* (Moscow: Progress, 1972); Sigmund Freud, *The Future of an Illusion, Moses and Monotheism, Totem and Taboo;* Friedrich Nietzsche, *Thus Spoke Zarathustra* and *The Genealogy of Morals.* The "totalization" problem in these classic analyses is discussed in chap. 4.

62. *Illuminations* [II/77], p. 253.

63. Sigmund Freud, "The Uncanny," in *On Creativity and the Unconscious* (New York: Harper, 1958), pp. 122–62.

64. See the citations of the work of Ernst Bloch, Walter Benjamin and Frank Kermode above.

65. In that sense, it is correct to speak of the great conservative thinkers as providing "retrospective Utopias" despite their antiutopian insistence. For an implicit example here, see Eric Voegelin, *Anamnesis,* ed. Gerhart Niemeyer (Notre Dame: Univ. of Notre Dame Press, 1978), esp. pp. 3–55. For a clear example of how flexible the category "conservative" can be, see Garry Wills, *Confessions of a Conservative* (New York: Doubleday, 1979), esp. pp. 187–231. For a devastating exposé of the reactionary (not conservative) character of the "new philosophers" in France (Levy and de Benoist) see Thomas Sheehan, "Inventing God in Paris," *New York Review of Books* (Jan. 24, 1980), 13–18.

66. The intellectual and spiritual journey of T. S. Eliot is particularly representative here: from the early modernity of *The Waste Land* through the Christian evocation of *Four Quartets.* The last phrase is from the reflection on incarnation in *Quartets.*

67. Quoted in Barrett, *The Illusion of Technique* [42], p. 325.

68. Ludwig Wittgenstein, *Tractatus Logico-Philosophicus* (London: Routledge and Kegan Paul, 1974), p. 73. Note, too: "There are, indeed, things that cannot be put into words. *They make themselves manifest.* They are what is mystical" (p. 73—emphasis his).

69. See Stephen Toulmin, "Contemporary Scientific Mythology," in *Metaphysical Beliefs,* ed. Alasdair MacIntyre (London: SCM, 1957), pp. 13–81; Robert Heilbroner, *An Inquiry into the Human Prospect* (New York: Norton, 1974).

70. Heilbroner's choice of the Atlas myth as a candidate seems more a move of desperation than a step forward into our uncanny situation. For a theological analysis of Heilbroner on myth, see Langdon Gilkey, *Reaping the Whirlwind* [II/2], pp. 79–88.

71. See *Deconstruction and Criticism* and *Textual Strategies* [III/70] for representative expressions here. For a recent philosophical "deconstruction" of the Western tradition of representation, see Richard Rorty, *Philosophy and the Mirror of Nature* (Princeton: Princeton Univ. Press, 1979); idem, "Philosophy as a Kind of Writing," *New Literary History* (1978), 141–61.

72. Roland Barthes, *The Pleasure of the Text* [III/61], and *Writing Degree Zero* (Boston, Beacon, 1967); see also Serge Doubrovsky, *The New Criticism in France* [III/31], esp. pp. 57–117. For some good examples of Barthean analyses of popular

culture, see *Mythologies* (New York: Hill & Wang, 1972) as well as for his semiological understanding of myth (ibid., pp. 109–59).

73. See Michel Foucault, *Language, Counter-Memory, Practice,* ed. Donald F. Bouchard (Ithaca: Cornell Univ. Press, 1977); idem, *The Order of Things* [III/32].

74. Inter alia, see Jacques Derrida, *Speech and Phenomena* (Evanston, Northwestern Univ. Press, 1973); idem, *Writing and Difference* (Chicago: Univ. of Chicago Press, 1976), esp. pp. 3–31; 154–69; 278–95.

75. See George Steiner, *Language and Silence* [VIII/21]; Arthur Cohen, *The Tremendum* [V/27]; Aleksandr Solzhenitsyn, *The Gulag Archipelago.* For a helpful study of Solzhenitsyn's roots in Russian Orthodoxy, see Niels Nielsen, Jr., *Solzhenitsyn's Religion* (Nashville: Nelson, 1975). On these issues, see also Lawrence Langer, *The Holocaust and the Literary Imagination* (New Haven: Yale Univ. Press, 1975).

76. Note Emil Fackenheim's analysis of the event of the Holocaust as a "negative root experience," in *God's Presence in History* [V/27], pp. 3–35.

77. For the development of the concept "caesura," see Arthur Cohen, *The Tremendum* [V/27].

78. Note how the work of both Elie Wiesel (on the Holocaust) and Solzhenitsyn (on the Gulag) achieve their force not by drawing morals but by telling the stories that cannot be forgotten.

79. See chap. 10 for details.

80. I add the expression "be likely to come" to indicate that the various traditions of the "extraordinariness of the ordinary" (see chap. 9) are not to be dismissed in the contemporary attention to the literature of extremity. Yet even there the extraordinariness of the ordinary bears its own negation of the merely ordinary and everyday—as in the work of Martin Buber.

Chapter 9

Christian Responses in the Contemporary Situation

Family Resemblances and Family Quarrels

i. Introduction

The focus of this chapter will be upon theological responses: more exactly those individual and communal Christian theological responses in the contemporary situation to the event of Jesus Christ as that event is mediated through the tradition in the situation. Those mediations are expressed in three paradigmatic forms: manifestation, proclamation and historical action. The primary response of any Christian systematic theologian remains a response in the present to the event and person of Jesus Christ. Whenever that event is experienced in the present situation through some personal sense of the uncanny, the event-character itself moves to the forefront of Christian theological attention. The primary Christian word designed to emphasize that event-character is the word "grace." Grace—the grace of Jesus Christ—is mediated through the ecclesial and cultural traditions and through the situation in the three principal forms of manifestation, proclamation and historical action. These forms of mediation, as the presently realized situational forms of the living tradition and its mediation of the event and person of Jesus Christ, exist as three distinct focal meanings upon the event and through it, upon all reality (self, world, God) in relationship to the event.

The event of Jesus Christ, experienced in the present uncanny situation by Christians as uncanny gift and command, a power not one's own—experienced as grace—elicits all these focussed, mediated theological experiences. When the Christ event is experienced as the religious event of grace in the present, when the full Christian tradition of manifestation-proclamation-action (and, therefore, the full Christian symbol system) is allowed by each theologian to work its corrective and expansive functions, when the sense of the uncanny alive in the situation is really attended to for its possible mediations, when the dangerous memory of Jesus of Nazareth functions in its critical and corrective role upon all past, present and future mediations of the event of Jesus Christ, then contemporary Christian systematics begins to approach relative adequacy.

Any observer of contemporary Christian theology cannot avoid noticing how pluralistic, how diverse, even how conflicting are the theological interpretations of Christianity in our period. Nor is that cause for either surprise or despair. If the systematic theologian must correlate an interpretation of Christianity with an interpretation of the situation, the interpretations, as personal responses, are likely to prove as conflicting as the situation itself, and as diverse as the Christian tradition. It is not merely that an interpretation of the situation is an "essentially contested concept." So too is an interpretation of Christianity. One major aspect of this conflict of interpretations is, of course, situational. Just as there is no *one* fundamental question to which all other questions must relate, so too with Christian systematic responses to that situation. There is no one response, no single journey of recognition and expression of the Christ event's transformation of the situation and its transformation by the situation. Rather each theologian finds some elective affinity between some interpretation of the questions and responses in the situation and some interpretation of the questions and the responses of the Christian tradition and hence to the Christ event.

The other major reason for this conflict of interpretations is the Christian tradition itself. To understand the full complexity of that tradition from the New Testament to the present would take several lifetimes of several Leibnitzes. To understand even partially some of the theological classics of the situation, to try to discern the "signs" in one's own situation, to try to listen to, learn from, converse with and argue with one's own contemporaries on the subject matter disclosed in this diverse, pluralistic, conflictual tradition is task enough for any theologian. As we saw earlier, the New Testament itself is internally pluralistic. As everyone knows, the later Christian tradition from the post–New Testament period to the present is yet more radically pluralistic in its interpretations of Christianity and often mutually contradictory. The history of the conflict of Christian interpretations on any single Christian symbol—God, Christ, grace, creation, redemption, eschatology, sacrament, word, church, faith, hope, love, sin—will document this clearly enough for any interpreter still infected by the impoverishing virus of an ahistorical, worldless "orthodoxy." The history of the conflict of interpretations within any single church tradition clarifies the same reality. Pluralism is not an invention of our present age. Pluralism is a reality in all the traditions. The conflict of interpretations is merely a new expression for the actuality and destiny of Christian self-interpretation. An appeal for a focus upon the classics is merely one strategy for clarifying some major paths through this conflict.

It is not perhaps a bad strategy. For attentiveness to the reality of the classic alerts all Christian theologians to note the singular fact that they are not called upon to invent a new religion, but to the more arduous labor of interpreting an already existing one. We find ourselves in Christianity as we find ourselves in the English language: an incredibly dense forest of syntax, grammar, history; a forest which grew not in the manner of the gardens of Versailles—the manner of theory—but in the manner of history itself into ever-changing, ever-stable possibilities of meaningful communication. We may, like the purists of the language, declare that no neologisms, no new metaphors, no new possibilities of meaning are either necessary or welcome. Or we may, as G. K. Chesterton somewhere remarks, realize that certain new "popular" expressions sound like "they were invented by Henry James in an agony of verbal precision." How one ever learns to pronounce English correctly, for example, seems largely a matter of mystery and memory. Fortunately, however, for reading and writing English at least, there is a syntax and a grammar which have remained relatively stable in this history-laden forest of a language—a forest which is in truth our primary home for whatever meaning we may grasp.

There also exists, again fortunately, a basic grammar for Christian systematic theology. The word "system" here is, of course, something of a misnomer. Indeed, except for individual "systems" like those of Aquinas, Gregory Palamas, Calvin, Schleiermacher or Hegel, the "system" in most Christian systematic theologies is more properly what Whitehead called an "assemblage," or what the medievals named a "book of sentences" as distinct from a "summa."[1] What most systematic theologians who attempt a systematic expression actually achieve is usually a form of "rough coherence" between the roughly coherent major symbols in the Christian symbol system and the even more roughly coherent analyses of the fundamental questions in a particular cultural situation.

Yet the basic grammar of Christian systematics endures. That grammar is constituted by the classic symbols and doctrines which every theology worthy of the history of the classic self-understandings of Christianity recognize as the paradigmatic candidates for Christian response and recognition—God, Christ, grace; creation-redemption-eschatology; church-world; nature-grace, grace-sin; revelation; faith, hope, love; word-sacrament; cross-resurrection-incarnation. *All* these symbols, like Everest, are simply there. They serve, minimally, as reminders that certain responses, certain moments of recognition, certain internal self-correctives, certain directions of thought and feeling have achieved paradigmatic, classic status. They cannot be ignored. In every cultural situation, an adequate Christian response demands that attention must be paid to the entire symbol system: through both critique and suspicion, retrieval and reinterpretation in and for the situation, yet controlled by some present experience of the event.

The range of responses to these symbols is also varied throughout the

Christian tradition, as H. Richard Niebuhr's study of classical Christian responses in *Christ and Culture* amply demonstrates.[2] The options Niebuhr analyzes under the rubric of certain classical "ideal types" for the relationships between "Christ" and "culture" (Christ Against Culture [e.g., Tertullian]; the Christ of Culture [e.g., Ritschl]; Christ Above Culture [e.g., Aquinas]; Christ and Culture in Paradox [e.g., Luther]; Christ the Transformer of Culture [e.g., Maurice]) have justly achieved something like the place of a contemporary classic of theological analysis of theologies. Niebuhr's analysis achieves its persuasive power, I believe, largely through its discriminating, generous, and just attention to *classic* expressions in each ideal type.[3] If Niebuhr had joined an analysis of the classics in one ideal type to polemical sketches of period pieces in the other types, he would have robbed his analysis of its magisterial power. Replace his analysis of Luther, for example, with a seventeenth-century example of Lutheran "orthodoxy" and you tear away the classic disclosure in Luther's type of "Christ and Culture in Paradox." Replace Aquinas with a nineteenth-century neo-Thomist manualist and the disclosive power of his "Christ Above Culture" paradigm collapses.

As I will suggest in this chapter, the major pluralistic theological options in our situation may be viewed as Christian responses of disclosive recognition to an uncanny power not our own. By its own disclosive force, that power transforms each theologian's interpretations of both situation and tradition. In fact, what one most often finds in contemporary Christian theology are what might be named variations on the final classical ideal type of H. R. Niebuhr: Christ the transformer of culture.[4] More exactly, one finds distinct interpretations via distinct foci of response and recognition in the Christian tradition critically correlated to distinct foci of fundamental questions and responses in the contemporary situation. Those mutually critical correlations between interpretations of the situation and the tradition-mediated event will and do work in both directions.

Underlying both situation and tradition will be some personal recognition of the presence of the uncanny as the presence of a power not one's own. The disclosure of that *power* has the classic force of some recognition of the whole. The sense of the uncanny in the situation discloses a religious dimension to the situation itself. The sense of the uncanny in the Christ event mediated through the tradition in manifestation, proclamation and action discloses the explicitly religious, the Christian experience of the uncanny as pure power, gift and command from the God whose decisive self-manifestation is recognized by the Christian in the event and person of Jesus Christ, whose reality is experienced anew in the situation as that power, gift and command named grace. That same religious disclosure, in further Christian responses to the full range of the classic symbols of the tradition, intensifies into fuller recognitions of the whole, the ultimate reality, as none other than the God of Abraham, Isaac, Jacob and

Jesus Christ. The recognition of the power of the whole, now acknowledged as given by the very power of God, is experienced as a happening, an event, a gift—a grace. The present experience of grace is acknowledged in Christian faith as the final reality with which we all must deal—the incomprehensible reality of the ultimate mystery named God; the God experienced, in the fundamental trust and loyalty evoked, elicited, even effected by that disclosure, as the encompassing, uncanny reality of an incomprehensible love.

The recognition of the uncanny in the questions disclosed in the situation is ultimately the recognition of the question I am to myself. It releases the interpreter to hear, to attempt some personal response. The recognition of the event-gift-happening reality of the response as not merely disclosive of, but elicited by the power of the whole, releases the interpreter to listen further. The power released by that event, gift, grace releases still other interpreters to a response of fundamental trust in the ultimate reality—a trust named faith. As the focus of that trust shifts in a response of Christian faith to the paradigmatic event of Jesus Christ, then the realities of God, the self, history and cosmos, the reality of the whole, begin to clarify, intensify and demand new—and now explicitly theological—responses. Then, in unfolding theological moments, new possibilities of response occur through new experiences of recognition, response, reflection upon all the major classic symbols. These further disclosures evoke, elicit, sometimes effect fuller transformations of the self and the self's interpretations of who one is, what meaning existence may bear in the light of that event and those symbols. And then, only then, the peculiar journey of Christian systematic theology begins: critical reinterpretations, empowered throughout their journey by some originating personal response of recognition, to the whole complexity of the Christian symbol system. Each theologian, partly influenced by the sense of the fundamental questions in the situation, partly influenced by the major focus of one's own traditions and response to the event, will then begin a personal journey of intensification into the interpretation of that symbol system in and for that situation.

Christian systematic theology is a personal risk of interpretation of the event (including the tradition and symbols which mediate it) and the risk of an interpretation of the situation. Ordinarily, both risks of interpretation will be guided by the belief that the theologian must correlate these two interpretations or collapse into rough incoherence. More exactly, the systematic theologian articulates mutually critical correlations between the interpretation of the situation and the interpretation of the event. The structure of systematic theology is the structure of a personal, risk-ridden response of participatory and critical interpretations of both situation and event. Involved in that response, sometimes at every moment in both interpretations, sometimes as a distinct moment following the two distinct interpretations, will be some personal theological articulation of the mutually critical correlations existing between these two interpreted realities (situation and event). The phrase "mutually critical correlations" functions here to indicate that the responses may take any form in the whole range of classic Christian responses analyzed by H. Richard Niebuhr. The particular form will be dependent upon the particular point at issue.[5]

At one time, an identity of meaning between situation and response may be the key; at another, confrontation between two opposed meanings; at most times, for myself, the major key for Christian systematic theology will be the transformation of both questions and the responses in the situation by the classic, paradigmatic, disclosive and transformative power of the event. Which route (identity, confrontation, transformation, paradoxical relationships or relationships of sublation from the "Christ above" culture) is needed for a particular critical correlation of the interpretations of situation and event cannot be decided *a priori*. The correct route can be found only in the process of a systematic theological understanding of the particular point at issue—an understanding guided heuristically by the general method of systematic theology. That general method takes the heuristic form enunciated above. That general method may guide but not control the specific demands of the particular theological point at issue in a particular instance of interpretation: the general method guides; particular interpretations rule.[6]

The pull of the inner event of some personal response of recognition (ordinarily named faith) will continue to encourage systematic theologians towards a developing recognition and response to all the outer events of the Christian symbols and their disclosive power in order to transform the inner event into a set of communicable meanings.[7] As Christian, the distinctive focus of the response will prove to be none other than the reality of Jesus Christ experienced as both decisive word and true manifestation. As involved concretely in some particular Christian ecclesial, spiritual or theological tradition, as grounded in some particular social, political and cultural situation, the individual theologian will find some particular way to focus her or his interpretation of the full complexity, the rough coherence, of the entire Christian tradition. Central among these focal meanings, as we saw earlier, are the realities of manifestation, proclamation and action. Within each major focus several paths lie open for interpretation. Within each and among all three there also exist family resemblances to assure that the principal focus on the event is kept in view.[8] To some of the journeys of contemporary theological response through manifestation, proclamation and action we now turn.

ii. The Trajectories of the Route of Manifestation

Earlier forms of manifestation as the sheer eruption of the powers of the cosmos—all those forms of originary, archaic religions analyzed by

Mircea Eliade—seem, in our day, relatively muted. This remains so even for those Christians whose religious experience is likely to move in the direction of vision, image, ritual, reflection, meditation—in a word, manifestation. Yet even though archaic immediacies seem now largely silent in urban Christianity, there do exist even now powerful expressions of the reality of Christian manifestation: manifestations bearing as many distinct journeys as there are different expressions of manifestation in both tradition and situation.[9]

The sheer immediacy of the power of manifestation, once overwhelming in our and other cultures, now seems rare. Instead we find many routes for the mediation of that immediacy. A first naivete seems impossible to most theologians. A second naivete—the route of mediation—seems our best hope to understand and experience the power of manifestation.[10] That mediated immediacy is present in many forms in contemporary culture and contemporary Christianity. In the contemporary age where the sheer immediacy of first naivete seems largely spent, where the foci for the journeys of mediation are as pluralistic as the questions and responses in both situation and tradition, the particular forms of the mediations of the power of manifestation assume a new religious importance.

The most familiar form of mediation in contemporary Christian theologies is a mediation of religious reality via philosophical reflection. Indeed, the critical power released by classical philosophy's primal wonder at existence still serves for many thinkers as their surest, sometimes their single, clue to the character of religious reality. From the urbane wonder and civilized cosmological reflections of Whitehead, through the self-assured, hard, logical passion of Hartshorne for a coherent concept of God, through the dynamic, restless reality of a contemporary "unhappy consciousness" pulled ineluctably toward transcendence, releasing itself, through its own transcendental reflection, towards that beckoning transcendence as a horizon of incomprehensible mystery in Karl Rahner or Louis Dupré, we see the same fundamental reality at work. We find the contemporary philosopher of religion and fundamental theologian taking ever new forms of the journey "within." That journey, initiated classically by Augustine, retrieved in our time by transcendental subjectivity and the "reformed subjectivist principle" alike, proves for many philosophers the surest intellectual route to the power of the whole—a power ultimately disclosed as empowering the journey itself. That route starts from some sense of wonder at existence, formulates that sense as a question of the whole through disciplined reflection to a renewed, religious sense of fundamental trust in the whole now reassured and reinforced by the mediation of philosophical reflection.

When these philosophies of religion, these cosmologies and metaphysics, these fundamental theologies, face their systematic theological tasks by their different, often conflicting routes, the same kind of spirit remains at work. That route of critical mediation of an original, an immediate wonder becomes a mediated immediacy. Recall, for example, Schleiermacher's classic disclosure of the manifesting experience of the feeling of absolute dependence in the *Speeches*.[11] That same route freed Schleiermacher in *The Christian Faith* to develop a postdogmatic method of systematic response, a *Glaubenslehre,* to interpret the entire range of symbols and confessions in the faith of the contemporary Christian church.[12] Schleiermacher's theological responses, like the responses of all Christian systematic theology, will prove harmonious with, yet never reducible to, the originating religious experience of the manifestation of the whole itself.[13] Rather that experience will inform the interpretations of the symbols, while simultaneously being itself transformed by them.[14] The religious experience of the manifested whole responds to the now believed-in religious realities disclosed in the Christian symbols experienced in the present Christian community. The theologian must move from the mediations of the *Speeches* to the fuller, concrete, transformative mediations of the *Glaubenslehre*. The original religious experience of manifestation, to be sure, does prove necessary for understanding all later systematic theological mediations and their relationships to common experience. Yet only the concrete, communal experience of the full range of the symbols of an explicitly Christian, indeed ecclesical, religious consciousness will prove *sufficient* for the task of a properly Christian systematics.

In a manner analogous to Schleiermacher's formulation of his *Glaubenslehre,* one may find in our own day Karl Rahner employing a transcendental systematic theology informed by, but never controlled by, his earlier transcendental reflections in philosophy of religion and "formal-fundamental" theology.[15] Rahner formulates the reality of a transcendental revelation whereby we recognize ourselves as always already in the presence not of an object but of a horizon of absolute mystery. Rahner's philosophical-transcendental mode of reflection mediates that reality and, in that very mediation, evokes and elicits the manifesting presence of the incomprehensibility within which we live as historical spirits-in-world.[16] That same transcendental mode of mediating reflection is again reformulated by Rahner as the human spirit's unceasing search for an absolute savior (a transcendental christology).[17] Then, in a categorical *systematic* christology,[18] Rahner will attempt to show how the high christology of Chalcedon, once reformulated into modern transcendental and existential categories, responds to the human drive for an absolute savior, to the same originating manifestation of radical mystery, to the same restless demand in the eros of the human spirit for fuller disclosure, more encompassing transformation and, ultimately, for the absolute.[19] To discover with Rahner—on the other side of that Christian systematic response—that the concrete is always-already graced and that the "purely natural" is a "remainder concept," is to find oneself temporarily startled at the surprising recognizability, the now disclosive and transformative force of the classical symbols and doctrines as mediated in their religious-existential significance through these philosophical-theological exercises in transcendental reflection. In the works of a Schleiermacher or a Rahner, a reader cannot but find—in their philosophies of religion and their "fundamental theologies"—a contemporaneously mediated retrieval of the manifesting power of an originating religious immediacy ("the feeling of absolute dependence," "the always-already presence of the horizon of radical mystery").[20] But the reader must also note that, in their systematic theologies, this originating experience is itself constantly transformed by, even as it informs, the theological interpretations of the symbols of a living, contemporary, ecclesial Christian faith experience. Only when that transformation occurs does there come into view the full reality of a recognizably Christian and believably contemporary *systematic* theology.

Although many seem puzzled by the phenomenon, it is really not so surprising that, despite their many obvious and crucial differences, the theological responses of many Catholic and Liberal Protestant theologians tend to be analogous in structure and in spirit: their similar trust in the mediating powers of critical and/or speculative reason, their openness to metaphysical inquiry, their love for the logos tradition of christology, their openness, however guarded, to mystical experience. All these forms of contemporary theology—from Schleiermacher to Cobb, Gilkey and Ogden in the Liberal Protestant tradition; from Aquinas to Rahner, Lonergan and major aspects of the theologies of Küng and Schillebeeckx in the Catholic tradition—reexpress through different methods and traditions of reflection the reality of some route of philosophical mediation to the religious-intellectual experience of the mediated immediacy of the power of manifestation. That power is rarely sensed as erupting from nature itself, as of old. Rather the power is now disclosed through the critical mediations of reason reflecting upon the original experience of wonder in existence only to yield through philosophical reflection to a mediated sense of a fundamental trust in the ultimate reality of God as well as an attendant trust in all reality as graced. Reflection upon that uncanny sense of wonder discloses the uncanny giftedness of all creation. It transforms the stuttering self into a creature alive to and with a fundamental trust in the ultimate reality manifesting itself/himself/herself as none other than an incomprehensible, a pure, unbounded, powerful love decisively re-presented as my God in the event of Jesus Christ.

For some theologians, therefore, philosophical reflection remains the main route of mediation to the disclosure of the power of manifestation. For others, however, the ordinary itself manifests itself in its true concreteness as extraordinary. The ordinary, the concrete, the everyday, not the "unhappy consciousness" of the metaphysician is for some the surer, as the more home-ly, route available in our situation of homelessness. In terms of human experiences, contemporary philosophical-theological routes to an event of manifestation tend to emphasize experiential limit-situations (guilt, finitude, death; fundamental trust, utopian and eschatological hope, agapic fidelity even unto death).[21] In terms of the experience of critical reason, critical philosophical theologies emphasize those limit-questions to scientific, moral and aesthetic inquiry present to the modern critical spirit since Kant. Other contemporary theologians, whose understanding of reason remains more traditionally speculative than modern-critical, retrieve in contemporary form the grand ascents and the speculative flights available to traditional speculative reason. They turn for their sustenance not to modern critical, experiential and linguistic philosophies, but to the great *exitus-reditus* schemata of the Christian neo-Platonic traditions as does von Balthasar and, in his own fashion, Teilhard, or to a retrieval for our day of Schelling's speculative cosmology and those of his more cautious, more critical, yet still speculative successors like Tillich.[22] The drive of reason, in both its classical speculative and its modern critical modes, issues forth into a series of transcendental and metaphysical systematic theologies. All these philosophical theologies are grounded in the unceasing dynamism of the human spirit to an absolute, to a manifestation of the whole, and to a retrieval of the classical experience of reason as ultimately a thankful, responsive thinking.[23]

For other Christian thinkers, however, the major locus of an experience of the event-character of manifestation is not found principally through those jarring limit-questions and shocking limit-situations of our modern critical experience of reason and history, nor in the great ascents out of the everyday and the ordinary distinctive of the speculative journeys of the neo-Platonic traditions. Rather, for these thinkers, the ordinary itself in its full concreteness is the major locus of a manifestation-event. Indeed, the ordinary, once really lived, embraced and loved, manifests itself as the extraordinary revelation of our primordial belonging-to, our radical participation in this body, this family, this people, this community, this church, this tradition, this history, this planet, even this cosmos.[24]

In sometimes unconscious fidelity to Wittengenstein's maxim "Look, don't think," these masters of the retrieval of the extraordinariness of the ordinary free their readers by their journey into the concreteness of particularity and through particularity to the whole as the concretely graced. They free one to reexperience the ordinary world of body, history, community, nature in all its concrete, shocking extraordinariness. Their major point of departure remains, with Scotus and Butler, the insistence that "everything is what it is and not another thing."[25] Their major discovery—or rediscovery from the mists of childhood memories—is the experience classically expressed by Gerard Manley Hopkins of "the dearest freshness deep down things." They know, with Heidegger, the disclosure of the dignity and common humanity of the ordinary world of the everyday manifested in van Gogh's painting of a peasant's shoes.[26] They know, with Martin Buber and Gabriel Marcel, the reality of community in this people, this tradition, this world.[27] They know without sentimentality how extraordinary ordinary "simple" people can be: their dignity, their uncommon common sense, their tolerance for the weakness of others, their compassion, concrete *caritas,* unquestioning sense amidst suffering of belonging to a people and a graced world. These theologians have not ceased to experience the surprise lurking in every particular, the recognition of the need "to guard and gild what is common."[28] By their taste for the concrete, these theologians possess and communicate an astonishing ability to bypass the usual narcissisms, to recognize the shocking, lovable, real otherness of all concrete others.

Their taken-for-granted rootedness in a people, community, tradition, history frees these theologians to develop systematic pastoral theologies disclosive of reality of the local, the extraordinariness of the ordinary. Their undomesticated sense of surprise and wonder frees them to a *sense* of the world as God's creation. Their theologies do not bring in the doctrine of creation as a dialectical afterthought. Rather, they seem to sense all creation—the body, sexuality, community, nature—as a gracious gift to be enjoyed in a natural, embodied, sensate, concretely human manner. In their best exponents, precisely the sense first experienced as a passion for the astonishing concreteness of the particular releases their affectivity and their reason to the full concreteness of the whole. Simone Weil's profound sense of rootedness in the concrete people to whom she committed her life freed her sense of life as a passionate sensitivity to the sufferings and the dignity of a global humanity.[29] Those whose actual involvement in ecology is grounded in this sense of the world in its astonishing concreteness do not enter into that struggle in the usual penitential fashion or for the usual, rational, utilitarian motives. Rather they enter the ecological movement because, unlike most of their fellow Christians and Jews, they need not retreat when they hear Eliade's pointed question to us all: "Do modern Christians and Jews any longer really *feel* the world as God's creation?"

For these theologians resonate to the disclosures of classical nature mystics like Francis of Assisi. They understand, without effort, a theology like Bonaventure's articulation of the Franciscan vision of the whole world as internally related, a vision of the universe itself as God's own sacrament.[30] The illumination and participation motifs of Eastern Christianity, the patristic vision of the natural goodness of all existence, the radical immanence of God in all nature, the sense of each human being as *imago dei*—all these classic and often half-forgotten symbols of the tradition take on new life in the theologies of the concrete, the ordinary, the everyday.

With Joseph Sittler, these theologies of the ordinary will refuse to restrict the scope of God's grace to the forgiveness of our troubled, introspective, Western consciences.[31] Rather, like the whole Eastern Christian tradition, like Bonaventure, Scotus, Butler, Hopkins, Wordsworth and Teilhard in the West, they will retain and develop this healing sense for the concrete, the particular, the everyday. They will embark upon a journey of intensification into the concreteness of each particular reality—*this* body, *this* people, *this* community, *this* tradition, *this* tree, *this* place, *this* moment, *this* neighbor—until the very concreteness in any particularity releases them to sense the concreteness of the whole as an internally related reality through and through. The sense of the utter gratuity of each concrete reality which *is* "what it is and not another thing," the astonishment at the contingency, the need-not-have-been-ness of each particular reality, the capacity for undiminishing surprise unite in these theologies to a sense for the whole of reality *as the concretely* graced whole. The entire journey is a classic expression of the liberating paradox in every classic and its strange union of intense particularity and a universality achieved only through particularity.[32] These theologies rearticulate one liberating route beyond our usual Western homocentrism by their rootedness in the event, the gift of manifestation disclosed decisively in Jesus Christ and now disclosed everywhere, in each particular. In that journey, the concrete is manifested as the intensified particular and *hence and by the same route* as ultimately the whole. By their distinct journeys into the extraordinariness of the ordinary, these theologians of the everyday free us all to rediscover the bodily, sensate, sexual, communal, mystical and cosmic realities toward which the rest of us act as sleepwalkers in our too-successful attempts to live at arm's length from real, concrete, ordinary life, unmindful that[33]

> *There lives the dearest freshness deep down things;*
> *And though the last lights off the black west went*
> *Oh, morning, at the brown brink eastward, springs—*
> *Because the Holy Ghost over the bent*
> *World broods with warm breast and with ah! bright wings.*

This sense for the extraordinariness of the ordinary often opens many of the same theologians to the sense of the extraordinary itself as the paradigmatic. For some thinkers, however, the emphasis falls elsewhere: not on the ordinary but on the extraordinary as the central clue to reality. One of the classic expressions in modernity of the power of manifestation in the extraordinary event, image, symbol, ritual is Mircea Eliade's revealing comment: "Only the paradigmatic is the real." As we saw earlier, Eliade's own *oeuvre,* from his scholarly articulation of the dialectic of the sacred and the profane in every paradigmatic manifestation to his novel *The Forbidden Forest,* vibrates with a disclosive sense of some paradigmatic, extraordinary experience of manifestation from the cosmos. The paradigmatic is out of ordinary time and space. Hence it liberates us to the "really real" world, the world of sacred time and sacred space. From the privileged moments releasing involuntary memories in Proust to the privileged rituals in Eliade, one finds in modernity this other path: a path where only the extraordinary—only the involuntary memory, only the sacred ritual, the icon, the privileged mountain, tree, rock, will free us from the burden of our imprisoning, banalized ordinariness. Only the paradigmatic will heal what has happened to the ordinary in our lives—our wasted, distracted lives in society, our ambivalent recognitions of the terror in our willful history. Only if we find some way, some paradigmatic ritual to reexperience how time may be recaptured and retrieved in its meaning, only if we can find some route to the sacred time of origins, the true time of repetition of origins outside the profaneness of our banalizations and distortions, will we enter again into the true realm of the sacred, the realm of origins and manifestation.

Some Christian thinkers like T. S. Eliot journey forth to experience all the "hints and guesses" of the extraordinary: from the lesser epiphanies erupting in the everyday—"the wild thyme unseen, or the winter lightning/ Or the waterfall, or music heard so deeply/That it is not heard at all." They move on, with Eliot,[34] to the great Christian epiphanies—the manifestations of the Christ as sacrament of both God and humanity, the church as sacrament of both Christ and world, the sacraments as the privileged manifestations, re-presentations, of that event, the Eucharist as the paradigmatic manifestation of all reality in the light of that event.

In every human life there are certain privileged places, times, events, rituals, images, persons, which each of us recognizes as paradigmatic in their disclosure of some central truth by which we live. In Christian life the same kind of sense for the privileged, the paradigmatic also occurs. For the sacraments can become for the sacramental Christian the major occasion to free the self from the reality of the overwhelming ordinariness we know too well as banal, distracted and disoriented; to free the self for the liberating rhythms of the major events in the passages of a life (birth, marriage, sickness, death, healing, eating, community, service); to free the self to the paradigmatic founding events of Jewish and Christian history (Exodus, exile, nativity, epiphany, advent and lent, Good Friday, Easter, Pentecost). In the Christian liturgical year those events live in celebration, in both tension and harmony, with the eternal rhythms and moods of the seasons of nature itself. In the paradigmatic moment of Eucharist, *memoria* redeems by uniting with hope and promise, nature heals by joining paradigmatic history. Even the explosive power of the proclaiming word unites with the erupting illuminations of manifestation to become in Eucharist the Christian paradigmatic experience of a privileged time and space, a necessary withdrawal from the everyday, an involuntary memory disclosing that only the paradigmatic is the real.

From the shock of truth in Mark Rothko's paintings of the sacred void to the great icons of the East, the same kind of experience of a releasement following a refusal to domesticate the paradigmatic occurs. Beneath all our necessary suspicions of, even destruction of, the sentimentalizing, mythologizing, hagiographical "lives" of the saints, lies the power of these lives in disclosing their singular truth: the truth of a life lived on the wager that only the paradigmatic is the real. To read, for example, Edith Sitwell's charming studies of British eccentrics is to be intrigued and amused by the wondrous possibilities of the human spirit. To read the autobiographies of Teresa of Ávila or even of the "little" Thérèse of Lisieux is to recognize another, a paradigmatic possibility for the human spirit: how beyond even their and our obvious neuroses, beyond even their and our imprisoning societies, beyond even the explosive passionate extraordinariness of Teresa of Ávila and the bourgeois ordinariness of Thérèse lies a common truth. For these two very different lives disclose their common secret: Really to live life, we must live it as if only the paradigmatic *is* the real.

In some lives today the experience of sexual love is the last outpost of the power of manifestation in the extraordinary. From those experiences to some sense, however feeble, of the extraordinary in the classic events, persons, rituals, images and myths scattered as paradigmatic signs of releasement throughout our culture, the shock of recognition in and by the power of a paradigmatic manifestation still reverberates in the culture and in the Christian tradition. That sense lives even in a world that has tried to conquer nature, deny the body, trivialize sexuality, and empty the mythic unconscious of all its healing powers.

Fortunately some thinkers yet prevail to teach us the truth that even now that journey through the paradigmatic may be taken. When we recognize the undeniable truths disclosed in the writings of Proust, Jung, Eliade, when we recognize that some persons can only be named "saints," that Dietrich Bonhoeffer is correctly honored with the titles "witness" and "martyr," when we recognize even in our battered liturgies and our domesticated sacraments their enduring, healing, privileged truths, when we find recognizability in the welcome works of fantasy in contemporary literature, in the liberating experiences of body, nature, dreams, the erotic, we all lay claim to the truth of this particular journey wherein the intensification of a sense of the extraordinary becomes an event of manifestation of and by the whole. In some matters, "only the paradigmatic is the real."

What characterizes all three of these distinct journeys to the event of manifestation is the importance in each of some form of mediation. Whether the mediating reality be the power of critical or speculative reason, or the ordinary in all its myriad forms and its real concreteness, or the re-presentative mediation of the extraordinary, the paradigmatic and the sacramental, the necessity for some mediation endures. Moreover, the temptation of all expressions of manifestation—the idolatrous temptation to allow the mediating vehicle to become identified with the power-event of manifestation itself—is never countenanced by any authentic expression of mediated manifestation. Schleiermacher's Christian and ecclesial experiences in the *Glaubenslehre* is not reducible to the religious experience of *Speeches,* much less to the philosophical and aesthetic reflections which helped to mediate that first recognition. Rahner's categorical revelation is not reducible to transcendental revelation. Von Balthasar's sense of God's glory is never reduced to the shock of the beauty of the Christ which initiated his journey. No systematic theology is finally reducible to a fundamental theology.[35] All the finite, natural, sensate mediators of the sacraments re-present but do not constitute the event of graced manifestation. Christian icons and saints disclose, never displace, the paradigmatic Christian manifestation of God and humanity alike, the event of Jesus Christ. In the authentic spirit of manifestation, ultimately all reality discloses the all-pervasive power of the grace disclosed by that event, the radical immanence of God in the epiphanies of nature, in the paradigmatic moments in every life passage, in the classical events of Jewish and Christian history, in the "inner journey" of each human being as an *imago dei,* in the decisive incarnation-as-self-manifestation of God in Jesus Christ.

Intrinsic to all these mediations, moreover, is the power of negation revealing the reality of the uncanny while leading to a common and radical affirmation of a graced universe. Through the negations of the "limit-to" in the limit-situations and limit-questions of critical philosophies and theologies through the radical negations demanded in all the classic ascents and descents of speculative theologies, to the negations of the ordinariness of the ordinary as ordinary in the concrete disclosures of the ordinary's genuine extraordinariness, to the initial negations of the ordinary itself as "profane" in the journeys of the paradigmatic, the same kind of negation power assumes some central role in the emergence of the event as graced gift of manifestation.

As the experiences of a mediated immediacy of the event of manifestation in Jesus Christ intensifies in each distinct journey, moreover, the reality of the mystical begins to come more and more clearly into view.[36] As critical and speculative philosophical theologians and artists learn to let go into the sensed reality of some event of manifestation, some experience of releasement and primal thinking, a sense of the reality of mystical experience can begin to show itself in itself. Even those with no explicit mystical experience, like myself, sense that thinking can become thanking, that silence does become, even for an Aquinas when he would "write no more," the final form of speech possible to any authentic speaker. As the sense of the extraordinariness of the concrete ordinary intensifies, the sense of the radical immanence of God in all reality frees the nature-mystic to respect, even when one does not experience, the realities disclosed in Francis, Bonaventure, the great Romantics and Teilhard. As the power of the paradigmatic explodes, the possibility of the kataphatic route of mysticism—a way classically expressed in the startling introduction of imagery in Ignatius Loyola's *Spiritual Exercises* and in the great iconic visions of Eastern Christianity—becomes alive again in ever new images and rituals. Latent in all these forms of the mystical journey is a yet more radical sense of the need for further negations, an intensification of the demands for negation already present in each former journey to the event of manifestation; the demands of negation to move beyond these words and images, this still too loud silence to the previously unreal reality of radical affirmation through radical negation expressed in the journeys of the apophatic mystical traditions and the negative, apophatic theologies. As the negative intensifies the sense of God's radical transcendence, a yet more intensified affirmation of God's radical nearness in each and to all can also be released in these apophatic traditions. At the end of all these journeys of manifestation, it would seem, all those carried along by the power of the event of manifestation in Jesus Christ cannot but recognize some pervasive yes at the heart of the universe, some radical mystery sensed as power, as an abiding love that undoes all our more usual senses of the futility and absurdity of existence. With Teilhard these theologians of manifestation acknowledge that yes, that manifestation of ultimate meaning in giftedness as the yes of a pure, unbounded, power of love manifested/re-presented in the Logos, pervading all history and nature in the Spirit, immanent as the transcendent God in all reality. These theologians find manifested in the event of Jesus Christ a new transformed self: a self freed for the freedom of some ultimate yes to reality in that event's disclosure of a gift, a graciousness come no longer as "medicinus," but as pure "favor." Through that freedom, the theologians of manifestation recognize and develop theologies designed to articulate their primal sense of the ultimate meaning of the event of manifestation: All is grace.

iii. The Trajectories of the Route of Proclamation

The experience of some Christians, especially the great Reformers and the major neoorthodox Protestant theologians in the contemporary period, shifted away from all experiences of manifestation into the empowering experience of God's decisive word of address in Jesus Christ. No depth experience, no quest for the ultimate, no mysticism, they urged, can save us in this situation. Only if God comes as eschatological event, as unexpected and decisive Word addressing each and all; only if God comes to disclose our true godforsakenness and our possible liberation can we be healed.

In all its forms, a word-centered neoorthodox theology has exploded upon the Christian consciousness from the post–World War I period to the present. The theologies of the Word are grounded in a profound religious sense of the power of the tensive subject matter revealed in the proclaimed word in the scriptures. They have attempted to retrieve that power by returning to the concerns and the power of that word-event of God's freedom, the Protestant Reformation.[37] They recognize both judgment and grace in the preached word. They live by the memory of Luther's theological innovation when preaching became sacrament. Those theologies communicate the forgiveness offered in the shocking and liberating message of justification by grace through faith. They are grounded, as well, in the sense of a vertical, a radically transcendent eschatological reality at the heart of distinctively Christian existence—a sense intensified by both the findings of contemporary New Testament research and a sense of profound cultural crisis, an apocalyptic "sense of an ending." Both forces united to expose and ultimately to destroy earlier Liberal beliefs in the relatively easy continuity, even harmony, between Christianity and secular culture. In H. Richard Niebuhr's splendid words—words which speak for all the Protestant neoorthodox theologians of that great period of upheaval in modern Christian reflection—earlier Liberal theologies must be negated because of their failure to disclose the negations at the heart of the Christian gospel: "A God without wrath brought men without sin into a kingdom without judgment through the ministrations of a Christ without a cross."[38]

A reader of this neoorthodox tradition from the earliest debates on Karl Barth's *Epistle to the Romans* through the most recent debates on Moltmann's *Crucified God* cannot avoid noticing one dominant fact: The unrelenting rigor in these theologies are struggles which characterize all theology that grapples with a subject matter that grasps one, that cannot be controlled. This same seriousness occasioned an often polemical style that carried with it more than a little of an *odium theologicum*. The internal quarrels of the neoorthodox—violent, powerful, always serious—bear all the marks of a family quarrel.[39] Has any theologian since Luther himself matched Karl Barth in his explosive and powerful style, ranging from the expressionist language of *Romans* to the classical, yet still tensive, calm of the *Church Dogmatics*? Can any theologian doubt the utter seriousness of Barth's hermeneutical struggle to allow the real subject matter of theology, the Word of God in Jesus Christ as event, to take over in all theology?[40] The singleness of vision of Barth through all his tortured shifts and self-assured turns, through all his polemical outbursts at other theologians and all his ironic self-distancings ("I am not a Barthian") were impelled by fidelity to the Word.[41] They demanded that the event of the proclaimed Word—the radical transcendence of God and the eschatological coming of God's word into this world in the triumph of grace in Jesus Christ—be kept steadily in view by all theology worthy of the name Christian.[42] Barth's hermeneutical triumph in *Romans* freed the inner dialectic of the biblical subject matter. Barth allowed that dialectic to confront and transform every theological interpreter into the risk of a reinterpretation bearing, for Barth, the marks of a language at once expressionist and proclamatory: "offense," "crisis," "dialectic," "tangent," the "crater of faith formed by the explosion of a shell."[43]

For Rudolf Bultmann[44] the same hermeneutical seriousness demanded that the dialectic of the authentic subject matter of the scriptures be allowed to take over, yet in a way ultimately distant from Barth's own. The kerygma, with its decisive claim upon us, releases the event of decision proclaimed and evoked by its judging, healing proclamation. That same kerygma, at the same time and by means of the same dialectic of the subject matter, demands the radical demythologizing of all traditional and biblical modes of expression. Modern interpreters of the scriptures must learn "to distinguish what is said from what is meant and measure the former by the latter." They must risk that their own preunderstanding will be challenged, confronted, transformed by the claim of the authentic, demythologized kerygma. They must recognize, in genuine kerygmatic preaching and in a word-centered Christian theology, the radical call to each in that paradoxical event of proclamation-address wherein God is recognized as gracious to a now-acknowledging sinner. They must spurn all complacency—all "theologies of glory," all attempts at self-justification—to allow, at last, the sheer event-character of the proclaimed word to claim them. Theologians, for Bultmann, must recognize, beyond the mythologies of biblical apocalyptic and liberal progress alike, the truth that, through the event of the proclaimed word, we may finally recognize as our own: "In every moment slumbers the eschatological moment. You must awaken it."[45] The kerygma, for Bultmann, always awakens that moment for all theologians who can hear its claim by the risk of a genuinely existential interpretation of its explosive power.

In that great and stormy period of the rediscovery of the power of proclamation, Paul Tillich[46] also forged several of his most powerful, original and proclamation-centered concepts: "The Protestant Principle," to unmask and destroy all idolatries, illusions and self-delusions; the concepts of "heteronomy" and "autonomy" and the need in our situation for their sublation by "theonomy"; the reality of religion in this situation as one of "ultimate concern"; the fact that this power is more likely to be found in avant-garde art and radical social and political movements than in the cozy enclaves of the churches which no longer feel the power of the proclaimed word; the need to discern in the situation those full, those classic, epoch-making moments hidden as *kairoi*; the need to recognize in the frightening events of twentieth-century history the reality of the "demonic"; the need to recognize in our unconscious nihilism a pervasive sense of meaninglessness.

The always unsteady alliances of Barth, Brunner, Gogarten, Bultmann and Tillich through their joint struggle with a complacent liberalism and their joint rediscovery of the explosive power in every word of proclamation lasted but a moment.[47] Each went his separate way.[48] Yet however different their later routes, no one of them would ever abandon their joint discovery of proclamation in that early heady period where the confronting power of the true as proclaimed word burst anew upon the Christian consciousness. Through their interpretations, the force of proclamation left a new crater in our midst: a crater which still focusses theological attention even as it evokes religious awe. These exemplary German Protestant theologians, along with their American praxis-oriented counterparts and equals, Reinhold and H. Richard Niebuhr, were indeed "giants amongst us." They command attention even now, perhaps especially now, when what E. M. Forster once named "poor, chatty little Christianity" seems to have forgotten the power of any word, much less the unmasking power of a word of authentic proclamation. If the word "classic" has any meaning, the neoorthodox theologians at their best achieved classic expressions of the power of the proclaimed word. If any theologian has since forgotten that no exercise in self-justification is countenanced by that proclaimed and judging word, they will remind us. For they recognized that the word liberates us from all our compulsive attempts at self-justification by its dialectic of an explosive judgment and healing grace. These theologians remain as rocks upon which crash all later attempts to forge a merely cultural Christianity, a *theologia gloriae,* whose real glory they exposed in all its pathology as yet another vain attempt at self-justification, whose true glory is to hear the liberating, accepting, forgiving, judging word that is proclaimed in Jesus Christ.

Their immediate successors in contemporary theologies of the Word, especially the "new hermeneutic" positions of Gerhard Ebeling and Ernst Fuchs, provided variations on the theme the neoorthodox first established.[49] These later theologians develop important variations, to be sure, on that theme. They do so insofar as the reality—now, note, the *manifesting* reality of all primal language—is allowed its necessary, grounding importance for understanding the power of the proclaimed word. Yet these later theologies of word, I believe, still draw their primary strength, not really from the reflections of Heidegger on primal language nor from Gadamer's interpretation theory. Rather they live on the resources of the explosive power of Word first released in the prophetic and eschatological strains of both Testaments, paradigmatically expressed in the parables of Jesus and the Pauline theology of the cross, retrieved in the word event which was the Reformation and recalled for and in our word-impoverished, wordy culture by those early twentieth-century classic exponents of the power of the Christian proclaimed word as that proclamation disclosed anew the event of Jesus Christ.

iv. From Manifestation and Proclamation to History and Praxis: Political and Liberation Theologies

For many in our period, the classic routes of manifestation and proclamation are not sufficient for the distinctively Christian journey in our situation. Instead many theologians initiate their journey from some sense of the power of manifestation or proclamation, or both, but then move on into the realms of action and history, of performative personal, social and political praxis. For these contemporary theologians, we are primarily neither hearers of the word nor seers of a manifestation. But because we have seen and have heard, we are freed to become doers of the word in history. What unites these highly diverse thinkers—usually named political and liberation theologians—is their attack on the "individualism" of past personalist, existentialist and transcendental journeys,[50] their insistence on the primacy of praxis in all theology, and their recovery of the political, historical, eschatological not-yet at the heart of the Christian vision of redemption.

That each of these theologians has first appropriated one of the earlier classic journeys of manifestation or proclamation seems clear. If the original appropriation has been one of manifestation (as in Metz and Gutierrez), then a reader notices the prevasive presence of the power of a fundamental trust hidden in their praxis, the disclosive reality of a manifesting sense of giftedness, an emphasis, even in the grip of the eschatological not-yet, upon creation and incarnation.[51] If the original appropriation has been one of proclamation (as in Moltmann, Soelle, Braaten, Ruether and Cone) then the different resonances of the journey of theologies of the word emerge: an emphasis upon loyalty to God's cause commanded by that gift, the eschatological emphases upon justifying redemption and the cross in their theologies. Above all, for all political and liberation theologians, the word event of proclamation commands, the gift event of manifestation demands a singular recognition: the recognition of the primacy of praxis, action in and for a church and a global society groaning to be set free from the alienating events and oppressive structures in the contemporary situation. What that praxis disallows is the temptation in all expressions of Christianity, whether manifestation or proclamation, to unduly interiorize, spiritualize, individualize the content of God's eschatological promises for history and the futural character of God's own reality as the absolute future.

Their social-political-historical praxis illuminates, in the manner of the left-wing Hegelians, the historical and societal character of reason itself. Here "reason" is neither "pure" nor speculative, nor purely critical, but always practical. Practical reason functions as transformative of all other uses of reason in theology through its emancipatory interest, its criticism of all unconscious ideologies, its unmasking of negations in particular sociopolitical structures in situation and tradition alike. Theological-practical reason grounded in the praxis of Christian faith through its eschatological "death-dealing" negations of the present situation and tradition in the light of the negations first expressed in the prophetic traditions, in the preaching of the reign of God to the poor and the outcasts by Jesus, and, above all, in the contradiction of the cross and the hope for all history revealed in the proleptic resurrection of Jesus Christ.

We must move, insists Gutierrez, from traditional notions of theology as "wisdom" and "science," and their disclosures of analogous harmonies, to the practical reality of actualizing the conflicts in society and church disclosed by the manifestations grounding both wisdom and science.[52] We must realize, insists Moltmann, that the word is a word of promise that commands action in and for history and a word of contradiction that unmasks the conflicts and contradictions existing now. We must free ourselves, argues Metz, from the privatization of our transcendental subjectivity to the emancipatory and communicative praxis demanded by Christian eschatological revelation. We must come to recognize, argue Cone and Ruether, that the interpretations of both word and manifestation in the dominant Euro-American theologies of the tradition do not respond to the actualities of historical and systemic oppression experienced by blacks, by women and by the oppressed and marginalized groups throughout the world.

All these theologies move from some originating experience of the power of word or manifestation to insist upon the primacy of historical action in the world.[53] By these means these theologians hope to retrieve all the subversive and liberating memories in the Christian tradition: the classical prophetic heritage, the preaching of the reign of God by Jesus to the poor and outcasts, the dangerous memory of Jesus of Nazareth himself, the contradictions and conflicts in situation and tradition exposed by the cross of the crucified one, the proleptic vindication of history disclosed by the resurrection of Jesus Christ, the formerly despised apocalyptic reality pervading the New Testament and exploding throughout Christian history in the "counterlogos" movements of radical Christians. Armed with that prophetic and apocalyptic heritage and with a radical, often Marxian sociological imagination, these theologians uncover the conflicts and contradictions in our contemporary situation and in the Christian tradition. They ground their theologies in personal journeys of intensification into the prophetic-critical, liberating and emancipatory *praxis* of the tradition. The bondage they wish to expose is not primarily the bondage of our private attempts at self-justification but the structural and systemic bondage of whole peoples. The liberation they seek is a deliverance from the fixations and distortions of our political, societal, and ecclesial past and present in all its alienating and oppressive forms by a deliverance to a praxis of faith in real history, the promise of the eschatological reality of God's future as commanding and empowering us to action now.

The "freedom of the Christian" they seek and find in the prophetic heritage is a freedom from all our cherished habits of privatization in an alienating and oppressive world. At the same time, our true freedom is a freedom from the world and thereby for the actual, concrete, political, historical world and its liberation. Christian freedom remains an existence in the praxis of faith that trusts in and is loyal to God and God's promises and commands for history. Above all, Christian freedom is a loyalty to God's own privileged ones—the ones whose voice has not been heard save in prophetic and apocalyptic movements, the ones privileged to Jesus of Nazareth, the ones whose voice is still not heard by the dominant theologies of the West: the oppressed, the alienated, the marginalized.

These journeys of the Christian prophetic spirit have entered into a route of intensification whose full reality is yet to unfold. The earlier confidence—the radical proleptic hope proclaimed in the resurrection in Moltmann's *Theology of Hope* has received its own internal dialectical corrective in his later negative dialectic of the cross in *The Crucified God*. The earlier world-hope in secularity disclosed by the symbols of incarnation and sacrament in Metz, Baum, Schillebeeckx and *Gaudium et Spes* has found its self-corrective in Baum, Metz and Schillebeeckx's retrieval of a historical eschatology, their retrievals of the narratives of the concrete histories of suffering, their insistence upon the subversive memories of both the prophetic tradition and Jesus. The earlier confidence in ongoing ecclesial reform expressed in Vatican II and the ecumenical movement has received, in the exemplary journey of the best ecclesial political theology of our day, Hans Küng's, a theology of the cross guided by the dangerous memory of Jesus to unmask ecclesial distortions.[54] As Küng continues his journey "through the institutions," he continues, as does Charles Curran in American theology,[55] the necessary Christian theological fight for a truly Christian church.

That same journey of intensification has been marked by a fidelity to the concrete. The power of the proclaimed word event reveals not the historicity of the individual authentic subject but the actual history of concrete histories of suffering of individuals and whole peoples and the prophetic, proleptic history of God's promises in Jesus Christ for those peoples, for that history. The logos of the intelligibility disclosed in the realities of manifestation discloses as well the counterlogos of cross and resurrection, the realities of conflict and contradiction lurking in a too easy pluralism, the subversive memories of the apocalyptic traditions and their demand for all the living and the dead. The power of constant critique upon both society and church in Metz, Schillebeeckx, Soelle, Moltmann, Küng, Curran, Ruether, Davis, Baum, Lamb, Elizabeth and Francis Schüssler Fiorenza and other ecclesial and societal "political theologians'' has released the power of a critical, prophetic consciousness upon concrete societal, political and ecclesial praxis. The power of that critique is expressed in both an ideology critique empowered by the emancipatory interests of critical reason along with the negative dialectics of their secular mentors in the Frankfurt School as well as the traditions of social justice in the North American Catholic and Protestant theological traditions.[56]

In political theologies, critique has maintained its theological center of gravity by means of the ''eschatological proviso'' upon all concrete political programs. That necessary proviso disallows any suggestion that the prophetic promise is concretely realized in only one societal-political form. That same power, at the same time, frees these theologians to propose some societal system as more relatively adquate (usually a democratic socialism), and to unmask the pretensions to fulfillment in the present alienating and oppressive economic, political, societal and ecclesial structures of both secularism and sacralism. The political theologians in both Europe and North America, like Reinhold Niebuhr in his day, have broken the grip of any ''transcendental irresponsibility'' upon theology, any purely privatized notion of religion preferred by both communist authorities in the East and secularism in the West. All privatization, all refusals to face action, praxis, politics, history are fatal not only to theology but to the proclamation and the manifestation of the event of Jesus Christ that empowers theology.

Nor has the emphasis upon the primacy of praxis in political theologians undone the permanent achievements of the great theologies of manifestation and proclamation of the recent past and the present. The latter will emphasize the powers of disclosure in manifestation and proclamation as the privileged paths for Christian theology. The former will insist that the transformative power of performative praxis releases the subject to be in the truth by doing the truth. Where criteria of transformation are not allowed, there remains the always present danger of ever more subtle theological articulations of a paradoxically ''private'' religious publicness. Where criteria of disclosure are not explicitly addressed, the powers of transformative praxis can lead their practitioners to ever more subtle refusals to engage in critical theological interpretations proper to any theology worthy of its vocation to authentic freedom.[57]

The political theologians achieve their journey of intensification into the concrete by means of an unyielding critique of the illusions and ideologies embedded in the concrete situations and structures of both society and church. They make that journey with the clear Christian warrants of a retrieval of the prophetic and apocalyptic strains in the tradition and the equally clear ''eschatological proviso'' upon all concrete political options. The insistence among political theologians upon concreteness frees them to the reality of the concrete: the concrete as the prolepsis of a global consciousness of an interdependent humanity and the concreteness of the eschatological future promised by God for all the living and the dead. That eschatological reality, whose force is the force of negation, the power of an exposure of the not-yet in society and church, is present even now—present for all proleptically in the cross-resurrection of the event of renewed promise, true word and decisive manifestation named Jesus Christ. The redemption from bondage proclaimed and manifested in that gift event, the political theologians insist, must include not only our redemption from the bondage of death, transitoriness, personal anxiety and sin. Redemption also must include our recognition that we are now empowered and commanded to enter the historical struggle for emancipation from the human, all-too-human bondage that our inhuman structures and systems have imposed upon history, society and church.[58]

The search of the Euro-American political theologians for the concrete in history and praxis is present in a distinct form in the analogous journeys of the liberation theologians. Here we find theology directly related to concrete histories of suffering and oppression. The central sign in our situation for the liberation theologians is an uncanny sign of contradiction and conflict: the massive, catastrophic suffering of whole peoples. Not wonder, not giftedness, not personal justification, not reconciliation, is the foremost clue to the contemporary situation: but the stark, system-enforced suffering of individuals and peoples trapped in concrete situations of systemic oppression. The liberation theologians do not focus upon the alienations experienced by those theologians in the "first world" experiencing and struggling against the alienating pain of the privatization of art and religion. Rather the liberation theologians shift their focus from alienation to oppression: an oppression enforced by means of all the life-killing structures—economic dependency, sexism, racism, classism, elitism. These structures concretize and solidify the sin and guilt of the oppressors even as they enforce and intensify the agony of oppressed individuals, peoples and traditions.

The contemporary situation will be addressed theologically, the theologians of liberation insist, only if two moves are made in theology. First, the primacy of praxis insisted upon by the political theologians must receive the new form of critical reflection upon concrete, actual situations of liberating praxis.[59] Grounded in the central call to discipleship of the New Testament by the memory of the Jesus who preached to and acted for the outcasts of his day, this praxis is now incarnated in God's "remnant" and "underground," the concrete communities of liberating praxis. These communities range from the "base communities" in Latin America, the tradition of liberating spirituals, songs and practices of the black churches in America, the holistic traditions of radical communion between nature and humankind in the native American traditions, the worldwide network of feminist groups, the realities of cultural oppression experienced by ethnic groups throughout the world.[60] These are the voices that have not been heard in theology. These are the voices of all those whose very powerlessness has included the final indignity that their experiences of both life and the Christian gospel could be ignored by the dominant theologies since those experiences were presumed to be already accounted for in the experiences and definitions of others. Through the theologies of liberation those voices are finally being heard by all theologians. The first step for all other theologians to take is to listen. In that sense the provocative title of Vine Deloria—a title which fits the first demand implied in all liberation theologies—hits the mark squarely: *We Talk, You Listen.*[61]

The second move of liberation theologians is equally clear. In direct relationship to the experiences of these concrete communities of praxis and their subversive memories of centuries of suffering in the struggle for liberation, certain central and relatively overlooked symbols of the Christian tradition must be retrieved and rethought. Those symbols—as in the case of "sin and grace" for Saiving and Plaskow,[62] will receive radical reinterpretations in relationship to the needs and demands for justice in the concrete communities of praxis. The actual practice of the community itself has been/is/will continue to be transformed by the living experience, the praxis, of the power and ideals of Christian faith. Central among the newly retrieved traditions is the prophetic-apocalyptic strain in Christianity: now understood, with Gutierrez, as the discovery by the theologian in the community of "the profound meaning of *historical events* to make Christian commitment within them more radical and clear" (emphasis mine).[63]

Central among the symbols of that prophetic tradition chosen for major attention is, of course, "liberation"—political, economic, cultural and thereby actual prophetic-religious liberation from the structures of systemic bondage destroying individuals, cultures and societies. The liberating God of Exodus and the ancient prophets, the reign of God proclaimed to the poor and outcast by Jesus, the reality of the crucified and risen Christ as Liberator disclosed in the Book of Revelation function as the primary symbols that allow the theologians of liberation to understand God as the God of the oppressed who suffers and works with all peoples for their fully human—their personal, political, societal, cultural, religious—liberation.

The Christ event as the liberating, gracious word, manifestation and, above all, action by this Liberating God[64] discloses as well the need to transform all individualist and personalist understandings of the dialectic of grace-sin into new interpretations. It is little wonder that one of the most striking contributions of liberation theologies to the Christian theological consciousness is their transformation of traditional understandings of sin. For just as traditional doctrines of grace—of justification and sanctification, of operative and cooperative grace, of salvation, redemption and reconciliation—are transformed by "critical reflection in the communities of liberating praxis" upon the central doctrine of "liberation," so too traditional understandings of sin are accorded similar transformations. For the Latin American liberation theologians, as for such North Americans as James Cone and Rosemary Radford Ruether, the theological emphasis will fall upon the realities of sin and guilt not as primordially individual but as embedded in "social" structures and systems whose full force is felt not in the private conscience of the introspective, alienated individual but in individuals and peoples caught in the binds of those social structures, institutions and systems that enforce the law of sin and guilt upon all humankind. For the feminist theologians, for example, theologians must call into question traditional theological understandings of sin.[65] The feminist theologians argue that the central understanding of sin in Western Christianity since Augustine has been an understanding of the sin of pride as sinful self-preoccupation become self-assertion. But pride may well speak to the experience of men, but is not, the feminist theologians argue, the dominant "sin" of women. Rather the primary sin of women has been their self-preoccupation not through pride but through a self-negation and self-dispersal enforced by their unconscious and conscious involvement in the sexist and patriarchical structures of church and society—structures that enforce a sinful self-negation under the rubrics of un-Christian understandings of "self-sacrifice" and "pride." These sins of self-negation demand a different kind of judgment from the usual Western, male-oriented interpretations of the primal sin as pride. The doctrine of sin, like its dialectical counterpart, the doctrine of grace, must not be allowed to encourage a self-negating passivity. An authentic theology of sin and grace will elicit the liberating freedom of responsible self-assertion with and for others.

The particularity of the concrete communities from which these different theologies of liberation emerge, moreover, seems to be leading each particular theology of liberation on the same kind of journey of intensification that we have seen in other theologies. A commitment to a particular community and its experience of one dominant mode of oppression—sexism, classism, racism, economic dependency, cultural injustice—and its particular expression of liberating Christian praxis should free the participants to see and hear the oppressions of all others—at the limit of the global community of "the wretched of the earth." Theologians should hear, as well, all the forgotten, even nameless dead whose lives and suffering must not be forgotten, whose story is not told in the history of the victors, whose memories should spur us to action now, whose ultimate vindication we trust to the God who raised Jesus from the dead. The liberation theologians demand that the voice snatched away from all these nameless ones in their own lifetimes by the victors of history be returned to them. As the contemporary Christian theological journey of Rosemary Radford Ruether demonstrates, a commitment to one particular community should free the theologian of liberation to recognize the needs and demands of all communities. For the linked realities of sexism, racism, classism, anti-Semitism are disclosed in the light of the empowering and commanding freedom and responsibility revealed by the God of Exodus, of Jesus, of Jesus Christ, by the God of all those prophetic and apocalyptic groups too long marginalized from the church's memory, the God of all those communities of the liberating praxis of faith existing even now.

As the journey of intensification into a particular community and its memories and hopes on behalf of the global community of humankind continues in the theologies of liberation, their demands for self-criticism also develop. Their earlier style of pure confrontation towards all other forms of theology seems now more willing to release its enraged grip and allow the real theological conflict of mutually respecting argument to occur. That development promises the real and liberating possibility of authentic conflict in the conversation among all forms of theology.

Moreover, the religious power of manifestation has also begun to surface in the theologies of liberation alongside the roots of most of these theologies in prophetic proclamation and action. Hence the movement of liberation from a particular community to a global humanity expands to include the nonhuman, nature itself. The emphasis in Gutierrez on struggle, solidarity and contemplation, the fight of Ruether against all forms of "dualism" including "nature" vs. "spirit," the emergence of the demand for the recognition of the powers of nature and body in Sheila Collins and others, the insistence by Charles Long that black theologies retrieve some of the nature wisdom of their ancestral African religious heritage, the conscious retrieval of holistic attitudes in native American religions by Christian theologians, the "second naivete" of Latin American and Spanish theologians towards the realities of Latin "popular religion," the use by liberation theologians of the findings on the importance of ritual and image by cultural anthropologists like Mary Douglas and Victor Turner[66]—all these signs of the presence of "manifestation" suggest that another crucial step forward is being taken by these prophetic theologies of proclamation and action: the homocentrism[67] of the Western proclamation—action traditions (a homocentrism shared by many of the earliest expressions of both political and liberation theologies) is now being recognized as yet another and more subtle form of entrapment demanding liberation. Homocentrism is recognized as the entrapment it is largely by means of a liberating retrieval of the traditions of manifestation within many of liberation theologies themselves.

For myself, besides their other obvious contributions, the theologies of liberation represent above all a classic event in search of a classic text. The sheer event-character of the great liberation movements of our time, both secular and religious, represent no fad, no fashion, no new consumer product. They represent rather the liberating reality of a classic, a kairotic event disclosing and transforming all. They expose central contradictions in both situation and tradition. They reveal the possibilities grounded in the eschatological actions and promises of the God of Exodus and Jesus Christ, for communal, societal and ultimately global liberation. They can be ignored only at the price of willful self-deception. These theologies encourage the powers of both suspicion and retrieval of the Christian tradition and its disclosure of the fuller reality of sin and the liberating transformations of politics and history by grace.[68] Above all, the liberation theologies allow all theologians to hear and see the tradition from a perspective faithful to its ownmost self-understanding: from that perspective privileged to the ancient prophets and Jesus alike—the perspective of the outcast, the powerless, the oppressed, the marginalized, all those whose story the rest of us have presumed to tell them. It is perhaps little wonder that I have not yet found the classic text of liberation theology that I have sought—that work that will explode with power as Barth's commentary on Romans once did in the neoorthodox theologies of proclamation. The search for the classic disclosed through and by these theologies, I have come to believe, will not end in any text. The classic of liberation theologies is the classic not of a text but of an event: the event of a liberating praxis wherein the actions of whole peoples whose disclosive, ignored, forgotten, despised story is at last being narrated and heard in ways which may yet transform us all.

Notes

1. On the medievals here, see Bernard Lonergan, *Grace and Freedom* [I/65], pp. 1–41; idem, *Method in Theology* [I/10], pp. 335–55.
2. H. Richard Niebuhr, *Christ and Culture* [I/99].
3. Indeed, the earlier analysis (chap. 3) of general criteria of relative adequacy for pluralism (viz., Wayne Booth's criteria of justice, critical understanding and vitalization) are applicable to H. Richard Niebuhr's analysis of the relative adequacy of the different models, and his own "concluding unscientific postscript" (pp. 230–57).
4. Ibid., pp. 190–230.
5. Recall the discussions in chap. 2 of how this general model shifts in emphasis in relationship to the distinct concerns of fundamental, systematic and practical theology and the specific criteria of relative adequacy relevant to each.
6. Recall the relationship between general criteria and particular (context-dependent) criteria for general interpretation theory in chap. 3.
7. It is for this reason, moreover, that ordinarily the systematic theologian will be a believer in the event which he or she is interpreting. In the case of Christian theology, this belief in (or faith as response and orientation) may be distinguished from the acceptance of particular beliefs implicit or explicit in that faith. Moreover, authentic "faith," on strictly Christian hermeneutical grounds, is a gift, not a

personal achievement (and so recognized in the individual response to the event). Therefore, it is more accurate to leave the question of the "faith" of the systematic theologian a factual not an in-principled one (hence my use here and in chap. 2 of the word "ordinarily"). The distinction in principle can be put this way: on general hermeneutical grounds the preunderstanding of the systematic theologian *must* involve at least a horizon open to the religious dimension of existence—i.e., a willingness to ask the kind of fundamental questions that are religious questions. Second, the systematic theologian must also recognize some claim to serious attention in the event under interpretation: a recognition that can occur across a wide spectrum ranging from some resonance to the event through the full-fledged shock of recognition of authentic, recognizably engifted faith. "Ordinarily" a reality closer to the latter ("personal faith") will be involved for most systematic theologians. In principle, however, the former "resonance" to the event and preunderstanding of the fundamental questions would suffice to allow the conversation (step 3) between interpreter and text event to prove a genuinely hermeneutical and systematic theological one. This is perhaps a better formulation of this question of the "faith" of the theologian than my earlier one in response to John Connelly: see John Connelly, "The Task of Theology" and my "Response," in *CTSA Proceedings* (1974), 1–59, 67–77. The position I defended then is proper to fundamental theology (see chap. 2). For systematic and practical theologies, however, the more nuanced position suggested here seems more relatively adequate to the hermeneutical character of systematic theology. Some formulations of the "necessity of faith" for theology are, in my judgment, too sweeping and unnuanced (often failing to employ even such basic distinctions as that between "faith or belief-in" and "beliefs," or failing to mention the full spectrum of possibilities from "implicit faith" [here some resonance to the event] to the gift of personal faith). The traditional Anselmian phrase "fides quaerens intellectum" continues to be the classic brief description of the matter-of-fact hermeneutical character of systematic theology. Here the Anselmian dictum can be translated as faith seeking an interpretation that retrieves its genuine publicness. The notion of the kind of "realized experience" elicited by the religious classic may also be used to state the kind of experience involved in the Anselmian motto used by Schleiermacher for his *Glaubenslehre*: "Qui expertus non fuerit, non intelliget." For historical reflections on how the category "belief" changed its meaning from "more than knowledge" (*pistis*—knowledge plus resolve for enactment) to less than knowledge, see Wilfred Cantwell Smith, *Belief and History* (Charlottesville: Univ. Press of Virginia, 1977). The earlier notion of "belief" seems to accord with the "realized-experience" hermeneutical position (in its full spectrum) taken here.

8. I assume here that the "family resemblances" are open to more mediation than Wittgenstein's own more discrete formulations seem to be. See *Philosophical Investigations* (New York: Macmillan, 1958), esp. pp. 31–49. In short, as mentioned in chap. 3, Gadamer's formulation allows for a mediation of the different languages bearing "family resemblances." To translate: the differences within and among the three principal language families here (manifestation-proclamation-action) are by definition mediatable since all are interpretations of the same event of Jesus Christ (all are, therefore, in the same "family") and each is open to further conversation with the other principal interpretations or modes of expression for that event.

9. See chap. 5, sec. 3.

10. Exceptions abound here, too, however, as in the revival of mystical theologies, the analysis of "popular religion," or the full-fledged realities of paradigmatic Christian rituals and festivals especially in Latin American, Asian

and African forms of indigenous Christianity. The analysis of this chapter, as of the whole book, relates principally to theologies—a realm where this generalization does hold.

11. *On Religion: Speeches to Its Cultured Despisers* (New York: Harper, 1958). For a helpful study of the Romantic background of the *Speeches,* see Jack Forstman, *A Romantic Triangle: Schleiermacher and Early German Romanticism* (Missoula: Scholars Press, 1977).

12. *The Christian Faith* [I/76], pp. 3–131. For an interpretation of *Glaubenslehre,* see B. A. Gerrish, "Continuity and Change: Friedrich Schleiermacher on 'The Task of Theology'" [II/36], pp. 13–49; and Martin Redeker, *Schleiermacher: Life and Thought* (Philadelphia: Fortress, 1973).

13. See Gerrish's response to Emil Brunner's famous (and representative) charge: ibid., pp. 22–48.

14. The structure, as I mentioned earlier, will prove one of moving from the relatively abstract ("First Part: The Development of our Religious Self-Consciousness which is always both presupposed by and contained in every Religious Affection") to the concrete ("Second Part: The Explication of the facts of Religious Self-Consciousness as they are determined by the Antithesis of Sin and Grace").

15. This structure can be seen most clearly in *The Foundations of Christian Faith* [IV/27].

16. Ibid., pp. 44–90.

17. Ibid., pp. 206–12.

18. Ibid., pp. 212–28.

19. It is interesting to note how the *eros* tradition of the ancient Greeks has been employed in manifestation-oriented theologies, both in Eastern Christian theologies and in Western theologies from Augustine through Rahner.

20. Alternatively, with Schubert Ogden or Hans Küng, "fundamental trust": see Schubert Ogden, *The Reality of God* [I/100], pp. 37–38; Hans Küng, *On Being a Christian* [I/96], pp. 57–83.

21. On these realities, see *BRO*, pp. 91–146.

22. See Hans Urs von Balthasar, *Love Alone* (New York: Herder and Herder, 1969); on Teilhard here, see Henri de Lubac, *Teilhard de Chardin: The Man and His Meaning* (New York: Mentor, 1965); on Tillich, see James Luther Adams, *Paul Tillich's Philosophy of Culture, Science and Religion* [VIII/3], esp. pp. 17–64; for a review of Schelling scholarship (including Tillich's two theses), see the review essay by Robert R. Williams in *RSR* 5 (1979), 116–23.

23. See Eric Voegelin, "Reason: The Classic Experience," in *Anamnesis* [VIII/65], pp. 89–116.

24. For representative Catholic pastoral theologies here, see the work of Mary G. Durkin, Rosemary Haughton, Bruno Manno and John Shea: inter alia, the articles by Durkin, Shea and Manno in *Toward Vatican III* [III/106]; see also Mary Durkin, *The Suburban Woman: Her Changing Role in the Church* (New York: Seabury, 1976); John Shea, *Stories of God: An Unauthorized Biography* (Chicago: Thomas More, 1978); Rosemary Haughton, *The Transformation of Man: A Study of Conversion and Community* (London: Chapman, 1967). The journal *Pastoral Psychology* often provides illuminating materials on this possibility. For a good study of the Catholic sense of community, see also Langdon Gilkey, *Catholicism Confronts Modernity* [I/100], pp. 17–20. The works of Eugene Kennedy are excellent on the psychological aspects of the communal humaneness and ambiguities of the Catholic sensibility; as representative, see his brilliant analysis, "Being A Catholic: Does It Make a Difference?" *CTSA Proceedings* (1974), 311–22.

25. See Nathan A. Scott, Jr., *The Wild Prayer of Longing: Poetry and the Sacred* (New Haven: Yale Univ. Press, 1971), p. 48; William Lynch, *Christ and Apollo* (New York: Sheed and Ward, 1961); idem, *Images of Hope* (New York: Mentor, 1965); Nathan A. Scott, Jr., "Poetry and Prayer," in *Negative Capability* (New Haven: Yale Univ. Press, 1969), pp. 89–113.

26. Martin Heidegger, "The Origin of the Work of Art," in *Basic Writings* [II/52], pp. 162–68.

27. See, Martin Buber, *I and Thou* and *Between Man and Man* [I/5]; Gabriel Marcel, *Being and Having* (Boston: Beacon, 1951) and *Homo Viator* [IV/46].

28. See Nathan Scott's analysis of this reality in Roethke and others, in *The Wild Prayer of Longing*, pp. 76–121; see also Teilhard de Chardin's little classic of spirituality *Le Milieu Divin* (London: Collins, 1957). For a brilliant and polemical defense of the option of the everyday and the concrete over the "sublime" and the "transcendental," recall T. E. Hulme's famous attack on the Romantics: "The essence of poetry to most people is that it must lead them to a beyond of some kind. Verse strictly confined to the earthly and the definite (Keats is full of it) might seem to them to be excellent writing, excellent craftsmanship, but not poetry. So much has romanticism debauched us, that, without some sort of vagueness, we deny the highest" (*Speculations* [New York: Harcourt, Brace, and World, 1924], p. 127).

29. Simone Weil, *The Need for Roots* (Boston: Beacon, 1952).

30. See Ewert Cousins, *The Coincidence of Opposites in the Theology of St. Bonaventure* (Chicago: Franciscan Herald, 1978); idem, ed., *Bonaventure: The Soul's Journey into God* (New York: Paulist, 1978), pp. 1–51. For an interesting study of Francis himself, see Edward Armstrong, *Saint Francis: Nature Mystic* (Berkeley: Univ. of California Press, 1973).

31. Joseph Sittler, *Essays in Nature and Grace* [V/64].

32. See chap. 3, sec. iii.

33. Gerard Manley Hopkins, *The Poems*, ed. W. H. Gardner and N. H. MacKenzie (London: Oxford, 1967), p. 31.

34. T. S. Eliot, *Four Quartets*, "The Dry Salvages," p. 136 in *Complete Poems and Plays*. For a study, see Helen Gardner, *The Art of T. S. Eliot* (New York: Dutton, 1959).

35. The general methodological reason can be stated as follows: the concrete is not reducible to the abstract. This does not deny, of course, our earlier point that the necessary abstractions of fundamental theology should play a corrective role upon the presuppositions and formulations of systematic theology.

36. One of the major positive signs of this is the splendid series of classical Western mystical writers presently being published by Paulist Press. For a well-earned tribute to this remarkable series, see Jill Raitt's review article in *RSR* 6 (July 1980). See also the informative work by Harvey Egan, "Christian Apophatic and Kataphatic Mysticisms," *TS* (1978), 399–427; and William Johnston, *The Inner Eye of Love: Mysticism and Religion* (London: Collins, 1978). I am especially thankful for guidance in this area to my friend and colleague, Bernard McGinn, whose careful scholarship on neo-Platonic and other Western forms of mystical theologies may be sampled in his many articles on these themes: for one example, see his article on Eckhart in *JR* 61 (Jan. 1981).

37. Representative here on the Reformation is Heinrich Bornkamm, *The Heart of Reformation Faith* (New York: Harper & Row, 1965); John H. Leith, *Introduction to the Reformed Tradition* (Atlanta: John Knox, 1977).

38. H. Richard Niebuhr, *The Kingdom of God in America* [I/85], p. 193.

39. For excellent representative articles of the major figures here in their earlier

period (especially Barth, Bultmann, Gogarten and Tillich), see *The Beginnings of Dialectic Theology* [V/48], especially interesting are the selections from the Harnack-Barth correspondence (pp. 165–91); see also *Revolutionary Theology in the Making: Barth-Thurneysen Correspondence, 1914–1925* (Richmond: John Knox, 1964).

40. For a non-Barthian tribute to Barth's hermeneutical accomplishment here, see James M. Robinson "Hermeneutic Since Barth," in *The New Hermeneutic* [III/21], pp. 1–78.

41. Representative scholarship here includes: Hans Urs von Balthasar, *The Theology of Karl Barth* (New York: Holt, Rinehart, and Winston, 1971); Herbert Hartwell, *The Theology of Karl Barth: An Introduction* (Philadelphia: Westminster, 1964); David Mueller, *Karl Barth* (Waco: Word, 1972).

42. See G. C. Berkouwer, *The Triumph of Grace in the Theology of Karl Barth* (Grand Rapids: Eeerdmans, 1956).

43. See Karl Barth, *The Epistle to the Romans* (London: Oxford Univ. Press, 1972); note also von Balthasar's sensitivity to the expressionist language of *Romans,* in *The Theology of Karl Barth,* pp. 67–68.

44. For references, see chap. 5.

45. *History and Eschatology* [VI/54].

46. For references, see chap. 8, no. 3.

47. For examples of how unsteady the alliance was even at the beginning, note the Tillich-Barth exchange in *The Beginnings of Dialectic Theology* [V/48], pp. 133–65; for a Barthian-oriented analysis of Barth and Bultmann, see James D. Smart, *The Divided Mind of Modern Theology: Karl Barth and Rudolf Bultmann, 1908–1933* (Philadelphia: Westminster, 1967).

48. For one of the clearest examples of how different those ways became, see Karl Barth, "Rudolph Bultmann—An Attempt to Understand Him," in *Kerygma and Myth,* II, ed. Hans Werner Bartock (London: SPCK, 1962), pp. 83–133.

49. See *The New Hermeneutic* [III/21], especially the essays by Ebeling (pp. 78–111) and Fuchs (pp. 111–47).

50. Representative here of the earlier period (on deprivatizing): Dorothee Soelle, *Political Theology* [V/52]; Jürgen Moltmann, *Theology of Hope* [IV/8]; Johann Baptist Metz, *Theology of the World* [I/94]; for some informative studies of these developments, see M. Douglas Meeks, *Origins of the Theology of Hope* (Philadelphia: Fortress, 1974); Carl Braaten and Robert Jensen, *The Futurist Option* (New York: Newman, 1970); Walter Capps, *Time Invades the Cathedral: Tensions in the School of Hope* (Philadelphia: Fortress, 1972); André Dumas, *Political Theology and the Life of the Church* (Philadelphia: Westminster, 1978); Claude Geffre, *The New Age in Theology* (New York: Paulist, 1972), pp. 63–111; Alistair Kee, ed., *A Reader in Political Theology* (Philadelphia: Westminster, 1974); Alfredo Fierro, *The Militant Gospel* [I/14].

51. See Johann Baptist Metz, *Theology of the World* [I/94], pp. 13–56; on Metz, see Roger Dick Johns, *Man in the World: The Theology of Johannes Baptist Metz* (Missoula: Scholars, 1976); Gustavo Gutierrez, *A Theology of Liberation* [IV/50], pp. 169–73 (creation), pp. 192–93 (incarnation).

52. Gutierrez, ibid., pp. 3–21. On theologies of liberation, see Robert McAfee Brown, *Theology in a New Key: Responding to Liberation Themes* (Philadelphia: Westminster, 1968); Rosino Gibellini, ed., *Frontiers of Theology in Latin America* (Maryknoll: Orbis, 1979); Rosemary Ruether, *Liberation Theology* [II/101]; Sergio Torres and John Eagleson, eds., *Theology in the Americas* (Maryknoll: Orbis, 1976); Brian Mahan and Dale Richesin, eds., *The Challenge of Liberation Theology: A First World Response* (forthcoming); Francis Fiorenza, "Latin American

Liberation Theology," *Interpretation* (1974), 119–31; Alfred T. Hennelly, *Theologies in Conflict: The Challenge of Juan Luis Segundo* (Maryknoll: Orbis, 1979). For constructive developments, besides the works of Boff, Cone, Gutierrez, Miranda, Ruether and Segundo referred to in earlier chapters, see, as representative, Hugo Assmann, *Theology for a Nomad Church* (Maryknoll: Orbis, 1976); Frederick Herzog, *Liberation Theology: Liberation in the Light of the Fourth Gospel* (New York: Seabury, 1972); José Míguez-Bonino, *Doing Theology in a Revolutionary Situation* (Philadelphia: Fortress, 1975). For a critical and constructive analysis of some forms of liberation theology, see Schubert Ogden, *Faith and Freedom* [IV/88].

53. This insistence is not, of course, confined to the political and liberation theologians—although emphasized by them more than by earlier "manifestation" and "proclamation" theologies. In the North American tradition, the praxis emphasis has been a major one from the beginning (see chap. 2, n. 82). For some recent North American expressions of this tradition, see Langdon Gilkey, *Reaping the Whirlwind* [II/2]; John C. Haughey, ed., *The Faith That Does Justice* [I/38]; and Langdon Gilkey, "The Political Dimensions of Theology," *JR* (1979), 154–69.

54. Inter alia, see Hans Küng, *The Church—Maintained in Truth?* [II/32].

55. Inter alia, see Charles Curran, *New Perspectives in Moral Theology* (Notre Dame: Univ. of Notre Dame, 1974); idem (with Robert Hunt et al.), *Dissent in and for the Church: Theologians and Humanae Vitae* (New York: Sheed and Ward, 1969).

56. See John Coleman, "Vision and Praxis in American Theology," *TS* (1976), 3–40; Charles Curran, "American and Catholic: American Catholic Social Ethics, 1880–1965," *Thought* (1977), 50–74; David Hollenbach, "Public Theology: Some Questions for Catholicism after John Courtney Murray," *TS* (1976), 290–303; Robin Lovin, "Covenantal Relationships and Political Legitimacy" [I/34]; Martin Marty, "A Sort of Republican Banquet" [I/8].

57. A major exception here is Juan Luis Segundo: see especially his revisionary notion of church as "sign" (vs. any ecclesiocentrism) in *The Community Called Church* [I/94], and his revisionary interpretations of "grace" and "love" in *Grace and the Human Condition* (Maryknoll: Orbis, 1973). For a good study of Segundo, see Alfred Hennelly, *Theologies in Conflict* [52].

58. See Francis Fiorenza, "Critical Social Theory and Christology," in *CTSA Proceedings* (1975), 63–111.

59. See José Míguez-Bonino, *Doing Theology in a Revolutionary Situation* [52]; and from the "political theology" side, see Jürgen Moltmann, "An Open Letter to Jose Miguez Bonino," *Christianity and Crisis* (1976), 57–63.

60. For examples here, see: Gustavo Gutierrez, *A Theology of Liberation* [IV/50]; *Black Theology: A Documentary History, 1966–1979,* ed. James Cone and Gayraud Wilmore (Maryknoll: Orbis, 1980); *Mission Trends 4: Liberation Theologies,* ed. Gerald Anderson and Thomas Stransky (New York: Paulist, 1979); idem, *Mission Trends 3: Third World Theologies* (New York: Paulist, 1976); James Cone, *God of the Oppressed* [IV/50]; idem, *A Black Theology of Liberation* [II/109]; J. Deotis Roberts, *Liberation and Reconciliation: A Black Theology* (Philadelphia: Westminster, 1971).

For representative feminist theologians see Rosemary Radford Ruether, *New Woman, New Earth* [IV/50]; Sheila Collins, *A Different Heaven and Earth* (Valley Forge: Judson, 1974); Letty Russell, *Human Liberation in a Feminist Perspective* (Philadelphia: Westminster, 1974); Elizabeth Schüssler Fiorenza, "Feminist Theology as a Critical Theology of Liberation," pp. 188–217, in *Mission Trends 4*; a "post-Christian" position may be found in the influential later work of Mary Daly,

Beyond God the Father (Boston: Beacon, 1973); a good and representative collection is *Womanspirit Rising: A Feminist Reader in Religion,* ed. Carol Christ and Judith Plaskow (San Francisco: Harper & Row, 1979). I wish to express my thanks to Mary Knutsen for her work in feminist theology, especially her work in process, "Shreiking Heaven," and her critical guidance through the growing literature. On ethnicity, see Andrew Greeley and Gregory Baum, eds, *Ethnicity* (=*Concilium* 107; New York: Seabury, 1977).

61. (New York: Macmillan, 1970); idem, *God Is Red* (New York: Grosset & Dunlap, 1973); see also Benjamin Reist, *Theology in Red, White and Black* (Philadelphia: Westminster, 1975).

62. See Valerie Saiving Goldstein, "The Human Situation: A Feminine View" [II/24]; and Judith Plaskow, *Sex, Sin and Grace: Women's Experience and the Theologies of Reinhold Niebuhr and Paul Tillich* (Washington: Univ. Press of America, 1979).

63. *Theology of Liberation* [IV/50], p. 13.

64. On the "God who acts" motif in these theologies, see chap. 2, n. 108.

65. See n. 61.

66. For references (in order) see: Gustavo Gutierrez, *A Theology of Liberation* [IV/50], pp. 203–13; Rosemary Ruether, *New Woman, New Earth* [IV/50]; Sheila Collins, *A Different Heaven and Earth* [60]; Charles Long, "Civil Rights–Civil Religion: Visible People and Invisible Religion," in *American Civil Religion* [I/39], pp. 211–22; the essays on "African Perspectives" in *Mission Trends 3* [60]; Benjamin Reist, *Theology in Red, White and Black* [61]; Segundo Galilea, "Latin America: The Debate on Popular Religion," *Concilium* 136 [IV/9]; and the articles by Virgil Elizondo, Joan Llopis, Vincent Garcia and David Power, in Herman Schmidt and David Power, eds., *Liturgy and Cultural Religious Traditions* (=*Concilium* 102; New York: Seabury 1977); and Robert Stark, "Religious Ritual and Class Formation" (Ph.D. diss., University of Chicago).

67. See Schubert Ogden, *Faith and Freedom* [IV/88], pp. 97–124.

68. See Leonardo Boff, *Liberating Grace* (Maryknoll: Orbis, 1979); Roger Haight, *The Experience and Language of Grace* (New York: Paulist, 1979), pp. 143–86; Juan Luis Segundo, *Grace and the Human Condition,* [57].

Chapter 10

A Christian Systematic Analogical Imagination

i. Classical Theological Languages: Analogy and Dialectic

As each Christian systematic theology within these three classical families of manifestation, proclamation and action—vision, hearing and act—moves forward into the particularity of its experience of the event of Jesus Christ, two realities take hold in the properly systematic theological journey. First, creative reinterpretations of the major classical symbols, texts, events, images, persons, rituals will occur in and for an understanding of the fundamental questions disclosed in the situation. Inevitably this involves the risk of a personal interpretation, not the false security of mere repetition. Inevitably, too, the power of critical reason and its emancipatory interest towards both tradition and situation will be employed. For all systematic theologies, like all fundamental theologies before and alongside them, live by the power of the critical freedom granted as grace and command in the originating religious event itself.

The theologian's sense of belonging to that event of manifestation, proclamation and action is the primordial ground releasing the power of the freedom of the theological search for the meaning and truth of Christianity in the contemporary situation. The symbol does "give rise to critical thought before returning to the symbol." Systematic theologians cannot simply repeat; they must critically interpret the tradition mediating the event. Theologians cannot collapse into, they must critically interpret the situation in the light of the event. From Schleiermacher's liberating insight into the modern critical need for a new form for systematics, a *Glaubenslehre,* through Karl Rahner's struggle against the neo-Scholastic manuals and for the risk of an authentic retrieval of the classical doctrines, through Karl Barth's reinterpretations of the Reformed tradition (interpretations which remain not orthodox but *neo*orthodox), to Rudolf Bultmann's recognition that demythologizing is demanded by both the subject matter of the kerygma and the contemporary situation, to Paul Tillich's masterful insight into the doubt at the heart of authentic contemporary faith, to Reinhold Niebuhr's insight—an insight shared by all the later political and liberation theologians—that the contemporary socioethical crisis and its demand for criteria of transformation and praxis is at least as vital a crisis for the Christian spirit as the cognitive crises posed by modernity, to Hans Küng's theological struggle with the distortions of the ecclesial traditions and society, the same recognition of the systematic theologian's ownmost task endures. That task is the risk of a creative, as both participatory and critical, interpretation of the event (and the traditions and forms mediating the event) in and for the interpreted situation. Each theologian articulates some personal theological response to that event: a response focussed upon some major form (or forms) expressing the event (manifestation-proclamation-action), a response articulating some series of mutually critical correlations between an interpretation of the event (and the traditions and forms mediating the event in the present) and an interpretation of the situation (and the traditions and forms mediating that reality). The particular response will be determined, above all, by the particular subject matter under analysis. The general, heuristic form of response will follow the pattern of mutually critical correlations between interpretations of situation and event as each reality influences (confronts, correlates, informs, transforms) the understanding of the other.

In the theology of Langdon Gilkey, for example, we may note this process at work with unusual clarity.[1] Gilkey always provides a theological interpretation of the "religious dimension" present in some major reality in the contemporary situation and then provides a new theological interpretation of the significance of the explicitly religious, Christian event and its major symbols for and in that situation. Mutually critical correlations between situation and event are established at every major point in the analysis. Yet Gilkey does not allow his general method a more than heuristic value. For the particular subject matter under study in both situation and event takes hermeneutical precedence over the method to allow for a whole spectrum of possible particular correlatives (confrontation, identity, transformation) depending on the subject matter itself. An informed reader of Gilkey's work soon learns his general theological method. The reader can, therefore, make an informed guess but never an *a priori* prediction on Gilkey's position on a particular issue. For there, as in all good interpretation, the particular subject matter takes over and the heuristic value of the method guides but ultimately yields to the subject matter itself.

A second reality also comes into play in properly systematic theologies. The full range of the Christian symbol system comes more and more clearly into view as demanding attention from each theologian in a struggle to articulate some envisionment of the heart of the matter in relationship to the whole symbol system. Each theologian also searches, therefore, for criteria of internal coherence among the symbols. Each theologian is obliged to develop criteria of internal coherence for that symbol system and is usually content to achieve some "rough coherence" among the major symbols. That coherence will basically be forged by a theologian's correlation of some personal interpretation of the core symbolism of the tradition (usually under the guidance of either manifestation, proclamation or action) and some interpretation of the situation. That initial coherence will demand the development of further criteria for the internal coherence of the whole range of symbols. Those latter criteria, in turn, will range from the "rough coherence" of Barth and Reinhold Niebuhr and most theologians to the rigorously systematic coherence of Aquinas, Palamas, Calvin, Schleiermacher and Hegel.

A theologian may prove so gripped by a particular original, revelatory insight in the event—as was Luther, as was Barth, as are many contemporary liberation theologians—that other classic theological alternatives cannot but seem sub-Christian, even "right, strawy" monstrosities. Yet what is dismissed in one's early work with a resounding "no" often returns in one's later reflections: now, to be sure, in a transformed, more relatively adequate form. Yet, however intense a particular experience of Christian manifestation or proclamation or action may prove for any theologian, all systematic theologians eventually find the initial experience of the event demands accountability to the fuller reality of the entire range of classics in the Christian tradition if one is to have a relatively adequate systematic theology. All the classic systematic theologies from Paul and John to our own day are de jure inadequate, de facto relatively adequate accounts of the fuller range of the entire symbol system from the dominating perspective of a singular stance of personal response.

Thus does the search for relative adequacy in any systematics occur: The search is always bounded by the theological knowledge of the intrinsic inadequacy of any theology in relationship to the event itself. That search, within that liberating sense of boundedness, is the fate become the welcome destiny of every systematic theology. The criteria of relative adequacy formulated by the forms of emancipatory and critical reason released by both situation and event—criteria of internal conceptual coherence, existential meaningfulness and adequacy to common human experience and language in fundamental theologies—join the major criteria for truth in systematic and practical theologies as disclosure and transformation. Each set of criteria plays its conscious or unconscious role in every systematic theology that risks its true task of creative, critical, practical, participatory interpretation of event and situation alike. The relatively internal criteria of relative adequacy demanded in all interpretation also hold firm: the hermeneutical criteria demanded for any interpretation of any classic; the criteria of internal coherence for the full range of the classic forms and symbols articulating the full significance of the event.

All these sets of criteria of relative adequacy come into play in explicit and implicit form, moreover, when the theologian also recalls that the language of theology is usually not the same kind of language as that of the originating religious experience and expression. Theological language is ordinarily a second-order, reflective language bearing further criteria for its reflective task. To develop a language that is both faithful to the tensive character of the religious language employed for the originating religious event and faithful to the demands of critical reflection is a major aspect of theology's task. The theologian, as theologian, develops a properly reflective language of critique and participation by means of the articulation of theological *concepts* that are neither mere categories nor simple replacements of the originating tensive religious language. In that effort for an adequate conceptual, reflective language, all the criteria of relative adequacy and all the tasks proper to a relatively adequate systematic theology as reflective upon the original religious language emerge as the final theological task. Two major conceptual languages have served as the principal candidates for this task in theology: analogical and dialectical languages. Both language traditions, I believe, continue to function as the classic *theological* languages par excellence.

The first of these languages, analogy, is a language of ordered relationships articulating similarity-in-difference. The order among the relationships is constituted by the distinct but similar relationships of each analogue to some primary focal meaning, some prime analogue.[2] A principal aim of all properly analogical languages is the production of some order, at the limit, some harmony to the several analogues, the similarities-in-difference, constituting the whole of reality. The order is developed by explicating the analogous relationships among various realities (self, others, world, God), by clarifying the relationship of each to the primary analogue, the meaning chosen as the primary focus for interpreting reality.[3] In Christian systematics, the primary focal meaning will be the event of Jesus Christ (usually mediated through particular forms and particular traditions). That focal meaning *as event* will prove the primary analogue for the interpretation of the whole of reality. The event will prove the major clue to the similarities-in-difference awaiting explication among the realities God, self, other selves and world (society, history, nature). These now articulated similarities-in-difference will prove clues to the possibly ordered relationships disclosed by the event as each analogue is focussed, interpreted, related through newly formed propositions to the other analogues as similarities-in-difference by the primary analogue, the Christ event.[4]

Where theologically exact, the resultant order is never purchased at the price of either intensity or variety. Any harmony present in the order is never forced (never, for example, cheaply affirmative) but recurs through and by means of the common focus upon the intensity of the originating tensive event releasing its focal meaning to guide the entire series of interpretations of real-similarities-in-real-difference. When the Christ event is acknowledged as the radical mystery of the self-manifestation of God, the guidance of a more particular focal meaning for the event (e.g., incarnation) will alert the theologian to the need for negations in the interpretation of each reality (God-self-world). Negations of any claims to full adequacy (for example, any attempts at exhaustive, univocal meanings in any analogue) are negations to assure that the similarities remain similarities-in-difference, to assure that the analogous relationships of proportion are related to the uncontrollable event, negations to keep the principles of order and harmony from becoming merely affirmative. The negations function as principles of intensification constituted by the tensive event-character of the focal meaning to negate any slackening of the sense of radical mystery, any grasp at control of the event and the similarities-in-difference of the realities (God, self, world) focussed upon and interpreted by that event.[5]

The negations with their disclosure of radical dissimilarity in similarity, by their concentration upon the tensive event-character in the focal meaning will also manifest the genuine similarities disclosed by means of the defamiliarizing difference exposed in the event. The presence of the negations continue in the real similarities articulated as similarities-in-difference. For these reasons, the major explicitly analogical traditions in theology have correctly insisted that in the theological use of analogies, the dissimilarities between God and world are as great as the similarities; the *via eminentiae* is possible only on condition of its constant fidelity to the *via negationis*.[6] In the more familiar contemporary formulation, God-language is by definition "perfection-language"; and the logic of perfection-language is grounded in the radical, irreducible logical difference of "all" from the logical alternatives "some" and "none."[7]

Systematic theological analogical language, therefore, is a second-order reflective language reexpressing the meanings of the originating religious event and its original religious language to and for a reflective mind: a mind searching for some order, yet recognizing, at every moment in its search, the irreducible tension at the heart of its own participatory and distancing experience of the originating event as an *event* of a disclosure-concealment to focus the entire search; a mind recognizing, therefore, the ultimate incomprehensibility of the event that provides the focal meaning for developing both analogies-in-difference and order from chaos; a mind also recognizing the self-constituting, dynamic demands of the spirit of inquiry's ownmost need for critical reflection and the human mind's and heart's need for some similarities-in-difference, some analogues, some principles of order, some ultimate harmony in the whole of reality.

All these realities assure that any moves to order and, at the limit, to harmony in systematic theology will be won only by a mode of reflection faithful to the power of the uncanny negatives disclosed in the event, won only by a mode of reflection faithful as well to the need for the negative in the very dynamism of critical reflection itself. Any analogical concepts that emerge from that constantly expanding, never-ending dialectical relationship between authentically critical reflection and real participation in the negating, defamiliarizing, disclosing event will be concepts that never lose the tensive power of the negative. If that power is lost, analogical concepts become mere categories of easy likenesses slipping quietly from their status as similarities-in-difference to mere likenesses, falling finally into the sterility of a relaxed univocity and a facilely affirmative harmony. The analogies will be produced by the reflective and imaginative power of an individual theologian involved in the dialectical relationships of participation and critique. For example, a first-order tensive religious language like the metaphorical language in the parables of Jesus may receive a distinct, but never separate, reflective sublation into the second-order reflective language of theological analogy—as they do in the Johannine tradition.[8]

The analogies-in-difference will express a whole series of somehow ordered relationships (the relationships within the self, the relationships of the self to other selves, to society, history, the cosmos) all established in and through reflection upon the self's primordial experience of its similarity-in-difference to the event. The analogies will bring to expression some production by means of a theological analogical imagination: a production produced by the power of an analogical imagination released by the religious event and reflected upon by the critical powers of each theologian. The power of an analogical imagination as imagination was honored by Aristotle in his famous dictum "to spot the similar in the dissimilar is the mark of poetic genius." That same power—at once participatory in the originating event of wonder, trust, disclosure and concealment by the whole, and positively distancing itself from that event by its own self-constituting demands of critical reflection—releases the analogical imagination of the systematic theologian to note the profound similarities-in-difference in all reality.

These now articulated analogues will be further developed into a pattern of ordered analogical relationships among God-self-world. The pattern, in turn, follows the same path. The pattern is first disclosed by the critical spirit's focussed attention upon the revelatory power of the constitutive event and its disclosure of radical, all pervasive grace. With grace, some order, some religious sense of the reality of cosmos informing what once seemed pure chaos, some fundamental trust in reality itself as constituting an order in spite of all absurdity and chaos ultimately emerges.

The theologian articulates those principles of order disclosed in the event by refashioning the original disclosure. First, the theologian articulates one particular theological focal meaning or prime analogate (e.g., incarnation). Then, by means of some principles of philosophical reflection (e.g., neo-Platonic emanation theory) that seem or, better, are argued to bear a real affinity to that focal meaning, the theologian develops a properly systematic theology. As systematic, that theology is now able to articulate the similarities in difference among God-self-world by formulating some ordering principle (e.g., the exitus-reditus scheme) to express the relations of proportion in that order, even the harmony, in the newly envisioned, theologically reinterpreted, analogically imagined whole of reality. Throughout its deliberate journey, the analogical imagination of the systematic theologian at its best is always guided by the original religious-theological focal meaning, its singular key, its prime analogue for understanding the ordered whole of an originally pluralistic, conflictual, chaotic reality. Any theological analogical vision retrieves in a second-order language proper to reflective thought the originating religious experiences of trust, wonder, threat and giftedness released by the event. The symbol has given rise to thought but thought now returns reflectively to the symbol expressing the event. But the reflective journey of a theological analogical imagination has not been in vain. For the theologian returns to the symbol bearing the fruits of that reflection: a now-ordered series of analogical relationships among God-self-world ordered to and by some focal meaning for the event (e.g., Jesus Christ as Logos), a focal meaning which has proved itself a relatively adequate reflective analogue for understanding the originating religious event and the similarities-in-difference that event discloses.

It is hardly surprising that the religious traditions focussed upon manifestation in the event are usually oriented, on the theological level, to explicitly analogical language systems. The great traditions of neo-Platonic, Thomist and later idealist speculative theologies have produced analogical envisionments of the whole of reality. Those envisionments are ordered by and to a particular focal meaning (e.g., the logos) which speculative reason believed it found in the originating event's disclosure of trust, wonder, threat, gift. That envisionment is enhanced by the daring traditions of ordering principles of proportionality produced by speculative reason (the exitus-reditus schema, the "great chain of being," the nature-spirit relationships of Schelling). The system is open to correction at every crucial moment in its analogical journey by the negations demanded both by the focal meaning and by the classical experience of reason that guides its reflections (the *via negationis,* the apophatic traditions, the powerful negations present in nature mysticism and in Schelling's speculative philosophy and theology).

The shift from the speculative reason of classical patristic, medieval and later idealist theologies to the more troubled, more modest reflections of the post-Kantian critical reason of modern theologies is, to be sure, a major shift. And yet even that profound shift should not becloud the continuing presence of the same kind of analogical imagination in postcritical systematic theologies. From the original impact of Schleiermacher's discovery of the nonreducibility, the primordial event-character of religious experience in the *Speeches* to his systematic delineation of the whole series of ordered relationships ordered to and by the transformation of that religious experience into the explicitly Christian religious event-experience of sin and grace in the *Glaubenslehre,* the presence of an analogical imagination in a now critical, not speculative mode is clear. A similarly critical and participatory analogical journey, I believe, may be witnessed in all the major Liberal and "post-Liberal" Protestant theologies from Schleiermacher to contemporary process theologies, experiential theologies and Wolfhart Pannenberg's daring analogical search for a theology focussed on a proleptic universal history. That analogical imagination was present as well in the distinct but related journeys of the courageous early twentieth-century Catholic modernists and their successors.

The same kind of theological journey may be witnessed in a distinctively Catholic and critically reflective form, as we saw above, in Karl Rahner. Rahner's early transcendental discovery of human being as a struggling, striving, restless, reflective, historical spirit-in-world, as always-already present to a horizon of radical mystery and real incomprehensibility, yields in his later systematics to an explicitly Catholic retrieval of the incomprehensibility of God and our own humanity in the light of the disclosure-concealment of both God and humanity in the Christ event, and in the further light of a systematic retrieval of the order, the rough coherence, hidden in the classical doctrines of the Catholic tradition. The obscure, for Rahner, is understood *as* obscure only on the other side of the clarity provided by those analogies and that order. The incomprehensible is theologically retrieved *as* incomprehensible only on the other side of a theological comprehensibility of those analogies and that order.[9] Radical mystery is theologically understood not as puzzle or problem but *as* mystery only on the other side of a critical, reflective retrieval of the intelligibility of the concepts in the doctrines and the ordered relationships among the major doctrines.[10] The unity achieved is never the deadening uniformity beloved by a univocal mind but a unity-in-difference disclosed by similarities-in-difference to an analogical mind. For Rahner, reality not merely has analogies but *is* analogy through and through. As the analogous journeys of the mystical *theologies* remind us, even the religious silence evoked by an intensified (i.e., mystical) religious experience of the originating event is *theologically* understood *as* silence only on the other side of that speech, that reflective, second-order, kataphatic speech proper to the mystical theologian as speaker.

Moreover, the distinct but related principles of order grounded in the focal meanings of the extraordinariness of the ordinary and the reality of the paradigmatic yield, in a genuinely theological-analogical imagination, their own patterns of ordered relationships. Indeed, as these two distinct streams of manifestation-experience expand into systematic theologies they tend to converge into a mutual self-recognition. Then the radical sense of "likenesses" in the gifted *variety* of the ordinary joins a sense for an *intensity* negating the "profane" and the everyday in the paradigmatic to yield, as in Bonaventure and Teilhard de Chardin, theologies empowered by a vision of a recognition of "a coincidence of opposites."[11] All reality is now understood theologically in Bonaventure as it was religiously experienced in Francis: The entire world, the ordinary in all its variety, is now theologically envisioned as sacrament—a sacrament emanating from Jesus Christ as the paradigmatic sacrament of God, the paradigmatic clue to humanity and nature alike.

In all these theologies in the explicitly analogical language traditions, just as in all the *religious* expressions of manifestation, experience will ordinarily focus upon the religious experiences of trust, wonder, giftedness. So too the theological emphasis, clarified by some manifested focal meaning, will focus upon the similarities-in-difference in the extraordinary variety of reality. They will also focus upon the possible order, and, at the limit, the emerging harmony disclosed to reflection by concentration upon the disclosures provided by the focal meaning of a manifestation event and by reflection's own manifestory dynamism towards that same event. Yet to interpret these theological traditions, the interpreter must note that the likenesses discovered in variety, the emerging harmony discovered in order are produced by the presence of those moments of intensity, the necessary negations: similarity-in-difference, the negation of any univocity, the manifestation in the event of sheer giftedness, the concealment in every disclosure, the absence in every presence, the incomprehensibility in every moment of genuine comprehensibility, the radical mystery empowering all intelligibility.

Where analogical theologies lose that sense for the negative, that dialectical sense within analogy itself, they produce not a believable harmony among various likenesses in all reality but the theological equivalent of "cheap grace": boredom, sterility and an atheological vision of a deadening univocity. Some such loss seems to have occurred in the Thomist tradition's later invention (in Cajetan) of a "doctrine of analogy": a "doctrine" historically unfaithful to the pluralistic uses of analogy and the sense for the importance of negations in Aquinas' own extraordinarily fruitful theological analogical imagination.[12] For the later Thomistic "doctrine of analogy" proved fateful in its consequences for Catholic theology by its antidialectical (and, finally its antianalogical) stance. That doctrine ultimately yielded[13] in the neo-Scholastic manuals to the clear and distinct, the all-too-ordered and certain, the deadening, undisclosive and untransformative world of the dead analogies of a manualist Thomism committed to certitude, not understanding, veering towards univocity, not unity-in-difference.

As the great twentieth-century retrievals of Thomas's own analogical vision show, however, the "analogy of being," if really grounded philosophically in Thomas' own original metaphysical insight into the radical dialectical otherness of *esse,* can prove a genuine philosophical analogy to the theological "analogy of grace" grounded in the Christian religious experience of the radical giftedness and all-pervasiveness of grace.[14] In spite of their important internal differences, the many movements of the post-neo-Scholastic Thomist revival in the modern period united to retrieve (whether metaphysically in Gilson, Maritain and Przywara, transcendentally in Maréchal, Rousselot, Rahner and Coreth, or linguistically in Burrell) the powerful negative dialectics and the pluralistic use of analogies at the heart of both Thomas' philosophical "analogy of being" and his theological "analogy of grace." With this Thomist method of some authentic retrieval of the analogical core of both Thomas' philosophy of *esse* and his theology of grace and nature, these modern interpreters of Thomas freed Thomism from its captivity to Cajetan's "doctrine of analogy." They retrieved the classic status of Thomas' analogical envisionment of all reality by way of his analogies of nature and grace, his reinterpretation of the *exitus-reditus* schema for some order into the grand architecture of the *Summa Theologiae*.

Most modern forms of Thomist theology have remained faithful to the liberating intellectual ideal of the Scholastic tradition: "to distinguish without separation in order to unite without confusion." That ideal does genuinely liberate the thinker by rendering explicit one clear set of criteria for all authentic conversation. All forms of authentic modern Thomism have lived by the power of Aquinas' own analogical imagination and his demands for a conversation held in fidelity to the ideal of that kind of unity-in-difference, not uniformity. Singly and together, these modern forms of Thomist theology have undone the fatal hold of an ahistorical neo-Scholasticism on the Catholic theological analogical tradition. The power in those diverse expressions of a Thomist analogical imagination eventually released the fuller dynamism and variety in the Catholic theological tradition as a whole and thus assured the existence of a pluralism of analogical conceptual frameworks in Catholic theology.[15] Within our now-wider pluralism, the various modern Thomist theologians—and, behind them, the still astonishing classic achievements of Thomas Aquinas himself—live as genuine options, as classic alternatives in the continuing theological conversation within Catholic Christianity, indeed within all Christian theology in our period.

The same kind of sense for the necessity of negation at the heart of all genuine analogy has received even sharper emphasis in the contemporary retrieval of the tradition of the mystical theologies, indeed, in any theology principally focussed upon some intensified experience of the paradigmatic character of the originating event as manifestation. In those theologies focussed upon the paradigmatic character of the proclaimed word and the prophetic action, moreover, a sense of the importance of negation, now become an intense sense for a theological negative dialectics, has exploded into the center of contemporary theological consciousness. It has produced new dialectical languages in theology—and eventually new analogical languages.

The religious experience of the explosive power in the proclaimed Word empowered Kierkegaard as it empowered Barth, Bultmann, Gogarten, Brunner, Niebuhr and Tillich in their early period to insist upon the irretrievably dialectical character of all authentically Christian theological language hermeneutically faithful to that word. Neither the participatory trust in similarities and continuities of the analogical language traditions nor the presumptuous *Aufhebung* of Hegel's positive dialectical language could account for the rupture at the heart of human pretension, guilt and sin—a rupture disclosed for Kierkegaard in the event of the "absolute paradox" of Jesus Christ proclaimed in that judging, negating, releasing word.

Amidst all the genuine differences in the formulations of theological language as dialectical language by the theologians of the word, one major characteristic unites them all into a genuine family resemblance: the necessity of radical theological negations to constitute all Christian theological language. What the proclaimed word reveals to authentic Christian faith, theological language must reexpress in the reflective form initially of a negative dialectics. Indeed, the dialectics of theological language is constituted by the negative dialectic inherent to the subject matter of the proclaimed word itself. To reflect this reality theologically is to develop a second-order language expressive of a negation of all human efforts to save oneself, the negation of all poisonous dreams of establishing any easy continuities between Christianity and culture, the negation of all claims to a deluded, self-propelling "progress" within society and culture, the negation of all aesthetic, ethical, and "pagan" religious possibilities. These negations in the proclamation must be reexpressed in any theological language that dares to claim hermeneutical fidelity to authentic Christian faith hearing the Word of Jesus Christ: a word disclosing the reality of the infinite, qualitative distinction between that God and this flawed, guilty, sinful, presumptuous, self-justifying self.

Thus does the theological language of the dialectical theologians of the word first emerge: expressionist in its defamiliarizing, negating, unsettling rhetoric; alive in its concepts with the tensive power of radical negations upon all claims to similarity, continuity, ordered relations. For the theologians of the word, all nondialectical language does not express Christian faith, for the Christian knows that "only God can speak nondialectically." "Let God be God" becomes the watchword of the theologians of the Word. Jesus Christ as Word-Event becomes the prime focus to disclose the delusions in Liberal Christianity. It matters little to these theologians what form that delusion takes: from the comic pathos of "cultural Christianity," through the self-confidence of Catholic philosophical-theological analogies or mystical ascents, to the arrogance of Hegel's claim to a philosophical sublation of all the negations in religious representations through the Absolute Concept.

The same power of a radically theological negative dialectics of the proclaimed word erupts in the works of most of the political and liberation theologians. Jürgen Moltmann concentrates on that word to attack both "analogies" and "epiphanies" in his appeal to the tradition of negative dialectics in Adorno and Horkheimer.[16] Moltmann reformulates their secular negative dialectic of the present as nonidentical to the rational into theological, reflective, negatively dialectical terms formulated in fidelity to both the explosive power of the positive word of promise in the resurrection and the prophetic negative word in a theology of the cross. The cross, as cross, exposes the contradictions in the present, the nonidentity of the present with God's word, the need for a theological negative dialectics. Johann Baptist Metz appeals to the interruptive power of the kind of temporality disclosed in apocalyptic to negate any present claims to identity between rationality and actuality. Metz conducts a sustained theological polemic against all "evolutionary" schemas for history and time. He even partly replaces his own earlier analogical language and its grounding in incarnation with a narrative language that, he argues, is better able to maintain the tensions, the interruptions, the negations and discontinuities in a Christian-as-eschatological vision of time, suffering and history.[17]

The liberation theologians' language also functions as a powerful theological form of negative dialectics through and through: explicit negations of oppressive systemic realities in church and society alike, practical negations of the "wisdom tradition" in theology in either its earlier or its present "academic" forms; radical, even enraged, negations of all theological theories and languages not purified and transformed in the crucible of concrete situations and communities of liberating praxis. So powerful does this concentration on negation by way of liberating praxis become that it can occasion deliberately extreme formulations—reminiscent of the early Karl Barth's denunciation of the tradition of the "analogy of being" as the "anti-Christ"—as when José Miranda feels free to dismiss Rahner's entire theology as nonbiblical.[18]

All these theological masters of prophetic suspicion and negative dialectics cling to the radical negative insight of Melville: "Say no with thunder, for all who say yes, lie." In reading these theologies no one need fear that the intensity embedded in all negation has lost its power. Like the German expressionist paintings of the 1920s, like the revolutionary art and action of the 1960s, the theologies of word and prophetic-apocalyptic action have retrieved that tradition of Christian intensity by recovering the necessity of some confrontational, conflictual *no* to any complacent self, culture or society. They will not let those negations disappear into the quicksand of an encompassing affirmative culture. With Bonhoeffer, they will struggle to unmask all "cheap grace," all too easy continuities and relaxed similarities between Christianity and culture, between God and the human, God and world.

When the purging fire ends, the reader of these contemporary theologies of negative dialectics wonders: What hope remains for any similarity, any continuity, any order? Yet an interpreter of these theologies need not construct hypotheses. The facts are clear enough. Each of the theologians of the dialectical word moved forward into the fuller range of the Christian symbol system and the fuller range of the contemporary situation. In making that journey, each developed alternative theological languages whose emphasis and power remained rooted in the power of proclamatory negation while rearticulating the similarities-in-difference, the continuities, even the order disclosed by the proclamation into new theological as analogical languages. Karl Barth, through his study of Anselm, released himself from a purely negative dialectics and articulated, in his *Church Dogmatics,* ever-new reformulations of a new theological language of analogy—his "analogy of grace" language.[19] Like all analogical languages, Barth's focussed on some primal meaning to provide the primary focus for interpreting all reality and for articulating the order implicit in the relationships among God, self, world. That focal meaning, to be sure, will never be allowed to admit any despised, negated "point of contact" between this God and this humanity.[20] Rather the focus will always prove to be the irrevocably dialectical reality of God's Revealed Word in Jesus Christ. That focus, constantly reformulated throughout the *Dogmatics,* will serve to reorder and transform the ordered relationships among all the major doctrines of the Christian church. To assure that this analogical language never becomes some "pagan" substitute, the language of the *Dogmatics* always includes a constitutive dialectical component within its general analogical form. As every reader of the *Dogmatics* quickly learns, for every yes in Barth, a no is lurking. For every no, there will soon follow some resounding yes. Yet grounding and eliciting all the negations in the *Dogmatics* is the yes of the gracious and merciful God disclosed in the event of Jesus Christ. Indeed, that pervasive "yes" so takes over as the *Dogmatics* moves forward through the entire range of Christian doctrines that some of his fellow Reformed theologians began to doubt whether Karl Barth really possessed an adequate doctrine of sin, whether Karl Barth, defender of Calvin, was in fact headed towards a universalism![21] Whatever the truth of those "charges," one fact is clear: In the *Dogmatics* of Karl Barth negative dialectics endures but does not prevail. To prevail is the role of the radical yes, the triumph of grace, which his dialectical-analogical theological language focussed on the event of Jesus Christ expresses over and over again. Symbolizing this classic Barthian journey, I believe, was Barth's own noble last message to his former adversary, Emil Brunner, once the recipient of one of the fiercest nos in Karl Barth's arsenal: "If he is still alive and it is possible, tell him again, 'Commended to our God', even by me. And tell him *Yes,* that the time when I thought that I had to say 'No' to him is now long past, since we all live only by virtue of the fact that a great and merciful God says his gracious Yes to all of us" (emphasis his).[22]

All the other "giants" of the theology of the word in that explosive period of theological tumult took their separate journeys to a theological language that was finally both dialectical and analogical. No one of them ever betrayed the focussed and intense original vision of the negations released by the word as necessary in all properly theological language. Rudolf Bultmann's kerygmatic theological program of demythologizing and existential reinterpretation did demand a negation of both biblical and doctrinal mythologies and all human cultural pretensions. Yet Bultmann also insisted that there is a proper, human, theological speech for God-talk—the language of analogy.[23] Without ever betraying his own dialectical vision of reality—a vision that sees that, because we are freed by God from ourselves and from the world, we are thereby freed for the world and for authentic decision and action, Bultmann articulated a genuinely theological as analogical-dialectical language correlating the reality of God and the reality of the human in existentially meaningful terms.

More than any other theologian from that period, Paul Tillich from his earliest work to the *Systematic Theology* forged a theological language that maintained fidelity to both the intensity of negative dialectics and the ambiguous, estranged, broken yet real continuities, similarities-in-difference and order in all reality. In developing his method of correlation and his ontological doctrine of the New Being, Tillich never yielded his original theological belief on the need for every correlation to include a moment of negative dialectics ("the Protestant Principle")[24] nor his profoundly analogical sense of the need for a *re*union of the really separated. With his now-familiar doctrine on how symbols as distinct from signs participate in the realities they signify, with his demand for ontological analyses in theology, with his unfolding dialectic of the ordered relationships among essence, existence and actuality in the basic structure of the *Systematic Theology,* Tillich explicated a theological language of symbol that bore, as he recognized, striking resemblances to the classical traditions of analogy.[25] Yet what makes the *Systematic Theology* so masterful an achievement is not the individual parts in the system but the pervasive presence throughout the whole of a theological imagination articulating a reflective, second-order, theological language designed to unite intensity, variety and order. That articulation included a new analogical language that never simply "sublated" the negative dialectical realities revealed in both our estranged "situation" and the proclaiming, confronting word of the "message."[26]

Tillich's *Systematic Theology* is a theological expression of the contemporary need to find mutually critical correlations between theologically informed interpretations of both situation and message, the need to attempt fidelity to *both* religious manifestation and proclamation—in Tillich's words, both "Protestant principle and Catholic substance."[27] As any reader of the *Systematic Theology* knows, whatever one's criticisms of Tillich's formulations on particular issues, his dialectical language of "both-and," unlike the compromising "both-ands" of theological "moderates," never yields to any easy, relaxed harmony. It admits of no easy "middle" position between "extremes." Rather, in Tillich, the analogies are always intrinsically dialectical, the negations are always present in the very expression of the equally real affirmations. Our essential goodness for Tillich *is* as real as our existential estrangement. Radical ambiguity and similarities-in-difference throughout all reality are as real as the graced event and the ordered relationships disclosed in and by the power of the New Being, the Spirit and the Kingdom. In a theological, reflective language at once dialectical and analogical, Tillich's *Systematic Theology* articulates the ideal of a contemporary search for some internal coherence among the major symbols of the Christian faith correlated to the major fundamental questions in the contemporary situation. Like his Catholic theological analogue, Karl Rahner, Tillich insisted upon the reflective, even ontological nature of theological language *as* theological. Again like Rahner, Tillich never hesitated to commit himself to develop a theological language that would attempt to retrieve the strength of the analogical traditions: a strength retrievable only through a contemporary appropriation of the necessary and constantly corrective truth in all the negative dialectical moments, in both situation and message.

In the political and liberation theologies the same kind of reminders of real similarities-in-real-difference elicited by the full Christian symbol system also emerge. Moltmann's negative dialectics in *The Crucified God* posits its theology of the cross only in relationship to the resurrection hope and promise of his earlier *Theology of Hope*. Metz's narrative theology of apocalyptic and its memory of suffering posits itself only in relationship to his own earlier theology of the world and the secular, and his still earlier and continuing relationship to the transcendental-incarnational theology of Rahner. Even Metz's most apocalyptic expression of negative dialectics posits itself as a political theology by its grounding in a political-mystical praxis. The negation of the individualism of earlier existentialist and transcendental theologies by Moltmann, Metz and Schillebeeckx is not purchased at the price of the loss of the personal, of the subject as subject. Their insistence, like Küng's, upon the reality of the not-yet in cross and apocalyptic posits itself only by also positing its own ground in the even-now of the prophetic promise disclosed in resurrection and incarnation.

As the manifestation-realities recently emerging in the liberation theologies take hold, it seems safe to predict that the force of the radical affirmations already empowering their liberating negations will become yet more prominent to reveal the actual similarities-in-difference implicit in their positions. The intrinsic dignity of the human being (a dignity *already* known as constitutive by the demand for authentic human liberation, a dignity already believed to be present in the proleptic reality of Christ the Liberator) was manifested, proclaimed and acted upon as both not yet here yet here even now in the prophets, in the teaching and ministry of Jesus, in the cross-resurrection-incarnation of Jesus Christ, in the great Magna Carta for a Christian humanity in Galatians 3:28, in the radical demands for all humanity in Matthew 25, in the hopes for a collective, historical, cosmic liberation in the Book of Revelation. All these favored biblical themes of the liberation theologies pulsate not only with the power of their negations upon our distorted present and fixated past, but also with the recognition of what, in God's liberating act in Jesus Christ, is present *even now* as a force let loose in history to undo even our sin, both personal and structural, as the power of God's future impinges and erupts upon the present.

As these realities come more and more to the fore in the political and liberation theologies, I believe, the similarities in dissimilarity, the possibility of theological conversation even in conflict, the order and continuity disclosed in God's liberating act for the oppressed as that act unfolds its meaning through the entire Christian symbol system (redemption *and* creation; cross *and* resurrection; and, yes, liberation *and* reconciliation) will release yet *new* analogical languages. Their new analogical ordered relationships will be so focussed upon the negating, judging reality of liberation that they will liberate even the healing similarities and continuities present *even now* in our sinful and graced state.

Each of these traditions—the religious traditions of manifestation, proclamation and action, the theological language traditions of analogy and dialectics, the experiential situational traditions of fundamental trust and suffering—posit themselves as theologies within an uncanny journey through and in the event-gift-grace disclosed in the entire Christian symbol system. The self-corrective process of that fuller reality may be trusted in the present and the future to continue to work its development, its corrections and confrontations of all Christian theological perspectives. The self-corrective nature of reflective reason, both critical and practical, proper to theology may also be trusted to work within each theological tradition and within the conflicts, confrontations, arguments and conversation among them all. Thus can we be assured of the never-ending emergence of new, more relatively adequate analogical languages: languages which have not lessened their demand for the incorporation of ever new, ever more intense negations in both situation and event and thereby the reformulation of new similarities-in-difference, continuities-in-discontinuity and ordered relationships-in-disorder. All similarities and negations must finally be controlled by a hermeneutical fidelity to the Christ event itself.

Without the ever-renewed power of the negative, all analogical concepts eventually collapse into the false harmony, the brittle sterility, the cheap grace of an all-too-canny univocity or an unreal compromise pleasing no one who understands the real issues. Without the similarities produced through differences and negations, without the continuities, the order and even the possible, actual *or* proleptic harmony produced by an internal theological demand for some new mode of analogical language, negative dialectics, left to itself, eventually explodes its energies into rage or dissipates them in despair. For alone, a theological negative dialectics leads into the uncanny whirlpool of the chaos of pure equivocity: a chaos whose own uncanny *fascinans et tremendum* power must one day discover that its own radicality and liberating power is ultimately empowered by, because rooted in, the same reality as its analogical counterparts: the always-already, not-yet event of the yes disclosed in the grace of Jesus Christ.

ii. A Christian Systematic Analogical Imagination: A Proposal

In an already lengthy work, it would be inappropriate and impossible to attempt a full systematics. And yet an outline of what the arguments and interpretations of this work suggest for the basic form of a Christian systematics seems in order. A schematic summary of what we have already seen allied with some suggestions on other symbols is all I can attempt here. Yet that much, at least, seems needed if the implicit ordering principles (and thereby the rough coherence of the "system") implicit throughout the present analysis of *systematic* theology may receive the kind of explication needed for the criticism of other theologians.

The major aim of all systematic theology is to formulate a theological understanding of the originating religious event into a theological focal meaning. The particular focal meaning chosen for that theological understanding will prove an "essentially contested concept." More exactly, the ultimate incomprehensibility of the religious event itself as well as the inability of critical intelligence to master either situation or event will yield a recognition that all theological proposals are necessarily and intrinsically inadequate. Karl Barth spoke for all theologians when he stated "the angels will laugh when they read my theology." Any claim to final adequacy masks a manipulative spirit which does justice to neither the irreducibility of the original religious event nor the real but finite powers of critical, discursive reason. Yet a relative adequacy for a particular theology in a particular situation can be hoped for. If the journeys of intensification and critique are allowed, that relative adequacy can sometimes be achieved. The classical theologies of the tradition, the various candidates for classical status in the contemporary period exist as firm reminders that relative adequacy is indeed possible. How well the initial focal meaning is formulated through interpretations of event and situation and in fidelity to criteria of both appropriateness and understandability, how fruitful that focal meaning proves as the journey through the entire range of Christian symbols occurs and as the relationships of the religious and Christian focus to the other moments of the human spirit (ethics, art, science, history, the other religions) ensue, will determine the relative adequacy or inadequacy of any systematic theology.[28] Whether explicitly formulated or not, criteria like those we have seen throughout this work will be employed: criteria for the interpretation of religious classics and other cultural realities; criteria of internal coherence among the major categories; criteria of a rough coherence in the whole; criteria of existential meaningfulness to the situation; criteria of truth as both disclosure and transformation; criteria for adjudicating the inevitable conflicts that emerge in the concrete exercise of the mutually critical correlations between the interpreted meanings of the tradition and the interpreted meanings of the situation. In sum, criteria are an essential moment in the reality of any authentically theological conversation: a conversation with the subject matter disclosed in the classical texts, events, images, rituals, symbols, persons expressive of the originating religious event.

The ideal of conversation signals to the theologian that, even at this initial systematic moment of personal choice and interpretation leading to a formulation of the paradigmatic focal meaning for a systematics, the theologian is embedded in the history of a religious tradition expressing and communicating the event and the history of the effects of a particular cultural history now newly expressed in the contemporary situation. The choice and formulation of a focal meaning is always highly personal yet never solitary. The fact that most systematic theologies are also called "church theologies" only serves to underline the historicity of every theologian. Tradition as *traditio,* as the living reality of that event in the present, is the major concrete social, historical and theological power in every systematic theology. That religious event comes to us as the living reality of Spirit in the proclamations, manifestation and actions of an ecclesial community. The event may, of course, come more through some movement in the world than through an explicit church tradition. Yet even there it may come indirectly *as* church: as the living reality of the originating religious event in the world of history.[29] The church as both sacrament of the Christ *and* eschatological sacrament of the world remains the primary concrete, social and theological locus of all systematic theologies.

Once a focal meaning is chosen and formulated, the rest of the journey of a systematic analogical imagination begins. For then each theologian strives—through critical interpretations of the core symbols in the full range of the Christian tradition and through critical interpretations of the realities of the contemporary situation—to find some ordered relationships for understanding the similarities-in-difference in the whole: the realities globally named God-self-world. By concentrating throughout this journey on a particular focal meaning to reinterpret both tradition and situation, each systematic theology risks its unfolding into a series of ordered relationships among the realities of God-self-world. The primary key to the order is provided by the focal meaning. At the same time, the understanding of the focal meaning itself is inevitably transformed by its exposure to the full range of the Christian symbols and the full range of questions in the situation.[30] The reformulations of the focal meaning as the systematic theology unfolds are sometimes a clue to the relative inadequacy of the original choice. More often, the reformulations prove not negations but transformations of that focal meaning as the fuller realities of the symbol system and the further critical questions in the situation disclose themselves to the critical consciousness of the theologian. As the ordered relationships emerge in their demands upon the focal meaning, the initial insights into God-self-world provided by the initial formulation of the focal meaning are inevitably transformed. For example, a further understanding of both the biblical symbols for God and a contemporary philosophical understanding of the internal relationships among God-self-world may cause a particular theologian to shift from an understanding of the reality of God in "classically theistic" terms to a panentheistic set of concepts. As the fuller reality of a particular symbol is retrieved by some contemporary, situational rediscovery of a half-forgotten classical theme in the tradition, the focal meaning is also reformulated: as when the symbols of eschatology are released from their earlier individualism to societal, political, historical reality in order to disclose that the originating redemptive event is both always-already here yet always-already not-yet here, not only to individual historicity but to history.

Through such developments does the search for relative adequacy occur: a choice of some focal meaning, the development of ordered relationships of God-self-world by means of the focal meaning; the continuous transformation of relationships and focus alike as the fuller reality of the symbols and the fuller demands of the situation are critically responded to in every systematic theology.

The present work, however unsystematic in form, has also risked the articulation of a focal meaning and an implied set of similarities-in-difference and ordered relationships for the whole, for the realities of God-self-world. The concrete focal meaning for a Christian systematics is the always-already, not-yet event/gift/grace of Jesus Christ. This focal meaning presupposes, by re-presenting, the always-already event of grace—the event experienced, even if not named, as from and by the power of the whole. The event is an always-already actuality which is yet not-yet: always-already, not-yet in experience and knowledge through a disclosure that is also a concealment; in praxis through its releasement of the pull to a right way of living in and by the power of the whole and its intensification in that very releasement of the counterthrust of a not-yet transformed human spirit, tempted always to disperse itself away from the whole, or even to stand in defiance against the encompassing whole.

For the Christian in responding to the event of Jesus Christ senses that the very concreteness of that focus intensifies, clarifies, transforms the experience always-already, not-yet present in all human experience. The principal focus remains on the event and gift of Jesus Christ now renamed grace. Yet the focus of radical grace is itself always focussed by and towards the event of Jesus Christ. For the Christ event lays hold upon an individual as pure gift. Through that sense of giftedness, in the Christ event, the Christian rediscovers an experience of the whole which is, in fact, the experience of the power of judging, healing love who is God. This experience intensifies the experience of a fundamental trust working as the same kind of love disclosed as the final power with whom we must all ultimately deal.

The Christ event is itself constantly refocussed for the tradition by a continual recall of its own grounding in the dangerous and provocative memory of Jesus of Nazareth, the one proclaimed and manifested as the Christ. In fidelity to the memories of this loving, suffering and vindicated Jesus of the earliest apostolic witnesses, the church focusses its present experience of that event not upon itself but upon the entire Christian tradition's experience of the event. That focus will constantly be reinterpreted by new interpretations in the present of the church's memory of the Jesus proclaimed as the Christ in the proclamation, narratives, symbols and theologies of the Christian scriptures. That memory—the memory of the one who preached the reign of God, who lived and ministered, who met the fate of crucifixion and was vindicated by God in resurrection—lives throughout Christian history as a presence transforming all Christian experiences of the event into the living praxis of an *imitatio Christi*. The Jesus the church remembers is none other than the Jesus remembered as the Christ by the early communities and proclaimed in the confessional narratives and theologies of the New Testament. The Jesus the Church must remember, as historical criticism in its liberating, even prophetic function makes clear, should include historical criticism's own portrait of that apostolic witness to Jesus. When thus remembered by a church open to the demands and gift of historical criticism, the temptations of the church to withdraw from the gift and demand of the kind of life disclosed in Jesus Christ, the temptations to domesticate and mythologize that reality are fought through the ever-renewed Christian focus upon the dangerous, provocative, subversive memories of this Jesus.

The always-already, not-yet event of grace named Jesus Christ mediated through the tradition serves, therefore, as the paradigmatic focal meaning for any Christian systematic theology. That event discloses the theological possibilities of a series of ordered relationships among God-self-world. And yet, as we have seen throughout this work, the history of Christian reflection on that event has also been shaped both by different situational questions and by three further major focal meanings for interpreting the paradigmatic focus of the Christ event. Each focus—whether manifestation, proclamation or historical action—both clarifies and intensifies some major aspects and emphases in the originating event. At the same time, each focus limits, occasionally even distorts, the vision of other major disclosures in the same paradigmatic event. In contemporary Christian systematics, moreover—in a situation where the hope that a global humanity may yet emerge from our pluralistic present and in an inner-Christian situation where the kairotic event of an ecumenical spirit has at last taken hold in most major Christian theologies—the need for all three focal meanings is clear. In the past, the emphasis upon one of these three focal meanings has ordinarily meant that each theology necessarily emphasized, even exaggerated, some dimensions of the event and obscured other dimensions. The self-respect necessary to Christian self-identity was present in all these classic Christian theologies. And yet the necessary dialectical counterpart to that self-identity—the necessary self-exposure to the full range of the Christian symbol system, to the full range of the theologies and spiritualities in the entire ecumenical Christian church, the full range of the fundamental questions in the situation—was too often disowned in the heady exhilaration occasioned by one particular individual or ecclesial focal meaning chosen to interpret *the* paradigmatic focal meaning for all Christians—the event of Jesus Christ.

In christology itself this reality is clear enough. When interpreting the reality of the Christ event through the focus of manifestation, theologians emphasize the reality of "incarnation" as God's radical immanence in all reality through the manifesting Logos. These christologies will ordinarily prove representative or sacramental christologies—re-presenting the original grace that is always already given to us by a gracious God, decisively given as gift and demand in Jesus Christ. So pervasive does that always-already reality become that its not-yet is relatively downplayed by the dominant note of re-presentation and the radical, fundamental trust disclosed by and to the journey of manifestation in the tradition of logos theologies from John through Justin to Rahner, Ogden and Cobb.

In interpreting the reality of the Christ event through the prism of proclamation, most "theologians of the word" will focus upon the radicalization of that judging-healing word of address in either the confessed parables of Jesus or the theology of justification in Paul's theology of the cross. The tensive, negating language of Paul will be retrieved in new forms to disclose the centrality of the cross, the recognition that Jesus Christ *is* the Crucified One, a judgment upon all human pretensions. Any "already" (much less any claim to the always-already character to that event) will come in these christologies of the cross only through the crucible of a radical Christian hermeneutics of suspicion upon all "works" as those works are confronted by the cross and the memory of this suffering, vindicated Jesus. Thus will Karl Barth speak of the "tangent" to the circle, Bultmann of the canonical priority of the Pauline proclamation of the eschatological event of Jesus Christ, Moltmann of the negative dialectics released by recognizing the God-forsakenness of the crucified one, Jüngel of the sense of absence present in the revelation of the crucified one, and Küng of the radical "not-yet" released in Paul's theology of justification—a "not-yet" dialectically related not to the "always-already" language of Rahner, but to the "even-now" language of Küng's own christology.

In interpreting the event through the paradigm of historical action, the political and liberation theologians formulate their christologies in relationship to the same not-yet power in the symbol "cross" united to the historical (prophetic and apocalyptic) proleptic, promissory reality of resurrection and the radical not-yet present in apocalyptic. The resurrection of the crucified one liberates our hope for all history, all the living and the dead: a hope promised as interruption of the suffering, alienated, oppressed—the overwhelmingly "not-yet"—actuality of history itself. To live the discipleship of a following of Christ through the cross of the present, empowered by the dangerous memory of Jesus and by the future hope promised to all through his resurrection is the route to a christology where the not-yet of the present, the hope of the future as God's future, and the need to enter the historical struggle for justice now are highlighted.

All these christologies possess their own disclosive truth. And yet the event of Jesus Christ, as most theologians eventually acknowledge, is expressed with relative adequacy only in the full range of the symbols cross-resurrection-incarnation. That event is genuinely understood as the focal meaning of Christian faith only by being interpreted as at once decisive manifestation, true word and authentic action of God by God. That event discloses simultaneously an always-already and yet a not-yet. That event demands that every christology allow the self-corrective, self-exposing journey through all three major symbols (cross, resurrection, incarnation), through proclamation, narrative, thought, symbol, doctrine and apocalyptic, through all three major focal meanings (proclamation, action, manifestation) of the classical christological journeys in the Christian tradition.

The reality of that Christ event is often refocussed and constantly judged and corrected in contemporary christology through its concentrated focus upon the memory of Jesus of Nazareth. That reality is disclosed through a spirituality, a praxis of discipleship employing appropriate Jesuanic imagery (as in Sobrino and Metz) or through the focus now available through the practice of historical-critical methods upon the earliest apostolic memories (as in Ogden) or through the focus of the present experience of a recognition of the whole tradition as mediating that event to us (as in Troeltsch or in this work).

Christianity does not live by an idea, a principle, an axiom but by an event and a person—the event of Jesus Christ occurring now and grounded in none other than Jesus of Nazareth. What memories do we have of the actual Jesus? The memory of the one proclaimed in all the confessions and forms of expression of the New Testament, the memory lived in the discipleship of an *imitatio Christi* throughout the history of Christianity, the memory proclaimed in word and manifested in sacrament in the Christian church. Those memories—all of them—are what exist to impel every christology to attempt relative adequacy. What is that memory in the New Testament? It is the dangerous and subversive memory of Jesus—dangerous, above all, for the church which confesses it: the memory of the one who proclaimed the coming reign of God, who taught and lived the truth that God's cause will prevail for the future belongs to God; who acted with a radical love towards all—a harsh love, both judging and healing; who lived with a freedom which did not hesitate to unmask human pretensions or to take the side of the outcast. That memory is the memory of this Jewish layman, this Jesus of Nazareth, who taught and ministered, who met rejection at every step, who received the fate of crucifixion, who was raised and vindicated by God. It is the memory of this one person which freed the earliest witnesses to believe that the Crucified One lives amongst us, that the Jesus *is* the Christ. The church's own memory of Jesus—a memory purified of early, late and present distortions by historical and social-scientific criticism, literary criticism and ideology critique, purified by the living praxis of discipleship and by the critical reflections of theologies—serves as the necessary focus for understanding and criticizing all christologies.

The christologies of manifestation need the dangerous memory of Jesus to keep their representative christologies grounded in the full event of Jesus Christ witnessed to by the church—as Rahner's move from a transcendental to a categorial christology testifies, as Ogden's theological development of Marxsen's analysis of the original apostolic Jesus-kerygma witnesses, as Troeltsch's uses of historical criticism on the whole tradition showed.[31] The christologies of proclamation and action need that full memory-image as well—as such distinct christologies employing historical criticism as those of Kasper, Küng, Pannenberg and Schillebeeckx indicate.[32] In developing an adequate christology, each Christian theologian is obliged to enter the seeming labyrinth of historical criticism, the radical demands of the praxis of discipleship and a sense of one's own historicity as an historical existence in this community and history.

What Christians *know* historically about the "Jesus of history" they know, like everyone else, through the ever-shifting results of historical criticism. *That* Christians believe in the actual Jesus as the Christ comes to them from some present experience of the Christ event: an experience mediated by the whole community of the Christian church. What Christians believe about Jesus comes to them, above all, from the tradition witnessing to Jesus and experienced now as a fundamentally trustworthy source. *What* any particular Christian may believe or disbelieve in the traditional christological formulations produced throughout the long history of that tradition, they will ordinarily believe because of their fundamental trust in the tradition mediating that event and person, or will disbelieve as a result of some exercise of critical reason or some new experience of the Christ event in some new situation.[33] Even the power to dissent is a power released by the freedom from and for the world disclosed in the very Christ event which the tradition mediates. History itself—for what is historical existence other than ethical life in a community and a tradition—can be trusted to sort out in the long run the truths and falsehoods for the Christian community, a community trusting in the Spirit's presence to it. The collaborative character of theology as a discipline can be trusted to sort out the theological aspects of those same realities in the short run of mutual, responsible criticism.

The results of these demands unite in every christology which performs its ownmost task wherein its chosen focal meaning for interpreting the Christ event will be continuously reinterpreted by its critical understanding, by its memory of the person of Jesus of Nazareth through historical criticism of the earliest apostolic witness, by personal discipleship, and by existence in the tradition. Without a focus upon the person of Jesus, the Christ event can lose its decisiveness by quietly disowning its distinctively Christian identity. Without the paradigmatic focus upon the present, mediated experience of the Christ event as decisive manifestation, proclamation, action, every christology is in danger of becoming either a Jesusology or a supernaturalist mythology. For the paradigmatic focal meaning of all systematic theology remains the event-gift-grace of Jesus Christ. In understanding that event through the interpretation of manifestation we grasp better its always-already character. In understanding that event through the distinct interpretations of proclamation and action, we grasp better the fuller dimensions of its not-yet reality. Through the full focus upon the event provided by the symbols cross-resurrection-incarnation (each focussed on some major aspect of the meaning of the apostolic memory-images of the life, preaching, ministry, death and resurrection of Jesus of Nazareth), Christians understand that their concrete and distinctive focal meaning for understanding the whole, the realities of God-self-world, is and must remain the decisive always-already, not-yet event of Jesus Christ as the decisive self-manifestation of God's own self.

iii. Christian Analogical Imagination: Ordered Relationships, God-Self-World

By concentrating attention upon that focal meaning, the always-already, not-yet event of Jesus Christ, Christian theologians develop ordered relationships for the whole of reality. The fundamental control, because it is the focal meaning for all those relationships, will be present in that event as the decisive self-revelation of God disclosing as well the nature of both the self and the world. The secondary, yet crucial, controls for articulating those relationships will be some particular fundamental question (death, transience, finitude, sin, alienation, oppression, trust, joy, love, order) and some particular form of critical reason and lived praxis to articulate those questions in critical correlation with a response to the Christ event itself. There is no ready-made recipe available before the encounter with the subject matter to guarantee success. What remains available for systematic theologians are the needs which the analogical imagination reveals: the need to keep the primary focus upon the concrete Christian focal meaning as the paradigmatic clue to the nature of the whole and the reality of intensification for Christian self-identity; the need to recognize and explicate the situational questions and the realities of critical reason and transformative praxis in each particular journey; the need to risk relating the first to the second by means of mutually critical correlations controlled by the demands of the subject matter; the need to allow these exercises to become the occasion for the imaginative risk of the production of ordered relationships for the similarities-in-difference of God-self-world.

The reality of God, to be sure, is no single locus of a single ordered relationship in any theology worthy of the name. Rather from the originating experience of the primal Christ event as the self-revelation of God to some analogous understanding of self and world, the reality of God pervades every expression of a systematic theology. So, too, in their distinct ways, do the other two primary candidates for ordered relationships: self and world. For every symbol, from the originating revelatory event to the final understanding of God disclosed by the entire symbol system, is also an understanding of self and world.[34] Every human understanding of God is at the same time an understanding of oneself—and vice versa. Every proper understanding of the self is never an understanding of some unreal, isolated self but an understanding of a self in internal relationships, in intrinsic coexistence with the reality of the "world." For "world" encompasses the realities of those other selves, of society, history, nature and the cosmos itself: all the realities which exist as the always present coexisting internal relationships for the emergence of any self. Any personal self exists as a person in direct proportion to an ability to explicate into consciousness its internal relationships to a coexisting world and to the reality of God which grounds and posits both self and world. It is impossible to separate these realities God-self-world. It remains possible to distinguish them, to understand them distinctly in order to unite these mutually reenforcing realities into the similarities-in-difference, the ordered relationships of a systematic theology.

For myself, the overwhelming reality disclosed in the originating event of Jesus Christ is none other than grace itself. From the first glimmers of that graciousness in the uncanny limit-questions of our situation through the amazing grace disclosed in all explicitly religious experiences to the decisive representation of that pervasive always-already, not-yet graciousness disclosed in the event of Jesus Christ, grace prevails for the Christian as the central clue to the nature of all reality. This grace prevails in spite of all else: the often overwhelming sense of the meaninglessness and absurdity of our existence lost, as Pascal reminded us, "in this remote corner of nature," the frightening spectacle of the massive suffering endured by human beings, indeed by all creation, from the beginning of history to the demonic outbursts of anti-Spirit and the realities of alienation and oppression in our own day. The theologian may never forget these actualities. Yet we can learn that we may honestly, *in spite* of all, now yield to that other clue, that other faith, disclosed in the fundamental trust we live in the everyday by going on at all, that trust disclosed decisively in the revelation of the graciousness of God and the graced reality of self and world in the event of Jesus Christ. As thus released, we are not freed to some new knowledge, some new gnosis which we now possess for ourselves alone. Rather we are finally freed to embrace a fundamental trust in the whole, to demand of ourselves, by that trust, a hope for the sake of the hopeless, to risk a life in the impossible gospel possibility of a faith and hope working through a love given as pure gift and stark command.

The not-yet always present in the always-already reality disclosed in Jesus Christ, moreover, undoes at the core any claims to gnosis, any temptations to triumphalism, any refusals of self-exposure, any complacency in ourselves as graced or God as gracious, any flight into sentimental notions of love untouched by the passion for justice.

Who, in this perspective, is God? God is the power not our own disclosing itself in philosophy as the one necessary individual, the power disclosing itself in all religious experience as the graced reality of the whole manifested by the power of the whole and in the Christian experience of the Christ event as the personlike yet transpersonal power of pure, unbounded love, that ultimate reality which grounds and pervades all reality, the reality with which we must ultimately all deal. As that power of graciousness God affects all and is affected by all.[35] Love, and love alone, is the surest clue to who God is and thereby to what reality, in its ultimate meaning, in spite of all else, finally always-already is. That always-already reality of gracious love is experienced religiously and understood theologically through its presence-in-union with the not-yet of its full presence to us in the light of God's decisive presence in the event of Jesus Christ. The power of that not-yet will yield theological understandings of the always-already reality of God as Love in all forms of theology. The theologies focussed upon manifestation, in understanding God as the always-already reality of Love and Grace will forge negations of any claims to control on that knowledge. They will develop understandings of the radical incomprehensibility of God on the other side of all our best comprehensible schemas of theological intelligibility. They will forge, for and in our actual situation, understandings of the presence of God in God's very absence in the situation. Above all, they will return, again and again, to the radical mystery who God as Love and Power is and must remain.

The theologies focussed upon proclamation, in fidelity to their experience of God's word of address in the Word of Jesus Christ, will intensify the Christian sense, present in Paul, Augustine, Luther and Calvin, that the gracious God can never be taken for granted. God's naked majesty and sovereignty, God's judgment and wrath, remain as radical not-yet reminders to all who would rest easily and complacently in any always-already presence of God's graciousness. Thus will the theologians of the word, from Luther to Moltmann and Jüngel, forge their theologies of the Hidden and Revealed God disclosed in the Crucified One as the God-forsaken One. Thus will the dialectic of the triumph of grace in all these theologies yield understandings of God as hidden in the very revelation releasing us to the risk of faith: in the God to whom, as Luther insisted, we must sometimes "dare against God to flee to God" (*ad deum contra deum*).

The theologians focussed upon prophetic historical action, with their ready sense of the actuality of the not-yet in our distorted history, will turn to the promises of God in history as their surest clue to God's gracious always-already reality. Thereby will they speak of the futural nature of God—a nature proleptically disclosed in God's renewal of the promises to humanity in the resurrection of Jesus Christ, a nature proleptically disclosing the not-yet, yet even-now reality of the God who comes and will come in Jesus Christ.

The only God there is is the God who is Love. To understand the reality of that God in a systematic theology, we must turn first to the paradigmatic clue of the event of Jesus Christ as the always-already, not-yet reality of that event transforms all our situational understandings of the reality of

God. We must then seek some internally coherent set of concepts for expressing the reality of that God in ways both coherent and resonant to our situation and its fundamental questions. We do so best when we develop conceptually coherent and existentially meaningful theological interpretations of God: interpretations that evoke the dialectical always-already, not-yet sense of radical mystery which must pervade every Christian understanding of the reality of God.

The reality of God as love releases the self to risk the Christian self-transcendence of faith working through love. The experience of grace as giftedness liberates the self to appropriate as one's own the fundamental trust which is the first experience of that gift. The gift of trust illuminates the always-already graced reality of the finite, created, graced self. In its manifestation-orientations, above all, the power of that giftedness as God's own radically gracious always-already presence frees the self to trust: to trust in the radical immanence of God in all reality, to trust in reason and its many paths, to trust in the profound *eros* in every self in all its quests for truth, for goodness, for beauty, for beatitude. In such manner, will the manifestation-traditions in Christian theology develop their trusting understandings of the graced, self-transcending self. As grounded in that gift of trust, *eros* will be transformed but not negated by divine *agape*. That transformation is *caritas*.[36] Reason will be sublated but never disowned by the faith which seeks understanding. That sublation is theology. The sensate, sexual, aesthetic reality of our embodied reality will be transformed but must not be negated in Christian spiritualities emerging from that experience of gifted trust. Those transformations become Christian understandings of the created giftedness of the body, sexuality, beauty, for understanding the real-as-embodied self.

Although the emphasis in all manifestation-focussed theological understandings of the self is clearly upon the always-already presence of God's radically immanent gift of grace to all reality, it is not the case that this emphasis disowns the reality of the not-yet. The sense for the not-yet, although often muted, is pervasive in the very sense of giftedness negating all pretensions to self-achievement, in the negations of sin and sins as failures "to hit the mark," as disorienting to the true *telos* of the self, in the negations of all rationalisms presuming to control or manipulate that gift, in the recognitions of the radical ambiguity of the self—a self graced and essentially good yet existentially disoriented, distorted by habit and vicious actions. The reality of the not-yet is present as well in all manifestation theologies in their refusal of any easy always-already optimism on the self in favor of a long-range, eschatological optimism and a short-range realism on the self's actuality. In the typologies of nature and grace so often employed in these theologies to understand the self, let us note, grace is the category employed to understand our concrete existence, grace and its giftedness is the reality which allows one to understand the giftedness of that "abstract remainder" concept in all its modalities, "nature." But its grounding in that concrete sense of pure grace, the freedom disclosed to the self never reaches the heights of Romantic and existentialist self-creation. An understanding of freedom, for the Christian, always returns to the understanding of freedom as a gift to the self-transcending self: a gift related to the orienting and disorienting, the liberating and distorting, influences of all reality upon the fragile, finite, gifted, free self.

For those theologies whose major focus for understanding the self is proclamation, the emphasis shifts radically. The seeming impossibility of authentic existence in the confrontational light of the actuality of radical sinfulness disclosed by the actuality of grace now haunts the shaken conscience of the faithful self. The terror of existence in all its forms is now felt with power: especially the terror of the self vainly, despairingly attempting to flee from its unwelcome recognition of its own twisted reality, attempting to justify itself before itself, others, God. This frightening self-recognition releases the dialectic of the self who has heard a Word of proclamation, this self *simul iustus et peccator* who has experienced the defamiliarizing force of a judging and liberating word from God. The hydra-like possibilities for self-deception and self-justification are relentlessly exposed by the hermeneutics of suspicion upon the self released by the word of proclamation. The always-already giftedness of *eros* will begin to be muted. Indeed, *eros* will fall under suspicion as those self-distorting, self-seeking, self-justifying actualities present in all human love, friendship, the human search for truth, beauty and goodness. The philosophers, Kierkegaard warns us, may build their palaces of speculation, but they live with the rest of us in the hut down the hill. Driven by the real power of the not-yet in our graced state, the theologians of the word will force their negations upon the consciousness of all selves: Reason may become a "whore"; images may become "idolatry"; a Christianity focussed on the manifesting giftedness of all creation will begin to seem "pagan"; *agape* will have nothing to do with *eros*; sins will become sin; teleological orientations will be dismantled and replaced with deontological commands; grace will be justifying and that justification forensic; what was once seen as cooperative grace now seems self-justifying "works."

Like all hermeneutics of suspicion, like all forms of negative dialectics, these theologies of the word—even in their most extreme statements, perhaps especially at their most extreme—illuminate the stark negativities, the actual not-yet at the heart of any claim to human authenticity. Yet as these theologies develop into fully systematic positions, a strange sea-change seems to occur. First, all is taken away from the self in its pretensions to authenticity. Then all is returned in the new transformation of grace worked by hearing the Word of God in Jesus Christ. We must continue to recognize our not-yet state in all its *simul iustus et peccator* reality, and yet, with Barth, we must also finally recognize, through that word, not only the reality of our humanness but even the humanity of God.[37] For the triumph of grace means triumph. However distorted the present not-yet reality of that grace in every present self, its always-already power is present and does transform all those willing to listen to that Word and its commands in every situation with the concrete other of the neighbor. The radical gospel command to constant self-transcendence released by that word is experienced by every self who has heard a word of real address from a Sovereign God. The dialectic of sin-grace intensifies, yet never removes, that always-already graced possibility of self-transcendence in the gift and command of *agape*.

For those theologians whose major focus for understanding the self is historical prophetic action, the ideal for the self is the futural, eschatological ideal of the future reign of God affecting and commanding every self to enter the struggle for justice now. That ideal, interpreted as radically historical and global, discloses the future reality of a kingdom of love and justice—the kingdom present in history through God's acts and promises to the people Israel and in the cross-resurrection of Jesus Christ. That ideal for our common humanity is present even now in the gift and demand for the liberation and emancipation of all humanity if any single human being is to be fully free. That eschatological ideal focusses its understanding upon the self as a social, indeed political and historical self: a self related to all, committed above all to the privileged ones of the prophets and the gospel, the outcast, oppressed, alienated. To be a self means to live for all those who have been robbed of their right to humanity by their entrapment in sinful social structures. That futural, eschatological ideal of a self committed to the reign of love and justice demands that concrete love for the neighbor now become a love that works through the struggle for justice. The love revealed in the reign of God preached by Jesus and decisively disclosed in the cross and resurrection of Jesus Christ liberates us to see the nonidentity of our present state with any real humanity. Indeed, that eschatological ideal serves to unmask the irreconcilable conflict between the humanity promised in Jesus Christ and its nonidentity with our present actuality in both society and church. The prophetic unmasking of our present inhumanity demands the development of a Christian negative dialectics—negating the present realities of sexism, racism, classism, economic and cultural oppressions and privatized alienations in the light of the gift and demand of the emancipatory and redemptive freedom for the self as a self related to all selves, the living and the dead, through the eschatological event of Jesus Christ.

Our task, as those empowered to become human beings by the gospel promise, is to face squarely the conflictual actuality of the present and commit ourselves, in that prophetic and apocalyptic hope which is faith's reality today, to the reality of God's reign by committing ourselves to the struggle for justice now. What is now both possible and necessary is a commitment to a cause greater than the self. This liberation dialectic of sin-grace in its now historical-political-prophetic and even apocalyptic forms lives by the power of its eschatological not-yet. Yet that not-yet is itself grounded in the even-now reality of God's promises and actions for humanity in ancient Israel and God's proleptic disclosure of humanity's future in Jesus Christ. The self-transcendence of this Christian ideal for the self becomes a constant self-transcendence of a self involved in concrete, liberating praxis in and for concrete historical communities in the inevitably conflictual reality of the present.

Amidst the real conflicts of Christian interpretation on the authentic self expressed in the inevitable clash of these three classical Christian ideals for true selfhood, one fact stands out. In spite of their otherwise real and perhaps even irreconcilable ideals for the self, all three are committed to a model of radical, because graced, self-transcendence; a self always-already gifted and commanded to a real self-transcendence towards the neighbor; a self always-already, not-yet free from and for this world. By attempting to live that gospel call and gift of an always-already, not-yet agapic self-transcendence, Christians realize that they cannot rest in the less radical demands of either self-fulfillment or self-negation. The *ressentiment* latent in the latter, like the narcissism latent in the former, are exposed as inappropriate ideals for the radical, agapic ideal of self-transcendence by the event of Jesus Christ. The route to authentic selfhood for the Christian, whatever the particular focus for interpreting that ideal, remains a route of the radical discipleship of an *imitatio Christi*. The demands for real mutuality expressed in the Christian ideal and reexpressed in the *caritas* tradition, the radical self-sacrificial love disclosed in the cross of the Crucified One are themselves expressions of the gospel agapic gift and command to the self to live a radical equal regard for every human being, for the neighbor, not only the friend. That demand for equal regard, for concrete agapic neighbor love, impels the transvaluation of all values by its risk of some form of a radical agapic self-transcendence. Only that kind of self-transcendence can ultimately define the heart of any Christian attempt to become a gifted, commanded, always-already, not-yet agapic self. The reality of God as love decisively revealed in the event of Jesus Christ is the central clue to the meaning of the self as a human self both loved and loving. In Christian systematics, there is no theology which is not also an anthropology. There is no Christian anthropology that is not also a theology. The Christian doctrines of God and the human rise and fall together. The key to both, and the key to their interrelationships, may be found in the harsh, demanding reality of radical agapic love.

In understanding the realities of God and self, the theologian is already understanding the reality named world. For the God who as Love affects and is affected by the self affects and is affected by all. And the self is never an isolated, private, worldless phenomenon. Rather the self at every moment is never substance but subject, affected by and affecting both God and world. Self and world are coexistents which can be distinguished, never separated. Both self and world are co-posited by God. They are always-already affected by that God who is Love and, as Love, is, in turn, always-already affected by both self and world.

The particular focus chosen to understand God and the self is, at the same time, the central clue to which some particular aspect of the world will be emphasized in a particular theology. Should it be any cause for wonder that those theologies with their major focus on the reality of manifestation will be most alive to certain signal realities in the complex phenomenon named "world"? With their sense for radical giftedness and thereby of God's radical, always-already, loving immanence in all reality, these theologies will be open to a pervasive sense of grace. Nature and body, not only history and spirit, will be felt as graced and thus interpreted in theologies of creation, incarnation and sacrament. The mutuality present in authentic friendship and real community, the character of all authentic *eros* will be recognized as the graced realities they are. The somehow ordered, fragile relationships of justice in society, like the ordering reality of authentic tradition, will be honored as the graced, gifted realities they are.

In our other two major focal meanings for interpretation, the emphasis will shift elsewhere. In proclamation-oriented theologies, the terror within the self struggling with its own internal conflicts and the leveling power of mass society and technology will shift the major focus of the self-world relationship onto the graced reality of the "authentic" individual. Yet even that tradition, as in Emil Brunner, can employ the interpersonal categories of the I-thou, or can employ, as in Karl Barth, the historical categories of covenant to disclose a Christian theological understanding of the interpersonal and historical world to which the self is intrinsically related.[38] Indeed the sense of civic responsibility in the Reformed tradition—a sense retrieved in H. Richard Niebuhr's model of "responsibility" and Reinhold Niebuhr's Christian interpretation of historical passage and the struggle for societal justice[39]—are ample testimony to the fact that theologians of the word, however focussed upon the reality of the authentic individual, do not lose themselves in the worldless trap of Romantic and existentialist individualism.

In prophetic action-oriented theologies, the major focus for the self is its relationship to the worlds of economy, society and history. The reality of the nonidentity of those realities to the eschatological reign of God empowers these theologies to focus upon the conflicts within the historical world with the sense that conflict itself is the key to history. In the left-wing Hegelian form of this belief (which most of the political and liberation theologians accept), the further emphasis will be upon the need for a negative dialectics of either constant critique or liberating praxis towards and in the conflicts and contradictions of the contemporary world. That critique and that praxis will bring to consciousness the actual and perhaps irreconcilable conflicts already present in society, church, history. Inspired by the proleptic eschatological hope disclosed in the event of Jesus Christ, these Christian theologians will eventually depart from any purely secular (usually Marxist) analogues to discern the presence, *even now,* of God's future reign struggling in God's "underground," remembered in the subversive reality of suffering of all the living and dead victims—the authentic if forgotten tradition of every society and every history. Often distrustful of the fundamental trust present in the manifestation theologies, usually suspicious of the emphasis upon the individual in the proclamation theologies, mindful of the radical conflicts and massive human suffering present in all history and societies, anxious for a victimless history, trusting in God's promises of liberation, these theologians will view the reality of the world as a world of conflictual history from their futurist, eschatological perspectives.

Within the conflict of Christian interpretations on the reality of world (as other persons, society, history, nature), certain factors emerge with clarity.[40] Each theology must maintain fidelity to its chosen paradigm but must also allow for the full reality of world—history and nature, society and interpersonal relationships, infrastructures and cultural superstructures. Each must be faithful to the journey of intensification into its own concrete particularity on behalf of the fully concrete reality of all. As the journey through the entire range of the Christian symbol system occurs,[41] the necessary self-corrections and expansions of concern for world are also likely to occur: eschatology and creation; word and sacrament; justification and sanctification; history and nature; the always-already *and* the not-yet of the power and scope of grace.

As greater ecumenical self-exposure takes firmer hold on all Christian theologies, the present conflict of interpretations may yet become a genuine conversation. As all theologies—whether focussed proximately upon manifestation, proclamation or prophetic action—focus ultimately upon the reality of the event of Jesus Christ, the full scope of the grace released by that event upon the world in its entirety will follow. What unites these conflicting understandings of world will prove none other than the singular clue which informs their different understandings of God and self. That clue remains the grace which is agapic love disclosed in and by the proleptic event of Jesus Christ. That love as healing gives and demands an opening of every Christian understanding of world to the full scope of the always-already presence of that grace, that love, in the worlds of history and nature alike. That love as judging gives and demands as well a recognition of the not-yet conflictual reality also present in every society, in all history and in a nature "groaning to be set free."

In a Christian theological perspective, the world and the self are really related as coexistents. Both are really related to the God who, as Love, is their beginning and their end. That God as Love affects all and is affected by all. That God, in the decisive self-manifestation of who God is in the proleptic event of Jesus Christ, also discloses who we are in our real-as-graced possibility and what the world is in its graced reality. By the emancipatory power of that revelation, the Christian faith is a risk taken in the trust that, in spite of all, the self and the world are held in the always-already, not-yet reality of God's redemptive love. With that trust, the Christian attempts to live a life of faith working through love and justice, a life of the discipleship of the *imitatio Christi,* a life which promises and commands the risk of that agapic, judging, healing love, that necessary, impossible possibility that judges and empowers every self, every society, all history and all nature. The final power with which both self and world must deal is none other than the harsh, demanding, healing power of the ultimate reality affecting and affected by all, the Love who is God.

Notes

1. Note, especially, the structure of the already cited works: *Naming the Whirlwind, Reaping the Whirlwind, Catholicism Confronts Modernity* and *Message and Existence* [I/100 and II/2].

2. For the fullest exposition on the "focal meaning" interpretation of analogy, see David Burrell, *Analogy and Philosophical Language* (New Haven: Yale Univ. Press, 1975). I have employed this "focal meaning" interpretation elsewhere to show the analogical character of my own Catholic theological language tradition: in *CTSA Proceedings* (1977), 234–45, and in "Theological Pluralism and Analogy" [I/107]. Two other studies of analogy are informative here: Niels C. Nielsen, Jr., "Analogy and the Knowledge of God: An Ecumenical Appraisal," in William March, *The Problem of Religious Knowledge* (Houston: Rice Univ., 1974), pp. 21–103; and the fascinating study of analogy as an *episteme* in Michel Foucault, *The Order of Things* [III/32], esp. pp. 46–78.

The literature on analogy is vast; the more important works (for the theologian) include: H. Leutkens, *The Analogy Between God and World* (Uppsala: Almquist, 1952)—a valuable historical survey; Battista Mondin, *The Principle of Analogy in Protestant and Catholic Theology* (The Hague: Nijhoff, 1968)—helpful on Aquinas and Thomism, far less so on Barth and Tillich; George Klubertanz, *St. Thomas Aquinas on Analogy* (Chicago: Loyola Univ. Press, 1960)—invaluable collection of texts in Aquinas; Ralph McInerny, *The Logic of Analogy* (The Hague: Nijhoff, 1961)—the groundbreaking study on the logical questions, influential on Burrell's linguistic work; Bernard Montagnes, *La Doctrine de l'analogie de l'être d'après St. Thomas d'Aquinas* (Louvain: Nauevelauts, 1963)—a valuable survey especially on "participation" themes, influential on Ricoeur's interpretation of Thomist analogy; Jennifer Rike is presently completing a valuable study of Rahner's relationship to this complex tradition of analogy. For myself, the major influence has been the careful and creative linguistic analyses of David Burrell in *Analogy and Philosophical Language,* and more recently, *Aquinas, God and Action* (Notre Dame: Univ. of Notre Dame Press, 1979). The latter book is a creative use of Burrell's understanding of analogy on such central terms of Aquinas as "esse," "actus" and "causality." Burrell is not, however, as helpful in that work on the process tradition, a tradition whose use of analogical language may also be interpreted as a distinct "focal meaning" one. The differences between these two analogical languages (process and Thomist—especially transcendental Thomist), in my judgment, would be aided by a focus on the differences in the candidates chosen for the "focal meaning" rather than by the more familiar charges and counter-charges largely based on "wooden" readings of the other tradition. The differences would remain. But the conversation might become far more fruitful.

3. In that sense, in more traditional language, the primary note is given to an analogy of attribution before the development of analogy of proportionality. The traditional Thomist "doctrine of analogy" has been challenged on historical grounds: see especially Klubertanz on Thomas' pluralistic use of forms of analogy and the distinct analyses of Ralph McInerny and David Burrell. However, for a creative contemporary retrieval of aspects of the traditional Thomist-Cajetan tradition here, see William Hill's important historical and constructive work *Knowing the Unknown God* (New York: Philosophical Library, 1971).

4. See chap. 10, sec. iii, for my own attempt.

5. Hence the traditions of the comprehensible-incomprehensible-God language of incarnation theologies, or the hidden-revealed-God language of theologies of the cross, or the distinct theological models of self-transcendence (e.g., Reinhold Niebuhr's in contrast to Bernard Lonergan's) for understanding the self in relationship to some primary evaluative focal meaning. These traditions are good examples of one of the major criteria for good *theological* use of analogical language: the ability to preserve the tension of the original symbolic language within the clarity of the concept.

6. For one account of the "grammar" here, see David Burrell on Aquinas in *Exercises in Religious Understanding* [IV/81], pp. 80–141, and in *Aquinas* [2]; for a creative but exaggerated claim for the role of negations in Thomas, see Victor Preller, *Divine Science and the Science of God* [II/56].

7. I discuss the relationship between process and Thomist understandings of different candidates for "focal meanings" for "perfection-language" (i.e., for analogical God-language) in two forthcoming monographs: (1) three lectures entitled "Process Theology and the Catholic Tradition" (the St. Michael's lectureship at Gonzaga University, Spokane); (2) three lectures entitled "The Character of God-Language" (the Tuohy lectureship at John Carroll University, Cleveland) to be published with the lectures of John Cobb in a book on the issue of God-language. Since I discuss the relevant texts on this complex issue and the differences and similarities between these two traditions there, I have not in this text. My own option is basically for the process theology tradition but not, I hope, without a more adequate treatment of some of the subtleties and complexities of the Thomist (especially transcendental Thomist) position than the latter was accorded in *BRO*. I continue to believe (as in *BRO*) that process theologies need to develop and be corrected by the symbolic (and, therefore, radical mystery) side of the tradition and need, as well, a profounder sense of the negative in their developments of analogical language. I remain convinced, however, of the greater basic adequacy of the process tradition for interpreting the central Christian understand-

ing that "God is Love" and for resonating to a contemporary sense of change, process and internal relationships (see *BRO*, pp. 187–204). Still, the symbolic, the negative and the sense of radical mystery (incomprehensibility, hidden and revealed God etc.) need more dialectical incorporation into a process *systematic theological* understanding of God. These realities do demand further attention from process theologians in order to assure that the use of process concepts is a genuinely theological use in the sense that the tensive character of the originating religious language is maintained in the clarity of the concepts used in the second-order theological analogical language. For somewhat similar suggestions, see Langdon Gilkey, *Reaping the Whirlwind* [II/2], pp. 330–34; and Philip Hefner's review of David Griffin's process theodicy in *JR* (1979), pp. 87–94.

In sum, if one holds (as I do) that the process understanding of God provides greater relative adequacy as an interpretation of both the scriptural and the contemporary-situational understandings of God than most "classically theistic" alternatives, then the *further* questions for that process understanding concern the relationship of symbol-concept, the reality of the negative (and evil) and the sense of radical mystery classically evoked in languages such as Luther and Calvin's hidden-and-revealed-God language, and Aquinas and Rahner's incomprehensibility language. For analyses of the hermeneutical appropriateness of process categories to the scriptural understanding, see Lewis S. Ford, *The Lure of God: A Biblical Background for Process Theism* (Philadelphia: Fortress, 1978), and the special issue on this theme of *JAAR* (March, 1979).

I have also come to realize how anonymously Marcionite Christian theological language for God (including my own) can unwittingly become. The Old Testament understanding of God (as Bruce Vawter has correctly emphasized) includes a complexity which sorely needs retrieval in contemporary Christian theology. The understanding of God in Amos, Hosea, Deuteronomy, Lamentations and the Wisdom literature, for examples, bespeaks a complexity (and often an ambiguity) that needs recovery by Christian theology. Here again Jewish theology can be enormously illuminating. A greater retrieval of *our* Jewish roots as Christians and a better understanding of the rich postbiblical Jewish traditions (rabbinic, philosophical, kabbalistic and post-Holocaust) could free Christian theologians to think anew the fuller complexity and reality of the negations and analogies in our own Christian theological language of God as Love. Indeed, the hermeneutics of suspicion which the event of the Holocaust casts upon Christianity could free a new hermeneutics of retrieval of our own Old Testament roots for understanding anew not only the doctrine of salvation (as in liberation and political theologies) but also the doctrines of Christ and God. I have tried to provide some initial reflections on these themes in the paper entitled "Catholic Theology and the Holocaust" (to be published, along with the other papers from the 1980 Holocaust Conference at Hebrew Union College, by Fortress Press), also in the paper entitled "History, Historicity and Holocaust" (to be published, along with the other papers from the conference at Indiana University, by the university press) and in my foreword to Arthur Cohen's *The Tremendum* [V/27]. In the present text, I regret to say, those themes are more implicit than explicit. In the future I hope they may become far more explicit.

8. See my "Metaphor and Religion: The Test-Case of Christian Texts" [VI/85] for the warrants for this claim.

9. Karl Rahner, "Thomas Aquinas on the Incomprehensibility of God" [V/21].

10. Karl Rahner, "The Concept of Mystery in Catholic Theology," in *Theological Investigations,* IV, 36–77.

11. See Ewert Cousins, *The Coincidence of Opposites* [IX/30], esp. pp. 199–

227. Cousins' work is also valuable for relating Bonaventure's position (as distinct from the more familiar and influential Thomist position) to the contemporary process discussion (see pp. 229–69).

12. See references in n. 3.

13. That the Cajetan tradition need not have so yielded is implied by the non-manualist retrieval of aspects of that tradition in William Hill, *Knowing the Unknown God* [X/3].

14. As an example, see Eric Mascall, *Existence and Analogy* (London: Longmans, Green, 1949); idem, "The Doctrine of Analogy," *Cross Currents* (1951), 38–57. For a helpful survey of distinct Thomist positions on "esse," see Helen James John, *The Thomist Spectrum* (New York: Fordham Univ. Press, 1966).

15. The major "schools" referred to are: the Gilson-Maritain traditions of a "metaphysics of esse," the "participation" emphasis of Fabro and Geiger, the Maréchal-Rousselot-Rahner-Coreth tradition of "transcendental Thomism," the generalized empirical transcendental method of Lonergan, the linguistic reformulations of Burrell and others. For an analysis of a pluralism of "conceptual frameworks," see Jean Marie Le Blond, "L'Analogie de la Verité," *Recherches de science religieuse* (1947), 129–41; Gerald McCool, *Catholic Theology in the Nineteenth Century* [I/65], pp. 260–63 (on Rahner and Lonergan). For an analysis of the more radical pluralism likely in the future of Catholic theology, see Jean-Pierre Jossua, "Changes in Theology and Its Future," in Jossua and Metz, eds., *Doing Theology in New Places* (=*Concilium* 115; New York: Seabury, 1978), pp. 102–13.

16. See Jürgen Moltmann, *The Crucified God* [IV/50], pp. 26–28. For informative analyses of the differences between classical Greek and Hegelian-Marxist notions of "dialectic," see *Dialectic,* ed. Chaim Perelman (The Hague: Nijhoff, 1975).

17. Johann Baptist Metz, *Faith in History and Society* [II/35], exp. pp. 3–14, 154–84.

18. José Miranda, *Marx and the Bible* [VI/31], p. 249.

19. Karl Barth, *Anselm: Fides Quaerens Intellectum* (Cleveland: World, 1962); idem, *Church Dogmatics,* I/1, pp. 260–83; *Church Dogmatics,* II/1, pp. 204–54 (Edinburgh: T. & T. Clark, 1936, 1957).

20. *Natural Theology* ("Nature and Grace" by Emil Brunner; and the reply "No!" by Karl Barth) [V/64].

21. C. G. Berkouwer, *The Triumph of Grace* [X/42]; on Barth's "universalism," see *Church Dogmatics,* II/2, pp. 415–49; on "sin," *Church Dogmatics,* IV/1, pp. 385–513; IV/2, pp. 378–498.

22. Quoted in Eberhard Busch, *Karl Barth: His Life from Letters and Autobiographical Texts* (Philadelphia: Fortress, 1976), pp. 476–77.

23. This Bultmannian suggestion is developed by Schubert Ogden in *Christ Without Myth* (New York: Harper & Row, 1961), pp. 146–53. The relevant references in Bultmann are provided there.

24. See James Luther Adams, "Paul Tillich on Luther," in *Interpretation of Luther: Essays in Honor of Wilhelm Pauck,* ed. Jaroslav Pelican (Philadelphia: Fortress, 1968), pp. 304–35.

25. See Paul Tillich, *Systematic Theology,* I, 235–41.

26. For the dialectical character of Tillich's analyses, see Robert Scharlemann, *Reflection and Doubt in the Thought of Paul Tillich* [VIII/3]. For a study of the full range of Tillich's life and interests, see Wilhelm and Marion Pauck, *Paul Tillich: His Life and Thought,* Vol. I (New York: Harper & Row, 1976). For an important

recent analysis of Tillich in relationship to Maréchal, Rahner et al., see John Robertson, Jr., "Tillich's Two Types and the Transcendental Method," *JR* (1975), pp. 199–220.

27. *Systematic Theology,* III, 11–30.

28. Recall, as relevant here, our earlier suggestions (chap. 2, n. 31) that the distinct sub-disciplines share the general theological model and may concentrate (in terms of criteria of intelligibility) on the relationship of the religious to the true (fundamental theology), the relationship of the religious to the beautiful as true (systematic theology), the relationship of the religious to the good as true (practical theology). The major disciplinary conversation partners will then be: dialectic and metaphysics for fundamental theology, rhetoric and aesthetics for systematic theology, ethics and politics for practical theology. Each theological discipline will, of course, attempt an interpretation of the "Christian fact" (the event mediated through the whole tradition). Each discipline will develop mutually critical correlations between the two interpretations in relationship to the relevant (and disciplinary and problem-related) criteria of relative adequacy (like the criteria of "disclosure" and "transformation").

29. This is especially the case for those theologies (e.g., Rahner, Ogden, Metz, Schillebeeckx, Moltmann, Cobb, Küng, Segundo, Gilkey et al.) that develop some formulation of the church-world relationship like that suggested in my own earlier suggestion of the relative adequacy of the "church as eschatological sacrament of world" model. See especially, Edward Schillebeeckx, "The Church, the Sacrament of the World," in *The Mission of the Church* [VII/73], pp. 43–51; for Karl Rahner, see article cited earlier [I/94] plus "The New Image of the Church," in *Theological Investigations,* X, 3–29; "The Church's Commission to Bring Salvation and the Humanization of the World," in *Theological Investigations,* XIV, 295–313. Even greater emphasis on "world" models for church are developed by Metz, Moltmann and Segundo [I/94]. For a good constructive summary of this alternative world-oriented model of church, see Roger Haight, "Mission: The Symbol for Understanding the Church Today" [I/94]. I prefer to remain with the "eschatological *sacrament* of world" model on the assumption that this model can account for these latter dominant and correct concerns with world and "mission" while still providing more adequately, through the notion "sacrament" (as distinct from mission), closer ties to the *representative* character of all theological forms of expression from christology through ecclesiology. Juan Luis Segundo's option on church as "sign" seems to bear an analogous insistence (*The Community Called Church* [I/94]). I presume that my own earlier remarks (chap. 1, sec. iii) on the need for sociological understandings of church related to more strictly theological understandings will be encompassed by any model of "church as sacrament of Christ and *world*." When that model is accepted, it follows methodologically that there is a theological need for interdisciplinary reflection between sociological and ecclesiological understandings of church. I assume, as well, that the model of "church as sacrament of Christ and *world*" should eliminate any vestigial ecclesial exclusivism or triumphalism sometimes present in earlier "sacramental" models of the church. As sacrament of Christ, the church mediates but is always under the judgment of the event of Jesus Christ (and, therefore, under the judgment of the Kingdom with which the church is not to be identified; the church is the *sign* or *sacrament* of God's coming Kingdom decisively represented in the event of Jesus Christ). As eschatological sacrament of world, the church *defines* (as sign or sacrament) that decisive Christ event in its always-already, not-yet reality in the world. But the event is not *confined* to the church by the church's ownmost sacramental self-understanding—as representative eschatological sacrament *of*

the whole world. The emphasis upon "sacrament," I recognize, can seem so to emphasize the always-already reality as to downplay the reality of the not-yet. Yet, in this use of the sacrament model, the church as eschatological sign re-presents and thereby mediates the eschatological always-already, not-yet reality of the event of Jesus Christ in the world. The ecclesial mediation, in sum, is defined by the eschatological event it mediates and is thereby itself an always-already, not-yet sign of that reality as always-already, not-yet present *in the world.* The familiar hermeneutical reflections on the differences between "sign" and "symbol" (the latter participates in the reality it signifies, the former does not) remain obviously relevant to any understanding of the representative character of sacrament as a *symbolic* form of expression.

30. I have not attempted here to show that fuller exposure. Yet the fuller range would be needed (the symbols of justification-santification, for example, or especially the distinctively Christian trinitarian understanding of God) for any full-fledged systematics. The bare structure is all I have attempted here. For an example of a fuller range in contemporary theology, see John Macquarrie, *Principles of Christian Theology* [VI/116].

In fact, a full Christian systematic understanding of God may properly begin with the distinctively Christian trinitarian understanding of God—as does that of Karl Barth and Eberhard Jüngel. For myself, the major Christian metaphor "God is Love" focussed on what love-in-suffering means in Jesus Christ would call forth in a full systematic theology: (1) first, a process understanding of the internal relatedness of God and world and an understanding of the "suffering" of God focussed on the ministry, cross and resurrection of Jesus Christ; (2) an interpretation of the traditional Christian understanding of God's trinitarian nature by means of that focus on suffering love. It is of some interest to note that even such nonprocess theologians as Karl Rahner (cited before) and Eberhard Jüngel in his commentary on Barth, *The Doctrine of the Trinity: God's Being Is in Becoming* (Grand Rapids: Eerdmans, 1976), and in his own constructive position, *Gott als Geheimnis der Welt* [V/64], resort to process-like language in their trinitarian language, whether focussed on the proclamation of the cross (Jüngel) or the manifestation of the Trinity in the incarnation (Rahner). Both books of Jüngel develop a new "analogy of faith" language for the trinitarian conceptuality for God (e.g., see *Gott als Geheimnis,* esp. pp. 450–511). I believe, in sum, that a distinctively Christian systematic theological language would, in fact, prove to be trinitarian, yet a trinitarian language that would follow from the central metaphor "God is Love" (not the "psychological analogy" of Thomas et al.). Hence a trinitarian understanding of God would employ process-language that would itself be *transformed* by the christological focus on both the dangerous memory of Jesus embedded in the scriptural narratives and the suffering in history and by the intensification principle of the actuality of suffering love *in* God disclosed in the cross of Jesus Christ.

31. I should add that the emphasis upon the dangerous memory of Jesus (and its disclosure of the negations, the not-yet and the eschatological future) in the christology of this systematic theological work is intended to complement the decisive representative always-already christology of the fundamental theology of *BRO.* There the *reality* of Jesus (as distinct from "the historical Jesus") was equally affirmed, but his dangerous memory did not play its fuller role because of a relative lack of development in *BRO* of the point that the always-already reality of God's grace in Jesus Christ is simultaneously a not-yet reality as well.

32. My criticism of the use of "the historical Jesus" (i.e., the Jesus as known by modern historical-critical methods, not the *actual* Jesus of Nazareth confessed

by the church as the Christ) in these christologies still holds—as does my belief (see chap. 7, n. 15) that, in spite of that difficulty, the use of historical criticism in these christologies still plays a corrective role for the present church by releasing in the present a historically retrieved Jesus-kerygma as a subversive memory for contemporary church and society.

33. The seeming inability of many church leaders to recognize at least their pastoral responsibility to the latter kinds of "dissent" remains one of the major scandals of Christianity to those both within and outside its tradition. It is sometimes difficult to trust a tradition which too often seems to distrust itself: by distrusting its own ability to hand on the event and memories entrusted to its care in ever *new* interpretations in ever new and diverse cultural situations. The kind of theological sense of responsibility represented in the actions of a classic pastoral leader like Pope John XXIII was present not only in his extraordinary praxis but in his words: "In essential matters, unity; in doubtful matters, freedom; in all matters, charity." On John XXIII, see the fine tribute of Hannah Arendt, "Angelo Guiseppe Roncalli: A Christian on St. Peter's Chair," in *Men in Dark Times* (New York: Harcourt, Brace & World, 1968), pp. 57–71.

34. Inter alia, see Friedrich Schleiermacher, *The Christian Faith* [I/76], esp. pp. 142–94; Karl Rahner, *Foundations of Christian Faith* [IV/27], esp. pp. 116–78; Paul Tillich, *Systematic Theology*, I, 163–86. An important recent study on the development of typologies for the God-self relationship is Wayne Proudfoot, *God and the Self: Three Types of Philosophy of Religion* (Lewisburg: Bucknell Univ. Press, 1976). Proudfoot's retrieval of Royce's theory of interpretation for the concept of a social self is a valuable addition to the present discussion of hermeneutical theory—despite Proudfoot's own seeming dismissal of the post-Romantic hermeneutics in the German and French traditions.

35. For the arguments why process categories express this central Christian understanding of God with greater relative adequacy, see *BRO*, pp. 146–204.

36. For the contrary, anti-*eros* and anti-*caritas* view, see Anders Nygren, *Eros and Agape* [V/64]. As I suspect is obvious from the text, I do not share Nygren's negative judgments on *eros* or *caritas*. For an informative defense of the traditional Augustinian view of *caritas*, see John Burnaby, *Amor Dei* (London: Hodder and Stoughton, 1947). For a careful analysis of different Christian understandings of *agape* and their ethical import, see Gene Outka, *Agape: An Ethical Analysis* (New Haven: Yale Univ. Press, 1972).

37. See Karl Barth, *The Humanity of God* (Richmond: John Knox, 1960).

38. For a relevant comparison of Barth and Rahner here, see James M. Gustafson, *Protestant and Roman Catholic Ethics* (Chicago: Univ. of Chicago Press, 1978), pp. 111–27.

39. See H. Richard Niebuhr, *The Responsible Self* (New York: Harper & Row, 1963); Reinhold Niebuhr, *The Nature and Destiny of Man* [II/24].

40. A word of clarification here: as employed earlier in this work, "world" was employed in a contrast to "church" and thereby referred to the *human* world that is not explicitly "church" (see, for example, n. 29 above). In this final section, "world" is used as in contrast to both "God" and "the self" and thereby includes not only society and history but also nature.

41. It is perhaps worth repeating at the end of this structural analysis the insistence mentioned at the beginning: the present analysis is merely one of a *basic structure* and makes no claims to providing a full systematic theology. Rather the present analysis merely explicates the *kind* of basic moves implied in this work as a whole. The journey through the whole Christian symbol system or the whole of the contemporary situation, or even through the full range of the symbols chosen

for analysis here (God, Christ, self, world, church) remains a future hope, not a present claim. The need for an explicitly trinitarian understanding of God, in keeping with the christological focus and the continuity of focus on "love," remains, for myself, the major further need that demands addressing for a distinctively Christian interpretation of the reality of God—a task I hope in the future to attempt along the lines mentioned in nn. 7 and 30.

Chapter 11

Epilogue

The Analogical Imagination

Entries

When I think no thing is like any other thing
I become speechless, cold, my body turns silver
and water runs off me. There I am
ten feet from myself, possessor of nothing,
uncomprehending of even the simplest particle of dust.
But when I say, You are like
a swamp animal during an eclipse,
I am happy, full of wisdom, loved by children
and old men alike. I am sorry if this confuses you.
During an eclipse the swamp animal
acts as though day were night,
drinking when he should be sleeping, etc.
This is why men stay up all night
writing to you.

James Tate

The Christian focus on the event of Jesus Christ discloses the always-already, not-yet reality of grace. That grace, when reflected upon, unfolds its fuller meaning into the ordered relationships of the God who is love, the world that is beloved and a self gifted and commanded to become loving. With the self-respect of that self-identity, the Christian should be released to the self-transcendence of genuine other-regard by a willing self-exposure to and in the contempory situation.

Indeed, the reality of self-exposure to the other is a condition for the possibility of authentic conversation in our day. The need for conversation—expressed in the differing strategies of confrontation, argument, conflict, persuasion and above all, concentration on the subject matter—should free the Christian theologian to the fuller contemporary possibility of an analogical imagination. Under the rubric of a comparative and critical hermeneutics, the real similarities and dissimilarities, the continuities and the discontinuities present in the contemporary pluralist situation should be allowed their necessary emergence. When the ability to listen is present, the fear of confrontation, conflict, argument are not shunned. Rather they are necessary dialectical moments in every serious analogical conversation. Even some form of therapy backed by critical theory and its strictly negative dialectics of suspicion may also be necessary at those moments when, in the course of conversation, the blockages caused by systematically distorted communication are spotted and demand healing if the conversation is to continue.

If Christian theologians are not to sentimentalize the reality of the harsh, demanding, healing love disclosed in the portrait of Jesus of Nazareth confessed in the New Testament, love as real other-regard will not shrink from the necessary moments of confrontation, conflict, argument demanded by all serious conversation on the fundamental questions of existence in the situation and the fundamental responses in every religious tradition. When that subject matter takes over, systematic theology becomes the attempt to establish mutually critical correlations between interpretations of both situation and event. That general, abstract, formal rubric acts as an initial heuristic guide for a genuine conversation with the concrete subject matter. The collaborative character of theology as a discipline should further ensure that no particular theological conversation be allowed to stop too soon, to announce relative adequacy too rapidly, to forget the fundamental inadequacy inevitably attendant upon any serious attempt to understand those kind of questions and those kind of responses.

If we are not to deny the witness of experience itself in the human search for love, then we also know that listening, argument, conflict, confrontation are internal dialectical necessities operative in the demands for self-transcendence present in every loving relationship. Real friendship, like the love which grounds and impels it, is that way. If we are not to domesticate the reality of conversation nor sentimentalize the ideal of an analogical imagination, we must remain sensitive to the need for new negations of present achievements—negations always needed for genuine analogy. If conversation is a reality, then conflict, confrontation, argument can prove liberating possibilities. Because an analogical, not univocal, imagination is the need of our radically pluralistic moment, the dissimilarities are as important as the similarities-in-difference, the ordered relationships will emerge from distinct, sometimes mutually exclusive, focal responses of the different traditions and the focal questions in the situation. Each of us understands each other through analogy or not at all.

For Christian systematic theology, the first clue for an appropriate response to the radical pluralism of the contemporary situation is the need to reflect upon the pluralism *within* the Christian tradition in order to reflect upon the pluralism *among* the religious traditions or the pluralism *among* the analyses of the situation. From the genuine pluralism in the Testaments through the conflicting, explosive mutual rejections of Christians by Christians in Christian history to the more hopeful contemporary ecumenical setting, the realities of different focal meanings (manifestation, proclamation, prophetic action) for interpreting the paradigmatic Christian focal meaning, the event of Jesus Christ, have made all the difference. The emergence of the sense of a need for the other experienced in each classic Christian tradition as now necessary even to understand one's own particularity is the kairos in the recent emergence of ecumenical Christian theologies. The recognition that no classic tradition should abandon its particular genius in its entry into conversation with the others is a central key for enhancing a genuinely ecumenical theology.

The scope of the entire Christian symbol system, like the reality of the event of Jesus Christ which decisively elicits and empowers the whole system, is the always-already, not-yet reality of grace as manifestation, proclamation and prophetic action. Any Christian systematic theology attempting its ownmost task of relative adequacy to the unity-in-differences in that symbol system and in that event must free itself to be transformed by the larger conversation of the classics of the entire Christian tradition. In the liberating paradox of the kairos in the contemporary situation, each Christian theology can now continue to intensify the journey of intensification into its own particularity only by its willingness constantly to expose itself *as itself* to the really other.

The second clue which the history of classical Christian systematics discloses is the reality of pluralism in the situational analyses of theology. From the concentration upon mortality and transience in the Greek Fathers, through the rage for order in Aquinas and the great Scholastics, through the impassioned search for forgiveness from guilt and sin in Luther to the courageous responses to the cognitive crises posed for Christian self-understanding by the Enlightenment and by the rise of historical consciousness in the classic Liberals and Modernists, to the facing of the linked crises of alienation and oppression, of global massive suffering in the mediating theologians of modernity and the recent political and liberation theologians, Christian systematics has lived a situational pluralism bearing its own clues for the radically pluralistic present. That pluralism of fundamental questions in the history of theology also suggests that the journey of particularity must now become the journey of self-exposure to all the fundamental questions posed in the uncanniness of our contemporary situation. The necessity for interdisciplinary methods in theology, like the need for collaborative practices among theologians themselves, was never more urgent. And yet, despite the persuasive pleas of great methodologists of theology like Bernard Lonergan, collaboration seems all too often absent in the privatizing chaos of the present. The cosmos that may emerge from that chaos may yet become an order disclosed by a communal analogical imagination. At least that would be the case for those Christian systematic theologians conversant with and committed to interpreting the pluralistic tradition and situation that is our own.

Each journey through the concreteness of a particular vision or tradition today must be undertaken on behalf of the proleptic concreteness of that future global humanity which the present suggests and the future demands. As participants in each religious tradition often sense, the journey of an analogical imagination within each tradition and among all the traditions must intensify. For no more than Christian theology can continue to confine its attention to the cognitive crises, the alienations and promises of the Euro-American cultural situation (all too often defined, it is true, as the situation of a white, male university professor of theology like myself) no longer can Christian theology confine its attention to Christianity alone. Christian systematic theology of the future cannot afford the traditional luxury of first interpreting Christianity and then quickly noticing and even more rapidly interpreting, via principles of Christian self-understanding, the "other religions."

If the always-already, not-yet reality of grace decisively disclosed in the Christ event *is* the focal meaning of Christian self-understanding, then that actuality must impel Christian theologians to enter into conversation with all the other religions and their classics. Where that conversation will lead no one yet knows. But that it must occur—at the beginning, not the end of a Christian systematics faithful to our situation and its hopes and demands for a global humanity—seems clear. If the clues provided by the pluralism within the Christian tradition are kept in view, the possibilities of approaching the conversation among the religious traditions through the use of an analogical imagination may prove real.[1] Then the autonomy of each will be respected because each will be expected to continue, indeed to intensify, a journey into her/his own particularity. Then the demand upon all to expose themselves to the really other in the listening, the confrontations, conflicts, arguments, conversation will be encouraged. Then the search for real similarities-in-difference and genuine dissimilarities, the search for correlates, contraries, and contradictions among the focal meanings of each tradition and, through those focal meanings, the development of ordered relationships for self, world and the ultimate reality will occur. Neither an earlier "indifferentism" nor its modern correlate, the "repressive tolerance" of a lazy pluralism, can be countenanced by the demands imposed by a conversation guided by an analogical imagination.

Consider, for example, the promise in the genuine conversation now alive in the Jewish-Christian theological dialogue. There the always-already, not-yet covenantal focal meaning of Judaism converses with the always-already, not-yet Christic focal meaning of Christianity. The analogies do not cancel out real differences. They clarify them. Genuine conversation between these two covenantal traditions now occurs: finally shorn, on the Christian side, of the revolting polemics and ignorant caricatures of the complex and pluralistic manifestation, proclamation and prophetic-action traditions of Judaism.[2] Consider, as a second example, how manifestation-oriented Christian theologies (like those of Pannikar and Cobb) hold real promise by their Christian entry into a genuine conversation with Hinduism (Panikkar) and Buddhism (Cobb).[3] The earlier and still relevant methodological reflections of Ernst Troeltsch, once shorn of his Europeanism, suggested analogy as a responsible way to the conversation among the religions.[4] Similarly, the demand by Wolfhart Pannenberg that Christian systematics incorporate within its horizon from the very beginning a theology of the history of religions holds the same kind of promise, now methodologically formulated, for an interdisciplinary analogical imagination.[5]

A religion like Christianity, a religion which includes as its paradigmatic focal meaning the always-already, not-yet event of the grace of Jesus Christ, a religion which includes within itself the additional focal meanings of manifestation, proclamation and prophetic action, should be willing to enter into the conversation among the religions which the emerging future of a global humanity demands. What will happen to all the traditions, including the Christian, when that conversation begins in earnest only the future will tell.[6] What should not happen, however, seems clear. At least for those who hold to the ideal of an analogical imagination, the dreams—the all too universal dreams—of Arnold Toynbee and other abstract universalists will not prove the route to follow. Rather the particularity of each tradition will gain in intensity as its own focal meaning becomes clearer to itself and others, as its ordered relationships for the whole come more clearly into analogical view. Each self-identity, in the self-respect of its own particularity, will find itself anew by releasing itself to a self-exposure of conversation with the others. That each will be changed by that conversation seems assured. To try to determine what concrete changes will occur before the conversation itself is a matter of literally idle speculation. In the meantime, each thinker can learn anew that the road to true concreteness—the concreteness which is the whole—is through the actual concreteness of each particularity and the deliberate, analogical, concrete conversation of all the traditions on the fundamental religious questions and the classical responses in the religions.

The realities expressed in analogical languages are not confined to those traditions which explicitly use analogical language. Rather all those involved in the contemporary struggle to achieve a personal vision open to the emergence of a global humanity sense the need for something like an analogical imagination. We can, of course, retreat into the heady experience of a relaxed pluralism of privacies. We can retire to our reservations and forget the increasing consumerization of all the classic experiences and expressions of our and every culture. Let philosophy retreat from its classical search for wisdom: A technological age will not discourage it. Let art and religion become purely private options, personal preferences, exotic consumer goods, let them renounce all authentic claims to truth and publicness: The bureaucracies of neither West nor East will discourage that harmless diversion.

We can also retreat into the righteous purity of a siege mentality where we alone possess the truth and we build our righteous worlds unsullied by the "invincible ignorance" of the alien others. Fundamentalists, traditionalists and dogmatists in every religion, monists in every movement of thought need not trouble with a messy pluralism. They already know the truth—a truth, it seems, that sets them free from the world but never for it. In their comfortable isolation, they can continue to preach a truth that can ignore all the truths disclosed in the classics of other religions and secular cultures, save the one truth the despised "world" has taught them all too well—the truth of power in its myriad forms, from the sword of religious wars to the bureaucratization of the spirit in contemporary fundamentalist and dogmatist empires. The corruptions of pluralist tolerance, like the corruptions of civil liberties, are real enough. Yet, as the too-easily-despised Enlightenment thinkers in their demand for tolerance and civil liberties should have taught us, these corruptions pale beside the outright oppression inflicted by the self-righteous upon all those who will not share their univocal ideologies.

For all those who cannot share either the easy answer of a relaxed pluralism or the hard answer of a brittle univocity, the reality of an analogical imagination becomes a live option in our day. That option lives by its belief that the route to the future concreteness of the whole—a truly global humanity—lies through the concreteness of each particularity. That option recognizes that it provides no ready theory by means of which anyone can deduce other options or arrange them in some preferred hierarchical chain of being.

That option recognizes as well that each of us understands each other through analogies to our own experience or not at all. What little, painfully little, I understand of the Buddhist notion of compassion, I understand through my own experience of compassion—an experience formed through my concrete involvement in my own religious and cultural heritages. I recognize that my focal meaning for compassion is likely to receive a liberating transformation through genuine contact and conversation with the Buddhist traditions. I cannot predict, much less deduce, the results of that conversation in advance. Yet if I have already lived by an analogical imagination within my own religious and cultural heritages, I am that much more likely to welcome the demand for further conversation. If I, as a Catholic Christian, have really faced the critique of the Catholic understanding of love as *caritas* by Protestant theologians, if I have actually experienced, in critical conversation, the force of the critiques of suspicion upon all Christian understandings of love as compassion, *agape* or *caritas* in Freud, Marx and Nietzsche, then I should have exited from those conversations transformed. I may, in fact I do find that the Catholic *caritas* understanding of Christian love remains the focussed ideal of my life. Yet I also know that my earlier willingness to try to understand alternative options for understanding love and to try to appropriate their critiques of certain realities in my own focal meaning have subtly transformed, purified and enriched my rootedness in my own *caritas* tradition. With T. S. Eliot, I may even recognize that only after that often heated conversation did I find that the self prior to the conversation had the experience but missed the meaning. Only by analogically reaching out to the hard concreteness of the other and through that expanding conversation to the proleptic concreteness of the whole, will any of us find that we arrive where we began only to know the place for the first time.

This may seem not only a strange paradox, but a painful destiny to us Westerners, with our engrained belief in the ideal of individuality (all too often corrupted into the hard dogma of individualism or caricatured into the soft doctrine of the narcissist self). Yet it is true: We understand one other through analogies to our own experience and we understand ourselves through our real internal relations to and analogous understandings of the other. We should not really need contemporary historical and social-scientific consciousness to remind us of the truth that every self is a radically social, historical, relational reality, for entry into any genuine conversation should teach this liberating insight.[7]

As we have seen, conversation occurs *only* where the conversation partners allow the subject matter to take over. Conversation occurs only when we free ourselves for the common subject matter and free ourselves from the prisons of our vaunted individualism (expressed in either the timidity of self-consciousness or the indecent desires for self-aggrandizement). As we may now add, only the realities of genuine self-respect and self-exposure to the other in conversation with the classic expressions of the human spirit is likely to free us all to the fuller reality of a liberating analogical imagination in this pluralist situation.

A Christian conversation partner aids no one if she/he lacks that self-respect: a journey, at once participatory and critical, into the particularity of the classics of the Christian tradition. The ever-new classical reexpressions of the Christian spirit from the New Testament to our own day witness to the de facto necessity of this self-respect in Christian self-identity. Those same classics, by their very rootedness in their own cultural and historical situation, witness as well to the necessity for constant self-exposure to the other. In our radically pluralistic situation, the forces of true suspicion and believable retrieval have been set loose in every secular and religious tradition. The actuality of variety and the demand for authentic particularity unite as the environment of all. An analogical imagination may yet free us to a communal conversation on behalf of the kairos of this our day—the communal and historical struggle for the emergence of a humanity both finally global and ultimately humane.

What, in this situation, is self-respect? It is the willingness to enter the journey of intensification into the concrete particularity of my own experience, history, tradition in all its classic expressions. What is self-exposure? It is the willingness to enter even my own journey of particularity on behalf of the concreteness of all, the willingness to listen to the other, to discover together the real similarities-in-difference and the real dissimilarities, to find what order may yet be possible in that variety of similarities and dissimilarities, continuities and discontinuities, negations and affirmations, to discover what analogies may free us all from the pathos of a fated history of competing monisms.

Conversation remains the ideal of any analogical imagination in any tradition. Conflict is just as often the reality. Nor should conflict be feared as the analogical imagination's own internal demand for ever-new negations of its always tentative order, its similarities-in-difference, must recognize. Self-exposure is nothing other than the internal demand of authentic self-respect. Self-exposure is nothing other than the demand for entering with the other into the subject matter of the back-and-forth movement of the conversation itself. If the subject matter discloses itself as so systematically distorted by the demonic forces of our or another's history, then the conversation must cease, for the moment. We must then allow some form of theory or therapy, personal or societal, to take place. Yet therapy, in individuals as in societies and cultures, is a practice designed to allow the conversation to begin anew. Therapy liberates individuals, as ideology critique liberates societies and traditions, to that minimal self-respect: the ability to release oneself anew to the subject matter of the conversation and the concrete otherness of the conversation partner.

Self-exposure is the willingness and ability to listen, to argue, to confront if necessary, to try to live the ideal of conversation even in the actuality of conflict. Self-respect includes the willingness to try to render explicit criteria for truth, warrants and backings in argument, rules for the interpretation of the classics of both tradition and situation, responsible personal wagers on the particularity of our own journey.

Concrete forms of both self-respect and self-exposure constitute the reality of all conversations where the subject matter is allowed to take over. In our pluralistic, conflictual, near chaotic situation, conversation may assume the form of an analogical imagination. Then everyone will be encouraged to risk his or her own journey of intensification into a concrete particularity and articulate some primary focal meaning. Everyone will be encouraged to take that journey on behalf of the really concrete—the all, the whole. Each will employ some focal meaning in a constant series of exercises of self-exposure designed to see what similarities-in-difference may be disclosed, what new negations—even of the most cherished aspects of my own particular focal meaning—are now demanded, what continuities, what order, what possible present or proleptic future harmony may yet be disclosed.

In the explicitly religious expressions of this analogical imagination, the focal meaning will prove some human response to a religious event—an event experienced as of and by the power of the whole—an event empowering every journey of intensification in every particular religious tradition. With some new personal voice or new envisionment of the whole each interpreter enters into the attempt to develop the similarities-in-difference and the dissimilarities, the negations and affirmations, the ordered analogous relationships disclosed by that focal meaning. In theology, the event is religious. The focal meaning articulated to interpret the event is theological.

Any theological focal meaning will find itself transformed, sometimes even negated, as the journey into the fuller range of classical expressions, the core symbols of the particular religious tradition goes forward. Any theological focal meaning will find itself further transformed (as will all or some of its attendant interpretations of the other core symbols) as the theologian moves, in honest and necessary critical self-exposure, into the fuller range of the situation. In such manner occur the peculiar journeys of systematic theologians: concentrated in some theological paradigmatic focal meaning employed to interpret the originating religious event, expanding that focal meaning into relationships with all reality—God, self, world—exposing all those understandings to the fuller range of the symbol system and the entire range of live options and questions in the situation.

Whether a thinker employs explicitly analogical language is not the real issue. What ultimately counts is the emergence of an analogical imagination for all those thinkers, secular and religious alike, who cannot accept either the brittleness of self-righteous ideologies masking some univocal monism or the privatized sloth of an all too easy pluralism masking either a decorous defeatism or some equivocal rootlessness. For all such persons, in fidelity to the concreteness of their own particularity, on behalf of the futural concreteness of all—of the concrete whole—there emerge, in both secular and religious form, the reality and the demands of a contemporary analogical imagination.

We understand one another, if at all, only through analogy. Who you are I know only by knowing what event, what focal meaning, you actually live by. And that I know only if I too have sensed some analogous guide in my own life. If we converse, it is likely we will both be changed as we focus upon the subject matter itself—the fundamental questions and the classical responses in our traditions. That analogical imagination seems and is a very small thing. And yet it does suffice.

For the analogical imagination, once religiously engaged, can become a clearing wherein we may finally hear each other once again, where we may yet become willing to face the actuality of the not-yet concealed in our present inhumanity in all its darkness—a deepening, encroaching darkness that, even now, even here, discloses the encompassing light always-already with us.

Notes

1. For an interesting development of this suggestion of pluralism within Christianity as an initial route to take, see George Rupp, *Beyond Existentialism and Zen* [VI/20], pp. 9–16. For important and diverse analyses of religious pluralism in contemporary American society, see the special issue of *Soundings* (1978) entitled "Dilemmas of Pluralism: The Case of Religion in Modernity," ed. F. Stanley Lusby and Charles Reynolds.

2. For exposures of that Christian polemic, see Rosemary Ruether, *Faith and Fratricide* [Pt. II Intro./8]; and Samuel Sandmel, *Anti-Semitism in the New Testament* [IV/6].

3. See Raimundo Panikkar, *Intra-Religious Dialogue* (New York: Paulist, 1978); also the special issue of *Cross Currents* on Panikkar (Summer 1979; includes bibliography); John Cobb, *The Structure of Christian Existence* (Philadelphia: Westminster, 1967), pp. 60–73, 137–51; idem, *Christ in a Pluralistic Age* [Pt. II Intro./2]; Langdon Gilkey, "The Mystery of Being and Nonbeing: An Experimental Project," *JR* (1978), 1–13; *Christian Faith in a Religiously Plural World,* ed. Donald Dawe and John Carman (Maryknoll: Orbis, 1978). For some philosophical reflections on the issues, see *The Question of Being: East-West Perspectives,* ed. Mervyn Sprung (Philadelphia: Pennsylvania State Univ. Press, 1978); Wilfred Cantwell Smith, "The Christian in a Religiously Plural World," in *The Faith of Other Men* (New York: Mentor, 1963), pp. 103–28; and Huston Smith, *Forgotten Truth: The Primordial Tradition* (New York: Harper & Row, 1977).

4. See here the essay by Michael Pye, "Ernst Troeltsch and the End of the Problem about 'Other' Religions," in *Ernst Troeltsch and the Future of Theology* [II/36], pp. 171–96.

5. See Wolfhart Pannenberg, *Theology and the Philosophy of Science* [I/51], pp. 297–346.

6. Note the remarkable "final" lecture of Tillich in *The Future of Religions* [V/44].

7. To repeat a comment made earlier: the discipline of cultural anthropology (especially when understood hermeneutically as in Geertz, Boon, Turner et al.) is the discipline most sophisticated in the kind of cross-cultural conversation now demanded of theologians. I wish to express my thanks to Mark Taylor for his informative work on the possible relationships between theology and cultural anthropology. Mr. Taylor is presently completing a dissertation (Univ. of Chicago) on aspects of the subject. The need for a conversation between theologians,

historians of religions and cultural anthropologists, especially those in all three disciplines who reflect upon the hermeneutical character of the enterprise, never seemed more urgent. My own brief reflections in this Epilogue and in chaps. 4 and 5 are at best initial steps of a methodological kind to clarify how the hermeneutically oriented systematic theologian might enter into the conversation. I hope in the future to be able to provide an attempt at such conversation rather than the present very general rubrics for the conversation itself. I assume, of course, that the explanatory methods in step 4 of the interpretative process as well as the "pluralism of readings" in step 5 would remain operative both within each discipline and in the conversation among religions and among disciplines reflecting on the religions. For some representative "historian of religion" reflections here, see *The History of Religions, Essays in Methodology,* ed. Mircea Eliade and Joseph Kitagawa [IV/12].

Index of Principal Names

Abrams, Meyer, 113, 134, 141n.42, 141n.48–49, 145n.73, 151n.106, 152n.108, 366n.24, 368n.59
Achtemeier, Paul, 295n.72
Adams, Charles, 180n.7
Adams, Hazard, 139n.35
Adams, James Luther, 23, 42n.78, 44n.95, 364n.3, 400n.22, 441n.24
Adorno, Theodor, 46n.106, 95n.103, 146n.76, 182n.21, 191n.75, 220n.11, 220n.17, 328, 356, 365n.15, 366n.27, 367n.33, 416
Ahlstrom, Gosta, 227n.54
Ahlstrom, Sydney, 36n.26, 38n.39
Allen, Douglas, 219n.5, 224n.33
Altizer, Thomas, 52, 84n.19, 186n.52, 224n.33
Arendt, Hannah, 35n.17, 37n.31, 135n.1, 146n.77, 156, 179n.4, 345, 359, 366n.21, 444n.33
Aristotle, 9–10, 37n.35, 71, 92n.78, 103–04, 108, 113, 119, 138n.18, 149n.96, 275, 298n.82, 352
Arnold, Matthew, 67, 123, 189n.68, 365n.8
Assman, Hugo, 403n.52
Audinet, Jacques, 180n.9
Auerbach, Eric, 251, 288n.16, 296n.81, 300n.94
Augustine, 33n.7, 33n.9, 49, 63, 83–84n.14, 84n.24, 104, 150n.106, 166, 187n.54, 187n.59, 201, 229n.73, 251, 310, 344, 349, 355–56, 396, 400n.19, 431
Avinieri, Sholomo, 95n.96, 366n.26

Baeck, Leo, 203, 222n.27
Balthasar, Hans Urs von, 99, 147n.82, 322, 335n.21, 380, 385, 400n.22, 402n.41, 402n.43
Barr, James, 135n.3
Barrett, William, 355, 367n.42–43, 368n.50, 369n.67
Barth, Karl, 42n.76, 60, 87n.36, 104, 107, 132–33, 138n.21, 157, 165, 180n.8, 185n.32, 196, 213–14, 220n.14, 221n.20, 226n.48, 227n.56, 228n.64, 251, 258, 288n.16, 294n.65, 297n.81, 304n.118, 313, 335n.17, 344, 387–89, 402n.39–43, 402n.47–48, 405, 407, 415–18, 421, 426, 434, 436, 438n.2, 441n.19–22, 443n.30, 444n.37–38
Barthes, Roland, 117, 120–21, 123, 139n.31, 144n.61–62, 145n.68, 145n.71, 146n.80, 296n.81, 360, 369n.72
Baum, Gregory, 31–32n.1, 44n.95, 93n.80–81, 179n.7, 180n.9, 392, 403n.60
Beardslee, William A., 292n.47, 292n.51, 296–97n.81, 298n.84, 301n.100, 301n.103
Beardsley, Monroe, 139n.35, 141n.47, 143n.60
Becker, Ernest, 41n.73, 119n.42, 164
Bell, Daniel, 7, 35n.16, 35n.21, 365n.6
Bellah, Robert, 36n.26, 38n.39, 182n.14
Benjamin, Walter, 95n.103, 96n.105, 123, 146n.76, 220n.17, 296n.81, 328, 351, 356–57, 366n.27, 367n.39–40, 368n.53, 368n.55, 369n.64, 404n.66
Bentley, Eric, 147n.82
Berger, Peter, 24, 31–32n.1, 33n.7, 37n.36, 42n.83, 43n.86, 179n.5, 182n.14, 183n.23, 227n.53, 365n.6
Berkouwer, G. C., 402n.42, 441n.21
Bernstein, Richard, 37n.28, 37n.30, 37–38n.36, 92n.78, 93n.82
Berrigan, Daniel, 60, 87n.40
Bethge, Eberhard, 147n.82
Betz, Hans Dieter, 289n.27, 333n.2
Biale, David, 222n.27, 368n.55
Bloch, Ernst, 137n.16, 146n.76, 220n.17, 226n.50, 296n.81, 356–57, 366n.27, 368n.53, 369n.64
Blondel, Maurice, 92n.75, 335n.19
Bloom, Harold, 145n.70, 146n.80, 356, 368n.55
Blumenthal, David, 223n.27
Boers, Hendrikus, 287n.3
Boff, Leonardo, 245n.24, 334n.10, 334n.15, 403n.52, 404n.68
Bonaventure, 135, 247n.27, 253, 381, 386, 401n.30, 413, 441n.11
Bonhoeffer, Dietrich, 147n.82, 157, 180n.8,

185n.40, 213–14, 227n.53, 228n.65–66, 384, 417
Bonino, José Miguez, 403n.52, 403n.59
Boon, James, 144n.64, 179n.5, 455n.7
Booth, Wayne, 86n.33, 113, 121–22, 141n.48, 143n.59, 146n.78–79, 149n.95, 366n.22, 366n.24, 398n.3
Bornkamn, Günther, 300n.95, 301n.97–98, 302–03n.110
Borowitz, Eugene, 222–23n.27
Bourke, Myles, 289n.20, 295n.79
Bowker, John, 179n.7
Braaten, Carl, 245n.21, 390, 402n.50
Braithwaite, Richard Bevan, 172, 191n.74
Brecht, Bertolt, 146n.76, 215, 294n.65, 366n.27
Brooks, Cleanth, 145n.70, 145n.73, 151n.106, 301n.104
Brown, Norman O., 139n.30
Brown, Peter, 147n.82, 187n.59
Brown, Raymond, 83n.6–7, 229n.72, 289n.20, 295n.79, 299n.92, 303n.113–14
Brown, Robert McAfee, 402n.52
Browning, Don, 138n.22, 147n.82, 367n.30
Brunner, Emil, 87n.36, 157, 180n.8, 227n.56, 228n.64, 389, 400n.13, 415, 418, 436, 441n.20
Buber, Martin, 33n.5, 84n.26, 222–23n.27, 358, 370n.80, 381, 401n.27
Buck-Morss, Susan, 94n.96, 368n.54
Buckley, Michael, 294n.57
Bultmann, Rudolf, 83n.6, 83n.10, 104, 107, 133, 138n.28, 154, 197, 225n.45, 226n.47–48, 226n.52, 227n.56, 243n.11, 245n.23, 246n.25, 251, 253, 256, 260–61, 265, 269–70, 289n.26–27, 290n.30, 291n.38, 291n.40, 293n.51, 293n.54, 294n.62, 295n.70, 301n.97, 302n.109, 304n.118, 304n.120, 313, 335n.17, 356, 388–89, 402n.39, 402n.47–48, 405, 415, 418, 426, 441n.23
Burke, Kenneth, 141n.48, 183n.22
Burnaby, John, 444n.36
Burrell, David, 94n.86, 191n.81, 414, 438–39n.2, 439n.3, 439n.6, 441n.15
Butterfield, Herbert, 352, 367n.41

Cajetan, 222n.27, 413, 439n.3, 441n.13
Calinescu, Martin, 145n.71, 224n.34
Calvin, John, 92n.69, 104, 195, 221n.20, 227n.58, 229n.73, 258, 373, 407, 417, 431, 440n.7
Cameron, J. M., 135n.1
Campenhausen, Hans von, 244n.16
Camus, Albert, 53, 164, 186n.45, 341
Carr, Anne, 184n.27
Cassirer, Ernst, 148n.87
Chadwick, Henry, 89n.48
Chardin, Teilhard de, 304n.119, 380, 386, 400n.22, 401n.28, 413
Childs, Brevard, 227n.55
Chomsky, Noam, 149n.97
Christian, William A., 66, 92n.72
Cioran, E. M., 6, 34n.13
Clebsch, William, 219n.8, 287n.4
Clifford, W. C., 86n.33, 165, 187n.56
Cobb, John, 138n.21, 180n.9, 181n.10, 228n.69, 242n.2, 251, 258, 288n.14, 300n.95, 310, 314, 317–18, 334n.8, 334n.14–15, 336n.25, 379, 425, 442n.29, 450, 455n.3
Cohen, Arthur, 39n.45, 91n.65, 222–23n.27, 365n.13, 370n.75, 370n.77, 440n.7
Coleman, John A., 32n.1–2, 34n.12, 34n.14, 43n.89, 44n.95, 88n.43, 93n.82, 403n.56
Coleridge, Samuel Taylor, 111, 141n.43
Collins, John, 179n.7, 292n.51
Collins, Sheila, 397, 403n.60, 404n.66
Cone, James, 57, 97n.109, 164, 186n.50, 247n.26, 251, 327, 390–91, 396, 403n.52 403n.60
Congar, Yves, 39n.51, 42n.83, 92n.75, 135n.1, 336n.26
Connelly, John, 399n.7
Conzelmann, Hans, 246n.25, 260, 291n.36, 295n.71
Coreth, Emerich, 414, 441n.15
Cousins, Ewert, 401n.30, 440–41n.11
Cox, Harvey, 61, 227n.53, 229n.72
Crane, R. S., 141n.48, 145n.70, 149n.97
Crites, Stephen, 33n.6, 150n.104, 296n.81
Cross, Frank Moore, 227n.54
Crossan, John Dominic, 191n.77, 251, 289n.17, 297n.81, 298n.85
Crowe, Frederick, 94n.94, 138n.23, 225n.45
Cuddihy, John Murray, 39n.45
Curran, Charles, 392, 403n.55–56

Daly, Mary, 403n.60
Danielou, Jean, 26, 76
Dante Alighieri, 132, 138n.29, 139n.31, 195, 200–01, 220n.9, 222n.27
Danto, Arthur, 297n.81
Davis, Charles, 95n.100, 392
Dealy, Glen, 36n.28
Delattre, Ronald, 221n.24
Deloria, Vine, 395
de Man, Paul, 145n.70, 149n.95, 220n.17
Derrida, Jacques, 117–18, 121, 144n.62, 145n.70, 145n.72, 148n.94, 149n.95, 220n.17, 291n.46, 357, 361, 367n.37, 370n.74
Despland, Michel, 180n.7, 221n.25
Detweiler, Robert, 153n.109
Dewey, John, 37n.30, 91n.65, 93n.82, 142n.53, 190n.71

Dickstein, Morris, 139n.30–31
Dillon, Richard, 299n.91
Dilthey, Wilhelm, 40n.61, 138n.25, 142n.57, 144n.60
Dodd, C. H., 265, 270, 295n.70, 298n.85, 303n.113, 313
Doubrovsky, Serge, 139n.31, 369n.72
Douglas, Mary, 150n.99, 397
Dudley, Guilford, 219n.5, 224n.33
Dulles, Avery, 43n.89, 44n.90, 338n.34
Dumas, André, 402n.50
Dunn, James D., 272, 287n.3, 288n.7, 295n.73, 295n.76, 295n.78, 296n.79
Dupré, Louis, 156, 179n.7, 182n.16, 186n.52, 191n.80, 377
Durkheim, Emile, 156, 159, 171, 182n.14

Eagleton, Terry, 146n.76, 365n.8
Ebeling, Gerhard, 16, 39n.57, 222n.27, 245n.23, 270, 294n.63, 334n.15, 356, 389, 402n.49
Edwards, Jonathan, 92n.69, 104, 221n.24, 228n.71
Eliade, Mircea, 41n.69, 135n.4, 139n.31, 150n.99, 154–56, 158, 168, 170–71, 179n.1–3, 180n.9, 181n.12, 182n.21–22, 186n.52, 188n.66, 189n.68, 190n.73, 193, 205–09, 213–15, 219n.1–3, 219n.5, 224n.33–34, 224n.36, 224n.39–41, 225n.42, 225n.44, 229n.73, 253, 360, 377, 381, 383–84, 456n.7
Eliot, T. S., 26, 35n.17, 76, 108, 120–21, 125, 138n.29, 139n.31, 139n.34, 145n.69, 146n.80, 147n.81, 189n.68, 201, 207, 220n.9, 222n.27, 303n.117, 341, 369n.66, 383, 400n.34, 452
Ellul, Jacques, 60–61, 75, 87n.40, 344, 353

Fackenheim, Emil, 92n.73, 222–23n.27, 224n.30, 366n.25, 370n.76
Farley, Edward, 39n.51, 45n.104
Ferré, Frederick, 179n.7, 343, 365n.17
Feuerbach, Ludwig Andreas, 137n.17, 156, 158, 172, 346
Fierro, Alfredo, 34n.14, 402n.50
Fiorenza, Elizabeth Schüssler, 247n.26, 392, 403n.60
Fiorenza, Francis Schüssler, 93n.80, 94n.83, 392, 402n.52, 403n.58
Ford, Lewis S., 440n.7
Forstman, Jack, 138n.25, 400n.11
Foucault, Michel, 108, 117, 139n.32, 146n.78, 146n.80, 220n.17, 361, 370n.73, 438n.2
Francis of Assisi, 135, 247n.27, 381, 386, 401n.30, 413
Frei, Hans, 251, 263, 288n.16, 291n.46, 297n.81
Freud, Sigmund, 33n.7, 53, 106, 109, 135n.4, 137n.16–17, 156–57, 159, 167, 171–72, 187n.62, 190n.71, 191n.75, 199, 220n.17, 346, 348–51, 354–57, 363, 366n.22, 366–67n.30, 367n.31, 368n.56–57, 369n.61, 369n.63, 452
Fromm, Erich, 37n.36, 220n.17, 367n.33
Fuchs, Ernst, 245n.23, 270, 356, 389, 402n.49
Fuller, Reginald, 271, 288n.8, 295n.73–74, 303n.115
Funk, Robert, 251, 270, 289n.17, 292n.51, 294n.63, 297n.81, 298n.85
Furnish, Victor, 295n.69, 302n.106

Gadamer, Hans-Georg, 66, 73–75, 87n.38, 90n.59, 92n.74, 94n.94, 96n.104, 101, 111, 113, 117, 127, 135n.5, 135n.7, 135–36n.8, 137n.12–13, 137n.16, 138n.25, 138n.27, 140–41n.39, 141n.40, 141n.50, 142n.52, 142n.57, 143n.58, 143n.59–60, 144n.62, 145n.67, 146n.80–81, 147–48n.87, 148n.92, 151n.106, 152n.107, 179n.2, 179n.5, 187n.65, 192n.83, 219n.1, 221n.19, 226n.45, 246n.25, 337n.29, 353, 359, 366n.23, 368n.49, 389, 399n.8
Gager, John, 291n.37, 332n.1
Galilea, Segundo, 180n.9, 228n.72, 404n.66
Galot, Jean, 292n.49
Gay, Peter, 365n.14
Geertz, Clifford, 7, 11, 35n.16, 35n.18–19, 39n.40, 41n.73, 95n.99, 144n.64, 147n.83, 163, 170, 179n.5, 185n.36, 288n.6, 455n.7
Geffre, Claude, 402n.50
Gerhart, Mary, 144n.60, 149n.97
Gerrish, B. A., 87n.35, 227n.56, 227n.58, 228n.62, 336n.22–23, 400n.12–13
Gilkey, Langdon, 17, 26, 40n.57, 45n.100, 82n.2, 84n.14, 89n.51, 93n.82, 96n.108, 227n.53, 289n.26, 301n.101, 336–37n.29, 364n.3, 369n.70, 379, 400n.24, 403n.53, 406, 440n.7, 442n.29, 455n.3
Gill, Robin, 24, 32n.1, 43n.86
Gilson, Etienne, 414, 441n.15
Goethe, Johann Wolfgang von, 140n.36, 142n.56, 207, 350
Goffman, Erving, 38n.37, 41n.73, 142n.52
Gogarten, Friedrich, 226n.48, 227n.53, 389, 402n.39, 415
Goldstein, Valerie Saiving. *See* Saiving.
Goodman, Nelson, 291n.46
Gottwald, Norman, 97n.108, 227n.54
Gouldner, Alvin, 32n.2, 95n.96, 95n.99, 302n.108, 366n.26
Grant, Robert, 89n.48, 244n.13, 244n.16, 261, 291n.37, 291n.42
Greeley, Andrew, 24, 32n.1–2, 38n.39, 42n.79, 42n.84, 43n.85, 44n.95, 45n.102,

87n.43, 93n.82, 96n.106, 229n.72, 333n.2, 365n.6, 403n.60
Griffin, David, 334n.15, 336n.25, 440n.7
Grillmeier, Aloys, 246n.25, 287n.4, 292n.49
Gunn, Giles, 113, 137n.14, 141n.49, 152n.109
Gustafson, James, 23–24, 42n.77–78, 42n.80, 44n.95, 92n.69, 221n.20, 228n.60, 287n.4, 444n.38
Gutierrez, Gustavo, 57, 95n.100, 164, 186n.50, 247n.26, 258, 390–91, 395, 402n.51–52, 403n.53, 403n.60, 404n.66

Habermas, Jürgen, 7, 35n.21, 36n.24, 36n.28, 38n.36, 42n.83, 73–75, 89n.54, 93n.82, 94n.96, 95n.103, 137n.16, 146n.80–81, 220n.17, 337n.29, 345, 348, 366n.21, 366n.23, 367n.33, 367n.48
Hahn, Ferdinand, 271, 288n.8, 295n.74
Haight, Roger, 44n.94, 97n.112, 404n.68, 442n.29
Happel, Stephen, 141n.43, 227n.56
Harnack, Adolf, 212, 244n.13, 321–22, 325n.18, 336n.22, 402n.39
Hart, Ray, 149n.96
Hartshorne, Charles, 159, 161, 183n.25, 185n.32, 221n.22, 377
Hartt, Julian, 149n.96
Harvey, Van, 17, 31–32n.1, 39n.57, 43n.86, 85n.32, 91n.68, 158, 185n.32, 187n.56, 242n.6, 245n.21–22, 251, 288n.14, 295n.77, 300n.97, 302n.107, 333n.4, 335n.17
Hauerwas, Stanley, 94n.88
Hegel, Georg Wilhelm Friedrich, 33n.9, 108, 140n.36, 141n.50, 142n.55, 146n.80, 150n.105–106, 157–59, 180n.10, 185n.34, 207, 221n.19, 223n.30, 253, 293n.57, 342, 346, 351–52, 356, 366n.25, 373, 407, 415–16
Heidegger, Martin, 61, 89n.52, 103, 127, 135n.6, 137n.16–17, 138n.25, 141–42n.50, 142n.54, 142n.57, 143n.59, 144n.65, 147n.85, 147n.87, 148n.87, 148n.92, 150n.101, 154, 179n.2, 182n.21, 190–91n.73, 191n.75, 192n.83, 199, 219n.1, 246n.25, 303n.113, 303n.116, 352–56, 360, 363, 367n.37, 367n.42–45, 368n.46–47, 368n.52, 368n.58, 380, 389, 401n.26
Heilbroner, Robert, 369n.69–70
Hennelly, Alfred T., 403n.52, 403n.57
Hennessey, James, 38n.39, 40n.65
Heschel, Abraham, 222–23n.27
Hill, William, 439n.3, 441n.13
Hirsch, E. D., 142n.58, 143n.58, 144n.60
Hodgson, Peter, 93n.82
Hollenbach, David, 34n.12, 37n.34, 403n.56
Homans, Peter, 219n.2, 367n.30
Horkheimer, Max, 36n.24, 36n.27, 46n.106, 95n.103, 220n.11, 220n.17, 328, 356, 365n.15, 366n.19, 367n.33, 416
Hügel, Friedrich von, 156, 168, 170, 183n.22, 188n.66
Hume, David, 186n.44
Hutchinson, William R., 97n.111
Huxley, Aldous, 172, 191n.74

Ignatius Loyola, 120, 145n.68, 195, 222n.27, 258, 386

James, Henry, 125, 147n.86, 373
James, William, 86n.33, 92n.82, 147n.82, 164–65, 167–71, 186n.48, 187n.54–55, 188n.66, 194, 360, 364n.2
Jameson, Frederic, 146n.76, 365n.8, 366n.27–28
Jaspers, Karl, 356–57, 367n.37
Jay, Martin, 94n.96, 367n.33, 368n.50, 368n.54–55
Jefferson, Thomas, 37n.29, 38n.39, 135n.5, 138n.20
Jensen, Robert, 277n.56, 402n.50
Jeremias, Joachim, 245n.23, 251, 260, 291n.35, 298n.85, 300n.97
John, 48–49, 65, 83n.8, 83n.11, 138n.28, 179n.6, 201, 213, 235, 243n.11, 246n.25, 250–51, 253–54, 260, 264, 270, 272–74, 282–87, 290n.29, 291n.38, 295n.79, 303n.113–14, 303n.117–18, 304n.120, 308, 310–13, 315, 317, 324, 330, 333n.3, 333n.5, 407, 425
John of the Cross, 174, 191n.81, 195, 201
Johnson, Lesley, 365n.8, 366n.27
Johnson, Samuel, 123, 147n.83, 154, 168, 189n.68
Jossua, Jean-Pierre, 441n.15
Joyce, James, 132, 207, 296n.81, 358
Jung, Carl J., 157, 159, 219n.2, 356–57, 360, 368n.57, 384
Jüngel, Eberhard, 91n.63, 227n.58, 298n.85, 303n.111, 431, 443n.30

Kähler, Martin, 243n.11, 245n.23, 276–77, 299n.87, 301n.97, 335n.17
Kant, Immanuel, 108, 110, 138n.20, 140n.36, 140n.38–39, 141n.47, 161, 164, 183n.22, 186n.44, 221n.25, 356, 365n.14, 380
Käsemann, Ernst, 245n.23, 246n.25, 251, 265, 288n.11, 289n.20, 292n.50, 292n.51, 293n.52, 293n.54, 293n.56, 301n.97, 313n.110
Kasper, Walter, 271, 295n.75, 314, 318, 322, 333n.6, 335n.21, 427
Katz, Steven, 223n.27

Kaufman, Gordon, 17, 39n.57, 43n.88, 92n.77, 223n.27
Kaufman, Walter, 302n.106, 367n.37
Keck, Leander, 245n.20, 300n.97
Kelsey, David, 287n.-2, 288n.15-16, 290n.28, 294n.64
Kermode, Frank, 108, 138n.29, 139n.34, 262, 291n.43-44, 291n.46, 296n.81, 299n.90, 345, 366n.21, 369n.64
Kierkegaard, Søren, 4-6, 33n.6, 34n.13, 84n.23, 103, 111, 126, 128, 133-34, 135n.4, 150n.104, 151n.105-106, 164, 185n.37, 186n.43, 199, 201, 221n.21, 221n.23, 321, 341, 346, 354-55, 415, 433
Kitagawa, Joseph, 34n.13, 87n.39, 181n.12, 187n.65, 219n.5, 224n.33, 456n.7
Knitter, Paul, 180n.9, 182n.20, 334n.14
Koester, Helmut, 289n.23, 303n.113
Kolakowski, Leszek, 95n.96, 366n.26
Komonchak, Joseph, 23, 42n.83, 43n.89, 44n.95, 135n.1
Kuhn, Thomas, 40n.60, 141n.48, 226n.46
Küng, Hans, 17, 24, 44n.96, 86n.32, 88n.44, 96n.106, 185n.33, 192n.90, 227n.57, 244n.15, 246n.24, 251, 288n.11, 291n.34, 292n.49, 293n.56, 300n.96, 301n.101, 311, 314, 319, 334n.9, 334n.15, 336n.29, 337n.29, 337n.31, 337n.33, 379, 392, 400n.20, 403n.54, 406, 419, 426-27, 442n.29
Kurrik, Marie, 368n.60

Lamb, Matthew, 31-32n.1, 37n.36, 40n.61, 46n.106, 93n.78-80, 93n.82, 94n.95-96, 95n.103, 96n.104, 142n.57, 180n.9, 392
Langer, Susanne, 140n.36, 147n.87, 192n.183
Lasch, Christopher, 33n.7, 34n.11, 38n.37, 364n.1, 365n.6
Lash, Nicholas, 335n.20
Lawler, Justus George, 134, 152n.108
Leeuw, Gerardus van der, 168, 170, 188n.66
Leith, John, 401n.37
Lévi-Strauss, Claude, 117, 144n.64, 151n.106, 189n.70, 361
Linge, David, 137n.12, 138n.27
Little, David, 182n.19
Loewe, William, 335n.21
Loisy, Alfred, 244n.13, 321-22, 335n.18-19, 336n.27
Lonergan, Bernard, 15, 19, 33n.10, 36n.28, 37n.36, 39n.54, 40n.64, 41n.66-67, 42n.83, 63, 70-72, 85n.30, 91n.65, 91n.68, 94n.84-90, 94n.92, 94n.94, 104, 110, 133, 135n.1, 137n.18, 138n.19, 138n.23, 164, 182n.17, 186n.51, 227n.56, 246n.25, 287n.4, 304n.118, 310, 335n.21, 337n.29, 343, 365n.17, 379, 398n.1, 439n.5, 441n.15, 448
Long, Charles, 34n.13, 397, 404n.66
Lovin, Robin, 34n.12, 37n.34, 185n.40, 403n.56
Lowe, Walter, 367n.30, 367n.35
Lubac, Henri de, 91n.65, 400n.22
Luckmann, Thomas, 32n.1, 34n.14, 42n.83, 43n.86
Lukacs, Georg, 146n.76, 187n.54, 366n.27-28
Luke, 97n.108, 252-53, 260, 274, 277-78, 280, 291n.36, 295n.71, 299n.87, 299n.91, 307, 311, 313, 333n.5
Luther, Martin, 65, 90n.62, 91n.63, 104, 142n.56, 164, 186n.43, 195, 197, 227n.58, 228n.61, 251, 253, 258, 269, 284, 304n.118, 321, 355, 374, 387, 407, 431, 440n.7, 441n.24
Lynn, Robert, 39n.51

McBrien, Richard, 43n.89, 44n.91-92, 289n.20
McCann, Dennis, 39n.48, 42n.78, 95n.103
McCarthy, Thomas, 94n.96, 95n.103, 368n.48
McCool, Gerald, 40n.65, 184n.27, 337n.30, 441n.15
McCready, William, 42n.79, 96n.106
McFague, Sallie, 153n.109, 251, 289n.17
McGarry, Michael B., 243n.8
McGinn, Bernard, 292n.51, 401n.36
McInerny, Ralph, 438n.2, 439n.3
MacIntyre, Alasdair, 366n.22, 369n.69
Mackey, James, 92n.75, 295n.77
Macquarrie, John, 189n.66, 289n.23, 302n.105, 303n.116, 443n.30
Malinowski, Bronislaw Kasper, 157, 170, 181n.13
Malraux, André, 35n.17, 242n.2, 258, 317
Mannheim, Karl, 32n.1
Marcel, Gabriel, 25, 45n.98, 164, 186n.46, 381, 401n.27
Marcuse, Herbert, 36n.24, 39n.43, 220n.12, 220n.17, 345, 352-53, 366n.20-22, 366n.29, 367n.33, 367n.40
Maritain, Jacques, 258, 414, 441n.15
Mark, 200, 250, 253, 260, 262, 266, 276-80, 298-90n.27, 291n.43, 295n.71, 296-98n.81, 299n.87, 299n.91, 301n.104, 313, 332n.1, 333n.5
Marty, Martin, 33n.8, 36n.26, 38n.39, 93n.82, 180n.9, 403n.56
Marx, Karl, 41n.74, 72, 92n.78, 95n.99, 109, 137n.16, 156, 159, 167, 172, 187n.62, 190n.71, 191n.75, 199, 346-51, 354-57, 363, 366n.26, 369n.61, 452
Marx, Werner, 137n.16

Marxsen, Willi, 243n.11, 244n.16, 245n.21, 246n.25, 251, 260, 271, 287n.3, 287n.5, 289n.27, 291n.36, 292n.48, 301n.97, 333n.3, 336n.29, 427
Matthew, 260, 274, 277–78, 280, 299n.87, 299n.91, 313, 333n.5, 420
Maurice, F. D., 212, 304n.118, 314, 374
Mead, Sidney, 36n.26, 37n.29, 38n.39, 190n.71
Meland, Bernard, 219n.8
Metz, Johann B., 17, 44n.94, 57, 71, 77, 86n.35, 93n.78, 93n.80, 93n.82, 94n.87, 95n.98, 95n.103, 96n.104–06, 97n.109, 164, 186n.50, 204, 246n.26, 251, 265, 289n.19, 289n.25, 292–93n.51, 293n.54, 294n.60, 296–97n.81, 301n.99, 314, 327, 337n.31, 390–92, 402n.50–51, 416, 419, 427, 441n.15, 441n.17, 442n.29
Miller, J. Hillis, 121, 145n.70, 145n.72, 366n.24
Mills, C. Wright, 32n.2, 34n.14
Minear, Paul, 289n.20
Miranda, José, 251, 290n.31, 314, 403n.52, 416, 441n.18
Misgeld, Dieter, 95n.102
Moltmann, Jürgen, 44n.94, 57, 76, 97n.109, 157, 164, 180n.8, 186n.50, 213, 226n.50, 251, 258, 265, 292–93n.51, 293n.54, 302n.107, 303n.112, 304n.118–19, 311–12, 314, 327, 334n.9, 334n.11, 387, 390–92, 402n.50, 405n.59, 416, 419, 426, 431, 441n.16, 442n.29
Montagnes, Bernard, 438n.2
Moore, George Foote, 179n.6
Moore, Sebastian, 229n.72
Morel, Georges, 191n.81
Moule, C. F. D., 295n.79
Murdoch, Iris, 39n.44
Murray, John Courtney, 8, 13, 34n.12, 36n.26, 37n.34, 39n.45, 39n.49, 93n.82, 403n.56

Neill, Stephen, 287n.3, 289n.23
Neusner, Jacob, 223n.27
Neville, Robert, 147n.82, 219n.6
Newman, John Henry, 87n.33, 92n.75, 201, 322, 335n.20, 360
Niebuhr, H. Richard, 37n.32, 42–43n.85, 43n.87–88, 44n.97, 45n.99, 45n.102, 65, 83n.7, 83n.11, 90n.61, 91n.64, 91n.67–68, 92n.70, 104, 133, 164, 186n.47, 191n.78, 226n.46, 241n.1, 335n.17, 374, 376, 387, 389, 398n.2–3, 401n.38, 436, 444n.39
Niebuhr, Reinhold, 13, 33n.8, 37n.34, 39n.45, 39n.48, 62, 82n.2, 89n.50, 93n.82, 104, 133, 164, 186n.49, 204, 335n.17, 389, 393, 404n.62, 406–07, 415, 436, 439n.5, 444n.39
Nielsen, Kai, 191n.74
Nielsen, Niels, Jr., 370n.75, 438n.2
Nietzsche, Friedrich, 5, 49, 52–53, 106, 130, 137n.16, 139n.32, 142n.55–56, 147n.82, 156, 167, 172, 186n.52, 187n.62, 190n.71, 191n.75, 199, 220n.17, 302n.106, 341, 346, 349–57, 363, 366n.25, 367n.37, 367n.45, 369n.61, 452
Nisbet, Robert, 135n.1
Novak, Michael, 37n.36, 187n.53
Nygren, Anders, 14–16, 32n.1, 39n.52, 39n.57, 85n.31, 92n.73, 228n.64, 444n.36

O'Collins, Gerald, 335n.21
O'Donovan, Leo, 44n.94, 184n.27
Ogden, Schubert, 17, 26, 39n.57, 45n.100, 82n.1, 82–83n.4, 83n.10, 86n.34, 89n.51, 96n.108, 135n.1, 164, 186n.46, 192n.88, 219n.8, 227n.53, 242n.6, 243–44n.13, 244n.16, 245n.21, 245n.23, 246n.26, 251, 291n.40, 292n.48, 301n.97, 310–11, 314, 333n.3, 333n.8, 379, 400n.20, 403n.52, 404n.67, 425, 441n.23, 443n.29
O'Meara, Thomas, 43n.89, 364n.3
Otto, Rudolf, 150n.102, 156, 168, 170–71, 183n.22, 188n.66, 189n.69
Outka, Gene, 444n.36
Outler, Albert C., 334n.8, 335n.19

Palmer, Richard, 138n.25
Panikkar, Raimundo, 450, 455n.3
Pannenberg, Worfhart, 15–16, 39n.51, 39n.53, 39n.57, 84n.26–27, 89n.55, 182n.20, 182–83n.21, 191n.78, 242n.5, 265, 292–93n.51, 293n.54, 301n.101, 314, 333n.6, 334n.11, 337n.29, 412, 427, 450, 455n.5
Pauck, Wilhelm, 97,n.111, 441n.24, 441n.26
Pauck, Marion, 441n.26
Paul, 53, 63, 65, 138n.28, 142n.56, 179n.6, 195, 201, 229n.73, 235, 243n.11, 246n.25, 250–53, 256, 258, 264, 266, 270, 272–73, 275, 282–86, 288n.7, 288n.12, 289n.27, 290n.29, 292n.50, 298n.85, 302–03n.110, 303n.111, 304n.118, 304n.120, 307–08, 311, 315, 317, 324, 330, 332, 333n.3, 333n.5, 407, 420, 426, 431
Pelikan, Jaroslov, 228n.64, 287n.4, 441n.24
Pelotte, Donald, 39n.49
Penner, Hans, 189n.66
Perrin, Norman, 245n.23, 246n.25, 251, 260–62, 287n.3, 288n.9, 289n.18, 289n.22, 289n.27, 291n.35–36, 291n.40, 291n.43, 295n.71, 295n.73, 298n.83, 298n.85, 299n.87–88, 299n.90–91, 301n.97, 333n.5
Peter, Carl J., 91n.65
Petersen, Norman, 262, 291n.43, 299n.91
Pétrement, Simone, 186n.49

Peukert, Helmut, 93n.78, 95n.103
Pieper, Josef, 141n.44, 191n.82
Pittenger, Norman, 336n.25
Plaskow, Judith, 395, 404n.60, 404n.62
Plato, 9, 12, 53, 123, 135n.7, 139n.35, 140n.38, 181n.13, 352
Plotinus, 111, 134, 139–40n.36
Poggioli, Renato, 39n.42, 141n.47
Polanyi, Michael, 343, 365n.17
Preller, Victor, 90n.56, 439n.6
Proust, Marcel, 135n.4, 206, 358, 383–84
Przywara, Erik, 414
Pye, Michael, 336n.22, 455n.4

Rad, Gerhard von, 293n.54, 299n.89
Rahman, Fazlur, 288n.6
Rahner, Karl, 37n.34, 43n.90, 44n.94, 82n.3, 91n.63, 91n.65, 104, 107, 132–33, 145n.68, 162, 165, 184n.27–30, 185n.31, 185n.34, 191n.78, 192n.87, 204, 221n.21, 227n.58, 244n.18, 251, 253, 288n.13, 294n.57, 294n.60, 304n.118, 310–11, 313–14, 318, 322–24, 333n.8, 334n.11, 335n.21, 336n.25, 336n.27, 337n.31, 356, 366n.30, 377–79, 385, 400n.19, 405, 412, 414, 416, 419, 426–27, 439n.2, 440n.7, 440n.9–10, 441n.15, 442n.26, 442n.29, 443n.30, 444n.34, 444n.38
Raitt, Jill, 401n.36
Ramsey, Ian, 63, 89n.52
Ramsey, Paul, 37n.32
Ratzinger, Joseph, 333n.8
Rawls, John, 9, 10, 37n.32–34
Redeker, Martin, 400n.12
Reist, Benjamin, 404n.61, 404n.66
Ricoeur, Paul, 13, 39n.47, 87n.38–39, 95n.102, 113, 118, 124, 127, 136n.8, 137n.18, 138n.24, 140n.36, 142–43n.58, 143n.59–60, 144n.62, 145n.67, 145n.75, 148n.90, 148n.92, 148n.94, 149n.96–97, 150n.98–99, 151–52n.107, 187n.61–62, 187n.65, 190n.70, 190n.72, 191n.77–78, 192n.83, 192n.89, 204, 221n.26, 224n.33, 228n.68, 228n.70, 229n.73, 246n.25, 291n.46, 296–97n.81, 298n.85, 303n.111, 348, 366n.22, 367n.30–31, 368n.49, 438n.2
Rieff, Philip, 33n.7, 364n.1, 366n.30
Roberts, Deotis, 403n.60
Robertson, Roland, 42n.77, 44n.97, 179n.7, 180n.9
Robinson, James M., 138n.21, 226n.48, 245n.20, 245n.23, 270, 287n.3, 289n.23, 303n.113, 402n.40
Robinson, John A. T., 61, 333n.7
Robinson, Paul, 220n.17, 367n.33
Roncalli, Angelo Giuseppi (Pope John XXIII), 444n.33
Rorty, Richard, 369n.21
Rosenzweig, Franz, 222n.27, 242n.3
Roszak, Theodore, 139n.30, 139n.33
Royce, Josiah, 25, 42n.82, 45n.98, 164, 186n.47, 241n.1, 444n.34
Ruether, Rosemary, 57, 95n.101, 164, 186n.50, 243n.8, 247n.26, 251, 327, 390–92, 396–97, 402n.52, 403n.60, 404n.66, 455n.2
Ruland, Vernon, 152n.109
Rupp, George, 45n.101, 97n.111, 182n.20, 287n.4, 455n.1
Russell, Letty, 403n.60

Said, Edward, 144n.64
Sainte-Beauve, Charles Augustin, 108, 139n.34
Saiving, Valerie, 84n.24, 395, 404n.62
Sanders, E. P., 303n.110, 303n.115
Sandmel, Samuel, 89n.48, 179n.6, 455n.2
Sanks, T. Howland, 44n.92
Santayana, George, 165, 172, 191n.74, 191n.76
Sartre, Jean-Paul, 125, 145n.66, 147n.84, 149n.96, 220n.17, 341, 353
Saussure, Ferdinand de, 361
Schafer, Roy, 291n.46, 367n.34
Scharlemann, Robert, 364n.3, 441n.26
Scheler, Max, 37n.32, 148n.89, 164, 168, 170, 186n.51, 188n.66
Schelling, Friedrich Wilhelm Joseph, 111, 140n.36, 335n.21, 346, 380, 400n.22
Schillebeeckx, Edward, 43n.90, 71, 88n.44, 227n.56–57, 242n.8, 251, 289n.21, 292n.49, 294n.59, 299n.86, 299n.93, 300n.96, 301n.101–02, 301n.104, 319, 334n.15, 336n.29, 337n.31, 337n.33, 379, 392, 419, 427, 442n.29
Schineller, Peter, 44n.94, 287n.4
Schleiermacher, Friedrich, 33n.9, 42n.76, 67, 82n.1, 87n.36, 90n.58, 106, 138n.25, 144n.60, 145n.75, 155–56, 158, 169, 171, 180n.10, 183n.22, 188n.66, 189n.68, 192n.87, 212, 221n.20, 227n.56, 253, 304n.118, 373, 378–79, 385, 399n.7, 400n.12, 405, 407, 412, 444n.34
Schneidau, Herbert, 83n.10, 219n.4, 226n.49
Scholem, Gershom, 203, 222n.27, 356, 360, 368n.55
Scholes, Robert, 296n.81
Schoof, T. M., 336n.28, 337n.30
Schoonenberg, Piet, 244n.18, 333n.7
Schopenhauer, Arthur, 130, 140n.36, 142n.55, 151n.106
Schroyer, Trent, 36n.24
Schweizer, Eduard, 289n.20
Scott, Nathan, A., Jr., 35n.17, 152n.109, 191n.76, 363n.3, 401n.25, 401n.28

Segundo, Juan Luis, 41n.74, 44n.94, 57, 95n.99, 164, 180n.9, 186n.50, 403n.52, 403n.57, 404n.68, 442n.29
Seliger, Martin, 95n.99, 367n.36
Sennett, Richard, 35n.17, 36n.28, 367n.36
Sharpe, Eric J., 180n.7
Shea, William, 93n.82, 190n.71
Sheehan, Thomas, 191n.73, 369n.65
Siebert, Rudolf, 93n.78
Sittler, Joseph, 228n.64, 381, 401n.31
Smart, Ninian, 39n.56, 179–80n.7
Smith, Huston, 455n.3
Smith, Jonathan Z., 36n.28, 182n.18, 219n.5, 224n.33, 227n.54, 291n.37
Smith, Wilfred Cantwell, 181n.10, 399n.7, 455n.3
Sobrino, Jon, 245n.24, 251, 295n.77, 312, 314, 327, 334n.10, 334n.15, 427
Søderblom, Nathan, 157, 168, 170
Soelle, Dorothee, 226n.52, 251, 289n.26, 314, 390, 392, 402n.50
Sokolowski, Robert, 369n.60
Solzhenitsyn, Aleksandr, 166, 219n.7, 258, 354, 370n.75, 370n.78
Sontag, Susan, 139n.30
Steiner, George, 191n.75, 226n.46, 345–46, 355, 366n.21, 367n.42, 368n.52, 370n.75
Steinfels, Peter, 35n.16, 365n.16
Stendahl, Krister, 288n.12, 302–03n.110
Strauss, Leo, 7, 35n.21, 36n.25, 37n.31, 94n.94, 359
Streng, Frederick, 180n.7, 189n.66
Stroup, George, III, 243n.12, 296–97n.81
Sullivan, John Edward, 180n.7
Sullivan, Lawrence, 180n.9, 181n.12

Tannehill, Robert, 246n.25
Tate, Allen, 147n.83
Taylor, Mark C., 150n.104
Terrien, Samuel, 222n.26
TeSelle, Eugene, 241n.1
TeSelle, Sallie McFague. *See* McFague.
Theisen, Jerome, 43n.90
Theissen, Gerd, 291n.37
Thibault, Pierre, 40n.65
Thom, Gary, 220n.12
Thomas Aquinas, 33n.9, 39n.54, 63, 90n.56, 90n.62, 94n.87, 104, 107, 138n.19, 164, 186n.44, 191n.81, 191n.82, 221n.21, 227n.58, 310, 373–74, 379, 385, 407, 413–14, 438–39n.2, 439n.6, 440n.7, 440n.9, 443n.30
Tillich, Paul, 53, 84n.22, 84n.25, 88n.44, 104, 133, 138n.22, 156, 158, 164, 168, 170, 173, 180n.10, 183n.22, 186n.45, 188n.66, 190n.71, 192n.85, 197, 204, 221n.21, 223n.27, 225n.44, 313, 334–35n.17, 340–41, 364n.3, 364n.5, 365n.7, 365n.9, 380, 388–89, 400n.22, 402n.39, 402n.47, 407n.62, 405, 415, 418–19, 439n.2, 441n.24–25, 441–42n.26, 444n.34, 455n.6
Todorov, Tzvetan, 149n.97
Tolbert, Mary Ann, 298n.85
Tolstoy, Leo, 50, 84n.16, 123, 200, 219n.7, 321
Torrance, Thomas, 63, 89n.50
Toulmin, Stephen, 17–18, 36n.28, 40n.58, 40n.60–61, 40n.64, 85n.30, 146n.75 343, 365n.17, 369n.69
Trilling, Lionel, 34n.11, 139n.31, 365n.12
Troeltsch, Ernst, 24, 44n.97, 83n.9, 87n.36, 90n.58, 157, 189n.66, 244n.13, 293n.56, 322, 336n.22–23, 427, 450, 455n.4
Turner, Victor, 41n.73, 150n.99, 180n.9, 185n.38, 397, 455n.7
Tylor, E. B., 157, 181n.13

Vaihinger, Hans, 226n.46
Vawter, Bruce, 440n.7
Via, Dan, 251, 289n.17, 297n.81, 298n.85
Voegelin, Eric, 37n.31, 70, 94n.84, 94n.94, 99, 126, 135n.2, 369n.65, 400n.23
Vogel, Manfred, 222–23n.27

Waardenburg, Jean J., 189n.66
Wach, Joachim, 41n.69, 156, 168, 170, 183n.22, 187–88n.65, 192n.84, 219n.6, 222n.26, 223n.28
Weber, Max, 24, 34n.14, 41n.74, 44n.97, 156, 159, 189n.66, 341, 352
Weil, Simone, 164, 186n.49, 201, 381, 401n.29
Weintraub, Karl, 34n.11
Wellek, Rene, 140n.36, 141n.39
White, Hayden, 291n.46, 296–97n.81
Whitehead, Alfred North, 159, 164, 185n.39, 186n.44, 310, 334n.9, 360, 373, 377
Wiesel, Elie, 223n.27, 370n.78
Wilder, Amos, 152n.109, 292n.47, 292n.51, 296n.80, 297n.81, 303n.115
Wiles, Maurice, 40n.57, 302n.108
Williams, Raymond, 39n.50, 146n.76, 365n.8, 366n.27
Wills, Garry, 37n.29, 138n.20, 369n.65
Wimsatt, William, 143n.60, 145n.73, 147n.83, 151n.106
Winquist, Charles, 226n.47
Winters, Yvor, 123, 145n.75
Wittgenstein, Ludwig, 80, 113, 137n.27, 159, 359–60, 369n.68, 380, 399n.8
Wood, Charles, 188n.65, 190n.70

Yearley, Lee, 335n.20
Yerkes, James, 224n.30
Yoder, John Howard, 60, 87n.40
Yu, Anthony C., 153n.109

Index of Principal Subjects

Analogy, 86n.34, 88n.45, 266–67, 312, 362–63, 408–13, 417–21, 446–55; and dialectic, 413, 415–21, 447–48; and theology, 408–14, 421–24, 429, 446–55
Apocalyptic, 265–66, 268, 292n.51, 293n.54, 306, 309
Art, 12–13, 109–15, 146n.80, 354–55; and artist, 109, 124, 147n.82; and game, 113, 126, 135n.8
Authority, 99, 135n.1, 155, 351; of Jesus, 278, 300n.95, 300n.96; of scripture, 248–49, 287n.2

Chalcedon, 235, 243n.12, 244n.18, 246n.25, 251, 264, 287n.4, 292n.49, 306, 317, 323, 333n.7, 336n.25, 378
Christology, 234–35, 242n.5, 249–87, 337n.34; and contemporary christologies, 235, 314, 425–29; criteria of relative adequacy for, 246n.25, 306–09, 312, 315, 318–22; of cross, 311–12; logos, 310–11, 314, 318. *See also* Jesus Christ; Jesus of Nazareth.
Church, 15–16, 43n.90, 235–37, 241n.1, 244n. 17, 251–52, 313, 320–25, 328–29, 392–93, 422, 424–25; as eschatological sacrament of Christ, 422, 442n.29; models for, 23, 43n.89, 43n.90, 442n.29; as a public for theology, 21–28, 50, 422; and world, 44n.94, 45n.104, 364n.5. *See also* Tradition; World.
Classic, 14, 68, 100–35, 140n.37, 147n.82, 248, 351, 363–64, 372–73, 397–98; Christian, 233–35, 248–49, 275, 309; cultural, 134, 144n.64, 340–42, 347; intensification in, 125–26, 133, 199, 248; interpretation of, 115–24; paradigmatic character of, 194, 196, 197; production of, 124–30, 199–200; religious, 154–78, 163, 173–74, 200–01, 234, 248, 255–57, 263, 340–42
Conversation, 101, 135n.8, 178n.1, 236, 345, 363, 422, 446–55, 455n.7; and conflict, 437, 447, 453; with religion, 167, 176
Cross, 281–87, 307–08, 314, 316, 331, 426
Culture, 7, 11–14, 347

Doctrine, 265–68, 293n.57, 294n.65, 306, 309

Enlightenment, 30, 67, 78, 156, 196, 327, 346, 349–52, 451; dialectic of, 342
Eschatology, 265–70, 393–94
Ethics, 9, 57; and interpretation, 121–23, 145n.75; and proclamation, 203–04; and social justice, 13, 38n.38. *See also* Theology, practical.

Faith, 47, 65, 164, 209, 329–32, 430; as praxis, 337n.32; as response, 258, 269, 286, 320–21, 329–30

Genre, 127, 133, 149n.97, 174, 241, 247n.28, 250–51, 257–58, 263, 318, 327. *See also* New Testament.
God, 51–54, 160–61, 209, 234, 241n.1, 248, 259, 276–82, 310–11, 316–17, 330–31, 375, 429–38, 443n.30
Gospel, 276–81
Grace, 285, 311, 371, 374–75, 386, 414, 417, 423–24, 430–32, 437–38, 448

Hermeneutics. *See* Interpretation.
History, 76, 106, 210, 215
History of religions, 449, 451, 455n.7
Holy Spirit, 241n.1, 317, 425

Ideology critique. *See* Reason, critical.
Imagination, 128, 149n.96, 263, 312, 327. *See also* Analogy.
Incarnation, 281–87, 302n.108, 307–08, 314, 316, 331, 425
Interpretation and Interpretation Theory, 59–60, 101–04, 115–24, 135n.8, 137n.12, 148n.92, 148n.95; and application, 135n.8, 137n.12, 242n.4, 364n.5; and distanciation, 127, 145n.95, 246n.25, 263; and explanation, 117–18, 127, 145n.95, 237, 244n.18, 246n.25, 255–56, 259–61; need for critical pluralism of, 112, 121, 141n.48, 143n.60, 151n.106; of religion, 59–60, 156–67, 189n.70, 190n.71, 193, 255–57;

and retrieval, 190n.71, 195, 199, 373; steps of, 118–21, 142n.58, 142n.59, 151n.107, 247n.28; and suspicion, 106, 137n.16, 190n.71, 194, 199, 220n.17, 346–50, 352–57, 363, 373
Islam, 248, 287n.6

Jesus Christ, 47, 162, 212, 218, 273, 276–81, 329–32; and apostolic witness, 235–38, 272, 312–15, 323, 326, 424; event and person of, 233–37, 248, 254, 258–59, 286, 308–317, 371, 423–24, 426–29; and "historical Jesus," 238–39, 245n.20, 245n.23, 245n.24, 295n.68, 300n.97, 326, 334n.15, 443n.32
Jesus of Nazareth, 234–35, 277–81, 286, 313, 329–32, 424, 427–29; and "new quest," 245n.21, 245n.22
John, 48, 235, 250–51, 253–54, 270, 272, 278, 280, 282–87, 303n.113, 311–13, 315
Judaism, 203, 210–12, 222n.27, 248, 287n.6; and anti-Semitism, 179n.6; and Christian theology, 222n.27, 439n.7, 449–50

Kerygma, 235, 269–72, 294n.65, 388

Limit. *See* Religion.
Luke, 252–53, 277–80, 307, 311, 313

Manifestation, 193, 195, 202–08, 213–19, 221n.26, 222n.27, 224n.41, 228n.72, 251, 253, 257, 286–87; and Christian theology, 227n.56, 376–86, 390–93, 397, 425, 427; and history, 213. *See also* Theology, manifestation-oriented.
Mark, 276–80, 313
Matthew, 277–80, 313
Metaphor, 151n.107
Method, theological, 15–21, 39n.54, 39n.57, 233–47; and criteria of appropriateness, 59, 238–40, 326; and criteria of intelligibility, 238–40, 326, 442n.28; and critical correlation, 24–27, 42n.85, 45n.104, 60–61, 64, 80, 88n.44, 340, 364n.4, 374–76, 405–08, 419, 447. *See also* Theology; Theology, Systematic.
Mysticism, 203, 360, 385

Narrative, 251, 275–81, 296n.81, 307–09, 313, 325
New Testament, 235–41, 240n.1, 248–52, 273, 310; and canon, 80; and genre, 241, 247n.28, 250–51, 263–64, 270, 274–87, 308, 312–13, 316–18, 325, 327, 334n.17; and historical criticism, 259–64, 313, 324–27, 332n.1; and interpretation of "working canon," 254–59, 264, 272–73, 290n.29, 309, 313–14, 333n.3; and literary criticism, 259–62, 313, 324–28; and religious understanding, 260–62, 271; and social scientific criticism, 259–62, 324–27, 332n.1
Nicaea, 235, 246n.25, 251, 264, 287n.4, 306, 317

Parable, 276–77, 298n.85, 325–26
Paul, 235, 250–53, 270, 272, 280, 282–87, 302n.110, 311, 315, 332
Pluralism, 4, 33n.7, 36n.26, 254, 308–10, 312–13, 318–19, 342, 366n.22; and Christian theology, 4, 226n.46, 372, 447–55
Polity, 7, 9–11, 35n.17
Praxis, 69–79, 93n.82, 95n.104, 122, 246n.25, 301n.99, 390–95, 398, 429
Proclamation, 203, 209–18, 221n.26, 222n.27, 225n.45, 250–51, 253, 257, 268–76, 281, 286–87, 307–09, 313, 386–88, 390–93, 425–26. *See also* Theology, proclamation-oriented.
Public, 3–6, 17, 28–31, 34n.12, 36n.25, 36n.26; and classic, 112, 130–31; and privateness, 6, 11, 13, 34n.14, 109; and theology, 3, 17–21, 28–31, 63, 79–82, 104, 233; three principal publics, 5, 22, 28–31, 31n.1, 51, 56, 33n.9

Reason, 30–31, 36n.28, 78, 195; critical, 73, 75, 106, 420, 429; instrumental, 8, 30, 350–54; practical, 390–91, 420; technical, 78, 195, 350–54
Religion, 4, 11, 13, 180n.9, 357; academic study of, 16, 19–20; civil, 38n.39, 182n.14; and classic, 156, 340–41; and dialectic, 156, 165–66, 174, 176, 202; and limit, 160–61, 163, 165, 174, 180n.10, 193, 380; phenomenology of, 168, 180n.8, 188n.66; philosophy of, 159–65; sociology of, 157, 181n.13, 182n.14, 261–2. *See also* Classic, religious.
Resurrection, 279, 281–87, 301n.101, 307–08, 313–14, 316, 331–32, 336n.29
Revelation, 173, 193, 310

Scripture, 248–49, 259, 275, 309; as normative, 249. *See also* New Testament.
Secularity, 61, 87n.43, 210–11, 215–16; distinguished from privateness, 34n.14, 87n.43
Self, 12, 33n.7, 53, 209, 256, 341, 429, 432–35, 438; artist as, 124; the single one, 4, 30, 253, 256, 342; social/historical, 118, 256
Situation, 242n.4, 252–58, 271, 305–06, 310, 315, 339–42; contemporary, 25, 27, 30,

60, 80, 234, 341–64; and sociological analysis, 340, 343–44; and theological analysis, 15, 340, 343–44, 355–57, 371–76. *See also* Uncanny; World.
Society, 6–14, 21, 26
Style, 129, 133, 150n.98, 174
Symbol, 7, 11, 13, 108, 139n.36, 205; religious, 205–06; theological, 281–87, 293n.58, 307–09

Theology, 3–6, 19–21, 28–31, 45n.104, 59, 282–83, 315–16, 328–29, 340; and academy, 14–21, 39n.57; and church, 15, 21–28, 50, 328–29; confessional, 3, 16, 64–65, 82; as discipline, 17–21, 428, 447–49; distinguished from religious studies, 20, 39n.57, 41n.70; historical, 56, 84n.28; and language, 407–21; manifestation-oriented, 286–87, 303n.118, 303n.119, 376–86, 405, 411–14, 425, 431–32, 436; neo-orthodox, 180n.8, 387–89; philosophical, 58, 89n.47, 377–80; political and liberation, 27, 37n.36, 41n.74, 70, 75–79, 228n.72, 246n.26, 290n.33, 390–98, 416, 419–20; process, 439n.7, 443n.30; proclamation-oriented, 286–87, 303n.118, 303n.119, 313, 386–89, 405, 415, 425–27, 431, 433, 436; prophetic/action-oriented, 390–98, 405, 425–27, 431, 434–37; as story, 239; theocentric quality of, 51–54, 82n.4; and world, 23, 25, 339. *See also* Method, theological.
Theology, Fundamental, 22, 56–59, 62–64, 85n.31, 97n.114, 160, 183n.26, 184n.29, 240n.1, 377–79, 385, 442n.28
Theology, Practical, 56–59, 69–79, 85n.31, 93n.82, 95n.104, 97n.114, 337n.32, 442n.28
Theology, Systematic, 56–59, 64–69, 79–82, 85n.31, 90n.58, 97n.114, 99–107, 178, 198, 233, 240n.1, 371–76, 378–79, 385, 425, 429, 447–48; and interpretation, 67, 104–07, 130–35, 155, 183n.26, 195, 233, 375–76; criteria of relative adequacy for, 18, 26, 371–72, 405–11, 421–23, 442n.28; and theologian as believer, 398n.7. *See also* Method, theological.
Tradition, 27, 68, 76, 80, 99–100, 234–41, 243n.9, 243n.10, 243n.13, 245n.19, 252, 313, 315, 319–22, 328–32, 339, 371–72; and authority, 99; and Catholicism, 13, 27, 217; Christian tradition as self-reformatory, 237, 246n.26, 324–27, 420; and church, 320–25, 424–25; and interpretation, 59, 137n.16, 146n.80; and Protestantism, 13, 27
Trinity, 443n.30, 444n.41
Trust, 47, 54, 236–37, 253–54, 306, 311–12, 323, 328, 330–32, 379, 428, 430–32
Truth, 20, 58, 61–62, 88n.45, 110, 157, 268, 353; and classic, 108, 115; and fundamental theology, 62–63, 86n.34, 407; and hermeneutics, 68; and practical theology, 71–79, 86n.34, 407; and systematic theology, 65–69, 86n.34, 407

Uncanny, 357–64, 371–74

Whole, 159, 163, 173, 182n.21, 200, 330–31, 374–75, 430
Word, 387, 389. *See also* Kerygma; Proclamation.
World, 23, 25, 31, 45n.104, 48–51, 211, 364n.5, 429–30, 435–38, 444n.40